Marx, Marxism and the Spiritual

Edited by
**Anjan Chakrabarti, Anup Dhar
and Serap A. Kayatekin**

 Routledge
Taylor & Francis Group

LONDON AND NEW YORK

First published 2020
by Routledge
2 Park Square, Milton Park, Abingdon, Oxon, OX14 4RN

and by Routledge
52 Vanderbilt Avenue, New York, NY 10017

Routledge is an imprint of the Taylor & Francis Group, an informa business

© 2020 Association for Economic and Social Analysis

British Library Cataloguing in Publication Data
A catalogue record for this book is available from the British Library

ISBN13: 978-0-367-85977-0
ISBN13: 978-0-367-50449-6 (pbk)

Typeset in Adobe Garamond Pro
by Newgen Publishing UK

Publisher's Note
The publisher accepts responsibility for any inconsistencies that may have arisen during the conversion of this book from journal articles to book chapters, namely the inclusion of journal terminology.

Disclaimer
Every effort has been made to contact copyright holders for their permission to reprint material in this book. The publishers would be grateful to hear from any copyright holder who is not here acknowledged and will undertake to rectify any errors or omissions in future editions of this book.

Contents

Citation Information   viii

Notes on Contributors   xi

Editors' Introduction   1
Anjan Chakrabarti, Anup Dhar and Serap A. Kayatekin

Theory

1. Rethinking Marx and the Spiritual   15
   Kevin M. Brien

2. Spirituality Beyond Man: Toward a Labor Theory of the Soul   29
   Oxana Timofeeva

3. Marx, Foucault, and the Secularization of Western Culture   51
   Vivek Dhareshwar

4. What Kind of "Life Affirmation"? Disentangling the Conflation of
   Spinoza and Nietzsche   64
   Jan Rehmann

5. Specter and Spirit: Ernst Bloch, Jacques Derrida and the Work of Utopia   85
   Jason Kosnoski

6. Ernst Bloch and the Spirituality of Utopia   102
   Peter Thompson

7. Reading Marx with Levinas   117
   Serap A. Kayatekin and Jack Amariglio

8. Liberation Theology and Marxism   138
   Enrique Dussel, Irene B. Hodgson and José Pedrozo

Practice

9. Saint Francis in Climate-Changing Times: Form of Life, the Highest Poverty,
    and Postcapitalist Politics   163
    Stephen Healy

10. Faiths with a Heart and Heartless Religions: Devout Alternatives to the
    Merciless Rationalization of Charity   181
    Cihan Tuğal

11. Gramsci's Concept of the "Simple": Religion, Common Sense, and the
    Philosophy of Praxis   201
    Marcus E. Green

12. Subalterns, Religion, and the Philosophy of Praxis in Gramsci's *Prison Notebooks*   222
    Fabio Frosini

13. Marxism as *Asketic*, Spirituality as *Phronetic*: Rethinking Praxis   239
    Anup Dhar and Anjan Chakrabarti

Social Context of Theory and Practice

14. Religion in Russian Marxism   260
    Ross Wolfe

15. Serving the Sighs of the Working Class in South Africa with Marxist Analysis
    of the Bible as a Site of Struggle   295
    Gerald O. West

16. Inner Life, Politics, and the Secular: Is There a "Spirituality" of Subalterns and
    Dalits? Notes on Gramsci and Ambedkar   320
    Cosimo Zene

Conversations

17. "I am sure that you are more pessimistic than I am...": An Interview with
    Giorgio Agamben   343
    Jason Smith

18. Crossing Materialism and Religion: An Interview on Marxism and Spirituality
    with the Fourteenth Dalai Lama   353
    Anup Dhar, Anjan Chakrabarti and Serap Kayatekin

Marx, Marxism and the Spiritual

While Marxian theory has produced a sound and rigorous critique of capitalism, has it faltered in its own practice of social transformation? Has it faltered because of the Marxian insistence on the hyper-secularization of political cultures? The history of religions – with the exception of some spiritual traditions – has not been any less heartless and soulless. This book sets up a much-needed dialogue between a rethought Marxian praxis of the political and a rethought experience of spirituality.

Such rethinking within Marxism and spirituality and a resetting of their lost relationship is perhaps the only hope for a non-violent future of both the Marxian reconstruction of the self and the social as also faith-based life-practices. Building on past work in critical theory, this book offers a new take on the relationship between a rethought Marxism and a rethought spirituality (rethought in the life, philosophy and works of Christian thinkers, anti-Christian thinkers, Marxian thinkers, those critical of Marxist statecraft, Dalit neo-Buddhist thinkers, thinkers drawing from Judaism, as well as thinkers drawing critically from Christianity).

Contrary to popular belief, this book does not see spirituality as a derivative of only religion. This book also sees spirituality as, what Marx designated, the "sigh of the oppressed" against both social and religious orthodoxy. In that sense, spirituality is not just a displaced form of religion; it is a displaced form of the political too. This book therefore sets up the much-needed dialogue between the Marxian political and the spiritual traditions.

The chapters in this book were originally published in *Rethinking Marxism – A Journal of Economics, Culture and Society.*

Anjan Chakrabarti, Professor of Economics, University of Calcutta, India.

Anup Dhar, Professor of Philosophy, Ambedkar University Delhi, India.

Serap A. Kayatekin, Professor, American College of Thessaloniki, Greece.

19. Transcendence, Spirituality, Practices, Immanence: A Conversation with
     Antonio Negri   368
     Judith Revel

     Index   377

Citation Information

The following chapters were originally published in various issues of *Rethinking Marxism*. When citing this material, please use the original page numbering for each article, as follows:

Chapter 1
> *Rethinking Marx and the Spiritual*
> Kevin M. Brien
> *Rethinking Marxism*, volume 21, issue 1 (2009), pp. 103–116

Chapter 2
> *Spirituality Beyond Man: Toward a Labor Theory of the Soul*
> Oxana Timofeeva
> *Rethinking Marxism*, volume 32, issue 1 (2020), pp. 66–87

Chapter 3
> *Marx, Foucault, and the Secularization of Western Culture*
> Vivek Dhareshwar
> *Rethinking Marxism*, volume 28, issue 3–4 (2016), pp. 354–366

Chapter 4
> *What Kind of "Life Affirmation"? Disentangling the Conflation of Spinoza and Nietzsche*
> Jan Rehmann
> *Rethinking Marxism*, volume 28, issue 3–4 (2016), pp. 397–417

Chapter 5
> *Specter and Spirit: Ernst Bloch, Jacques Derrida, and the Work of Utopia*
> Jason Kosnoski
> *Rethinking Marxism*, volume 23, issue 4 (2011), pp. 507–523

Chapter 6
> *Ernst Bloch and the Spirituality of Utopia*
> Peter Thompson
> *Rethinking Marxism*, volume 28, issue 3–4 (2016), pp. 438–452

Chapter 7

Reading Marx with Levinas
Serap A. Kayatekin and Jack Amariglio
Rethinking Marxism, volume 28, issue 3–4 (2016), pp. 479–499

Chapter 8

Liberation Theology and Marxism
Enrique Dussel, Irene B. Hodgson, and José Pedrozo
Rethinking Marxism, volume 5, issue 3 (1992), pp. 50–74

Chapter 9

Saint Francis in Climate-Changing Times: Form of Life, the Highest Poverty, and Postcapitalist Politics
Stephen Healy
Rethinking Marxism, volume 28, issue 3–4 (2016), pp. 367–384

Chapter 10

Faiths with a Heart and Heartless Religions: Devout Alternatives to the Merciless Rationalization of Charity
Cihan Tuğal
Rethinking Marxism, volume 28, issue 3–4 (2016), pp. 418–437

Chapter 11

Gramsci's Concept of the "Simple": Religion, Common Sense, and the Philosophy of Praxis
Marcus E. Green
Rethinking Marxism, volume 30, issue 4 (2018), pp. 525–545

Chapter 12

Subalterns, Religion, and the Philosophy of Praxis in Gramsci's Prison Notebooks
Fabio Frosini
Rethinking Marxism, volume 28, issue 3–4 (2016), pp. 523–539

Chapter 13

Marxism as Asketic, *Spirituality as* Phronetic: *Rethinking Praxis*
Anup Dhar and Anjan Chakrabarti
Rethinking Marxism, volume 28, issue 3–4 (2016), pp. 563–583

Chapter 14

Religion in Russian Marxism
Ross Wolfe
Rethinking Marxism, volume 32, issue 1 (2020), pp. 6–40

Chapter 15
Serving the Sighs of the Working Class in South Africa with Marxist Analysis of the Bible as a Site of Struggle
Gerald O. West
Rethinking Marxism, volume 32, issue 1 (2020), pp. 41–65

Chapter 16
Inner Life, Politics, and the Secular: Is There a "Spirituality" of Subalterns and Dalits? Notes on Gramsci and Ambedkar
Cosimo Zene
Rethinking Marxism, volume 28, issue 3–4 (2016), pp. 540–562

Chapter 17
"I am sure that you are more pessimistic than I am...": An Interview with Giorgio Agamben
Jason Smith
Rethinking Marxism, volume 16, issue 2 (2004), pp. 115–124

Chapter 18
Crossing Materialism and Religion: An Interview on Marxism and Spirituality with the Fourteenth Dalai Lama
Anup Dhar, Anjan Chakrabarti, and Serap Kayatekin
Rethinking Marxism, volume 28, issue 3–4 (2016), pp. 584–598

Chapter 19
Transcendence, Spirituality, Practices, Immanence: A Conversation with Antonio Negri
Judith Revel and Arianna Bove
Rethinking Marxism, volume 28, issue 3–4 (2016), pp. 470–478

For any permission-related enquiries please visit:
www.tandfonline.com/page/help/permissions

Notes on Contributors

Jack Amariglio, Merrimack College, Massachusetts, USA

Arianna Bove, Queen Mary University of London, London, UK

Kevin M. Brien, Washington College, Maryland, USA

Anjan Chakrabarti, University of Calcutta, Kolkata, India

Anup Dhar, Ambedkar University, Delhi, India

Vivek Dhareshwar, Srishti School of Art, Design and Technology, Bangalore, India

Enrique Dussel, National Autonomous University of Mexico, Mexico City, Mexico

Fabio Frosini, University of Urbino, Urbino PU, Italy

Marcus E. Green, Pasadena City College, California, USA

Stephen Healy, Institute for Culture and Society, Western Sydney University, New South Wales, Australia

Irene B. Hodgson, Xavier University, Ohio, USA

Serap A. Kayatekin, American College of Thessaloniki, Thessaloniki, Greece

Jason Kosnoski, University of Michigan-Flint, Michigan, USA

José Pedrozo, translator of Chapter 8, 'Liberation Theology and Marxism'

Jan Rehmann, Union Theological Seminary, New York, USA, and Free University of Berlin, Berlin, Germany

Judith Revel, Université Paris Ouest Nanterre La Défense, Paris, France

Jason Smith, University of California-Irvine, California, USA

Peter Thompson, Institute of Modern Languages Research University of London, London, UK

Oxana Timofeeva, European University, St. Petersburg, Russia

Cihan Tuğal, University of California, Berkeley, California, USA

Gerald O. West, University of KwaZulu-Natal, Durban, South Africa

Ross Wolfe, High school special education teacher in the South Bronx, USA

Cosimo Zene, SOAS, University of London, London, UK

Editors' Introduction

Anjan Chakrabarti, Anup Dhar and Serap A. Kayatekin

Religious distress is at the same time the *expression* of real distress and also the *protest* against real distress. Religion is the sigh of the oppressed creature, the heart of a heartless world, just as it is the spirit of spiritless conditions. It is the opium of the people.
> —Karl Marx, introduction to *A Contribution to the Critique of Hegel's Philosophy of Right*

We are apt to forget that all systems produce evil sooner or later, when the psychology which is at the root of them is wrong... Therefore, I do not put my faith in any new institution, but in the individuals all over the world who think clearly, feel nobly, and act rightly, thus becoming the channels of moral truth. Our moral ideals do not work with chisels and hammers. Like trees, they spread their roots in the soil and their branches in the sky, without consulting any architect for their plans.
> —Rabindranath Tagore, *Creative Unity*

> Not Christian or Jew or Muslim, not Hindu
> Buddhist, sufi, or zen. Not any religion
> or cultural system. I am not from the East
> or the West, not out of the ocean or up
> from the ground, not natural or ethereal, not
> composed of elements at all. I do not exist,
> am not an entity in this world or in the next,
> did not descend from Adam and Eve or any
> origin story. My place is placeless, a trace
> of the traceless. Neither body or soul.
> I belong to the beloved, have seen the two
> worlds as one and that one call to and know,
> first, last, outer, inner, only that
> breath breathing human being.
> —Mawlana Jalaluddin Rumi, "Only Breath"

Marxism has conventionally found itself on the side of "materialism." There has also been a hyperseparation, as against the overdetermination of "matter" and "spirit," in much of Marxian thought and praxis. One of the aims of this edited volume comprising articles published in *Rethinking Marxism* is to explore why and how this separation happened and how Marxism historically found itself to be heavily tilted toward materialism while the mutual constitutivity of matter and spirit was relegated to the background. One can ask in this context whether

Karl Marx is responsible for this tilt and this hyperseparation, or is it later Marxism that made this tilt and hyperseparation deeply entrenched? When and why and how did Marxism come to be marked by such a defensive response to all talk of spirit, spirituality, religion, and theology? Among other things, this volume uncovers some of the historical and textual background of this tilt and hyperseparation. How did this disavowal of anything spiritual creep into Marxism? Was it there in Marx's thoughts? Was it always there in Marxism? Is Marxism constituted by this disavowal? Is Marx's work premised on a simple rejection of religion as the "opium of the people"? Is religion simply "false consciousness"? Is religion a mere instrument of manipulation in the hands of the ruling classes? Or is Marx's relation with spirituality and religion much more sophisticated and complex, as shown in the two lines preceding the oft-quoted infamous line, that religion is the "opium of the people."

One of the more influential philosophers of postwar Europe, Michel Foucault, in his capacity as the genealogist of Western thinking has tried to show how, in spite of their avowed disavowal of questions of spirituality or religion, many of the modern secular sciences have secret spiritual, religious, or even theological moorings. In fact, religion and secularism may not be opposite poles; they may be two sides of the same coin. We bring some of Foucault's insights regarding philosophy and spirituality to bear on Marxism in this volume. Is much of Marxism also, somewhat secretly, tied to spirituality in spite of its disavowal of anything spiritual and its equally aggressive and narrow materialism? What does the invocation of the "spectre" or the "ghost" (so reminiscent at times of the Holy Spirit) in Marx's writings gesture toward? Does this unsettle or problematize the rather stark demarcation between matter and spirit in much of Marxism? Is there also in Marxism's turn to the "commune" and to communitarianism (as against individualism)—read by Jean-Luc Nancy as a kind of creative "being-in-common" grounded in principles of fairness, justice, and equality—a turn toward the rather deeper tenets of the spiritual being, a being that foregrounds the interconnectedness and interdependence of all species? Even in its apparent scientism, is there then in Marxism a "secret spirituality," all the more because many faith-based orders share with Marxism similar or apposite principles?

In some ways, this volume explores and tries to put to dialogue two significant movements: that of the praxis of Marxism and that of "practical philosophy." In the praxis of Marxism, activist scholars have indeed set up interesting connections between on the one hand, spirituality, religion, and on the other, liberation from exploitation-oppression. How should contemporary Marxism respond to such movements in both praxis and in the conceptualizations of ethics? As Marxism traveled eastward, it encountered first Islam and then pagan practices and Buddhism; as well, it encountered animistic and spiritual orders in Africa and perhaps Latin America. Marxism's troubled relation to societies and cultures with deep roots in "faith-based orders" is a history we need to face. Nonetheless, in this encounter we should not rest our analyses on easy and unproblematic divisions between a Europe that is safely secular and a non-Europe that is religious and spiritual. Perhaps Marxism came face to face with theology in Europe more than in the rest of the world. This volume explores the troubled history of Marxism's relation with theology, religion, and spirituality in both Europe and the non-European world.

Why does a dialogue between Marxism and spirituality matter for Marxism? For one, almost all the essays in this volume are troubled by distrust in the question of the self in Marxism and suggest in the process a need to seek new ground for its connection with social and political transformation. The interrogation of self and of self-transformation unlocks a trail of questions that opens in turn the question of Marxian praxis, allowing us to address a host of hitherto uncomfortable moments within Marxism, moments that have been inerasable blots in its history. Here we are referring to the inflexion point at which Marxism—a supposed theory of emancipation—becomes a system of oppression and violence.

The history of Marxism draws attention to the seminal importance of this issue, and Marxism, if it is to remain relevant in the twenty-first century, cannot avoid interrogating it. In this context we draw attention to Marxism's relationship with largely religious or spiritual cultures, including those in other nationalities and communities that did not or do not fit its model of progress. What happens when the other of capital—the proletariat—faces its other? This other has emerged as Marxism's other, and history shows that Marxism has not found a way to deal with this outside. For example, what happened when the Soviet Union, armed with Marxism (as the self-proclaimed defender of proletarian rule), faced the others that appeared unfamiliar and strange to it? What happened when China and Tibet came face to face—one armed with Marxism and the other (dis)armed with spirituality, nonviolence, and faith-based practices? At the moment of its encounter with the other, why does Marxism become oppressive and violent? Why does it lack self-reflection?

In any genuine evaluation of the past and present, Marxists need to face the violence inflicted by Marxism and Marxists, and the structure and technology of oppression it gave shape to. The well-known argument that what happened was not Marxist or socialist or communist does not absolve those of us identifying with Marxism in any way we care to define. It does not absolve us because the fact remains that such oppressive structures and violence were created and made operational in the name of Marxism. Therefore, questions about the contexts in which Marxism has become violent and even dystopian need to be asked with courage and answered with honesty. Can there ever be a "social humanity" (as Marx suggested) without an emancipatory self wherein "free development of each is the condition for the free development of all"? Can an emancipatory self ever be produced in disconnect with some sort of spirituality? This volume was partly driven by a desire to explore whether a rethought relation between spirituality and Marxism would help the latter to self-reflect on its possibility of becoming oppressive and to temper the violence and aggression that have become part of the history and practice of Marxism. The point is not to give up on Marxism's emancipatory project of shaping a social humanity but rather to produce it in connection with a self-reflective gaze that forces it to reflect on its "standpoint of human society."

As mentioned before, almost all the essays, in various kinds of engagement between Marxism and spirituality, draw attention to the need for self-refection in Marxism and address the question of self and self-transformation as an essential condition for endogenizing the vexed problems of modes of oppression and violence that continue to persist in "socialist" systems and in communist subjects. As an extension, does spirituality offer us a mirror for addressing the self, for producing self-self dialogues, not with the purpose of demoting social and political transformation but rather to make way for a new kind of praxis that works through their mutual constitutivity? We suggest in this volume that the question of modes of oppression and violence is not incidental or a derivative of Marxism but is fundamental to what Marxism is.

Moreover, this volume is also an exploration of the troubled interface between Marxism and spirituality—not only to reimagine Marxism but to reimagine spirituality itself. Would a turn to (Marxist) materiality bring to spirituality a new hue, a new imagination? Would a turn to materiality and the political make spirituality more engaged in terms of human suffering and rescue it perhaps from individualist and "pop" versions circulated through "gurus" in the logic of global capital?

It needs to be said that in all the questions that have shaped this volume, understanding the complicated and many-layered relation of Marxism's relation to spirituality is not the only path that can be taken. The contemporary and historical place of oppression and violence in Marxism is not something that can be approached merely by exploring the troubled relation of Marxism to spirituality. None of the themes that this volume deals with are themes of religion, spirit, and spirituality only. So we have to admit from the start that the conversations that are had in this volume are not the only ones to be had. But we are convinced that they are among those conversations that are imperative to be had nonetheless.

This volume was born out of the conviction that any Marxism that feels the need to "rethink" itself has to be ready for conversations, for dialogues with systems of thinking that are different from it. It should be open to the idea of talking to the "other" and the outside and always be vigilant of its own potential for obliterating the other and the outside. Marxism should not fear its own change in the course of these conversations that will possibly also transform the other and the outside.

Kevin M. Brien, in his essay, "Rethinking Marx and the Spiritual," points to the importance of discussing the spiritual in the work of Marx, because, he argues, the spiritual crisis born in the context of capitalism contains revolutionary potential. Starting with the claim that the spiritual as "a domain of the psyche having to do with certain sorts of lived experience" has a very broad spectrum, Brien goes back to Marx, who, disagreeing with Feuerbach, argued that alienation is not caused by religious self-alienation, but is rather caused by class, ethnic, and sectarian conflicts. The author claims that while Marx may have dropped the word "spiritual" from his writings after his earlier work, he never dropped the concept of the spiritual as an essential aspect of the human, and thus his or her existential needs. He argues that Marx's work contains a notion of spirituality that is this-worldly and goes beyond theism, but also beyond atheism.

Starting with a similar argument that Marx and spirituality are not antithetical, Oxana Timofeeva in "Spirituality Beyond Man: Towards a Labor Theory of the Soul," takes the initial steps of developing a materialist theory of the soul, weaving a thread that starts with Hegel's *Phenomenology of the Spirit*. The author argues that in this work the spirit emerges as a splitting of reason which tries "to grasp its truth as a material object" and realizes itself in social life, which Hegel calls the "kingdom of animals." Timofeeva claims that it is the individual that the philosopher refers to as animal. Marx, in his 1844 *Manuscripts*, develops Hegel's thought through his study of estranged labor, which estranged reason has become in bourgeois society. Using Negarestani's argument that challenges the equation of "human" with "homo sapiens" and that seeks to extend to anything that can become a rational being, Timofeeva makes the claim that that the essence of human is free labor, or universal production, detaching it from our particular species. She then derives her notion of what the soul is based on the oeuvre of the great Soviet author Platonov. The soul is the bridge, Timofeeva argues, between the animal and the spiritual; it is the human essence but conceptualized in a non-essentialist and non-anthropocentric way. Spirituality, she says, "is the work of the soul." And, its liberation requires hard and concerted labor which, however, is imperative for addressing the funda-mental problems of contemporary society.

Vivek Dhareshwar, in an essay entitled "Marx, Foucault, and the Secularization of Western Culture," explores the "secularization of Western culture" and the "disappearance of spiritual knowledge" in the Western tradition. The secularization argument is premised on a somewhat perplexing and intriguing claim of Marx in "On the Jewish Question," that the truly religious/

Christian state is not the state that professes or embraces Christianity but the one that is secular. The essay accesses the question of spirituality from the perspective of "experiential knowledge." It argues that Marx's works (with what the author feels is "the partial exception of some early fragments")—largely inspired by Enlightenment perspectives—do not leave much room for such knowledge. This foreclosure of experiential knowledge qua spirituality happens primarily because Marx conflates experiential knowledge qua spirituality with theoretical knowledge qua theology. This then leads to another mistake: science emerges as the common interlocutor for both experiential knowledge/spirituality and theoretical knowledge/theology. Dhareshwar argues that it is only in Foucault's late work—when he was largely focused on highlighting the difference between the Christian (and not just the Enlightenment) notion of truth and the Hellenic-Romanic notion of truth—that spirituality is opposed not to *science* but to *theology*: "The conflict was not between spirituality and science, but between spirituality and theology." The essay then rewrites the spirituality/theology distinction in terms of "problematization" (which was the route spiritual movements used to seek to access truth) and "normativization" (defined by the author as the combination of theological rationality or truth seeking—whose secular embodiments are Descartes and Kant—and morality). Dhareshwar sees normativization as the unique contribution of Christianity; however, it is this substratum of normativization that provides the context for so-called secular knowledges, such as psychiatry, criminology, and the moral sciences, which are in effect secular theologies or theological secularisms. The author thus manages to demonstrate that secularization, usually thought of as that which contributes to the decline of theology, in effect and somewhat paradoxically strengthens the grip of theology on the modern and in the Enlightenment modern. What gets foreclosed in this secret pact between theology and secularism is the spiritual. The distinction between the theological and the secular is then an internal distinction, the very claim indeed made by Marx in "On the Jewish Question." The essay argues that Marx is both hostage to/ victim of and also free from this internal distinction: free from it because Marx does see the secret connection between Christian theology and capitalism; hostage to it because Marx mistakenly converts the spiritual/theology distinction to the idea/matter distinction and, at times, to the religion/secular distinction; victim of it because Marx misses out on the larger (Christian) narrative of normativization, which Foucault manages to see, and renders explicit only one subplot—that pertaining to "class"—and hence Marx sees the class politics of the proletariat as the only counterplot to (capitalist) alienation, reification, and fetishism. The essay argues that (Marxian) critique and (Foucauldian) genealogy perhaps need to be brought into dialogue to recover a *disavowed* spirituality in the secular-theological tradition on the one hand and a *missed* spirituality in the Marxian tradition on the other hand.

In "What Kind of 'Life Affirmation'? Disentangling the Conflation of Spinoza and Nietzsche," Jan Rehmann explores Marxism's attempts to look for a spirituality that is embedded in everyday life and can be connected to transformative practices. He believes this tradition coexists with another one emanating from orthodox Marxism, founded on a strict separation between matter and spirit and science and religion. He does this by what he names a philosophical "detour" of subjecting the widespread conflation of Spinoza with Nietzsche, which he thinks is absolutely necessary to our current understanding of "life-affirming" spirituality. The problem here for Rehmann is our route to Spinoza: "one of the most democratic" philosophers goes through Nietzsche who, as one of the most "elitist and aristocratic" philosophers, distorted our knowledge of the former. Crucial to this distortion, argues the author, is the notion of power that Spinoza uses, which in a long and winding genealogy became associated with Nietzsche's "will to power," which later on, via the work of Gilles Deleuze, led to a confusion of collective power from below with power as domination from above. By going through a layered analysis, Rehmann reveals this conflation, which has had serious implications in left thinking. He does this first by revealing the fundamental difference in the notions of power that Spinoza and Nietzsche use; in this usage, Rehmann argues, Nietzsche's reliance on a particular translation by Kuno Fischer—who translated Spinoza's concept of *potential* as power in general—played a very important role as well. Rehmann then shows that, while the "middle Nietzsche" was indeed influenced by Spinoza, in his later works Nietzsche strongly opposed Spinoza's conatus with his notion of will to power. In the next layer of his analysis, Rehmann directs his attention to the work of Negri, an influential thinker in revitalizing the significance of Spinoza for the Left, and he argues that while Negri's posing of an opposition between *potential* and *potestas* is a simplification, his argument on the ontological priority of *potential* is correct. In the final layer of his analysis, Rehmann argues that *potentia agendi* describes collective power geared to cooperation while Nietzsche's will to power "naturalizes" relations of domination and oppression, thus being fundamentally different from the former. Rehmann argues that leftist politics should not be based on resenting those at the top, as such sentiments can be co-opted into populist movements with potentially destructive results. Instead, he argues, a resilient Left should base its imaginary on notions of the "good life" developed by the people themselves. In building this imaginary, Spinoza's concepts of *potentia*, hilarity, and joy can be very valuable sources.

Any discussion of Marxism's relation to spirituality, without a doubt, has to consider that tradition which revolves around the concepts of utopia and the messianic. It is the work of Ernst Bloch, one of the most prominent representatives of that tradition, that the next essay discusses.

In "Specter and Spirit: Ernst Bloch, Jacques Derrida, and the Work of Utopia," Jason Kosnoski sets up an imaginary encounter between the two thinkers with the aim of developing a notion of utopian work based on Marx's understanding of unalienated labor. Kosnoski argues that the concept of "not yet conscious" in Bloch's work suggests that even the most basic efforts to fulfill mundane needs contain the potential for reimagining the larger structures of society. As society is always in flux, the utopia is forever incomplete and always entails an element of disappointment. But the melancholy coming from this realization of inherent incompleteness, for Bloch, is invigorating and not necessarily disabling. Kosnoski then moves on to Derrida's work to discover his relation to the messianic. He shows how his work on mourning for the specters of the past can activate the desire to project "that sense of justice into the future and hence the messianic." The author argues that considering the work of Bloch and Derrida together offers us the processes of how to imagine possible futures.

As the previous essays looked for the sources of spirituality in different traditions, the next argues that spirituality is an essential element of Marxism and not something external to it. Peter Thompson, in "Ernst Bloch and the Spirituality of Utopia," delves into the intellectual world of Ernst Bloch, on the question of spirituality. He initiates a productive engagement of Bloch's insights with those of contemporary thinkers, especially Žižek. This leads to a process of rethinking Marxism as an open system that is a combined existence of spirituality and materiality, produced by making both the subject (Hegel) and object (Marx) open-ended. The central category is the "not yet" that in turn opens the space for an introduction of the necessity of contingent events in the movement of both subject and object, therefore making the transition nonteleological and yet necessary for Marxists to intervene in a certain way.

The importance of class antagonism and unequal ownership are the material conditions that keep Marxists and Bloch interested in an open-ended historical process wherein that process itself embodies a spiritual event. Here, the dialectic of contingency plays a central role since it contains within it an anticipatory moment that enables us to both plan for the unforeseen and also to map out what we think this unknown known might possibly hold for us. This unknown known includes a fascism that mobilizes both religious categories from the past as well as a messianic Führer-fixated model of the future. But if this not-yet-ness is correlated with metaphysical materialism, then it is possible to unpack an alternative space into which anticipatory consciousness, liberated from both *re-ligio* and reductionist materialism, can be projected while at the same time rejecting neither religious development toward atheism nor materialist development toward complexity and the "multiversal." This requires, however, a shift not just to rethinking Marxism but also to bringing spirituality back into Marxism by dredging a Christian route to atheism along the lines of Bloch and Žižek, who contend that, unlike any other religion, Christianity is based on an idea of God as the son of man rather than the son of God.

The continuous questioning of Western philosophical traditions finds a different angle in the following essay. In "Reading Marx with Levinas," Serap A. Kayatekin and Jack Amariglio set up an imaginary encounter between Emmanuel Levinas, arguably the most influential philosopher of ethics of the post–World War II era, and Karl Marx. A relentless critic of ontology within the Western philosophical traditions, Levinas argued that any ethics based on ontology erases the alterity of the "Other" by rendering it the "Same." For him, every ethics based on ontology is thus fundamentally flawed since doing an act of "good" on the basis of the argument of the humanity of the other simultaneously defines what a human being is and therefore instantly what or who a human being is not. Against the background of the Holocaust, Levinas's life's work was to build an argument about the violence of ontology and an antihumanist ethics of "otherwise than being," a transcendence through infinite responsibility for the other, a decidedly nonreciprocal, noncontractarian view wherein I and only I am responsible for the other, and the responsibility of the other toward me is the other's concern only. Drawing from the work of Judith Butler, Kayatekin and Amariglio argue that Levinas's troubling notion of "infinite responsibility" for one's persecutor can be explained by the idea of an impingement of the other on oneself by the fact that we are all part of a sociality. This is persecution precisely because we don't have a choice over this impingement. This argument, for Kayatekin and Amariglio, sets one of the important differences between Levinas and Marx, in that Levinas's ethics belongs to the preontological while Marx's analysis is that of a specific, that is capitalist, ontology, leading to the conclusion that the two thinkers thus theorize on different levels. Despite this difference in the levels of theorization, Kayatekin and Amariglio argue that the spirituality of these thinkers resides in their other-oriented thinking.

The authors then go through an extended discussion of the antihumanism embedded in Marx's *Capital*, after which they pose the difficult but necessary question: "Am I infinitely responsible for my exploiter?" Levinas has categorically rejected this possibility, which however remains an issue for Marxism. Kayatekin and Amariglio argue that the question of infinite responsibility, when applied in the context of class exploitation, presents us with the imperative about the conditions of class transformation. The authors conclude that a reconsideration of Levinas's work in the context of class exploitation will, on the one hand, render it more solid; on the other, Marxism with Levinas's question considered will be rendered more humane.

Just as Brien points to the broad spectrum of the spiritual ranging from theism to atheism, the next contribution discusses one of the most significant revolutionary forms of theistic spirituality of the modern era. Set in the Latin American context, the essay by Enrique Dussel, Irene B. Hodgson, and José Pedrozo titled "Liberation Theology and Marxism" historicizes the rise and evolution of liberation theology as the first political theology to systematically connect the methodology of Marxism with that of a critical-concrete theological reflection, namely Christian theology that grows out of Christian praxis based on faith for bettering the condition of the poor and oppressed. It defends its association with Marxism by arguing that Christian theology has always imported methods from the appropriate resources of its time, from symbolic rationalism of Adamic myth in Babylonia to the science of Plato during the Greek period to the philosophy of Aristotle during the Middle Ages and so on. The authors reject criticism by a section of Church orthodoxy saying that liberation theology has surrendered to the non-Christian features of atheism and demotion of human person, seen as features of Leninist-Stalinist Marxism with its method of dialectical materialism. What is emphasized instead is Marx's take on work-bread-life and the critical method of Marxism derived from scholars-practitioners like Gramsci-Althusser-Che Guevera and others, the dependency school of Latin America, and sociopolitical movements such as the Nicaraguan revolution. Likewise, distancing itself from the emphasis of Christian orthodoxy on abstract questions of truths, doctrines, and liberty, liberation theology focuses upon the concrete condition of human misery of the poor and oppressed, which it argues is the central focus of faith-based Christianity. Since the present state of human misery is structured by the historical context of capitalist-driven exploitation and modes of oppression, there is a need to integrate Marxism—the most sophisticated critical method against capitalism—from the standpoint of Christian faith-based praxis of the poor and oppressed.

As Dhareshwar attempts the delinking of religion and spirituality in the evolution of secularism in the West, Stephen Healy turns to a search for contemporary relevance in what Foucault would call experiential practices of Catholicism; taking off from the philosophy and practice of poverty and austerity of Saint Francis and from the expansion of the way of life of Catholic monastic orders in the eleventh and twelfth centuries (most notably that of the Franciscans, who harbored an implicit critique of the Church as an earthly power), Healy's essay "Saint Francis in Climate-Changing Times: Forms of Life, the Highest Poverty, and Postcapitalist Politics" makes an interesting connection between "forms of life," the "practice of highest poverty," and postcapitalist politics in climate-changing times as *context*. Forms of everyday life attuned to the collective material practice of the highest poverty, however, do not mean, for Healy, renunciation and asceticism but something more radical: namely, *ascetic* (à la Foucault) exercises of the self and a refusal to turn natural and human reality into an object to be used. The essay thus inaugurates a different "return" and a different relationship of Marxism with Christianity—one that aligns with contemporary postcapitalist explorations of the contained consumerism of the "developed" minority world, with cooperation and collectivity, including efforts to live with less, to care for what we hold in common, or to invest in an ecologically habitable future. Healy's essay deserves to be placed in the larger corpus of the Marxian return to Christianity, returns that are housed under such names as Derrida, Agamben, Žižek, Negri, and Badiou. Such returns counter the end-of-history condition and post-ideological cynicism and usher in the revolutionary movement/moment "to come" as against nonevental times. The Franciscan "form of life," with the spiritual as its ground, helps Healy conceptualize the postcapitalist project of pursuing a different "mode of humanity" in which one might develop the capacity to survive in the Anthropocene. Healy sees the contemporary explosion of social movements—as with the eleventh- and twelfth-century explosion of monastic movements and critiques of the Church—as predicated upon experimental practices that redefine what is necessary for us to survive and how we care for things in common that we cannot own, including "simple living," "downshifting," and "cheapskating" (i.e., living cheaply), which is somewhat akin to the long tradition within Christianity (and within many other traditions) of voluntary simplicity. Cheapskating, however, is not a renunciation of ownership but a desire for a life where consumption is thoughtful and deliberate. In that sense, Healy offers in such postcapitalist praxis the glimpse of an evental everyday or an everyday event.

Among the new life forms we want to build, is there a place for charity, that notion that is central to all religions and that has been criticized heavily, especially by the Left? Through a detailed reading of charity, Cihan Tuğal's essay entitled "Faiths with a Heart and Heartless Religions: Devout Alternatives to the Merciless Rationalization of Charity" rehabilitates the concept of charity as a weapon for the poor and oppressed to be wielded, as a critique and as an act of social transformation, against the capitalist system. This overturns the conventional reading of Marxists who condemn charity as a way of managing, legitimating, and maintaining capitalism, of perpetrating and hiding the exploitation, dependence, and degradation of subordinate classes by the rich. This view is present in the thought of Marx, Engels, and Kautsky and has been reiterated more thoroughly in recent times by Žižek and Badiou who, Tuğal argues, fatally and quite misleadingly separate *agape*—the true nature of love— from charity and, following that, condemn charity as a concept of reaction. Tuğal's essay undermines this one-dimensional rendition of charity by showing the Christian reading of *caritas* to be multidirectional: it can be traditional and conservative (philanthropic love based on the individual giving of the rich to the poor and on responsibility for the poor, thereby separating *caritas* from its social moorings and from questions of the structures of oppression and poverty); it can be liberal (challenging the idea that giving to the poor is undesirable and that the poor are undeserving); and it can be emancipatory (charitable love is where *agape* and *caritas* cannot be separated). To this end, the essay traces Lucien Goldmann's take on Pascal as capturing a reformulation of *caritas* within Christianity, after the rise of liberalism and political economy as a demotion of *caritas* and with the recent battle in the Catholic Church between the conservative and the more emancipatory strands. Particularly important for the latter is Pope Francis's invocation of *caritas* to uphold the Christianity of the poor against the current world order, thereby shifting the focus once again from the individual to the social and collective. Tuğal finds a trace of this present antiliberal, anticonservative turn in the insights of liberation theology and particularly in those of Gustavo Gutiérrez, who instead of treating charitable love as opposed to structural transformation considers such love as an investment in it. Reading charity as political charity entails understanding the poor as an exploited and oppressed mass, which resituates charity as redistribution of wealth in favor of the poor and in opposition to the proprietor class and to institutions of inequality favoring the rich. As against holding onto state-sponsored top-down ideas of socialism, an argument is made in favor of social transformation in which the welding of processes of redistribution with processes of the heart—that is, charitable love—is considered a necessary supplement to class struggle, the self-organization of the oppressed, and state planning in the struggle against poverty and the subordination of the poor that the capitalist system upholds.

The next two contributions in this volume engage the work of another seminal thinker in the history of Marxism, that of Antonio Gramsci, one of the first thinkers who attempted to comprehend in depth the phenomenon of religion and its relevance to understanding subalternity and social change.

Marcus E. Green in his essay "Gramsci's Concept of the 'Simple': Religion, Common Sense, and the Philosophy of Praxis" shows how the very first note Gramsci entered in the *Prison Notebooks* concerns the Catholic Church's treatment of poverty and inequality as natural conditions ordained by God. Through a diachronic analysis of the composition of the *Notebooks*, Green shows how Gramsci's early focus on religion developed finally into the concept of the "simple," which Gramsci utilized as a category to examine the Catholic Church's paternalistic view of common people and peasants as "simple and sincere souls," in contrast to superior cultured intellectuals; as also to develop a "renewed common sense" (or "good sense") that contains critical and reflective philosophical foundations transcending the passivity and paternalism of religion. Such a movement requires articulating and disseminating a new conception of philosophy and culture that possesses a critical grounding and provides a basis of struggle in which the "simple" plays a predominant role in the direction of political lives and in the creation of a new hegemony. As against the Church's condescending portrayal of the "simple," Gramsci thus argues for a conception of "common sense," renewed, albeit, tied to conditions of "subalternity." For Gramsci, determinist Marxism, like the Catholic Church, presents a worldview, which is largely incapable of addressing the political aspirations of the "simple" and the "subaltern." Hence both Marxism and religion require rethinking. The editors of the volume would like to add in this context that Tagore's turn to the *sahaj* or the *sahajiya* (as against the theological or religious) is akin to Gramsci's turn to the "simple."

In "Subalterns, Religion, and the Philosophy of Praxis in Gramsci's *Prison Notebooks*," Fabio Frosini offers an interpretation of how Gramsci's understanding of religion relates to the conditions of subalternity. As Frosini explains, the capacity of subaltern classes to construct autonomous political institutions transformed with the formation of the modern state. The autonomous political institutions of subaltern classes in ancient and medieval states were replaced with so-called private organizations of civil society in the formation of the modern state, wherein subaltern classes confronted the hegemony of the dominant class. With the birth of mass society, the masses entered political life, yet religion ordered their way of thinking, resulting in a situation in which the masses were included in the state but neutralized. But as Frosini argues, Gramsci viewed religion as a conception of the world that formed thought and action by a search for coherence (or "good sense"). Thus, according to Frosini, to confront the hegemony of the modern state, subaltern classes require the formulation of a coherent unity of theory and practice in their religious ideas, which present the opportunity to translate into forms of self-organization and self-emancipation.

The ongoing reflections between spirituality and Marxism take on yet another historical and theoretical angle, engaging the philosophies of thinkers from the non-West in the next contribution. Focusing on the uneasy *and* between Marxism and spirituality, Anup Dhar and Anjan Chakrabarti, in their essay entitled "Marxism as *Asketic*, Spirituality as *Phronetic*: Rethinking Praxis," try to rethink "praxis" by displacing and grounding Marxism in self-reflection and self-transformation (which it largely lacks) and rethink spirituality in the "material social" and in transformative social action (which it largely lacks). The essay moves beyond the paradigmatic "matter/spirit" binary and brings each arm of the binary and their interlocutors to overdetermination and contradiction; by building on the relationship of four unconventional notions of "truth" in the thought of Marx, Gandhi, Heidegger, and Foucault. Through a rereading of the "Theses on Feuerbach," Marx is shown to have shifted focus from the matter/object-spirit/subject binary to "human sensuous activity" or "practice," from the (theological) "Word" to the (proletarian) "deed," and from the "secular critique of religion" to the "critique of secularism." Keeping the human in focus, Gandhi spiritualized religion in terms of *how* one *lived* religion and not in terms of "what" one *believed*. The experience of religion is thus shifted from "God is truth" to "truth is God," wherein truth is a moral experience of self-transformation and action.

The key to moving Marxism beyond the binary of simple materialism and simple spiritualism is opened through a Derridean-Heideggerian reading of *Geist*: *Geist* not as "speculative idealism" but as uncanny supplement to the material social. Moving away from the cold reason of Enlightenment that *Sophia* (the desire for ultimate and absolute knowledge of first principles) represents, Heidegger seeks truth in the "other reason" of *phronesis*. Phronesis is the concrete encounter of "being-related to the with-which," such that truth lies not in ultimates but rather in the relation between actually existing beings, between self and other, as well as in action, in practice. Practical reason and an attention to our modes of being in the world foreground the inalienable relation between matter/social and spirit/individual, which both Marx and Gandhi had sought in their respective pursuit of truth.

The turn to *askesis* in the later work of Foucault paves the way for the question of the utter neglect of self-transformation in Marxism, a problem practically amplified by Marxism's history of violence and state repression. Shifting the discussion from the matter/spirit binary, Foucault pits spirituality against philosophy. Truth, for Foucault, is not for knowledge but for the subject and can only be achieved through and in self-transformation, the labor of *askesis*. But why can't Marxism be asketic? To seek possible answers, one needs to first address the question of traces of fascism in ourselves—even among militant revolutionaries—which in turn calls for what the authors term an "anti-Oedipal Marxism." The authors argue that when social and political transformations are undertaken without reflection on the anti-Oedipal imperative of ethical action, all kinds of dystopias, including violence, result. The essay asks: can there be an anti-Oedipal Marxism? The authors invoke Resnick and Wolff's turn from class as noun to class as process as providing one possibility, implying that the struggle for social and political transformation (say, for ending class exploitation) need not be violent since it fundamentally involves a change in process and not the actual annihilation of people. By showing that the exploited in one site can be exploiter in another, this turn brings self-reflection right into the heart of Marxian practice and argues for the indispensability of asketic self-transformation in sociopolitical transformation. This opening is used to reread Gandhian praxis, wherein self-social-political transformation was historically attempted in interrelation with one another.

The discussions around the connection of Marxism with spirituality have been part of some of the most significant social movements of the twentieth century. In the following four essays it is this connection that the contributors analyze.

In "Religion in Russian Marxism," Ross Wolfe delves into the god-building episode in Russian Marxism during the revolutionary period to explore the broader question of the dichotomy between mind and spirit and between Marxism and spirituality. Particularly important is the cluster of ideologies known as Vperëdism, within which god-building was one strand. Taking off from Vperëdism, the aspects of god-seeking (conventional religion), god-building (such as in Gorkii's deep humanism), and religion (such as in Lunacharskii's religion of labor) and also their uneasy relations are unpacked. This strand of revolutionary thought tried to introduce a "religion without God" by separating the question of spirituality from god-seeking religion, and through that built an association with Marxism. In developing his position over time, Gorkii contends that there is no God but dream about God, which is materialized through the union of universe with man's inner nature, initially pathos and then labor. Lunacharskii deals with humanism and historical progress to critically engage with

Gorkii and places labor at the center of his analysis of religion. A complex debate is shown to unravel within and outside Russian Marxism. On the other side was Lenin who considered all worship of divinity, both god-seeking and god-building, to be obfuscating the real conditions of exploitation and oppression and blunting "social feelings" by "replacing the living by the dead." The irony of Lenin's mummification is also discussed.

There is no doubt that the South African anti-apartheid struggle was one of the most important social movements of the twentieth century. Liberation theology's reach was not confined to Latin America. It played a defining role in the anti-apartheid struggle in South Africa, without a doubt one of the defining social movements of the twentieth century.

"Serving the Sighs of the Working Class in South Africa with Marxist Analysis of the Bible as a Site of Struggle" by Gerald O. West builds, on the one hand, on Marx's notion of religion as "the sigh of the oppressed" (this, West sees as paradigmatic of African forms of Marxism) and on the other, on the work of the South African biblical scholar Itumeleng Mosala (*Biblical Hermeneutics and Black Theology in South Africa* [1989]) to argue that "the Bible was intrinsically a site of class struggle" as against the analysis of black theologians who see biblical *interpretation* as the site of struggle. West shows how Mosala emerges as an "editor" of the text of the Bible and where "the embodied sigh of the oppressed is the 'first text' and the Bible is the 'second text.'" In tune with the methodology of "redaction criticism," Mosala reads the Bible "backwards," which helps Mosala recognize "the final form [or the second text] of the Bible as the oppressor's form." Marxism takes Mosala to an understanding of the historical modes of production (MPs) antecedent to the production of the Bible, namely, the sites of class struggle within "the sacred economy of ancient 'Israel,'" in the context of the "conflict between the village commune and the city-temple complex" and the consequent emergence of the "state" and the "ancient 'system of *theo-economics*, and its constituent *regimes of allocation* and *regimes of extraction*.'" Mosala also creates the ground as to why decolonization need not necessarily be accompanied by de-christianization in black contexts. Black theology must employ the progressive aspects of black history and culture to liberate the Bible from the second text or the oppressor's form, so that the first text of the Bible may in turn liberate black people. That is the hermeneutical dialectic between Marxism and the spiritual West proposes through Mosala.

Gramsci's work on spirituality informs yet another contribution to the volume through the concept of inner life. As Cosimo Zene argues in his essay "Inner Life, Politics, and the Secular: Is There a 'Spirituality' of Subalterns and Dalits? Notes on Gramsci and Ambedkar," the formation of critical consciousness is one of the central elements in the struggle for the self-emancipation of subaltern groups and Dalits. Returning to the notion of the "inner life" in Gramsci's writings, Zene points out that dominant culture often denies inner life and spirituality to subalterns and Dalits. While religion tends to fall under the control of dominant groups—with structured laws, hierarchies, and sanctions—inner life and "secular spirituality," present opportunities to escape the grasp of hegemonic power. This notion in Gramsci's thought, as Zene shows, overlaps with the reclamation and recognition of Dalit spirituality in the work of B. R. Ambedkar. Both Gramsci and Ambedkar opposed the notion of some form of future religious salvation for subalterns and Dalits and in contrast advocated instead for their empowerment. Thus, rather than denying inner life and spirituality, Zene argues that critical consciousness and historical self-awareness are paramount to overcoming the subordination of subaltern groups and Dalits alike.

The final part of the volume comprises three interviews with two prominent thinkers and a global spiritual leader.

In the interview titled "I am sure that you are more pessimistic than I am..." Giorgio Agamben sets up a "subtle parallel" between "messianic actuality" (*kairos*) in Paul and Benjamin and the political in Marx; where the messianic does not coincide with religion; where messianic time is neither the time to come (the eschatological future, the eternal) nor is it exactly historical or profane: "it is a bit of time taken from the profane that, all of a sudden, is transformed." Building on Pauline, "usages" as "conducts of life" and on "practice that cannot be assigned a subject," the question of the "classical political" and the "the revolutionary subject," posed in the "old sense," i.e., "in terms of class, of the proletariat," are rethought. The subject in is turn conceived in terms of subjectivation (the Pauline "as" or "is") and desubjectivation (the Pauline "as [if] not"; where desubjectivation is not the destruction of all subjectivity, but where the subject is the subject of its own desubjectivation). Even the question of "care of the self" in late Foucault is tied to an "apparently opposite theme," the letting go of the self. The political terrain is reframed as a kind of battlefield in which two processes unfold: "the destruction of all that traditional identity was" and "its immediate resubjectivation by the State," "but also by the subjects themselves." Paul is presenced as a thinker who, instead of proposing a universal principle, "divides the division." And what remains is the new but undefinable subject, who is always *left over* or *behind*. It is a kind of *resisting, through remaining*; through the *remainder*. This is not to lose hope but to find that which is "given to the hopeless" ("the desperate situation of society in which I live fills me with hope").

In the following contribution, we present an interview carried out with the fourteenth Dalai Lama, one of the most prominent spiritual leaders who, on a number of occasions, has openly expressed sympathy with Marxism. Anup Dhar, Anjan Chakrabarti, and Serap Kayatekin's conversation/interview with the Dalai Lama explores on the one hand what it means to *be* "Marxist"—why the Dalai Lama would like to assert that he is a (*true*) Marxist—and on the other how to find/found a religion of earthly hope and worldly relief from suffering and not an otherworldly belief in the cessation of oppression-exploitation-humiliation thus redefining both Marxism and religion. This redefinition sees Marxism as a philosophy and praxis of ending exploitation and achieving equality in this world and not as an exercise of paranoid statecraft; it sees religion as *lived ethic among interdependent sentient beings*. In the process, the Dalai Lama translates the conventions of religion into the spiritual experience and brings religion qua the spiritual closer to the Marxian political.

The conversation also explores the interface between what could be called the *political consequences of a rethought spirituality* and the *spiritual consequences of a rethought Marxism*. Dalai Lama in the process brings to contention a somewhat "atheist" and "this-worldly" spirituality, a reflexive Marxian materialism of attention to human suffering, and a Marxian praxis of equal distribution and social transformation not totally stripped of compassion, empathy, and love. He also distinguishes between two kinds of spirituality: one premised on belief and the other premised on concern for the other's well-being. He calls the second kind of spirituality *secular spirituality*, which includes even the nonbeliever. He sees such spiritual imagination as ground for the ethical construction of this-worldly happiness. He also raises two questions, one for Marxism and the other for religion: How would Marxism take form in a largely democratic country like India? Would its form be different from the form it took in largely feudal-monarchical Russia and China? With respect to religion, he sees religious organizational imagination as tied to the feudal spaces in which and from which the early religions originated. He is hence in search of a religious imagination and an imagination of religious organization that is in tune and in sync with a contemporary democratic ethos; religion hence will have to democratically take into consideration the nonbeliever or the atheist.

The conversation ends with a discussion on violence and the violent history of both Marxism and religion. The discussants agree on the fact that, while the oppressed suffers, it is the oppressor who gets dehumanized: the oppressor is the one losing human compassion, losing touch with love. And if Marxism or religion puts on the cloak of an oppressor or begins to take the standpoint of the oppressor, they lose touch with the spiritual.

In the final interview, a concept central to the thinkers discussed by Healy and Dhareshwar, that of transcendence in the thought of Saint Francis and Foucault, becomes the topic of conversation between Antonio Negri and Judith Revel. Building on the two meanings of transcendence—"blind obedience to God, which Francis defends, and that which establishes the worldly power of the Church, which Francis hates"—and Foucault's concept of "spiritual exercises" (such exercises help to build oneself and build relationships with the other) culled in turn out of Greek Stoic philosophy, the dialogue "Transcendance, Spirituality, Practices, Immanence," between Antonio Negri and Judith Revel, asks two sets of related questions. On the one hand it asks: can there be spirituality without transcendence? Or more specifically, can there be an "immanent spirituality" (or a spirituality with at least a "critique of transcendence")? On the other hand it asks: "In the class struggle experienced in the shadow cone of Marxism," is there a kind of "secret spirituality"? Would some experiences of communist militancy, such as the practice of the virtues of solidarity, of prophecy, or of poverty, gesture toward spiritual experience? In the process, the dialogue inaugurates an understanding of spirituality as something concerning "gestures, bodies, materiality of the world, intersubjective relations and the relationship with oneself." The dialogue also refers to spirituality as to a "making" in the world, to an "immanent practice" (that does not preclude an appreciation and awareness of power), and not to some sort of "disembodied spiritual ether." The setting up of a spiritual perspective that is not oblivious to the question of power stems from the need to find political forms radically different from the old transcendent models of metaphysics or, in political terms, of sovereignty. The dialogue between Negri and Revel thus brings to trialogue Marx, Spinoza, and Foucault in the form of a conversation and the marking of a not too overt connection among (1) a "political ontology of power" (which is different from and is opposed to a metaphysics of sovereignty), (2) a philosophy of immanence (as putting to question religious transcendence), and (3) spirituality as a set of practices as well as relationships, gestures, and structures (which is different from and is opposed to a "spirituality of acceptance as a renunciation of oneself and the world in the name of another life").

One of the overlapping themes in this volume cohered around the matter of spirituality in relation to collective life forms. The hope in this particular collective effort is that an unconditional willingness to face the past—a common desire to talk with Marxists and non-Marxists alike, exposing ourselves to other ideas while accepting the possibility of the transformation of our ideas without fear—will make for a more humane Marxism that is more engaged with the reality that surrounds it and that is more relevant to a contemporary modernity that is tearing itself apart. It is in this somewhat dystopian terrain that Marxism and spirituality must bring one another closer together in order to imagine, propose, and construct what Marx designated a new "social humanity" or "human sociality" in the making. In the creation of this social humanity, as Tagore suggests in the epigraph above, what we need is not a set of rational guidelines that will shape our morality but rather a way of being that grows and flourishes. In this mode of sociality, it matters not where we come from and who we are. As the great Rumi writes in his sublime poetry, it is the breath that all being takes. It is perhaps an existence that is "otherwise than being," in the words of Levinas.

Rethinking Marx and the Spiritual

Kevin M. Brien

dedicated to Robert S. Cohen

This essay explores the "the spiritual" in Marx's thought and, in so doing, interprets that thought as an integral whole. A metalevel characterization of the spiritual, oriented toward a broad spectrum of specific modes of the spiritual, is given. Various citations from Marx's texts open up, in a preliminary way, a vista on a humanistic Marxist mode of the spiritual. Feuerbach's views on religion are examined, followed by Marx's critical appropriation of them, that construes religion as an alienated form of the spiritual that tears it away from its this-worldly home in the secular domain. An analysis of Marx's religion in "the opium of the people" passage is given—with special concern for the meanings of "imaginary flowers" and the "living flower." The essay argues that implicit in this passage is Marx's recognition of an array of fundamental existential needs that all people have. Finally, an exposition of how each of these needs would be manifested in the specific mode of the spiritual at play in Marx's thought concretely brings it into focus.

My explorations concerning Marx and "the spiritual" in this essay presuppose that there is *not* a sharp conceptual break between the early and late Marx. The argument that could plausibly establish such a case is much too long and complex to be given here but, in my judgment, the strongest case for holding that Marx's life work actually is an integral whole involves bringing into play Marx's mature method of dialectical explanation *that moves from the abstract to the concrete* to show the interconnection between the early and late Marx.[1] In what follows I adapt this method to my explorations of the spiritual in Marx.

To orient my readers let me give the following characterization of the "spiritual" at a metalevel that abstracts from the specific contents of any particular mode of the spiritual. At such a level I project the spiritual as that *domain of the human psyche having to do with the lived experience* of existential meaning and value, of wholeness and love, of creative agency, and of interconnection with other humans, nature, and reality at large. I interpret this formulation as being intentionally oriented toward a

---

1. For those interested, I refer them to my book where I present a sustained case (Brien 2006).

very wide spectrum of specific modes of the spiritual that could be elaborated on more concrete levels of analysis.

Furthermore, I hold that the specific modes of the spiritual at one end of such a spectrum would mostly be oriented toward "inner realms" that have little to do with everyday outward practice, while at the other end of the spectrum would be modes of the spiritual having the potential of fully suffusing everyday human practice in the world. In my view, the degree to which any specific mode of the spiritual would suffuse ordinary everyday practice in the world (or fail to do so, as the case may be) would depend entirely on the specific mode considered. It will come out in what follows that the mode of the spiritual I associate with Marx is one that can fully suffuse everyday human practice.

My discussion begins on quite an abstract level, where I explain Marx's distinction between "spiritual forces" and the "religious form" they so often assume. Moving to a less abstract level, I cite pasages where Marx uses phrases like "spiritual life" (*das geistege Leben*) that suggestively point toward his own positive notion of "the spiritual." Moving to a still less abstract level, I turn to a brief exploration of Feuerbach's view of religion, which influenced Marx so significantly. In this context I draw from Marx's "Theses on Feuerbach" to clarify the specific way Marx disagreed with Feuerbach's view of religious self-alienation. I argue that Marx interprets the alienation of "spiritual forces," that for him have their proper home within the secular basis, in terms of the *secular basis becoming alienated from itself*; and that he also points to the practical necessity of transforming the secular basis in a way that involves "spiritualizing" the secular basis itself. I next discuss the "opium of the people" passage where Marx speaks of religion as "people's illusory happiness" and holds that criticism of religion "has plucked the imaginary flowers from the chain ... [so that people] will throw it off and pluck the living flower" (1997, 250). Going to an even less abstract level, I give an exposition of what Marx likely means by "imaginary flowers" and the "living flower," arguing that these metaphors point toward Marx's own positive understanding of the spiritual.

Following this I argue that implicit in the "opium of the people" passage is Marx's recognition of an array of fundamental needs all people have, which I interpret as existential needs. On a still more concrete level, I specify the particular way in which each of these needs would be manifested in the specific mode of the spiritual at play in Marx's philosophical paradigm. However, I do not mean to imply the spiritual can be reduced to such needs, especially when seen abstractly. Rather, I construe Marx's positive notion of the spiritual in terms of the specific concrete form these needs should take as they suffuse associated modes of human practice and are dialectically shaped by such practice. Finally I argue that suffusing a revolutionary praxis with such a this-worldly mode of the spiritual would, on a wide-enough scale, have some real hope of transforming the secular basis in the direction of social justice and a more human future.

Before proceeding, however, a rationale for addressing the spiritual in connection with Marx is appropriate. Why is it important? What is the benefit? In my view, a pandemic crisis of the human person pervades much of planet earth: a crisis of the human spirit manifesting itself in so many diverse ways, a spiritual crisis! Not altogether a new crisis, though, for Nietzsche explored the existential breakdown of traditional Western modes of the spiritual (but without addressing the role of capitalism in generating this breakdown) and codified it in his projection of the "advent of nihilism." Unfortunately, the crisis of the human person has greatly intensified in many ways and spread very widely in the past hundred years, largely due to the ongoing impact of capitalist systems on peoples throughout the world. In the United States itself, the capitalist system has so warped the human psyche that a looming meaninglessness now hangs over much of the country. Yes, it is blunted and masked somewhat by the torrential gush of consumer goods and services that the system spews out to mollify the people—the contemporary opiate for many of the people. But the system also systematically generates increasing alienation as a very significant dimension of its gross national product. The notion of the spiritual that I associate with humanistic Marxism has the potential not only to address the intensifying crisis of the human person, but also to help in generating a revolutionary agency that could transfigure the system. So far as I am aware, this paper constitutes a creative breakthrough in thinking about the spiritual in relation to Marx.

The Spiritual in Marx

What meanings do the terms "religion" and "the spiritual" have for Marx? Do they have basically the same meaning, or is there a fundamental difference for him between his notion of religion and his notion of the spiritual? Here let me first refer to a section of *Capital* where Marx is talking about the historical necessity of material production developing through an alienated and antagonistic transitional phase in which the human subject is transformed into an object. In this connection he writes, "It is necessary [for material production] to go through this antagonistic form, just as it is necessary at first to give man's *spiritual forces* [*die geistigen Kräfte*] a religious form by erecting them into autonomous power over against him" (1977, 509; emphasis added). It seems quite clear that Marx is here making a distinction between the "spiritual forces" of human beings, on the one hand, and what he takes to be the alienated "religious form" that these forces can have when they involve the projection of an "independent realm in the clouds" from which they seem to stand over human beings as an alien and autonomous power. In using the phrase "religious form" in this way, Marx seems to be suggesting that religion itself, in the sense in which he means it, carries with it the connotation of an associated alienation of the spiritual forces of the human being and of the spiritual dimension itself. What positive view of the spiritual might Marx embrace, then, and what would constitute an unalienated expression of the spiritual forces for him?

To open some conceptual space, let me first say that there is no philosophically justifiable reason to rigidly limit the term "spiritual" to the relatively narrow ways it is often used in traditional Western settings—especially ways that see spirituality and the spiritual as necessarily involving beliefs in a creator god, a soul, and a supernatural world. I contend that the general term "spiritual" must be seen as orienting one to a very wide spectrum of specific modes of the spiritual that manifest "family resemblances" with one another, rather than some common quality or set of qualities that can be captured via an abstract universal or some Platonic-like essence

(Wittgenstein 1953, sec. 67). I mean a spectrum that includes not only theist and dualist modes, but also nontheist, nondualist, naturalist, animist, and even atheistic modes of the spiritual.

Considering the following passages, let us reflect upon what Marx himself might mean by "the spiritual" and whether he embraces some positive notion of the spiritual. Here, though, it is important to note a caveat concerning the term "spiritual" (whether in English translation or in the original German). The term itself does not really matter for a rose by any other name is still a rose. I take the term "spiritual" to abstractly connote a domain of the psyche having to do with certain sorts of lived experience, and I take the passages that follow as Marx's *pointers toward* his way of concretely elaborating the *particular mode of the spiritual* he embraces. So then, some of Marx's formulations.

> Man lives by nature. This means that nature is his body with which he must remain in perpetual process in order not to die. That the physical and *spiritual life* [*das geistige Leben*] of man is tied up with nature is another way of saying that nature is linked to itself, for man is a part of nature. (1997, 293; emphasis altered)

> [Alienated labor] alienates his *spiritual nature* [*sein geistiges Wesen*], his human essence, from his own body and likewise from nature outside him. (295; emphasis altered)

> For not only the five senses but also the so-called *spiritual* [*die geistigen Sinne*] and moral *senses* (will, love, etc.), in a word, human sense and the humanity of the senses come into being only through the existence of their object through nature humanized. (309; emphasis altered)

These passages make explicit references to "spiritual life," "spiritual nature," and "spiritual senses," and they do so without any implication for Marx that spirituality and religion are synonymous or that his use of the term "spiritual" in these contexts suggests anything like a creator god, a soul substance, or a supernatural world. Moreover, far from being a rejection of the spiritual, these passages seem to point to what Marx believes to be an unalienated expression of this very dimension. To develop this, let me next explore some of the views of Ludwig Feuerbach who had such a significant influence on Marx, especially concerning religion.

In *The Essence of Christianity*, Feuerbach argues that the notion of God is an external projection of man's inner nature, and that the humanly projected aspects of God correspond to human needs. According to his account of the origin of belief in a transcendent God, our early Judaeo-Christian forebears noticed in themselves certain qualities that they regarded as very special—qualities like reason, will, and love.

> What then *is* the nature of man, of which he is conscious, or what constitutes the specific distinction, the proper humanity of man? Reason, Will, Affection. To a complete man belong the power of thought, the power of will, the power of affection. The power of thought is the light of the intellect, the power of will is the energy of character, the power of affection is love … Reason, Will, Love, are not powers which man possesses, for he is

nothing without them, *he is what he is only by them;* they are the constituent elements of his nature. (Feuerbach 1957, 3; emphasis added)

As Feuerbach sees things, our early forebears abstracted these qualities in their imagination from their own situation and, after removing in thought the limitations such qualities had in their own case, they projected the notion of an all-knowing reason, an all-powerful will, and an infinite love. They then projected a metaphysical subject to which they attached these projected qualities, and the name they gave to the resulting complex made in their own image was "God." The various attributes of this "divine being" were all attributes of human beings, but with the human attributes "purified" and their limitations transcended. Other projected attributes included God "as a being of the understanding" and "as a moral being" (33–49). Moreover, for Feuerbach all these attributes corresponded to various needs in human nature. All this is the "true or anthropological essence of religion" for Feuerbach: "The divine being is nothing else than the human being, or rather, the human nature purified, freed from the limits of the individual man, made objective—i.e., contemplated and revered as another, a distinct being. All the attributes of the divine nature are, therefore, attributes of the human nature" (14).

Feuerbach also construes God as the alienated personification of the powers of human beings standing over them as an external threatening force: their own "rejected nature" now purified, objectified, hovering over them in a menacing way, calling for submission, and promising retribution if submission is not forthcoming. "As the action of the arteries drives the blood into the extremities, and the action of the veins brings it back again, as life in general consists in a perpetual systole and diastole; so it is in religion. In the religious systole man propels his own nature from himself, he throws it outward; in the religious diastole he receives the rejected nature into his heart again" (31). Feuerbach's remedy for this alienated situation goes something like this. Recognize that humans have created God in their own image; do away with the imaginary metaphysical subject that humans have projected; draw back into the human context the powers that they had attached to this metaphysical subject; recognize and embrace the limited nature of these powers in the human context; and then redefine "God" in reference to the context of human relations. Consider, for example, Feuerbach's attitude toward God and Love.

> Who then is our Saviour and Redeemer? God or Love? Love; for God as God has not saved us, but Love, which transcends the difference between the divine and human personality. As god has renounced himself out of love, so we, out of love, should renounce God; for if we do not sacrifice God to love, we sacrifice love to God, and in spite of the predicate of love, we have the God—the evil being—of religious fanaticism. (53)

For Feuerbach, God is not an ontologically real, transcendent being; rather, God is the love that is at play in human relations when these relations are really human. Moreover, for him the I-Thou relationship is confined exclusively to the human community so he redefines "God" as something like the unity of I and Thou, you flowing into me and me flowing back into you. Moreover, what is really special, sacred, and holy for him *is love itself*: not love as an abstract ideal, but love as a concrete reality. This is what is sabotaged when God is made into a transcendent, threatening force standing over humans. And this, for him, is the vital heart of Christianity, hence Feuerbach's paradoxical stance that atheism is the essence of Christianity.

Turning back to Marx, I draw from his famous "Theses on Feuerbach" for some of his critical stances on positions that Feuerbach adopted. Marx writes:

> Feuerbach starts out from the fact of religious self-alienation, the duplica-tion of the world into a religious and secular world. His work consists in resolving the religious world into its secular basis. But the fact that *the secular basis becomes separate from itself* and establishes an independent realm in the clouds *can only be explained by the cleavage and self-contradictoriness of the secular basis.* Thus *the latter* must itself be both understood in its contradiction and *revolutionized in practice.* (1997, 401; emphasis added)

Marx would fully agree with Feuerbach that religious self-alienation involves the duplication of the world into an otherworldly religious world and a this-worldly secular world. Presumably Marx also would agree that the humanly projected attributes of God are linked to human needs that find some kind of compensatory fulfillment in the belief in an imaginary divine being. But Marx does *not* agree with Feuerbach that alienation is *caused* by religious self-alienation. Rather, religious self-alienation for Marx is a symptom of concrete, historically conditioned circumstances in which human beings are enmeshed in very secular class conflicts that cause human beings to be alienated from one another.

Here let's look carefully at Marx's formulation from the above citation: "the secular basis becomes separate from itself and establishes an independent realm in the clouds." What is it *within* the secular basis that could possibly become separate from itself (i.e., the secular basis) and establish an independent realm in the clouds? There seems to me to be only one plausible answer to this question: namely, that the spiritual dimension of human being, as Marx understands this dimension, is in reality a dimension of the secular basis. However, this dimension undergoes an alienated orientation away from the secular basis, which is its ontologically real home, and toward an imagined otherworldly reality that is projected by the religious imagina-tion.

Remember that Marx sees the human being as a natural being. Thus, ontologically speaking, man *is* a secular being for Marx: a this-worldly being interacting with other human beings and with the nonhuman natural world. The alienated orientation of the spiritual dimension away from the secular basis presumably occurs when the secular basis is so riven with class, ethnic, and sectarian conflicts that it cannot fully manifest and express itself in an unalienated way *within* the secular basis and therefore retreats to an imaginary religious world. Well, then, if Marx can indeed embrace some notion of the spiritual, just how is the spiritual dimension to be construed within Marx's philosophical framework? What is its content? I begin by citing the famous passage where Marx writes:

> The struggle against religion is ... indirectly the struggle against that world whose spiritual aroma is religion. *Religious* suffering is the *expression* of real suffering and at the same time the *protest* against real suffering. Religion is

the sigh of the oppressed creature, the heart of a heartless world, as it is the spirit of spiritless conditions. It is the *opium* of the people. The abolition of religion as people's *illusory* happiness is the demand for their *real* happiness. The demand to abandon illusions about their condition is a *demand to abandon a condition which requires illusions* ... Criticism has plucked the imaginary flowers from the chain, not so that man will wear the chain that is without fantasy or consolation but so that he will throw it off and pluck the living flower. (1997, 250)

Why would Marx speak in such ways if he did not believe that human needs of some sort are at play in the human construction of religion? I suggest that at play in these striking formulations (and in many others) is an implicit recognition by Marx of an array of human needs that are, in his sense of the term, spiritual in character, and that call for fulfillment from the very depths of the human being.[2] Moreover, I suggest it is *spiritual* needs that are at play in the "spiritual forces" that assume a "religious form" in historical conditions of a sort that prevent the full, many-sided, unalienated expression of human powers. Marx is critical of religion because, in his view, what usually counts as religion constitutes merely a compensatory "fantastic realization" of spiritual needs that, while giving people some kind of consolation in the context of oppressive social conditions, also functions like blinders that prevent people from recognizing the real possibility of the unalienated fulfillment of these needs in concrete social life.

Next let's consider Marx's formulation that criticism "has plucked the imaginary flowers from the chain, not so that man will wear the chain that is without fantasy or consolation but so that he will throw it off and pluck the living flower." What are the imaginary flowers Marx has in mind here, and what is the living flower?

Above we saw Feuerbach argue that God is "human nature purified, freed from the limits of the individual man, made objective—i.e., contemplated and revered as another, a distinct being." In Feuerbach's view, our early human forebears, faced with all the terrors of existence and aware of such terrors once full self-consciousness had developed, projected a divine being with unlimited Reason, Will, and Love, a divine being on whom they could depend in the face of the trials and tribulations of life and in whom they could find comfort and consolation. What did belief in such a divine being, with all its other associated attributes (a moral being, etc.) and its assorted metaphysical attachments (substantial soul, afterlife, divine justice, etc.), provide to human beings? Among other things it provided an orienting belief system: an orienting perspective within which humans could view themselves and try to understand themselves in relation to nature, to other human beings, and to the Divine Being of religious belief, and it provided them some kind of value orientation as well, some kind of "moral" guidance.

Furthermore, however fragile human existence might be, such a belief system provided a divine ground on which these special attributes of humankind, now "purified," would stand forever secure against the ravages of time, beasts, and other humans. If one's particular historical circumstances were cruel, unjust, and lacking in

2. Many formulations with similar import are concentrated in Marx's early writings (see especially Marx 1997, 265–336).

any genuine community, any I-Thou feeling, one could nonetheless be sure of God's love and of having community and interconnection with God. One could also be sure that God would in the long run mete out divine justice to all human beings who ever lived so that everyone got their just deserts. Furthermore, if one's individual historical and social conditions allowed one no, or very little, opportunity for manifesting creative agency, one could nonetheless be sure that the urge to free agency would be forever sanctified via God's all-powerful creative will sustaining all of creation in existence without let or hindrance.

If these are some of the "imaginary flowers" to which Marx most likely made implicit reference, what did he mean by the phrase that the criticism of religion would prepare the soil so that one could "pluck the living flower"? What is the living flower that Marx means here? I believe that the "living flower" Marx had first and foremost in mind is what he calls "free conscious activity," which he takes to be "the species character of human beings" (1997, 294). Importantly, such activity must be construed not simply as "inner consciousness," but rather, as the dialectical interface between consciousness and human practice.

There are many formulations throughout Marx's work that point toward the same "living flower." Consider these, for example.

> [Free activity is] the creative manifestation of life arising from the free development of all abilities, of the 'whole fellow'. (Marx and Engels 1968, 246)

> [Socialism is] a higher form of society, a society in which the full and free development of every individual forms the ruling principle. (Marx 1967, 2:592)

> Free individuality . . . is founded on the universal development of individuals. (1972, 67)

> The rich man [in a socialist context] is simultaneously one who *needs* a totality of human manifestations of life and in whom his own realization exists as inner necessity, as *need*. (1997, 312)

If "free conscious activity" is the primary "living flower" Marx had in mind when he spoke of plucking the living flower, what, then, about other, associated "living flowers"—or perhaps various aspects of the primary living flower? Let me point to what I believe are perhaps the most significant of these other living flowers: (*a*) genuine community with other people, as opposed to various sorts of segmental relations to others—what Marx called "the illusory community in which individuals have come together up till now" (1997, 457); (*b*) the felt need to be related to other human beings as a human being; (*c*) a many-sided, all-round development of one's potentials; (*d*) experiencing the development of one's energies as an end in itself; (*e*) the experience of joy and spontaneity in one's practice; and (*f*) an experience of wholeness. The brief excerpts from Marx's text that follow are but a few sample formulations of Marx's thoughts along these lines, taken from a pool of countless companion formulations one might cull from Marx's writings. (Allow me to continue with the flower metaphor.) If one takes the above factors (*a*) through (*f*) as symbolizing the stems of flowers, and then takes the citations from Marx below as symbolizing the blossoms of these flowers, one might then take the whole flowers from stem to blossom as symbolizing Marx's notion of a *humanized and spiritualized secularism*.

> Only in community do the means exist for every individual to cultivate his talents in all directions. Only in the community is personal freedom possible. (1997, 457)

> In this relationship [of man to woman] is also apparent the extent to which man's *need* has become *human*, thus the extent to which the *other* human being, as human being, has become a need for him, the extent to which he in his most individual existence is at the same time a social being. (303)

> Man appropriates to himself his manifold essence in an all-sided way, thus as a whole man. Every one of his *human* relations to the world—seeing, hearing, smelling, tasting, feeling, thinking, perceiving, sensing, wishing, acting, loving—in short all the organs of his individuality ... are an appropriation of the object in their *objective* relation or their *relation* to it. (307)

> Beyond it [the realm of necessity] begins that development of human energy which is an end in itself, the true realm of freedom, which, however, can blossom forth only with the realm of necessity as its basis. (1967, 3:820)

Now that I have given some sense of what I consider Marx to mean by "imaginary flowers" and "living flower," I want to suggest that these metaphors point toward Marx's recommended way of addressing *fundamental spiritual needs* that all humans have, and I wish to refer to such needs as *existential needs*. The existential needs I have in mind include the following: the need for some kind of orienting world-view, the need for some kind of value perspective to guide one's actions, the need for existential meaning, the need for interconnection with nature, the need for community with others, the need for creative expression of potentials, and the need for wholeness.

But why call these existential needs? Why not just psychological needs? I respond that such needs are a special class of psychic needs associated with the peculiar existential situation of human beings that is, in turn, based on the particular kind of biological organisms humans happen to be. Humans are the sort of biological organisms whose distinctively human physical and mental practices are *not* narrowly programmed by determinate instincts. Rather, humans have reflective self-con-sciousness and the underlying biological potential for "making themselves" in an enormously vast spectrum of different ways of being human, all associated with different modes of the spiritual, depending on the concrete historical conditions which obtain in a given situation at a given time. This means that the *spiritual dimension is itself historically variable* in some important ways (see Brien 1996, 222–59).

But, then, how to understand *the particular form of the spiritual*, the particular manifestation of the spiritual forces, that humanistic Marxism would associate with the sort of revolutionary practice that would have some real possibility of revolutionizing the secular basis, and of cultivating a cultural transition in the direction of a genuine, humanistic socialism? Inasmuch as I view the spiritual as the domain of the psyche having to do with the *lived experience* of the various existential needs indicated above, I go on now to present a sketch of some of the *main contours of a humanistic-Marxist spiritual mode* in accordance with Marx's own recommended way of addressing the various existential needs he distinguished. It will be seen that this mode of the spiritual has the potential of *fully suffusing everyday human practice in the world* for this mode of the spiritual cannot be reduced to "inner consciousness," but must be interpreted as the dialectical interface between human activity and consciousness. I now turn to a sketch of the specific ways of addressing the various existential needs that, in Marx's view, would not be alienated. I ask my readers to bear in mind, though, that since such needs are not discrete atomic needs, there will necessarily be some overlaps in the vignettes that follow.

The existential needs for some kind of *orienting world-view* and for *inter-connection with nature* would be expressed in a humanistic-Marxist spiritual mode via an experiential recognition that the human being is a being of nature interacting with other human beings and with nature, "not an abstract being squatting outside the world" (Marx 1997, 250) but essentially a natural being immersed in the world. By acting in and upon the natural and social environments in specific ways, human beings make themselves in specific ways and constitute their powers as real objective powers. Thus, there are ontological bonds among human subjects as well as between them and the natural world. Moreover, naturally given resources are shaped by human beings into a vast multiplicity of objects, which become thereby the repositories of human powers and energies. In the spiritual mode under discussion, all these ontological interconnections would be experienced in ways that are life affirming rather than life negating. Thus, individuals interrelating with one another via the mediation of objects would be *respectful of them as embodiments of the energies of social individuals* (see Marx 1967, 1:41–6; 1997, 325–7), and would reciprocally affirm each other as they interrelate (see Marx 1997, 281).

For Marx, the existential need for *community with others* would be manifest in an active interrelation between people such that there is an experiential recognition of human individuals as social individuals—both the recognition that individuals become the particular kind of social individuals they are by virtue of the particular ways they interact with each other and the recognition that the most positive development of human individuals is dynamically bound up with the most positive development of their social relationships (see Marx 1997, 457). Such a manifestation of the need for community does not see the connection with others as a hindrance to individual development, but rather, as a pathway toward full human development. It is a need for reciprocal, many-sided, life-affirming relations on the part of individuals with many-sided, life-affirming counterparts in order that everyone may become fully human.

In a humanistic-Marxist practice, the existential need for *creative expression of potentials* would be manifested in a many-sided, freely flowing, creative unfolding of individual powers. This, of course, is not to be understood as anything like the typical egotism of Western culture for it is qualified by the practical recognition of oneself and others as social individuals and by the recognition that the freedom of each is bound up with the freedom of all. Thus the many-sided, creative unfolding of individual powers is an unfolding that does not seek to dominate the other, but does not let itself be dominated by the other, either. Nor is Marx's affirmation of individual powers to be understood as an affirmation of the kind of possessive individualism that has been so dominant for so long—with all its emphasis on having and on possessing (money, things, property, etc.). Marx's concern is not with having much, but with being much (see Marx 1997, 307–9).

The existential need for meaning would be addressed by adopting modes of activity that are experienced as meaningful rather than as an onerous means to some end that is to be realized by the activity—that is, some wished-for goal that lies outside the activity itself. Such activity is experienced as an end in itself, even if it may also be activity that is a means to something in fact (see Marx 1997, 294–5). Thus it is experienced as intrinsically meaningful, as spontaneously creative, and as joyful. As Marx puts it, such activity is "a free manifestation of life and an enjoyment of life" (281). The need for meaning is also manifested and concretely expressed in direct personal relations when people relate to each other as whole human beings and treat each other as ends. Marx highlights the existential importance of such meaningful relations among people when he writes, "Not only the wealth but also the poverty of man equally acquire—under the premise of socialism—a human and thus social meaning. It is the passive bond which lets man experience the greatest wealth, the other human being, as need" (312).

Some of the ways a humanistic-Marxist spiritual awareness would address the existential *need for wholeness* have already been suggested in the remarks above concerning the need for a totality of human manifestations of life and a many-sided, all-round development. But it would also be manifested in the need for a transformation of the various dimensions of the human psyche—cognition, conation, sensuousness, intuition, sensation—as they obtain in alienated modes of consciousness, and their subsequent harmonious integration in more holistic modes (308–10). It also includes the need to experientially integrate the spiritual with nature in a holistic way, and to overcome the alienated separation of the spiritual dimension from the body that has been characteristic of much of the Western cultural tradition (295).

The existential need for some kind of *value perspective* would be manifested in a humanistic-Marxist practice that is committed to freely and fully developing one's potential. This connotes an active freedom that involves a need for a many-sided creative activity that constitutes a totality of human manifestations of life, including, of course, the need to be related to the other as a whole human being in concrete practice. In such activity one treats others, and oneself also, as whole human beings, a practice that involves the recognition that the fully developed freedom of each is tied up with the fully developed freedom of all. A corollary of this is "*the categorical imperative to overthrow all conditions* in which man is a degraded, enslaved, contemptible, [exploited, dehumanized] being" (257–8). Thus, it is the sort of activity that does not imply or involve the denial or repression of the other as it affirms itself.

Conclusion

Following this sketch, I now address apprehensions that might be felt by those who are uncomfortable with the term "spiritual" in connection with Marx. Earlier I mentioned the strong association the term "spiritual" has with theistic religion in Western cultures, but I brought out that there is not an exclusive association of the term "spiritual" with theism and that Marx used the term "spiritual" many times in his earlier writings in very positive ways, with no connotation of any otherworldly reality. It is true that Marx used the term "spiritual" much less often in his later writings than he did earlier, but I suggest that Marx had reasons for this that for him were compelling. Here I have in mind positions that Marx and Engels vehemently criticized in *The German Ideology*, which used the term "spirit" and "spiritual" with Hegelian connotations from which Marx and Engels wanted to dissociate themselves (Marx and Engels 1968, 157–74). I contend, however, that Marx never dropped the *concept* of the spiritual at play in his early writings, even though he used the term "spiritual" [*geistige*] much less frequently.

Let me also mention another consideration that might make it easier to embrace the secularized form of the spiritual I have outlined above in association with Marx. In view of the strong association of the term "spiritual" with theistic religions in Western cultures and a consequent reluctance to associate the term "spiritual" with *atheism*, it might be well to take the following cue from Marx, when he says that "atheism no longer makes sense."

> *Atheism* as the denial of this unreality [an alien divine being beyond man and nature] no longer makes sense because it is a *negation of God* and through this negation asserts the *existence of man*. But socialism as such no longer needs such mediation. It begins with the *sensuous perception, theoretically and practically*, of man and nature as *essential beings*. It is man's *positive self-consciousness*, no longer attained through the overcoming of religion. (1997, 314)

I believe it is culturally important for our time not only to go beyond traditional interpretations of theism, and also beyond atheism, but even beyond secular humanism as it is commonly understood and to adopt what might be called a *spiritualized and humanized secularism* for which the question of atheism no longer arises in an existential way. The solution to the problem that "the secular basis becomes separate from itself and establishes an independent realm in the clouds" is, for Marx, not a complete suppression of the spiritual (Marx 1997, 401), but rather, a revolutionary practice that successfully transforms the secular basis so that the spiritual dimension can be fulfilled in a this-worldly way that does not require recourse to an imaginary being.

Let us remember that, in Marx's view, one of the most essential practical prerequisites for a successful transition to genuine socialism is "the formation of a revolutionary mass ... a mass which revolts not only against particular conditions of the prevailing society but against the prevailing 'production of life' itself, the 'total activity' on which it was based" (432). But such a revolutionary mass doesn't drop out of the sky like a *deus ex machina*. Rather, it comes to be on the basis of a new practice—*a new praxis* guided by right understanding of the real possibilities of a humanistic socialism, and committed to right effort to cultivate a transition to such a socialism. As Marx says, it is necessary "to expose the old world to full daylight and to shape the new along positive lines" (211). In order for this to happen, it is necessary for theory to grip the masses: "The weapon of criticism obviously cannot replace the criticism of weapons. Material force must be overthrown by material force. But theory also becomes a material force once it has gripped the masses. Theory is capable of gripping the masses when it demonstrates *ad hominem, and it demonstrates ad hominem* when it becomes radical. To be radical is to grasp things by the root" (257).

I suggest that, for Marx, the *root of the spiritual* is not to be found in some otherworldly reality. Rather, it is to be found in this world. Our era is one of those momentous historical junctures during which the shifting tectonic plates of world history can induce enormous and unpredictable changes. To emerge from this historical juncture without degenerating into something like international fascism, I believe it is practically imperative for the peoples of our era *to embrace* the spiritual anew and *reclaim* it from the clutches of authoritarian, dogmatic, and fanatic fundamentalist theists, and most especially from extremist and violent religious fundamentalists—whether Christian, Hindu, Muslim, Jewish, or whatever.

Our era represents the time to radically transform the secular basis. Moreover, I believe a growing understanding of how humanistic Marxism can accommodate the spiritual dimension could go a long way toward nurturing such a development, especially in the case of that vast number of people for whom traditional modes of the spiritual are not viable. Our era is the time to suffuse a revolutionary praxis with a this-worldly mode of the spiritual that has some real hope of transforming the secular basis in the direction of social justice as all of humanity faces the daunting crises that loom throughout planet earth. Our era is the time to *humanize the spiritual, and to spiritualize the secular.* Our era is the time for the peoples of the world to unite! Let the living flowers bloom!

Acknowledgments

I want to gratefully acknowledge Jacinda Swanson and Cecilia Rio for their very helpful criticisms of earlier drafts of this paper.

References

Brien, K. M. 1996. Marx and the spiritual dimension. *Topoi: An International Review of Philosophy* 15: 211–23.

———. 2006. *Marx, reason, and the art of freedom.* 2d ed. Amherst, N.Y.: Humanity Books.

———. 2007. Marx's dialectical-empirical method of explanation. *Utopía y Praxis Latinoamericana* 39: 9–32.

Feuerbach, L. 1957. *The essence of Christianity.* Trans. G. Eliot. New York: Harper and Brothers.

Marx, K. 1967. *Capital*. 3 vols. Ed. F. Engels. New York: International Publishers.
———. 1972. *The Grundrisse*. Trans. and ed. D. McLellan. New York: Harper and Row.
———. 1973. *Grundrisse*. Trans. M. Nicolaus. Middlesex: Penguin.
———. 1977. *Karl Marx: Selected writings*. Ed. D. McLellan. New York: Oxford University Press.
———. 1997. *Writings of the young Marx on philosophy and society*. Trans. and ed. L. Easton and K. Guddat. Indianapolis: Hackett.
Marx, K., and F. Engels. 1968. *The German ideology*. Trans. and ed. S. Ryazanskaya. Moscow: Progress.
Wittgenstein, L. 1953. *Philosophical investigations*. Trans. G. E. M. Anscombe. New York: Macmillan.

Spirituality Beyond Man: Toward a Labor Theory of the Soul

Oxana Timofeeva

This essay analyzes Marx's materialist understanding of spirituality within the context of the Marxian conception of the essence of the human developed in the Economic and Philosophic Manuscripts of 1884. *The relevance of this work is demonstrated through references to Hegel and classical Marxists, such as Georg Lukács or Evald Ilyenkov, and also to recent discussions in contemporary philosophy on the problems of labor, the unconscious, artificial intelligence, and depression. The essence of the human is identified with the soul as understood by Andrei Platonov, as a kind of secret human being inside the body of any species and thus detached from* Homo sapiens, *or "man" in its traditional sense. This allows us to disengage the human from both essentialism and anthropocentrism. Instead, this impersonal essence is defined by an ambiguous concept of labor that supposes both alienation and emancipation.*

We are the miners of your heart.
We dig the ore of your soul
And bring to the surface
From out of your depths
Your songs, Tanya.

—Chto Delat, *A Border Musical*

At first sight, the spiritual dimension of Marx's thought is not so obvious: spirituality might seem to be incompatible with his strong materialist stance. However, if we get them right, materialism and spirituality do not create a contradiction. Instead, they must be taken together: without spirituality, materialism remains vulgar, and without materialism, spirituality is held hostage by religion, esotericism, spiritism, and other kinds of "opium of the people."

The very idea of an incompatibility of spirituality and materialism in Marx is the result of a general misunderstanding. On one hand, as noted by Erich Fromm (1961), Marx's materialism is often reduced to the earthbound attitude that sees the general motive of humans' activity in a "wish for monetary gain and comfort" and "striving for maximum profit." In his book *Marx's Concept of Man*,

Fromm refutes "a widespread assumption that Marx neglected the importance of the individual; that he had neither respect nor understanding for the spiritual needs of man, and that his 'ideal' was the well-fed and wellclad [sic], but 'soulless' person." On the other hand, an inevitable confusion is inserted by a stereotyped equation between the spiritual and the religious, due to which Marx's criticism of religion is read as a denial of all spiritual values.

Since 1961, when Fromm criticized these misconceptions or "falsifications" of Marx's thought coming from the humanist perspective, materialism has gained much more respect in widespread opinion. Most of today's intellectuals would likely claim themselves materialists, whatever such a qualification would imply. Contemporary philosophy develops a whole range of materialist theories and doctrines to fit every taste—new materialisms: agential, transcendental, dialectical, and so on. Materialism is no longer a foul term for a lack of spiritual values but is both an ontology and an epistemology that accounts for differences, for alterity, and for the heterogeneous materiality of the world while opposing itself to the old metaphysics that treated matter as secondary and subordinate to the spiritual or ideal. Incidentally, this materialist trend began with Marxism: although today's new materialisms generally strive for the nonhuman, it was Marx who, already in 1845, in his *Theses on Feuerbach*, used the term "new materialism" to designate an orientation toward "a human society, or social humanity."

Spirituality, however, still resists being immediately grasped in Marxist terms. As far as spirituality is associated with idealism and religious worldviews, it seems to be alien to the historical- and dialectical-materialist tradition in which "the criticism of Heaven turns into the criticism of Earth" (Marx 1970). Focused on the critique of political economy, material relationships, and concrete social structures, Marxism seems to leave any spiritual dimension beyond its scope. However, if we restrict ourselves to superficial opinions of this kind, we miss the very core of Marx's project: that is, its orientation toward not interpreting but changing the world according to a universal demand for a new, better society.

As Fromm (1961) puts it: "Marx's aim was that of the spiritual emancipation of man, of his liberation from the chains of economic determination, of restituting him in his human wholeness, of enabling him to find unity and harmony with his fellow man and with nature." Today, along the lines of the growing radical critique of humanism and anthropocentrism, Fromm's claim might sound a bit problematic, first of all because of his use of the term "man" where one could say "woman," "animal," "plant," "robot," or anything else. It is as if he, the man, was already a thing of the past: his claim's relevance is dubious. Yet, as I will argue, a spiritual emancipation is still at stake, as spirit goes beyond man. In order to clarify this point and develop a materialist account of Marx's spirituality, I will begin by taking a closer look at its genesis in Hegel's thought, and then, through an analysis of the spiritual dimension of the working activity of human beings, I will come to the outline of a labor theory of the soul.

The Genesis of the Spiritual: The Thing Itself

In the first place, the spiritual must be released from all of its commonplace, otherworldly, and obscure connotations. Spirit is not something ephemeral. At least, not in Hegel's philosophy, which is constitutive for Marx (2015), who after a serious criticism of Hegel avowed himself "the pupil of that mighty thinker" and performed a dialectical negation of his theory, turning it right side up by its head. We have to keep in mind that spirituality in Marx is an heir of the Hegelian dialectics of spirit, and spirit in Hegel is neither transcendent nor divine: it emerges through human activities and unfolds in the historical process.

Hegel's *Phenomenology of Spirit* narrates the unfolding of the spirit as an experience of consciousness that comprises six steps, or levels: consciousness (chap. 1–3), self-consciousness (chap. 4), reason (chap. 5), spirit (chap. 6), religion (chap. 7), and absolute knowing (chap. 8). I prefer to call them levels, as in a computer game where each new level repeats the preceding one but with increasing complexity so that the repeating levels are never the same. Spirit is discussed in chapter 6 within the dialectics of the ethical order, culture, and politics. However, the realm of spirit is actually opened up earlier, in chapter 5, titled "Reason," where consciousness experiences itself as individuality and reaches the limits of this experience. The spirit is not individual; it starts where individuality is sublated.

The emergence of spirit in Hegel's *Phenomenology* deserves to be considered at greater length. First, in chapter 5, while trying to figure out where spirit comes from and searching for the origin of thought in the material reality that spirit thinks is external to it, consciousness in the shape of reason comes to an infinite judgment: "The being of spirit is a bone" (Hegel 2018, 201). Hegel refers to phrenology, which seeks the explanation of spiritual phenomena in the formation of a skull bone. Just as cognitive scientists today explain all emotional and intellectual activity through the movement of brain neurons, phrenologists of Hegel's time believed that thought literally *emerged* from the head. From Hegel's perspective, they were right inasmuch as they represented a certain formation of consciousness: this judgment, in which spirit as the origin of thought appears as a material object (a bone), was the truth for the so-called observing reason, or positive science. The reason looks for itself outside of itself, in the nonhuman and in human nature, and ultimately finds itself in the other-than-itself—that is, in objective material reality. If the spirit *is*, it is some*thing*: it is observed by reason as a thing (*ein Ding*) but presents at the same time its essence. At this stage, consciousness splits into two: into the observing and the observed, the life of thought and the deadness of the bone. Spirit emerges from this split, from reification or, better said, from the ossification of reason, the dialectical redoubling of consciousness.

"The being of spirit is a bone" is not only the truth but also the deadlock of reason, which must be overcome in the next step, when reason ceases to observe reality and plunges itself into active life. The deadlock of observation is sublated when we switch from theory to practice. However, there is already

another impasse just around the corner: the *passage-à-l'acte* of rational self-consciousness results in desperate and disappointing attempts of individuality to establish itself in the world from which it feels separated. It wants to enjoy but
only finds death beyond the pleasure principle; it wants to act freely according
to the law of the heart but feels limited by the rules of society; it wants to
change the order of things according to its idea of the good, but the way of the
world always prevails over virtue. What is wrong with this consciousness is that
it thinks it stays outside and against the world without acknowledging its place
within the world. In other words, individuality does not understand its social
predicament.

The pivotal point is the next section of chapter 5, entitled "The Spiritual
Kingdom of Animals and Deception; or, the Crux of the Matter" (Das geistige Tier-
reich und der Betrug oder die Sache selbst). Here, Hegel shows that what individuality *does* is not only its act but also its work, a thing that is produced (*die Sache*).
Consciousness in the form of individuality can only express and actualize itself
through its work. It might have an idea, an image of a thing in mind, but it still
has to make the idea real using necessary materials and tools. The work is the
truth of individuality and is at the same time external to it. I am not an author if
I only have an idea of a book, but when I write and publish it, the book leaves
me and begins to live a life of its own that I cannot control. My individuality is
in it: it *is* what *it* does, and it is so not only for me but also for others. This "perme-
ation of individuality and objectivity which has objectively come to be" (Hegel 2018,
236) is the crux of the matter, or the thing itself (*die Sache selbst*).

What really matters is not the work I produced but the way it exists among
others and for others. It acquires a social existence in which it is never alone.
There are always already other things that are better or worse, that are compared
to each other and contested by others. The objective truth of a subjective action
thus belongs to the intersubjective domain of circulation and exchange. This is
where spirit appears not as a bone—that is, as a particular, natural thing (*ein
Ding*)—but as a social thing (*die Sache*) that becomes universal. By the end of
this section of chapter 5, Hegel (2018, 241) gives the following definition of the
thing itself: "Rather, it is an essence whose *being* is the *doing* of *singular* individuals
and of all individuals, and whose doing is immediately *for others*, or it is a *fact* and is
only a fact insofar as it is the *doing* of *each* and *all*, the essence that is the essence of
all essence, that is *spiritual essence*."

What happens here is no less than the birth of spirit. With Hegel, we find that
the spiritual originates in social practice, in sublating individuality through the
processes of labor. The work mediates between the individual and the social, or
spiritual, in its initial, simple "animal" form. Here it should be noted that, except
for the title, animals are not mentioned in this significant chapter. Why is it
then called "The Spiritual Kingdom of Animals"? With what connection is animality here? At least two very brief explanations can be found in Marx. In his essay
"Debates on the Law on Thefts of Wood," written in 1842, he speaks about

feudalism as the spiritual animal kingdom divided into castes or classes as if by different species; within a single species there can be justice and equality, but not between them: "One species feeds at the expense of another" (Marx 1996). Much later, in one of his letters to Engels, Marx (1962) refers to Darwin and uses the Hegelian metaphor of the spiritual animal kingdom in relation to the civil society: "It is Hobbes's *bellum omnium contra omnes*, and one is reminded of Hegel's *Phenomenology*, where civil society is described as a 'spiritual animal kingdom,' while in Darwin the animal kingdom figures as civil society" (McLellan 2000, 565).

The civil society depicted by Hegel in *Phenomenology* is an animal kingdom because it is a society of individuals, regardless of the species. An individual is an individual everywhere—among humans or other mammals or birds, bees, jellyfish, and so on. What differs for both Hegel and Marx—the spiritual animal kingdom from the natural animal kingdom—is the thing itself, sociality constituted by labor. Those who work nevertheless remain individuals for themselves; their consciousness is restricted by their private interests, and they neither control nor understand the crux of the matter. Therefore, they necessarily deceive each other even if they try to be honest (in fact, one cannot stay honest in the spiritual animal kingdom). Notwithstanding, the whole thing works well. Individuals think that they pursue their own interests, but what really benefits from their mutual deception is the thing itself. Applying Hegel's description to contemporary capitalist society ruled by the market, Slavoj Žižek (2012) comments: "The properly dialectical tension emerges here when we become aware that, the more individuals act egotistically, the more they contribute to the common wealth. The paradox is that when individuals want to sacrifice their narrow private interests and directly work for the common good, the one which suffers is the common good itself." It is precisely from the chaos of private interests that the public doing of each and all, or spiritual essence, emerges.

Furthermore, not only is the spirit born from the blind interactions of private individuals—or as Alain Badiou calls them, human animals—but these very individuals with their interests are produced by configurations of spirit. Žižek (2012) writes, "This fact in no way entails that ridiculous conclusion that we are somehow 'regressing' to the animal level: the animality with which we are dealing here—the ruthless egotism of each of the individuals pursuing his/her private interest—is the paradoxical result of the most complex network of social relations (market exchange, social mediation of production)." It appears that the animality of individuals within the market system is not as natural as it might seem. Behind their animality is a complex network to which individuals remain blinded. This network results from an abstraction and constitutes an ideal, spiritual substance: "In the civil society structured by market, abstraction rules more than ever in the history of humanity. In contrast to nature, the market competition of 'wolves against wolves' is thus the material reality of its opposite, of the 'spiritual' public substance which provides the background and base for this struggle among private animals."

From Hegel to Marx: Alienation and Abstraction

There is a dialectics between the animal (individual) and the spiritual: they present two sides of the same process, in which they reflect and define each other. In multiple interactions of individuals, the spirit is actualized and materialized, which means that it becomes its opposite, becomes matter. This moment is crucial for Georg Lukács: in contrast to such interpreters as Alexander Kojève, who focuses on the more popular chapter 4, dedicated to the dialectics of master and slave, Lukács emphasizes chapter 5, "Reason." In the description of the spiritual animal kingdom, or, as he puts it simply, capitalist society, Lukács sees the turning point not only of Hegel's book but of modernity in general. Translating Hegel into the language of Marxism in his essay on the structure of *Phenomenology*, Lukács (1975, 333) explains that "the world of economics which dominates man and which utterly controls the life of the individual, is nevertheless the product of man himself." In the passage on the spiritual kingdom of animals, subjective spirit becomes objective: through the externalization of spirit, an individual consciousness integrates within objective social reality. Of all Hegelian concepts, externalization, or alienation, is for Lukács the most important as it constitutes the very essence of capitalism.

The one who starts reading Hegel from *Phenomenology* would perhaps not recognize him in Lukács's strong adaptation. In *Phenomenology* Hegel does not use words like capitalism, bourgeois society, market, money, value, commodity, and so on, and he is writing about the work and the thing itself, so that a naïve reader can conclude that at stake is the work of art or something else. What gives Lukács grounds for translating, for instance, the relation of individuals to the thing itself as commodity fetishism is a good knowledge of Hegel's earliest works, from the Jena period. If we open *Jenaer Realphilosophie*, we will find there not only all the categories of political economy but also a kind of outline of the critique of the capitalist system.

In his Jena lectures of 1803–4, Hegel portrayed what would shortly receive the name of the spiritual kingdom of animals but did so in terms of labor and money. He explained that single laborers work for their own needs, but at the same time this labor contributes to the universal and ideal domain of public life. The thing the laborer produces is not the thing that the laborer really needs and not the one the laborer actually uses. Instead of immediately satisfying these needs, the work gives the laborer a formal possibility of such satisfaction. This is how Hegel (1979, 247) introduces the idea of exchange: "Between the range of needs of the single [agent], and his activity on their account, there enters the labor of the whole people, and the labor of any one is in respect of *its contents, a universal labor for the needs of all*, so as to be *appropriate for the satisfaction of all of his needs*; in other words it has a value; his labor, and his possessions, are not [just] what they are for him, but what they are for everyone; the satisfaction of needs is a universal dependence of everyone upon one another." In this formulation we now indeed recognize "the doing of each and all," which in chapter 5 of *Phenomenology* would be called spiritual substance, and we see that Lukács is right that at stake is actually the idea of abstract labor, better known in its later Marxian materialist version: abstract, formal, universal, but above all estranged labor, the product of which does not belong to the laborer but contributes to the universal value, which "itself, as a thing, is *money*" (Hegel 1983, 122).

Interestingly enough, in these early lectures, Hegel (1979, 249) compares a civil society ruled by money to the living dead: "Need and labor, elevated into this universality, then form of their own account a monstrous system of community and mutual interdependence in a great people; a life of the dead body, that moves itself within itself, one which ebbs and flows in its motion blindly, like the elements, and which requires continual strict dominance and taming like a wild beast." Why is this system of mutual interdependence called a life of the dead body? Because through the process of the production of value out of labor power, the living self is externalized, or reified, in the objective money-commodity complex. In exchange, the estranged self of laborers return to them as money. Hegel (1983, 123) explains: "(a) In laboring, I make myself immediately into the thing, a form which is *Being*. (b) At the same time, I externalize this existence of mine, making it something alien to myself, and preserve myself therein." Moreover, I am not the only one who thus preserves myself in the products of self-alteration; there is an entire system of the alienated thinghood of individualities, the objective spirit that now appears not as a bone but as money (money makes up the "bones" of the economic body). This comparison cannot but evoke a famous Marxian figure of the living dead: "Capital is dead labor, that, vampire-like, only lives by sucking living labor, and lives the more, the more labor it sucks" (Marx 2015).

A monstrous body that is created by individuals and at the same time constitutes them through setting the parameters of their needs is a system of alienation. However, in Hegel's dialectics, there is nothing "bad" about it: alienation is just that necessary negation of the individual through which the spirit as sociality has to come to itself. As noted by Jamila Mascat (2018) in her essay dedicated to the concept of abstraction in Hegel's philosophy:

> Individual *alienation* that stems from the mechanisms of abstract socialization underlying the economic, the juridical as well as the political spheres does not represent in Hegel's view a loss to recover. On the contrary, already in the Jena lectures, Hegel remarks that 'this alienation [i.e., the alienation of individuals' self-dependence into the magma of abstract sociality] is an acquiring (*Erwerben*),' inasmuch as it constitutes a peculiar form of *Bildung*, a deprivation that nevertheless guarantees a gain, which is precisely the surplus value of universal socialization.

A nonalienated existence of the individual is only an abstract universal, which is almost nothing, a pure statement. It still has to be activated in the experience, where it becomes its opposite: an abstract self becomes a concrete thing (reification). The thing in turn becomes money, and now we have another kind of abstraction—one that later, in Marxism, would be called real abstraction (Sohn-Rethel 1977). There are thus two abstractions: one is as yet not real, which is the abstraction of the individual self, and another is real, or social, which results in alienation. Replying to Roberto Finelli—in whose opinion only the late Marx "managed through his labour theory of value to accomplish the process that Hegel could not bring to completion; namely, transforming logical abstraction into an abstraction that is 'true in practice' and behaves as the 'highest factor of reality and universalisation' in modern society"—Mascat (2018) claims that "actually Hegel already fulfilled this task," but with a reservation: "Although manifestly Hegel is no Marx and *has no Capital*, i.e. he doesn't elaborate a critique of political economy." I find this claim, strengthened by its reference to the early Hegel, entirely convincing: yes, the true abstraction emerges already in Hegel, but no, he is not Marx and has no *Capital*.

Why does Hegel not have a *Capital*? Because of the limitations imposed on his method by idealism, with its primacy of spirit. Thus, in *Phenomenology* he discusses the spiritual animal kingdom not as a social formation but as a specific form of consciousness. One might say that, for Hegel himself, idealism is a form of fidelity to truth, fidelity to the notion: it is reality that has to come to the notion, and not the other way around. The shift between Hegel and Marx is precisely the shift within dialectics between idealism and materialism. However, I do not think that Hegel would be unhappy to learn that, in some two hundred years, someone like Žižek would call him a materialist. This can be understood pretty much as a dialectical twist, comparable in a sense to the gesture of Evald Ilyenkov, who tends to portray Marx almost as an idealist—but in an unusual sense, which he develops through an analysis that reconstructs the concept of the ideal in Marx. Indeed, Ilyenkov does not really call Marx an idealist—in the Soviet philosophy, idealism meant something totally outdated, reactionary—but he makes a considerable though untimely step toward the reevaluation and rehabilitation of the ideal within Marxist tradition, which, I think, against the backdrop of the rapid inflation of the concept of materialism in contemporary continental philosophy, is yet to come. Along with Lukács, Ilyenkov provides perfect guidance into Marxist spirituality as mediated by Hegel.

According to Ilyenkov (2012, 149), idealistic doctrines explain history and knowledge through the conception of the ideal "as consciousness or will, as thought or as the mind in general, as 'soul' or 'spirit,' as 'feeling' or as 'creativity,' or as 'socially-organised experience.'" The ideal is neither "mental in general" nor something that sits in your head or flies in the empyrean. It is objective. Beyond the concept of the ideal is a philosophical problem already grasped by Plato: "The problem of the objectivity of universal knowledge, the objectivity of universal (theoretical) definitions of reality, i.e., the nature of the fact of their absolute independence from humans and from humanity, from the special constitution of the human organism—its brain and its mind with its individual-fleeting states" (154). Ilyenkov calls this objectivity "the truth-value of the universal knowledge" and insists on its impersonal and collective character.

Ideal relates to "a collectively built world of intellectual culture, an internally organised and disjointed world of historically established and socially established ('institutionalised') *universal representations* by people about the 'real' world—as opposed to the individual mind." It is not reducible to an individual mind but constitutes "sensuous-suprasensuous" reality that is more than the separate states of separate minds. This reality is indeed a representation. What it represents is the real, or material, world "in historically established and historically changing *social (collective) consciousness*, in 'collective' impersonal 'reason,' in historically established forms of expression of this 'reason.'" In contrast to individuals, with their minds, souls, and so on, this spiritual content is stable; it "persists despite the fact that individual selves arise and vanish, sometimes leaving a trace in it, and sometimes without a trace, not even touching 'ideality,' 'spirit'" (Ilyenkov 2012, 155–6).

What, according to Ilyenkov, is truly materialist in Marx's solution of this problem—which (after Hegel) we may call the problem of the spirit—is that Marx brings to light a real social process in which genuine human activity, labor, "begins to produce not only a material, but also an *ideal* product" (Ilyenkov 2012, 158). Labor transforms the "material" into the "ideal," which not only becomes real and objective but also actively determines people's lives. Interpreting the ideal this way, Marx connects it to the value form. The latter is ideal "in the most strict and precise sense" (160), as it can be assumed by any use value—that is, any material object that can satisfy a human need. The value form is abstract; it does not have its own body, but it dwells in the bodies of things that are thus transformed into commodities, things that cost something independently of what they materially are and that can be exchanged on these grounds. Without having a body, this reality "easily changes one material form of its incarnation for another, persisting in all of its 'incarnations' and 'metamorphoses'" (161).

The Soul of the Commodity and the Essence of the Human

Thus, the ideal, or spiritual, essence persists over material things that come and go and passes from one of them to another—as do viruses, bacteria, parasites, (evil) spirits, or, in Marx's parlance, souls. Remember that at the beginning of *Capital* he compares a commodity to a human being whose body appears to be its use value and whose soul appears as an exchange value (or simply value). "The use values, coat, linen, &c., i.e., the bodies of commodities, are combinations of two elements—matter and labour," says Marx (2015, 31), repeating William Petty: "Labour is its father and the earth its mother." However, this is not a material use value but an ideal exchange value that pretends to be the very essence of things.

Marx (2015, 52–3) gives voice to commodities as if they were talking to each other: "Our use value may be a thing that interests men. It is no part of us as objects. What, however, does belong to us as objects, is our value. Our natural intercourse as commodities proves it. In the eyes of each other we are nothing but exchange values." What we learn from this attentive listening to things is that there was not only already a new materialism in Marx but also a kind of object-oriented ontology that, in contrast to today's theory, dialectically reflected upon its social core —reification, commodity fetishism. Contemporary ontology, with its sensibility aimed toward a general thinghood, adjusts thought to a general dehumanization of life: it fixes that everything and everybody are nothing but objects and that we have to get used to it. Marxist-oriented object ontology would compliment this assertion with a clear understanding of why it is so: because in capitalism as a form of organization of existence, everything and everybody is getting objectified as a commodity or labor force. Existing as a heap of objects might be an effect of reification. Endowed with numeric souls of value, all objects create commodities, and all of us fall into this tunnel: "There it is a definite social relation between men, that assumes, in their eyes, the fantastic form of a relation between things" (48).

As a commodity among many other commodities, I would claim: "My soul is what I cost—and such is my spiritual essence." Chatting in the language of value, the numeric souls of commodities sum themselves into the voice of objective spirit that, in Walter Benjamin's (2005, 260) words, "speaks from the ornamentation of banknotes." I must add, however, that what this voice says might be true, but only for one particular form of consciousness—and this form has to be overcome. At another level of the same game, I can equally claim that my soul—that is, my own little share of the spiritual essence—is not the above. What connects me to the spiritual essence is in fact my living labor, whereas money is a dead thing, a pile of "bones," which presents my labor in its negated, objectified, and reified form. Just as Hegel's infinite judgement "The being of spirit is a bone" is a deadlock of reason, the "labor-money" cluster is a deadlock of the capitalist system wherein all elements are bound to the commodity form.

It appears that for both Hegel and Marx, spirituality is a contradictory notion. On one hand is an actual spirit of labor, and on the other an objectified spirit of money (a bone, the living dead, the vampire of capital). These two spirits are tied to each other in the knot of alienation. Well ahead of *Capital*, in which he deduced the idea of the soul of a commodified thing, Marx, in his remarkable early book, the *Economic and Philosophical Manuscripts of 1844*, developed his concept of the essence of the human—a grim cocktail of humanism and essentialism for which he would indeed be criticized in the postmodern era, but which is able to persevere through this critic.

Human essence is, according to Marx, labor—not any labor, however, but a universal production. In their genuine conscious working activity, people express their freedom. They are essentially free producers, whereas other animals only produce when they have need (Marx 2009, 28–36). If I could only understand it literally, I would never agree with this definition: I think that the activity of other animals can also be considered as free, conscious, or universal production; we only lack the conceptual tools that at some point would allow us to grasp it. In my view, the essence of the human, as opposed to other animals, of course creates a limitation. However, this limitation can be overcome if we take the risk of adopting some new idea of the human—detached from one particular animal species.

I got this insight from Reza Negarestani's conception of inhumanism: while for Marx the essence of the human is labor, for Negarestani the human is defined through reason, which would sound almost a sort of old-school metaphysics if not for an interesting point in Negarestani's (2018) neorationalist approach, in which the human qua intelligence is an attribute that does not belong to one particular substance that is our species but can pass to anything else, such as to robots. Today we call ourselves humans; tomorrow this mantle will be taken by intelligent machines or some other beings. Anything can be intelligent, or human, says Negarestani, and we are not exceptional. We just have to admit that as reason grows into its universality, it will leave us behind, and we have to get ready to transmit our humanity to the ones who come after:

> Through the growth and maturation of reason, the definition and the significance of the human is freed from any purported substantive essence or fixed nature. The formal appellation to "humanity" becomes a transferable entitlement, a right that can be granted or acquired regardless of any attachment to a specific natural or artificial structure, heritage, or proclivity, since being human is not merely a right that is simply obtained naturally at birth through biological ancestry or inheritance. The title "human" can be transferred to anything that can graduate into the domain of judgments, anything that satisfies the criteria of minded and minding agency, be it an animal or a machine. The entwinement of the project of human emancipation—both in the sense of the negative freedom from the limitations established in advance or created by ourselves and the positive freedom to do something or become something else—with the artificial prospects of human intelligence is the logical consequence of the *human as a transferable right*. (62)

One can see that, in contrast to contemporary posthumanist criticism of the anthropocentric paradigm that denies all previous humanist tradition, Negarestani radicalizes humanism by turning it inside out. What I find the most relevant here is precisely this insistence on the idea of reason, and the human as reason, which was exposed, criticized, and deconstructed in the twentieth century to the extent that the baby seemed to be thrown out with the bathwater. Instead of dehumanizing the world, Negarestani's project suggests further humanization and expansion of reason beyond the anthropocentric horizon, which indeed echoes a Hegelian project of substance becoming subject. Additionally, in my view, such a transfer of the human to nonanthropomorphic things can create a basis of empathy and solidarity between human and nonhuman animals, machines, and other subjects that would thus be included in the domain of spiritual life. The universalizing of humanity can provide the basis for what Timothy Morton (2017) calls "solidarity with nonhuman people." Instead of getting rid of the human, keeping and developing the best from it and altering its potentials seems to be an important element of the struggle for the future, or, in Negarestani's (2018, 73) words, "*geistig* struggle."

Estranged Labor: A Worker and a Horse

From the Hegelian perspective, there is a clear coherence between reason (intelligence) and labor. Reason as a form of consciousness plays the same role for the spirit as labor for the society. Reason and labor reflect each other on two levels of the same structure: while reason belongs to the level of epistemology, labor refers to the realm of social ontology, or, closer to Marx, to the critique of political economy. Therefore, I suggest applying an inhumanist optics to Marx's definition of labor as human essence—that is, to detach the human qua labor from the body of *Homo sapiens*, just like Negarestani detaches reason from its (so to say) temporary biological repository.

Of course, Marx himself could not make this step. He did not question an essential anthropomorphism of the human. Let it be my modest contribution to the Marxist humanism dismissed by so many contemporary readers: if humans are those who produce universally—and not necessarily those with a larger brain, thirty-two teeth, or DNA with twenty-three pairs of chromosomes—then anything that for whatever reason begins to produce universally—that is, not only for itself but for others—deserves to be recognized as human. Therefore, I will not reject Marx's use of the character of labor as a criterion for the human-animal or, more broadly, human-nonhuman divide, as it actually does have a deeper sense within the logic of his argument, which I am trying to reconstruct in order to outline the contours of the spiritual that go beyond human in its traditional sense of "man."

Equipped with this optics, we can now shed a new light on Marx's vision of the human essence introduced in his *Manuscripts* of 1844. I suggest reading this work as if the laboring essence of the human was already detached from *Homo sapiens*; as if the main character of this book was not a "man" as we know him from our anthropocentric and patriarchal culture but a human in this innovative constructivist sense of the one who, one way or another, got to the point of the universal production. This could equally be a dog writing a philosophical treatise with its hind legs or an ape making a report for an academy, both coming from Kafka's prose, or a robot that arrives at an understanding of the sense of the work he does. From this perspective, what is essential for the human is not a particular form of bodily life but a universal form of labor. Let us imagine that it is to this indefinite creature whom he calls "man"—perhaps in order to make it easier for us to identify

with it—that Marx (2009, 31–2) applies the term species-being, *Gattungswesen*, borrowed from Ludwig Feuerbach. It would not be totally wrong to say that Marx's
Gattungswesen is a kind of soul that dwells in a laboring body. In contrast to a multiplicity of biological species, a species-being is not clearly determined by its environment, not specialized in something particular, like hunting, or fishing, or
digging the earth. Being initially indeterminate, it can instead freely choose any
of these or other activities, combine them, and so on.

The problem is, however, that within the capitalist mode of production, which is
based on estranged labor, this essential freedom cannot be fully realized. The
failure of a proper realization of the essence of the human is embodied here in
a specific anthropological type of the worker, whom bourgeois political economy
treats not as a human being, but as cattle: "Political economy knows the worker
only as a working animal—as a beast reduced to the strictest bodily needs"
(Marx 2009, 7)—who, "the same as any horse, must get as much as will enable
him to work" (6). However, as Marx emphasizes—and this emphasis is extremely
important for his theory of the essence of the human—there is a tiny difference
between a worker and a horse: in contrast to his comrade animal, the worker is
paid for his work. Even if his salary can only provide a very modest, partial satisfaction of his basic needs—for example, survival as a horse—the crucial moment is
here: he does not *work for free*, as the horse does; he *works freely*. Once the horse is
bought from the market, it belongs to the owner, and the slave labor of the horse,
too, belongs to the owner by default. In turn, the worker is free, and he freely goes
to the market himself to sell his own labor. His labor for someone else's profit is his
conscious activity, or, as is said, his free life choice—and this is precisely what
renders this system of social relations so deeply pathological. He consciously
and freely makes himself a working animal in order to survive as a working
animal: "It is only because [man] is a species being that he is a conscious being,
i.e. that his own life-activity is an object for him. Only because of that is his activity
free activity. Estranged labor reverses this relationship, so that it is just because
man is a conscious being that he makes his life-activity, his essential being, a
mere means to his existence" (31).

What is thus estranged is not only the product of his labor but, in the first place,
the very freedom that is his essence: it becomes a means of a mere biological survival. In order to stay alive as an animal—that is, to satisfy my basic natural needs
(food, accommodation, etc.)—I freely choose to convert my human essence—my
soul—into working hours and sell it to the owner of the means of production.
In this process, my essential freedom turns into its opposite—slavery:

> First, the fact that labor is *external* to the worker, i.e., it does not belong to his
> intrinsic nature; that in his work, therefore, he does not affirm himself but
> denies himself, does not feel content but unhappy, does not develop freely
> his physical and mental energy but mortifies his body and ruins his mind.
> The worker therefore only feels himself outside his work, and in his work

feels outside himself. He feels at home when he is not working, and when he is working he does not feel at home. His labor is therefore not voluntary, but coerced; it is *forced labor*. (30)

Estranged labor deploys a dialectical process between the worker and the animal: "As a result, therefore, man (the worker) only feels himself freely active in his animal functions—eating, drinking, procreating, or at most in his dwelling and in dressing-up, etc.; and in his human functions he no longer feels himself to be anything but an animal. What is animal becomes human and what is human becomes animal" (30). In this reality, depicted by Marx, we can thus discern another version of the spiritual kingdom of animals. It is, of course, different from the Hegelian, but not completely. For both Hegel and Marx the word "animal" designates an individual with its natural or private needs, and the "spiritual" (in Hegel) or "human essence" (in Marx) points to the laboring activity that connects us to the universal. Both demonstrate that what mediates between these two terms are closely related processes of externalization, estrangement, reification, and alienation that Marx in his *Manuscripts* also characterizes as dehumanization.

However—and this is a crucial point for understanding how progressive Marx's account on the question of the human actually was—thinking of the estrangement of labor qua the alienation of the human essence in some trivial sense of a mere reduction of human beings to the so-called animal condition is not quite accurate; it is a pity that the humanism of the *Manuscripts* can be interpreted in such a naive way. The fact is that what remains of workers when their human essence is taken out of them and put into a product that does not belong to them is not really an animal, not a natural individual. What happens to workers in the process of capitalist production (i.e., the production of value, the production of the monetary bones from the essential freedom that is the workers' living souls, when labor, which once transformed a monkey into a human being, now makes a human being a monkey again) is by no means a reverse evolution. Political economy treats workers as horses, but workers are not horses, and this not-being-a-horse is not in the sense that workers are still somehow *more than* horses—as if a worker allegedly still keeps reason, language, awareness of death, or some other attributes of dignity notoriously ascribed to men through the whole anthropocentric tradition—but is in the sense that, in deliberately selling their labor, workers are *less than* horses.

Alienation does not return us to mother nature, even if we take a holiday and honestly try to relax. The freedom we are designed for is (from a Marxist perspective) not only the freedom of eating, sleeping, and having fun, but is also —and mainly—the creative freedom of work, of transforming the world, of making things happen. It is precisely this indeterminate species-being that must be sold out so that we can have things to eat and places to sleep. I would like to write a book on that but, alas, not now—because what I have to do right now is to write a report of my academic activities, upon which my salary is based. I understand, however, that my personal household might be in better condition than many people, those I know and those I do not know. Not only do I have a warm house and a salary that allows me to buy vegetables and fruits, but also, between the reports, I still have an opportunity to write that book, for which I might not receive money but which I consider my essential and ultimately free production. My personal alienation within the system of academic routine of course makes me suffer, but it looks much less brutal than, for instance, the conditions of today's migrant workers, who live in the basements of buildings in the cities where they work, sometimes illegally, with no papers, and sometimes without being recognized as human beings. They are now keeping the place of the proletarians depicted by Marx (2009, 50) in the *Manuscripts* chapter entitled "Human Requirements and Division of Labor under the Rule of Private Property"—not only as dehumanized but also, so to say, as deanimalized beings:

> Man returns to a cave dwelling, which is now, however, contaminated with the pestilential breath of civilization, and which he continues to occupy only *precariously*, it being for him an alien habitation which can be withdrawn from him any day—a place from which, if he does not pay, he can be thrown out any day. For this mortuary he has to *pay*. A dwelling in the light, which Prometheus in Aeschylus designated as one of the greatest boons, by means of which he made the savage into a human being, ceases to exist for the worker. Light, air, etc.—the simplest animal cleanliness—ceases to be a need for man. Filth, this stagnation and putrefaction of man—the *sewage* of civilization (speaking quite literally)—comes to be the *element of life*—for him. Utter, unnatural depravation, putrefied nature, comes to be *his life-element*. None of his senses exist any longer, and (each has ceased to function) not only in its human fashion, but in an inhuman fashion, so that it does not exist even in an animal fashion.

Thus, estranged labor makes a free worker less than an enslaved animal: this very important detail of Marx's analysis is emphasized by Frank Ruda, who in his groundbreaking reading of Marx's *Manuscripts* goes against the grain of its antihumanist and posthumanist critics:

> Man is the only animal that can be less than an animal. Animal needs know objective minima, precisely because animals do not know their limitation. But man is an entity whose substance and whose needs are plastic, because what one knows (say, one's limits) one can redetermine. Knowing no objective limit, he is able to become less and less. His minimum is subjective and thus up for limitless redetermination. Man is the only animal that can therefore live at an absolute minimum; only man can live as if he does not live—this is the worker. (Žižek, Ruda, and Hamza 2018, 87)

One would perhaps object that man is in fact not the only animal that can live at the very minimum, as if he does not live. Suffice to recall a laboratory tick—described by Jacob von Uexküll—that was kept in isolation without nourishment for eighteen years and then came back to life as if nothing had happened (Agamben 2002, 45–7). What if we try, however, to embrace the previously mentioned strategy of detaching the human from the body of *Homo sapiens*, as what is really at stake here is not the body but, so to say, the essence of the worker, or the soul that dwells in one's animal body in this infinitely reduced mode?

Toward a Labor Theory of the Soul

I deliberately choose the word "soul" in order to designate that individual part of the spiritual, in both the Hegelian and Marxian sense, that constitutes not the result of the production of value (capital) but its source (living labor). In the manifold of cultural traditions, "soul" meant many different things: a kind of consciousness that belongs to every piece of nature; the essence of life that passes from one human, animal, or plant body to another; the divine element within the human body that flies to the heavens upon death; and so on. Although today, within the framework of a general materialist turn, this might sound like an anachronism, I seriously think that the idea of the soul is becoming more and more relevant and can open a new perspective on the main problems discussed by Marxism, such as alienation and emancipation.

My conception of the soul derives from the reading of Andrei Platonov, a Soviet Marxist writer who had the greatest compassion toward all living creatures. Platonov envisaged suffering not only in society but also in nature, which also had to be, according to him, liberated toward a universal communist horizon. The suffering of animals and plants is similar to the suffering of poor people, peasants, and workers, but most of the people just cannot recognize it; they do not see in the animal a comrade, a fellow being who might have a different body, like that of a dog, but whose soul is the same as ours. Only emphatic communists can understand the desperate feelings and desires of animals and plants, such as the desire for happiness, for a better world, or for communism, which, according to Fredric Jameson (1994, 97), still has not found its Freud or Lacan.[1]

To put it briefly, through the lens of Platonov's radical revolutionary humanism, the soul is a kind of human being inside the body of an animal of any species. Everybody can have a human soul, as in animism and ancient metempsychosis, in which the souls of the dead can relocate to the bodies of different animals: "On seeing the dog, Lichtenberg immediately understood that it was a former man who had been reduced by grief and need to the senselessness of an animal, and he was not frightened by it any more"; likewise, "Nikita decided that the shepherd had not liked being dead and had become a cock; so this cock was a man—a secret

---

1. Also see Timofeeva (2018, 167) and Flatley (2008, 180).

man. There were people everywhere, only they seemed not to be people" (Platonov 1999, 79, 167).

Just such an impersonal, secret soul constitutes—according to my version of Marxian humanism beyond anthropocentrism or spirituality beyond *Homo sapiens*—the essence of the human. We have to remember that Marx's *Manuscripts of 1844* are not only a work of social theory but also a brave exercise in philosophical anthropology that does not really know limits and taboos: nothing here is forbidden, even the parallels that I am trying to make between Marxism and animism, and especially regarding contemporary discussions on animism and indigene knowledge (De Castro 2009; Kohn 2013). From the perspective of Marxist humanism and spirituality, the soul can be understood as the bridge between the individual ("animal") and the universal ("spiritual"). If the individual (animal) and the universal (spiritual) are the two terms of a dialectical contradiction, then the soul is a mediator, a third term between them. It is the soul of an intelligent or working animal that connects it to the spiritual. The problem is that within the capitalist regime this bridge is always already broken. We cannot pass it: that is, we cannot realize ourselves not as individuals having basic private needs but as really free and universal beings. Who or what undergoes alienation? The answer is simple: the soul. The soul is broken.

In his novel *Soul*, Platonov (2007, 59) writes: "Slave labor, exhaustion and exploitation never just use up a man's physical strength, never just his hands and arms. No, what they appropriate is the entire mind and heart; first the soul gets eaten away, then body fades, and then a man hides away in death, slipping into the earth as if into some fortress and refuge." This slipping of an exhausted body into the earth is, again, a variation of a Marxian cave dwelling that is not natural but presents what Ruda called "becoming less and less." Later in the same novel, Platonov returns to this line: "Any exploitation of a human being begins with the distortion of that person's soul, with getting their soul so used to death that it can be subjugated; without this subjugation, a slave is not a slave. And this forced mutilation of the soul continues, growing more and more violent, until reason in the slave turns to mad and empty mindlessness" (103).

I would like to pay attention to the state of madness evoked by Platonov (1990, 294) not only in the *Soul* but also in other writings, such as the *Sea of Youth*, where one of the characters comes to the idea that communists must change the world as soon as possible because even animals are already becoming insane. In his writings madness is not some individual misfortune but rather an effect of catastrophic social or natural exhaustion. The idea that estranged labor mortifies workers' bodies and ruins their minds comes from Marxian anthropology. We can see that Platonov expands this logic toward nonhuman creatures. Individuals lose their minds when their lives become unbearable. Whereas emancipation would mean increasing the levels of consciousness in all animals (everybody could grow toward a conscious life), insanity is a sign of despair with which souls react to the injustice and absurdity of their situation. Today, when we have all the premises to claim that capitalism is an institutionalized madness, this point is clear and does not need additional argumentation. Deleuze and Guattari called it schizophrenia and elaborated ways to live and think through it, to reinforce it toward a multiple cosmic production. Today, we would rather call this depression: multiplicity turns into a narcissistic collapse and, honestly, we see no way out of it.

My friends on Facebook compete in reporting on their depressive episodes, comparing the chemicals they take and impatiently claiming not to have devalued their personal experiences of mental disorders. We are imprisoned in our depressions, as Platonov's souls in dumb, suffering bodies, and, thinking of it in terms of the uniqueness of our personal troubles—poverty, burnout, solitude, the absence of love, professional and social failures—we tend to forget that depression is a social phenomenon. I cherish the memory of Mark Fisher (2009, 37), who wrote in his *Capitalist Realism*: "If it is true, for instance, that depression is constituted by low serotonin levels, what still needs to be explained is why particular individuals have low levels of serotonin. This requires a social and political explanation; and the task of repoliticizing mental illness is an urgent one if the left wants to challenge capitalist realism."

Depression is the pain of the alienated soul. In 1915, Kafka described it as "metamorphosis": a human soul finds itself locked in the body of an insect on a morning when a salesman called Gregor Samsa has to wake up and go to his unloved work. He escapes into a gigantic beetle and afterward never really leaves the room that becomes his dirty *Höhle*—a cave, a den, a burrow. Treated as a parasite by his family, he dwells in this inhuman but also unnatural habitat, just as a Marxian worker in his rented apartment, and becomes less and less, until he dies and a housemaid removes him with the garbage. Now, after more than one hundred years, when such phenomena as hikikomori and modern types of depression have grown massively, we are getting used to this state of mind. "Don't leave your room, don't make a mistake," we say to each other, quoting a famous poem by Joseph Brodsky, who was sentenced to hard labor for his "social parasitism" (basically, for his refusal to "work," when being a poet was not considered proper employment by Soviet officials).

In his book *The Soul at Work*, published the same year as Fisher's *Capitalist Realism* and in the same Marxist line of politicizing mental illness, Franco "Bifo" Berardi discusses depression in the context of alienation within contemporary neoliberalism and cognitive capitalism. He suggests understanding the soul in a materialistic way and echoes Spinoza: "What the body can do, that is its soul" (Berardi 2009, 21). Finding coherence between the economic, the social, and psychic depression, he argues that depression comes from the return of the repressed, from the emotional, dark part of the soul that does not come through a censorship of the ideology of rationality and the harmony of the market system: "Desire is involved in the process, and the unconscious is speaking behind the curtains of every investment scene, of any act of consumption and economic exchange. This is why the supposedly perfect balance of the market has become a catastrophic mess.

Euphoria, competition, and exuberance were all involved in the dynamics of the bull market years. Panic and depression were denied, but they were always at work" (208).

The unconscious is indeed the right word and can be taken here as another name for the soul, as I understand it: exploited and alienated, the soul at work is the unconscious, beneath the ground of representation—an underground laborer, a Marxian worker in the cave, an illegal migrant in the basement, a miner with a black face. The work of the unconscious is one of the main points explored by Samo Tomšič, who elaborates a theory of labor and enjoyment between Marx and Lacan. Tomšič emphasizes the importance of the concept of labor in Freud's theory of the unconscious and suggests taking it literally: an energetic notion of labor power must be taken as a basis of a labor theory of the unconscious (Tomšič 2015, 11). Coming into line with this claim, I would like to broaden it in the direction of an outline of a labor theory of the soul, which can be understood both as a Marxian human essence designed for a universal free production and as a Freudian unconscious sweating in its coal mines. The soul is the dialectics of the two, so to speak, the dialectics of the bright and the dark sides of labor.

These reflections bring us closer to the materialist sense of Marx's spirituality: spirituality is the work of the soul. Marx called it human essence, but we should not be misled by this term and its heavy metaphysical connotations. In this regard, an important remark is needed: on the surface it can seem that for Hegel the essence (the crux of the matter) emerges as a result of alienation, whereas for Marx human essence (soul, in my definition) if precisely what is being alienated. However, the latter is only half true. Yes, the soul experiences alienation, but there is no nonalienated soul before this experience.

"For Marx the history of mankind is a history of the increasing development of man, and at the same time of increasing alienation. His concept of socialism is the emancipation from alienation, the return of man to himself, his self-realization," writes Fromm (1961). Today, this traditional humanist sentence needs a considerable correction: apart from the disturbing word "man," the crucial thing is that there is nowhere to "return"; the spiritual emancipation is not about getting back to some sheer essence. As emphasized by Tomšič (2019, 121), "The subject is brought into existence through the process of alienation, together with the fiction of full subjective being, non-alienated self, consciousness of ego-cogito, whose apparent primacy results from a retroactive projection." If there is a return, then this is a return to what has never been, to the unprecedented, to the spiritual as a free universal production of the soul. The liberation of the soul is a hard path through alienation in which we animals can perhaps realize our essence—why not call it, after Marx, the human?

How can we get there? Or what is the main obstacle on the road to freedom, the sight of which we always tend to lose? I think that the heart of the system of capitalist alienation is individualism. It is not only ideology, and Hegel is here even more explicit than Marx: the individual is the basic element of a social ontology that creates an entire system of the public humiliation of living labor by dead capital. A private individual, or human animal, is what must be overcome, and the soul—that is, human essence—de-privatized, detached from one particular species and set free. "Don't let the soul be lazy," says Russian poet Nikolay Zabolotsky. In spite of the ideology of idleness, procrastination, and staying in bed (depression) that is praised by many on the contemporary left, we still have to work on this.

Conclusion

This essay has tried to elaborate a Marxist (i.e., materialist) account of spirituality. Tracing its genesis to Hegel's dialectics of reason, explicated in chapter 5 of his *Phenomenology of Spirit*, I emphasized that the spirit first emerges as a splitting of reason, which tries to grasp its truth in observation of itself as a material object (a bone) and then actualizes itself in social life, depicted by Hegel as the spiritual kingdom of animals. What Hegel here calls the animal relates to private individuals with their egotistic interests that make them exchange labor for money. Thus, reification of the so-called observing reason of positive science turns into alienation of the actual reason of bourgeois society; estranged reason becomes the estranged labor that would become the main topic of the *Economic and Philosophic Manuscripts of 1844*, where Marx introduced the idea of the essence of the human. What follows then is my conceptual step, reinforced by Negarestani's neorationalist argument, that the human does not equal "man" in its traditional anthropocentric sense of a particular animal species, *Homo sapiens*, but that it can and does go beyond our species to whatever can become a rational being, from animals to smart machines. I apply a similar logic to the Marxian understanding of free labor or universal production, as the essence of the human, and suggest detaching it from our biological species: that is, to consider as human anything or anybody who can potentially become a free producer. I then reflect on the Marxian figure of the worker as a specific configuration of the laboring being in the capitalist mode of production, along with workers' psychic lives, affected by the estranged character of their work. I reflect upon their status between the animal (which in a Hegelian animal remains for a separate individual of any species) and the spiritual (which points to the universal dimension of social life). The third term, the bridge between the two, is what I call the soul, referring to Platonov's idea that the soul is a kind of human being hidden in an animal body. "Soul" becomes the name for the human essence understood in a nonessentialist and nonanthropocentric (i.e., a materialist) way. I address Bifo's theory of the soul at work and Fisher's claim about the political sense of mental disorders, analyzing the state of the alienated soul, of depression as the exhaustion of the soul together with the impossibility of overcoming its animal (i.e., individual) predicament in getting out of its own self and heading toward a realization of its essential freedom as a universal, spiritual being. Depression is the state of the alienated or broken soul, depicted by Kafka in the *Metamorphosis* as a human insect that cannot leave the room. However, this state of alienation cannot be released through a simple coming back to some preexistent organic human essence. Agreeing with Tomšič, who writes about the labor of the unconscious, and with other authors who continue a Hegelian line of understanding alienation as the main and necessary step in the formation of the spiritual, I suggest that such a spiritual essence does not exist naturally but must be created, for which the work of the soul is needed.

References

Agamben, D. 2002. *The Open: Man and Animal*. Stanford, Calif.: Stanford University Press.
Benjamin, W. 2005. "Capitalism as Religion [Fragment 74]." *The Frankfurt School's Critique of Religion*, ed. by E. Mendieta, 259–62. New York: Routledge.
Berardi, F. [Bifo]. 2009. *The Soul at Work: From Alienation to Autonomy*. Los Angeles: Semiotext(e).
De Castro, E. V. 2009. *Cannibal Metaphysics: For a Post-Structural Anthropology*. University of Minnesota Press.
Fisher, M. 2009. *Capitalist Realism: Is There No Alternative?* Zero Books.
Flatley, J. 2008. *Affective Mapping: Melancholia and the Politics of Modernism*. London: Harvard University Press.
Fromm, E. 1961. *Marx's Concept of Man*. New York: Frederick Ungar. https://www.marxists.org/archive/fromm/works/1961/man/ch01.htm.
Hegel, G. W. F. 1979. *System of Ethical Life and First Philosophy of Spirit*. Albany: State University of New York Press.
———.1983. *Hegel and the Human Spirit: A Translation of the Jena Lectures on the Philosophy of Spirit (1805–6)*. Detroit: Wayne State University Press.
———.2018. *Phenomenology of Spirit*. Trans. T. Pinkard. Cambridge: Cambridge University Press.
Ilyenkov, E. 2012. "Dialectics of the Ideal." *Historical Materialism* 20 (2): 149–93.
Jameson, F. 1994. "Utopia, Modernism and Death." *The Seeds of Time*. New York: Columbia University Press.
Kohn, E. 2013. *How Forests Think: Toward an Anthropology Beyond the Human*. Berkeley, Calif.: University of California Press.
Kojève, A. 1969. *Introduction to the Reading of Hegel: Lectures on the Phenomenology of Spirit*. New York: Cornell University Press.
Lukács, G. 1975. *The Young Hegel: Studies in the Relations between Dialectics and Economics*. Trans. R. Livingstone. London: Merlin.
Marx, K. 1970. *Critique of Hegel's Philosophy of Right*. Oxford: Oxford University Press. https://www.marxists.org/archive/marx/works/download/Marx_Critique_of_Hegels_Philosophy_of_Right.pdf.
———. 1996. "Debates on the Law on Thefts of Wood." Marxists Internet Archive. https://www.marxists.org/archive/marx/works/download/Marx_Rheinishe_Zeitung.pdf.
———. 2009. *Economic and Philosophic Manuscripts of 1844*. Marxists Internet Archive. https://www.marxists.org/archive/marx/works/download/pdf/Economic-Philosophic-Manuscripts-1844.pdf.

————. 2015. *Capital*. Vol. I. Marxists Internet Archive. https://www.marxists.org/archive/marx/works/download/pdf/Capital-Volume-I.pdf.

Mascat, J. 2018. "Hegel and the Advent of Modernity: A Social Ontology of Abstraction." *Radical Philosophy* 2 (1). https://www.radicalphilosophy.com/article/hegel-and-the-advent-of-modernity?fbclid=IwAR0SV-L3R_Fec1LJauW5KoMBiv1zdj9s3NYiJ9voRWcGZsSCJ42efK1H4VY#fnref63.

McLellan, B., ed. 2000. *Karl Marx: Selected Writings*. Oxford: Oxford University Press.

Morton, T. 2017. *Humankind: Solidarity with Nonhuman People*. London: Verso.

Negarestani, R. 2018. *Intelligence and Spirit*. Cambridge, Mass.: MIT Press.

Platonov, A. 1990. *На заре туманной юности: Повести и рассказы* (On the sunset of a hazy youth, novels and stories). Moscow: Soviet Russia.

————. 1999. *The Return and Other Stories*. Trans. R. Chandler and E. Chandler. London: Harvill.

————. 2007. *Soul and Other Stories*. Trans. R. Chandler and E. Chandler. New York: NYRB.

Tomšič, S. 2015. *The Capitalist Unconscious*. London: Verso.

————. 2019. *The Labor of Enjoyment: Towards a Critique of Libidinal Economy*. August Verlag.

Sohn-Rethel, A. 1977. *Intellectual and Manual Labor: A Critique of Epistemology*. Atlantic Highlands, N.J.: Humanities Press.

Timofeeva, O. 2018. *The History of Animals: A Philosophy*. London: Bloomsbury.

Žižek, S. 2012. "Welcome to the Spiritual Kingdom of Animals." https://blogdaboitempo.com.br/2012/09/18/welcome-to-the-spiritual-kingdom-of-animals-slavoj-Žižek-on-the-moral-vacuum-of-global-capitalism.

Žižek S., F. Ruda, and A. Hamza. 2018. *Reading Marx*. Cambridge, UK: Polity.

Marx, Foucault, and the Secularization of Western Culture

Vivek Dhareshwar

Although Marx's critique of capitalism, especially his theory of fetishism, requires experiential knowledge (my term for "spirituality"), his framework does not leave any conceptual room for such knowledge. The idea that spirituality is (perhaps the better) part of religion is a deeply held assumption of secular Western thought. Only in Michel Foucault's late lectures do we find a Western thinker realizing that what opposed spirituality, and subsequently suppressed it, is not science but religion. This essay reconstructs Foucault's reasons for making that startling claim and then explores how Marx's early insight into the secularization of European culture can be deepened with the help of Foucault's genealogical analysis of the disappearance of spiritual knowledge in the West. Equipped with a framework to understand the secularization of Western culture in a radically different way, the essay then tackles the question of reformulating Marx's theory of reification with the resources provided by experiential knowledge (spirituality).

Two Interpretive Problems

Let me begin with two textual or interpretive problems, taken from the works of Marx and Foucault, respectively. I propose a conceptual frame to bring the two problems face to face in such a way that the problems and the solution to them have the potential to throw entirely new light on how we must understand the secularization of Western culture. The interpretive problems will thus be shown to have a significance that far transcends their exegetical context.

The first problem has to do with remarks in which Marx persistently draws analogies between Christianity (as a religion) and (features of) capitalism. These analogies begin to appear in an intriguing light when we try to make sense of Marx's (1975, 222) claim, in "On the Jewish Question," that the truly religious/Christian state is not the state that professes or embraces Christianity but the one that is secular. Exegetically, we cannot set apart the latter claim and the recurring analogies. Since my aim is not exegetical, I will not be making any attempt to pursue in detail these analogies to speculate about the underlying pattern in Marx's thought. Moreover, exegesis will not solve our problem even when we take into account the analogies that Marx continued to draw, throughout his life, between capitalism and Christianity. Instead, I will focus on his characterization of the secular state as the truly Christian/religious state and explore its theoretical presuppositions.

We will need to ask: what theory of religion and secularization would give coherence to Marx's intriguing intuition? For at this stage, his remarks are nothing more than intuition. But his remarks taken in conjunction with his witty and insightful character-ization of what Luther's Protestantism accomplished will set the stage for our concep-tual exploration. In a set of remarks written using the rhetorical device of inversion that was so characteristic of his early writings, Marx (1975, 251, 342) says that Luther abol-ished the distinction between priests and laymen by turning all laymen into priests. Unlike many of his purely rhetorical inversions, this one is a gem of an insight that, if framed rightly, has the potential to throw light on the process of secularization in the West.

Where does spirituality fit in this story? To answer that question we need to take up the second textual problem: nearly as intriguing—and needless to say, as enigmatic— as the early Marx's claim about the secular state is the late Foucault's (2005, 27) claim that what opposes spirituality in European thought is not science but theology. Spirituality disappears from, or gets radically transformed in, European thought and sociality[1] under pressure from theology—that is to say, from religion. He further claims that this transformed spirituality finds expression in nineteenth-century European thought, especially Hegel and Marx. Doubtless, one manifestation of that presence, however transformed, is precisely Marx's intuition regarding the secular state and its political treatment of religion and civil society.

Having stated how one intriguing and enigmatic intuition can be supported and clarified by another similarly intriguing and enigmatic claim, it is time to see how we can go about seeking a theoretical defense and elaboration of these claims. Let me start with the second problem: that is, with Foucault (2005) and his extraor-dinarily rich lecture series for the year 1981–2, made available to us as *The Herme-neutics of the Subject*.

In the same way as Marx never makes clear what in Christianity (as religion) makes him characterize the secular state as the truly Christian state, Foucault never address-es the question of what in Christianity (as religion) makes it hostile to experiential knowledge. Notice that I have used "experiential knowledge" in place of "spirituality." Since the latter term retains its Christian monastic roots, it is important, for the pur-poses of this paper, to signal a radically different sense of the term by using it inter-changeably with experiential knowledge. Why is theology—the discourse, the science, or the self-description of religion—opposed to spirituality or experiential knowledge? Although this question is waiting to be asked, there is a reason why it does not occur to Foucault to raise it in this form. I will come back to it. Let me instead focus on "spir-ituality," which Foucault discusses with great clarity and richness of detail. Spirituality or experiential knowledge has to do with exploring the conditions for the access to truth. Let us note this careful formulation: *access to* truth, not *knowing* truth (*connaissance*).

---

1. I put it this way rather than saying "European culture" for a reason that will become clear later on.

Access versus Knowing

The claim, which is both systematic and historical, is that "care of the self" and "know thyself" were linked motifs in the long summer of Hellenic and Roman thought, which brought into being a flourishing culture of the self for about a millennium, starting in the fourth century B.C.E. The startling discovery for Foucault is that this remarkable period has simply disappeared or been driven underground by the two other models that have come to dominate the historical account: namely, the Platonic and the Christian. In the Platonic model, both the motifs are present, but "know thyself" acquires a distinctly or exclusively epistemic character, so much so that anyone who has not read Foucault's discussion of what that dictum means will be baffled by this sentence! Well, it meant something completely nonepistemic: before you undertake a vow to the Delphic oracle, make sure you have the ability to fulfill it. While the Platonic model still gave a central place to the "care of the self," this motif totally disappears from the Christian model, to be replaced by something unknown to both the Greek and the Roman cultures: namely, faith.

The major task Foucault sets himself is to document the delinking of the access to truth from the condition of spirituality, from the practices that prepared subjects for the truth that would transform them in their being. The access to truth becomes transformed into knowing/having truth. The transformation was complete, with no trace of the condition of spirituality for access to truth, when Descartes formulated the proposition *ego cogito* and when Kant later went to the extent of denying that the structure of the knowing subject is knowable at all. The ground for this transformation was prepared by Christianity:

> This theology, by claiming, on the basis of Christianity of course, to be rational reflection founding a faith with a universal vocation, founded at the same time the principle of a knowing subject in general, of a knowing subject who finds both his point of absolute fulfillment and highest degree of perfection in God, who is also his Creator and so his model. The correspondence between an omniscient God and subjects capable of knowledge, conditional on faith of course, is undoubtedly one of the main elements that led Western thought —or its principal forms of reflection—and philosophical thought in particular, to extricate itself, to free itself, and to separate itself from the conditions of spirituality that had previously accompanied it and for which the *epimeleia heautou* was the most general expression ... During these twelve centuries the conflict was not between spirituality and science, but between spirituality and theology. (Foucault 2005, 26–7)

For the "care of the self" culture, subjects are not capable of truth unless they undergo a transformation or conduct certain operations on themselves. But the self to which these subjects are seeking access, the truth, is not the self—empirical or transcendental—of the philosopher. Nor is it the other world or the kingdom of the Christians being sought. The access sought was to a dimension of consciousness itself—self-consciousness, if you like, so long as it is not understood egoistically, as having the structure of the ego. If the access to the self or truth needs transformation through spiritual practices, then in a very different way this access also transforms subjects in their very being.

So the element that is neither the subject nor the object but that can be accessed in multiple and multiply diverse ways, all attempting a transformation of the subject, the element that is both the beginning and the end, that initiates the transformation and that completes the journey, brings about a complex relationship between culture and sociality. The innumerably diverse modes of access—all the many philosophical schools and "cults"—generate cultural learning in the different practical modes that are elaborated throughout what Foucault calls the golden period of the Hellenistic/ Roman model of the self. Thus, sociality—the relationship between people, the different socializing structures—begins to be modulated and articulated by the cultural learning that emerges in the practical exploration of the conditions of spirituality. Different groups or schools will bring in different domains of life—economics, medicine, art, erotics—within the ambit of the care of the self. The tendency is for the care of the self to "become coextensive with life" (Foucault 2005, 86). Even intellectual knowledge (*connaissance*) is here in the service of or subordinate to the practices of the self. Any aspect of life—love, old age, friendship—or any activity—economics or dietetics—can become the domain of application for the care of the self. This knowledge, this learning, is the cultural that articulates or modulates the social, which in its turn sustains the cultural.

It may seem that "cultural learning" is in some sense a pleonastic expression. I use it nevertheless to formulate the deep concern that explicitly subtends both Marx's and Foucault's inquiries into forms of knowledge that articulate or disarticulate the social.[2] Marx's concern with finding a richer notion of practice than what philosophy is able to provide converges with Foucault's investigation of how the quasi-theoretical or scientistic modes of discourse produce distortions of intersubjective relationships. Both open up a new field of inquiry by showing how a certain kind of knowledge

---

2. Foucault (2005, 179) is emphatic about this point:

> While having trouble with the word and putting it in inverted commas, I think we can say that from the Hellenistic and Roman period we see a real development of the "culture" of the self. I don't want to use the word culture in a sense that is too loose and I will say that we can speak of culture on a number of conditions. First, when there is a set of values with a minimum degree of coordination, subordination, and hierarchy. We can speak of culture when a second condition is satisfied, which is that these values are given both as universal but also as only accessible to a few. A third condition for being able to speak of culture is that a number of precise and regular forms of conduct are necessary for individuals to be able to reach these values. Even more than this, effort and sacrifice is required. In short, to have access to these values you must be able to devote your whole life to them. Finally, the fourth condition for being able to talk about culture is that access to these values is conditional upon more or less regular techniques and procedures that have been developed, validated, transmitted, and taught, and that are also associated with a whole set of notions, concepts, and theories etcetera: with a field of knowledge (*savoir*).

What we see in this work is how the "culture of the self" *enables* the sociality of the period, which in turn *sustains* the care of the self or helps experiential knowledge to flourish. My own formulation of the relationship between culture and sociality owes much to an exchange with Balagangadhara (1994) on a series of insightful notes he produced to clarify his proposal to look at culture as a configuration of learning.

that does not fit the model of theoretical or intellectual knowledge is intertwined and interarticulated with sociality. Because their work goes a long a way toward illuminating the mutual dependence and support of sociality and spirituality, it can also be mined for understanding how secularization, the normativization of different domains of sociality, strips sociality bare of its rich articulations, its ability to act as the condition for the emergence of experiential knowledge.

Normativization

The context is now set for understanding how Christianity, born in this milieu, sharing on the face of it many of the motifs and problematics pursued by the schools, communities, and groups that practice the care of the self—motifs such as conversion, salvation, return to self, self-knowledge—nevertheless radically and unrecognizably transforms those motifs and problematics. In fact, as Christianity begins to be ascendant, theology on its behalf begins to separate the condition of spirituality from access to truth, transforming the latter into an autonomous development of intellectual knowledge (*connaissance*). This separation or uncoupling takes the form of an attack on the activities and domains—love, friendship, economics, dietetics, politics—that the "care of the self" culture had sought to integrate or to bring within its ambit. In other words, the sociality that was nurtured and articulated by the "care of the self" begins to be stripped of its cultural knowledge. The separated domains are subjected to a process of what we might call "normativization," since the activities in these domains get transformed by subsuming them under moral norms so that theology can examine the "truths" of these domains.

Here is Foucault's (2005, 255–6) analysis of the Christian model and its difference from the "care of the self" model:

> How is this Christian model ... characterized? I think we can say that in this model knowledge of the self is linked in a complex way to knowledge of the truth as given in the original Text and Revelation: knowledge of the self is entailed and required by the fact that the heart must be purified in order to understand the Word; it can only be purified by self-knowledge; and the Word must be received for one to be able to undertake purification of the heart and realize self-knowledge. There is then a circular relation between self-knowledge, knowledge of the truth, and care of the self. If you want to be saved you must accept the truth given in the Text and manifested in Revelation. However, you cannot know this truth unless you take care of yourself in the form of the purifying knowledge (*connaissance*) of the heart. On the other hand, this purifying knowledge of yourself by yourself is only possible on condition of a prior fundamental relationship to the truth of the Text and Revelation. This circularity is, I think, one of the fundamental points of the relations between care of the self and knowledge of the self in Christianity. Second, in Christianity self-knowledge is arrived at through techniques whose essential function is to dispel internal illusions, to recognize the temptations that arise within the soul and the heart, and also to thwart the seductions to which we may be victim. And this is all accomplished by a method for deciphering the secret processes and movements that unfold within the soul and whose origin,

aim, and form must be grasped. An exegesis of the self is thus required. ... Finally, third ... [turning around on the self in Christianity] is essentially and fundamentally to renounce the self. With Christianity then we have a scheme of a relation between knowledge and care of the self that hinges on three points: first, circularity between truth of the Text and self-knowledge; second, an exegetical method for self-knowledge; and finally the objective of self-renunciation.

I had remarked in the beginning that Foucault never asks why theology attacks spirituality. This extended analysis is one place where we can begin to speculate what might be his answer to that question. There is little doubt that, in the last decade of his life, Foucault's research focused on highlighting the radical difference between Christianity and Hellenic-Romanic thought. Truth, of course, is at the heart of what he uncovers. With Christianity emerges a conception of truth totally at odds with the conception that had organized the "care of the self" culture. If self-knowledge in the latter was access to a reality that was not the object of knowing, then knowing (*connaissance*) in Christianity is entirely and exclusively intellectual or theoretical. The examination of conscience, for example, is a knowing of the kind that Christianity brings into being, as is the endless decipherment of the self as an object, a domain. When Christianity began to attack domains like economics and erotics that had been integrated into the conditions of spirituality as part of the access to truth, those domains were opened up for knowing through the rational reflection of theology. A peculiar combination of rationality and morality began looking for "truths" in these domains, truths that allegedly provide subjects with knowledge about how they ought to act or what they ought to avoid. This combination of rationality and morality is what I would like to term "normativization," the unique contribution of Christianity. If problematization was the route that many spiritual movements used to seek access to truth, Christianity fashioned normativization as the route for the salvation of souls.[3]

---

3. Greek ethics worries about whether it is appropriate to do certain things: for example, when to assert self-mastery, when to give in to the erotic approaches of young boys, or to take an example from the domain of dietetics, whether eating certain things is conducive to one's well-being. Such worries are termed "problematization" by Foucault. This contrasts with what Christian morality does to actions: it begins to norm them—that is, make them "wrong." The early Christians begin to classify a whole range of activities as morally wrong (Foucault 1985).
    The most difficult problem here is the relationship between truth and norm. Can that be investigated philosophically? It is clear that part of the reason for Foucault's rejection of philosophy in favor of genealogy has to be that the philosophical route to that question will lead back to theology. Instead, he thought he could show how the ethical reflections of Greek and Roman schools and their exploration of the condition of spirituality as access to truth had nothing in common with the universally binding property of Christian morality (or its secularized versions) or with the Christian concept of Truth. Whereas the secularized version of Christian morality is relatively easy to track (think of Nietzsche's work), the secularized version of truth has posed a far more difficult challenge. Although Foucault did not always formulate his earlier inquiry as tracking secularization, this tracking was evident, for example, when he discussed vertical or in-depth Christianization (as distinct from its horizontal spread through proselytization) or when discussing the welfare state as a pastoral form of power; however, once he began his inquiry that produced the volumes on the history of sexuality, it was clear that he was indeed explicitly investigating the relationship between truth and norm as that which structures the secularization process.

It is this normativization that provides the subject matter for the so-called secular knowledges such as psychiatry, criminology, and the moral sciences. Foucault's later investigation into the conception of truth and knowing that Christianity developed thus clarifies the questions with which his earlier investigation into madness, delinquency, and sexuality were concerned. More importantly, his later work provides us with a novel hypothesis about how we can understand the process of secularization. Secularization is usually thought of as a process that registers either the decline of religion or, what is the same thing, a liberation from religious thinking (some even reviving the Weberian thesis of disenchantment as part of the process). If, however, we focus on the Truth of Revelation in the Text and see the effects of the truths that the subsequent normativization process generates, then we begin to understand secularization very differently.

This focus forces us to think about how secularization continues in an intensified fashion the religious attempt to transform access to truth into knowing truth(s). It is important to grasp what this transformation does to the sociality of the golden age of the care of the self. That sociality was richly articulated because it embodied the learning that the "care of the self" culture produced through its diverse explorations of the condition of spirituality. Secularization strips sociality of that cultural learning. Christianity as religion creates a religious-secular world. Secularization is, if you like, another face or garb of religion. The secular may once have contrasted with the religious—for example, when Christianity began to oppose itself to the entirely secular pursuit of spiritual knowledge in the Hellenistic-Roman culture. In the Roman world the secular began to contract and, eventually, as the process of the Christianization of the Roman world was completed, the secular world was absorbed within the religious world (MacMullen 1984; Markus 1990; Balagangadhara 1994). The distinction between religious and secular, then, is a distinction drawn within religion. The distinctions between man and citizen, civil society and political society presuppose theology for their intelligibility. Higher, universal interests are to be embodied in the state; base, particular passions are pursued in civil society. Marx unerringly pins this secular, liberal doctrine that enshrines the secular state as the ultimate human achievement for what it truly is: namely, secularized theology. Secular*ism* is thus the way the secular state—that is, the truly religious state—deals with what it construes to be religions.[4]

Fetishism through Genealogy

The above is indeed the claim Marx makes in his "On the Jewish Question." Most commentators of that text and of the early Marx have found Marx's claim puzzling (Leopold 2007). But now that we have the historical, theoretical, and above all, the spiritual presuppositions for understanding his remarks in place, we will be in a position not only to

4. If the direction I am suggesting is persuasive as well as illuminating, we will have a coherent alternative to the current ways of thinking about the secular, secularization, and secularism (which have found expression in a spate of recent books and anthologies discussed with great fanfare on the website of the American Social Science Research Council).

appreciate the full force of Marx's characterization of the secular state but also to give a different dimension to his understanding of alienation and fetishism. Let me quickly redraw the picture necessary for supporting my claim from the discussion of Foucault above. What I aim to do is something far more complicated than the usual sketching of the intellectual context; I'm staging this encounter between Marx and Foucault by seeking an alignment of their problems through their own conceptual story.

Let us ask how European sociality, as Foucault's genealogy would have us sketch it, looked to Marx, who was fashioning his own concepts to understand it. It is important that this move is understood in the right way in order to grasp the significance of the argument I am building. I am not only eschewing the standard or default way of situating thinkers in their own times, I am also steering clear of the way Marxist scholarship has tended to look at the early and late Marx. I do not have the space here to explain why that is necessary or how I see that scholarship; the theoretical yield, I am hoping, will be enough justification. My strategy amounts to the suggestion that Marx's critique needs to be situated within Foucault's genealogy of Western normativizing culture (Dhareshwar 2014). From Foucault we have a twofold description of the secularization of the West. There is the disappearance, or at any rate subjugation, of spiritual knowledge, which leaves the domains of sociality stripped of their cultural learnings; the latter process is captured through the normativization of domains such as the economy, the polity, and erotics.

The same process also throws light on another significant phenomenon: philosophically, the subject as such becomes capable of truth:

> The subject only has to be what he is for him to have access in knowledge (*connaissance*) to the truth that is open to him through his own structure as subject. It seems to me this is very clear in Descartes, with, if you like, the supplementary twist in Kant, which consists in saying that what we cannot know is precisely the structure itself of the knowing subject, which means that we cannot know the subject. Consequently, the idea of a certain spiritual transformation of the subject, which finally gives him access to something to which precisely he does not have access at the moment, is chimerical and paradoxical. So the liquidation of what could be called the condition of spirituality for access to the truth is produced with Descartes and Kant; Kant and Descartes seem to me to be the two major moments. (Foucault 2005, 190)

This liquidation process, I argue, while it produced a different conception of truth and the subject, also effected a reduction of the complex articulation of sociality that the "care of the self" culture had produced. Foucault hints that the condition of spirituality resurfaces in the revolutionary movements of the nineteenth century and in the thought of Hegel and Marx (and also Freud), but this is in some sense a distorted attempt to reunite conditions of spirituality and truth. It is distorted because the transformation of the access to truth into the autonomous development of truth(s) is retained intact or at any rate is not seriously interrupted. Hegel's phenomenological account of the movement of consciousness and self-consciousness into absolute knowledge would be a good, paradigmatic example. His account of family, ethical life, and the state is conceptually rich and nuanced, but it still presupposes the normativized stripping of sociality in these domains. Marx in a way recognizes this, but his critique also misdiagnoses the problem, as one of offering a materialist account in place of the idealist dialectic of concepts (hence, his demand for an account of practice and sensuous activity that is as rich as the Hegelian account of concept formation). Marx's early concept of alienation and his later theory of fetishism (the reification of social relationships and the personification of things) both obliquely register the process that has created a sociality separated from the cultural learning that had articulated it. The analogy that Marx so frequently and insistently draws between capitalism and Christianity shows that somewhere in his theorizing he glimpses a pattern, a link that eludes the explicit conceptual framework. That is the source of the philosophically uncertain status of alienation in his early work. While it seems to indicate something more than the physical separation of the product of labor, there was no conceptual room for Marx to see it as an expression of the experiential or spiritual condition, an experience-occluding structure. In the later theory of fetishism, we have one of the most profound understandings of the autonomization of the reified social relationship, yet Marx fails to realize that his own theory of class and productive forces succumbs to that process.[5]

From Foucault's genealogy we have been able to extract a picture of how culture and sociality are interrelated: in that picture, culture as learning enables sociality and the latter in its turn sustains the former. That was what produced the long summer of the Hellenistic-Roman model of the care of the self. Christianity as religion and capitalism both separate the two and tend to destroy cultural learning. Alienation as a certain kind of experience expresses not the separation of the objectification of labor when the latter becomes labor power; instead, alienation is the separation of action—any action—from the condition of spirituality. Culture, as I have said, enables the social, and the social sustains the cultural. When culture is separated from the social, the latter is poised for reification in many ways. In Foucault's (2003) account "race," "class," and "the nation" are prime examples of the process of reification: the "truth" of blood and history producing the nation, the "truth" of interest producing class.

Although I have deliberately switched to the Marxian term "reification" to render the link transparent and poignant, what creates this condition of sociality is the process that Foucault abstractly characterized as the autonomization of a certain conception of knowing and the forging of the link between truth and subjectivity. Once the domains that were the conditions of application of the care of the self were destroyed, sociality came under the purview of truths that the secular human sciences began to uncover. That process, the one I am calling secularization, transforms the practical domains—domains that had come under the ambit of the condition of spirituality—into spheres that appear autonomous. The practical/ethical sphere of erotics/economics/dietetics is thus unrecognizable in the domain of sexuality (Foucault 1985), whose

5. This may seem enigmatic but only if we fail to see that "class" itself is a product of normativization. Although sexuality is the fully worked-out example of a normativized entity in Foucault's mature work (Dhareshwar 2014), he had opened up other inquiries that we can retrospectively see as attempts to demonstrate how "race," "nation," and "class" too emerge as products of normativization (Foucault 2003). The implication is clear: "class" is a theoretical term that cannot be used in social-scientific explanation everywhere in the world.

truths begin to form subjects; the problematic of self-governance and government of the other morphs into the pastoral project of the welfare state, transforming people into normed subjects or citizens. This, I suggested earlier, is a religious-secular world. The process that Foucault terms govermentalization is what I have been calling normativization. In the same way as monasticization minutely governed the life of the monk, the state, the judiciary, psychiatry, and other such quasi-scientific disciplines, including the human sciences, generalize the mechanism underlying the monastic life to different domains of sociality (Foucault 2007).[6]

Marx is indeed recognizing this world when he says that the truly Christian state is the secular state and not the theocratic state. The state, in the theological picture, had always laid claim to be the true Vicar of Christ, a claim that was at the bottom of the prolonged church-state conflict. In the secular-religious world, the state and politics come to represent the "higher" aspiration of the subject as citizen, with the subject's "lower" or base aspirations being confined to civil society. The secular state deals with Judaism politically by making it part of civil society, and hence belonging to the baser side (Marx 1975, 222). Consistent with this stance, Marx seeks liberation from politics itself, for politics is after all, in this religious-secular world, a form of pastoral power (to switch to Foucault's terminology). For Marx then, emancipation is emancipation from the secular-religious world. It is this picture that lies behind the recurring analogy between Christianity (as religion) and capitalism in Marx's work (both early and late).

Here is an example where the analogy is so drawn that something more than an analogy is straining to break through:

> Therefore the supporters of the monetary and mercantile system, who look upon private property as a purely objective being of man, appear as fetish-worshippers, as Catholics, to this enlightened political economy, which has revealed—within the system of private property—the subjective essence of wealth. Engels was therefore right to call Adam Smith the Luther of political economy. Just as Luther recognized religion and faith as the essence of the external world and in consequence confronted Catholic paganism; just as he transcended external religiosity by making religiosity the inner essence of man; just as he negated the priest as something separate and apart from layman by transforming the priest into the heart of the layman; so wealth as something outside man and independent of him —and therefore only to be acquired and maintained externally—is abolished [auf-gehoben]. I.e., its external and mindless objectivity is abolished inasmuch as private property is embodied in man himself and man himself is recognized as its essence—but this brings man himself into the province of private property, just as Luther brought him into the province of religion. (Marx 1975, 342; emphasis in the original)[7]

---

6. Foucault does not always distinguish governmentalization as a mechanism from government as a domain. It is quite clearly the former that is of crucial importance for understanding secularization. Perhaps the only place where Foucault does explicitly use the term secularization to designate the phenomenon of governmentalization is in his lecture "What is Critique" (Foucault 2007, 44).

7. In *Capital*, the analogy is turned into a relationship of "fitting": "For a society of producers, whose general social relations of production consists in the fact that they treat their products as commodities, hence as values, and in this material form bring their individual, private labours into relation with each

The image of the priest in every layman not only captures what Protestantism accomplishes but as an image also throws light on the normed/norming citizen of the secular-religious republic insofar as this priestliness consists in the assumption of the normative attitude. This passage from Marx is straining to argue that the creation of the province of religion and the province of private property—in which the essence of man as the subject of labor, of sexuality, of madness, of delinquency is lodged—that creation may not be two distinct processes. It is better regarded as two different descriptions of the same process.

Spirituality as Experiential Knowledge

Without an explicit conception of spiritual knowledge, which as Foucault says was driven underground by this time, Marx could only articulate the condition of spirituality by succumbing to the reification of the social. In his case, it turned out to be class. The class politics of the proletariat, he thought, would allow it to transform itself and the sociality that created it. As he was unable to explicitly theorize either alienation or, later, fetishism as the expression of the loss of the condition of spirituality, he could only think of combining intellectual knowledge and reified sociality as an alternative to the religious-capitalist world. As we look back on the tragic results of that experiment in the last century, the pressing question is how else to rediscover the conditions of spirituality and the access to truth in a world whose sociality seems insulated from any cultural learning that may be capable of such a rediscovery? That seems to me at the heart of Foucault's later lectures, from which I have liberally drawn. And yet, he does not explicitly ask why religion/theology is hostile to spiritual knowledge. By way of a conclusion, let me return to that question.

It may be that Foucault takes himself to have answered this question insofar as his discussion of how truth as it figures in the conception of access to truth is radically different from truth in the conception of the subject capable of truth, explicitly talking about the "liquidation" of the condition of spirituality by the dominance of the latter conception. This is entirely right since Foucault associates the emergence of the epistemic concept of truth with Christianity. He fails, however, to explicitly conceptualize this conception of truth as what distinguishes (Christianity as) religion. He often slips into categorizing the "care of the self" schools or groups as religious.

The problem here is not simply one of classification. The failure to distinguish religion from those practicing the care of the self has the disastrous consequence of ignoring one of the major ways in which the secular-religious world deals with those groups pursuing the conditions of spirituality: namely, by construing them as (false) religions. This of course may not be a problem in contemporary Europe (where the "care of the self" groups have disappeared) except in a marginal way, even though early Christianity did indeed deal with the pagan practices by casting them as rival or false religions. But in the non-Western world—as in India, which has been brought into the province of the secular-religious world through colonialism—the way the state deals with

other as homogeneous human labour, Christianity with its religious cult of man in the abstract, more particularly in its bourgeois development, i.e., in Protestantism, Deism, etc., is the most fitting form of religion" (Marx 1976, 172).

traditions of spirituality is reminiscent of Marx's description of how the secular-religious state would deal with the Jewish question. So there is the obvious danger of how the secular-religious world may use familiar strategies of normativization to liquidate surviving traditions of spirituality, if they have not already done so.[8]

If, however, spirituality is knowledge—what I have been calling experiential knowledge—then the issue cannot be only one of resistance and preservation. Are there new ways of interarticulating cultural knowledge and sociality? I have been using the term cultural learning (Dhareshwar 2015) whenever I have spoken of spiritual or experiential knowledge. The reason for that should be obvious: that is, learning is intrinsically linked to happiness. As Foucault too makes clear in his rich reconstructions of the culture of the "care of the self," the conditions of spirituality and access to truth have no one path. There are innumerable ways and heuristics to discover or invent to seek access to truth that brings about transformation in the subject, bringing about happiness. Consequently, the sociality articulated by that cultural learning also tends to be richly layered and pluralized. When, therefore, the religious-secular world of capitalism has begun to strip sociality of all cultural learning, the urgent question for both practical-spiritual knowledge and intellectual knowledge is: how can we articulate new cultural learnings that find expression in the articulation of sociality itself? Perhaps both critique and genealogy will be of service in clarifying what that question demands.

Acknowledgments

I wish to thank Anjan Chakrabarti, A. P. Ashwin Kumar, and Serap Kayatekin for their responsive criticism and for pressing me to clarify my arguments. If obscurity still remains, it is entirely due to my obduracy.

References

Balagangadhara, S. N. 1994. *"The heathen in his blindness ... "*: *Asia, the West and the dynamic of religion.* Leiden: Brill.

Dhareshwar, V. 2014. Critique, genealogy and ethical action. In *Marx, Gandhi and modernity: Essays presented to Javeed Alam*, ed. A. Bilgrami, 98–126. New Delhi: Tulika.

———. 2015. Sites of learning and intellectual parasitism: The case for new humanities. *Journal of Contemporary Thought* 41 (Summer): 57–78.

Foucault, M. 1985. *The use of pleasure.* Trans. R. Hurley. New York: Vintage Books.

———. 2003. *"Society must be defended"*: *Lectures at the Collège de France, 1975–76.* Trans. D. Macey. Basingstoke: Palgrave Macmillan.

8. This is what is taking place in non-European and nonreligious contexts, such as in India. Concealed just beneath the superficial problem of terminology lies the biggest problem, which has gone unnamed. While taking the tolerant policy of "let's ignore what people mean by religion so long as we know what they are referring to," we pass over the problem of saying what exactly happens in this move. We repeat the way secular-religious culture (the state) treats spiritual traditions by misconstruing them as religions, thereby initiating at least one major way of liquidating them.

————. 2005. *The hermeneutics of the subject: Lectures at the Collège de France, 1981–1982*. Trans. G. Burchell. New York: Palgrave Macmillan.

————. 2007. What is critique? In *The politics of truth*, trans. L. Hochroth and C. Porter, 41–82. Los Angeles: Semiotext(e).

Leopold, D. 2007. *The young Karl Marx: German philosophy, modern politics, and human flourishing*. Cambridge: Cambridge University Press.

MacMullen, R. 1984. *Christianizing the Roman Empire (A. D. 100–400)*. New Haven: Yale University Press.

Markus, R. 1990. *The end of ancient Christianity*. Cambridge: Cambridge University Press.

Marx, K. 1975. *Early writings*. Trans. R. Livingstone and G. Benton. Harmondsworth: Penguin.

————. 1976. *Capital*. Vol. 1. Trans. B. Fowkes. Harmondsworth: Penguin.

What Kind of "Life Affirmation"? Disentangling the Conflation of Spinoza and Nietzsche

Jan Rehmann

As we think about how to develop a life-affirming spirituality, we need to be attentive to the social perspectives from which we are speaking. This essay attempts a critique of the widespread conflation of Spinoza and Nietzsche in both mainstream research and poststructuralist interpretations. The assumption of a continuity of their concepts of power overlooks that the late Nietzsche took a sharp anti-Spinozian turn and introduced his "will to power" against Spinoza's conatus. Whereas Spinoza's potentia agendi designates a collective and cooperative capacity to act, Nietzsche's "will to power" naturalizes the principle of domination. A spirituality inspired by Nietzsche's philosophy can never get rid of its inherent "pathos of distance," which manifests itself even in its most "leftist" forms as a celebration of social distinctions against ordinary people. Recourse to Spinoza can help redefine life affirmation in a democratic-socialist way, constituting a dynamic component of counterspirituality from below.

It is certainly true that Marxism, in particular in its dogmatized forms, has introduced a hyper separation between "matter" and "spirit," "science" and "religion," that has made it difficult to rescue any kind of spirituality. It is no less true that many Marxists have made serious efforts to understand and conceptualize a spiritual dimension that is not severed from everyday life but linked to transformative practices in the world. But notwithstanding some one-sided and polemic formulations that have provoked the accusation of materialist reductionism and "objectivism," Marx was mostly interested in what has been later described as a "philosophy of praxis," and he considered the Geist (mind or spirit) not as secondary but as an integral part of "sensuous human activity," subjective practice, and the "language of real life" (see Marx 1845, 3; Marx and Engels 1845–6, 36, 43–4).

For Gramsci,[1] faith/belief (*fede*) designates a worldview that transcends small circles of intellectuals and becomes a popular ethico-political force and part of an "intellectual and moral reform." Ernst Bloch (1986, 1280) distinguished between a traditional *theistic religion* and *faith* as a belief in "what is germinating ... still unfinished in the world" but

---

1. See Gramsci (Q10I§5, Q10II§41.I, Q11§12, Q11§67, Q13§1, 1975).

not yet "spilled out before our eyes."[2] He developed a Marxist concept of spirituality as a "transcending without any heavenly transcendence but with an understanding of it" (1288). It might be a surprise for many to hear that similar perspectives have been developed within theology as well, most famously by Dietrich Bonhoeffer, who in a fascist prison cell shortly before his execution outlined his vision of a "religionless Christianity." Authentic transcendence does not mean a "'religious' relationship to the highest, most powerful, and best Being imaginable" but "a new life in 'existence for others'" (Bonhoeffer 1972, 280, 381–2). Another source of inspiration for critical philosophers and theologians alike is Walter Benjamin's (2007, 254) "weak messianic power" that enables each generation to redeem its defeated ancestors by remembering and reproposing their liberatory projects and hopes in the presence of the now. Indeed, instead of waging the old battles between "atheism" and "religion," "secularism" and "faith," "reason" and "spirituality," progressives (both atheistic and religious) need to learn the skills to mutually *translate* the different discourses.

We need to be aware, however, that the concept of spirituality is no more "innocent" than what is usually described as "religion." For one thing, it is burdened with the long history of a "spirit" that is understood as distinct from and opposed to body and matter. In order to deconstruct this ideological dichotomy, it is imperative to go back to the ancient meanings of spirit as "breath" (Hebrew *ruah*, Greek *pneuma*), which explains, for example, why Agamben (2005, 46–47, 49–51) translates Saint Paul's juxtaposition of *sarx* and *pneuma* not as one of "body" and "spirit" but rather of "flesh" and "breath." For another thing, throughout our bourgeois era of possessive individualism, spirituality has been held captive by an ideology of power-protected "inwardness" that seals it off from communal and political commitments. To counter this tendency, the notion of a "spirituality of the common" has been proposed that helps create and sustain connections of solidarity with one another and with nature (see Kahl and Rehmann 2013). And finally, not dissimilar from religion, the dimension of spirituality is again and again captured by the existing class system and is structured by social distinctions between cultural elites (claiming to develop a "deeper" ontological sense of being) and the "masses" (considered to live a superficial life of mere survival or blind consumption). To a large degree, spirituality has become a distinctive marker for the educated segments of the upper and middle classes. Leftist intellectuals are of course not exempt from reproducing an elitist perspective that conceives of the subaltern masses as being submerged in a conformist and meaningless way of life, not dissimilar to Nietzsche's portrayal of the "last men" that are to be overcome by the "overman." As we think about how to design an embodied, life affirming, and transformative concept of spirituality, we need to be attentive to the social positions and perspectives from which we are speaking.

This brings me to the subject of this essay, a philological and philosophical critique of the widespread conflation of Spinoza and Nietzsche in both mainstream research and poststructuralist interpretations. Though the connection to the title of this special issue, "Marxism and Spirituality," may seem far-fetched at first, this philosophical detour is relevant for a clear awareness about what we mean when we talk about a

---

2. The English edition that translates the German *Glaube* (faith/belief) as "religion" is of course fundamentally flawed.

life-affirming spirituality today. We are confronted with the problem that our access to one of the most democratic philosophers of early modernity is to a large degree mediated and thus distorted by one of the most elitist and aristocratic thinkers. More specifically, I will oppose what has become a commonplace opinion in the literature: namely, the assumption that Nietzsche's will to power is identical with or congenial to Spinoza's concept of power. It was primarily via Gilles Deleuze that this line of continuity became influential within the academic Left, contributing to a widespread confusion between collective power from below and power of domination from above. I will try to show that this confusion is philologically untenable and politically devastating. It belongs to a grand narrative in Nietzsche research that is characterized by a "hermeneutics of innocence" (Losurdo 2004)—that is, by an interpretative paradigm that dissimulates the elitist and antidemocratic perspectives of Nietzsche's philosophy.

Since I try to peel off the different layers of the continuity thesis, I need to develop my argument through a series of textual analyses. My philological findings can be summarized in five points: (1) the widespread juxtaposition of Spinoza's "static" and Nietzsche's "dynamic" notions of power is untenable and diverts attention from the fundamental qualitative difference between their respective concepts of power; (2) Nietzsche relied on a philosophical handbook (Kuno Fischer) that translated Spinoza's concept of *potentia* as "power" in general and thus facilitated a semantic shift from a collective agency from below to a domination/power from above; (3) it is true that the "middle" Nietzsche was influenced by Spinoza, but the continuity thesis overlooks that the late Nietzsche took a sharp anti-Spinozian turn and introduced his "will to power" against Spinoza's *conatus*; (4) rethinking Spinoza's concepts of *potentia* and *potestas* in the framework of Gramsci's theory of hegemony allows us to reassess Antonio Negri's groundbreaking interpretation of Spinoza; whereas his assumption of an "absolute antagonism" between *potentia* and *potestas* was a simplification, his observation of an ontological priority of *potentia* is still accurate; (5) whereas Spinoza's *potentia agendi* designates a collective and cooperative capacity oriented toward relations of synergy with others, Nietzsche's "will to power" naturalizes the principle of oppression and domination. When he adopts some Spinozian descriptions of *potentia*, he is in fact operating a hostile takeover that turns a potentially democratic agency into an elitist notion of aristocratic domination that he fantasizes further into the annihilation of the weak.

Even if the different meanings of "power" might intersect in empirical phenomena, it is important to keep them apart on an analytical level. Such conceptual discernment allows us to recognize Spinoza's importance for the development of a progressive and life-affirming spirituality that does not fall into the trap of reproducing the traditional Western dichotomies of matter and spirit, body and mind, reason and emotion, knowledge and imagination.

"Hermeneutics of Innocence" as a Grand Narrative of Nietzsche Scholarship

The equating of Spinoza's and Nietzsche's power concepts is indeed overwhelming. William Wurzer (1975, 171, 200–1) has argued that even though Nietzsche abandoned

Spinoza's goal of an eternal rest in God, both believed that power is the source of movement and therefore of existence. According to Deleuze's (1986, 62) classic book *Nietzsche and Philosophy* of 1962, Nietzsche's will to power can be derived from Spinoza's capacity for being affected so that it can be defined as the "determined capacity of force for being affected" or as an "affectivity, a sensibility, a sensation." Absent in this equation, of course, is Nietzsche's hierarchical obsession that motivates him to define power in terms of an aristocratic rule *over* the popular classes. The assumption of a continuity between Spinoza's and Nietzsche's concepts of power is then reaffirmed in Michael Hardt's (1993, 34–8) study on Deleuze. It is therefore hardly a surprise to see it emerge again in Hardt and Negri's (2000, 358–9) *Empire*, which describes Nietzsche's power concept in terms of an "expansive power," so that its difference to Spinoza is reduced to an "omnilateral expansiveness of the power to act." This assumption is quite astonishing because it contradicts Negri's (1991, 137–9, 220–1, 228–9) own finding in *The Savage Anomaly* that Spinoza's concept of power is characterized by expansiveness and is thereby to be mediated with Marx's concept of productive forces.

It is not an exaggeration to describe this line of continuity as a powerful "grand narrative" that has been dominating the research on Spinoza and Nietzsche for decades, with only a few voices objecting to it. From there, the equation seeped into innumerable studies in philosophy and social theory, so that (for example) Manuel Vasquez's (2011, 46–7) substantial book *More than Belief: A Materialist Theory of Religion* contains the questionable assumption that Spinoza's "*conatus* as self-affirming and identity-constructing striving ... foreshadows Nietzsche's even more radical notion of the will to power." A 2013 conference on "Spinoza and Nietzsche in Dialogue" at the University of London was marked by the commonly shared opinion that there is a "remarkable affinity" between Spinoza's and Nietzsche's concepts of power (Wiesmann 2013) and that the ethical position of Nietzsche's will to power is the same as Spinoza's *potentia* (Rutherford 2013). As Domenico Losurdo (2004, 563–4) has demonstrated in detail, the predominant interpretation is based on a "hermeneutics of innocence" that considers any historical-political reconstruction of Nietzsche's propositions to be a violation of his philosophy. It subjugates even Nietzsche's bluntest statements—from the support of slavery to the annihilation of the weak and degenerate—to an allegorical interpretation and thereby depoliticizes one of the sharpest masters of suspicion, who was proud of his uncompromising "aristocratic radicalism," as Nietzsche himself called it.[3]

I take as an example the way Deleuze's *Nietzsche and Philosophy* deals with Nietzsche's "pathos of distance." In the *Genealogy of Morals*, Nietzsche had defined this pathos as a "pathos of nobility ... the feeling of complete and fundamental superiority of a higher ruling kind in relation to a lower kind, to those 'below,'" and it was also clear that for him the terms "noble" and "master" as well as "base" and "slave" were to be understood not in a moral sense but in a caste or estate sense (*im ständischen Sinn*)—that is, in the sense of an aristocratic classism from above. His examples were the ancient Greek aristocracy, the Roman "warrior," the "Aryan" conquering and master race, and the "magnificent blond beast" (Nietzsche 1999, 5:259–65, 5:275) In a first move, Deleuze (1986, 2) renders Nietzsche's "pathos" quote as "pathos of difference and distance," thus associating it with the seemingly innocent term "difference";

---

3. See also Losurdo (2004, 781, 798) and a book review by Rehmann (2007).

then he interprets Nietzsche's class oppositions as a "differential element" that distinguishes between the "active force" or "affirmative will" on the one hand and the "reactive force" or "negative will" on the other (55–7, 61, 86). By this allegorical interpretation, the staunch antidemocratic and antisocialist aristocrat morphs into a "nomadic rebel" who is much more radical and subversive than Marx and Freud because he "decodifies" the state and the family and helps us develop a "war machine" against the state (Deleuze 1995, 142–4, 148–52). Paradoxically, the depoliticization of Nietzsche was the precondition for a new repoliticization that positioned him among the "radical Left" during and after 1968. The basic philosophical operation that underlies this shift is to disguise Nietzsche as Spinoza, and the cornerstone of this rapprochement is the equating of their power concepts.[4]

Let us next try to peel off the different layers of the continuity thesis.

"Static" versus "Dynamic" Power?

So far as this grand narrative considers the differences between Spinoza and Nietzsche, it does so in the framework that the latter has developed further the former's concept of power in two respects: (1) that Nietzsche freed the Spinozian concept of power from its connection to "reason," which was in turn oriented toward the knowledge of God; and (2) that he transformed Spinoza's "static" model of self-preservation into a dynamic model of power enlargement.

The first difference can be justified by numerous quotes in which Nietzsche criticizes Spinoza's orientation to reason as a rationalist "prejudice" (Nietzsche 1999, 9:517, 9:490) that destroys affects by analysis and vivisection (118). This contradicts, however, Spinoza's (2001, pt. 4, prop. 7 and 14, dem.) observation in the *Ethics* that knowledge (*cognitio*) cannot restrain at all an affect except if it becomes itself an affect and furthermore a stronger one. Nietzsche (1999, 9:517) is aware of this, since he summarizes in his Spinoza excerpt that cognition must "be an affect, in order to be a motive." Contrary to Nietzsche's criticism, Spinoza's *reason* is a quite subtle concept. Instead of "destroying" affects, it rather surfs on conflicting emotions. Its role is to "arrange and connect" the existing affections of the body so that, for example, hatred is to be conquered by love or generosity and is not to be met with hatred in return (Spinoza 2001, pt. 5, prop. 10, schol.); Spinoza's reason is concerned with balancing the differences of affects, and this balancing act is in particular achieved by cheerfulness or hilarity (*hilaritas*), which entails that "all the parts of the body are equally affected, that is to say, the body's power of action (*Corporis potentia agendi*) is increased" (pt. 4, prop. 42, dem.).

The second difference addresses the difficulty that Spinoza does not define the affects in a static way but is rather interested in their dynamics. He even defines the affects according to the criterion of whether they increase or diminish the body's

4. For a critique of this left-Nietzschean shift, see Rehmann (2004, 52–60). At the same time as Deleuze transforms Nietzsche in a kind of rejuvenated Spinoza, he submits Spinoza to a Nietzschean interpretation, inspired by life philosophy (Oittinen 1994, 65). As Karl Reitter (2011, 350) has shown, he replaces Spinoza's free community with Nietzsche's "strong individual" and thus gives his philosophy an "a-social turn."

capacity to act (Spinoza 2001, pt. 3, def. 3), and it is in particular the affect of joy that increases the body's power of action (pt. 4, prop. 41, dem.). Contrary to any dualism between body and spirit, the same motives that increase our body's power of action also increase our power of thought (pt. 3, prop. 11 and 12). And again Nietzsche is completely aware of this dynamic character of Spinoza's power concept when he summarizes in his Spinoza excerpt that "we do what we do, in order to preserve and to increase our power" (Nietzsche 1999, 12:261). But this knowledge does not prevent him from criticizing in *The Gay Science* the self-preservation principle of the "consumptive Spinoza" from the point of view of his own concept of power enlargement as an expression of "people in distress" caused by their descent from the popular classes (3:585).[5] He thereby has set his readers on a wrong track, and a large part of Nietzsche scholarship has lost its way in this maze.

The consequences of this paradigm can be seen when scholars cannot but recognize that Nietzsche's juxtaposition is misguided. As Günter Abel (1998, 51) observes, Nietzsche empties Spinoza's concept of power of its dynamic moment and thus reduces it to the static principle of self-preservation. But instead of criticizing Nietzsche for this deceptive manipulation, he praises it as philosophically productive because it overcomes the still remaining "teleology" in Spinoza's *conatus* and thus gets to a "completely a-dualistic concept of process-events" (53). But why should Nietzsche's will to power not be "teleological"—namely, oriented toward the increase of power? We should also consider that a philosophical critique of "teleology" needs to differentiate between different levels: are we dealing with the construct of a predesigned teleology in nature or in history or with the fact that human beings in different spaces and time periods anticipate goals and perspectives? The latter designates a capacity that according to Spinoza in the *Ethics* (2001, pt. 1, appendix; pt. 2, prop. 40) belongs to the nature of our imagination. Without developing capacities of anticipation and hope, emancipatory social movements can neither emerge nor maintain themselves.[6] Negri (2013, 8, 78–9) speaks in this regard of a "teleology of praxis" from below, oriented toward the construction of the common.

Similar to Abel, Hannah Grosse Wiesmann proves in detail how Nietzsche deliberately and one-sidedly reduced Spinoza's concept of power to a static notion of self-preservation. But instead of inquiring why Nietzsche did this, she simply reiterates the standard assumption that the two concepts of power are closely related. The only difference is that, according to Nietzsche, it is not the *subject* but the *will to power* that wants to preserve itself (Wiesmann 2013). Even though we have learned from Althusser that history is a "process without a subject" (i.e., it is not driven by a unitary mover of history, which of course is not a denial that there are innumerous subjects involved in the process), the idea of a "will" without willing subjects is an oxymoron. The argument gets lost in uttermost abstractions.

---

5. English Darwinism, which Nietzsche considers to be heavily influenced by Spinoza, stemmed from "poor and lowly folks who knew all too intimately the difficulty of scraping by"; also, it "exudes something like the stuffy air of English overpopulation, like the small people's smell of indigence and overcrowding" (Nietzsche 1999, 3:585).
6. For the significance of "anticipation" in Marxism and particularly in the philosophy of Ernst Bloch, see Rehmann (2012).

I'd like to propose instead to read Nietzsche's fallacious distinction between a static and an expansive concept of power as a symptom of the fact that the real difference between Spinoza's *potentia agendi* and his own concept of power is to be found somewhere else. Already the terminological coincidence is questionable and goes back to a problematic translation.

Power as a Sociologically Amorphous Concept

It is very likely that Nietzsche had never read Spinoza's writings themselves. He had only a secondhand knowledge, in particular through Kuno Fischer's (1880) *Geschichte der neuern Philosophie*, which translated the Spinozian concept of *potentia* simply as "power."[7] Most Anglo-Saxon translations did the same. In some German editions based on the translation of Jakob Stern, the term *potentia agendi* is translated as "capability of activity" (*Tätigkeitsvermögen*). Similarly, the *Historical-Critical Dictionary of Marxism* decided to translate *potentia agendi* as "capacity to act" (*Handlungsfähigkeit*) and thus associated it with the respective concept of the critical psychology school founded by Klaus Holzkamp—a subject-theoretical key concept that is designed to connect individual and social reproduction in a nonreductionist way.[8]

We get a similar basic signification, however, when we look at the etymology of the Germanic and Romance-language terms for power. The German term *Macht* goes back to the Gothic terms *mahts* and *magan*, which mean "to be capable." This corresponds to the French verb *pouvoir*, or *poder* that underly the Romance nouns *(le) pouvoir, puissance*, and *poder*. In both language families, *Macht*/power is connoted with *Möglichkeit*/possibility, which explains why Zedler's *Universal-Lexikon* of 1739 (quoted in Röttgers 1980, 585) can define power as a capacity "to make the possible real." When Michael Hardt and Antonio Negri (2000, 407–8) describe the "power of the multitude" in terms of its "becoming subject," they refer to the Latin verb *posse*: "power as a verb, as activity," part of the Renaissance triad *esse-nosse-posse*, being-knowing-having power, expressing "what a body and what a mind can do."

This etymology is theoretically relevant in that it supports the idea that power is, as Max Weber (1978, 53) put it, "sociologically amorphous." Tied to a complex of capacities, it might express both reciprocal relationships and unequal ones (such as in a pedagogical constellation), both competencies monopolized by elites or cooperative capacities to act from below. Whereas *power* is in principle open to democratization, the concept of *domination* is formed around the ancient figure of the *dominus* ("master"; in German, *der Herr* in *Herrschaft*), which embodies the intersection of patriarchal and class rule. It cannot therefore be conceived without its constitutive meanings of hierarchy and verticality. Whereas *power* is to be found on opposite sides of class, gender, and race divides, *domination* is an "institutionalized, structurally anchored asymmetric power relation of superiority and subordination" (Goldschmidt 2004, 83). Max Weber (1978, 53–4) defines it by the successful issuing of "commands" to others, bolstered by an "administrative staff" ready to exercise the "necessary compulsion."

7. See the detailed philological studies of Brobjer (2004) and Sommer (2012).
8. See Reeling-Brouwer (2001) and Markard (2001).

The analytical distinction between power and domination is of course not to be understood as an empirical distinction of two separated domains. What the capability of "making the possible real" is actually *capable of* in the framework of antagonistic class societies depends to a large degree on the respective social position in this system of domination. The general meaning of capacity can therefore morph easily and unnoticed into the meaning of a particular capacity made possible by a privileged social position, and this might occur without the need to change the term "power." This ambiguity traverses the entire conceptual history of power, which in turn needs to be deciphered as a field of hegemonic power struggles. It circulates in an ellipse around the two poles of the general capacity *of people* to act and of the narrow signification of the power of domination *over people*, in which the capacity to act is monopolized by the ruling classes and power elites.

When we try to locate Spinoza and Nietzsche on this ellipse, we need to be aware that the usage of the ambiguous *terms* representing "power" does not coincide with the underlying *concepts*. Before we reconstruct these concepts from their respective combinations, we will take a closer look at where Nietzsche was indeed inspired by Spinoza and where and why he took his distance from him.

The Late Nietzsche's Departure from Spinoza

That Nietzsche (1975, III) was influenced by Spinoza already in July 1881 can be shown by his famous postcard to Overbeck in which he enthusiastically described Spinoza as his predecessor because "he denies free will—; purpose—; a moral world order—; the nonegotistical—; evil—." This positive reception of Spinoza coincides with Nietzsche's so-called "middle" period, which stretches from his break with Wagner around 1876 to the end of 1882, when he started preparing *Thus Spoke Zarathustra* (published in 1883). It is often called the "enlightened" period, characterized by Nietzsche's (1999, 6:322, 6:325) attempt to rid himself from what he describes in *Ecce Homo* as "the opiate Wagner," a peculiar combination of romantic idealism, German nationalism, and anti-Semitism. During this middle period, Nietzsche intensely collaborated with and befriended Paul Rée, a Jewish moral philosopher who was in turn influenced by Spinoza. It was also Rée who introduced Nietzsche to the French moral critics de Montaigne, de La Rochefoucauld, de Vauvenarges, de La Bruyère, and Stendhal. It seems that Nietzsche's friendship with the Jewish intellectual helped him to overcome his earlier anti-Semitism, at least partially and temporarily (see Losurdo 2004, 206, 272). It was not only Wagner himself but also other contemporaries around him who blamed Rée's "destructive" influence for Nietzsche's separation from those who saw his critique of "ideals" as an embarrassing aberration—Nietzsche's "milieu" responded to Nietzsche's ideology-critique by mobilizing anti-Semitic stereotypes.[9] Indeed, in *Human, All-Too Human*, Nietzsche (1999, 2:310) combined his naturalist materialism with praise of the Jewish people for having provided humanity not only with Christ as the noblest

---

9. See Pfeiffer (1970, 252, 286, 310). Cosima Wagner (quoted in Treiber 1999, 515) notes in her diary of 1 November 1876: "Dr. Rée pays us a visit in the evening, but his cold and blunt character does not appeal to us. On closer examination we find out that he must be an Israelite."

man but also with Spinoza as the "purest sage." One should, however, not overlook the inconsistencies: at the same time as the middle Nietzsche praised the nomadic rootless cosmopolitism of the Jews (2:309–11), he maintained the anti-Semitic stereotype of the "Börsen-Jude" (stock-market Jew) as the "most disgusting invention of the human species" (2:310; see also the analysis in Losurdo 2004, 252–8). Spinoza's influence can be seen in particular in the criticism of free will, teleology, morality, and "life negation." The middle Nietzsche also uses the Spinozian concept of "self-preservation" (2:95), which he later denounced as an outcome of Spinoza's physical weakness and "phthisis" (3:585).

The advocates of continuity between Spinoza and Nietzsche overlook, however, that Nietzsche's relationship to Spinoza undergoes a fundamental change when he transitions to his late period. This late period, starting about the end of 1882, is characterized by a radicalization of his antidemocratic aristocratism. Also, the anti-Semitism of his early Wagnerian period comes back with a vengeance, but it is now integrated more consistently into a radical classism from above against all subaltern classes.[10] This transition is a highly overdetermined process that comprises manifold social, political, and biographical aspects. Toward the end of 1882, Nietzsche's friendship with Paul Rée turned into hostility and contempt because both fell in love with Lou Andreas-Salomé. This crisis of unhappy love coincided with the composition of *Zarathustra*, by which Nietzsche (see 1975, 324) had "elevated himself 'vertically' from this low point to [Nietzsche's] altitude," as he writes in a letter to Overbeck.[11] This new and precarious "altitude" would accompany Nietzsche during his late period, until his breakdown in 1889.

In November 1882, again at the time of his break with Salomé and Rée, Nietzsche introduced for the first time his concept of a "will to power" (1999, 10:187), which from then on replaced the Spinozian concept of "self-preservation." From spring 1883 onward, we can observe a growing distance to Spinoza that turned into open hostility. He attacked Spinoza's *conatus* of self-preservation as the plebeian foundation of "English empiricism" (1999, 11:224). Spinoza was depicted as a sneaky advocate of vengeance and resentment, an insidious preparer of poison.[12] The climax of anti-Semitic stereotypes was reached when Nietzsche wrote a skit on Spinoza, which says among other things:

> Yet secretly beneath this love, devouring
> A fire of revenge was shimmering
> The Jewish God devoured by Jewish hatred ...
> Hermit! Have I recognized you? (11:319)

The fact that Nietzsche broke with Spinoza at the very time when he developed his famous "will to power" shows already that the assumed linearity between Spinoza's and Nietzsche's power concepts is erroneous. But how can we then

---

10. According to Domenico Losurdo (2004, 823–5, 851–2, 877–8), the position of the late Nietzsche is to be analyzed in the framework of a transversal racialization (*razzizzazione trasversale*) directed immediately against the popular classes and the poor.

11. "If I don't find this alchemist trick to transform these feces into *gold*, I am lost," Nietzsche (1975, 312) writes in a letter of 25 December 1882.

12. See Nietzsche (1999, 3:585, 3:624, 5:43, 6:126, 6:184, 10:350, 11:226, 13:504, 13:537).

explain that both Spinoza and Nietzsche seem to equate virtue and power, power and ethics?

An "Absolute Antagonism" between *Potentia* and *Potestas*?

It is important to realize that Spinoza used two different terms for what is usually translated as "power": namely, *potentia* and *potestas*. The relationship between these two terms has become a contested issue in the scholarly debate. Antonio Negri (1991, 229) has described it as a relationship of "absolute antagonism." According to him, *potentia* expresses the creative capacity and collective praxis of the many and thus founds a "metaphysics of production" in which the productive forces free themselves from the relations of production (218, 228–9); on the other hand, *potestas* designates a power that subordinates multiplicity, the mind, freedom, and *potentia* (190–1). The thesis of an "absolute antagonism" is connected to a second argument: *potentia* has ontological priority in that it is the constitutive power that connects the singular and the multitude, whereas *potestas* is a secondary, reactive force/violence that tries to channel *potentia* into rigid and ossified forms.[13] We can already see in this reading the conceptual arrangement of *Empire*, *Multitude*, and *Commonweath*, according to which a "biopolitical" productive force of the multitude is exploited and manipulated by the parasitic apparatus of Empire.

Against this interpretation Marin Terpstra (1990, 80–8) has objected that Spinoza did not consistently maintain such a terminological opposition but instead tried to integrate the concept of *potestas* into that of *potentia*. Martin Saar (2013, 175–6) challenged what he saw as Negri's "over-interpretation of a terminological distinction," claiming that Spinoza used the concept of *potestas* often not as an antagonism to *potentia* but rather in the sense of its intensification. According to him, Negri's dichotomy overlooks that there is no fundamental anti-institutional impulse in Spinoza's work and that Spinoza considers the establishment of institutional and procedural regulations of the *potestas* as a core issue of political thought (178).

Negri's thesis of an "absolute antagonism" between *potentia* and *potestas* is indeed a simplification of a more complex relationship. In Spinoza's (2007, 197–9) *Theological-Political Treatise*, the term *potestas* is used in the context of higher state powers (*superiores potestates*), whereas *potentia* designates the competences that individuals transfer to such a higher governmental power. Spinoza indeed does not oppose such a transfer from the multitude to the state and even supports a strong *potestas* of the state—not least in order to secure some protection from the Jewish and Christian religious apparatuses that had excommunicated him or denounced him for atheism.

But Spinoza does keep the two concepts at a distance. People will not be able to transfer their power (*potentia*) to other persons in such a way that they cease to be human beings, and there will never be a sovereign power (*potestas*) that can dispose of everything just as it pleases (2007, 208). Contrary to Hobbes, Spinoza thinks this

---

13. Similarly, for Frédéric Lordon (2014, 160), "There is no *potestas* that does not emanate from *potentia* (*multitudinis*)—but in the form of hijacking and to the advantage of the most powerful of master-desires, the desire of the sovereign."

power to act is to be transferred to the entire society: democracy is for him the "most natural" form of state because it "approaches most closely to the freedom nature bestows on every person ... no one transfers their natural right to another in such a way that they are not thereafter consulted but rather to the majority of the whole society of which they are a part. In this way all remain equal as they had been previously, in the state of nature" (202). This corresponds to the ideal that "the whole of society ... should hold power together, collegially, so that all are subject to themselves and nobody must serve their equal," with the result that all "are acting ... by their own proper consent" (73). The ultimate purpose of the state is therefore "not to dominate or control people by fear or subject them to the authority of another" but rather to allow people's "minds and bodies to develop in their own ways in security and enjoy the free use of reason"—that is, "in fact freedom" (252).

It is important to notice that Spinoza's *potentia* of the many is never fully surrendered to the *potestas* of the state. In the context of the "absolutistic" seventeenth century, it articulates a significant democratic counterweight. Matheron (1997, 214–5) argues that there is no power transfer in the proper sense because sovereignty remains defined not by the *potestas* of the sovereign but by the *potentia* of the multitude. According to Balibar (1997a, 174–6), Spinoza's conflict-ridden state of nature is not abolished by a homogenous state law; the conceptual arrangement maintains a dialectical openness to the opposition between the established *summae potestates* and the multitude: the *potestas* can only put its power into practice effectively if the people, who constituted it, consider it as a law that corresponds to their will. Obviously, Spinoza struggles with a key problem of hegemony as later elaborated by Marxist theories: in the long run, the *potestas* of the state—its characteristics as *società politica*, as Gramsci would call it, or as "repressive state apparatus," as Althusser would reformulate—depends ultimately on the consensus of the people and thus remains bound to their *potentia agendi* (in whatever illusory and displaced manner). It is obvious that Spinoza has no elaborate theory of how such a mass consensus is fabricated by ideological apparatuses from above.

Where Negri Is Nevertheless Right

The fact that Negri reduces the contradictory relationship between *potentia* and *potestas* to an "absolute antagonism" is due primarily to his sweeping rejection of any dialectics and of social mediations. This leads Negri and Michael Hardt to the illusory assumption that the "immaterial labor" of the multitude and the Empire confront each other in an immediate opposition and without any civil society mediations.[14] Negri is absolutely right, however, when he insists on the ontological priority of *potentia*. Even if Spinoza employs the notion of *potestas* in different ways, he uses the notion of *potentia* consistently. The different usage in regard to *potestas* can in turn be explained by an ambiguity of social and political reality itself: the question of whether or to what extent a state power is actually backed by the

14. See Hardt and Negri (2000, 25–7, 2004, 108–10, 114). For a critique of the concept of "immaterial labor," see Haug (2004).

potentia of the many depends on the concrete conjuncture and cannot be decided beforehand. It also needs to be mentioned that Negri (2013, 13, 25) in his later book *Spinoza for Our Time* distanced himself from the assumption of an "absolute antagonism" and argued that *potentia* and *potestas* are characterized not by an "ontological dualism" but rather by both an interaction and a dissociation, so that *potentia* can work both within and against *potestas*.

In Spinoza's *Ethics, potentia* first emerges at the center of his concept of God. It is conceived not in terms of transcendent religion as power over human and nonhuman beings but rather in the sense that God does and thinks an infinitude of things in an infinite way: the "power of God is nothing but the active essence of God" (Spinoza 2001, pt. 2, prop. 3, dem. and schol.), a "substance consisting of infinite attributes" (pt. 1, def. 6), "existing from the necessity of its own nature alone," and determined to action by itself alone (pt. 1, def. 7). It is the active essence of *potentia* that mediates and holds together Spinoza's equation God = substance = nature (*natura naturans*). God is conceived as a universal potentiality of production that operates within each individual reality. The notion of God as a depersonalized, subjectless productive force is also the foundation of a critique of transcendent religion, which in its anthropocentrism ascribes human affects to God (pt. 1, prop. 8, schol. 2). Seduced by this anthropocentric teleology, humans "assert that the gods ordained everything for the use of man" and thus degrade the gods to an instrument of their own "blind cupidity and insatiable avarice" (pt. 1, app.). Althusser (1976, 135), who uses Spinoza's ideas to de-Hegelianize Marxism, links Spinoza's concept of an immanent God to his philosophical critique of teleology: "Spinoza, because he 'begins with God,' never gets involved with any Goal"; not only did he refuse such a Goal but he also explained it "as a necessary and therefore well-founded illusion," which leads Althusser to the conclusion that Spinoza formulated the "first theory of *ideology* ever thought out."[15]

Looking at Spinoza's usage of humans' *potentia agendi*, one can see that it is never employed as dominating power *over* people. The difference with God's *potentia* is that it is "infinitely limited by the power of some other object, and … infinitely surpassed by the power of external causes" (Spinoza 2001, pt. 4, prop. 3, dem.). That's why humans need to adapt to nature and are subjected to sufferings, or *passionibus* (pt. 4, prop. 4, cor.). To translate the Latin term *passio* as "passion" without any specification, as many Anglo-Saxon editions do, is of course misleading. Spinoza uses the terms *passio* and *pati* for something of which we are not the "adequate cause" and that is therefore done to us. It designates a passive attitude, the state of being subjected to alienating powers, or to reformulate it in Gramscian terms, to be held in subalternity by "foreign hegemonies";[16] to this imposed subalternity he opposes the notion of *acting*, which means that we are the adequate cause of our actions (pt. 3, def. 2). This emphatic notion of acting, caused by itself and self-determined although always limited by external causes, is the starting point for the "geometrical method" that characterizes

---

15. Althusser (1976, 135) then specifies three characteristics of Spinoza's ideology-theory: "(1) Its *imaginary* 'reality'; (2) its internal *inversion*; (3) its 'center': the illusion of the *subject*"; for a critical evaluation, see Rehmann (2014, 160–5).

16. See Gramsci (Q6§38, 1975).

Spinoza's *Ethics*, a method that describes affects and virtues according to their enhancing or inhibiting potentials—just as if he were considering "lines, planes, or bodies" (pt. 3, preface).

We can well imagine why Nietzsche in his middle "ideological-critical" period was impressed by this "geometrical" critique of morality, and some traces of this approach can also be discovered in his later work. But the "power" from which Spinoza criticizes morality is conceived as a cooperative capacity. Contrary to Nietzsche's elitist cult of heroic loneliness, Spinoza is interested in a processual "transindividuality" oriented toward relations of synergy with others (Balibar 1997b). The *potentiae* of the individuals are realized in a social collaboration: even if satirists, theologians, and melancholiacs scoff at human communities, people find out that they are "social animals" equipped with the experience that "far more advantages than disadvantages arise from the common society of men" and that "by mutual help they can much more easily procure the things they need, and that it is only by their united strength they can avoid the dangers which everywhere threaten them" (Spinoza 2001, pt. 4, prop. 35, schol.). Spinoza's *potentia agendi* is embedded in these cooperative arrangements. If people are placed among those who agree with their nature, their "power of action will by that very fact be assisted and supported" (pt. 4, append., num. 7). *Potentia* is the capacity that makes people agree with each other, whereas *impotentia* and passive suffering separates people and turns them against each other (pt. 4, prop. 32–4); the virtue resulting from this *potentia* is oriented toward what is common to all and can be equally possessed by all (pt. 4, prop. 37).

One of Martin Saar's (2013, 161–2) objections to Negri's interpretation is that Spinoza's *potentia* covers all meanings of power, the enhancement as well as the endangerment, empowerment as well as its opposite, and the dispossession of power. It is no coincidence that he does not back up this assumption by any reference, for Spinoza does not actually use *potentia agendi* in the sense of destruction and dispossession. Saar confuses the level of theoretical concepts with the level of description of the concrete, which according to Marx's (1857–8, 100) methodological self-reflection in the *Grundrisse* is a "rich totality [Zusammenfassung] of many determinations and relations." One of the main tasks of social theory is to develop analytical concepts that grasp specific dimensions underlying social life and its meanings. These dimensions cut across the concrete realities of societal relations and surface in different contradictory combinations. It is beyond dispute that the capacity to act of the many is regularly and continuously appropriated, accumulated, and instrumentalized by the powers of domination. It is not possible, however, to conceptualize these modes of appropriation/dispossession and alienation if one sneaks them already beforehand into the concept of *potentia* itself. Saar (2013, 163) argues that one should not give Spinoza's concept of power a "sharpness of differentiation" that "artificially tears apart related problems." I would suggest to proceed the other way around: to define the concepts both of *potentia agendi* and of domination in an analytically sharp manner, as "ideal-types," as Max Weber would say, so that we can use them for an investigation of the complex and ambiguous mixture ratios of power and domination in empirical reality.

Nietzsche Turns Spinoza's *Potentia Agendi* into Its Exterministic Opposite

When the early Nietzsche demands that one should have the courage of Hobbes and derive moral precepts from the *bellum omnium contra omnes* and the prerogative of the strongest (Nietzsche 1999, 1:194, 1:772), he positions himself already at the opposite pole of the power ellipse. In his late writings, he portrays power as conquest, suppression of the weak, exploitation, and the will to violation and rape, all of which "belong to the nature of the living being," as he explains in *Beyond Good and Evil*.[17] Nietzsche's syntagm "will to power" has the function to naturalize the principle of oppression and domination and to anchor it in the "essence of life" itself. Inheriting the capacity of the Kantian transcendental subject to bring order into the sensual chaos, Nietzsche's "will to power" constructs an ontological identity between the social relations of domination with the strictly hierarchized insides of the subject (divided into "commanding" and "obeying" parts), between organic and inorganic nature, human beings and protoplasm, which Nietzsche describes in terms of slavery and castes.[18] All of these levels are determined by the same principle: it is solely the "ruling role of the highest functionaries ... in which the will to life emerges as active and form-giving" (Nietzsche 1999, 5:316). Whatever is active and creative is described as an effect of aristocratic rule, which is in turn disguised as the "affirmation of life."

If one omits reconstructing the meaning of Spinoza's *potentia agendi* from its connections with cooperative production and relationships, one cannot understand the fundamental transformation that happened when the term was appropriated by Nietzsche. Whereas Spinoza's concept is meant to lead to common activities and thus to produce a "power-accumulation in each part of the aggregate" (Röttgers 1980, 597–8), Nietzsche's concept of power is oriented toward power accumulation by the very few and the disempowerment of the many. His terminological adoptions of some of Spinoza's terms are part of a hostile takeover by which the elements are severed from their original context and integrated in an opposite arrangement.

Let us examine this shift of meaning with a famous example: when Spinoza (2001, pt. 4, def. 8) argues that *virtue* and *potentia* are the same, we can interpret this in the sense that one cannot discuss moral values and attitudes detached from the development of collective and cooperative agency. It is not too far-fetched to translate this into Gramsci's ethico-political perspective that the subaltern classes need to develop their own hegemony. Nietzsche summarizes this definition in his Spinoza excerpts as follows: "Virtue and power are identical ... Good is what heightens our power; evil is the opposite" (Nietzsche 1999, 12:261). We can see already that the translation of *potentia* as power as such introduces a slippery ambiguity into the statement that opens the way to a hierarchical notion of power. Nietzsche then transfers this sentence almost verbatim to his *Der Antichrist*: "What is good? Everything that heightens the feeling of power in man, the will to power, power itself. What is bad? Everything that is born of weakness." Some readers might still fancy from this a general deliberation on virtue, power, and weakness as such, but the philosophical abstraction is suddenly disrupted when

17. See Nietzsche (1999, 5:207–8, 5:313–4) and compare also Nietzsche (1999, 13:258).
18. See Nietzsche (1999, 9:490, 12:92, 12:424, 13:360).

Nietzsche continues: "The weak and the failures shall perish ... and they shall even be given every possible assistance" (6:170; and see 13:192). In fact, both his appeal to the weak and failures committing suicide in order to show at least a remainder of virility and also the eugenic fantasy to "assist" them by killing them altogether belong to the ongoing obsessions of the late Nietzsche, for whom the creation of the future man requires on the one hand his systematic breeding and on the other hand the "annihilation of millions of failures" (11:98).[19]

I will not try to summarize or resolve the numerous debates on the relationship between Nietzsche's philosophy and the regime of German fascism. A differentiated analysis would certainly take its distance from both a "hermeneutics of innocence," which severs Nietzsche from his political context and puts the blame on his sister Elizabeth, and the assumption of a direct continuity, which flattens out the differences between Nietzsche's "aristocratic radicalism" and the right-wing populism that undergirds the ascent of fascist ideology (see Losurdo 2004, 654–6, 660–1, 768–72). But if it is methodologically questionable to treat Nietzsche as an immediate forerunner of German fascism, one cannot but take notice that Nietzsche's hostility to the French Revolution, his condemnation of a Judeo-Christian and in particular Pauline "slave revolt in morality," his polemics against Christian "pity," and his exterminist hatred of the poor and suffering were avidly picked up by Nazi leaders in order to justify their mass murder of the handicapped and other "subhuman beings" (875, 880–2).

By all means, Nietzsche has overpowered Spinoza's capacity to act, incorporating it into a power of domination, which he fantasizes further to the annihilation of the weak. What is eliminated and repressed in the equation of Nietzsche and Spinoza is nothing less than the "difference" between social cooperation and projected genocide. To overlook this glaring opposition is utterly irresponsible and scandalous, intellectually and ethically. Unfortunately, this applies to Negri as well. In his *Spinoza for Our Time*, he cannot but realize that Nietzsche's critique of Spinoza is "extremely harsh and combative" (Negri 2013, 72–3, 80), but he does not even try to explain this hostility. This is due to the prejudgment, inherited from Deleuze, that "there is nothing in Nietzsche that thrusts toward reaction" (67). The blindness regarding Nietzsche's open stance of radical aristocratism, and thus regarding his fundamental opposition to Spinoza, provides in turn the precondition for his triumphal success in poststructuralism and postmodernism—disguised as Spinoza! Geoff Waite (1996, 337) is right when he points out that Nietzsche has been "remarkably effective in pulling the wool over the eyes of what he himself called the 'lower' or 'working class' or ... 'caste' ... over the eyes, then over the bodies and, if need be, over the corpses." "Hence," he writes, "a philosophically coherent and politically emancipatory project must forge its way *back* to Spinoza *past* the Nietzschean self and only then ... *into* the future" (14).

A Leftist Project Needs Appealing Images of a "Good Life" for All

When Walter Benjamin (2007, 255) in his "Theses on the Philosophy of History" formulates the task for every generation "to wrest tradition away from a conformism that is

19. See, for example, Nietzsche (1999, 9:250, 11:75, 11:102, 11:547, 13:13, 13:220, 13:611).

about to overpower it" and to fan "the spark of hope in the past," this is in particular important for our approach to Spinoza. By overcoming some of the deeply ingrained Western dualisms between matter and spirit, body and mind, affect and reason, acting, and feeling and thinking, he can be used for the development of a progressive ethics and a corresponding embodied spirituality. His concept of *potentia agendi* is also important for a renewal of critical theory because neither the ideology-critique of the early Frankfurt School around Horkheimer and Adorno nor the ideology-theory of the Althusser School were actually interested in the practical impulses to resist or to subvert the ideological interpellations from above. Althusser and his followers based their general concept of ideology primarily on Jacques Lacan's psychoanalysis, according to which the constitution of a subject coincides with its subordination under the "law of language." Taken up by Judith Butler and many others, this explanation has contributed to a widespread a priori equation of subjectivity/subjectivation and subjection, which flattens out the contradictory composition of people's agency and dissimulates their attempts at self-socialization and self-conduct.[20] Without conceptualizing the dimensions of a horizontal and cooperative capacity to act, it is impossible to understand the everyday motivations that are constitutive of a counterhegemony from below. Since Spinoza's ethics is directed against everything that turns life activities into attitudes of passivity, it can provide a philosophical foundation for our critique of alienating conditions and for our initiatives to counteract and overcome them. To this purpose Spinoza's *potentia agendi* could be combined with Gramsci's concept of "good sense" (*buon senso*), the "healthy nucleus" characterized by a sense of experimentalism and of "direct observation of reality," from which a philosophy of praxis can start to render common sense more coherent.[21] Enrique Dussel (2008, 78–82) proposes a similar combination of Spinozian and Gramscian arguments when he describes the power of the people, which he calls "hyperpotentia," as being composed of three components: (1) the "will-to-live" and to preserve life, which is continuously negated by the "will-to-power" of the powerful; (2) the unifying force of critical consensus; and (3) the feasibility of achieving a new hegemony.

Experience has shown that leftist politics cannot be based upon resentment, not even upon the resentment against "those on top," which can be easily diverted and hijacked by right-wing populism. A sustainable leftist project needs to be centered on conceptions and images of a "good life" that are developed, spelled out, and debated by the people themselves. A case in point is the South American notion of *buen vivir*, which designates a well-being within communities that is egalitarian and ecological. Based on the indigenous Quechua-Aymara traditions of *sumak kawsay* and *suma qamaña*, and repositioned against the U.S.-imposed concept of "development," the concept became such a powerful mobilizing perspective in social movements that it was incorporated into two new constitutions, in Ecuador (2008) and Bolivia (2009). Whenever we go beyond the usual laundry lists of progressive demands and develop a politics centered upon projects of a good life for all, Spinoza's combination of potentia, hilarity, and joy can provide an invigorating philosophical support.[22] It can encourage us to

---

20. See the critiques in Rehmann (2014, 165–78, 314–8) and in Kaindl and Rehmann (2008).
21. See Gramsci (Q11§12, Q15§22, 1975) and compare with Rehmann (2014, 126–31).
22. In a similar vein, Ted Stolze (2014, 569–70) has argued that Spinoza's concept of *fortitude* as one's internal power consisting of *generosity* and *courage* is an important building block for a Marxist ethics.

show that the shiny promises of commodity aesthetics and consumerist ideologies are nothing more than the sad manifestations of the restless gearbox of capitalist accumulation and the social distinctions it entails. Spinoza's coupling of *potentia agendi* and *potentia cogitandi*, which is ultimately oriented toward the knowledge of *deus sive natura*, should not be overhastily denounced either as a naive faith in reason or as "religion." It could rather be used for our attempts to live an examined and examining life that overcomes the dualisms of "matter" and "spirit."

It is beyond dispute that Nietzsche developed a "life-affirming" vision of "strong," self-confident individuals who free themselves from mediocrity and narrow prescripts of morality—this is in fact one of the reasons for his appeal among rebellious movements. But we have to add immediately that his utopia was built upon the horrible dystopia of an enslaved and despised multitude. A spirituality inspired by his philosophy can never get rid of its inherent "pathos of distance," which manifests itself even in its most "leftist" forms as a celebration of social distinctions against ordinary, unenlightened people. Ishay Landa (2007, 79–85) has shown that Nietzsche's enormous influence on popular culture has created an elective affinity between an "outright elitism" on the right and a "critical elitism" on the left.[23] If we follow Antonio Negri and Judith Revel's (2016, 477) proposal of an immanent spirituality that is tied to a "doing" in the world, breaks through the bourgeois confines of a power-protected "inwardness," and seeks "common joy" and the "ethical construction of happiness," we will need to be aware that such a spirituality of the commons can only be developed against the overwhelming *potestas* of social distinctions that reproduce the class relations of neoliberal capitalism. For that, we need to be able to distinguish between exclusivist and democratic versions of spirituality: that is, philosophically speaking, between Nietzsche and Spinoza. The "affirmation of life," which Nietzsche tried to fuse with and hijack for his aristocratic class position, is to be released from its entanglements with privilege and elitism. This recourse to Spinoza can help to redefine life affirmation in a democratic-socialist way so that it constitutes a dynamic component of a counterspirituality from below. It describes the philosophical and ethical foundation of what the *Communist Manifesto* anticipated would become "an association in which the free development of each is the condition for the free development of all" (Marx and Engels 1848, 506).

This discernment might also help to open up new avenues to religion. Spinoza's critique of religion was to a large extent still framed by a rationalism that focused on logical and factual inconsistencies in the Hebrew Bible and in religious beliefs. Rationalist frameworks have continued to haunt later criticisms as well. Even though Marx and Engels had an intuitive sense for the "sigh of the oppressed creature," they were ultimately less interested in unpacking its potentials than in confronting the "misty creations of religion" and its "shibboleths" with "science" and rational analysis. But a critical approach informed by materialist theories of ideology must acknowledge that religions can no longer be defined by a fixed and homogenous "essence" but instead are to be analyzed as ideological fields traversed by contradictions and struggles. A fine-tuned and de-essentialized approach to religions consists primarily in the

23. Landa (2013, 429–30) discusses this tendency with the example of Badiou's "Nietzschean Communism," which he sees as characterized by a "transcendental disdain" against the masses that are considered as only superficially alive.

analytical task of deciphering both the oppressive functions and also agential potentials in religious fields, as well as in the strategic task to oppose the former and to construct alliances with the latter (see Rehmann 2011, 150–1).

Such a fine-tuning can in turn rely on Spinoza's distinctions between enhancing or inhibiting affects and virtues. What is missing in Marx and Engels's critique is an analytical distinction between religion and faith, the latter describing a complex of relations and attitudes that can be found both inside and outside religion. But Spinoza's *potentia agendi*, understood as collective agency, is in need of "faith" in the sense of its ancient usages (the Hebrew '*mn*, Greek *pistis*, and Latin *fides*) that cover the semantic field of trust, faithfulness, truthfulness, reciprocity, and reliability.[24] A trace of this meaning is still visible in the English term "faithful," which has nothing to do with religious beliefs. A collective capacity to act also needs "faith" in the Blochian sense of grasping what is not yet "spilled out before our eyes" but that "is germinating ... still unfinished in the world" (Bloch 1986, 1280).

The late Derrida (1999, 253, 255–6) insisted that "faith in general" is part of the structure of the social bond to the other, and it is thus an "undeconstructible" precondition for the deconstruction of religions.[25] We do not know how later generations will experience the spirituality by which they celebrate and sustain community with each other, with life, and with nature. They might conceive of it as liberation *from* religion or *of* religion (from the strictures of capitalist alienation), depending on how they understand the term. They would certainly not hesitate to "inherit" and claim back all spiritual and cultural potentials they find suitable, whether transmitted by religious or nonreligious traditions, through literature, poetry, music, or dance. What is relevant is not the labeling according to a sterile religious-secular dichotomy but rather the possibilities emerging from people's democratic power to decide about their conditions of work and social life and to develop a spirituality of the commons that expresses and celebrates their new capacities to act, to connect, to enjoy.

References

Abel, G. 1998. *Nietzsche: Die Dynamik der Willen zur Macht und die ewige Wiederkehr.* 2d ed. Berlin: De Gruyter.

Agamben, G. 2005. *The time that remains: A commentary on the Letter to the Romans.* Stanford: Stanford University Press.

Althusser, L. 1976. *Essays in self-criticism.* Trans. G. Lock. London: New Left Books.

Balibar, É. 1997a. *Jus-pactum-lex*: On the constitution of the subject in the *Theologico-political treatise.* In *The new Spinoza,* ed. W. Montag and T. Stolze, 171–204. Minneapolis: University of Minnesota Press.

———. 1997b. *Spinoza: From individuality to transindividuality.* Delft, Neth.: Eburon.

24. Of course, faith in these ancient usages is not an "innocent" and homogenous essence either; it can relate to both horizontal relations of reciprocity and friendship and to vertical relationships between authorities and subordinates.

25. Derrida's (1994, 168, 1999, 253) concept of faith is closely linked to what he describes as a nonreligious "messianicity without messianism" designating an opening to the future "without horizon of expectation."

Benjamin, W. 2007. Theses on the philosophy of history. In *Illuminations: Essays and reflections*. New York: Schocken Books.

Bloch, E. 1986. *The Principle of Hope*. Trans. N. Plaice, S. Plaice, and P. Knight. Cambridge, Mass: MIT Press.

Bonhoeffer, D. 1972. *Letters and papers from prison*. New York: Macmillan Publishing Company.

Brobjer, T. 2004. Nietzsche's knowledge of Spinoza. In *Spinoza in Nordic countries: Spinoza im Norden*, ed. V. Oittinen, 203–16. Helsinki: University of Helsinki Press.

Deleuze, G. 1986. *Nietzsche and philosophy*. London: Continuum.

———. 1995. Nomadic thought. In *The new Nietzsche: Contemporary styles of interpretation*, ed. D. B. Allison, 142–9. Cambridge, Mass.: MIT Press.

Derrida, J. 1994. *Specters of Marx: The state of the debt, the work of mourning, and the new International*. Trans. P. Kamuf. New York: Routledge.

———. 1999. Marx & sons. In *Ghostly demarcations: A symposium on Jacques Derrida's "Specters of Marx,"* ed. M. Sprinkler, 213–69. Verso: London.

Dussel, E. 2008. *Twenty theses on politics*. Trans. G. Ciccariello-Maher. Durham, N.C.: Duke University Press.

Fischer, K. 1880. *Fortbildung der Lehre Descartes' Spinoza*. Vol. 1, pt. 2 of *Geschichte der neuern Philosophie*. 3d ed. Munich: Verlagsbuchhandllung von Fr. Bassermann.

Goldschmidt, W. 2004. Art: "Herrschaft." In vol. 6, pt. 2 of *Historisch-Kritisches Wörterbuch des Marxismus*, ed. W. F. Haug, F. Haug, P. Jehle, and W. Küttler, 82–127. Hamburg: Argument-Verlag.

Gramsci, A. 1975. *Quaderni del carcere*. 4 vols. Ed. V. Gerratana. Turin: Einaudi.

Hardt, M. 1993. *Gilles Deleuze: An apprenticeship in philosophy*. Minneapolis: University of Minnesota Press.

Hardt, M., and A. Negri. 2000. *Empire*. Cambridge, Mass.: Harvard University Press.

———. 2004. *Multitude: War and democracy in the age of empire*. New York: Penguin Books.

Haug, W. F. 2004. Immaterielle Arbeit. In vol. 6, pt. 1 of *Historisch-Kritisches Wörterbuch des Marxismus*, ed. W. F. Haug, F. Haug, P. Jehle, and W. Küttler, 819–32. Hamburg: Argument-Verlag.

Kahl, B., and J. Rehmann. 2013. A spirituality of the commons: Where religion and Marxism meet. *Tikkun* 28 (1): 45–71.

Kaindl, C., and J. Rehmann. 2008. Subjektion und Subjektivierung: Einekritisch-psychologische Auseinandersetzung mit der lacanschen Psychoanalyse. In *"Abstrakt negiert ist halb kapiert": Beiträge zur marxistischen Subjektwissenschaft—Morus Markard zum 60. Geburtstag*, ed. L. Huck, V. Lux, T. Pappritz, K. Reimer, and M. Zander, 235–49. Marburg: BdWi-Verlag.

Landa, I. 2007. *The overman in the marketplace: Nietzschean heroism in popular culture*. Lanham, Md.: Lexington Books.

———. 2013. True requirements or the requirements of truth? The Nietzschean communism of Alain Badiou. *International Critical Thought* 3 (4): 424–43.

Lordon, F. 2014. *Willing slaves of capital: Spinoza and Marx on desire*. London: Verso.

Losurdo, D. 2004. *Nietzsche, il ribelle aristocratico: Biografia intellettuale e bilancio critico*. Torino: Bollato Boringhieri.

Markard, M. 2001. Art: Handlungsfähigkeit II. In vol. 5 of *Historisch-Kritisches Wörterbuch des Marxismus*, ed. W. F. Haug, F. Haug, P. Jehle, and W. Küttler, 1174–81. Hamburg: Argument Verlag.

Marx, K. 1845. Theses on Feuerbach. In *Marx-Engels complete works*, vol. 5, ed. K. Marx and F. Engels, 3–5. London: Lawrence & Wishart.

———. 1857–8. *Grundrisse: Foundations of the critique of political economy*. London: Penguin.

Marx, K., and F. Engels. 1845–6. *The German ideology*. In *Marx-Engels complete works*, vol. 5, ed. K. Marx and F. Engels, 19–539. London: Lawrence & Wishart.

———. 1848. *The manifesto of the Communist Party*. In *Marx Engels complete works*, vol. 6, ed. K. Marx and F. Engels, 477–519. London: Lawrence & Wishart.

Matheron, A. 1997. Spinoza and Hobbes. In *The new Spinoza*, ed. W. Montag and T. Stolze, 207–16. Minneapolis: University of Minnesota Press.

Negri, A. 1991. *The savage anomaly: The power of Spinoza's metaphysics and politics.* Trans. M. Hardt. Oxford: University of Minnesota Press.

———. 2013. *Spinoza for our time: Politics and postmodernity*. Trans. W. McCuaig. New York: Columbia University Press.

Nietzsche, F. 1975. *Nietzsche Briefwechsel: Kritische Gesamtausgabe*. Vol. 3, bk. 1, ed. G. Colli and M. Montinari. Berlin: De Gruyter.

———. 1999. *Sämtliche Werke: Kritische Studienausgabe*, 15 vols. Ed. G. Colli and M. Montinari. München: De Gruyter.

Oittinen, V. 1994. *Spinozistische Dialektik: Die Spinoza-Lektüre des französischen Strukturalismus und Poststrukturalismus*. Frankfurt: Peter Lang.

Pfeiffer, E., ed. 1970. *Friedrich Nietzsche, Paul Rée, Lou von Salomé: Die Dokumente ihrer Begegnung*. Frankfurt: Insel Verlag.

Reeling-Brouwer, R. 2001. Art: Handlungsfähigkeit I. In vol. 5 of *Historisch-kritisches Wörterbuch des Marxismus*, ed. W. F. Haug, F. Haug, P. Jehle, and W. Küttler, 1169–74. Hamburg: Argument Verlag.

Rehmann, J. 2004. *Postmoderner links-Nietzscheanismus: Deleuze & Foucault, eine Dekonstruktion*. Hamburg: Argument Verlag.

———. 2007. Review of Domenico Losurdo's *Nietzsche, il ribelle aristocratico: Biografia intellettuale e bilancio critico*. *Historical Materialism* 15 (2): 173–93.

———. 2011. Can Marx's critique of religion be freed from its fetters?. *Rethinking Marxism* 23 (1): 144–53.

———. 2012. Antizipation. In *Bloch Wörterbuch: Leitbegriffe der Philosophie Ernst Blochs*, ed. B. Dietschy, D. Zeilinger, R. Zimmerman, 3–13. Berlin: De Gruyter

———. 2014. *Theories of ideology: The powers of alienation and subjection*. Chicago: Haymarket Books.

Reitter, K. 2011. *Marx, Spinoza und die Bedingungen eines freien Gemeinwesens: Prozesse der Befreiung*. Münster, Germ.: Westfälisches Dampfboot.

Revel, J. 2016. Transcendence, spirituality, practices, immanence: A conversation with Antonio Negri. *Rethinking Marxism* 28 (3–4): 470–8.

Röttgers, K. 1980. Macht I. In vol. 5 of *Historisches wörterbuch der philosophie*, ed. J. Ritter and K. Gründer, 588–603. Basel, Switz.: Schwabe Verlag Basel.

Rutherford, D. 2013. Perfectionism in Spinoza and Nietzsche. Backdoor Broadcasting Company. http://backdoorbroadcasting.net/2013/05/donald-rutherford-perfectionism-in-spinoza-and-nietzsche.

Saar, M. 2013. *Die Immanenz der Macht: Politische Theorie nach Spinoza*. Frankfurt: Suhrkamp.

Sommer, A. U. 2012. Nietzsche's readings on Spinoza: A contextualist study, particularly on the reception of Kuno Fischer. *Journal of Nietzsche Studies* 43 (2): 156–84.

Spinoza, B. de. 2001. *Ethics*. Trans. W. H. White. Hertfordshire: Wordsworth Editions.

———. 2007. *Theological-political treatise*. Ed. J. Israel. Cambridge: Cambridge University Press.

Stolze, T. 2014. An ethics for marxism: Spinoza on fortitude. *Rethinking Marxism* 26 (4): 561–80.

Terpstra, M. 1990. *De wending naar de politiek: Een studie over die begrippen "potentia" en "potestas" bij Spinoza*. Nijmegen, Neth.: Eigen beheer.

Treiber, H. 1999. Nachträge zu Paul Rée. *Nietzsche-Studien: Internationales Jahrbuch für die Nietzsche-Forschung*, no. 27: 515–6.

Vasquez, M. A. 2011. *More than belief: A materialist theory of religion*. Oxford: Oxford University Press.

Waite, G. 1996. *Nietzsche's corps/e: Aesthetics, politics, prophecy, or The spectacular technoculture of everyday life*. Durham, N.C.: Duke University Press.

Weber, M. 1978. *Economy and society: An outline of interpretative sociology*, vol. 1, ed. G. Roth and C. Wittich. Berkeley: University of California Press.

Wiesmann, H. G. 2013. Spinoza's conatus and Nietzsche's will to power: Self-preservation vs. increase of power? Backdoor Broadcasting Company. http://backdoorbroadcasting.net/2013/05/hannah-grosse-wiesmann-spinozas-conatus-and-nietzsches-will-to-power-self-preservation-vs-increase-of-power.

Wurzer, W. S. 1975. *Nietzsche und Spinoza*. Meisenheim, Germ.: Anton Hain.

Specter and Spirit: Ernst Bloch, Jacques Derrida, and the Work of Utopia

Jason Kosnoski

In this paper I contend that both Ernst Bloch's theory of Utopia and Jacques Derrida's interpretation of the messianic promise of Marxism contain an underappreciated emphasis on the concept of work that can act as a basis for a novel synthesis of the two perspectives. When both theories are interpreted through this lens, they may be seen as representing two "moments" of a flexible Utopian "work" that closely resembles Marx's understanding of unalienated labor. Such a synthesis would be practiced as the alternation of Derrida's negative and Bloch's positive "Utopian work" with individuals engaging in the diverse, developmental, and collective production of Utopian visions of the best society. This process closely mirrors the creative, artisan-like work that Marx envisioned as flourishing after the eradication of the division of labor. When individuals practice it, they may gain an appreciation for this fundamental Marxist value even while existing in alienated, capitalist society.

Despite the Left's long-established role as a prime generator of visions of the best society, Marxism has possessed an ambiguous relationship with Utopia. Marx and Engels vigorously criticized such "Utopian socialists" as Saint-Simon, Charles Fourier, and Robert Owen, claiming they believed that "historical action is to yield to their personal inventive action" (1976, 515). In other words, they generated their models of better societies out of their own desires, not the concrete, material possibilities presented by the contradictions of political economy.[1] Although he did voice skepticism, Marx occasionally provided glimpses of his Utopian vision, with one of the most prevalent themes in these musings being that of labor evolving from a material necessity characterized by alienation and exploitation to a "prime want" that allowed for solidarity and self expression (see Marx 1989).[2] Due to these

---

1. Engels gives a more elaborate critique of "Utopian socialists" in *Socialism: Utopian and Scientific* (1989). Despite these denunciations of Utopia, Kamber stresses Marx's ambivalence toward the concept, stating that "all his life Marx incorporated deeply utopian impulses into his theory yet attacked the same ideas (when led by others) as sentimental, seeking phantom images of harmony, or simply bourgeois" (1997, 112).
2. Kamber in particular stresses how Marx sees labor as transformed from toil to desire as an important part of his understanding of Utopia (1997, 108).

contrasting sentiments, the status of Utopia within contemporary Marxism remains contested, with some disparaging the concept as pejoratively idealistic while others claiming that Utopian thinking could lead to political action, especially when the material and political prospects for radical political action seem difficult to discern.[3]

Both Jacques Derrida, in his *Specters of Marx,* and Ernst Bloch, in his entire corpus (but especially *The Principle of Hope*), explore how envisioning the contours of an ideal future constitutes a salutary, and even necessary, endeavor for Marxists. But unlike many who advocate Utopian thought, they do not attempt to outline a concrete plan for the best society, and instead present procedures that orient individuals toward envisioning a future that embodies Marxist principles. Despite this shared interest, Derrida and Bloch take significantly different views of the process and outcomes of such activity, with Bloch contending that inspiring Utopian images that could support Marxist politics lie within both seemingly insignificant daily activities and discredited bourgeois ideology, and Derrida claiming that through critical examination of the instabilities and exclusions of past political action, a messianic promise of justice and redemption can act as inspiration for a "New International." Thus the question arises, how can such seemingly disparate under-standings—a formless promise of future messianic justice, and a concrete search for Utopian "pearls" (Benjamin, quoted in Arendt 1968, 38) embedded within the detritus of history and daily life—contribute to a coherent theory of Marxist Utopian thought?

Although certain details of Bloch's and Derrida's positions remain quite discordant, when one examines the *process* that each recommends for producing their orientation toward a just future, they suggest a common Marxist focus centering on the concept of work. Due to their shared interest, it is possible to imagine a synthesis of the two Utopian perspectives embodying the values of diversified, developmental, collective work that Marx envisions as the result of the abolition of the capitalist division of labor. Not only does focusing on these theorists' use of the concept of work tie their Utopian thought together in new and interesting ways, but such a combined account of both theorists' "Utopian work" suggests practices that, if repeatedly performed, could cultivate appreciation for unalienated labor itself and subsequently invigorate the motivational power of Marxist ideals. Through practicing the simultaneously frustrating yet liberating labor of investigating the possibilities for perfecting the world, individuals could cultivate hopeful Utopian enthusiasm through experiencing techniques of unalienated labor, which they cannot gain through their actual, exploitative existence within capitalist society.

My argument proceeds in three steps. First, I read the process by which Bloch believes that individuals "educate their hope" as necessitating a "work of mediation" that produces "concrete" Utopian images exhibiting both emotionally inspiring and truly Marxist visions of the future. Second, I contend that Derrida can also be seen as articulating a vision of Utopian labor, which he calls the "work of

3. See Zeitlin (1996) and Singer (1993) for strong endorsements of the need to invigorate the concept of Utopia in Marx's thought.

mourning," that entails individuals working to recognize the historical exclusion created by the performative acts of naming. Third, I explore how, through combining the two analyses around this work-centered interpretation, one can imagine the actual practice of imagining a better future that remains faithful to the Marxist tradition. Imagining a fusion of the two theorists' understanding of Utopian work represents an innovation because, while some have noted the general similarity between Bloch and Derrida, through this synthesizing strategy they gain both a stronger tie, conceptually and procedurally, to a fundamental Marxist concept while simultaneously providing insight into reimagining these two theories as tangible practices that could play a role in Marxist praxis.

Bloch and the Work of Utopian Mediation

The entry point that facilitates interpreting Bloch through his use of the concept of work lies in his claim that, although any particular situation is structured by a historical, material, and linguistic framework that encourages some possibilities and disallows others, he still asserts that hiding within every moment is an undetermined horizon of possibility that humans perceive on the edges of their consciousness. Bloch refers to this perception as the "not yet" conscious, and suggests that even the most basic efforts at fulfilling needs contain the potential for reimagining the grand structure of society. For example, simple hunger, he notes, can often inspire greater and more systemic desires for fulfillment: "Out of economically enlightened hunger comes today the decision to abolish all conditions in which man is an oppressed and long-lost being. And in human work, undertaken for the purpose of satisfying needs, transforming raw materials into richer and richer utility values, runs as a consciousness which overhauls the available world in the imagination" (1986b, 76). Such manifestations of the "not yet," Bloch emphasizes, embody not simply human desire, but also an actual perception of the *dynamis*[4] and undetermined potentiality lying within all situations. Also, note how he observes that the physical work of addressing hunger leads to a work that transforms "consciousness" and one's perception of the world. Thus, he ties the experience of mundane work to the expansive potentialities of the future, a theme that, as will become apparent, permeates his thought.

This prelinguistic "not yet" comes to be expressed through "little daydreams." Bloch emphasizes that these seemingly minor exercises of the imagination both embody concrete visions of the world and serve as a general reminder that the possibility of radical social transformation always remains present, even within periods when reform seems utterly unlikely. Such "little daydreams" take their specific shape within the context of the "surplus" generated through the interaction of specific situations with the surrounding cultural matrix. Although it might seem that both past and current society remain rife with ideology, Bloch stresses that even the most blatantly, bourgeois concepts (such as "man," "economics," and "rights") contain the seeds of potential visions of the best world. The always present possibilities stemming from the "not yet" lead Bloch to present a long catalogue

4. See Kellner and O'Hara on Bloch's "Left Aristotelianism" (1976, 23).

within *The Principle of Hope* outlining the Utopian surplus in objects as grand as the Cathedral of Reims and in acts as mundane as cooking dinner. Although Bloch's evaluations concerning the Utopian potential within various pieces of art and historical events are questioned by some,[5] the important point remains that the ubiquitous phenomenological potential of the "not yet" can be wedded to the specific surplus within a particular cultural artifact that acts as the raw "material" used for the construction of the particular Utopian image.

Bloch claims that the perception of the "not yet" and the generation of daydreams constitute only the preliminary stages in a longer process of active development of Utopian images he refers to as "educating hope." In this effort of explication, Bloch notes that, in order to educate hope, individuals must consciously mediate the raw material of their sensed "not yet" with the Utopian surplus inherent in their cultural environment in a dialectical process to develop "the mediated *novum*" (1986b, 197). Such development requires a further level of mediation because Bloch insists that "really possible" Utopias require that the opportunities provided by any cultural surplus be evaluated in light of the material and economic contradictions inherent within the contemporary social landscape.[6] Although Bloch claims that all situations ontologically contain indeterminacy and are amenable to imaginative reformulation, the necessary exertion required by mediation connects what would otherwise be flights of fancy with possible, but not inevitable, possibilities for advancing social transformation.

Such a process of mediation of the ideal potentiality and material constraints of concrete situations leads to a method necessarily characterized by false starts, frustrations, and errors. In addition, no matter how congruent they seem with the concrete economic and social trends of a period, Bloch emphasizes the partiality and provisionality of Utopian visions. He claims that even edifying and inspiring images initially produce vague, incomplete, and even false hopes in need of refining, and thus "the formation of ideals is by no means restricted to obligations and spells ... even if this brighter side also displays strong negative aspects: those of substitution, overblownness, abstractness" (167). It is important to note that Bloch is stressing that the process of imagining a better world does not entail simply wishful thinking. Even the most powerful Utopian images that are thoroughly mediated with the most exacting evaluation of "real possibility," if actualized, must disappoint through incompleteness. Bloch calls this the "melancholy of realization" and notes:

> The blind spot, this not-seeing of the immediately entering Here and Now, also in fact appears in every realization ... Everywhere else there is a crack, even an abyss in the realizing itself, in the actuated-topical entrance of what

5. See Webb, who states that "whilst hidden beneath a bewilderingly complex set of categories, Bloch's method for distinguishing the concrete from the abstract and reactionary boiled down to nothing more than distinguishing between his own personal likes and dislikes" (2000, 160).
6. For the best elaboration of Bloch's understanding of the relationship of historical materialism to Utopian idealism, see his excursus on the *Theses on Feuerbach*, especially the sections "Epistemological Group: Perception and Activity—Theses 5, 1, 3" (1986b, 255–62) and "Theory-Practice Group: Proof and Probation—Theses 2–8" (267–74).

has been so beautifully foreseen, dreamed out; and this abyss is that of the ungrasped *existere* itself. So the darkness of nearness also gives the *final reason for the melancholy of fulfillment:* no earthly paradise remains on entry without the shadow which the entry still casts over it. (299)

Thus, Bloch claims that even if social interventions could bring about desired changes—even the final realization of a successful revolution—these successes would not result in a static finality, but instead would always fall short of idealized expectations. No matter how seemingly radical and complete, an idealized Utopia can never capture the indeterminate, dynamic totality of society and vice versa. Hence the desire for both imagining and creating the "perfect" society will always be accompanied by disappointment and require effort and exertion to produce.

Bloch argues that such melancholy, or "pathos," does not undermine the effort to imagine and strive toward Utopia. It should simply loosen the individual's investment in any individual Utopias s/he produces and instead shift their focus to what Bloch deems to be the general perspective of the "front." He states that "the site for both kinds of self-apprehension and their *Novum,* the *Ultimum,* is however located solely on the 'front' of the process of history and is predominantly confronted with only mediated-real possibility. *This remains that which corresponds to exact anticipation, concrete utopia as objective real-correlate*" (205). Bloch's focus on the "front" positions consciousness toward a process of mediation, negation, and pathos as opposed to a concrete, static vision.[7] He writes that "man and process, or rather: subject and object in dialectically materialist process, consequently both stand equally on the 'front.' And there is no other place for the militant optimist than the place which the category of the 'front' opens up" (200). The melancholy and pathos that come from the realization that all specific Utopias are partial, Bloch claims, actually motivate individuals to engage in the process of hopeful projections of the "perfect" future even more vigorously.[8]

Because of the indeterminate forward orientation and the mixture of euphoric imagination and the pathos of disappointment, Bloch stresses that maintaining an orientation to a "utopian front" truly constitutes "work" and not simply an individual flight of fancy. In discussing the repeated mediation of ideal and material that pushes individuals toward the perspective of the front, Bloch exclaims— somewhat counterintuitively for a process that he characterizes as rife with

7. Jacoby makes a similar point, arguing that the theorists of the "Jewish messianic tradition" (as he calls it), like Bloch, regard the vagueness of any Utopian vision as its strength. He states that "like Wittgenstein, they concluded that what was truly important could not be uttered... 'as soon as we really have something to say we are forced to be silent'" (2005, 104). For an argument that places Bloch in the "messianic" tradition and thus ties him to Derrida through Jewish themes, see Rabinach (1985).

8. Bloch's focus upon the undetermined front as opposed to specific visions of the future does not end with the individual, and extends to his theory of history and totality. Jay contends that, in contrast with Georg Lukács, Bloch argues that "history should thus be understood not as the objectification of a metasubject...but as an experimental process driven by the goal of a possible future totalization. Lukács fails to grasp the utopian dimension of reality, he underplays the still unfinished quality of the whole" (1984, 182).

"melancholy" and "pathos"—that one might begin "finally the blissful work of explication" (198). In another of many such examples of his usage of the term "work," he claims that all "previous materialism lacks the *constantly oscillating subject-object relation called work*" (257). Through many such references to work, he contends that Marxist speculation concerning the future cannot simply focus upon the macrodialectical movements of history and economic structures, but must also investigate "the human sensory activity" where individuals actively form and reform their ideas and ideals. When read this way, the phenomenological work process of cultivating Utopian images becomes equally, if not more, important than the individual images produced. Bloch makes this emphasis upon process as opposed to substance very clear. For example, he writes, "However the effect of the positive aspect of the subject-related theory of value, that which is switched to *production* is quite different. Then nothing is finished and pre-ordered in ready made packages, man himself builds his house according to his own measurements in an inhospitable world" (1986b, 1331). Such a focus on "production" valorizes not the specifics embedded in the particular vision, but the process of constructing the vision in itself. In other words, "building a house," where the house is the whole of one's future society, significantly alters the status of Utopia away from the traditional view of Utopia as blueprint. But most significantly, the acknowledgment that such a process occurs in an "inhospitable world" grounds this account in a Marxist understanding of work, where individuals construct their visions within the context of the material realities that surround them while retaining the optimism and sense of efficacy accompanying the process of constructing visions of the best society.

Even if Bloch's Utopia is interpreted as procedure rather than as a list of substantive commitments, he still faces the charge leveled by some Marxists that Utopia and Marxism remain incompatible. Darren Webb argues that, in fact, any attempt to articulate a vision of the perfect society undermines revolutionary praxis. He states, "For if one believes that the revolutionary hope of the masses depends upon a vision of a better future then one will be led to proclaim that this vision is not a utopia, and one will be led to proclaim this because, quite simply, the revolutionary hope of the masses has never been ignited by mere utopia" (2000, 162). Webb argues that Bloch's only contribution consists of (and all any Marxist understanding of Utopia should provide is) a "restless future oriented longing for that which is missing" (Webb 2007, 71), devoid of any content.[9] If any attempt to articulate methods and principles of Utopian "work" must end in a totalitarian desire to impose a "correct" interpretation of the desired future, then perhaps examining another "Marxist" Utopian thinker who seems to eschew any positive content for his Utopian procedure, such as Jacques Derrida in *Specters of Marx*, might provide a provocative contrast with Bloch.

9. For other works advocating a left-leaning "orientation" toward hope, see Rorty (1998, 1999), especially his discussion of "the unpatriotic Left." For a thorough articulation of the benefits and phenomenology of "hope" at the expense of Utopia, see Shade (2007). This work briefly attempts to draft Bloch into its campaign for the advocacy of hope by tying him to the nontheistic, "hopeful" practices of religion (225 n. 11).

Derrida and the Work of the Mourning

Although Derrida goes out of his way to deny any relationship between his "messianic" interpretation of Marxism and Utopia, striking similarities exist between his understanding and Bloch's, especially when viewed through their mutual interest in how the concept of work might be fundamental for Marxist imagining of the best society. As with Bloch, Derrida commences his account through analyzing the structure of human apprehension and creation of meaning. He claims that radical social critique always remains a possibility even amidst the most stultifying ideology, due to the instability inherent in all acts of signification. Derrida argues that Marx's withering criticism of classic bourgeois concepts such as value, money, and exchange employs a similar strategy to that of deconstruction in that both valorize the undefined, always possible arrival of the disruption of seemingly totalized systems of meaning that both mask and justify power. He describes this acknowledgment of the constant possibility created by internal semantic contradictions as the "messianic promise" contained within Marxism because, although the opportunity for disruption of settled meaning constitutes an always present prospect for realizing goals, no one can predict the time, place, or manner of the opening. He explains: "Now if there is a spirit of Marxism which I will never be ready to renounce . . . It is even more a certain emancipatory and messianic affirmation, a certain experience of the promise that one can try to liberate from any dogmatics and even from any metaphysico-religious determination from any messianism" (1994a, 89). This acknowledgment, even hope for the prospect of disruption and critique of both current ideology and future "progressive" social innovation suggests that individuals possess the agency, within particular contexts, to play an active role in reimagining their relationship to their future.

Derrida claims that in order to capitalize on this messianic possibility, one must turn attention toward an underappreciated aspect of Marx's approach to both the past and the future. Occasionally, he notes that Marx, as opposed to trying to banish the ideological specters of the past through critique, instead adopts a "hospitable" attitude, graciously opening doors to unexpected and even frightening guests who might seem strange, threatening, or antiquated.[10] Hospitality requires that the specters of the excluded past, present, and even future be not only welcomed but integrated into one's experience as polite company, allowing them to stay in one's "home." Derrida points out that in recounting the "specters" of the past evoked in this revolutionary time of disjuncture, Marx "takes pleasure in it, the pleasure of repetition; on seeing him so sensitive to these compulsive waves one gets the impression that he is not just pointing his finger: he is taking the pulse of history" (112). This hospitable attitude toward specters exhibited by Marx produces a profound feeling of the *Unheimlich* (uncanny), the simultaneous feeling of being home and not at home, or feeling strange in the familiar. The messianic hope of a better future must,

---

10. Derrida states that, although occasionally Marx grounds his critique in a "predeconstructive ontology" that focuses on the possibility of "dissipating the phantom," he also "insists on respecting the originality and the proper efficacity, the autonomization and automatization of ideality as finite-infinite processes of difference (phantomatic, fantastic, fetishistic, or ideological)—and of the simulacrum which is not simply imaginary in it" (1994a, 170).

at least initially, cause discomfort, not only because of its seeming autonomy and independence from the will of the individual, but also because the uncanny leads one to question the status of one's most basic conceptual assumptions: "One may deem strange, strangely familiar and inhospitable at the same time this figure of absolute hospitality whose promise one chooses to entrust to an experience that is so impossible, so unsure in its indigence to a quasi 'messianism' so anxious, fragile and impoverished" (168). Thus, the messianic does not produce grand plans for reformulating society or suggest the form of a single figure, party, or social group sweeping away the detritus of a previously fallen era. Instead, Derrida suggests that adopting a hospitable attitude toward the specters of experience leads to the messianic through constant cultivation of an attitude of "dis-ease" with one's surroundings, a willingness to embrace the "out-of-joint-ness" produced through the disjuncture between the rigidity of reification and plasticity of existence. Although Marx expresses ambivalence toward these specters, Derrida asserts that only through actively welcoming the discomfort of hectoring specters will individuals engulfed in a culture of depoliticizing reification truly perceive the messianic possibilities that surround them.

Derrida characterizes this embrace of the *Unheimlich* through hospitality to specters as "the work of mourning."[11] Mourning for Derrida requires that one embrace the injunction to recognize the existence and the previous political act that conjured the specters in the first place. Invoking the performative violence he sees as constituting the "mystical foundation" of authority (Derrida 1994b), he claims that the "work of mourning" "consists always in attempting to ontologize remains, make them present, in the first place by identifying the bodily remains and localizing the dead" (1994a, 9). To mourn entails spending time with the dead, but not attempting either to resurrect them or dispel them. One does not ask for the specter's presence, but one does not attempt to push it away, either. Derrida states, "One should not rush to make of the clandestine immigrant an illegal alien, or what always risks coming down to the same thing to domesticate him. To neutralize him through naturalization. To assimilate him so as to stop frightening oneself with him. He is not part of the family, but one should not send him back, once again, him too, to the border" (174). What Derrida seems to be saying through passages such as this is that in working to create new strategies and visions of the future, one must first acknowledge and, in fact, realize how one is constituted by the ideas and values that one rejects. In imagining what one would like to become and criticizing what one once was, one must acknowledge what one leaves behind. If this does not occur, the "fear" of the contingency and irreducible unfixity of both individual identity and the values, hopes,

---

11. Sezman picks up on this theme of work by noting that Derrida's Marxist spectrology implies "the continual work of un-doing everything that tries to hide its specters—in other words the work of deconstruction, a work that does not try to banish ghosts but keeps them close by" (2000, 110).

and visions for a better world that underlie identities will ironically bring about clinging to the supposed certainties of the past.[12]

Although difficult, this work of mourning does not preclude the possibility of overcoming such reservations concerning imagining the new. In fact, the work of mourning that appears within Marx's seeming fascination with "invoking" ghosts can create a sense of the appreciation of contingency, otherness, and fluidity that Derrida sees as leading individuals to reimagine their society. Derrida claims that mourning is "[i]n fact and by right interminable, without possible normality, without reliable limit, in its reality or in its concept, between introjection and incorporation. But the same logic, as we suggested, responds to the injunction of a justice which, beyond right or law, rises up in the very respect owed to whoever is not, no longer or not yet, living, presently living" (97). Thus, the work of mourning not only assists individuals in acknowledging fear of instability, especially in revolutionary times, inducing them not to find comfort in the past, but also opens them to the respect of indeterminate otherness that lies at the root of Derrida's conception of justice. This account of the outcome of mourning, hidden within Marx's attempts to exorcize the specters of history, philosophy, and bourgeois political economy, suggests that, ironically, a focus on the past can create an attitude toward the future—and not simply an attitude, but an active desire to project that sense of justice into the future and hence the messianic.[13] The desire to bring healing to the world and imagine possible permutations of time without injustice can spring from the work of mourning. Although this mournful work seems different from a Utopian gesture, it remains integral to Derrida's messianic thought and ties the concept firmly to that of Bloch's work. Both working to mourn and educating hope through the work of mediation require the individual to undergo trying processes of confronting their desires with external forces they cannot control, but both contend that such efforts to work with Utopian images and urges, ironically build eagerness to engage in the world through radical political praxis.

Derrida admits that this interpretation represents a departure from most Marxist thought, but many state that his reinterpretation has eviscerated any resemblance between his work and dialectical materialism. In *Ghostly Demarcations, a Symposium on Jacques Derrida's* Specters of Marx, theorists criticize what they see as the idealism and lack of class analysis in Derrida's reinterpretation. Terry Eagleton's response is perhaps the most stinging: "Derrida has now taken Marxism on board, or at least dragged it halfway up the gangplank, because he is properly enraged by liberal-capitalist complacency; but there is also something unavoidably opportunist about this political pact, which wants to exploit Marxism as critique, dissent,

12. Such a conscious act of capitalization and embrace of the messianic remains necessary, according to Derrida, because the epistemic instability that undergirds this concept can cause irrational attachment to tradition and authority. As Lewis explains, "recognition of the flawed or incomplete nature of being, Derrida suggests, can trigger emotional reaction aimed at denying or exorcizing such a recognition" (1996, 26).
13. Kochi, for one, emphasizes how the messianic can act as an inspiration for radical political activity, stating that it results in a "radical form of ethics structured upon otherness which acts as a critique of the rule of capital and as motivation of new forms of action and political association/disassociation" (2002, 30).

conveniently belaboring instrument, but is far less willing to engage with its positivity" (Eagleton 1999, 86). Objections such as these raise serious doubts as to whether Derrida's work of mourning can lead to any type of positive political action, much less action that works toward a classless society.[14] Derrida does call for a "New International" comprised of all who suffer from injustice and degradation, which he claims will encompass agitation against class oppression.[15] But whether such a concept constitutes an engaging vision, and whether the work of mourning would lead individuals to embrace that new international, remains an open question.[16] Furthermore, such an indeterminate understanding of where the "work" of Utopia might lead raises the question, suggested by Derrida himself, of whether his understanding can be called Utopian at all.

Bloch, Derrida, and the Work of Utopia

Although both Derrida and Bloch individually provide provocative understandings of Utopia that can be fruitfully interpreted through their mutual invocation of work, when combined, the amalgam suggests a more concrete relationship with Marxism than either has on its own. Furthermore, integrating the Utopian work processes outlined previously allows one to imagine how the two theorists' accounts, each addressing the flaws of the other, might produce a powerful and motivating set of practices that could assist concrete Marxist political praxis.

Before commencing this synthesis, one must acknowledge that a number of theorists have already explored similarities between Bloch and Derrida. Wayne Hudson briefly suggests the contours of an interaction between the two before publication of *The Specters of Marx*, commenting, "Bloch ... develops a concept of traces which could be usefully challenged in light of a Derridian semantics with its emphasis upon difference and erasure. Bloch's work as a whole is subject to a Derridian critique; it also contains elements for a positive deconstruction of Western metaphysics against Derrida, based on the insight that the meaning which is never

14. Spivak makes a critique similar to Eagleton's, but adds that Derrida's position "cannot know the connection between industrial capitalism, colonialisms, so-called postindustrial capitalism, neocolonialism, electronicified capitalism, and the current financialization of the globe, with the attendant phenomena of migrancy and ecological disaster" (1995, 68). In other words, she claims that Derrida suffers from lack of analysis of contemporary events.

15. He states, "Whenever I speak of the new international in *Specters of Marx* emphasizing that in it solidarity of alliance should not depend fundamentally and in the final analysis on class affiliation, this in no way signifies for me the disappearance of classes or the attenuation of conflict connected with class differences of oppositions ... At issue is simply another dimension of analysis and political commitment, one that cuts across social difference and opposition of social forces" (1999, 239).

16. One final indication of Derrida's commitment to both class and party structure can be found in an account of his reaction to the Paris student uprisings of 1968, which he criticizes with a "*crypto-communist inheritance*, namely the condemnation of 'spontaneism' in Lenin's *What is to Be Done?*" (Smith 2008, 626).

completely present has positive rather than negative connotations" (1982, 216).[17] Diverging from this relationship of complementarity, Tarik Kochi interprets Bloch and Derrida, despite their similarities, as presenting visions of Utopia that stand in tension with one another. Kochi sees the always never defined, always open potentiality of Derrida's messianism as unable to provide any specific direction to those wishing to apply it in practice, even those whose only wish is to acknowledge the call of the other who might be wronged through the closure represented by a political decision. He claims that Bloch, by grounding his Utopian urge (an urge that he contrasts with Derrida's messianism) in the concrete general ethic of "humanism" and the more concrete images provided by history, provides the ability to apply the general ethic of Utopia to the concrete situations involved in political action. He states: "Further, Bloch's future leaning ethic, human dignity, which is the source of the 'not yet' demonstrates the importance of a particular grounding of the ethical command, if any translation into the political is at least to be attempted. This runs contrary to Derrida's approach, where the absolute openness to the other evades any con-ceptualization of the good" (Kochi 2002, 31).

Kochi goes on to argue that "Bloch operationalizes Derrida" (44) through a relationship of "active tension" resulting in a "process philosophy" (47) of mutual conceptual competition. He asserts that "what the messianic tension assures us is that intervention cannot amount to justice, but we may legitimately work towards this goal, the impossible event when our work stems from below and when it is tied to the image of the human face belonging to community" (47). But is a constant reminder of the impossibility of Utopia an adequate result of the encounter of these two authors? Can one imagine a relationship that both acknowledges the difficulties of Utopia and provides concrete principles pointing toward a plausible communist future?

To envision such a combination, it is necessary first to articulate more fully what Marx might have meant by his invocation that labor could become a "prime want" in a communist Utopia.[18] Bertell Ollman describes such work as possessing three main characteristics: (1) the division of labor has been abolished and "people now feel the need and have the ability to perform many types of work"; (2) not just work but communal "activity with others" has become a prime want with common, coordinated organization in the manner of an "orchestra leader who directs a willing orchestra"; and (3) one's entire environment becomes the material one uses to actualize one's projects, or, "the entire world becomes the product of [individuals'] conscious effort to bend things to [their] own purposes," including themselves (1977, 21). Shlomo Avineri builds on this description by interpreting art as the paradigm for work in a communist Utopia:

17. Geoghegan expresses a similar interpretation that suggests that both theorists offer complementary "reconfigurations of the modern secular project" (2002, 16) unified around the concept of "non-contemporaneous" time (14).
18. Although Marx discusses alienation throughout his works, the most thorough discussion of the nature of unalienated labor occurs in *The Economic and Philosophical Manuscripts of 1844* (Marx 1975) and *The German Ideology* (Marx and Engels 1975). See also Ollman's *Alienation: Marx's Conception of Man in Capitalist Society* (1976, 97–103).

> Marx mentions on several occasions that work activity in future society will be much more like art than labor... there never exists, strictly speaking, an "object" of art: for a piece of music to become an artistic experience it does not suffice that it has been "produced" by the composer. It has to be reproduced by an orchestra or an individual, performed and "reproduced" again by the listener, otherwise it is merely a piece of dead wood. (1973, 330)

This "artistic" account of Utopian labor casts the activity in terms of both collective production and consumption, activities which encourage that dialogue and creative tension that lead to multiple visions of the good life and the best institutions. And as with art, this labor process requires effort and entails frustration yet still results in the production of edifying images produced through autonomous, creative action.

Using these parameters, if one imagines the actual performance of Bloch's, then Derrida's Utopian work, then a process emerges where Bloch's "work of mediation" builds images from the material of concrete political-economic possibilities and cultural surpluses while Derrida's "work of mourning" encourages individuals to accept the exclusions and failures produced through the possible actualization of any Utopian cultural material.[19] But in imagining these processes as a tangible, "operationalized" practice, as suggested by Kochi, one must introduce phenomenological properties of work, particularly that of time. Work, especially creative, autonomous "craftsmanship" of the type that would most likely flourish in any communist Utopia lacking alienation and exploitation, would be undertaken using a process characterized by rhythm and resistance.[20] While performing a craft, individuals possess a general vision of what they want to construct, yet depending on the nature of the material with which they work, they creatively modify their goals in a reiterated process of construction and evaluation. This constant alternation between the positive experimentation and negative criticism creates a rhythmic process that actually stokes the motivation of the craftsperson to move the process forward and persist in the face of resistance. Richard Sennett, in his study of craftwork, claims that "doing something over and over is stimulating when organized as looking ahead. The substance of the routine may change, metamorphose, improve,

19. One example of the material used by both Bloch and Derrida in their Utopian work is the citizen as invoked by the French Revolution. Bloch states, in a productive interpretation, that "the abstract citizen of the state who is wrenched away from secular man, although still contained in him the true man, brought into relief is the citoyen; but he is also this as the 'political power' the bearer of socialized freedom" (1986a, 176–7). Derrida notes how Louis Bonaparte could capitalize upon the spectral remainder of this concept to make the revolution "disappear like a phantasmagoria, by means of a perverse diabolical and non-appeared exorcism" (1994, 119).

20. This characterization of unalienated work as "craftsmanship" comes from Sennett, who contends that the "utopian core" of Marxism centers on a society where all production takes the form of practicing crafts. He states that "the young Karl Marx thought of himself as a secular Hephaestus whose writings would set the modern craftsman free" (2008, 29). In fact, craft work constitutes a better description of unalienated, Utopian labor than art, with its combination of both the creative and the reproductive.

but the emotional payoff is one's experience of dong it again" (2008, 175). Thus creative, unalienated labor must be understood as a time-bound process where different types of labor are not simply combined or seen as existing in tension, but are repeatedly and rhythmically performed to encourage the development of resistant and propulsive energies. Imagining the combined work stemming from the two theories suggests that those practicing it would engage in rhythmic alternation between the work of mourning and the work of mediation that would actually stoke one's motivation to persist in the process itself.

Furthermore, the tempering of positive propulsive mediation with the resistance of mourning acknowledges not only that unalienated craftwork necessitates resistances over time, but also that this practice cultivates these resistances. When imagining Bloch's positive with Derrida's negative ideological Utopian deconstruction as concrete work, such a process over time conserves and even increases the level of tensions. Craftwork consciously generates such resistances, leading Sennett to comment that "in the production process, introducing complexity is a procedure that addresses the suspicion that things are not what they seem" (225). Derrida's and Bloch's mutual concern with the difficulties that accompany work accord well with Sennett's claim that the "path of least resistance" often leads to a "corruption" that is avoided through craftwork's cultivation of resistances and difficulty. Thus, with the introduction of time, rhythm, and resistance as necessary properties for conceptualizing the performance of a combined "work of Utopia," one can begin to conceptualize the additional benefits of imagining Bloch's and Derrida's not simply as perspectives concerning Marxist Utopia, but as phases within a difficult yet rewarding process of actually generating Utopian images.

Although the actual activities envisioned by these alternate accounts entail quite distinct attitudes and activities, these differences further endow a combined interpretation of Bloch's and Derrida's Utopian work with the characteristics of unalienated labor. Bloch's "not yet" and the "work of mediation" propel forward while Derrida's "work of mourning" holds back. While the "front" indicates possibilities for new descriptions and actions, the work of mourning preserves and even cultivates the Unheimlich that reminds individuals of the exclusions of their forward motion. It is these differences—the act of simultaneously engaging in both constructive and deconstructive Utopian work—that approximate the plural, productive styles lacking an imposed division of labor better than either Derrida's "work of mourning" or Bloch's "work of mediation" can do individually. Alternating between the construction and criticism of Utopian visions provides individuals with a holistic, developmental experience of work where individuals undertake varied "activities" and use multiple skills. Unlike work organized in capitalist firms where the relations of production force individuals into a rigid hierarchy between distinct types of labor, when undertaking both the "work of mediation" and the "work of mourning" individuals engage in such diverse activities as creatively interpreting the vague Utopian potentialities in everyday situations, critically assessing whether these potentialities accord with the material potentialities within society, and emotionally mourning the exclusions and failures of past Utopian efforts. Although the fusing of these two understandings of the "work of Utopia" does not literally require "hunting in the morning" or "criticizing at night," the diverse forms of labor suggested through this amalgamation strongly resemble, at least in their diversity, Marx's hopes for unalienated labor in communism.

Additionally, through constituting both a constructive and deconstructive phase, the combination of the two modes of work suggests increased flexibility and plasticity of the individual Utopian visions. Individuals will come to expect that the products of their Utopian work will and should be revised, producing an ever expansive Utopian urge where the "entire world" becomes both material and subject for one's efforts to imagine a world without exploitation. Rigid, separated, and reified Utopian images would be constantly subject to rounds of construction and criticism, and the exertion of engaging in these diverse labors while cultivating Utopian urges (whether of the messianic or of hope) intermingles frustrations with inspiration and augments difficulty with motivation.[21] The cultivation of such a general longing consisting of constructing and deconstructing of particular Utopias, dialectically building toward ever more "realistic"[22] yet expansive visions will constantly long for new "material," whether such substance originates in diverse cultures and experiences or within the present or past. Instead of projecting a single vision that might become mired in particular values, images, or goals, this constant revising and longing ensures truly expansive visualization of a socialist world and truly motivates individuals to search out material for building these visions from every possible location and time period.

Finally, with such alternation between different modes of work, individuals will be drawn to outside sources, whether historical, material or the perspectives of those around them, that they can use as inspirations for their own efforts. Thus, as opposed to envisioning Utopia as a flight of individual fancy, this synthesized work of Utopia envisions a process where groups use each other as resources for their collective or individual efforts. As Avineri (1973) states, Marx sees unalienated Utopian labor as akin to a group organized in the manner of a "willing orchestra," and he stresses that art's production is meaningless without its reception by others. Imagining the actual practice of construction and criticism, mediation and mourning, suggests a further collectivization of Utopian work, with individuals simultaneously mourning and mediating, and each both producing and experiencing such labor. If one thinks of the different modes of collective work as corresponding to different modes of political organization, the "work of mediation" can be seen as a form of class-based politics, attempting to cull visions of solidarity from the past, while Derrida's work of

21. This focus on Utopian work as creating a multiplicity of images of the perfect society is also endorsed by Jameson, who observes, "A new formal tendency, in which it is not the representation of utopia, but rather the conflict of all possible utopia, and the arguments about the nature and desirability of utopia as such, which move to the center of attention. Here the new form seems to reach back and to incorporate within itself all the opposition and antinomies we have identified in an earlier chapter; to reorganize itself around the increasingly palpable fact and situation of ideological multiplicity and radical difference in the field of desire" (2005, 216).

22. In an account that mirrors Bloch's seemingly ironic call for a "realistic" Marxist Utopia, Geras describes his Utopia as "conceived in a minimalist spirit. And it grows not out of any overreaching optimist, but out of a bleak view of the currently prevailing moral culture, and a not very sanguine view of either, regarding some of the more negative characteristics in the make-up of human beings" (2002, 2).

mourning corresponds to a more indeterminate, constantly changing political imaginary.[23] In combining these two political strategies, Marxist political organizations would be open to new members, strategies, and guiding Utopian visions while retaining a strong base in the working class. Just as individuals would draw on many sources in their individual work to imagine Utopia, groups would draw upon many cultures, perspectives, and values to ground their collective construction of their Utopian goals.

Conclusion

The work of imagining how the constituents of a perfect world lie within the mundane details of our daily surroundings seems not only disconnected from traditional Marxism, but disconnected from traditional political organization and activity. Working to form an attitude toward a Utopian "front" or engaging in the work of mourning that welcomes messianic specters constitutes a precondition for how those most mired in alienated labor can muster the collective strength to change their situation. Without some concrete means of generating even a weak vision of the future that stokes desire, passion, and eventually action, Marxism faces a difficult task in combating the ideologies of individualism, skepticism, and fundamentalism so prevalent in contemporary culture. Cultivating the "craft" of building Utopias through the difficult, exciting, reiterated practice of the work of mourning and the work of mediation could act as a potent generator of realistic, motivating Marxist hope. And with the collective work of imagining, individuals might be more likely to engage in the collective work of social transformation. Even when the present seems to hold very little promise for improvement, in contradistinction to the realities of daily work life and the lack of freedom within capitalist existence, such a Derridian/ Blochian "work" of Utopia provides an inspiring yet rooted, critical and plural method for formulating images of the future.

Acknowledgments

A version of this paper was given at New Marxian Times, the Seventh International Conference of Rethinking Marxism, held 5–8 November 2009 at the University of Massachusetts Amherst. I would like to thank the participants and audience of the "Utopia, Religion and Violence" panel, and especially my co-panelist, Manuel Yang, for an engaging discussion that greatly improved the essay. I would also like to thank Dana Levin and Sierra Fox for careful, compassionate copy editing.

23. See Hardt and Negri (2000) and Laclau and Mouffe (1985) for visions of radical social movements that exhibit the flexibility of such "work of Utopia." Although Lewis suggests that both theories put forth "an argument that class-based politics—particularly the revolutionary politics of the classical Marxist tradition—are no longer relevant under conditions of postmodernity" (1996, 32), it could also be said that they imply class will play an important, if not singular, role in political organization, and that class will play a constitutive and even necessary role in any Left movement, if not sufficient or singular.

References

Arendt, H. 1969. Introduction to *Illuminations: Essays and Reflections*, by W. Benjamin. New York: Schocken.

Avineri, S. 1973. Marx's vision of future society. *Dissent* 40 (Summer): 323–31.

Bloch, E. 1986a. *Natural law and human dignity.* Trans. D. Schmidt. Cambridge, Mass.: MIT Press.

———. 1986b. *The principle of hope.* 3 vols. Trans. N. S. Plaice and P. Knight. London: Basil Blackwell.

Derrida, J. 1994a. *Specters of Marx: The state of the debt, the work of mourning and the New International.* Trans. P. Kamuf. London: Routledge.

———. 1994b. Force of law: "The mystical foundation of authority." In *Deconstruction and the possibility of justice*, ed. D. Cornell, M. Rosenfeld, and D. Carlson, 3–67. New York: Routledge.

———. 1999. Marx & Sons. In *Ghostly demarcations: A symposium on Jacques Derrida's* Spectres of Marx, ed. M. Sprinker, 213–69. New York: Verso.

Eagleton, T. 1999. Marxism without Marxism. In *Ghostly demarcations: A symposium on Jacques Derrida's* Spectres of Marx, ed. M. Sprinker, 83–7. New York: Verso.

Engels, F. 1989. Socialism Utopian and scientific. In *Marx-Engels collected works*, vol. 24. New York: International Publishers.

Geoghegan, V. 1996. *Ernst Bloch.* London: Routledge.

———. 2002. "Let the dead bury their dead": Marx, Derrida and Bloch. *Contemporary Political Theory* 1 (1): 5–18.

Geras, N. 2002. The ideal of multivious care (Utopia and inequality). *Rethinking Marxism* 14 (1): 1–7.

Hardt, M., and A. Negri. 2000. *Empire.* Cambridge, Mass.: Harvard University Press.

Hudson, W. 1982. *The Marxist philosophy of Ernst Bloch.* New York: St. Martins.

Jacoby, R. 2005. *Picture imperfect: Utopian thought for an anti-Utopian age.* New York: Columbia University Press.

Jameson, F. 2005. *Archaeologies of the future: The desire called Utopia and other science fictions.* London: Verso.

Jay, M. 1984. *Marxism and totality: The adventure of a concept from Lukács to Habermas.* Berkeley and Los Angeles: University of California Press.

Kamber, T. 1996. Marx, tragedy, and Utopia. *Rethinking Marxism* 9 (1): 101–15.

Kateb, G. 1972. *Utopia and its enemies.* New York: Schocken.

Kellner, D., and H. O'Hara. 1976. Utopia and Marxism in Ernst Bloch. *New German Critique* 9 (Autumn): 11–34.

Kochi, T. 2002. Anticipation, critique and the problem of intervention: Understanding the messianic: Derrida through Ernst Bloch. *Law and Critique* 20 (13): 29–50.

Laclau, E., and C. Mouffe. 1985. *Hegemony and socialist strategy: Towards a radical democratic politics.* London: Verso.

Lewis, T. 1996. The politics of "hauntology" in Derrida's *Specters of Marx. Rethinking Marxism* 9 (3): 19–39.

Marx, K. 1975. *The economic and philosophical manuscripts of 1844.* In *Marx-Engels collected works*, vol. 2. New York: International Publishers.

———. 1989. *Critique of the Gotha program.* In *Marx-Engels collected works*, vol. 24. New York: International Publishers.

Marx, K., and F. Engels. 1975. *The German ideology.* In *Marx-Engels collected works*, vol. 5. New York: International Publishers.

———. 1976. *The manifesto of the Communist party.* In *Marx-Engels collected works,* vol. 6. New York: International Publishers.

Nelson, C., and L. Grossberg, eds., 1988. *Marxism and the interpretation of culture.* Urbana: University of Illinois Press.

Ollman, B. 1976. *Alienation: Marx's conception of man in capitalist society.* Cambridge: Cambridge University Press.

———. 1977. Marx's vision of communism: "A reconstruction." *Critique* 8: 4–43.

Rabinach, A. 1985. Between enlightenment and apocalypse: Benjamin, Bloch and modern German Jewish messianism. *New German Critique* 34 (Winter): 78–124.

Rorty, R. 1998. *Achieving our country: Leftist thought in twentieth century America.* Cambridge, Mass.: Harvard University Press.

———. 1999. *Philosophy and social hope.* New York: Penguin.

Sennett, R. 2008. *The craftsman.* New York: Penguin.

Shade, P. 2001. *Habits of hope: A pragmatic theory.* Nashville, Tenn.: Vanderbilt University Press.

Singer, D. 1993. In defense of Utopia. *Socialist Register,* 249–56.

Smith, J. 2008. Jacques Derrida, 'crypto-Communist?' In *Critical companion to contemporary Marxism,* ed. J. Bidet and S. Kouvelakis. New York: Haymarket Books.

Spivak, G. 1995. Ghostwriting. *Diacritics* 25 (2): 65–84.

Szeman, I. 2000. Ghostly matters on Derrida's Specters. *Rethinking Marxism* 12 (2): 105–16.

Webb, D. 2000. *Marx, Marxism and Utopia.* London: Ashgate.

———. 2007. Modes of hoping. *History of the Human Science* 20 (3): 65–83.

Zeitlin, M. 1996. In defense of Utopia. *Monthly Review* 48 (7): 23–8.

Ernst Bloch and the Spirituality of Utopia

Peter Thompson

This essay outlines the significance of the unknowable and the spiritual in the works of Ernst Bloch. Bloch argued that Marxism needed to generate a "warm stream" of analysis to complement the "cold stream" of socioeconomic categories. His major works, The Principle of Hope *and* The Spirit of Utopia, *represent attempts to provide this warm stream. This means that he was one of the few Marxist thinkers who took religion and faith seriously and attempted to find within them and within communism a common root of the anticipatory consciousness of a different world. His central operator was the Not-Yet, meaning that the tendencies latent in human development cannot be fully realized under current conditions. It is therefore spirit that carries these latent tendencies.*

Marxism is the depleted uranium of political philosophy. Its hardheaded materialist analysis is still good at punching through the armor plating of bourgeois ideology to reveal the soft internal contradictions of the system, but it no longer has the power to generate the revolutionary heat it did in the nineteenth and twentieth centuries. Too many people feel they have been burnt by that heat. Of course, this contradiction is not necessarily new, and Ernst Bloch had already argued in the 1930s that the struggle against fascism needed not only the "cold stream" Marxism of socioeconomic analysis but also the "warm stream" of utopian desire and human liberation in order to be successful. It needed a *spiritual* dimension (Bloch 1977, 141). At a time when it is the Right that is once again using leftist and anticapitalist rhetoric to paint a picture of a pristine Golden Age that needs defending, it is the Left that is struggling to find an alternative vision for the future. Without that alternative vision, it is questionable—possibly for the first time in human history—whether there can be any future. Just at the point when there appears to be various crises coming together in one headlong rush, it is Marxism—which offers universal historical analysis, if it offers anything—that is found wanting.

Alain Badiou (2012) has maintained that the true crisis we are facing in the twenty-first century is not that of capitalism but of socialism. More precisely, he maintains that this is a "crisis of negation." By this he means that the objective crisis of capitalism, which showed its full force in the Second Great Crash (of 2008) and which is still ongoing, has not given rise to its own negation in the form of an alternative social vision. Fredric Jameson's (2003) take on this crisis of negation is to state that "it is easier to contemplate the end of the world than it is to see a better one in its place."

If the whole point of Marx's work was to sketch out possibilities for the transcendence of the existing and for the establishment of a better world, we have to ask why it is that just at this point he is condemned by so many—not least by those who sincerely wish for a better world—as surplus to requirements.

Of course, on one level the answer to that question is obvious: it is precisely because the world is in crisis that radical answers, which go beyond mere tinkering with some of the symptoms, are bound to come under attack. Psychologically, it is not always the case that things have to get really bad before we are prepared to make a change, but sometimes the worse things get, the more likely it is that we will resist change and hark back to previous, apparently golden ages. Bloch (1934) was aware of this when he argued in his *Erbschaft dieser Zeit* that National Socialism was a modernizing but also a deeply reactionary and backward-looking phenomenon. He called this *Ungleichzeitigkeit* (nonsimultaneity). For him, the Conservative Revolution was summed up by fascism. It was a revolution to restore a supposed lost order. But that is not the only level on which we have to operate. There are serious questions about Marx and Marxism that do need to be addressed, particularly by those who wish to see a reinvigoration of Marxism as a serious contender in the battle for hegemonic ideas.

The question I shall be addressing here is therefore whether Marxism has any relevance to the twenty-first century, a century in which one Stalinist state has completely disappeared to be replaced by greater Russian neo-nationalist chauvinism and in which a Maoist state has completely transformed itself into the most nakedly capitalistic country under control of a Communist party the world has ever known. Cuba still functions to a certain extent as a romantic pole of attraction to many on the left, but it too has questions to answer about how it has developed and what the legacy of Stalinism has done to its own revolutionary tradition, regardless of the pressure exerted on it by American imperialism. Likewise with Venezuela, as Chavism declines into a form of authoritarian left-Peronism.

The question is whether it is possible to stand outside our prejudices and to conduct a rigorous critique of everything we believe in. This does not mean a capitulation in the face of what appear to be overwhelming political difficulties, but it should be the default position of anyone who follows Marx's famous dictum: *de omnibus dubitandum*. To paraphrase Ernst Bloch (1972, 125), the great thing about Marxism should be that it creates its own heretics.

To be sure, the crisis of negation has indeed led, to a certain extent, to a rediscovery of Marx.[1] His face has appeared on the cover of many incongruous publications, almost always asking the question of whether he was right or not about capitalism. Given that the crisis that emerged in 2008 is due to head down into its second phase at any moment, it is likely that there will be further renewed interest. The activities of French students and workers on the streets in the Nuit Debout—a sort of "Paris Spring" 2016—may well be a new harbinger of social transformation similar to the one in 1968. Equally we could argue that the limited socialist demands made by

---

1. In recent years Marx and Lenin have appeared on the cover of the *Economist*, where their theories of capitalism have been (inadequately) discussed, and David Harvey has enjoyed a period of fame alongside Thomas Piketty and others. That the prescriptions delivered are at best left-Keynesian is not the issue here.

Bernie Sanders has helped invigorate his challenge for the Democratic presidential nomination in the United States. But whether Marx and Marxism will play any role in this transformation is questionable, at least.

The conclusion is often that, yes, in part Marx was right in his analysis, but any prescriptions he may have made turned out to have been worse than the original disease, and therefore the doctrine itself has to be rejected because of its supposedly universal consequences. Any concession that he may have been right about globalization and the tendency of profit rates to fall is offset by constant references to the gulags in the Soviet Union or Pol Pot's genocidal regime in Cambodia or the general and specific disaster that is North Korea.

In this essay I will seek to explain why Marxism—despite all the complications and difficulties—remains worth pursuing, but only if we see it as a means of analysis and not as a universal truth. Of course this contention itself has become a universal truth, but often it is something that is mouthed as an exculpatory catechism, with very little honest power behind it. This essay will be an investigation of the works of Ernst Bloch, a Marxist who in his later years described himself as "not a non-Marxist," as a result of the guilt by association that all Marxists suffer. When rethinking Marxism, we have to turn the title and the slogan on its head and point out that Marxism itself is a process of rethinking. The very use of the substantive "Marxism" belies an adherence to something that does not exist, per se.

The nonexistence of the subject under discussion leads to two possible paths. The first is an untrammelled commitment to the original project regardless of its suitability to current conditions. The second path is to open up the original project into what Ernst Bloch called an "open system." There are then two further dangers—one lying at the end of each of these paths. The first path tends to end either in dogmatism or burnout and the second in either collusive resignation or confused indecision. I would contend that most of the global Left finds itself at one of those four dead ends. The outcomes range from hyperactive ultraleftism and ideologically empty identity politics to total withdrawal from the field.

But an interest in Marx and the insights his works provide are still able to lead us into an understanding of the way in which the world fits together and of where the points of friction are within that fit. It remains the case that any attempt to interpret the world, let alone change it, is made more difficult by a refusal to engage with Marx. I hope to avoid, however, any dogmatic or reductionist assertions about why Marx still matters. An adherence to Marx must be one based on the merits of the case rather than the fullness of his beard. We need an open and self-critical defense both of the Marxist method and of many Marxist conclusions. To use a Hegelian word much loved by Marx himself, the point is that of *Aufhebung*, a term that means to transcend something through its absorption and overcoming and not simply its rejection or negation. It does no good to simply maintain an adherence to a pure strain of Marxism—one untainted by the dirty business of how to take power and how to hold onto it. This sort of platonic bolshevism leaves those using Marx's ideas open to dismissal as pure idealists.

On the other hand, if we *do* stand up to questions of taking power, then we are equally accused of harboring the authoritarian tendencies inherent in all "totalitarian" systems of thought and action. We are damned as vague utopian idealists if we don't have a plan for power and as potential mass murderers if we do. The only permissible political stance in these times appears to be what Richard Rorty (1982, 14) has called a "North-Atlantic bourgeois liberalism" complemented by weary cynicism and disavowal, in which we say that we know full well that socialism is not possible but nevertheless continue to believe in its ultimate inevitable triumph. What is required is a far more open dynamic in which Marx and Marxism can play a role alongside other political strands. Of course, one of the main characteristics of depleted uranium is that it leaves behind a toxic legacy that is very hard to clean up. That legacy in the Stalinist tradition—as well as other strands that consider themselves revolutionary and yet also carry deep within them the Stalinist bacillus—must be confronted.

Ernst Bloch and Open System Marxism

Ernst Bloch attempted to address this with what he called an "Open System" of Marxism in which all movement toward stasis and dogma is to be challenged in a processual dynamic that relies upon an interaction between contingent events and the tendencies and latencies toward progressive change that inhere in human history. These nonsimultaneous tendencies may shift and disappear, but there remained for Bloch a sort of quasi-Kantian "invariant of direction" toward human liberation, which could be suppressed but never extirpated.

For Bloch, the narrative of the future is, by definition, incomplete and under constant and often aimless construction. But any future must have sublated within it all past figurations. The present moment does not exist in that it is taken up with both the distorted past and the disavowed future colliding to create a convincing chronological narrative. Memory construction is part of the construction of history and, married to the anticipation of the future, aids the metaphysical dimension of human past and future. Taken together with the darkness of the lived moment, there is no alternative to the construction of all three temporal elements of existence. The result is metaphysics, but it is a materialist metaphysics that I have elsewhere called the metaphysics of contingency (Thompson and Žižek 2013, 82).

The problem with much traditional Marxism is that it has never really gone beyond dialectical materialism in its most vulgar forms. There are of course thinkers who have attempted to do this. As soon as they leave the trusted path of Marxist orthodoxy, however, they are immediately written off as renegades, revisionists, or even heretics. But wherever belief gangs up with orthodoxy in order to persecute thought, dogmatism is always the result. In Marxist discourse there is too often a desire to return to the safe ground of reductionist materialism—what Bloch called *Klotzmaterialismus* (a *Klotz* being a lump of dead and inert stuff). For this reason, any Marxism worth its salt has to be heretical in its discussion of the role of the imagination and spirit. Within Bloch's Marxism there was always a heretic trying to get out. Just as he believed that the human being is not yet complete, so he maintained that Marxism was an approach that was not yet complete, as for all its insights, the objective conditions that would allow it to flourish were not yet complete or even visible. This combination of the subjective and the objective conditions, which puts neither above the other but combines them into a Hegelian dialectical unity of opposites, is central to his thought and sets him apart from but also places him within both subjectivist idealism and objectivist

Marxism without needing to abandon either. Contingent responses to emergent processes require flexibility and even inconsistency.

To paraphrase Alain Badiou (2005) and to combine his ideas with those of Ernst
Bloch, what Marxism needs is fidelity to an event that has not yet happened. This
by definition requires commitment to the *spirit* of a utopian future and not to any
sort of fixed reality hanging over from a glorified past—what we might call a *specter*
of utopia. Bloch called this recognition of the "Not-Yet" an "invariant of direction" embodied in a principle of hope, not merely as a blind optimism but as an educated hope
(*docta spes*) based in the human desire for a better life. Whereas Spinoza saw hope as an
inconstant quantity, Bloch saw hope as the fundamental element of what it means to be
human. Indeed, the ability to develop an anticipatory consciousness based on the principle of hope is the very thing that separates us from all other species. But what made
Bloch a Marxist rather than just another romantic philosopher is that he saw material
objective reality in the form of class antagonism and the uneven ownership of the
means of production as that which stands in the way of human liberation rather
than the problem being simply one of inadequate individual consciousness. Hope
thus develops a metaphysical and spiritual dimension without ever leaving the
ground. Hope emerges not from the mind of God but from the mind of a species
adapted to and constantly involved in developing ways to overcome material
hunger. Bloch agreed with Brecht when the latter said, "First comes the bread, then
the morality," but the search for morality (*Moral*, to give the proper German term,
which is not necessarily the same as "morality") is not something separate from
bread but rather emerges from it. Only when we can build a society through collective
human labor can we arrive, as Bloch (1995, 1376) says, at a home that we all recognize
from our childhoods but in which we have never yet been:

> Humanity lives everywhere still in pre-history, indeed each and everything is
> waiting for the creation of a just world. *The true genesis is not at the beginning, but
> at the end*, and it will only start to come about when society and existence
> [*Dasein*] become radical, i.e. take themselves by their own roots. The root of
> history, however, is the laboring, creative human, engaged in reshaping and over-
> coming given conditions. Once he has grasped himself and that which is his,
> without alienation and based in real democracy, so there will arise in the world
> something that shines into everyone's childhood, but where no one has yet
> been: *Heimat* [homeland].

The Brechtian sense that "something's missing"[2] is about trying to define what a
utopian *Heimat* really is and how it might be possible to attain it. For Bloch, the
spirit of utopia and the principle of hope are to be understood as tendencies and latencies, endlessly open possibilities dependent on the dialectical interplay between contingency and necessity, between what is and what might be. The utopia he wanted was not
a programmatic one laid down in any blueprint but was processual and autopoietic: it
would emerge out of the process of its own becoming. As Bloch (1977, 171) put it,

2. See Bertolt Brecht's libretto and the character Jimmy Mahoney in *Rise and Fall of the City of Maha-
gonny*, an opera by Kurt Weill.

"Processus cum figures, figurae in processu" (The process is made by those who are made in the process). He called this a "concrete utopia," not because it already concretely existed but because the Hegelian origin of the term concrete goes back to its root as *con crescere*, a growing together and emergence of utopia out of reality. He called this a form of transcendence without the transcendent, a readiness to start from that which is possible—Aristotle's *Kata to dynaton*—but also a readiness to embrace that which might become possible—*dynámei on*. In dialectical terms this is the shift from quantity into quality, the movement from the gradual accretion of quantitative changes to a tipping point where everything changes. As Hegel (1977, 6–7) puts it:

> Besides, it is not difficult to see that ours is a birth-time and a period of transition to a new era. Spirit has broken with the world it has hitherto inhabited and imagined and is of a mind to submerge it in the past, and in the labour of its own transformation. Spirit is indeed never at rest but always engaged in moving forward. But just as the first breath drawn by a child after its long, quiet nourishment breaks the gradualness of merely quantitative growth—there is a qualitative leap and the child is born—so likewise the Spirit in its formation matures slowly and quietly into its new shape, dissolving bit by bit the structure of its previous world, whose tottering state is only hinted at by isolated symptoms. The frivolity and boredom which unsettle the established order, the vague foreboding of something unknown, these are the heralds of approaching change. The gradual crumbling that left unaltered the face of the whole is cut short by a sunburst which, in one flash, illuminates the features of the new world.

This new world—note here how close the Hegelian "Geist" is to the Christian "spirit"— is also at the root of much Marxian thought. This is not to agree with those who have always maintained that Marxism is just another religious doctrine but, on the contrary, to posit that religion has always been a self-misunderstood form of anticipatory, and therefore communist, thinking. To be a Marxist—or at least not to be a non-Marxist —therefore requires a degree of speculative thought that, though based in materialism, has to go far beyond the merely contingent. It means one has to develop an understanding of the unknowable and speculative elements of human existence as a metaphysics of contingency.

Marxism and Spirituality: The Dialectics of Contingency

In his discussion of Hegel in *Absolute Recoil*, Žižek (2014, 21) points out that as part of the process of sublation, the vanished mediator returns in a form in which "there is a moment of contingency in every emergence of meaning." Žižek here emphasizes the retrospective nature of this meaning. It is not that a specific contingent event is carried into the future on a fully conscious layer of meaning but that, when a contingent event emerges, its meaning has to be reconstituted from a historical process of which the event itself was largely unaware. This means that contingency cannot be equated with mere chance. It is not just that an event emerges out of nowhere but that the conditions that give rise to that emergence are largely forgotten or ignored.

This self-unconscious determination is therefore often based—in a nonmaterialist form—on the idea of the miracle and that of a religious understanding of the emergence of meaning. In this way meaning itself is handed over to the process and the process becomes a fully spiritual one. This is, of course, the meaning of the idea that "God moves in mysterious ways." In this version of history, not only is there no meaning to be adduced but also (in the more orthodox versions of religious understanding) the search for an underlying or causative meaning is itself blasphemous.

It is not that we are constantly dealing with the arbitrary nature of an emergent reality but that the process of emergence itself is not conscious and therefore needs —in order to be able to emerge properly—to develop a self-conscious narrative of its own necessity. The dialectic of contingency is therefore the interplay between chance and necessity, with necessity being redeemed only at a later juncture. In order for me to have been born, it was necessary for all previous generations of my family to have come together in the way that they did in order to produce me. But there is no substantive necessity for all those previous generations to have come about in the first place. This means that the dialectic of contingency is one in which we find unnecessary necessity working together with contingent reality. The interaction between conscious human intervention into history and the contingent emergence of new circumstances means that any plan must itself be a purely contingent one. A plan that cannot both react to and be part of the metaphysics of contingency remains a dogmatic blueprint.

Expanding this principle out into evolution itself makes this conundrum slightly clearer. The interaction within and between species emergence forms the basis of an unnecessary evolutionary dynamic. Any species that emerges from evolution does so in a way not determined by the outcome but by the process itself. As Marx (1973, 105) puts it in the introduction to the *Grundrisse*, "Human anatomy contains a key to the anatomy of the ape. The intimations of higher development among the subordinate animal species, however, can be understood only after the higher development is already known." In other words, the development of any species can only be known retrospectively. There is no point looking into the anatomy of "lower" species for what might come next. But evolution is not necessarily a smooth transition, and development of one form into another proceeds by what we might call dialectical disruption. Traditionally, this is seen in Hegelian terms as the dialectic of quantity into quality. Today, we would probably be advised to avoid such categorizations and speak instead of a "tipping point" (Gladwell 2000).

This tipping point is actually the juncture where subject and substance come briefly into alignment. Of course, as Hegel, Bloch, and Žižek point out, there is no distinct difference between subject and substance, the one being entirely enmeshed with the other within the dialectic.

This enmeshing only becomes visible at opportune, usually revolutionary moments. This is why revolutions form such an important background to the works of Hegel (1789), Bloch (1917), and Žižek (1789, 1917, 1989, ... ?). Revolutions are the point at which contingency produces a disruptive rather than stabilizing narrative. As Wordsworth (1970, 196) famously put it and as Hegel undoubtedly felt:

> Bliss was it in that dawn to be alive,
> But to be young was very heaven! Oh times,
> In which the meagre, stale, the forbidding ways

Of custom, law, and statute, took at once
The attraction of a country in romance!

The "times" he posits here are precisely the point in time at which contingent events emerge out of that which already exists to put a new complexion on "things" that already exist. It is the point at which Aristotle's *kata to dynaton*, that which is possible, flows over qualitatively into *dynaméi on*, that which may become possible. In other words, subject becomes substance, if only for a fleeting moment, inevitably to be disappointed and resundered. But as Žižek (2014, 29) reminds us, "The subject does not come first—it emerges through the self-alienation of the Substance. In other words, while we have no direct access to the substantial pre-subjective Real, we also cannot get rid of it." Seen in revolutionary terms, this is precisely the moment at which forbidding ways take on the attraction of a country in *romance!* In modernity, revolution transforms what would have been a religious phenomenon of God moving in mysterious ways into a phenomenon in which romantic love takes the place of God. Revolutionary developments, by the same token, always take on a romantic dimension that has a quasi-religious and messianic expression. The surplus of human consciousness always requires a form. This quasi-religious dimension is then reified into the worship of revolutionary iconography in which the subject is transformed back into substance as the Real of revolutionary transformation refuses to emerge fully.

Bloch (1970, 219) has a quasi-mathematical formula for this revolutionary and emotional transformation: "S is not yet P; the Subject is not yet Predicate." In saying this, he is inscribing the transitional and processual dynamic back into the relationship between subject and substance, or subject and object. What stops S from becoming P is only a question of time and appropriate conditions. But in order to insert the dialectics of contingency into this equation it is necessary to point out that all historical development is the emergence of contingent reality out of preexisting real conditions. These contingent events then work back on real conditions in order to create movement. Once again, the Not-Yet between the S and the P becomes more important than either the S or the P, both of which will themselves be transformed, either retrospectively in the case of the subject or proleptically in the case of the predicate. For this reason the very invisibility of the Not-Yet, its motivating negativity, becomes the force that will take us from an unfixed S to an unfixed P.

Žižek (2014, 29) arrives at a remarkably similar conclusion when he says, "The subject does not come first: it is a predicate-becoming-subject, the passive screen asserting itself as a first principle, i.e., something posited which retroactively posits its presuppositions." Using the thought of both Bloch and Žižek, we can therefore see that contingency—namely, the active yet unconscious process of emergence from the predicate-becoming-subject—is both a foreshadowing of the Aristotelian *dynaméi on* and a retrospective view of *kata to dynaton*. Bloch is important in this context because he gives central importance to this blind spot between the two forms of possibility, calling it the *Dunkel des gelebten Augenblicks*, the "darkness of the lived moment." Indeed, Bloch's (1977) last book, *Experimentum Mundi*, is a treatment of the inaccessibility of this gap between S and P. Bloch summed up the whole of his philosophy as "S is not yet P," meaning that the dialectical movement of history *and nature* is that of a processual dynamic, the future of which can only be guessed at. Tendency and latency, subject and object, are present in indeterminate dialectical form in this gap. It is here that one can perhaps see a reflection of Marx's wariness about laying down a blueprint for what a future society might look like. In his *Negative Dialectics*, Adorno (1966) later equated this with the old Judaic tradition of refusing to create graven images of god.

This darkness of the gap or, to give its more Hegelian expression, of negativity becomes the motivating force behind change because it contains within it an anticipatory consciousness that separates us from all other species. To be human is to anticipate a different future as well as one's own finitude. At the same time, this gap continues to carry within it memories of the past that are bent and shaped into the form that is required, regardless of whether or not the memories are true. As we know from Nietzsche (1999, 86), in the battle between pride and memory, memory is always the loser.

It is at this point that Bloch warns us against anamnesis: that is, the danger of looking backward merely in order to recover ideas from the past that can be refunctioned for the future. This category, which emerges in the Platonic dialogs, has the appearance of being forward looking but is in fact wedded to the uncertainties of the past. Plato asks how it is that we are to know what it is that we don't know. Anamnesis needs to rely only on past experience in order to project into the future. Bloch, however, asks us to trust our anticipatory unconscious, which knows that something has to be better than that which exists or has existed but does not yet know what that thing might be. As he points out, there is only a *spirit* of anticipatory consciousness rather than a fixed and teleological endpoint, the presence of which would lead us into the temptation of Kantian moralism (Bloch 1971, 447). From our past we might have an inkling of what lies ahead, but it is not a past that is correctly and accurately remembered; rather, it is a past that only exists in the indeterminate future. We tend as a species not only to hark back to a golden past but to use that (misremembered) past as a way of harking forward to a glorious future.

As Bloch (1971, 474) explains in *Subjekt-Objekt*, however, an idea that is simply transmitted from the past becomes old as soon as it is thought. This is, of course, the fate that awaits the owl of Minerva, who can only take flight when it is already dark. Bloch uses this Hegelian motif as the prime example of the problems of anamnesis. In the section "Hegel and Anamnesis," he writes: "The power of memory, indeed the desire to look behind the curtain of that which has passed, only increases when in service of the future" (473; translation mine).

Contingency therefore has not only a contemporary function but also one that looks backward in order to anticipate the future, and in a way that is only partially determined. Our contingent existence and the way in which we interact with contingencies from the past also inform the way we anticipate the future. We know that it is impossible to leap over contingent events, but we also know that we are able to shape the future on the basis of contingencies, which arise at all points but which may arise in a way not predicted by some dogmatic theory. Within the Marxist debate, for example, this leaping over of contingencies became central to the struggle for the legacy of the October Revolution. Stalin stuck strictly to the stagist interpretation not only because this allowed the Communist Party of the Soviet Union to determine by central diktat what stage of history a given country was in but also because it was central to Stalin's stagist, self-serving, and vulgar reading of the Hegelian dialectic.

But the dialectic of contingency contains within it an anticipatory moment that enables us both to plan for the unforeseen and also to map out what we think this unknown known might possibly hold for us. Bloch's interpretation of fascism, for example, falls precisely into this anticipatory and contradictory gap. He saw it as something that not only mobilized an anamnetic memory of a supposedly glorious past but at the same time, and possibly more importantly, painted a picture of the future that could be easily expressed and understood. In this context it was necessary for fascism to mobilize against contemporary liberal-democratic and bourgeois morality both in the name of the restoration of old values as well as the implementation of a new order. Fascism both conserved and revolutionized all existing values. The dialectic of contingency requires not simply a leaping over of the liberal-democratic stage but its utter annihilation as a precondition for the emergence of the new.

It is for this reason that Bloch saw fascism as an essentially religious movement, mobilizing both religious categories from the past (Joachim di Fiore's Third Reich, for instance) as well as a messianic führer-fixated model of the future. It is this nonsimultaneity of political impetuses that was at the center of Bloch's political agenda, especially during the 1930s when the appeal to past formations was exploited to the full by the fascists. It can be argued that current debates about "taking back control"—by leaving the European Union, for instance—appeal to a similar anamnetic desire to return to a pristine and safe world of spitfires on the village green, warm beer for tea, and the certainties of empire.

Marxism and Spirituality: Materialist Metaphysics

It is in this gap opened up by the transition from subject to predicate that not only anamnetic memories of past events but also an anticipatory imagination of what might and should come next take up a central position. Having established that the nonsubstantial difference between subject and predicate produces the gap into which the Not-Yet rushes, we must further examine what form this Not-Yet-ness takes.

At this point it might be objected that what I am doing here is merely a continuation of Plekhanov's famous contention (although he doesn't demonstrate quite how this happens) that Hegel's thought is the point at which philosophical idealism shades over into a materialism that was simply waiting to emerge.[3] But rather than looking back to d'Holbach, Plekhanov, and the various other philosophers whose metaphysics remained determinedly mechanistic, Bloch attempted to liberate matter from the given and put it in the service of the what-might-be, or *dynaméi on*. This anticipatory consciousness means that—as he argued in his 1968 book *Atheism in Christianity*—even etymologically, just as religion (*re-ligio*) means a tying down or tying back to a preordained message, so too materialism finds it difficult to liberate itself from its very deterministic and vulgar form. By returning to an Aristotelian conception of *potentia* within matter, Bloch sought to show that a religious understanding of the universe is constrained merely by the times that produce it. At the same time, however, such an understanding also contains within it an appeal to a future beyond the contingent.

3. For a discussion of this, see Pavlov (2016).

Equally, materialism became stuck in its own times and was unable to see beyond given parameters. It too developed a future dimension but one that was strictly laid down by the Party, which, as we know, is always right. It is for this reason that Bloch developed a very close interest in quantum theory and the ways in which it promised liberation from the *Klotzmaterialismus* of previous scientific models. In today's terms his atheism would be profoundly opposed to that of the "new atheists" who see reality as some fixed quantity against which religious forces are pitted. Bloch was keen to understand what it was in religion that continued to exert such gravitational force on human consciousness. A simple frontal war with religion would be counterproductive. Instead, as the title of his 1968 book shows, atheism could only be developed from within the religious traditions of a particular country. For Bloch, coming from a Jewish heritage within a family that had converted to Christianity, the latter faith provided the springboard from which it was possible to understand and implement an open atheism. He maintained that "only an atheist can be a good Christian; only a Christian can be a good atheist" (Bloch 1972, 9).

Žižek today argues similarly that he is a Christian atheist, not merely because he has been socialized in the Christian West but because the Hegelian concept of the social development of humanity sees Christianity as the final—effectively secular—form of religious belief. Perhaps declaring their Eurocentrism, it is only through Christianity that it is possible to move forward to atheism, all other religions still being bound back into a more or less dogmatic ideological fidelity to certain traditions and ideas. Bloch says that Christianity requires nothing but a commitment to an absent God. Indeed, Christianity itself is based upon the idea that God is not to be found in any metaphysical realm but is represented as the "son of man" rather than the "son of God" (see Bloch 1968). That, after all, is the very purpose of the crucifixion. The point at which Christ asks "Why hast thou forsaken me?" is the very point at which Christ himself becomes God and immediately dies.

Metaphysical materialism becomes a necessary correlate to the dialectics of contingency as it describes the space into which anticipatory consciousness, liberated from both *re-ligio* and reductionist materialism, can be projected while at the same time rejecting neither religious development toward atheism nor materialist development toward complexity and the "multiversal." This process also liberates Aristotelian *potentia* from its own theological limitations (Bloch 1952).[4]

Hegel, in a late development, spoke of an intermediary *objektiver Geist* located somewhere between subjectivity and the Absolute. It is in the workings of this objective spirit that we find the emergence of practical arrangements for civil society. In philosophical terms, this spirit also provides a conceptual framework for the interaction between contingency and necessity in that structures that emerge also need some sort of metaphysical underpinning. In his *Philosophy of Right* as well as in the *Encyclopaedia*, Hegel points out that in order to be able to break out of the immediate subject of circumstances and move toward the Absolute, it is necessary to develop a narrative of transition and change. In dialectical terms, however, the narrative adopted in order to

4. See also the translation by Loren Goldmann and Peter Thompson of Bloch's *Avicenna and the Aristotelian Left*, forthcoming from Columbia University Press.

explain transition and change itself becomes the motivating force behind transition and change.

Hegel—no less a product of his time than any other philosopher at any other time, confronted with the reality of his age, which was one of revolution in both society and science—played no other role than to help construct this narrative. He remains one of the most important philosophers of the late eighteenth and early nineteenth centuries precisely because his overarching narrative was that of transition from one historical state to another. The objective spirit that emerges, he contended, fills in the gap between what is and what might be. It is this transitional role of the objective spirit that Marx and Bloch took and turned on its head, arguing that it is the material conditions of production that revolutionize society and not simply the ideas of "men." In order to be able to take conscious control of transition, it is necessary to wrest that control from the hands of metaphysical gods and put it in the hands of humanity.

The agency of the proletariat was central to this philosophical step in that it remained the only class that could become universal. The partial and particular interests of all other classes stood against a development toward human control of society, regardless of their ideological commitment to a scientific narrative of progress. In the end their material interests prevented them from recognizing the categorical imperative of a totalizing revolution. And though it was not the purpose of this essay to argue about the positive and negative aspects of this Marxist position, I argue that the Marxist narrative of historical change is itself part of metaphysical materialism in that it posits the possibility of unknown and unknowable change out of existing material conditions.

For Hegel this change in social being is brought about by changes in self-consciousness. For Marx, as we know, it is being that determines consciousness. Somewhere between the two positions—the idealist and the materialist—there exists an indeterminate and unknowable realm in which the interplay of ideas and reality produces what I call the metaphysics of contingency. Objective spirit is actually the product of contingent reality taking place at the "decisive moment" in historical development, the *Augenblick* that gives us access to the ability to construct both a retrospective narrative and an anticipatory consciousness. As we know from Bloch, however, this *Augenblick* is distorted and unfocused and requires an oblique look.

This theoretical and ideological development remains an open one in which any attempts to tie thought back to dogmatic certainties can only be negative. The key operator here becomes once again the Not-Yet. It would be a mistake to imagine, however, that Bloch uses the Not-Yet as some sort of anticipatory stand-in for the Real or the Absolute. That which is Not-Yet is also that which *is*. In a classical Hegelian reversal, we can say that the Not-Yet is the true confluence of subject and substance. If we take the Not-Yet as defining something (in structuralist terms) that is present through its absence, then it becomes akin to Hegel's *Geist*. Just as with Bloch's Not-Yet, Hegel posits that the spirit is not something that is inflicted upon the subject by substance but is something present from the very beginning of the subject. Indeed, the subject is nothing without the substance of its own spirit. In order to be able to overcome this absent spirit, it is necessary to see the spirit as a central part of its own existence rather than as something external to and imposed upon substance. As the AA

(Automobile Association) puts it in more prosaic terms, "You are not stuck in traffic, you are traffic."

This unmasks the religious dimension in the thought of both Hegel and Bloch in that the Not-Yet-ness in the latter and the self-healing nature of the spirit in the former have clear parallels in Christian theology. In this reading, original sin is not some external substance that is done to an otherwise pristine natural subject to which we are always attempting to return but is an essential part of the subject's desire and movement toward its sublation into the Absolute. For Hegel, the fall is not something done to us through the sinfulness of the individual subject (in this case, Eve, in the patriarchal tradition) but is an essential part of what it is to wish to rise up. But rise from what and to what? What is the self-liberating dynamic that human beings have conceived for themselves?

In the thought of both Hegel and Bloch, we find the idea that an entity arises out of its own loss. *Etwas fehlt*, "Something is missing," is the phrase Ernst Bloch borrows from Brecht in order to illuminate this point. The *thing* of the *some*thing is only constituted by the fact that it is missing. Negativity, or the absence of something, is the very means by which that something is constituted. Not-Yet-ness is the space in which this gradual constitution takes place. But at the same time, appearance is the only way that essence can be discerned. Both Bloch and Žižek constantly shy away from the use of Nietzsche's thought, but this point can be best explained with Nietzsche's famous dialectical comment (later disavowed as a youthful mistake) that Apollo and Dionysus speak in contradictory and complementary unity through each other.

Of course, in a historical sense, the Kantian line of the gradual establishment of human freedom is a continuation of the progressive narrative that emerged in the eighteenth century and can be argued to have arisen out of the Christian narrative of salvation. What is important here, however, is not the progressive but the narrative element. It is only by recognizing the active tendencies and latencies in human consciousness and the material world that the spiritual dimension within materialism can be discovered and put to good conscious use. The spiritual is not a bit of useless historical junk DNA that is surplus to requirements but rather carries the principle of hope within it.

The spiritual is to be found in mathematical terms too. The symbol for infinity is in fact a Möbius strip. The square roots of -1 and infinity are both imaginary numbers that can only exist as concepts and not in reality. In his recent play, *X and Y*, Marcus du Sautoy plays with exactly this gap between what can exist as a concept against the reality of the existence of the thing. In Ernst Bloch's thought, the point of the Not-Yet is that it stands in for the Not-Ever. Rather than arrive at infinity, we are condemned to wait for Godot, again a concept that can exist only as an imaginary number. Equally with God, we can imagine "his" existence as a concept, but even those who believe in him cannot ever attain closeness to God other than through death, and in some traditions even to depict him is declared a crime. This is what Heidegger meant by *moribundus sum*, that the reality of our existence is limited on the ontic level by our individual death and on the ontological level by entropy and the absolute death of the universe. Ernst Bloch posited that death is the greatest of all anti-utopias. Given that death is inevitable, both ontically and ontologically, this implies that an "out," as du Sautoy puts it, is not possible. In his play he seeks to make a Möbius strip from a page of Shakespeare. There can be no better representation of the metaphysics of contingency in that, in order to be able to express the impossible, we have to turn from mathematics to literature, culture, and the intangible—to the spiritual. In order to be able to express the impossibility of attaining a future utopia, we are equally required to turn from reality to theory. This is the reason that thinkers such as Badiou and Žižek turn to either imaginary numbers or imaginary realities that stand in for the Real.

Žižek (2014, 352) shows how Hegel does this:

> Hegel's point here, predictably, is that such a limitation leads to what he calls the "bad" (or "spurious") Infinity: I know there is something beyond, but all I can do is replace one phenomenal determination with another in a process that goes on endlessly. In short, I merely replace one finite entity with another without ever reaching Infinity itself, so that Infinity is present only as a void that pushes me from one to another finite determination. In effect, I find myself in the world divided into Something(s) and Nothing, and all that is left to me is to produce more and more new Somethings to fill the void of Nothing.

This, I maintain, is the metaphysics of contingency: the constant construction, conscious or otherwise, of the contingent conditions for an infinity that can never be reached. As Adorno said, the great contribution that Ernst Bloch made to philosophy was to restore honor to the word "utopia." He did this precisely by changing it from a finite concept into a reality that can never be achieved but toward which we must always strive. This is what he meant by the *spirit* of utopia.

References

Adorno, T. 1966. *Negative dialektik*. Frankfurt: Suhrkamp Verlag.
Badiou, A. 2005. *Being and event*. London: Verso.
———. 2012. The crisis of negation: An interview with Alain Badiou. *Berfrois*, 2 March. http://www.berfrois.com/2012/03/the-80s-i-think.
Bloch, E. 1934. *Erbschaft dieser Zeit*. Frankfurt: Suhrkamp Verlag.
———. 1952. *Avicenna und die Aristotelische Linke*. Frankfurt: Suhrkamp Verlag.
———. 1968. *Atheismus im Christentum*. Frankfurt: Suhrkamp Verlag.
———. 1970. *Tübinger Einleitung in die Philosophie*. Frankfurt: Suhrkamp Verlag.
———. 1971. *Subjekt-Objekt: Erläuterungen zu Hegel*. Frankfurt: Suhrkamp Verlag.
———. 1972. *Atheism in Christianity*. Trans. J. T. Swan. New York: Herder and Herder.
———. 1977. *Experimentum Mundi*. Frankfurt: Suhrkamp Verlag.
———. 1995. *The principle of hope*. Vol. 3. Cambridge, MA: MIT Press.
Gladwell, M. 2000. *The tipping point: How little things can make a big difference*. New York: Little, Brown.
Hegel, G. W. F. 1977. *The phenomenology of the spirit*. Oxford: Oxford University Press.
Jameson, F. 2003. Future city. *New Left Review* 21 (May–June): 65–79. https://newleftreview.org/II/21/fredric-jameson-future-city.
Marx, K. 1973. *Grundrisse*. Harmondsworth, UK: Penguin.
Nietzsche, F. 1999. *Jenseits von Gut und Böse*. Berlin: De Gruyter.
Pavlov, E. V. 2016. Comrade Hegel: Absolute Spirit goes east. *Crisis and Critique* 3 (1): 157–89.

Rorty, R. 1982. *Consequences of pragmatism*. Minneapolis: University of Minnesota Press.
Thompson, P., and S. Žižek, eds. 2013. *The privatization of hope: Ernst Bloch and the future of utopia*. SIC 8. Durham: Duke University Press.
Wordsworth, W. 1970. *The prelude*. Oxford: Oxford University Press.
Žižek, S. 2014. *Absolute recoil*. London: Verso.

Reading Marx with Levinas

Serap A. Kayatekin and Jack Amariglio

Emmanuel Levinas is a profoundly influential figure in several post–World War II continental European philosophical traditions. A growing scholarship has started to explore the links between his work and Judaism and, inter alia, phenomenology, feminism, and deconstruction, but very little has been written in the English-speaking world on the connections between his thought and that of Marx. This essay is an attempt at an encounter between the two thinkers, exploring how Levinas's radical critique of ontology in the Western philosophical traditions can be brought to bear on Marx's antihumanist critique of capitalism as a way to think of an alternative ethical stand that starts from alterity, which is where the essay finds the spirituality of both thinkers to reside. While the theoretical planes on which they operate are different, through a difficult but necessary conversation, Levinas and Marx can pose to one another fundamental questions with crucial implications for their orientation.

When I spoke of the overcoming of Western ontology as an "ethical and prophetic cry" in "God and Philosophy," I was in fact thinking of Marx's critique of Western idealism as a project to understand the world, rather than transform it.
    —Emmanuel Levinas, "Dialogue with Emmanuel Levinas"

Humanism has to be denounced because it is not sufficiently human.
    —Emmanuel Levinas, *Otherwise than Being, or Beyond Essence*

If money, according to Augier, "comes into the world with a congenital blood-stain on one cheek," capital comes dripping from head to toe, from every pore, with blood and dirt.
    —Karl Marx, volume 1 of *Capital*

Why Levinas and Marx?

The thought of Levinas has enjoyed a growing influence in the last decades across a broad spectrum of academic fields. An increasing number of scholars have begun to engage with his work in an ever-widening field of disciplines such as philosophy, theology, psychology, linguistics, sociology, and social work. Although Levinas has also been explored in relation to different philosophical strands, especially phenomenology, enquiries about any possible connection to Marx have been negligible, at least in the

English-speaking world. At first sight this relative silence is somewhat inexplicable. For example, it can be argued that Marx's relentless critique of capitalism has ethical underpinnings. Given that Levinas was possibly the twentieth century's foremost ethical philosopher (Bauman 2000, 5) it seems natural that comparisons between these two thinkers should abound. Strangely, this is not the case.

Marx launched his criticism of capitalism as a historically and specifically unjust, unfair society that had to be transformed. People, he thought, and especially those largely denied the benefits of bourgeois economy and society, would build a society better serving their needs. This project of building a better society was primarily dependent on the extent to which humans could transcend class exploitation, which was central for Marx to the social forms that perpetuated injustice and subjugation. One of the conditions of existence of a more just society in a class-based social formation, like capitalism, was therefore the transformation of the processes of the production, appropriation, and distribution of economic surpluses.

While not an ethicist, Marx's fundamental concerns led him to consider ethical stances appropriate to opposing capitalism and, on a grander scale, any social system in which the laboring classes were "robbed" by nonlaboring owners of "their" labor. Marx located one source of the "violence" of capitalism in these processes of separation through which the laborer was alienated from the means and product of labor, the creation of a society enveloped by the presence of capital. One source of spirituality in Marx's thought has to be looked for here, in the creation of the other, in the processes of class, and in the desire for the transformation of these processes of exploitation: the efforts to bring about noncapitalist forms of existence and, perhaps, communist modes of existence.

One of our themes in this essay is an exploration of if and how Marx's critique of bourgeois values, and his own antipathy to universal, "humanist" ethical positions, some of which derive from his later writings, especially *Capital*, are in line with Levinas's more consistent and persistent ethical critique as first philosophy with the world as received. Our concern here is to explore how Marx's critique of bourgeois values and his radical critique of universal, humanist ethical positions, based especially on a reading of *Capital*, can be seen as kindred in spirit to Levinas's position that ethics are prior to philosophy.

As a radical critic of ethical positions based on ontology, Levinas was deeply suspicious of the moral positions that emerged from the proposition of the other's humanity. He believed and argued with zeal that the history of violence has a direct connection to the history of ethics based on ontology. The idea and practices of doing good on the basis of rational reasoning and the humanity of the other, for Levinas, are fundamentally flawed and fatal: every definition of a human being simultaneously brings together the definition of a non- or a subhuman being. An ethics is ethics as long as it respects and preserves the radical alterity of the other. It is this thinking oriented to the other that, for us, delineates the spirituality of his thinking.

If Marx is the radical critic of capitalism's specific ontology, then Levinas is the radical critic of Western ontology *in toto*. Can we bring one to bear on the other to further enrich their criticism? Can Levinas's general critique of ontology be used to interrogate Marx's critique of capitalist modernity? Can Marx's critique of class exploitation be deployed to provide further texture to Levinas's critique of ontology? These are the questions that guide our basic exploration of these two great critics of modernity.

Levinas and the Critique of Humanism: Ontology and Violence

The core of Levinas's work can be interpreted as a radical critique of ontology—all ontology—in Western philosophical traditions. For Levinas, argues Simon Critchley (2002a, 11), ontology is the "general term for any relation to otherness that is reducible to comprehension or understanding." In both its idealist and empiricist variations, philosophy is first based on the idea of Being: it is first and foremost the endeavor and the process of understanding, of comprehending, Being. In this act of understanding, there is a very particular relation between the "I" and the "Other." In trying to understand the "Other," the "I" takes it and appropriates it, rendering it "the Same." Philosophy, for Levinas, is all about this reduction of the other. Understanding the other, knowing the other, is the process of utilizing particular knowledge procedures to make the other, in thought and action, like myself. When I know the other, when I understand the other, the other has become like me, has shed any specificity that remains unknown or anything deemed central to the other's being, which is a form of Being's existence.

Levinas's work starts from this observation: in fact, the history of Western philosophy reveals to us that the attempt to understand, to comprehend, is identical with that of taking the other and making it the same. This has all the force of a Nietzschean "will to know" and all of the (perhaps) pent-up, tense, and aggressive power of the adage and encouragement to "understand." To understand the other at all costs involves violence. The desire to comprehend is imposing. This appropriative nature of philosophy, of its ontological phase and its nature of reducing the other to the Same, led Jean-Paul Sartre, to declare it "digestive philosophy" (Critchley 2002a, 16).[1]

Developing his critique of ontology as the basis of ethics, Levinas (1985, 95) distanced himself from Martin Heidegger in particular, whose work he singled out as one of the seminal moments of the Western philosophical tradition: "In [*Otherwise than Being*] I speak of responsibility as the essential, primary and fundamental mode of subjectivity. For I describe subjectivity in ethical terms. Ethics, here, does not supplement a preceding existential base [as Heidegger would have it]; the very node of the subjective is knotted in ethics understood as responsibility." In other words we can say that, for Levinas, philosophy, as the understanding of Being, culminates in the elimination of alterity. The essential quality of Western philosophy, which eradicates all alterity in order to construct a conception of human commonality and the unlimited right and access of the understanding, was Levinas's utmost concern and the driving force of his lifelong work. He argued that it is possible to derive ethics from ontology—and some specific notion of common, shared existence—but it is not desirable. Let us see this argument in detail.

---

1. Treanor (2007, 19) argues that according to Levinas it is impossible to sustain alterity in ontology: "Levinas's arguments assert that philosophies based on ontological foundations do not allow the self to encounter anything truly foreign, anything other than that which merely orbits the self as a satellite."

Levinas believed that ontology's inherent quality to eliminate otherness—via the dual work of appropriation (thereby reducing the difference) and by its not being able to apply understanding to that which is finally judged to be irrevocably different and therefore outside of the norms that reason has created for a common practice based on a shared ethics—is a fundamental source of violence in this world. He argues that an ethics based on ontology, which reduces alterity to sameness, is fundamentally fatal. Levinas's antihumanism has its source exactly in this same observation: if we base our ethics on the sameness of humanity—that is to say, on the idea that we are all human—and if this implies rules of moral etiquette from which we should not deviate, we open the door to violence.

It is not too difficult to see why. For if ethics derives from the notion that we are all human, an essential condition for the possibility of intraspecies violence arises: the belief that some people are not "really" human—that is, their species-being is held in abeyance, at best, and is determined to be nonconforming to a basic definition of life and species-life. If the motivation in ethical behavior is the understanding that the other is really not the other but in fact is the same, then those circumstances in which we are not able to see the same in the other—the "me" in the other—have proven over the course of modern history to lead to potentially deadly circumstances. In this quest for noninclusive all-ness, a turbulent history was made: indifference to the other, at best; genocide, at worst.

Western history is made of constant confrontations with the ontologically determined or ontologically defined other. The planters of the antebellum South of the United States considered their slaves as chattel. For many, slaves were human but also not quite so, and therefore they were subhuman. This was the perception that partly legitimized the ownership and thus the purchase and sale of human beings. This perception did not much change after the Civil War. In the sharecropping relations of the postbellum era, former slaves were still looked upon as belonging to a stratum below that of human beings, which perception justified their place at the bottom of a hierarchy reminiscent of medieval Europe. Similarly, in Victorian England of the nineteenth century, working classes did not always make it to fully human status. They were somewhere below that "privileged" point. It is precisely due to their subhuman status that they did what they were doing—labor—and that their fate as laborers could be hardened into one more hereditary trait.

And without a doubt the Holocaust, which is the primary background to all of Levinas's work, is one period in modern history where the failure to acknowledge the humanity of an other did result in genocides.[2]

2. Levinas was taken as a prisoner of war with the Tenth French Army in June 1940 and was sent to a military prisoners' camp where he did forced labor. Most of his family was killed by the Nazis (Critchley and Bernasconi 2002, xix). In the dedication of his magnum opus, *Otherwise Than Being, or Beyond Essence*, he wrote the following words: "To the memory of those who were closest among the six million assassinated by the National Socialists, and of the millions on millions of all confessions and all nations, victims of all the same hatred of the other man, the same anti-semitism" (Levinas 1999).

In a more piercing reference that links ontology to the Holocaust, Levinas (1990, 292) says the following: "Is the Being of being, which is not in turn a being—phosphorescence, as Heidegger has it? Here is the path taken by the author of this book: an analysis which feigns the disappearance of every existent—and even of the *cogito* which thinks it—is overrun by the chaotic rumbling of an anonymous 'to exist,'

The deeply radical nature of Levinas's critique was noted by Derrida (2001, 102) in his seminal work on the thinker, where he argued that ontology's quest for the same is at the root of all oppression:

> A thought which, without philology and solely by remaining faithful to the imme-
> diate, but buried nudity of experience itself, seeks to liberate itself from the Greek
> domination of the Same and the One (other names for the light of Being and of the
> phenomenon) as if from oppression itself—an oppression certainly comparable to
> none other in the world, an ontological or transcendental oppression, but also the
> origin or alibi of all oppression in the world.

If philosophy is the search for ontological truth, then for Levinas ethics comes before philosophy. This reversal allows us to consider Being not as driven first and foremost by a will to know but instead as a relation to the other, which is not reducible to com-prehension (Critchley 2002a, 12). Ethics is therefore "otherwise than knowledge" (11). It does not come from knowledge. It is not knowledge. It is a relation of "otherwise than being." This "otherwise than being" is not a suggestion of the alteration of being. It is far more radical than the transformation of being into another being. It is a transcendence.

Let us try to understand this in further depth. In articulating his endeavor at the start of *Totality and Infinity*, Levinas (1969, 47) wrote the following:

> For the philosophical tradition the *conflicts* between the same and the other are re-
> solved by theory whereby the other is reduced to the same—or, concretely, by the
> community of the State, where beneath anonymous power, though it be intelligi-
> ble, the I rediscovers war in the tyrannic oppression it undergoes from the totality.
> Ethics, where the same takes the irreducible Other into account, would belong to
> opinion. The effort of this book is directed toward apperceiving in discourse a non-
> allergic relation with alterity, toward apperceiving Desire—where power, by
> essence murderous of the other, becomes, faced with the other and "against all
> good sense," the impossibility of murder, the consideration of the other, or justice.

This is how Levinas, in these obscure lines, announced the point of what became his lifelong labor: to develop a discourse about the experience of not being violent ("the impossibility of murder") when confronted with the "Face" of the other, even if this goes against reason ("against all good sense"). All of this sounds disconcerting, against the grain, and deeply troubling. Yet this enigmatic statement, which has vexed thinkers all along, is at the core of Levinas's thinking. We will try to explore this point while arguing that the spirituality of Levinas's thinking emanates precisely

---

which is an existence without existents and which no negation manages to overcome. *There is*—imper-sonally—like *it is raining* or *it is night*. None of the generosity which the German term *'es gibt'* is said to contain revealed itself between 1933 and 1945. This must be said! Enlightenment and meaning dawn only with the existents rising up and establishing themselves in this horrible neutrality of the there is. They are on the path which leads from existence to the existent and from the existent to the Other, a path which delineates time itself."

from this point of the idea of an absolute Other, the infinity of the Other for which I am (infinitely) responsible.

Not "I" but "Here I Am": Infinite Responsibility for the Other

In a fascinating essay on Levinas's thinking and its relation to Judaism, Putnam argues that, *to be* human in the normative sense means to say *hineni*: "Here I am." Levinas (1999, 114) states this clearly in *Otherwise Than Being*: "The word *I* means *here I am*, answering for everything and for everyone." This is a command without a commander; it is a primordial obligation that is not grounded on any reasoning. Putnam (2002, 39) argues that if you have to ask the question "Why?" for this obligation, if you wonder, "'Why I should put myself out for him/her?,'" you are not yet human."[3] This command (without a commander) to say *hineni*, the ethical command, is not reciprocal and is infinite. It is something one feels or intuits rather than arrives at by reasoning (54).[4] It has no contractual dimension.

The ethical relation, for Levinas, needs to be asymmetric: it is not based on reciprocity but is characterized by "radical nonreciprocity" (Ciaramelli 1991, 88). In fact, ethics should precede reciprocity because a search to found ethics on reciprocity is to seek, once again, a "sameness" with the other (Putnam 2002, 39). This is exactly what Levinas avoids, and for good reason, in his ethical formulation. In making oneself available to the other, in saying *hineni*, I, and only I, am obliged without any expectation whatsoever of a similar obligation from the other.[5]

In stretching my hand to the other, I expect nothing. The other's obligation is the other's affair only. My responsibility for the other is infinite, without any inquiry. The infinite responsibility is a *calling*; it comes from within. It is not the application

3. For Levinas, holiness in the Bible has to do with this. In a fascinating interview with Chalier, he says that holiness in the Bible is "the position where the other is more important, where, as a result, the subject, at this moment doesn't think of itself. It is absolutely absorbed by the other. It is, uniquely, alterity. It's about taking charge, of being responsible, of preserving something and reassuring it. That's holiness, in as much as it is the situation par excellence, where the other comes before me." See "Levinas: The Strong and the Weak," section 3 of "Penser aujourd'hui: Emmanuel Levinas," YouTube video, 7:44, from an interview with C. Chalier in 1991, posted by Eidos84, 26 June 2011, http://www.youtube.com/watch?v=8AGDjpg72ng.

4. Putnam (2002, 54) goes on to argue that Levinas is more like Hume in thinking of ethics as a relation, a reaction. But there is an important difference: for Hume, since the essence of ethics is one's ability to *sympathize* with others, it still relies on the perception of the sameness of the other with oneself. We may be able to sympathize with some but not all. And if we fail to sympathize with some but not others, then we are not ethical. Ethics in this sense is a universal position, yet it is not based upon a humanist first principle or assumption. Sympathy works on the basis of our ability to think the other like me: "What would I do if I were in his/her position?" The necessity of understanding the other, of positing the Other in terms of a Being that is similar to Me, reveals the inherent cracks in ethics, which derive from philosophy based on ontology.

5. This responsibility is my responsibility and mine only. Zygmund Bauman (1999, 183) sees this non-reciprocity as the core of subjectivity: "Indeed, according to Levinas, *responsibility is the essential, primary and fundamental structure of subjectivity*. Responsibility, which means 'responsibility for the Other' and responsibility 'for what is not my deed, or for what does not even matter to me.' This responsibility, the only meaning of subjectivity, of being a subject, has nothing to do with contractual obligation. It has nothing in common either with my calculation of reciprocal benefit."

to human relations of a principle arrived at with the aid of rationality. It does not derive from an ability to empathize or sympathize.

Levinas's insistence on the nonreciprocity of infinite responsibility is one of the most troubling points of his thinking. His vehemence on this point is unconditional and radical, arguing that the persecuted has a responsibility for the persecutor (Levinas 1999, 126). How can we be responsible for acts we haven't committed? How can I be responsible to someone who is persecuting me? How can I, the persecuted, be responsible for the one who commits the persecution? This anxiety-provoking idea goes deeply against the grain of how we think about responsibility. To be able to come to terms with this, we need to understand what Levinas means by "persecution."

In *Giving an Account of Oneself*, Judith Butler (2005) articulates a nuanced reading of "responsibility for the persecutor." This responsibility, she argues, rises not because of the consequences of the acts of my free will that I have performed. It is not a state one can trace to one's deeds.[6] Quite to the contrary: it is persecution, an original trauma precisely because it is unwilled. It has no relation whatsoever to what I have intended or done. "Persecution is precisely what happens *without the warrant of any deed of my own*. And it returns us not to our acts and choices but to the region of existence, the primary, inaugurating impingement on me by the Other, one that happens to me, paradoxically, in advance of my formation as a 'me' or, rather, as the instrument of that first formation of myself in the accusative case" (85). There is a very clear suggestion here that this impingement of the other comes before the emergence of the "I."[7] The responsibility for the other that comes with this original trauma is thus preontological.[8] It is not something over which the "I," as free will, exercises choice. It comes before "I," before free will. It is in this sense as well, Levinas states (1999, 114), that ethics comes before philosophy: "Responsibility for another is not an accident that happens to a subject, but precedes essence in it, has no awaited freedom, in which a commitment to another would have been made. I have not done anything and I have always been under accusation—persecuted." It is possible to think of what Levinas articulates in

<hr>

6. Blanchot (1995, 25) gives us one of the most illuminating explanations of responsibility in the work of Levinas: "Responsible: this word generally qualifies—in a prosaic, bourgeois manner—a mature, lucid, conscientious man, who acts with circumspection, who takes into account all elements of a given situation, calculates and decides. The word 'responsible' qualifies the successful man of action. But now responsibility—my responsibility for the other, for everyone, without reciprocity—is displaced. No longer does it belong to consciousness; it is not an activating thought process put into practice, nor is it even a duty that would impose itself from without and from within. *My* responsibility for the Other presupposes an overturning such that it can only be marked by a change in the status of 'me,' a change in time and perhaps in language. Responsibility, which withdraws me from my order—perhaps from all orders and from order itself—responsibility, which separates me from myself (from the 'me' that is mastery and power, from the free, speaking subject) and reveals the other *in place* of me, requires that I answer for absence, for passivity."
7. Butler (2009, 77) repeats this elsewhere: "Importantly, there is no self prior to its persecution by the Other. It is that persecution that establishes the Other at the heart of the self, and establishes that 'heart' as an ethical relation of responsibility."
8. Ciaramelli (1991, 88) states that the ethical relation of radical nonreciprocity is prior to ontology, to "I am." As written earlier, this relation does not derive its meaning from the universal logos. What imposes this command on me is the transcendence of the other. It is the immediate presence of the other, which I cannot comprehend, that impels me to present myself to the other.

the form of this impingement by the other as *sociality*. We are all at all times encroached upon, as we are all at all times part of a sociality. There are no exceptions to this.

At this point we can already note an important difference between Levinas and Marx. While the other in Levinas's work is the other that belongs to all sociality, Marx's lifework was the theorization of a specifically capitalist sociality. The other in capitalist sociality is produced in multitudinous and historically specific ways, one of which is the creation of the other in the course of class processes of exploitation.

Let us pause here and ask the question: Can we contemplate a similar argument for exploitation? Can we propose that the exploited is infinitely responsible for the exploiter?

Am I, the producer of surplus labor, responsible for the other who exploits me by appropriating my surplus labor? Levinas's answer to this question will reveal the difference between persecution and exploitation and an instance of differentiation—but not, we think, as an instance of contrariness.

One of the most evocative images of infinite responsibility is offered by Catherine Chalier (1994, 126) through the metaphor of the maternal body:

> As the maternal body answers for the Other and makes room for him or her inside itself, it is evicted from its harbor and disturbed so far as to be out of breath, and this is precisely the signification of subjectivity. It is the ethical signification of the maternal saying. The "pre-original not resting on oneself" of the maternal body entails anxiety and listening but it lacks free choice. It is the time for an inalienable mercy for the Other, an infinite patience when facing an election that gives birth to the self in the very moment that it interrupts its essence.

The maternal body does not exercise choice in the way that it makes way for the other within it. The relation of the mother's body to the other within does not depend on a conscious decision. It has nothing to do with desire, want, or need. It is not the mother's purposeful "service" to the other. I am infinitely responsible for the one that impinges on me, without my choice or free will or decision.

Levinas (1999, 136–7) insists that the ethical relationship is not an expression of commitment. For "commitment refers ... to an intentional thought, an assumption, a subject open upon a present, representation, a logos." Commitment assumes an ego that, upon reflection, has made the conscious decision to serve the other. Commitment to the other reflects the acting upon of a principle arrived at through different thought processes.

This way of relating to the other is not an act of goodness deriving from principles. It is an act that is beyond the ego, in which the ego goes beyond itself and becomes something other than itself. The ethical act is the radical act of *substitution* for the other.[9]

---

9. Zygmunt Bauman (1999, 183) argues that for Levinas morality "*is the primary structure of the intersubjective relation*" and that "society starts when the structure of morality ... is already there." So for Levinas, "*Morality is not a product of society. Morality is something society manipulates*—exploits, re-directs, jams." Bauman then goes on to argue that the Holocaust was made possible by the *neutralization* of the attitudes of ordinary Germans rather than the traditional arguments, based on German exceptionalism, that point at the unique intensity and murderousness of German anti-Semitism in the long history of European anti-Semitism (185).

Levinas and Marx: Preliminary Questions

We know that Levinas was intrigued by Marx, yet references to Marx and Marxism are very sparse in his writing. Nonetheless, it is clear from these few allusions that what drew Levinas (2006, 102–3) to Marx was his conviction that Marxism, too, had given the other a serious consideration:

> Q.: Can your thought, which is a thought of love, be reconciled with a philosophy of conquest, such as Marxism?
>
> E.L.: No, in Marxism, there is no such conquest; there is the recognition of the other. True enough, it consists in saying: We can save the other if he himself demands his due. Marxism invites humanity to demand what it is my duty to give it. That is a bit different from my radical distinction between me and others, but Marxism cannot be condemned for that. Not because it succeeded well, but because it took the other seriously.

Levinas here is signaling to the importance of the place of the other in Marxism. His remark that Marxism is not a philosophy of conquest is also noteworthy. But is the other in Marxism really the same as in Levinas? Levinas points to a difference in the quote above. It is this question we will ponder in what follows. This is crucial for our exploration because the roots of spirituality in Marx's thinking lie precisely in this notion of the other, as well.

More than in any other text, possibly, it is in "Judaism and Revolution" that Levinas (1994, 97–8) engages with Marx's thought:

> Our text upholds the right of the person, as in our days Marxism upholds it. I refer to Marxist humanism, the one which continues to say that "man is the supreme good for man" and "in order that man be the supreme good for man he must be truly man" and which asks itself: "How could man, the friend of man, in specific circumstances, have become the enemy of man?" and for whom the anomaly called alienation is explained by the structure of the economy, left to its own determinism.

So Marxist humanism, intimates Levinas, stands for the necessity of human for fellow human, a "truly" human community that can be realized only through the transformation of humanity. Marxism also questions, Levinas says, the "specific circumstances" under which human beings become alienated from their fellows. These specific circumstances refer to the economic structure of the society in which they live.

These lines are deeply resonant with the processes of alienation that Marx depicts in the *Economic and Philosophic Manuscripts of 1844*. In going through a detailed depiction of how man is alienated from his labor and the product of his labor, Marx (1959, 32) theorizes the emergence of the deep separation between men. Let us see:

> It is just in his work upon the objective world, therefore, that man really proves himself to be a *species-being*. This production is his active species-life. Through this production, nature appears as *his* work and his reality. The object of labour

is, therefore, the *objectification of man's species-life*: for he duplicates himself not only, as in consciousness, intellectually, but also actively, in reality, and therefore he sees himself in a world that he has created. In tearing away from man the object of his production, therefore, estranged labour tears from him his *species-life*, his real objectivity as a member of the species, and transforms his advantage over animals into the disadvantage that his inorganic body, nature, is taken from him ... .

... An immediate consequence of the fact that man is estranged from the product of his labour, from his life activity, from his species-being, is the *estrangement of man* from *man*. When man confronts himself he confronts the *other* man. What applies to a man's relation to his work, to the product of his labour and to himself, also holds of a man's relation to the other man, and to the other man's labour and object of labour.

As I am separated from production, which is the very activity in my becoming a species-being, I become estranged from myself as well as my fellow humans. These processes of alienation, of being torn apart, create a deep disunion between me and my species-being and between me and my fellow humans. As I concede the product of *my* labor to the person who has not performed the labor, I confront this person as the other. In demanding the surplus labor I have produced, in appropriating the fruits of my labor from me, does my fellow, who is now the appropriator of my (surplus) labor, become my enemy? If we were to read the two texts by Levinas and by Marx in tandem, could we say that Levinas is alluding to a similarity between the other in a class relation and the other who persecutes me? Is there a similarity? If so, would the transformation of the conditions from which alienation arises also transform the conditions of persecution?

Let us remember at this point that the other for Levinas is an other that belongs to the preontological level; it brings about the originary trauma prior to the emergence of the self. The other in Marx, however, is one that emerges in an ontology and in fact, more specifically, the modern capitalist ontology. As the earlier quote indicates, Levinas is cognizant of the difference between Marx's way of thinking of the other and his own. Yet there is not a clear response in his texts as to what this difference may be. This difference thus needs to be excavated from his work through interpretation.

The descendants of Abraham, Isaac, and Jacob are human beings who are no longer childlike. Before a self-conscious humanity, no longer in need of being educated, our duties are limitless. Workers belong to this perfected humanity, despite the inferiority of their condition and the coarseness of their profession. But, strange as it may seem, humanity is nevertheless not defined by its proletariat either. As if all alienation were not overcome by the consciousness that the working class may achieve from its condition as a class and from its struggle; as if revolutionary consciousness were not sufficient for disalienation; as if the notion of Israel, people of the Torah, people as old as the world and as old as persecuted mankind, carried within itself a universality higher than that of a class exploited and struggling; as if the violence of the struggle were already alienation. (Levinas 1994, 98)

The descendants of Abraham, Isaac, and Jacob in this passage correspond to a human-ity that has found its true humanity. Levinas insists that here he is referring to all those who are no longer childlike and all those who have responded to the call of the other, who have accepted the infinite responsibility for the other, not to the Jewish people in particular.

When Levinas thinks of workers in this category of "perfected humanity," is he won-dering that the working class has reached this state of full humanity, as Putnam refers to, of having responded to the call of the face? While Levinas first thinks of those who are exploited as having reached this full humanity, he is careful to not equate all of hu-manity with the exploited. The revolutionary consciousness is not adequate to over-come "all alienation." The violence of persecution overrides the violence of exploitation. The persecution of mankind, which is as old as mankind, has a higher uni-versality than that of exploitation. Critchley (2002b) interprets this text as the prioriti-zation of persecution before exploitation; the persecution that comes with submission to the law of the responsibility for the other comes prior to my freedom and to justice. This is in keeping with our earlier argument that persecution corresponds to the pre-ontological level and holds for all sociality while exploitation holds to that of (capitalist) ontology.

So while the working classes belong to this category of "true" humanity, humanity is larger than its working class. Is Levinas here suggesting that revolutionary class strug-gle is but one aspect of a full transformation of sociality? That overcoming exploitation is not enough for overcoming one's alienation from the other at large? Is there a sug-gestion here that only when the revolutionary consciousness is conceived within the ethics of a change that is directed at the sociality as a whole can we talk about overcom-ing full alienation? This point is not really resolved.

At this point, we can ask the question: Even if we accept Levinas's position that per-secution is prior to exploitation, are they disconnected? How would an ethics that speaks to persecution also tend to exploitation? The difference in the level of the planes from which Levinas and Marx theorize creates a difficult problem for placing these two thinkers in dialog. This difficulty, however, does not imply an impossible task.

The Other in Levinas, the Other in Marx: An (Im)possible Dialog?

Robert Gibbs's (1992, 1994) work stands among the handful of efforts in the literature to explore the parallels between Levinas and Marx. In his article entitled "A Jewish Context for the Social Ethics of Marx and Levinas," Gibbs reveals similarities of polit-ical concern that underlie the work of both thinkers. His analysis is based on interpre-tations of the "early Marx." Let us see, briefly, his reflections on the kinship between the two thinkers.

Gibbs argues that Marx's work is a critique of the view that persons are self-suffi-cient, competitive individuals who freely maximize their satisfaction, the interest-seeking "economic man." According to Gibbs, Marx's analysis is based on the notion of socially constituted human beings. Marx in his early work argues that, while human beings in any society have been socially constituted, only under communism does humanity experience true sociality because only in a communist society do we en-counter the situation "where one exists for the others and they exist for me" (Gibbs 1992, 175). For Marx, writes Gibbs, the basic injustice of capitalism is that "people serve commodities"; the materialism unleashed in capitalist societies is a kind of "animal materialism." Communist society will be different from capitalist society: people will no longer look at things merely as commodities with a price but will see them as products with a social use. This way, as the use value of a commodity takes precedence over its exchange value, objects will cease to be things "in which we lose ourselves through our labour" and become, in the sense Levinas gives, "expressions of ourselves."[10] Thus: "Each person's hunger will be that of his fellow, and so the sat-isfaction of those needs will be a social action. In civil society, the satisfaction is social, but only in the modes of oppression (the banker's profit on the farmer's loan is part of the cost of the bread we eat)" (180).

Gibbs argues that in this vision of a society where people are *for* each other, Marx also reveals a Jewish vision that, for Gibbs, is a very important source of parallel with Levinas. Both thinkers in their vision of a different (and better) society draw upon an ethics that is decidedly nonindividualistic. Marx and Levinas both reject the view of a society comprising individuals who "use their freedom to enter a contract." Gibbs (1992, 184) draws fascinating parallels between the "Jewish people" of Levinas and the Judaic thought and the "proletariat" in the work of Marx described in expres-sions such as "a class with *radical chains*, a class of civil society, which is not of civil society," "a sphere which possesses a universal character through its universal suffer-ing," and "can win itself only through the *complete redemption of humanity*."

According to Gibbs (1992, 183), there is also a fundamental similarity between Marx and Levinas in what drives their work; this is found in the way they approach "knowl-edge": "The primary concern of both thinkers is the transformation of praxis, not the cognition of truth. By this I do not mean that truth is not also a goal, but it is a practical goal—even theory receives practical justification. For each thinker, social ethics is the focus and indeed the fulcrum of their work." Here we see yet again the precedence ethics takes over understanding in Levinas's work, and this accords well with Marx's famous remark in the "Theses on Feuerbach" that the significance of theory—its "point"—is the desire to transform reality. For both thinkers, truth is not an end in itself; its relevance is determined by the necessity to change truth. Gibbs's analysis is thus very important to uncovering the significant similarities between the works of Marx and of Levinas: their insistence on a particular sociality, their shared rejection of individualism, and their view that the motivation to change the world precedes the comprehension of it.

In a later and more textured essay published in 1994, Gibbs develops Marx's links to Levinas more fully through an analysis of the former's discussion of alienation under capitalism. Here, alienation is the experience of full externalization where capital em-braces everything and everyone, including capitalists. All forms of existence become enslaved to this omnipresent force. But Gibbs in this essay draws attention to a specific form of alienation (specific to capitalism), which is the separation of laborers from their labor. The one point that he could pursue but doesn't is however insinuated when he

10. For a different take on the relevance of Levinas for Marxism, see Horowitz and Horowitz (2003).

refers to the transformation of the object through labor and thus of "increasing its value," offering a connection to the appropriation of surplus value, the particular form class takes under capitalism.

Yet as Gibbs himself notes, the shortcoming of this work is that the "historic dialectic and economic analyses" have been pushed aside. While Marx certainly discusses both the historical dialectic and economic and class analysis in his "early work," their contours are not as fully developed, nor are they well distinguished from the theoretical humanism that guides much of his early writing. Marx's work can indeed provide us with crucial insights about the content of that sociality on which Levinas reflects, earlier in his work, yet it recedes further into the background later in his life (Gibbs 1994).

Without a doubt, in a more complete analysis, one of the central concepts in all of Marx's work, and certainly for the Marx of *Capital*, is that of class, which has to take central stage. This is the missing link in Gibbs's analysis, which we want to pursue here. Those processes of production, appropriation, and distribution of surplus labor[11] have to be part of the analytical consideration if we are to bring to bear a comparison of Marx and Levinas at the mature height of their respective work.[12]

In yet another intriguing passage from *Otherwise than Being*, Levinas confronts the inescapable questions: Can the infinite responsibility of being for the other lead to oppressive relations? Does this exposure, this "pure susceptibleness," mean that the ethical relationship can turn into forms of slavery? Just how meaningful is infinite responsibility if my unconditional exposure (subjection) to the other can be transformed into a relation of exploitation? How responsible are you being if you take my unconditional exposure to you and turn it into a relation of exploitation and appropriate what I produce? How responsible are you if you use my infinite "vulnerability" to you and make me your slave?

Levinas (1999, 117) argues that posing these questions in themselves already indicates a problem: "Why does the other concern me? What is Hecuba to me? Am I my brother's keeper? These questions have meaning only if one has already supposed that the ego is concerned only with itself, is only a concern for itself." The ego that asks the question "Why should I do this for the other?" while looking for a reason, a motivation for the act, is still an ego trapped in itself and is assumed to operate first and primarily for itself. Here, we are still in the realm of traditional ontology. That granted, we can ask: if infinite responsibility is unconditional exposure, how can it invigilate against oppression, persecution, and exploitation?

---

11. The reading of Marx's analysis along the lines of the overdetermined processes of fundamental and subsumed class processes was proposed by Stephen Resnick and Richard Wolff (1987) in their groundbreaking work, *Knowledge and Class*. Fundamental class processes refer to those economic processes through which surplus labor is performed and appropriated. Subsumed class processes are those that constitute the distribution of the surplus labor that has been appropriated.

12. Gibbs's work insinuates the importance of this without taking up the task. His analysis draws on the fundamental differences between capitalist and communist societies. This observation is sufficient to notice the necessity of class, since one of the most important differences that mark a capitalist society from a communist one in traditional readings of Marx is the existence of exploitative class relations in the former and their absence in the latter.

Levinas is well aware of these questions. He doesn't answer them. But he does make a categorical statement that the relation of responsibility does not include slavery. "No freedom, no commitment undertaken in a present, a present among others, recuperable, is the obverse of which this responsibility would be the reverse, but no slavery is included in the alienation of the same who is 'for the other'" (Levinas 1999, 135). Perhaps it is in this, more than in any other statement, that Levinas insinuates a warning about the dilemma that infinite responsibility poses, that the unconditionality of responsibility should not include slavery. Perhaps Levinas was weary of the limitations of an infinite responsibility. Because how meaningful for the other is infinite responsibility if the person I am responsible for is my slave? Alternatively, if I offer myself to you and you make me your slave, can a third person not ask the question, "What kind of a world is this?" This unexplained assertion, in our view, constitutes an important and intriguing gap in Levinas's work.

Here we can pose a question to Levinas about how he can make this "categorical" statement, that no slavery is included in infinite responsibility. Perhaps Levinas is able to say this because just as his ethics does not depend on ontology, and so there is no "Why?" asked for ethical action, so it is with slavery. Because once we pose the question "Why should slavery not be included?," we are once again in the realm of ontology. But we already know that Levinas's ethics precedes ontology. So Levinas can invoke the different planes of theorization between him and Marx as a response.

Yet it is also intriguing that Levinas seems compelled to address this issue of slavery, which, here, we take to be a euphemism for class relations. So while he doesn't go further than to assert that there is no place for slavery in infinite responsibility, that he makes this statement perhaps indicates a certain unease. Possibly this is an instance of him hailing Marxism's concern for the other in the context of class relations. Just as he notes that the revolution by the working class is not sufficient to overcome persecution, does he here, passingly, point at the possibility that where there are relations of exploitation the notion of infinite responsibility is affected? That it is altered and rendered problematic?

Enrique Dussell (2008, 2013) has taken what we consider to be this ambivalent position of Levinas and transformed it into a philosophy of the other in what he calls the ethics of liberation. Dussell, among other things, also draws from Marx's analysis of capitalism, giving Levinas's concept of the other a distinct sense wherein the other is "the widow, the orphan, and the stranger" (Paradiso-Michau 2008). The other is all those who are excluded by the totality: the poor, the women, the indigenous, the working class, the periphery of global capitalism.[13]

In this context of a clear asymmetry, Dussell then argues that the one who wants to transform this system—the "political actor"—is persecuted, is a hostage (Paradiso-Michau 2008, 94). Such actors obey the command of the victim for which they have infinite responsibility. Dussell's (quoted in Paradiso-Michau 2008, 95–6) notion of ethics is very similar to how Levinas sees ethics as a response to a call, to the face:

13. Chakrabarti, Dhar, and Cullenberg (2012) develop a very sophisticated and radical analysis of the other, drawing from the work of Levinas, among others, in the context of a novel notion of development.

Conscience is not so much about the application of principles to concrete cases, but a listening, a hearing the voice calling to me from outside, from beyond the horizon of the system: the voice of the poor calling for justice, calling from deep within their absolute sacred right, the right of the person as person. Ethical conscience consists in knowing how to "open up" to the other and to take that other in charge (take responsibility for him or her)—for the sake of the other, vis-à-vis the system.

We know that Levinas was very sympathetic to this extension of his work,[14] which, as mentioned, crystallizes the notion of the other as that of the oppressed, exploited, and marginalized, and although this reading is a clear possibility, we think that the notion of the other in Levinas is more ambivalent, as we have tried to indicate thus far throughout this essay.

Let us stop here for the time being and reconsider the threads of the argument so far. Levinas's notion of the other and of infinite responsibility for the other is a radical statement against the humanist ontology that besets Western thought and that, he argues, presents a problematic basis for an ethics. Levinas points to a preontological basis, for an ethics based on an original impingement of the other. This is a sociality in which we all exist. While Levinas gestures at the other-oriented thinking of Marxism in different texts, his gestures are ambivalent. His response to the possibility of infinite responsibility taking place in an exploitative context is one of assertion, that infinite responsibility does not include slavery.

For Marx, we think this would not suffice. We would need to go beyond a mere assertion. Marx would ask the question of why infinite responsibility cannot include slavery. Why can we not think of class exploitation in the context of infinite responsibility?[15]

There is an axis in Marx's work that finds its parallel in the radical antihumanism of Levinas on the grounds that the history of humanism has proven something quite different, that it is "not human enough." In fact, this parallel is the profound critique of bourgeois humanism that Marx develops fully in *Capital*, his class analysis of a capitalist sociality. What Marx reveals throughout this work is a fundamental critique of the bourgeois notion of sameness.

Marx and the Critique of Bourgeois Humanism: Humanism as Sameness

The first volume of *Capital* is a profound critique of bourgeois humanism, a passionate argument that establishes how exploitation takes place under conditions of free will

14. "I knew Enrique Dussel, who used to quote me a lot, and who is now much closer to political, even geopolitical thought. Moreover, I have gotten to know a very sympathetic group of South Americans working out a 'liberation philosophy' ... There is a very interesting attempt in South America to return to the spirit of the people ... I am very happy, very proud even, when I hear the echoes of my own work in this group. It is a fundamental approval. It means the other people have also seen 'the same thing'" (Levinas 2006, 102).

15. We thank Anjan Chakrabarti for helping us develop this point.

and equality. The power of Marx's argument derives from establishing how humanism in fact conditions and shapes the processes of exploitation. The foundations of the argument are first laid in his discussion of the sale and purchase of labor power, when the laborer and the capitalist face one another in the first phase of a long and involved relationship: "He and the owner of money meet in the market, and enter into relations with the sole difference that one is a buyer, the other seller; both, therefore, equal in the eyes of the law" (Marx 1977, 271). The laborer who comes to the labor market to sell labor power is the equal of the individual who is there to buy that labor power. Nothing separates them in terms of legal rights. On the face of it, the only difference that marks this transaction is that one is a seller and the other a buyer of labor power.

The two parties in this fateful exchange are "free" individuals: the laborer is "free" to sell labor power, and the buyer is "free" to buy it (or not). No political or legal compulsion exists for the laborer to sell; neither is the capitalist forced in any way imaginable to buy.

Yet the freedom Marx refers to is not merely legal freedom. This freedom emerges as the culmination of historical processes at the end of which the laborer has nothing else to sell. Stripped of every other possibility to make a living, labor power remains as the only source of the laborer's survival. Disentangled from precapitalist feudal obligations, severed from the means of production and the land, the capacity to work, thus "liberated," is now free to be offered on the market. For Marx there are two sides to this freedom: there is legal equality and there is the commodification of the capacity to work. In a passage loaded with irony, Marx (1977, 874) writes about this "double sense" of freedom[16] in his discussion of primitive accumulation in volume 1 of *Capital*: "Free workers, in the double sense that they neither form part of the means of production themselves, as would be the case with slaves, serfs, etc., nor do they own the means of production, as would be the case with self-employed peasant proprietors. The free workers are therefore free from, unencumbered by, any means of production of their own."

This stripping of the direct producers, their transformation into those who have nothing but their capacity to labor to sell, is a long, brutal, and violent process. When the bourgeois order is established and legitimizes itself as the eternal order that has always been, or as the "right" one, the one that is the best and most developed, this history of violence, of which it is the culmination, is lost to amnesia. Falling deeper and deeper into this slumber, capitalism starts representing itself as a universal form existing outside of history. Yet this forgotten long and violent history of the becoming of the free bourgeois individual is the history of *expropriation*. Violence is built into the class ontology of capitalism, of the laborer and the capitalist.

> The immediate producer, the worker, could dispose of his own person only after he had ceased to be bound to the soil, and ceased to be the slave or serf of another person. To become a free seller of labour-power, who carries his commodity wherever he can find a market for it, he must further have escaped from the regime of the guilds, their rules for apprentices and journeymen, and their restrictive labour regulations.

16. "For the transformation of his money into capital, therefore, the owner of money must find the free worker available on the commodity market; and this worker must be free in the double sense that as a free individual he can dispose of his labour-power as his own commodity, and that on the other hand, he has no other commodity for sale, i.e. he is rid of them, he is free of all the objects needed for the realization [*Verwiklichung*] of his labour-power" (Marx 1977, 272–3).

Hence the historical movement which changes the producers into wage-labourers appears, on the one hand, as their emancipation from serfdom and from the fetters of the guilds, and it is this aspect of the movement which alone exists for our bourgeois historians. But, on the other hand, these newly freed men became sellers of themselves only after they had been robbed of all their own means of production, and all the guarantees of existence afforded by the old feudal arrangements. *And this history, the history of their expropriation, is written in the annals of mankind in letters of blood and fire.* (Marx 1977, 875; emphasis added)

This freedom, the central pillar of humanism, which Levinas also relentlessly criticizes, for Marx is the end of a violent process, and is an end that nurtures further violence.

Everything that takes place in the market for labor power happens in accordance with the rules of the freedom of will, of rights, and of equality. In a well-known paragraph, Marx ends his discussion of this "bourgeois heaven" with free individuals meeting other free individuals, where a transaction takes place between people acting on their free will. The exchange that thus takes place is between equals and is also of equivalents: the wage that is paid to the laborer is equivalent to the necessary labor time required to produce the commodities the worker requires to survive. At the point of departure from the sphere of exchange, Marx (1977, 280) takes one final look at what we are leaving behind:

> The sphere of circulation or commodity exchange, within whose boundaries the sale and purchase of labour-power goes on, is in fact a very Eden of the innate rights of man. It is the exclusive realm of Freedom, Equality, Property and Bentham. Freedom, because both buyer and seller of a commodity, let us say of labour-power, are determined only by their own free will. They contract as free persons, who are equal before the law. Their contract is the final result in which their joint will finds a common legal expression. Equality, because each enters into relation with the other, as with a simple owner of commodities, and they exchange equivalent for equivalent. Property, because each disposes only of what is his own. And Bentham, because each looks only to his own advantage. The only force bringing them together, and putting them into relation with each other, is the selfishness, the gain and the private interest of each.

The Eden that is the realm of the exchange of equivalents is the prelude to the exploitation described in the rest of the volume. This is the first link between bourgeois humanism and violence in Marx's analysis: the freedom of having nothing else but one's capacity to labor; the freedom of selling that special commodity, one's labor power, is a "freedom" that has been acquired in the course of a long and brutal history of dispossession. The seller of labor power, the laborer, and the capitalist become what they are as consequences of this violence. They confront one another as free and equal persons ready to exchange equivalents only because the violence of dispossession has created a class of laborers and a class of capitalists. This exchange of equivalents thus marks the first moment of violence in Marx's account and analysis of capitalist humanism.[17]

17. Jeffrey Reiman (1999, 160) makes an interesting observation of how the sense of "freedom" liberalism forges comes to be internalized and accepted as the norm in time: "Furthermore, because capitalism requires freedom (in the sense of an absence of overt violence) in exchange, capitalism will survive only if exchange relations are normally free in this way. Thus, members of capitalist societies will naturally

Marx then extends and deepens his critique of bourgeois notions of freedom and equality in his analysis of the extraction of surplus labor in the form of value under capitalism. Laborers who sell their labor power to capitalists in an exchange of equivalents among individuals who are equals and of free will enter the sphere of production. In the process of production, laborers produce the equivalent of the value of their subsistence but also something beyond that. This surplus value produced by laborers is appropriated by capitalists in a fundamental class process. The moment of appropriation of surplus value, the very source of capitalists' profit, is another moment of violence in the ontology of capitalism. Marx's critique of this appropriation, the stripping of laborers from what they have produced under the pretext of the ownership of the means of production, or of the offering of the employment opportunity, or of the capitalist's risk taking, is one of the most powerful statements against the ideals of bourgeois individualism.

Here, Marx gives us a unique thesis: that notions of individual free will and equality do not counter but in fact nurture relations of exploitation. For him, humanism and class in the form of the processes of surplus-labor appropriation and distribution are not mutually exclusive; to the contrary, the violence of class is predicated on humanism. Perhaps it was a certain feel for this radical critique of liberalism in Marx that led Levinas to refer to "a liberal politics and administration that suppresses neither exploitation nor war." In fact, it could as well be Marx talking in Levinas's interpretation of the Mishnah where, in reference to the labor contract, Levinas (1994, 100) states: "The contract does not put an end to this violence of the other."

In Marx's analysis we find a radical critique of the bourgeois notions of "sameness" of the producers and the appropriators of surplus value, which becomes the cloak over the fundamental alterity, the essential difference between them. In this way Marx's class analysis is also his most developed theoretical assault on bourgeois humanism's idea of sameness. While Levinas is deeply suspicious of the violent potential in Western ontology's search for sameness, Marx is equally critical of bourgeois humanism's sameness under individualism, freedom, and equality, all of which nurture a fundamental alterity created by capitalist class relations.

Let us here rephrase an earlier question and ask: Is the kind of alterity created in the class processes of capitalism desirable for Levinas? Does this alterity need to be kept intact? What follows if we move away from Dussell's identification of the other with those who are excluded, oppressed, and marginalized? What if, for a moment, we considered another possibility? What if the other is my exploiter? Am I infinitely responsible for my exploiter? Am I infinitely responsible for the one who appropriates the surplus labor I have performed?

Marx and Marxists would insist, we believe, on an argument rather than an assertion. A possible Marxist response to this question would be that we actually should ask the question: can infinite responsibility be posed in the context of exploitation? And if the answer to that is a "yes," then this concept is very problematic.

---

come to see such freedom as the (at first, statistical) norm and to see overt violence as something to be resisted or corrected. As people come to expect it, the statistical norm will be subtly transformed into a moral norm. And then people will naturally assume that the content of the freedom they value is the absence of violence ... The moral doctrine of liberalism is then arguably 'read off' the face of capitalism."

It is not possible to think of exploitation in the same way that Levinas thinks of perse-cution. While persecution is the original trauma, the preontological impingement charac-teristic of any sociality, exploitation takes place in a specific sociality. There is a connection, however, between persecution and exploitation: to the extent we can transform that social-ity which imposes persecution, we can change the conditions of exploitation.

Responsibility for my persecutor is this exact responsibility for the other at all times. It is paying heed to a primordial call. It is like stretching your hand instinctively to a stranger who topples and is about to fall.

Marx after Levinas/Levinas after Marx

In the quote at the beginning of this essay, Levinas suggests that, in his philosophical call to overcome ontology as the basis of ethics, he was thinking of Marx's critique of idealism as a project to understand rather than change the world. When we read this quote carefully, it is clear that what Levinas refers to is the core of his project of severing the ontological ground of Western ethics. We read this as the insinuation that Levinas saw in Marx a kindred spirit in the critique of the ontology of modernity. Both thinkers were critics of the notions of human being, free will, and individualism that pervade Western philosophical traditions.

Despite rare references to him, we believe Levinas was more than intrigued by Marx. He was drawn to Marx's analysis of the suffering created within this system that has a specifically exploitative dimension to it. Marx held an attraction for him due to the former's concern for the other. Yet it would be fair to say that this attraction was an ambivalent one. We see this most clearly in Levinas's interpretation of the Mishnah in "Judaism and Revolution," where he refers to the liberatory potential of Marxism for the working class. Yet he is anxious to add to this that the liberation of one class is not the same thing as the liberation of the whole of humanity.

Levinas's work lends itself to the interpretation of the other as the marginalized, the op-pressed, and the exploited. But there is nothing imperative about this interpretation. So we can ask the questions: What if the other is my exploiter? Am I infinitely responsible for the one who appropriates my surplus labor? This is a difficult but necessary question. Al-though Levinas states that infinite responsibility cannot include slavery—which we take as synonymous with exploitative relations—this is only a categorical statement and not an argument. Any Marxist perspective would require more. It is true that the notion of in-finite responsibility leaves us very uncomfortable when the face of the other is the face of the exploiter. Perhaps it is a similar discomfort to what Levinas felt that pushed him to make this assertion.

In the processes of the transformation of sociality, is it possible that we should not lose sight of the fact that we are all bound up with one another, without choosing it, without willing it? Perhaps recognition of this unconditional imposition of the other at all times will render more likely a nonviolent transformation of exploitative class re-lations. Because of the original violence of the other, my preoriginary persecution can keep me alert at all times to respond to this call. In that sense, yes, I am responsible for my persecutor. In building a communist homeland, a constant awareness of this pri-mordial social attachment can prevent repetitions of the Stalinist purges of the 1930s, the labor camps of Kolyma, the famine during the Great Leap Forward (1959–61), the genocide engineered in Cambodia by the Khmer Rouge, the Communist invasion of Tibet, and countless other instances of violence inspired by interpretations of Marxism.

In an interview with Chalier, Levinas refers to the "malignancy of Being," the "sadness of self-interest." He believes that there is a certain "joy" and "accomplishment" in the return to "losing interest in oneself" (se dis-intéresser).[18] Could it be that Levinas's human being, who exists in infinite responsibility for the other, is the postcapitalist human being in Marx's communist utopia?[19]

We believe that Levinas after Marx is a more solid Levinas. Marx after Levinas, on the other hand, is a more humane Marx. In that sense, we think that Levinas's ethics confers a deeper spirituality to Marx's vision. With this deeper spirituality, perhaps the vision of a communist sociality would be more desirable and more resonant.

Let us end with Levinas's (1994, 107) words:

> We are told that each of the just shall have his home. Isn't the proletarian condition, the alienation of man, primarily the act of having no home? Not to have a place of one's own, not to have an interior, is not truly to communicate with another, and thus to be a stranger to oneself and to the other. After the world of night, after existence as a perpetual threat, after existence as wild beasts, not only threatening but also threatened, after fear and anxiety, what is announced here as the triumph of the just is the possibility of a society in which everyone has his home, returns home and to himself, and sees the face of the other.

In finding this home, which has no specific location, in transcending beyond Being, we need to be mindful of the alterity of the other—that we are all beings wrapped in this sociality. While transforming class relations and the otherness created by class, can we not heed to the call of the other? Can we not respond to the face? Can we not respond to the call "Thou shall not kill"? Marxism after Levinas can indeed be "humane" Marxism.

Acknowledgments

We are grateful to our friends Anna Challenger, Antonio Callari, Anjan Chakrabarti, George DeMartino, Anup Dhar, Rob Garnett, and Stephen Healy for incisive comments. Thanks are also due to Howard Caygill for helpful suggestions. The usual disclaimer applies.

References

Bauman, Z. 1999. *Modernity and holocaust.* Ithaca, N.Y.: Cornell University Press.
———. 2000. Am I my brother's keeper? *European Journal of Social Work* 3 (1): 5–11.

18. See "Emmanuel Levinas: Being in the Principle of War," section 1 of "Penser aujourd'hui: Emmanuel Levinas," YouTube video, 11:01, from an interview with C. Chalier in 1991, posted by Eidos84, 10 June 2011, http://www.youtube.com/watch?v=-1MtMzXNGbs.
19. In this primordial obligation toward the Other, in going beyond ourselves, we realize our true humanity. In freeing ourselves from the ego and presenting ourselves without any expectation to the Other, we find our true "homeland": "A homeland which has nothing to do with becoming rooted or with being the first owner" (Chalier 1991, 124).

Blanchot, M. 1995. *The writing of the disaster*. Lincoln: University of Nebraska Press.

Butler, J. 2005. *Giving an account of oneself*. New York: Fordham University Press.

———. 2009. Ethical ambivalence. In *Nietzsche and Levinas: "After the death of a certain god,"* ed. J. Stauffer and B. G. Bergo, 70–80. New York: Columbia University Press.

Carver, T. 1999. *The Cambridge companion to Marx*. Cambridge: Cambridge University Press.

Chakrabarti, A., A. Dhar, and S. Cullenberg. 2012. *World of the third and global capitalism*. Delhi: Worldview Publications.

Chalier, C. 1991. Ethics and the feminine. In *Re-reading Levinas*, ed. R. Bernasconi and S. Critchley, 119–29. London: Athlone.

Ciaramelli, F. 1991. Levinas's ethical discourse between individuation and universality. In *Re-reading Levinas*, ed. R. Bernasconi and S. Critchley, 83–105. London: Athlone.

Critchley, S. 2002a. Introduction to *The Cambridge companion to Levinas*, ed. S. Critchley and R. Bernasconi, 1–32. Cambridge: Cambridge University Press.

———. 2002b. Persecution before exploitation—a non-Jewish Israel? *Parallax* 8 (3): 71–7.

Critchley, S., and R. Bernasconi, ed. 2002. *The Cambridge companion to Levinas*. Cambridge: Cambridge University Press.

Derrida, J. 2001. *Writing and difference*. London: Routledge.

Dussel, E. 2008. *Twenty theses on politics*. Durham, N.C.: Duke University Press.

———. 2013. *Ethics of liberation in the age of globalization and exclusion*. Durham, N.C.: Duke University Press.

Gibbs, R. 1992. A Jewish context for the social ethics of Marx and Levinas. In *Autonomy and Judaism: The individual and the community in Jewish philosophical thought*, ed. D. H. Frank, 161–92. Albany: State University of New York Press.

———. 1994. *Correlations in Rosenweig and Levinas*. Princeton: Princeton University Press.

Horowitz, A., and G. Horowitz. 2003. An ethical orientation for Marxism: Geras and Levinas. *Rethinking Marxism* 15 (2): 181–95.

Levinas, E. 1969. *Totality and infinity: An essay on exteriority*. Pittsburgh: Duqueyne University Press.

———. 1985. *Ethics and infinity: Conversations with Phillipe Nemo*. Pittsburgh: Duquesne University Press.

———. 1990. *Difficult freedom: Essays on Judaism*. Baltimore: Johns Hopkins University Press.

———. 1994. *Nine Talmudic readings*. Bloomington: Indiana University Press.

———. 1999. *Otherwise than being, or Beyond essence*. Pittsburgh: Duquesne University Press.

———. 2006. *Entre nous: Thinking-of-the-other*. London: Continuum.

Marx, K. 1959. *Economic and philosophic manuscripts of 1844*. Moscow: Progress Publishers. https://www.marxists.org/archive/marx/works/download/pdf/Economic-Philosophic-Manuscripts-1844.pdf.

———. 1977. *Capital*. Vol. 1. New York: Vintage Books.

Paradiso-Michau, M. R. 2008. The widow, the orphan, and the stranger: Levinasian themes in Dussel's political theory. *Radical Philosophy Review* 11 (2): 89–97.

Putnam, H. 2002. Levinas and Judaism. In *The Cambridge companion to Levinas*, ed. S. Critchley and R. Bernasconi, 33–62. Cambridge: Cambridge University Press.

Reiman, J. 1999. Moral philosophy: The critique of capitalism and the problem of ideology. In *The Cambridge companion to Marx*, ed. T. Carver, 143–67. Cambridge: Cambridge University Press.

Resnick, S. A., and R. D. Wolff. 1987. *Knowledge and class: A Marxian critique of political economy*. Chicago: University of Chicago Press.

Stauffer, J., and B. Bergo, eds. 2009. *Nietzsche and Levinas: "After the death of a certain god."* New York: Columbia University Press.

Treanor, B. 2007. *Aspects of alterity: Levinas, Marcel, and the contemporary debate*. New York: Fordham University Press. Adobe e-book.

Liberation Theology and Marxism

Enrique Dussel

Translated by Irene B. Hodgson and José Pedrozo

A description of how liberation theology and Marxism are related should include at least four dimensions. First, the presuppositions of praxis: the political dimension consisting of the relationship of faith to recent Latin American historical reality. Second, the epistemological dimension or the presuppositions of theory: the relationship between faith and the social sciences in Latin America. Third, the criticism, from both within and outside the Church, of the linking of liberation theology and Marxism, especially since the *Instructions* (1984 and 1986) of the Congregation for the Doctrine of the Faith. And fourth, the paths that are presently opening for a fruitful use of Marxism by liberation theology.

Latin American Historical Praxis: Faith and Politics

Theology emerges from Christian praxis and, for that reason, we should first look at historical praxis, at the relationship between Christians and Marxists, in order to determine the possibilities for the theoretical use of Marxism in liberation theology.

Historical Lack of Encounter

The social doctrine of the church has prevented Christians from arriving at any real understanding of Marxism. From the early encyclical *Noscitis et nobiscum* (1849) to *Rerum Novarum* (1891),[1] in which Marxism was condemned because its followers "excite in the poor hatred of the rich, [and] intend to do away with private property and replace it with common ownership,"[2] and even later in *Quadragesimo Anno* (1931), the Vatican's position has remained unchanged: unmitigated condemnation.[3] Similarly, in Latin America anticommunism was the general position of all Christians—remember that Chardin founded the JOC (Young Catholic Workers) to fight Marxism; Father Hurtado in Chile launched social action as an anticommunist crusade; also Bishop Franceschi in Argentina and, in Mexico, even in the turbulent year 1968 Father P. Velázquez, continued along the same line (and these are the most "progressive" figures). Perhaps no one criticized Marxism as passionately as Bishop Mariano Rossell y Arellano (1938–1964) in Guatemala who, with his pastoral messages "On the Communist Menace" (1945) and "On the Excommunication of the Communists" (1949), encouraged the fall of the populist movement of J. Arbenz. Bishop Victor Sanábria (1899–1952) of Costa Rica was a notable exception—creating ties between the church and the Communist party in 1948.

The Marxists themselves (since the founding of the Communist parties in 1920) were not ready for any dialogue either, given their theoretical dogmatism (atheism and philosophical materialism) and their historical errors.[4] Christians who participated militantly in Catholic Action from 1930 onwards or in the Christian Democratic Party (after 1936 in Chile) concentrated much of their "apostolic" work in fighting Communist youth organizations (when these existed).[5] The confrontation lasted a century and was total.

Initial Phase of Encounter, 1959–1968

In January of 1959, Pope John XXIII called for the Second Vatican Council, and in that same month Fidel Castro entered triumphantly into Havana. It was a new era. The worldwide, and especially Latin American, Catholic renewal coincided with the death of Stalin and with the Twentieth Party Congress in Moscow (1956) under

1. Pope Pius IX indicated that there are some who accept "the criminal systems of communism and socialism." On socialism and Marxism in Latin American, see G. D. Cole, *Historia del pensamiento socialista*, vol. 3 (Mexico: Fondo de Cultura Económico, 1959), vol. 4 (1960), and vol. 5 (1961); Robert Alexander, *Communism in Latin America* (Rutgers University Press, 1959); Victor Alba, *Historia del comunismo en América Latina* (Mexico: Ed. Occidentales, 1954); Michael Loewy, *El marxismo en América Latina* (Mexico: Era, 1982); Sheldon B. Liss, *Marxist Thought in Latin America* (University of California Press, 1984); and my article "Encuentro de cristianos y marxistas en América Latina," *Christianismo y Sociedad* 74 (1980): 19–36. See also Héctor J. Samour C., "Valoración del marxismo en la teología de la liberación" (Universidad Nacional Autónoma de México, Ph.D. Thesis in Philosophy, 1988).
2. *Rerum Novarum*, nos. 11–12. Also, see my *Ethics and Community* (Maryknoll: Orbis Books, 1988), chap. 19, "The Gospel and the Social Teaching of the Church."
3. "Communism . . . teaches and desires two things: class struggle incarnated and the complete disappearance of private property," *Quadragesimo Anno*, no. 120. See also *Divini Redemptoris* (1937), nos. 8–14, as well as *Humani Generis* (1950) of Pius XII.
4. See my article previously cited, "Encuentro de cristianos y marxistas en América Latina." The Latin American Communist parties, upon participating in some of the popular movements after 1936 (as directed by Moscow) lost their worker base (for the workers were at times absorbed by the popular movements); in 1941, the Communist parties were given a new order to join with the "Allies" against Nazism. In 1945 they were found allied with Anglo-Saxon imperialism. These were irreparable mistakes.
5. See my *Los últimos 50 años (1930–1985) en la historia de la Iglesia en América Latina* (Bogotá: Indo-America Press, 1986), pp. 13ff.

the leadership of Khrushchev. The crisis of populism (Vargas, Perón, Rojas Pinillas, et al.) also led to that of Catholic Action. The JOC (Young Catholic Workers) and the JUC (Catholic University Students), which were more specialized groups, had ears better tuned to the new developments. The Movement of Popular Education began in northeast Brazil. In 1959 a Christian university group founded Popular Action in Sao Paulo, the first to declare itself to be socialist-inspired.[6] Here we have the beginnings of radical Christian commitment to politics. The question of "faith and politics" became a central concern. It is true that many Christians upon entering the political arena "lost" their faith. The issue is: why did they "lose" their faith? Should there not have been some other expression of faith that could have survived the "test" of politics? The "foquist" experiment—to which many young people committed themselves during the '60s—ended with the total commitment of Camilo Torres and his death in 1966.[7] Another path had to be found.

Even so, dialogue with the Marxists was possible in praxis. The New Left itself had lost much of its dogmatism and opened itself to new positions which allowed it to come to a better understanding of the "popular" problem. Shortly thereafter, Althusserianism would provide new motivation for post-Stalinist Marxism.

The failure of economic "development" (Kubitschek in Brazil, Frondizi in Argentina, Rómulo Betancourt and Caldera in Venezuela, López Mateo in Mexico, and Frei in Chile) similarly provided arguments for new kinds of Christian commitment. It was now the poor, the people, the historically oppressed, who were calling both Christians and Marxists to their service.

Convergence, 1968–1979

Events during 1968 profoundly affected Latin America. From Tlatelolco in Mexico (with the deaths of more than 400 students) to the Argentinian "cordobazo" (with the fall of Onganía), there were student and popular movements in all countries. Also of enormous historical importance was the success of the Conference of Latin American Bishops in Medellín, together with the failure of the Chilean Christian Democrats (1964–1970). For its part the Instituto Social para América Latina (ISAL), which is tied to the World Council of Churches, brought to Latin America the experience of revolutionary Christians of Africa and Asia.

The first significant instance of Christians and Marxists working together took place during the government of Salvador Allende (1970–1973) within the Frente Popular (Popular Front) which included MAPU (a Christian movement that grew out of the Christian Democrats). This movement was the fruit of two processes: the

6. See E. Kadt, *Catholic Radicals in Brazil* (London: Oxford University Press, 1971); S. Silva Gotay, *El pensamiento revolucionario cristiano en América y el Caribe* (Salamanca: Sígueme, 1981).
7. See *Camilo Torres por el Padre Camilo Torres Restrepo (1956–1965)* (Cuernavaca: CIDOC, 1967); *Obras escogidas* (Montevideo: Provincias Unidas, 1968). See also Rodolfo de Roux, *Historia general de la iglesia en América Latina* (Salamanca: Sígueme, VII, 1977), chap. 7; V. Bambierra et al., *Diez años de insurrección en América Latina* (Santiago de Chile, Prensa Latinoamericana, I–II, 1971); R. Goot, *Las guerillas en América Latina* (Santiago: Universitaria, 1971); and INDAL, *Movimientos revolucionarios en América Latina* (Brussels, 1972).

already emerging theology of liberation and the Christians for Socialism movement. The latter was related to the crisis in ILADES (the Latin American Institute of Social Studies), when in 1969 the Bigo-Vekemans group opposed the Marxist-based analysis proposed by the Arroyo-Hinkelammert group.[8] University and labor Catholic action groups (JOC and JUC) followed these events closely and identified themselves with them throughout Latin America—from Mexico and Central America to the Caribbean and South America (even Brazil).

Furthermore, the kind of dialogue that took place between Christians and Marxists in France (which began during the "Weeks of the Intellectuals" in the 1950s), which included the leaders of Catholic Action (such as Fathers Blanquart and Cardonnel), also occurred in Latin America. Such dialogue was popularized in the 1970s by the Althusserian work of Marta Harnecker who, although a so-called structuralist Marxist, was president of the Chilean JUC. Around this time Fidel Castro declared: "I believe that we have arrived at a time in which religion can enter the political arena in response to the people and their material needs."[9]

And in the declaration of Christians for Socialism, we read:

> Christians are clear that their political practice cannot be derived directly from their faith. Revolutionary Christians use the mediations of science and of revolutionary theory in order to open a historical path for action together with the working class and the Latin American people.[10]

In Argentina, because of the return of Peronist populism (1973), the theme of the "people" became central and, although not easily categorized as Marxist, was rapidly assimilated by liberation theology.[11] Luis Corvalán, Secretary of the Chilean Communist party, wrote from exile:

> In these conditions religion loses its character of opiate of the people and, on the contrary, in the measure to which the Church commits itself to humanity, one can say that, instead of alienating, religion is a source of inspiration in the struggle for peace, liberty and justice.[12]

8. Ives Vaillancourt, "La crisis del ILADES," *Víspera* 22 (1971): 18–27; Pablo Richard, *Cristianos para el socialismo* (Salamanca: Sígueme, 1976); *Cristianismo, lucha ideológica y racionalidad socialista* (Salamanca: Sígueme, 1975); Roger Vekemans, *Teología de la liberación y cristianos para el socialismo* (Bogota: CEDIAL, 1976). Richard Shaull brings in elements from the experience of struggles for liberation in Africa and Asia and from the ecumenical movements; he must be considered one of the founders of liberation theology. See his "Consideraciones teológicas sobre la liberación del hombre," IDOC (Bogota) 43 (1968) and "A Theological Perspective" in *Cultural Factors in Inter-American Relations*, ed. Samuel Shapiro (Notre Dame: University of Notre Dame Press, 1968).
9. See my *Religión* (Mexico: Edicol, 1977), pp. 212ff.
10. *Los cristianos y el socialismo. I Encuentro latinoamericano* (Buenos Aires: Siglo XXI, 1973), pp. 18–29. See Raúl Vidales's mimeographed anthology, *Praxis cristiana y militancia revolucionaria* (Mexico: CEE, 1978). For the context of the whole epoch, see my *De Medellín a Puebla* (Mexico: Edicol/CEE, 1979).
11. It is interesting to note that, beginning in approximately 1974, the "classist" position in liberation theology (in Chile, Peru and Brazil) accepted the category "pueblo" in political and sociological analysis. Finally, "pueblo" became a *historical subject*. See Giulio Giraldo, *Sandinismo, Marxismo y Cristianismo en la nueva Nicaragua* (Managua: CEE/CAV, 1986).
12. Raúl Vidales, *Praxis Cristiana*, doc. I, IV.

The year 1973 was somber: Allende fell and generalized repression spread through all of Latin America. Amid the darkness, the "base communities" would illuminate a path for the people, the poor, the oppressed. The dynamic we have been analyzing would grow stronger.

Beyond the Strategic Alliance, 1979–1984

The triumph of the Sandinista revolution provided the first historical test of the feasibility of dialogue between Christians and Marxists. Theory became reality. In their declaration of 7 October 1980, the FSLN (Sandinista Front for National Liberation) clearly moved beyond the worldwide period of misunderstanding between Christians and postcapitalist revolution—and this lesson would be learned not only in Africa and Asia but also in Cuba and the Soviet Union:

> We, the Sandinistas, affirm that *our experience demonstrates* that when Christians, *supported by their faith*, are capable of responding to the necessities of the people and of history, their own beliefs impel them to revolutionary militancy. Our experience shows us that one can be a believer and at the same time a committed revolutionary and that there is no unresolvable contradiction between the two commitments.[13]

The use of social analysis by liberation theology allowed the Nicaraguan episcopate to write:

> If socialism means, as it should mean, preeminence of the interests of the Nicaraguan majority and a nationally planned economic model that is solidly and progressively participative, we have no objection.[14]

During the ensuing years, the deaths of hundreds of Latin American Christian martyrs, especially that of Archbishop Oscar A. Romero on 24 March 1980, sealed these affirmations. However, although great progress was made in opening channels of communication between Christians and revolutionary movements, there were still clear tensions within the respective institutions themselves, that is, a traditionalist church opposed to the new openings, and dogmatic revolutionaries who continued to insist on atheism and materialism.

New Contradictions Guaranteeing Past Achievements, Post-1984

The criticism of liberation theology contained in the 1984 *Instruction*[15] of the Congregation for the Doctrine of the Faith centered its argument on the fundamental Marxist contamination of that theology. This produced a new debate but, at the same time, it basically convinced Marxists and the countries with "real socialism" (that is, avowed Communist countries) that liberation theology was not merely a fad

---

13. *Communicado oficial de la Dirección Nacional del FSLN sobre la religión* (1980), sec. 2.
14. *Compromiso cristiano para una Nicaragua nueva* (17 November 1979), p. 9.
15. An *Instruction* is a document unveiled by the Congregation of the Doctrine of Faith in the Vatican (the old Inquisition), with less importance than an Encyclical or a Bull.

but rather a deeply rooted current within the church that could provide people with convictions that enabled them to defend themselves publicly, even before the highest tribunal of the church. The persecutions that liberation theology suffered after 1972, especially of figures within the Latin American Bishops Conference, were now coming from Rome. In response to criticism, liberation theology reaffirmed its basic principles: that the preferential option for the poor and the oppressed demands of theological discourse instruments of analysis that permit it to carry out an authentic, pertinent, adequate reflection. The use of the social sciences (and of Marxism, if necessary) is analogous to the need for a scientific instrument that has been felt by all schools of theology since the second century of the Christian era when the School of Alexandria used Platonism, which was also considered satanic by many Christians of the time.

We shall see that the use of Marxist analysis by liberation theology, in a manner fully consistent with the tradition and the doctrine of the Church, was to continue and intensify.

The Epistemological Dimension: Faith and the Social Sciences

We want to establish that theology is a reflection that grows out of praxis and needs some form of theoretical analysis to carry out its own discourse. We will then have to take up three other issues: Why use Marxist analysis? Which Marxism are we talking about? How do liberation theologians make use of Marxism?[16] This last question merits particular consideration.

Theology and Scientific Discourse

Since the question of methodology has been amply treated in recent theological discussions, all we need to do here is review certain key ideas and situate them in the framework of our analysis.

All theology, in any given historical moment, uses some specific scientific discourse to construct its reflection.

Faith is the fundamental moment of theological discourse. But faith is an aspect of *praxis*, of *Christian* praxis. Christian action (praxis) includes the "light" that illuminates all action considered "Christian." That is, existential faith, ordinary or prophetic, illuminates the daily praxis of Christian living, following Jesus of Nazareth. In the same way, praxis (which includes faith as its Christian base) is the constituent antecedent of theology. Theology is nothing but a theoretical discourse (for Thomas Aquinas, it is spiritual, sapiential, and methodical but, at the same time, practical) that starts from Christian praxis and uses the light of faith to reflect on, think about, and describe rationally the reality of the problems that such a praxis daily faces.

---

16. Kenneth Aman criticizes liberation theology for "using" Marxism as an "instrument" (like the medieval *ancilla theologiae*); see his *"Using* Marxism: A Philosophical Critique of Liberation Theology," *International Philosophical Quarterly* 4 (1985): 393–401.

Whether as an ordinary or a prophetic reflection, theology characteristically seeks to provide a "methodical" reflection for the Christian life of any period both in that life's daily routine and in its extraordinary and innovative moments; and it seeks to elaborate this reflection according to the time's most developed rules or demands for rationality. In Babylonia during the sixth century B.C., the "Adamic myth" was a theological construct corresponding to the best of the symbolic rationalism of its time (for example, as compared to the myth of Gilgamesh). Jesus used the theological instruments of his time—those of the rabbinic and Pharisaic schools, and so on. Since the second century A.D., with the appearance of the Greek Christian theological schools (first among the Apostolic Fathers and later the Apologists or the Alexandrines), Christian belivers constructed a theological discourse with the "science" *(episteme)* of their time: Platonic philosophy (and theology).[17] Platonic "categories" allowed the construction of a Christian theology using instruments that in the first century had been considered part of "pagan" culture and, as such, intrinsically perverted. In the twelfth century, Albert Magnus and Thomas Aquinas made use of Aristotle at a time when his philosophy was explicitly condemned. This resulted in a theological discourse that has dominated Catholic theology to our days.

In the nineteenth century, the German theologian Moehler used philosophical instruments of his time to profoundly renovate German Catholic theology which greatly lagged behind Protestant theology which was already using the best philosophical insights from the Enlightenment and Hegel. It would not be until the twentieth century that Rahner could make use of a Heideggerian existentialism and Metz could draw on the Frankfurt "critical school" to bring theology up to the level of the best contemporary philosophical thought.

So it is clear that theology has always needed a method of analysis (traditionally, almost always a philosophical one) in order to fashion praxis and faith into a methodical, rational, scientific discourse.

Why Use Marxist Analysis?

Liberation theology grows out of the experience of Christian praxis, out of faith. Juan Luis Segundo tells us that it was in 1953, with the help of Melevez in Louvain, that he came to this fundamental insight. In my case, it was during the years 1959–1961 that Paul Gauthier in Nazareth made me see the necessity of evangelizing the poor, since the Christian rule for life was based on Isaiah 61:1 (*Luke* 14:18): "The Spirit of the Lord God is upon me, because the Lord has annointed me to bring good tidings to the afflicted."[18] In 1959 Comblin wrote his *Fracaso de la Acción Católica*, which opened a new current of theological thought in Latin America.

---

17. See my *El dualismo en la antropología de la cristiandad* (Buenos Aires: Guadalupe, 1974).
18. J. L. Segundo, *Theology and the Church: A Response to Cardinal Ratzinger and a Warning to the Whole Church* (New York: Seabury, 1985); Paul Gauthier, *Jésus l'église et les pauvres* (Tournai: Ed. Universitaire, 1962).

Gutiérrez remembers that already in 1964 he had his first intuitions into experience as spirituality and theology as wisdom.[19]

Historically speaking, before the formation of liberation theology as theology, it existed in the praxis and faith of the church, that is, in Christian communities, and in those who would later shape it as a theology. In order to serve militant Christians, this Latin American theology from its beginnings had to explain the theological justification for the "political commitment" of these Christians. But why should Christians commit themselves politically in the first place? The answer is evident: in order to effect social, economic, and political changes that would allow the exploited classes (on a first level), the poor (on a theological level), and the Latin American people (ultimately) to achieve a just, humane, fulfilled life.[20] It was this double necessity of thinking theologically about the "political commitment" to serve the oppressed, the poor, the people, that required the nascent theology to use analytical and interpretative instruments other than those known by previous theological traditions. Faced with the absence of an adequate established philosophy, the new theologians had to turn to *critical Latin American* social sciences. These were not just sciences that were "social" (such as sociology, economics, etc.), but also "critical"—because they tried to reveal and contextualize the reality of injustice—and "Latin American"—because our continent had so many of its own issues to resolve. The turn to these sciences was not, then, an a priori, dogmatic, or epistemological decision. Rather, on the basis of Christian praxis and faith, with essentially spiritual and pastoral criteria stemming from Christians' commitment to fight politically against injustice, according to the social doctrine of the church, new categories for adequate analysis had to be found.

And so the nascent Latin American theology developed its use of Marxist categorical tools of analysis, proceeding historically from the French Marxist tradition, which used them with groups of students and workers. Juan Luis Segundo, José Comblin, Gustavo Gutiérrez, and I were part of the generation that studied in France (or Belgium). These tools—we will soon see which ones and how they were used—permitted the new theology, which after 1968 began to be called Liberation (in Rubem Alves's Princeton thesis),[21] to achieve unexpected results in the analysis of historical, social, and political realities (as well as in other areas such as sexism and racism for, once discovered, the methodology was applicable to other areas of thought). All this produced, if you will, an "epistemological revolution" in the history of Christian theology. For the first time, the critical social sciences were used. Political economy and sociology, which had begun in the mid-nineteenth century, were now being used by Christian theology. As "modernism" gave rise to a crisis because of the use of history in theology (from Renán to Blondel), in the same way liberation theology created a crisis when it adopted the social sciences, of

19. See Roberto Oliveros, *Liberación y teología* (Mexico: CRT, 1977).
20. For the semantic evolution from "pobre" to "pueblo," see my "El paradigma del éxodo en la teología de la liberación," *Concilium* 209 (1987): 99–114.
21. *Theology of Human Hope* (Washington: Corpus Books, 1969).

which Marxism forms the critical nucleus. When we look at this crisis from the perspective of the twenty-first century, we will realize how important its missionary function was in the contemporary world—at the end of the twentieth century—that is, in the world of the poor of Latin America, Africa, and Asia, and especially in the real socialist nations for whom liberation theology was the only intelligible and prophetic theology possible.

Which Marxism Does Liberation Theology Use?

As is commonly known, liberation theologians use a "certain kind" of Marxism—and implicitly or explicitly exclude another kind. We will come back to this point later when we explain the reasons for the *Instruction* against liberation theology of the Congregation for the Doctrine of the Faith in 1984.

First of all, in assessing the variety of Marxisms, liberation theologians universally reject "dialectical materialism." No liberation theologian accepts the materialism of Engels (in *The Dialectics of Nature*) or of Lenin, Bukharin, or Stalin as philosophically coherent.[22] Marx is accepted and used as a social critic. The contact with Marx occurred in two ways: first, through secondary sources (as seen in the works of Yves Calves in France and Bernhard Welte in Germany); or second, especially at the beginning of liberation theology, through reading the "young" Marx directly, that is, up to the 1848 *Manifesto*. The influence of French thinkers was dominant in the first generation of liberation theologians (Segundo, Comblin, Gutiérrez, Dussel, at the beginning of the 1960s); after J. Maritain, there was E. Mounier and then Lebret. Teilhard de Chardin also provided inspiration for this period. The Cuban Revolution (1959) drew attention to Marx; people began to read the young Marx together with "Che" Guevara, Gramsci, and Lukács. Later we shall see how each of these writers influenced theologians' use of a "humanist" Marx (in the terminology of the time)—a Marx who is not dogmatic nor "economistic" nor naively materialistic. The French priests Cardonnel and Blanquart were also influential in the "reception" of Marxism by the future liberation theology. There was no systematic direct contact with the "definitive" Marx (after 1857), nor is there much use of this Marx today.

While such thinkers as Korsch, Goldmann, and even Trotsky have not directly affected liberation theology (although Trotsky has had an indirect effect), other schools of thought have been influential since 1968. Besides Antonio Gramsci, whose influence was present from the beginning and grew even stronger, the first significant Marxist impact was that of the Frankfurt School through the works of the "North American" Marcuse—who clearly influenced Rubem Alves's work in 1968 and had a more diffuse effect on other liberation thinkers (including J. B. Metz in Germany). Ernst Bloch also had a widespread impact—especially in Moltmann's studies on utopian vision and hope. Even more significantly, the work of Althusser,

---

22. See my *La producción teórica de Marx: Un comentario a los Grundrisse* (Mexico: Siglo XXI, 1985), pp. 36–37.

translated for the classroom by Martha Harnecker,[23] would exercise a strong influence not only on liberation theology (especially on the second generation of theologians)[24] but also on the entirety of Latin American Marxist thought.

Along with the French thinkers already mentioned, Italian liberation theologian Giulio Girardi has also had a significant influence, mainly in the way his clearly Marxist position evolved from a decidedly "classist" posture at the beginning to a later view that incorporated the "people" as the historical subject of liberation praxis.

Of the Latin American Marxists, not only "Che" Guevara, but also Mariátegui and Sánchez Vásquez have influenced the thought of some liberation theologians. Of course, the ideas of Fidel Castro since 1959 are required reading, especially his views on religion (similar to those of Rosa Luxemburg, who influenced the Popular Action movement in Brazil).

But the kind of Marxism that has most affected liberation theology has not been the "theoretical" kind we have been considering but rather the Latin American sociological and economic Marxism of "dependency theory," as elaborated by such thinkers as Orlando Fals Borda, Theotonio dos Santos, Faletto, Cardoso (many of whom, in reality, were not and are not Marxists). It is this sociology of "dependence," in its strong criticism of functionalism and developmentalism, that brought about the epistemological rupture of liberation theology from the dominant theology. Therefore, the position of Gunder Frank—despite all the criticism it has received—must be viewed as a determinant factor in liberation theology before 1972. Likewise, the views of Hinkelammert—as a Marxist and a theologian—are perhaps the only representative of the "definitive" Marx. At the end of the 1960s in Santiago a certain group at the Center for Studies of the National Reality did a serious study of *Das Kapital* which made possible a unique opening to Marxism within one of the most creative currents of liberation theology during the 1980s.

To date, there has been no adequate study of this entire complex history; nor is there a history of contemporary Latin American Marxism, much less of its presence in Christian movements.[25] Our brief historical review shows, however, how simplistic it is for conservatives to accuse liberation theology of being ideologically "Marxist." Long before its critics mounted their charges, liberation theology accepted, with complete Christian responsibility, the difficult task of incorporating a "kind" of Marxism that was compatible with the Christian faith of the prophets and Jesus and with ancient and recent ecclesiastical (which means ecumenical) traditions. Stalinist dogmatism, textbook economics, and "philosophical" Marxism are not at all part of liberation theology's use of Marxism.

---

23. *Conceptos elementales del materialismo dialéctico* (Mexico: Siglo XXI, 1974).
24. See Clodovis Boff, *Theology and Praxis: Epistemological Foundations* (Maryknoll: Orbis Books, 1987), originally published in 1978.
25. See the works of S. Silva Gotay and R. Oliveros cited in notes 6 and 19.

How Do the Liberation Theologians Incorporate Marxism?

An adequate answer to the above question would require a lengthy treatise. In these few pages, we offer only a preliminary sketch of how some theologians make use of Marxism; our intent is to provide a few examples rather than an exhaustive discussion.

The elaboration of the theory of development was pre-Marxist; so were the early works of Segundo and Comblin.[26] The theology of revolution, however, did use Marxist tools for its analysis, but not in the same way as liberation theology did.[27] I believe that the historical difference between these theologies is to be found in dependency theory, in the way that it "Latin Americanized" Marxism and gave it a sociohistorical dimension. Hugo Assmann was the first to explain adequately the "demarcation line" between such theologies as those of development, of revolution, of hope (Moltmann), and of politics (Metz).[28] We must not forget a book that made history—*Marx and the Bible* by Porfirio Miranda—which presented the encounter of Marxism and Christianity in a direct and biblical manner.[29] But, paradoxically, it is a Christian examination of Marx and not a Marxist interpretation of the encounter.

Rubem Alves, in his Princeton thesis of 1968 ("Toward a Theology of Liberation"), analyzes the North American situation at that time from the perspective of Marcuse using, but at the same time transcending, the Protestant tradition of theology of revolution.[30] For Alves, the "political humanism" of a Marcuse surpasses mechanistic technologism and shows the importance of the political; on the other hand, "humanistic Messianism" (philosophical Marxism) does not grasp the element of transcendence present in all liberation movements, as does Christian "messianic humanism."[31] Alves's quotes from the young Marx, from Marcuse, from Alvaro Viera Pinto *(Conciência e Realidade Nacional)*, from Bloch, and from Paolo Freire reveal the kind of Marxism he is using.[32] It does not yet involve social analysis.

26. F. Houtart-O. Vertrano, *Hacia una teología del desarrollo* (Buenos Aires, 1967); Vincent Cosmo, *Signification et théologie du développement* (Paris, 1967); J. L. Segundo, *Función de la iglesia en la realidad rioplatense* (Montevideo, 1962), *¿La cristianidad, una utopía?* (Montevideo, 1964), and *Teología abierta para el laico adulto* (Buenos Aires, 1968); and José Comblin, *Théologie de la paix* (Paris, 1960–1963) and *Théologie de la revolution* (Paris, 1970–1974).
27. See, for example, Helmut Gullwitzer, *Die reichen Christen und der arme Lazarus* (Munich: Kaiser, 1968); Ernst Bloch, *Thomas Münzer* (1969); Carlos Pinto de Oliveira, *Evangelho e revolucão social*, (São Paulo: Duas Cidades, 1962); and Jean Cardonnel, *L'évangile et la révolution* (Paris, 1968). See also R. Vekemans, *Teología de la liberación y cristianos para el socialismo*, pp. 100–112.
28. *Teolgía desde la praxis de la liberación* (Salamanca: Sígueme, 1973), chap. 2.
29. See the first edition in 1969 (Mexico), 1972 (Salamanca, Spain: Sígueme), and 1974 (Maryknoll: Orbis Books).
30. See note 21.
31. Rubem Alves partially hides the meaning of these categories: "political humanism," "humanistic messianism," "humanist messianism," etc.
32. ISEB (Río de Janeiro, 1962).

Hugo Assmann says:

The language of "liberation" is language that articulates socio-political, revolutionary consequences to be drawn from the analytical language of "dependence." It is directly linked with an analytical focus on the phenomenon of underdevelopment.[33]

This is a criticism of the "developmentalist" language used by certain Latin American social scientists—not necessarily Marxists—intent on explaining the poverty and oppression of the Latin American peoples. Although Assmann accepts the paradigm of super- and infrastructure, he is making a new use of Marxist categories by adopting the antieconomistic theory of ideology proposed by Gramsci and Lukács. From his broad background in Marxist thought, as well as in the German tradition, Assmann analyzes the "truth" of a statement on the basis of the praxis that grounds it. Nevertheless, again critical of traditional Marxism, he shows the revolutionary importance of the ideological struggle in which theology also takes part. For this reason, as we have said, he is the first to carry out the task of "marking" or distinguishing clearly between liberation theology and postconciliar European theologies (such as the theology of hope, political theology, and the theology of Third World revolutions). His analysis of the symbolic structure as superstructure is very clear.[34] He also criticizes Stalinist dogmatism and even Althusserian thought for not adequately treating the question of fetishism and the relationship between theory and praxis.

Juan Luis Segundo, formed by the rather functionalist sociology of the 1950s, also uses Marxist categories for analysis—in particular, the concept of ideology.[35] He used the social sciences in his early work *(Función de la iglesia en la realidad rioplatense)* and he is a master of the practice of "criticism." He lays bare the hidden and falsified parts of the European and North American—and even Roman— theologies (for instance, in his critical work *Theology and the Church: A Response to Cardinal Ratzinger and a Warning to the Whole Church).*[36]

Gustavo Gutiérrez, who in 1964 had already begun his pioneering work, quotes Gramsci in the first note of his *A Theology of Liberation* (the first parts of which appeared in 1968 as a criticism of developmentalism). He thus makes clear which kind of Marxism interests him: not a dialectically materialist Marxism but one that is economically critical, decidedly political, and culturally analytical.[37] From this comes the fundamental idea that theology (like philosophy in a Gramscian sense) is

---

33. ISEB, p. 122.
34. See H. Assmann, "Teología de la liberación: Una evaluación prospectiva" (1971); also note 28. The following article by Assmann is a classic: "El cristianismo, su plusvalía simbólica y el costo social de la revolución socialista" (in op. cit., 171–202), in which the "symbolic" blindness of the Left is criticized.
35. Leading to an extensive analysis in a complete volume at the beginning of his Christology, *Faith and Ideologies* (Maryknoll: Orbis Books, 1984). On our point, he wrote: "Evangelio, política y socialismo" in *Actualidad Pastoral* (1972), pp. 303–6, 327–31, 356–57; "La iglesia chilena ante el socialismo (Talca, Chile: Fundación Larráin, 1971), p. 25, mimeo.
36. See note 18.
37. (Maryknoll: Orbis Books, 1973), p. 15.

a "critical reflection" on Christian praxis.[38] Like all liberation theologians in the
'60s, Gutiérrez starts with the criticism of the "notion of development" and presents
liberation as its antithesis.[39] He quotes authors such as Althusser, Kosik, Lukács,
Mariátegui, Sánchez Vásquez, and, of course, Marx himself.[40] All of this shows
how liberation theology uses a Marxism that is critical, Latin American, and
antieconomistic to aid in political analysis. Gutiérrez also includes this quote from
"Che" Guevara:

> Let me say, at the risk of seeming ridiculous, that the true revolutionary is guided by
> strong feelings of love . . . They (revolutionaries) must struggle every day so that their
> love of living humanity is transformed into concrete deeds.[41]

Among the pertinent social sciences Marxism is used, also indirectly, by Gutiérrez as an instrument to discover and describe the reality of the poverty of the Latin
American people and the concrete projects of liberation. Gutiérrez's work "Marxismo y Cristianismo," never published as a book, shows his thoughtful and profoundly theological use of Marxist categories (such as class struggle, revolution,
and utopia).

José Míguez Bonino's study *Christianity and Marxism*, subtitled "The Mutual Challenge of Revolution," is perhaps the only work dedicated explicitly to
discussing the links between Marxism and Christianity among liberation
theologians (although Miranda also took up this theme in *Marx and the Bible*).[42]
The Argentine theologian's knowledge of Marx was not new, for it could already be seen in his prologue to the work of Rubem Alves when he wrote in
1969:

> Doesn't the renaissance of humanist Marxism grow out of the situation of the de-
> veloped countries . . . ? Isn't our situation very different, in that the humanization we
> need requires a more elemental and "materialist" basis that effectively incorporates
> political, scientific, and technological analysis, without which liberation becomes a
> mere dialectical game?[43]

Here Bonino indicates the "sacramental" framing of the discussion that occurred
during that period. We shall return to this point below.

As a theologian of the Christians for Socialism movement in 1972, Pablo

---

38. Ibid., p. 6
39. Ibid., pp. 21ff.
40. Althusser, ibid., pp. 39, 97, 249, 277; Kosik, pp. 38, 40; Lukács, p. 40; Mariátegui, pp. 18, 97, 98;
Sánchez Vargas, p. 18. He also uses Marcuse (pp. 31–32, 233) and Ernst Bloch (pp. 216–17, 220, 224,
243).
41. Ibid., p. 98. He quotes Castro on pp. 98, 120, 123.
42. Published only in English (Grand Rapids: Eerdmans, 1976).
43. In the prologue to R. Alves, *Religión: ¿opio o instrumento de liberación?* (Montevideo: Tierra
Nueva, 1972), pp. x–xi.

Richard, together with its founder Gónzalo Arroyo, made use of Marxist categories.[44] For Richard, Gramsci is required reading, especially his thesis on "Muerte de la cristiandad y nacimiento de la Iglesia," which Richard used systematically to construct the theoretical framework of his analysis.[45]

For Leonardo Boff, the rejection of capitalism "is oriented toward a liberation within a different society."[46] Theology is constructed from two sources: faith (biblical, according to the magisterium and tradition) and social reality.[47] In order for the theologian to understand that reality, "it is necessary to turn to the human social sciences, such as anthropology, sociology, psychology, political science, economics and social philosophy."[48] Marxism takes its place on this list, but Boff makes it clear that Latin American theology "does not make servile use of the analytic instrument developed by the Marxist tradition (that is, Marx and the different elaborations of socialism, of Gramsci, of French academic Marxism, and others); liberation theology separates the analytic instrument from its philosophical presuppositions (that is, dialectic materialism) and considers Marxism as a science, not as a philosophy."[49]

Clodovis Boff's *Teología do político e suas mediacões* (Theology and Praxis: Epistemological Foundations) is perhaps the most systematic theological attempt to incorporate the theoretical structure of Althusser.[50] It is a rigorous theoretical study and use of the French Marxism of the 1970s. It shows how a Marxist categorical framework can be used in a strictly Christian theology of the political. An analogous study in the 1980s is needed, this time using Marx himself as referent. We will return to this topic later.

Jon Sobrino states that many of the European theologies respond to the objections of the "first Enlightenment," that of Kant, which questions the relationship between faith and reason, while the "second Enlightenment," that of Marx, questions the relationship between faith and historical change. What role does religion play in historical transformations? Faith is used as justification both for domination and liberation.[51] This is where liberation theology makes use of Marxism: theology must not only interpret reality but also justify its transformation—even a revolutionary one.

Otto Maduro has done some innovative studies on the question of religion in the young Marx and in the young Catholic Engels.[52] Juan Carlos Scannone, as well as

---

44. "Racionalidad socialista y verificación histórica del cristianismo," *Cuaderno de la Realidad Nacional* 12 (1972): 144–53. See *Origen y desarrollo del movimiento Cristiano por el Socialismo: Chile, 1970–1973* (Paris: Centre Lebret, 1975).
45. (São Paulo: E. Paulinus, 1984).
46. *La fe en la periferia* (Santander: Sal Terrae, 1981), p. 125.
47. Ibid., p. 127.
48. Ibid., p. 12.
49. Ibid., pp. 75–76.
50. See note 24.
51. *Liberación y cautiverio* (Mexico, 1970), pp. 177–207.
52. See especially *Religión y conflicto social* (Mexico: CRT, 1980).

Lucio Gera, formed part of the school of liberation theology that opposes Marx- ism—because of conditions specific to their national reality.[53]

We must not forget how Marxism has been used in the deeper currents of spirituality and mysticism, for example, by Arthur Paoli, who studied Hegel and Marx in Italy, together with the future Paul VI then serving as advisor to the Italian Catholic Action. There is also Ernesto Cardenal's *Santidad en la revolución*, which marked a historical clearing of the path to revolutionary processes, which in the case of the guerrillas of Teoponte reached a truly mystical level—disregarding its political or nonpolitical implications (Néstor Paz Zamora).[54]

We could name many others, such as Raúl Vidales, Luis del Valle, Jorge Pixtley, Elsa Tamez, Beatriz Melano Caouch, Julio Santana, Luis Alberto Gómes de Sousa, Gilberto Giménez, and Alex Morelli.[55] We will leave for later my own position and that of Hinkelammert.

In summary, we have seen that liberation theology uses a *certain part* of Marxism in a *certain way*, never incompatible with the foundations of faith. Some liberation theologians have a more clearly "classist" position; others are more "populist." Some use only the instrument of ideological criticism; others social and even economic criticism. Some also oppose global Marxism—although it is diffi- cult to define them as members of a theological movement. Some are inspired by a more French current of Marxism; others by the Italian or German currents. Most move in different currents simultaneously. All of these theologians, however, use the thesis of dependency advanced by the Latin American current—defined with great care, conscious of the criticism it has received. Taking into account all of the indicated limitations, we can conclude that liberation theology is the first theologi- cal movement in the history of Christian thought worldwide to use Marxism (and in doing so it is ahead of other world religions).

53. Scannone, *Teología de la liberación y praxis popular* (Salamanca: Sígueme, 1976); Gera, "Aspectos eclesiológicos de la teología de la liberación," in CELAM, *Liberación: diálogos en el CELAM*, pp. 381–391 and *La iglesia debe comprometerse en lo político* (Montevideo, 1970).
54. Arturo Paoli, *Diálogo de la liberación* (Buenos Aires: Lohlé, 1970), *Meditazione sul Vangelo di Luca* (Morcelliana: Brescia, 1972); Ernesto Cardenal, *Santidad en la revolución* (Buenos Aires: Lohlé, 1971); and Paz Zamora, ed. by Hugo Assmann, *Teoponte, una experiencia guerrillera* (Oruro, Bolivia: CEPI, 1971).
55. Vidales, *La iglesia latinoamericana y la política después de Medellín* (Bogotá: Indo-America Press, 1972) and *Práctica religiosa y proyecto histórico* (Lima: CEP, 1975). Luis Del Valle has numerous publications in the journal *Christus* (Mexico) since 1968 and is organizer of the Centro de Reflexión Teológica (Mexico). Jorge Pixtley's *On Exodus* (Maryknoll: Orbis, 1987) and his work on *God's Kingdom: A Guide for Biblical Study* (Maryknoll: Orbis, 1984) open new paths in the exegesis of liberation. Elsa Tamez is a pioneer of exegesis and Latin American feminist theology. Milano Caouch is an Argentine feminist and theologian. Santana, "ISAL: un movimiento anti-imperialista y anti- oligárquico," in *NADOC*, 95 (1969); "Teoría revolucionaria: Reflexión sobre la fe como praxis de liberación," in *Pueblo oprimido, Señor de la historia*, pp. 225–242; and many other works. Luis Alberto Gómes de Sousa, "El futuro de las ideologías y las ideologías del futuro," *Víspera* 12 (1969): 23–31 and "Condicionamiento socio-político de la teología," in *Christus* 479 (1975): 14–18. Gilberto Giménez, "El golpe militar y la condenación de CPS en Chile," *Contacto* 1–2 (1975): 12–116 and *Cultura popular y religión de Anahuac* (Mexico: CEE, 1978). Alex Morelli, *Libera a mi pueblo* (Buenos Aires: Lohlé, 1971) and "Fundamentación teológica de la acción por la justicia," *Vida espiritual* 47–49 (1975): 36–63.

The Accusation of Marxism

The Christian option for the poor and the oppressed, together with the use of social sciences as an epistemological tool, was interpreted by many—both inside and outside the Church—as a Marxist "manipulation" of or "infiltration" into theology. This accusation, unjust in what it intends, is not new; it is almost as old as liberation theology itself.

The 1984 Instruction

One of the earliest accusations of the Marxist nature of liberation theology was made by Jaime Serna in October 1972 on Bogotá television and in the newspapers.[56] *El Tiempo* of 5 November declared: "CELAM accused of Marxism." In the same year, the Conference of Latin American Bishops changed orientation. In the first issue of the magazine *Tierra Nueva*, the first article by Bishop López Trujillo was titled "La liberación y las liberaciones." The Vatican *Instruction* also included the issue of "liberation theologies," even though in reality there has never been more than one liberation theology[57] (although there are undeniable differences from country to country). The Rockefeller Report in 1969 discussed Marxist infiltration in the church. And the Santa Fe Document of 1980, which read like an early political platform for Ronald Reagan, referred explicitly to the dangers of liberation theology.[58]

In 1975, R. Vekemans published his attack on liberation theology, *Teología de la Liberación y Cristianos para el socialismo;* in 1978, Bonaventura Kloppenburg also tried to link liberation theology and Christians for Socialism. Javier Lozano in *La Iglesia del pueblo* mounted an even more partisan criticism.[59] For Vekemans, the Christians for Socialism movement inspires liberation theology and results in a Marxist option for armed, violent struggle. According to Kloppenburg, for Marxists both movements eventually combined to form a "popular church," a new sect. According to Lozano, although the starting point for the new movement is to be found in the "popular church" inspired by liberation theology, the origins of liberation theology are located in a Leninist-Stalinist Marxism.

Part seven of the 1984 *Instruction* begins a discussion of "Marxist analysis." (We are omitting any comment on the theology that underlies the *Instruction*.)[60] The central idea with respect to our theme is formulated in the following way:

> The thought of Marx is such a global vision of reality that all data received from observation and analysis are brought together in a philosophical and ideological

56. *De Medellín a Puebla*, pp. 282ff.
57. *Instruction*, 1984, IV, 3.
58. *Department of State Bulletin*, (Washington D. C., 8 December 1969), pp. 504ff. See Ana María Ezcurra, *El Vaticano y la administración Reagan* (Mexico: Nuevomar, 1984).
59. Vekemans, see note 8; Kloppenburg, "Informe sobre la iglesia popular" (Mexico: CEM, 1978); and Lozano, Centro de Estudios y Promoción Social (Mexico, 1983).
60. See J. L. Segundo, *Theology and the Church* (see note 17), which shows the contradictions between the theology of the *Instruction* and that of the Second Vatican Council.

structure, which predetermines the significance and importance to be attached to them
. . . Thus no separation of the parts of this epistemologically unique complex is
possible. If one tries to take only one part, say, the analysis, one ends up having to
accept the entire ideology.[61]

The "thought of Marx" itself (leaving aside the interpretations of Engels, Lenin,
and Stalin) is philosophical-economic and, in his mature and definitive works,
"scientific,"[62] from the perspective of the later tradition. We can find nothing of
what the *Instruction* claims, when, for example, it states that "atheism and the
denial of the human person, of his/her liberty and rights, are at the core of Marxist
theory."[63]

In a careful line-by-line reading of the volumes that compose section 2 of Marx's
Collected Works, I have found nothing to substantiate such a description of his
views.[64] On the contrary, Marx opposed the militant atheism in the International—
Bakunin attacked Marx for directing the International that "negated atheism."[65]
Marx wrote to Friedrich Bolte, on 23 November 1871, stating that in 1868 he
could not accept Bakunin's proposal to "dictate atheism as a dogma for the
members," because "the International does not recognize theological sections
(theologische Sektionen)."[66] On 4 August 1878 he wrote to George Howell
indicating that a "Section on Socialist Atheists" that Bakunin tried to force
through was never accepted—and neither was that of the YMCA, because the
International did not recognize "theological sections."[67] Marx was specifically
opposed to militant atheism. The *Instruction* clearly ignores these facts, and ignores the differences among Marx, Engels, Lenin, Stalin, Gramsci, Lukács, and
Bloch.

With regard to the human person, we can state that for Marx it is the "person"
(*Person* in German) who is the starting point and constant referent for the establishment of his categories and his criticism. The "living work" *(lebendige Arbeit)* is the
person who, when "subsumed under" or "alienated" by capital (by "sin" for the

61. *Instruction* VII, 6. I leave aside the *Instruction*'s ambiguities in formulation (because if it is a
"hybrid amalgam" several conclusions can be drawn and not just one) and its contradictions (because in
VII, 8, it says: "Marxist thought has diversified to create different currents that *diverge notably,* some
from the others").
62. "Science" for Marx has a precise meaning; see my *Hacia un Marx desconocido: Un comentario a los
manuscritos del 61–63* (Mexico: Siglo XXI, 1988), chap. 14.
63. *Instruction* VII, 9.
64. Proposed complete edition of the works of Marx, in more than 100 volumes, still incomplete. Section II will contain all the materials on *Das Kapital* and will comprise 17 volumes. Marx
wrote *Das Kapital* in four drafts. We are finishing a commentary—in the style of Saint Thomas—
on these "four drafts" (from 1857 to 1880) in three volumes, two of which we have quoted in notes
22 and 62.
65. Letter from Marx to Liebknecht on 15 November 1872 (*MEW*, vol. 33, p. 402).
66. *MEW*, vol. 32, p. 328.
67. *MEW*, vol. 19, p. 144.

Christian), becomes a "thing," an "instrument," merely a "commodity"[68]—as John Paul II also teaches in *Laborem Exercens*.[69]

This means that, if we demonstrate that there are different traditions in Marxism, and even profound contradictions, the entire argument of the *Instruction* is wiped out at the roots.[70] Liberation theologians have been able to take from Marxism those elements that are not incompatible with their faith (as we have shown above). For this reason, the *Instruction*'s conclusion is false:

> This all-embracing conception thus imposes its logic and leads the "theologies of liberation" to accept a series of positions that are incompatible with the Christian vision of humanity.[71]

The Second Instruction of 1986

The 1984 *Instruction* evidently condemned liberation theology but was unable to demonstrate its unorthodoxy. However, the *Instruction* did achieve a practical intraecclesial effect: it provided justification for all those who wanted to exclude liberation theology from the training centers (whether for seminarians, nuns, or lay people), universities, journals, and so on. The practical effect was to prevent liberation theology from becoming the dominant theology of the Latin American church, as well as of the churches in Africa, Asia, and the socialist countries—let alone Europe and the United States. Consequently, the effect of the *Instruction* was "political."

As the title indicates, the *Instruction on Christian Liberty and Liberation*, dated 22 March 1986, deals principally with the problem of liberty, in particular, religious liberty. Its significance for the socialist countries (especially for Poland) was direct, while its bearing on the real issue of liberation in Latin America was rather tenuous. The 1986 *Instruction* opens with biblical passages such as "the truth will make us free" and not with "I am the bread of life" or "blessed are the poor." Liberation theology has as its starting point real, physical misery: that of hunger. The *Instruction*, on the other hand, concerns itself with truths, doctrines, with the struggle for liberty—assuming that the basic needs for food, drink, sleep, clothing, and health have already been met (the "criteria" for the Final Judgment of Matt. 25). With such an attitude, the *Instruction* can announce:

68. "Labour as *absolute poverty* . . . not separated from the *person [Person]*" (*Grundrisse*, CP 28, p. 222; German edition, Berlin: Dietz, 1974, p. 203). See my *La producción teórica de Marx*, chap. 7, pp. 139ff. "As such, according to his concept, *the poor man [pauper]* as person, is the bearer of the capacity for labour" (*Manuscritos del 61–63*, MEGA II, 3, pp. 34–35). See my *Hacia un Marx desconocido*, chap. 3.2.b. "By capacity for labour . . . we understand *corporality*, the living *personality* of a human being" *El Capital*, I, 4.3 (Mexico: Siglo XXI, 1980) and I, 1, p. 203, MEGA II, 5 (1983), 120. It would be easy to prove the "misinformation" and even superficiality of the *Instruction* on these issues.
69. Nos. 13–15. See my *Ethics and Community* (note 2), chap. 11–12 and 19.
70. See my *La producción teórica de Marx*, pp. 34, 36–37, 177–79. Here are examples of two serious questions for theology: the negation of militant atheism by Marx and the solid affirmation of militant atheism by Stalin; and the lack of dialectical materialism in the early Marx and his clear affirmation of it later.
71. *Instruction*, VIII, 1.

In its different forms . . . human misery is a manifest sign of the *congenital* weakness found in humanity after the fall.[72]

The response to this misery is "charitable works" or alms."[73]

Still, one can say that the *Instruction* did not explicitly repeat the first *Instruction*'s accusations with respect to Marxism, although in its frequent reference to the 1984 document it indirectly sustains those accusations. Theologically the position of this *Instruction* is very similar to that of the first one.[74]

Paths Opening in the Present

In line with Thomas Aquinas's teaching that theology is a "science" insofar as it uses a definite *method* (for Aquinas, an Aristotelian method), liberation theology uses its scientific tools methodically and according to the tradition of previous theologies, starting with the Apostolic Fathers and continuing through the Fathers of the church, the medieval Latin theologians, and so on. Liberation theology is, however, *the first theology* to use Marxism as a valid mediation, in a way that does not contradict Christian faith. The church Fathers made use of Platonism, Saint Thomas of Aristotelianism, and Rahner of Heideggerianism. In the nineteenth century, use of the "science" of history caused the crisis of modernism; today, however, this crisis has been resolved and all theology is "historical." The same process will occur with Marxism in the twenty-first century.

It is noteworthy that the marginalized nations of the world have been the first to adopt liberation theology, clearly because of their need for its practical and liberating option. Although liberation theology has suffered so much criticism, incomprehension, and even apparent condemnation, the paths have remained open, and future generations will be able to travel them safely, orthodoxly, and justly. In the remaining pages, we shall consider only some of the current challenges that lead the way to a promising future.

The Reception of Marxist Categories in the Magisterium

I offer only one, though a highly indicative, example (from among many) of how the Magisterium has made use of Marxist categories. Until recently, the church, in millions of its members, lived in a noncapitalist world—that is, in the nations of real socialism. In that world, Marxism and its categories were part of day-to-day life—of what Husserl or Habermas would call the *Lebenswelt*. John Paul II, in his 1981 encyclical *Laborem Exercens*, uses numerous Marxist categories and paradoxically presents, on one hand, an intelligent description of Marx yet, on the other, a portrayal of Marxism as ingenuous, economistic, and Stalinist.

72. *Instruction*, 1986, No. 68.
73. No. 67.
74. Because of which it would be the object of a criticism similar to the analysis previously mentioned in note 61.

The fundamental orientation of the encyclical is to explain the interrelatedness of *work-bread-life*.[75] *Life* stands at the origin of the relationship. *Human persons* are living beings; by living they consume and thus have needs;[76] these needs demand the creative activity of work that produces *bread* (the "fruit" as defined in biblical thought); by being consumed, bread *satisfies* needs and aids and increases life. This is the "vital cycle."[77] Marx offers a prototypical explanation of this cycle:

> In my production [read: my bread], I would have objectified my *individuality*, its specific character and therefore enjoyed not only an *individual manifestation of my life* during the activity, but also when looking at the object [the bread], I would have the *individual* pleasure of knowing my *personality* to be objective . . . and hence a power beyond all doubt . . . My work would be a free manifestation of life, hence an enjoyment of *life*.[78]

Marx, speaking of the relationship between work or production and consumption or satisfaction, clearly indicates his "personalism":

> In the first [production] the person becomes objectified as a *thing;* in the second [consumption] the thing created by him/her is *personified* [*personifiziert*].[79]

And in this famous text he repeats:

> The commodity [read: bread] is . . . an external object, a thing which through its qualities *satisfies human needs*.[80]

Needs are human for Marx. According to the encyclical: "Work is one of the characteristics that distinguish man from the rest of creatures."[81]

In accordance with Catholic social doctrine, the encyclical explains that the dignity of the human person is the foundation of the dignity of work. On this point it coincides with Marx almost word for word:

> Different sorts of work that people do can have greater or lesser objective *value* . . . nevertheless . . . each sort is judged above all by the measure of the dignity of the subject of work, that is to say, the person, the individual.[82]

---

75. "With his *work*, man has to obtain his daily *bread*" (first line of the encyclical and Nos. 1, 9, etc.). For "maintenance of life," see Prologue, nos. 1, 2, 3, 8, 10, 14, 18, etc.
76. "in order to *satisfy* one's own *needs*" (No. 4); "adapting it to his *needs*" (No. 5).
77. See my *Filosofía de la producción* on the "pragmatic circle" and the "poietic" or productive circle, the first need-consumption, the second, need-production-product-consumption.
78. CP 3, pp. 227–28; MEGA I, 3 (1932), 546–47 (emphasis added).
79. *Grundrisse*, I (Spanish edition, p. 11; German edition, p. 12).
80. *Capital*, I, 1, trans. B. Fowkes (New York: Random House, 1977), p. 127.
81. Prologue to *Laborem Exercens* (henceforth *LE*). In *Manuscrito I* of 1844, Marx explains clearly the difference between human work that involves consciousness and freedom and that of mere animal action.
82. *LE* 6.

Marx says explicitly that:

> Labour as *absolute poverty* [*absolute Armut*] . . . existing without mediation . . . can only be one [objectivity] not separated from the *person* [*Person*]; only one coincident with his/her immediate *corporality* [*Leiblichkeit*].[83]
> Labour . . . is [the] not-objectified, therefore, nonobjective, i.e., *subjective* existence of labour itself. Labour not as an object but as *activity* . . . as the living source of value.[84]
> We mean by labour power or labour capacity the aggregate of those mental and physical capabilities existing in the *physical form*, the *living personality* [*lebendigen Persönlichkeit*] of a human being.[85]

In some parts of the encyclical, the author seems to know Marx's work very well. He speaks of the *"capacity for labor" (Arbeitsvermöge)*, an expression that Marx uses in the *Grundrisse* (1857–1858) and in the *Manuscripts of 1861–1863* and *1863–1865*, but that he later replaces with *"labor power" (Arbeitskraft)* in *Das Capital* of 1867. (For that reason later Marxism stopped using the term.)[86] For Marx, "labor" in itself has no (economic) value; only the "capacity for labor" does[87] because such capacity is the "creative source of value" and has dignity (as an end) and so is not a means (the value of the commodity).[88] And for Marx, as in the encyclical, the person, subjectivity, the dignity of work ("living work")[89] constitute the source of the value of all things: even the thing called *capital*.[90]

Marx and the encyclical coincide completely in that *"objective* labor"[91] (a Marxist category) receives its value from *"subjective* labor"[92] (also a Marxist

83. See note 68. See also *La producción teórica de Marx*, chap. 7, pp. 139ff.
84. Ibid. The same text is found in the *Manuscritos del 61–63* (MEGA II, 3, p. 147); see also my *Hacia un Marx desconocido*, chap. 3.1.
85. *Capital*, p. 270. (1873), I, 4.3; Spanish edition, 203: MEGA II, 5, p. 120 (from 1866). We will explore this issue in a work in progress which will discuss *Das Kapital* in the manner of a scientific commentary.
86. For example: "as capacity for work or aptitude for work" (*LE* 5); "the capacity for work" (*LE* 12).
87. "The only thing opposed to objectified work is the non-objectified work—living work . . . The one has the value of use that is incorporated, the other exists as a human activity in process; the one is/has value, *the other is a creator of value*. It exchanges value for the *creative* activity *of value*" (*Manuscritos del 61–63*, Cuaderno I; MEGA II, 3, p. 30). See *Hacia un Marx desconocido*, chap. 3.1.
88. For Marx, the "creation" of value is "from the nothingness" of capital: "How can one get out of production greater value than he put in it, unless he believes that *something can be created from nothing* [*aus Nichts*]" (*Das Kapital*, III, chap. 1; edition in Spanish III, 6, 43; MEW 25, 48).
89. See my *Hacia un Marx desconocido*, chap. 14.2: "Crítica desde la exterioridad del *trabajo vivo*." Marx criticizes the reified objectivity of capital from the personal subjectivity of the worker.
90. "Fetishism" is only an inversion: the *person* of the worker becomes a thing; and the thing-capital is personified. See my "El concepto de fetichismo en el pensamiento de Marx," in *Cristianismo y sociedad* 85 (1985): 7–60.
91. Marx speaks of "objectified" labor or of the objective sense of labor.
92. Marx indicates that "living work" is work as an act, as activity, as subjectivity or subject; it is the individuality of the person of the worker, poor, naked, that is the constant reference of all of his critical thought. All of his work is an *ethic:* "if one wanted to choose to be an ox [*animal*], one could, of course, turn one's back *on the sufferings of humanity* and look after one's own hide. But I should really have thought myself unpractical *if I had pegged out* without finally completing my book [*Das Kapital*], at least in manuscript" (CP 42, p. 366; MEW 30, p. 452; letter of 30 April 1867).

category), for labor is described as subject and as subjectivity in the texts quoted from the *Grundrisse* and many of Marx's works.

The encyclical affirms "the primacy of humankind in the *production process*,[93] the primacy of humankind with respect to things" and thereby "the principle of the priority of work versus capital," because capital is only work objectivized and accumulated.[94]

Finally, the encyclical criticizes the isolation of people in capitalist societies, in contrast to the existence or "the sign of active persons within a community of persons,"[95] which reminds us of a text in the *Grundrisse:*

> Free individuality, based on the universal development of the *individuals* and the subordination of their *communal,* social productivity which is their social possession . . . is the third stage . . . *social* production [*gemeinschäftlische*] is not subsumed under the *individuals* who *manage it as their common wealth* . . . [It is] the *free* exchange *of individuals* who are associated on the basis of *common* appropriation and *control* of the means of production.[96]

For Marx, as for the encyclical, human work ("living work" or the "subjectivity of work"), as individuality in community, is the starting point of ethical criticism; that is, the starting point is the human person of the worker. To talk about the "means of production," or about "objective" work as technology, or to state that "we cannot *separate* capital from labor, and in no way can we oppose labor to capital"—all these are, *strictly* speaking, categories or distinctions made by Marx himself; and the encyclical rightly uses these categories to criticize Stalinist Marxists as dogmatic and economistic. The encyclical, like liberation theology, uses Marxist categories in the same way that Saint Thomas used Aristotle.[97]

Theology and Economic Criticism

While liberation theology, from the beginning, has used sociological and political categories for its ideological analysis, a *theology of the economy,* consistent with the *sacramental nature* of bread (the product of work)[98] as a means of establishing social relationships and of building up or negating the Kingdom, is relatively recent. In this regard, the work of Franz Hinkelammert, *The Ideological Weapons of*

93. For Marx, "living work" subsumed under capital is used, consumed as "process of work" in the heart of capital itself (in the *Grundrisse, Manuscritos del 61–63* and *63–65,* and in *Das Kapital*).
94. *LE* 11.
95. Ibid., prologue.
96. *Grundrisse,* I (CP 3, pp. 227–28; edition in Spanish, p. 86; German edition, pp. 75–77).
97. *LE* 5, 12, 13, 14, etc. At the beginning of the *Cuaderno de Paris* (1844), Marx notes that it is "not possible to separate" work from capital as if they were two autonomous "things," because all capital is only objectified labor. They are not two *things:* there is *one* "subjectivity" (the labor) and capital is only that same subjectivity *objectified.* Thus, he overcomes the "Trinity" (the three factors: labor, capital, land) which he criticized in *Das Kapital* (chap. 7 of the *Manuscrito del 65,* original folios 528ss., in the Amsterdam archives). For all of this, see my forthcoming work on the *Manuscritos del 63–65* (third version of *Das Kapital*).
98. See my "El pan de la celebración eucarística," in *Concilium* 172 (1982): 236–49.

Death, written to further a theology of life, has opened new perspectives.[99] Here Marxism is used adequately and on its own grounds (that is, economic and philosophical) and is incorporated from the perspective of a Christian faith that loses none of its own tradition. Hinkelammert points out that the criticisms leveled against fetishism by Marx are the same as those leveled against idolatry by Jesus and the prophets. Hinkelammert's reevaluation of "carnality" (*basar* in Hebrew and *sarx* in Greek, which is not merely the "body")[100] is consistent with Christian experience:

> However, the enormous value placed on real life in historical materialism has a critical correlate in the Christian message. In the Christian message the resurrection means a resurrection of human beings in their real life . . . Contrary to the way the forces of domination absolutize values, esteem for real life has always been the starting point for the ideologies of the oppressed . . . The specific element in Marxism is praxis that leads to trancendence within real life. The specifically Christian element is hope in the potentialities of praxis, going beyond what can be calculated to be humanly achievable. The connecting link between them is real material life as the ultimate basis for all human life.[101]

No longer is it a question of separating a Marxist philosophy that has to be rejected from a Marxist analysis that can be accepted. Now it is a question of a complete and fitting *rereading* of Marx himself from a Christian, theological perspective. As Thomas Aquinas *entered* into the field of "Aristotelianism" and "from within" began a *creative* process, the same thing has happened with this last, most recent and most promising, phase of liberation theology.

In my *Ethics and Community*,[102] I have tried to create a theological Christian discourse that is essentially biblical and, *at the same time*, strictly Marxist. The concept of "community" in *Acts* (2: 42–47) and in the *Grundrisse* (and in the later manuscripts up to *Das Kapital*) have served me as guides. Concepts (and categories) such as person, social relationship, work, value, and "blood," product or "bread," are strictly Christian and traditional and are strictly in accord with the "categories" that Marx established in the definitive period of his life (1857–1880). A comparison of my two studies *La producción teórica de Marx* and *Ethics and Community* will show that the epistemological hypothesis of the latter is the systematic and precise use of Marxist categories (as contained in the works published in MEGA by the West Berlin Marxist Institute), together with the use of the biblical categories in their Hebrew, Greek-Christian contexts. I have tried to overcome the dualism between the use of Marx's philosophy and analysis without losing the clear *difference* between the two modes of discourses. In future years, liberation theology will make creative advances in both a *missionary* and prophetic

99. (Maryknoll: Orbis Books, 1986), originally published in 1977. See also his *Crítica a la razón utópica* (San José: DEI, 1984).
100. See my *El dualismo en la antropología de la cristiandad*, n. 16.
101. *The Ideological Weapons of Death*, pp. 272–73.
102. (Maryknoll: Orbis Books, 1989).

sense, and will make itself comprehensible among ordinary people, especially among the exploited, as well as among real socialists.

Religion in Real Socialism

As just stated, one of the missionary virtues of liberation theology, was its ability to be understood in a world that until recently was considered atheist (actually, it was antisuperstitious) or materialistic (actually, it was concerned about the oppressed). The declaration of the Sandinista Government *Sobre la religión* in October of 1980 opened a new path for "real" worldwide socialism (see above). From then on, being a believer and a revolutionary were not two contradictory subjective (and objective) positions. The contradictions between faith and politics in the year 1968 were overcome—and liberation theology was a fundamental theoretical factor in bringing this about. In this context, Frei Betto's book *Fidel and Religion* is a historic work.[103] Providing more of a personal witness than a theoretical statement, the Cuban leader declared:

I think that the enormous historical importance of Liberation Theology, or the Liberation Church—whatever you want to call it—lies precisely in its profound impact on the political views of its followers. It constitutes a point of contact between today's believers and those of the past—that distant past of the first few centuries after the emergence of Christianity, after Christ. [Fidel shows here his Luxemburgian position.] I could define . . . Liberation Theology . . . as Christianity's going back to its roots, its most beautiful, attractive, heroic and glorious history. It's so important *that it forces all of the Latin American left* to take notice of it as one of the *most important* events of our time.[104]

The critics of liberation theology, *from within* the church, totally forget the prophetic-missionary function of this theology.

If we add to these considerations the "crisis" that occurred in the Soviet Union because of the low level of productivity (which calls into question the previous naive economistic theory of Soviet Marxism), the significance of liberation theology, *because it has known how to use Marxism in a Christian fashion*, became universal. It was not only useful for Latin America, Africa, or Asia, but also for real socialist countries. Mikhail Gorbachev, in his book *Perestroika*, harshly criticized bureaucracy and dogmatism.[105] He put forward a positive view of religion, of "spiritual" values; he defended "humanism" and democracy, demanding that "Lenin be read in a new way."[106]

It has been a long road: from the justification of a Christian praxis committed to the liberation of the poor and oppressed (by means of liberation theology), through

103. (New York: Simon and Schuster, 1988), originally published in 1985.
104. Ibid., p. 245.
105. (Mexico, ed. Diana, 1987), pp. 46, 49, 50, 52, 61, 102, 128, 138, 191, etc.
106. Ibid., pp. 8, 30, 31, 33, 34, 36, 37, 39, 44, 59, 78, 84, 90, 150, 169, 171, 179, 191, 223, 347, etc. On 29 April 1988, in the synod of the Orthodox Church, Gorbachev acknowledged that it was an error to have persecuted the church (*Los Angeles Times*, 5 May 1988, p. 9).

the Nicaraguan Revolution, the improvement of church-state relations in Cuba, the discovery of religion not just as an "opiate of the people" but also as a "miraculous remedy"—to the elaboration of a theology fully conscious not just of using but of *rereading and discovering the internal creativity of Marxist thought itself.*[107]

Conclusions

Liberation theology originates and learns in a organized way from the praxis of the Latin American peoples, from the Christian base communities, from the poor and the oppressed. It first justified the political commitment of militant Christians in order later, through praxis, to provide that same justification for the praxis of all the impoverished people of Latin America. It is therefore a critical theological discourse that analyzes traditional themes (sin, salvation, church, Christology, the sacraments, etc.) on a *concrete* relevant level. It does not reject *abstraction* (sin *in itself,* for example), but it situates such abstractions in a *concrete* historical reality (the sin of *the system of dependency,* for example).

The use of the human sciences, and particularly of Marxism, was made necessary by the need for a critical-concrete theological reflection based on the experience of the poor and the oppressed. It is the first theology in history to use this kind of analysis, and it does so based on the demands of faith, avoiding economism, naive dialectical materialism, and abstract dogmatism. It can then criticize capital or dependency as sin. Without recommending political positions—which is not the function of theology—it keeps from falling into a "third position" (neither capitalism nor socialism, but a Christian political solution). That does not keep it from being a theology that is orthodox (growing out of orthopraxis) or traditional (in the strongest sense of the word). It enters into a missionary dialogue with Marxism—a dialogue that Latin American parties or political movements and even persons in countries of what had been real socialism could understand.

In a few decades, the prophetic calls of liberation theology will be passed on as the "common" and "long established" beliefs of Christianity. This is the message of liberation because of which prophets are criticized and persecuted. As Jeremiah, imprisoned in his own Jerusalem, recognized: "O Jerusalem, you kill the prophets and stone those who are sent to you!" (Luke 13:34).

107. Op. cit., of F. Castro by Frei Betto, p. 276.

Saint Francis in Climate-Changing Times: Form of Life, the Highest Poverty, and Postcapitalist Politics

Stephen Healy

This paper considers the relevance of Franciscan monastic practice to contemporary postcapitalist politics in the time of the Anthropocene. Giorgio Agamben's reflections on the monastic revolution of the eleventh and twelfth centuries explores the different relationships between the rules governing monastic life and materiality, wherein the renunciation of property and the practice of highest poverty give the greatest expression of a collective, monastic form of life. The embodied connection between having a rule and living it contrasts starkly with emergent Church doctrine that introduced a cynical split between the sacred and the material: good or bad, the priest only need say the words. Centuries later, a version of this cynical split seems operative in contemporary "green consumerist" responses to the Anthropocene, amounting to a palliative gesture when what is required is revolutionary transformation. In contrast, this essay considers how contemporary postcapitalist politics, like monasticism, rests upon embodied forms of collective life.

Francis in opposition to a nascent capitalism refused every instrumental discipline, and in opposition to the mortification of the flesh (in poverty and in the constituted order) he posed a joyous life, including all being and nature, the animals, sister moon, brother sun, the birds of the field, the poor and exploited humans, together against power and corruption. Once again in postmodernity we find ourselves in Francis's situation, posing against the misery of power a joy of being.
—Michael Hardt and Antonio Negri, *Empire*

The poverty and austerity of Saint Francis were no mere veneer of asceticism, but something much more radical: a refusal to turn reality into an object simply to be used and controlled.
—Pope Francis, *Laudato Si': On Care for Our Common Home*

For the first time, what was in question in the movements was not the rule, but the life, not the ability to profess this or that article of faith, but the ability to live in a certain way, to practice joyfully and openly a certain form of life.
—Giorgio Agamben, *The Highest Poverty: Monastic Rules and Form-of-Life*

Both religious and secular thinkers identify Saint Francis as a revolutionary figure. On the secular side, Michael Hardt and Antonio Negri (2000) make Francis the last word of *Empire* and their discussion of the multitude as a revolutionary subject. On the religious side, Pope Francis (2015) similarly refers to his namesake's "radical refusal" to reduce reality to an "object simply to be used and controlled," as stated at the beginning of his encyclical *Laudito Si'*, on the interlinked issues of environment and inequality. Finally, Francis features prominently in Giorgio Agamben's engagement with the eleventh- and twelfth-century explosion of monastic movements grounded in the communal practice of the highest poverty: use without ownership. It is Agamben who identifies a radically different, joyful "form of life" connected to a different relationship with things—one that breaks with a dominant tradition that structured Francis's time and still structures our time.

Agamben's engagement with Francis and the monastic explosion is one element in a larger Marxian return to Christianity, a conversation involving Foucault, Derrida, Žižek, Negri, and Badiou among others (see Roberts 2008; Kaufman 2008).[1] The main focus of this conversation has been on Saint Paul's triadic theorization of temporality wherein Christ has already redeemed the world but the Second Coming has not yet happened and we live in the interval between. For these theorists, Paul's temporality becomes a means of recovering a revolutionary Marxian politics: both a recovery from the disasters of the twentieth century and, more centrally, recovery as a means of breaking from the interminable, depoliticizing end of history. While Agamben has been part of this conversation, his writings on Saint Francis push the Marxian-Christian turn in a direction that foregrounds a different problematic: the question of how to live in common. In this paper I will argue that Agamben's exploration of common life in the context of the Christian monastery provides a crucial perspective on how to answer this question.

This special issue is addressed to the relationship between Marxism and spirituality. My aim for considering these two things together through the figure of Saint Francis is quite pragmatic: to answer the question of how to live with others in the face of an emerging scientific consensus that human communities in the "developed" minority world will need to make 80 percent reductions in their carbon emissions to have any chance of avoiding the consequences of runaway climate change (Lenton 2014). The IPCC (2014) claims that this reduction must be achieved by 2050 to avoid catastrophic climate change. Some argue that these reductions must be achieved within a more immediate time frame (see Spratt 2015; McKibben 2012). Still others ominously conclude that it may be too late to keep global ambient temperature change below the two-degrees-Celsius threshold and thereby to possibly avoid the worst consequences of a warming world (Meinshausen et al. 2015). With luck, some of the changes required will be achieved through large-scale policy shifts—toward renewable energy, reuse economies, and reorganizing the infrastructure in cities and food and transportation systems, but all of these structural changes imply a changed relationship with daily

---

1. Michel Foucault's history of sexuality, genealogy of confession, and identification of the priest as the template for the exercise of pastoral power in the secular age (the host of experts that care for the self) constitutes a different sort of return to Christianity that is also crucially important for this conversation. See for example Hardt (2011).

life and consumption in particular. In the minority world, we need to do less consuming, and there is clear evidence that simply "greening" consumption is not a sufficient response (Alexander 2014).

Given the scale of change required, reducing the footprint of life in the minority world is unavoidable: flying less, driving less, eating and entertaining ourselves differently than we do now. While this represents a massive adjustment to material existence in the minority world, there is an equally daunting psychological challenge as well. Rosemary Randall (2009; see also Weintrobe 2012) argues that forced changes in habit and loss of "freedom" are likely to engender both vociferous denial and resentment-fueled efforts to raise the drawbridge around privileged life, to cling to the entitlements of mobility and comfort long after it becomes clear that it's not possible to do so. In her view, the only way around this psychic roadblock is for large numbers of us to *learn* to want to do what we have to do—to freely mourn and then give up a high-impact, high-consumption way of life sustained by economic growth. Randall's response has been to form support groups, patterned in part after the Twelve-Step movement, in which people can help one another to work through these losses and to voluntarily internalize and practice a new, less energetic way of life as an animating ethic. It is here perhaps that Agamben's reflections on a "voluntary," joyful, collective "form of life" might prove helpful in forging what Gerda Roelvink and J. K. Gibson-Graham (2009),[2] following Val Plumwood (2007), call another "mode of humanity": one capable of seeing us through a climate-changing time. There are, of course, innumerable differences between Francis's time and our own, but Agamben opens his reflections on monastic life with an observation that parallels our own time. The monastic explosion of the eleventh and twelfth century was complemented by a profusion of experiments in collective life among the laity and attempts at escaping from the dominant social order and the violence that defined the era.[3] The present moment seems likewise defined by innumerable experiments in other ways of living collectively and organizing economies, ecologies, and societies.

The essay that follows has four parts. In the first part, I contextualize Agamben's engagement with Francis in the context of a larger Christian (re)turn in Marxism and explore what is at stake for Žižek, Negri, and Badiou in their focus on Pauline temporality—the promise of an "emancipatory break" that will deliver us from the postpolitical end of history. Germane to my efforts here, I explore how "green consumerism," for Žižek and others, is a definitive symptomatic expression of the end of history as a cynical, postideological condition. However cogent their analyses, we are left in a familiar spot, waiting for a return of emancipatory politics while the question of how to live is left unanswered. In part two, I give a close reading of Agamben's analysis of the explosion of monastic movements and in particular how monastic practice constitutes a different "form of life" wherein life lived by monastic rules becomes inseparable from the collective material practice of the highest poverty. Agamben sees in this monastic movement an implicit critique of the Catholic Church as an earthly power, which has

---

2. See also Roelvink (2010).
3. As Agamben points out, these movements among the laity were all too often branded heretical and met with violence. The monastic movements, in contrast, stayed just enough inside the confines of the Church as an earthly power that they were allowed to persist.

implications for us in the present. In part three, I use this conception of the Franciscan "form of life" to understand the postcapitalist project of pursuing a different "mode of humanity" in which we might develop the capacity to survive in the Anthropocene. As in the time of Francis, I point to the contemporary explosion of social movements around the world and to how the success of these movements is predicated upon experimental practices that redefine what is necessary for us to survive and how we care for things in common that we cannot own. Finally, I conclude with some thoughts about what we might gain in thinking together the monastery and its form of life with the current efforts of enacting a different mode of humanity.

The Christian Turn, Green Consumerism, and the Limits of Messianic Marxism

> The Pauline tradition that has attracted the Left is central to the "return to religion" in political philosophy and theory. This is because, despite the widespread conservative reading of Pauline apocalypticism in orthodox Christianity and Christian fundamentalism, Pauline Christianity imagines a radical collective break with the prevailing order.
> —John Roberts, "The 'Returns to Religion': Messianism, Christianity and the Revolutionary Tradition"

John Roberts (2008, pt. 1, 59) argues that Marxian left political philosophers have returned, once more, to Christianity as "that which embodies the memory or prospect of a universal emancipatory politics." Roberts points out that this return is not new. Marx and Engels had their own complicated relationship with Christianity, and there have been other Marxian returns to Christianity, particularly in the writings of Lukács and Bloch.

For Roberts, in the present moment the work of Žižek, Badiou, Agamben, and Negri constitutes an important strand in this return to Christian thought. Each of these writers (re)cast Paul as a theologian of temporality in which the resurrection represents a break in temporality that allows for the emergence of a revolutionary subject. Paul's understanding of Christianity operates within a "triadic framework of Judeo-Christian transcendentalism: 'the already,' 'the not yet,' and the 'to come'" (Roberts 2008, pt. 2, 80). For Paul, the most significant event in history—the resurrection—has already happened. In the resurrection the old law that dictates the relationship between God and man is over and a new relationship has begun. But the Second Coming has "not yet happened," in a way that requires the faithful to act as if the return "to come" could happen at any moment.

It is not difficult to see in contemporary Marxist theory this same triadic temporality: "the already" (failed) revolution that has happened, the event "not yet" transpired that might inaugurate a new revolutionary potentiality, and the necessity of living in what Žižek (2010) calls nonevental times, attuned to a revolutionary moment "to come." Equally important, Paul's triadic temporality offers a way of understanding the present moment as a depoliticizing "end of history" in which the new law is still to come and—"after the Russian Revolution, the collapse of the Soviet Union, and the public destitution of Marxism and historical materialism—become a widespread crisis of political subjectivity itself under postmodern pacification and 'democratization' of the political process" (Roberts 2008, pt. 2, 75). Agamben, Badiou, and Žižek have developed various ways of describing the present "end of history" condition: the reduction of governance to the administration of bare life, the privatization of politics through its "democratization" (the postpolitical reduction of politics to the private expression of preference through voting), or the dominance of postideological cynicism. In each case there is a vision of the end of history in which society is forever captured by the existing state of affairs. What is required is a resurrection in the form of an emancipatory return of politics—some rupture or event that will restart the flow of history. In the absence of this break, the present state of affairs—the trinity of technology, markets, and (economic) rationality—continue as a world without end, what Agamben has referred to as "catastrophe" (Whyte 2013).

Žižek's (and others') analysis of green consumerism offers a quintessential example of why the "end of history" is seen in such catastrophic terms: a world in which real transformation becomes impossible. Žižek (2014, for example) describes green consumers as subjects caught up primarily in the process of the buying and selling of an "experience" central to cultural capitalism. Green consumerism, for Žižek, represents a packaging of ecological conscience—specifically, the belief that ordering fair-trade pumpkin spice lattes at Starbucks from the window of your Prius is all that's required to bring about a better world. When you indulge in this fantasy, you're buying not just a set of products but also the cultural experience of being a force for good.

Central to Žižek's analysis is the post-Lacanian distinction between pleasure and enjoyment. Pleasure, he explains, is by its very nature moderate. In the minority world, pleasure is a regime of moderation that conserves health where one can have sugar-free sweets, coffee in moderation, low-calorie beer, and so on. To this list we might add "green consumption" as a moderate pleasure, one designed to exculpate our guilt while not challenging our way of life overmuch.

Enjoyment, in contrast, is excessive. The function of enjoyment is not to conserve the subject but rather to annihilate it through, for example, the toxic flight of addiction—cigarettes, alcohol, and drug abuse, which illustrate the Lacanian observation that enjoyment serves nothing (Loose 2011).

Žižek argues that the ecological "brand," when it's pursued all the way, crosses the threshold from pleasure to enjoyment. Here he asks us to consider a fictional green-minded executive who purchases a larger "energy efficient" house in the country. This purchase is only available to a select few, coming at great economic and ecological cost, and is ultimately far less ecologically sound than living in a densely populated urban environment, and yet this is the "green consumer" fantasy when pursued to its individualist end.

Žižek is not alone in regarding "green" as the new opiate of the masses, as that which promises life only to betray it. Mark Davidson (2012), drawing on the same Lacanian framework, describes this same dynamic operating at a much larger scale in which the sustainable city functions as a cynical "palliative fantasy." In Davidson's view, model ecological cities, developed by planners around the world to showcase "green technology," take the form of a gentrified green district that exists alongside and is sustained by commitment to growth as usual. Erik Swyngedouw (2010) likewise argues that carbon markets also function as a fetishist fantasy in which anthropogenic CO_2 emissions are positioned as the *emergency* but also, conveniently enough, can be *controlled* through expert-led market-based technocratic approaches. This fetishist fantasy indulges the desire to imagine that we can deal with the ecological contradictions of industrialism through a technical fix without confronting the uneven, inequitable distribution of its consequences.

What each of these fantasy frames share in common is a subject—of green consumerism, sustainable urbanism, or CO_2 technofetishism—constitutively and cynically split between pleasure and enjoyment. On the one hand is investment in solutions that "act out" a response to ecological challenges (pleasure), and on the other hand is an unconscious commitment to economic growth (enjoyment).[4] Žižek, Davidson, and Swyngedouw each argue that this cynical ideology sustains an imaginary self-image where we can "act out," exculpating our guilt through green indulgence while at the same time unconsciously avoiding a traumatic confrontation with a real(ity): the fundamentally unsustainable pattern of life in the minority world and our complicit investment in an economy predicated on endless growth.

Žižek's, Davidson's, and Swyngedouw's analyses end with a call to break with the existing order. In their view we need a revolutionary subject that will inaugurate a new law in place of a cynical green consumerist subject and the "old law" governing pleasure and enjoyment. In keeping with Paul's triadic temporality, these theorists position this event as yet to come, contingent upon some future revolutionary rupture. However cogent their analysis, this deferral to the future is deeply troubling. We are left waiting at precisely a moment when scientific research on the multivalent ecological crisis tells us we are out of time. If Timothy Morton (2013) is right that the end of history has now coincided with the end of the world—as a stable predictable background against which we may measure human progress—then I am not sure how much longer we can wait. It is here that Agamben's analysis of the eleventh- and twelfth-century monastic explosion offers a different return to Christianity and a different politics centered on the question of how to live in common.

Monasticism, Highest Poverty, and Form of Life

Agamben (2013) describes the eleventh and twelfth centuries as a period of explosive growth in Catholic monastic orders—most notably the Franciscans but also a variety of lay communal movements. His engagement here constitutes, in my view, a very different "return" to Christianity, one that aligns with contemporary postcapitalist explorations of various forms of cooperation and collectivity—efforts to live with less, to care for what we hold in common, or to invest in a habitable future. To establish this parallel it is worth going through his argument in detail. Agamben represents monasticism as an attempt at producing communal life in the here and now rather than waiting for the hereafter. He sees, particularly in the Franciscans, a kind of indirect protest against the

---

4. One form that this enjoyment takes is the way in which even "environmental problems," when they are acknowledged, "are transformed into an engine of growth and innovation" (Neimanis, Åsberg, and Hedrén 2015).

Church's authority by practicing "joyfully and openly a certain form of life" (Agamben 2013, 93).

What defines these monastic movements more than anything else for Agamben is the production of a new genre of writing—rulebooks that mark out every aspect of the life of the brethren who obey them. The rules are exhaustive in their account of how to live life in the monastery. The hours of the day are marked by the recitation of the Psalms. Work, prayer, and rest are prescribed. Each garment that adorns the monk's body is saturated with significance. Three crucial, interrelated features are discernible in Agamben's analysis of this blending of life and rule: the voluntary participation of the novice, the joyful nature of collective life, and finally, the practice of the highest poverty.

Agamben begins his analysis with what cannot appear as anything but contradictions to many of us: the freedom that is to be found when the novice voluntarily submits to the strictures of the rule, the authority of the abbot, and the practice of highest poverty. He describes a formal process by which the novice is inducted into the life of the monastery and the cenobitic community (those who live the common life). But what distinguishes monastic life from ordinary life is *how* these detailed rules are positioned in relation to those who live them. "The rule is not applied to life, but produces it and at the same time is produced in it. What type of text are rules, then, if they seem to performatively realize the life that they must regulate? And what is a life that can no longer be distinguished from the rule?" (Agamben 2013, 69).

How does this work in practice? How do life and rule emerge together? Writing in a similar vein, Michelangelo Paganopoulos (2009) writes about the Eastern Orthodox monastery of Vatopaidi where he lived and worked as a researcher and monk for a time. Paganopoulos submitted himself to the rules and life of the order: working during the day and having no possessions apart from a small notebook in which to write his sins for confession to the Cypriot father each night. His job was a menial one—trimming the wax from already burnt candles so that the residue might be re-formed into candles and ultimately sold in religious shops. As one monk explained, they were recycling the wax "just like Jesus recycled His body" (366). The task, though simple, was painful since it involved holding a knife for long hours and trimming the burnt wax without cutting the candle.

> Because my wrists were already hurting after cleaning only a few candles, the verger asked me loudly to repeat the words of the prayer "Lord Jesus Have Mercy on Me the Sinner" while cutting the melted wax from the candles, as a technique to develop rhythm in the movement of my hands, and in relation to my breathing. Indeed after an hour of reciting the words, I was automatically moving the knife on the wax, breathing according to the rhythm of the words of the prayer. (366)

The verger explained that the rhythm, the words of the prayer, allow one to concentrate on God. The moments where the mind lapsed or wandered were the "sins" to be confessed in the evening to the priest. In contemporary parlance we might identify the performative power of these prayers, both words themselves and the cadence of their repetition, as integral to what makes a monk a monk, including the performance of his mundane duties.

Agamben in his analysis also underscores the importance of repetition, particularly of the Psalms, in constituting monastic life. Rather than being (only) functional to the sacraments associated with the Mass, the Psalms were frequently sung together by the monks to mark the cadence of collective life. For this reason, monastic life—which in both the Eastern Orthodox and Catholic Church emerged between the ninth and the twelfth century—is in stark contrast to the tradition of hermitage that existed prior to this period. In place of the ascetic privation of the hermit, life in the monastery was necessarily collective. The monks work, sleep, pray, are silent, or sing together.

Just as the Psalms establish the cadence of monastic temporality, it is the practice of the highest poverty that, in Agamben's terms, gives the greatest (spatial) scope to monastic life. Writing after Francis's death, Bonaventure (in Agamben 2013, 124) distinguishes between four types of property in *Defense of the Mendicants*: ownership, possession, usufruct, and simple use (also called poor use). The first three of these are familiar to us today as different ways of holding, having, or using property. The last category of simple or poor use is what is practiced in the monastery as the highest poverty: the right to use something without the right to own it.[5]

Along with celibacy, the vow of poverty is perhaps the most widely known aspect of the monastic tradition, and yet the highest poverty in Francis's time and after was a source of theological controversy. Pope Nicholas III, writing in 1279, endorsed the practice of the highest poverty by creating a distinction in which the Church owns the property, the monastery ground, and all that is within it, while the monks may make use of it. This is still practiced today as contemporary Franciscans continue to make a symbolic payment annually for the use of the monastery. Pope John XXII later argued, contra Nicholas and Francis, that in the case of consumables that are destroyed in their use, what he calls *abusus*, it is impossible to maintain the distinction between poor use and ownership (Agamben 2013, 131). That is to say, it is impossible in the final analysis to be in the world without laying some claim to it, exerting some ownership over it, if only through consumption of necessities. Agamben mentions in passing that in using the special case of things that are consumed completely in their use, Pope John XXII "furnishes the paradigm of an impossibility of using that was to find its full realization many centuries later in consumer society" (131). Behind this theological dispute over the philosophical soundness of the highest poverty is a much larger story about the Church as an evolving earthly power, one that has its own relationship to the ownership of property, life, and law, which Agamben starkly contrasts with life in the monastery.

5. Why is the vow of poverty, as it has come to be known, central to monastic practice? Contemporary Franciscan monk and progressive activist Father Richard Rohr offers a historical explanation. In Francis's time the ownership of land was an important part of identity since land title was connected to the family name. Francis's family was part of a then emergent merchant class that disrupted the traditional ownership schema, particularly in areas around Italy's protoindustrial cities, laying the conditions for a cycle of violence, dispossession, and reprisal. Francis's conversion moment came after spending a year as a hostage in one such conflict. The experience set him on a path to renounce not only patrilineal land title but also all personal property in an effort to escape the cycle of ownership, covetousness, and violent retribution endemic to his times.

Agamben argues that the monastic "form of life" is constituted by the indissociable relationship between monastic life, the rules that define it, and the practice of the highest poverty, which give this life its greatest scope. What makes form of life important for Agamben (2013, 72) is what the concept does to the central terms that organize ethical (and political) thought: "The cenobitic practice (communal life in the monastery), by shifting the ethical problem from the level of relation between norm and action to that of form of life, seems to call into question the very dichotomy of rule and life, universal and particular, necessity and liberty, through which we are used to comprehending ethics." In the monastic form of life, there is no difference but rather what Agamben terms a zone of indifference that runs through all of these central oppositions. To have a rule is to live it. What is universal is to be found only in the particular. To be a monk is to freely give up the liberty to own property and, in so doing, to enter into common and joyful life with the practice of the highest poverty.

Following Francis, Agamben argues that a life lived in imitation of Christ and the apostles was also a protest against the historical evolution of the Church as an earthly power. In specifying the coordinates of the monastic form of life, Agamben (2013, 117) traces the opposed developments shaping the Church during this same period of time, particularly in the divine office of priestly authority in which the Church

> decisively affirms the sharp distinction between life and liturgy, between individual and function, that will culminate in the doctrine of the *opus operatum* and the sacramental effectiveness of the *opus Dei*. Not only is the sacramental practice for the priest valid and efficacious *ex opera operato* ("from the work done") independently of the unworthiness of this life, but as is implied in the doctrine of the character indelible, the unworthy priest remains a priest despite his unworthiness.

In contemporary parlance we might say that the Church was arguing that the clothes make the man or that the cloth "doeth the work." Instead of the form of life in the monastery, a sharp division between life and law is being codified during this period in the Church and in the divine office of the priesthood. The effect of this radical separation is that it allows the sacraments the priest is empowered to perform, from baptism to unction, to have miraculous properties *independent of* the person performing them. The priest, whether good or wicked, merely becomes a conduit to their performance. It is this same split that allows the Church to venerate Christ while at the same time participating in the ordinary politics and economics of the day—to own property and collect taxations from those working church lands.

The priest is able to do what he likes in private because it is only required that he says the words in public, which means that ordinary people are free to do as they like in their own privacy—to indulge ordinary sins and ordinary lives—by virtue of this same split. As Žižek (2010) has argued elsewhere, this is the secret appeal of the Catholic Church: the Church can bear belief for you while you are free to doubt or sin in your private life so long as you consent to this arrangement. Could it be that in the separation between the liturgy and life in the Church is found the template for dominant cynical ideology that, Žižek argues, structures our own time? This seems to be exactly what Agamben (2013, 130) argues, as he concludes his essay with the assertion that the Church's radical separation between liturgy and life became the "ontologically operative paradigm," the "mould" into which secular society was forced.

What this might mean is that there is nothing particularly new about the cynical green consumer subject. It has been observed by others that when we buy swirly light bulbs and live in the hope of safe nuclear power to come, we can then go about business as usual just as wealthy Catholics could buy indulgences in prior centuries (Monbiot 2006). But what this also means is that the form of life practiced by Saint Francis *may* have relevance to our own time as the basis for a different response to the Anthropocene. I see in contemporary postcapitalist praxis an attempt to develop a form of life that travels under a different name. Inspired by burgeoning social movements, this project is an attempt to answer to the question of how to live in common.

Contemporary Experiments in Common Life

For the past twenty years, Gibson-Graham (1996, 2006) have argued that we no longer need wait for the end of capitalism to practice a postcapitalist politics. Though they do not draw explicitly on Saint Francis, like him they seem to have faith that we can create a common life (and even joy) now and that there is no need to wait for a time to come. In the years since making this initial argument in *The End of Capitalism (As We Knew It)*, there has been an explosion of social movements and scholarship focused on a postcapitalist politics: solidarity economies, economic democracy, peer-to-peer economies, degrowth economies, *buen vivir*, indigenous economies, transition towns, downshift and simple-living movements, and cooperative economies, to name but a few of the attempts at enacting another world that reassembles what already exists in the present one (Roelvink, St. Martin, and Gibson-Graham 2015).

J. K. Gibson-Graham, Jenny Cameron, and Stephen Healy (2013) further elaborate a postcapitalist politics by drawing on examples of collective action throughout the world taking back the economy for people and planet. The efforts and initiatives highlighted in the book attempt to answer some of the central ethical dilemmas of common life. What is necessary for survival? How do we organize economies and distribute surplus? How do we engage in ethical exchange with others? How do we care for commons? How do we invest in a future worth having? These concerns are expressed as questions both to invite the readers into a shared space of collective reflection and action and also because there is no final answer: no matter what answer is given, the question remains.

There are two ethical questions that have special resonance with Agamben's reflections on monasticism: "What does it take to survive well?" and "How do we care for what we hold in common?" The question of what's necessary for survival and how to care for common property are long-held concerns in Marxian theory.[6] What the phrase "surviving well" is meant to signal is the way in which we can no longer understand survival as "necessity" in human terms alone. In the Anthropocene, concerns about our individual and collective survival have to be read against the needs of the more-than-human planetary community (see also Gibson-Graham 2011).

6. See Jean–Luc Nancy (2009) for a history of the latter.

It might be enough to say that the explosion of contemporary movements that attempt to live differently, simply, lightly, and with less impact echoes the Franciscan ethos of simplicity and Francis's fabled regard for plant and animal life. Through Agamben's analysis we can go much further than this. Following Plumwood (2007), Roelvink and Gibson-Graham (2009) describe a central aim in postcapitalist politics, to "go forward in a different mode of humanity"—one that recognizes what is at stake in a time of accelerating ecological crisis (see Steffen et al. 2015). This "mode of humanity" is at once connected to a different way of thinking (reframing economy, humans, ecology) and a different way of being in the world (actually doing things).

The parallel that I wish to explore here is one in which we might consider this postcapitalist mode of humanity, though secular, as a "form of life" and in which the former shares with the latter an indifferent relationship between life and rule, given greatest scope through a different relationship with things. To do this, I want to explore some of the examples used in *Take Back the Economy* and elsewhere that provide an answer to the questions of what's necessary for survival and under what conditions we can survive well together by caring for what we hold in common. I focus my attention initially on the household as a space like the monastery where a different mode of humanity might be practiced "joyfully and openly," as Agamben put it. Broadening out from the household, I draw on the work of postcapitalist theorists to find other examples in which surviving well in the age of the Anthropocene finds greatest-scope in forms of collective experimentation.

In *Take Back the Economy*, we describe Cathy as a representative of a diffuse social movement in countries across the minority world focused on "simple living," or what Hamilton and Mail (2003) call "downshifting." Cathy, the founder of Cheapskates.com, has a passion for living cheaply. While there is a long tradition within Christianity (and many other traditions) of voluntary simplicity, at first blush Cathy's motivations are quite different, avowedly secular. "Cheapskating" is a commitment to an array of home-economic practices: self-provisioning DIY, continually auditing the household budget, and eliminating unnecessary expenditures. Cheapskating is not a renunciation of ownership but a desire for a life where consumption is thoughtful and deliberate. Cathy's devotion to cheapskating stems from a personal crisis when an unfinished housing renovation project coincided with the birth of twins and an unexpected job loss. Her initial response was to curtail her family's discretionary spending, but that was followed by a progressive reengineering of virtually every aspect of her household economy: cooking, cleaning, child care, entertainment, and home repair. She does this by means of both a rigorous household accounting process as well as experimentations in household provisioning—not just cooking but the use of home chemistry to produce better, safer, and cheaper supplies for laundry and household cleaning. She details these experiments and shares them with likeminded subscribers to her website, where she has parlayed her passion into an online business. On the site, Cathy describes herself as a cheapskate and not a miser. When she does buy something, she uses her savings and sense of discernment to buy things that are truly useful, durable, beautiful, or enjoyable—and she's in a position to do so because she's not spending money when she doesn't have to. The goal is not to live life in fear of spending, she explains, but to avoid wasting money on things that do not matter, in the service of creating a life she describes as "debt free, cashed up, and laughing."[7]

It is in Cathy's insistence that there is "joy" to be found in this life of frugality that I begin to hear a deeper resonance with Francis's form of life. What if we were to risk taking this comparison a bit further? Agamben says that it was the materiality of poor use that gave form to the free, joyful collectivity of monastic life, while Father Richard Rohr,[8] in a complementary fashion, says the monastery provided freedom and relative security from the violent struggles over property that defined Francis's moment in history. The joy and freedom that Cathy and her fellow cheapskates pursue is of a different kind: freedom from crushing consumer debt common in the minority world. Thus it is not so much the renunciation of property but rather the feeling of being owned by things, through debt, that is at issue here.

At this point it might be objected that the promise of living debt free is, in a sense, the experience of "individual salvation" in relation to consumer society. That may be the case, but even with the example of Cathy one can see the contours of a more collective practice through the sharing of information. Likewise, while Cathy is concerned with cheapness and her own sense of joy, her cheapskating ways have ecological implications that connect with critical scholarship focused on household sustainability. Gibson et al. (2011) argue that our conception of sustainable households must move beyond merely greening consumption practices. "Green," in their view, has the effect of siloing environmental concerns, generally confining them to the most affluent class of consumers who are in a position to buy "green." Ironically, the affluence of these consumers remains an overriding factor, and they still end up consuming more green food, energy, and electronics than those less affluent. In contrast, Cathy's focus on cheapness has a very different starting point than the green, middle-class sensibility. Though the aim is "cheapness" and not "greenness," Cathy's practical advice on frugality might speak to a broader socioeconomic spectrum while accomplishing the same ends: reduced consumption.

Gibson et al. (2011) argue that sustainable householding needs to place household economies into a broader interhousehold context. Writing in a speculative vein, Gibson-Graham (2011) follow along in the spirit of Dolores Heyden's "grand domestic revolution," asking us to imagine suburbanites that knock down the backyard walls, creating a common space for gardening and neighborhood water and biodiversity conservation. Other postcapitalist theorists have further explored the interhousehold as the context for experimentation in more equitable and sustainable living. To name but a few, Oona Morrow (2012) reimagines households as spaces of collective economic, social, and ecological embodied experimentation, including the collective recovery of the lost arts of self-provisioning. Kelly Dombroski (2016) tracks efforts by mothers to adopt less ecologically damaging practices of infant care, such as the adoption of elimination communication practices that eliminate the need for nappies. Louise Crabtree (2006) reviews existing cohousing and land-trust communities throughout Australia

7. See Cathy's blog: *Debt Free, Cashed Up, & Laughing: The Cheapskate Way to Living the Good Life*, http://www.debtfreecashedupandlaughing.com.au/p/about.html.
8. See more on Father Rohr at the website of the Center for Action and Contemplation, accessed 16 July 2016, https://cac.org/richard-rohr.

that disintegrate household functions—from meal preparation to childcare and security—into the context of larger collectivities, such as housing in the context of community land trusts.

Gibson-Graham (2011, 4) use the term "experimental orientation" to partly describe this different engagement with the matter that comprises common life: "The experimental orientation is another way of making (transformative) connections; it is a willingness to 'take in' the world in the act of learning, to be receptive in a way that is constitutive of a new learner-world, just as Latour's concept of 'learning to be affected' describes the formation of new body-worlds. In experimentation there's no active transformative subject 'learning about' a separate inert object, but a subject-object that is a 'becoming world.'" Part of what the use of this term "experiment" implies is a connection with laboratory science. Cathy, in her various DIY approaches to householding, embodies this experimental orientation. But what Gibson-Graham describe above goes further than that—the "experiments" involve learning from and being transformed by the objects you encounter in the course of learning to survive well. These encounters can take place in the household but also outside of it. Jenny Cameron, Craig Manhood, and Jamie Pomfrett (2011) detail the way in which urban and community gardeners are affected by their collective provisioning practices and in particular how they learn by doing with others. Ann Hill (2015) describes kindred experiments in community survival through peri-urban farming practices in flood-vulnerable portions of the Philippines where gardeners improvise and learn to be affected by the social and ecological dynamics of a climate-altered world.

What all of these efforts share in common is a shift in the ecological problematic from individual to surviving well in a collective context, and there is also a different kind of engagement with the matter—households, food, home canning, gardens, nappies—that shapes life. Following Roelvink (2010), Jenny Cameron, Katherine Gibson, and Ann Hill (2014) in their further explorations of urban farming in flood-prone urban areas of the Philippines describe this intimate, experimental engagement as the formation of a new subjectivity: a hybrid collective. They see the experiments in adapting to life in the Anthropocene as a joining with all elements that compose that space: "Children, chickens, citizens, carrots, commitments, compost, commons and computers along with microbes, rainfall, secateurs, seeds, fences and so on" in an "experiment" that is already underway (120).

At this point we can state more formally the parallel between Francis's "form of life" and the other "mode of humanity" being developed in the context of postcapitalist politics. For Agamben it was the material practice of the highest poverty that gave greatest scope to the indifferent relation between life and law in monastic life, joyful and collective. For postcapitalist theorists, intimate experimental engagements with matter in households, gardens, and communities are the most capacious context for the emergence of a hybrid collective. In contrast, the hybrid collective subject of a postcapitalist politics requires not so much a renunciation but an attenuation of properties: a willingness not just to question what we own or how we relate to others but an attenuation of the properties that define us as human. In the context of this collectivity, the question of how to survive well admits more than human necessity into consideration.

The concept of hybrid collective postcapitalist political theory, as it has been developed by Gibson-Graham (1996) and others, extends the post-Althusserian antihumanist tradition (see also Gibson-Graham 2014). In a similar way, could we not also see a process of "self-forgetting" that appears in some versions of the eponymous prayer of Saint Francis? Could it be that form of life, as Francis developed it, drew on a different tradition but arrived at a similar understanding of the (post)human condition? At this point it might be rightly objected that it is all very well to talk about a different mode of humanity but, insofar as it has been described, this different mode has moved no further than from the household to the garden, a space no bigger than the monastery. But there is nothing in postcapitalist scholarship that confines this new mode of humanity to a particular scale. Indeed, the political project would be to extend this other mode of humanity in the household outward into the city, the countryside, the infrastructure that links them, the forests, the oceans and atmosphere—attenuating the properties that separate them and establishing larger hybrid collectivities that experiment in enacting other worlds. This is not hypothetical—there is both a scholarship and a practice that seeks to understand this other world by building it: municipal solidarity economies (Utting 2015), community-based enterprises (Cameron 2010), open-source food systems, various forms of peer-to-peer financing, community-owned solar and alternative energy systems, and so on (Cameron and Hicks 2014). More recently, Gibson-Graham, Cameron, and Healy (2016) describe a new practice of solar commoning that links "solar citizens" to a large financial and physical infrastructure in order to sustain a postcarbon energy system. And what sustains this initiative is what solar activist and community entrepreneur Danny Kennedy (2014) refers to as the "audacity of an inevitable idea": what's required to transform the system already exists and merely needs to be moved into place.

Conclusion

> It is the problem of the essential connection between use and form of life that is becoming undeferrable at this point. How can use—that is, a relation to the world insofar as it is inappropriable—be translated into an ethos and a form of life? And what ontology and which ethics would correspond to a life that, in use, is constituted as inseparable from its form?
> —Agamben, *The Highest Poverty: Monastic Rules and Form-of-Life*

In the conclusion of his essay, Agamben (2013, 145) suggests that form of life is not only to be understood as a form of protest against the Church, whose authority came to depend upon the radical separation between liturgy and life, but is in fact a confrontation with the "operative ontological paradigm" that structures "Western" thought and consumer society. In the final pages, he asks the questions quoted above: How can use without ownership be translated into "an ethos and form of life?" And "what ontology and which ethics would correspond to a life that, in use, is constituted as inseparable from its form?"

In my view, the questions he asks here are different versions of the same questions that animate postcapitalist politics: the question of what's necessary for us to survive (use) and the question of how we care for what we hold in common (the world insofar as it is inappropriable). Both our individual and collective survival depends upon what we must use but can never wholly own: the atmosphere, hydrosphere, biosphere, and lithosphere. Pope John XXII concludes that the total consumption of a thing—what he calls *abusus*, which destroys the thing in the process of consuming—cannot be separated from owning such a thing. Using the simple example of food and drink to undermine the philosophical position of Saint Francis, his argument does, eerily, describe a truth humanity must now realize about itself: we possess the capacity to so thoroughly consume the world, to *ab-use* it so completely, that it will matter little whether or not we lay claim to it as individuals, enclose it, or continue to degrade it as an unmanaged open-access commons.

There is an urgent need to connect us to what's necessary for surviving well on a planet kept within a tolerable global ambient temperature—a steep learning curve for the collective actions required and little time in which to do it (perhaps none). What it might mean is not so much using the world without owning it but caring for it through our engagements with it, large and small. Even the smallest of experiments I describe here may yet enable larger transformations. For example, it would be easy for some in the critical left to dismiss Cathy's cheapskating as yet another instance of consumer subjectivity, green or otherwise, someone who has fully internalized life in pursuit of the bargain while adjusting to a declining standard of living. All of that might be true, but we are still left with the question of what is necessary for our survival, with how and how much to consume, and it is here that Cathy's efforts may prove instructive.

A better place to start might be to recognize that we understand only a little of what might be: it could be that Cathy's struggle to free herself from consumer debt might enable her, and millions like her, to be less economically insecure and less fearful, more open to other forms of collective practice, or even inclined toward greater solidarity with people in the majority world—more receptive to collective action and more inclined, as Pope Francis suggests, to follow his namesake in not reducing the world to a thing to be abused. What climate science makes clear is that people in the minority world have to change their patterns of consumption. Psychoanalysts like Randall suggest that unless this transformation is attended to willingly, it will engender resentment. From my perspective, the collective reflection of the carbon conversations Randall advocates could be complemented by a postcapitalist politics of experimentation on multiple fronts—directed at household and community, food security and infrastructure. Here the emphasis could be placed on the joyful possibilities of surviving well in a collective context.

In light of these other collective possibilities, the problem with "green consumerism" is not its emphasis on green consumer goods but that it asks too little of us. Indeed, that there is little room in such a vision for us to do anything *other than consume* the idea of a just and sustainable world. The split cynical conscience that Žižek, Davidson, and others identify places our green-conscious pleasure in what we do to "do good" while continued economic growth and the promise of more consumption remains unconsciously aligned with our enjoyment. This is a problem, and our enjoyment will indeed "serve nothing" if we cannot develop a different mode of humanity. What form of life allows us to imagine is a different relationship between ethical intention and everyday practice as that which constitutes common, joyful life. Francis saw it as a form of protest against the Church's authority, which was instituting its own cynical split between liturgy and ordinary life. In the present moment, "breaking the mold" and "confronting the paradigm" requires more than a critical awareness of the cynicism and insufficiency of green consumerism: it requires us to *practice* a different mode of humanity. Practice it, not wait for it "to come."

History makes its own argument against the vain nature of this hope for an emancipatory return, but what's missing is an alternative form of redemption. Both Agamben's version of Saint Francis, via form of life, and a postcapitalist politics with its process of material experimentation, transforming, and being transformed offer us an alternative version of the story in which we participate in redeeming ourselves. In *The Coming Community*, Elanor Kaufman (2008, 38) begins her discussion of Agamben's version of messianism with his retelling of a Hasidic rabbi who explains that "to establish the reign of peace it is not necessary to destroy everything nor completely begin the world anew. It is sufficient to displace this cup or this brush or this stone just a little, and thus everything." The messiah is required (to come, or come again), Agamben explains, because it isn't clear what cup, or brush, or stone is in question or which way to move it. What if, by means of experimentation and collectivity, we were to enact other worlds more just and less damaging, ways of living less all consuming and more reparative? We may move *the* cup, brush, or stone required, or we may not, but we cannot wait.

Acknowledgments

Many thanks to the Sydney-based members of the Community Economies Research Network for comments on an early draft. Thank you as well to Anup Dhar, Serap A. Kayatekin, Jared Randall, and Ceren Özselçuk for their detailed comments and encouragement. Usual disclaimers apply.

References

Agamben, G. 2013. *The highest poverty: Monastic rules and form-of-life.* Trans. A. Kotsko. Stanford: Stanford University Press.

Alexander, S. 2014. A critique of techno-optimism: Efficiency without sufficiency is lost. MSSI Working Paper 1/14, University of Melbourne, Melbourne.

Cameron, J. 2010. Business as usual or economic innovation?: Work, markets and growth in community and social enterprises. Special Issue on Social Enterprise and Social Innovation, ed. J. Barreket and S. Grant. *Third Sector Review* 16 (2), 93.

Cameron, J., K. Gibson, and A. Hill. 2014. Cultivating hybrid collectives: Research methods for enacting community food economies in Australia and the Philippines. *Local Environment* 19 (1): 118–32.

Cameron, J., and J. Hicks. 2014. Performative research for a climate politics of hope: Rethinking geographic scale, "impact" scale, and markets. *Antipode* 46 (1): 53–71.

Cameron, J., C. Manhood, and J. Pomfrett. 2011. Bodily learning for a (climate) changing world: Registering differences through performative and collective research. *Local Environment* 16 (6), 493–508.

Crabtree, L. 2006. Disintegrated houses: Exploring ecofeminist housing and urban design options. *Antipode* 38 (4): 711–34.

Davidson, M. 2012. Sustainable city as fantasy. *Human Geography* 5 (2): 14–25.

Dombroski, K. 2016. Hybrid activist collectives: Reframing mothers' environmental and caring labour. *International Journal of Sociology and Social Policy* 36 (9–10): 629–46.

Francis (pope). 2015. *Laudato si': On care for our common home.* http://w2.vatican.va/content/dam/francesco/pdf/encyclicals/documents/papa-francesco_20150524_enciclica-laudato-si_en.pdf.

Gibson, C., L. Head, N. Gill, and G. Waitt. 2011. Climate change and household dynamics: Beyond consumption, unbounding sustainability. *Transactions of the Institute of British Geographers* 36 (1): 3–8.

Gibson-Graham, J. K. 1996. *The end of capitalism (as we knew it): A feminist critique of political economy.* Minneapolis: University of Minnesota Press.

———. 2006. *A postcapitalist politics.* Minneapolis: University of Minnesota Press.

———. 2011. A feminist project of belonging for the Anthropocene. *Gender, Place and Culture* 18 (1): 1–21.

———. 2014. Being the revolution, or How to live in a "more-than-capitalist" world threatened with extinction. *Rethinking Marxism* 26 (1): 76–94.

Gibson-Graham, J. K., J. Cameron, and S. Healy. 2013. *Take back the economy: An ethical guide for transforming our communities.* Minneapolis: University of Minnesota Press.

———. 2016. Commoning as a postcapitalist politics. In *Releasing the commons: Rethinking the futures of the common,* ed. A. Amin and P. Howell, 378–90. London: Routledge.

Hardt, M. 2011. The militancy of theory. *South Atlantic Quarterly* 110 (1): 19–35.

Hardt, M., and A. Negri. 2000. *Empire.* Cambridge, Mass.: Harvard University Press.

Hamilton, C., and E. Mail. 2003. Downshifting in Australia: A sea-change in the pursuit of happiness. TAI Discussion Paper 50, Canberra.

Hill, A. 2015. Moving from "matters of fact" to "matters of concern" in order to grow economic food futures in the Anthropocene. *Agriculture and Human Values* 32 (3): 551–63.

IPCC (Intergovernmental Panel on Climate Change). 2014. *Climate change 2014: Synthesis report—Contribution of Working Groups I, II and III to the Fifth Assessment Report of the Intergovernmental Panel on Climate Change.* Ed. R. K. Pachauri and L. A. Meyer. Geneva: IPCC.

Kaufman, E. 2008. The Saturday of messianic time (Agamben and Badiou on the Apostle Paul). *South Atlantic Quarterly* 107 (1): 37–70.

Kennedy, D. 2014. The audacity of certainty: How the rooftop revolution is winning and why Australia needs to back the trend. Keynote address, Sydney Ideas series, University of Sydney, 23 October.

Lenton, T. M. 2011. Early warning of climate tipping points. *Nature Climate Change* 1 (June): 201–9.

Loose, R. 2011. Modern symptoms and their effects as forms of administration: A challenge to the concept of dual diagnosis and to treatment. In *Lacan and addiction: An anthology,* ed. Y. G. Baldwin, K. Malone, and T. Svolos, 1–39. London: Karnac.

McKibben, B. 2012. Global warming's terrifying new math. *Rolling Stone,* 12 August: 43.

Meinshausen, M., L. Jeffery, J. Guetschow, Y. R. du Pont, J. Rogelj, M. Schaeffer, N. Höhne, M. den Elzen, S. Oberthür, and N. Meinshausen. 2015. National post-2020 greenhouse gas targets and diversity-aware leadership. *Nature Climate Change* 5 (December): 1098–1106.

Monbiot, G. 2006. Selling indulgences. *George Monbiot,* 19 October. http://www.monbiot.com/2006/10/19/selling-indulgences.

Morrow, O. 2012. Home economics for the Anthropocene. Paper presented at The Society for Applied Anthropology 72nd Annual Meeting, 27–31 March, Baltimore.

Morton, T. 2013. *Hyperobjects: Philosophy and ecology after the end of the world.* Minneapolis: University of Minnesota Press.

Nancy, J.-L. 2009. Communism: The word. In *The idea of communism*, ed. C. Douzinas and S. Žižek, 145–53. New York: Verso.

Neimanis, A., C. Åsberg, and J. Hedrén. 2015. Four problems, four directions for environmental humanities: Toward critical posthumanities for the Anthropocene. *Ethics & the Environment* 20 (1): 67–97.

Paganopoulos, M. 2009. The concept of "Athonian economy" in the monastery of Vatopaidi. *Journal of Cultural Economy* 2 (3): 363–78.

Plumwood, V. 2007. A review of Deborah Bird Rose's *Reports from a wild country: Ethics for decolonisation*. *Australian Humanities Review* 42 (August): 1–4.

Randall, R. 2009. Loss and climate change: The cost of parallel narratives. *Ecopsychology* 1 (3): 118–29.

Roberts, J. 2008. The "returns to religion": Messianism, Christianity and the revolutionary tradition. Pts. 1 and 2. *Historical Materialism* 16 (2): 59–84; 16 (3): 77–103.

Roelvink, G. 2010. Collective action and the politics of affect. *Emotions, Space and Society* 3 (2): 111–8.

Roelvink, G., and J. K. Gibson-Graham. 2009. A postcapitalist politics of dwelling: Ecological humanities and community economies in conversation. *Australian Humanities Review* 46 (May): 145–58.

Roelvink, G., K. St. Martin, and J. K. Gibson-Graham, eds. 2015. *Making other worlds possible: Performing diverse economies*. Minneapolis: University of Minnesota Press.

Sprat, D. 2015. Recount: It's time to "do the math" again! A Breakthrough Online report. http://media.wix.com/ugd/148cb0_bb2e61584dbb403e8e33fd65b1c48e30.pdf.

Swyngedouw, E. 2010. Apocalypse forever? Post-political populism and the spectre of climate change. *Theory, Culture & Society* 27 (2–3): 213–32.

Steffen, W., W. Broadgate, L. Deutsch, O. Gaffney, and C. Ludwig. 2015. The trajectory of the Anthropocene: The great acceleration. *The Anthropocene Review* 2 (1): 81–98.

Utting, P. 2015. *Social and solidarity economy: Beyond the fringe*. London: Zed Books.

Weintrobe, S. 2012. *Engaging with climate change: Psychoanalytic and interdisciplinary perspectives*. London: Routledge.

Whyte, J. 2013. *Catastrophe and redemption: The political thought of Giorgio Agamben*. Albany, N.Y.: State University of New York Press.

Žižek, S. 2010. *Violence: Six sideways reflections*. London: Picador.

———. 2014. Fat-free chocolate and absolutely no smoking: Why our guilt about consumption is all-consuming. *Guardian*, 21 May. https://www.theguardian.com/artanddesign/2014/may/21/prix-pictet-photography-prize-consumption-slavoj-zizek.

Faiths with a Heart and Heartless Religions: Devout Alternatives to the Merciless Rationalization of Charity

Cihan Tuğal

The Left usually dismisses charity as demeaning intervention into the lives of oppressed classes, an obfuscation through which exploitation is legitimated. Few arguments by Marx and Engels are as deeply ingrained in Marxism as their statements on charity. This can be traced back to Marxism's common roots with liberalism. Marketization, religious reform, and liberal political economy undermined traditional conceptions of poverty and relief, which upheld interdependence between God, the rich, and the poor as sacrosanct. Marxism thus inherited an unshakable suspicion of heartfelt poverty alleviation, whereas today's liberalism has moved beyond its classical vulgarity to invigorate charity with a new spirit. Exploring Lucien Goldmann's take on Blaise Pascal and the ongoing reformulation of caritas within Christianity, this essay contends that a radically different conception of charity is possible and that charitable love is a battleground between conservative, liberal, and emancipatory understandings of religion, as recent developments within the Catholic Church demonstrate.

The sole aim of the Scripture is charity ... All bodies together, and all minds together, and all their products, are not equal to the least feeling of charity.
—Blaise Pascal, *Pensées*

To what extent want and suffering prevail among these unemployed ... I need not describe ... The philanthropy of the rich is a rain-drop in the ocean, lost in the moment of falling.
—Friedrich Engels, *The Condition of the Working Class in England*

Playing on Marx's comments on religion, this essay explores faith's contribution to the "merciless" thrusts of rationalization, liberalization, and capitalist development, as well as to their criticism. Some religious revivals have attacked traditionalist modes of generosity. These revivals have met resistance from religious circles in their quest to subordinate generosity to the making of the liberal subject. Neglecting such dimensions of charity, the Marxist criticism of philanthropy has narrowly focused on generosity's role in perpetrating and hiding the exploitation, dependence, and degradation of subordinate classes. This thinness of accepted Marxist wisdom on charity can actually be traced back to Marxism's common roots with liberalism and their shared distrust of interdependence. But the historical and contemporary struggles within charitable fields require a radical rethinking (if not total rejection) of Marx's and Engels's theses on charity, which remain unchallenged aspects of their theorization of religion.

Right before labeling religion the opium of the masses, Marx (2008a, 42) called it "the heart of a heartless world" (as well as "the spirit of a spiritless situation")—a once less emphasized twist in his essay "A Contribution to the Critique of Hegel's Philosophy of Right." When we scrutinize modern religion, however, we face a more complex reality. For instance, from the standpoint of modern volunteers and providers of charity, their actions indeed integrate "heart" and "spirit" with care. But the irony is that today's volunteering spirit deepens capitalist spiritlessness by pervading *religion itself* with means-ends calculations and an obsession with individual independence. Can we still call religion the spirit of a spiritless world? Was it always so in the nineteenth century? Can today's religion even be labeled "the opium" when it cultivates sober responsibility rather than drowsiness?

A second relatively neglected point in Marx's (2008a, 42) essay is the recognition that religion offers (not only an inverted expression but) a "protest" of the soulless (capitalist) world. Marx soon followed this with the claims that *real* criticism would replace spirited criticism and that religious protest only leads to an illusory happiness. Marx's statements were poetic, but his conclusions were hasty. We could rather look at religious protest of "soulless conditions" as *one kind of valid criticism that does not necessarily invalidate other kinds of criticism.* Some charitable practices constitute not simply the heart of a heartless world but rather a heart yearning for a different world order. A fresh look at the Salvation Army, Pascal, liberation theology, and today's Vatican could contribute to a strategy of sustainable redistributive transformation that would integrate love.

In recent philosophy, *agape* (the ancient Greek word for love) has indeed gained traction, suggesting that some Marxists now take "the heart" to be a necessary agent in socialist transformation rather than a distracting impediment in real criticism's path. But such realization has come at the expense of a further attack on charity, as both Badiou (2005) and Žižek (2010), today's foremost theorists of agape, have defined love in contradistinction to charity. This essay, in contrast, draws attention to the historical kinship between agape and charity by tracking the evolution of the concept of caritas in Christian thought and practice.

Charity in the Marxist Legacy

Marxists have learned from many aspects of faith. They have even contributed to the rehabilitation of some facets of religion.[1] In the past century and a half, however, charity has received only passing mention. Boer's (2007, 2009, 2011) massive three volumes, possibly the most comprehensive and in-depth discussion of Marxist debates on religion, mention charity less than a dozen times, even though they examine in depth the works of twenty-five key Marxists in some eleven hundred

1. These facets include the organization of the Catholic Church, the role of the clergy, and moral reform (Gramsci); messianism as well as the myths, stories, themes, theology, and doctrines of the Bible (Bloch 2009, 27); religion's role in protest, local autonomy, and community and class formation (Thompson 1966, 26–54, 118–20, 391–3, 397–9, 422–3); and last but not least, controversial religious figures such as Saint Paul (Badiou 2003, 4).

pages.[2] Is this simply a coincidence or is it because the original attack against charity by Marx and Engels is so ingrained in the social ethos of Marxism that it has remained unquestioned?

Rejection of charity is arguably at the foundation of the proletariat as an emancipatory class. When faced with the suggestion that a true practice of the social principles of Christianity would obviate communism, Marx (2008b, 83–4) fired back:

> The social principles of Christianity preach the necessity of a ruling and an oppressed class, and all they have for the latter is the pious wish the former will be charitable ... The social principles of Christianity preach cowardice, self-contempt, abasement, submission, dejection, in a word all the qualities of the canaille; and the proletariat, not wishing to be treated as canaille, needs its courage, its self-reliance, its pride and its sense of independence more than its bread. The social principles of Christianity are sneakish and the proletariat is revolutionary.[3]

In this poignant passage, Marx equated charity with cowardice and dependence. He opposed these to the rising (liberal) value of his age: self-reliance. Charity was so degrading that it should not taint the class that would liberate society; in fact, this class was defined by its lack of need for charitable acts.

Engels provided a much more empirically based critique of charity. He was indeed a firsthand observer of charity in a very specific and dramatic historical context: England of the Industrial Revolution, with its Malthusian liberalism. Under the influence of political economy and the increasing clout of the business class, much of traditional English poor relief had been recently dismantled. The remaining public relief and private philanthropy were only raindrops in an "ocean" of misery (Engels 1987, 117, 122). Engels perceived these relics of cross-class care as strong indicators of "hypocrisy" (224). And what could be a closer parallel to our own liberalizing global context and the mushrooming of philanthropies therein, as well as to the current critical perception of the latter?

Under these circumstances, Engels turned to the ethical consequences of philanthropy, since its actual financial impact was so little. The conclusions he reached about these effects resonate with what Marxism has come to regard as the essential traits of charity. Philanthropy is a hypocritical and diminished returning to "the plundered victims the hundredth part of what belongs to them" (Engels 2001, 391), but its real significance lies in the way in which it weakens the proletariat's spirit and restricts its mobility. It not only legitimates ill-gotten wealth by hiding the fact that what is being given to the poor was extracted from them in the first place but it is also used to further enslave them:

> Charity which degrades him who gives more than him who takes; charity which treads the downtrodden still deeper in the dust, which demands that the degraded,

---

2. This otherwise extensive survey mostly neglects Marxist theorization of non–Judeo-Christian religion, but Marxists seem to be thin on Islamic charity too. For instance, *Marxism and the Muslim World* (Rodinson 1972), arguably the major classic in this field, mentions *zakat*, *sadaqa*, and charity only a few times and quite dismissively.

3. This is a modified translation based on Draper (1971).

the pariah cast out by society, shall first surrender the last that remains to him, his very claim to manhood, shall first beg for mercy before your mercy deigns to press, in the shape of an alms, the brand of degradation upon his brow ... The English bourgeoisie is charitable out of self-interest; it gives nothing outright, but regards its gifts as a business matter, makes a bargain with the poor, saying: "If I spend this much upon benevolent institutions, I thereby purchase the right not to be troubled any further, and you are bound thereby to stay in your dusky holes and not to irritate my tender nerves by exposing your misery." (276–7)

Marx's and Engels's generalizations about charity were oft repeated across generations of Marxists. Kautsky (2001) traced the emergence of charity to the breaking up of primitive communism among the early Christians and to the emergence of classes and exploitation among them. In early Christianity, mutual aid societies had fostered collective property, but these mutated into charitable institutions as the community came to depend on rich members; class hatred against them was abolished within it.[4]

After these classical contributions to the discussion of religion, there has been even less focus on charity, almsgiving, and related topics[5] as Marxists and neo-Marxists became more concerned with other aspects of religion. Antonio Gramsci (1992, 100), even though he was among the handful of Marxists to have written extensively on religion, reproduced this orthodoxy regarding the social doctrine of Christianity. That alms is a Christian *duty*, he pointed out, implies that there will always be poor people. The timelessness of this duty also implied that class distinction and inequality too were inseparable parts of human existence.[6] As a consequence, Gramsci concluded, charity is simply a way to moralize social questions and thereby avoid political interventions.

In what seems to be the only explicit Marxist theorization of charity after Marx and Engels, Žižek (2010, 117, and see 4, 356) constructs it as the absolute other of proper love: "Charity [is] one of the names (and practices) of *non-love* today. When, confronted with the starving child, we are told: 'For the price of a couple of cappuccinos, you can save her life!,' the true message is: 'For the price of a couple of cappuccinos, you can continue in your ignorant and pleasurable life, not only not feeling any guilt, but even feeling good for having participated in the struggle against suffering!'" For Žižek, the ultimate function of charity is reproduction—that of the consumerist individual, but that of the economy as well: capitalism needs to be injected with charity to postpone its crisis (240). Charity is reduced, in this account, to a functional instrument of capitalist domination.

Even when Marxists have stumbled upon the emancipatory potential of charity (and upon elements of it that cannot simply be reduced to capitalist control), they have sought to dismiss it. Badiou (2003, 87) singles out a term that is key to Paul's epistles, "agape," which he laments has been "translated for a long time as 'charity,' a term

---

4. Also see Luxemburg (2003) on the classical Marxist criticism of early Christian communism and its charity/alms.
5. An essay by Hal Draper (1971), which treats charity as the negative reference point against which the Marxist idea of self-emancipation develops, is an exception.
6. For a criticism of the argument that Christianity assumes that inequality and poverty are immutable, see Collier (2001, 89–101).

that no longer means much to us." In a quite compelling way, Badiou reconstructs agape as the subjective operation that would allow a revolutionary intervention in the situation. But who is the "us" in this quote? Marxists? Christians? (Post)modern wo/men? And why was agape translated as charity for a long time?

A quick look at the numbers reveals that charity is increasingly central to our era. In the world's leader of giving, the United States, around 95 percent of households contribute to charity. Lest this be perceived as an essentially American practice, it should be noted that within the United States charitable giving has also sharply increased in the last decades. The total amount of dollars donated to charity has climbed from roughly $50 billion in 1980 to $325 billion in 2014. The number of charitable organizations in the United States is nearly a whopping one and a half million.[7] While the statistics might not be as impressive in much of the rest of the world, the numbers of people who donate to charity and who volunteer worldwide have increased from 2009 to 2013 (Charities Aid Foundation 2014, 15). Charity clearly means a lot to many people. Badiou's ambiguous "us" is symptomatic of the Marxist (and modern, sometimes even Christian) downplaying of charity.

Nevertheless, the linguistic confusion that Badiou points out is not accidental. By the early fourth century, Christians had exchanged the Latin word *caritas* in place of the Greek *agape* (Lindberg 2008, 16). The issue at stake was not just translating a word. For the Greeks, agape connoted love of family, friends, and the motherland. But in biblical usage, it came to be identified with the love of God and of one's "neighbor." The Bible used the word "neighbor" metaphorically: in reality, it urged Christians to reach beyond their immediate networks and care for excluded groups, which were usually neglected by the Romans (see Gutiérrez 1988, 116; Lindberg 2008). Behavioral transformations paralleled this etymological shift. In the classical Greco-Roman world, "philanthropy" involved help among and between the nobles; it further distinguished them from the rabble. Charitable "love" replaced philanthropic "love" to mark the common humanity of the rich and the poor (Lindberg 2008, 46). In sum, love came to mean something new for the Christians, and this necessitated a transformed vocabulary with novel connotations.

In many recent translations and exegeses, the biblical agape is indeed rendered as love (since it involves more than almsgiving). This is a remarkable break from, for example, the King James Version, which used love and charity interchangeably. Nevertheless, this clarification has introduced another potential misunderstanding: for centuries, charity did not *simply* mean almsgiving. It rather suggested the inseparability of aid and divine love.[8] If one strong window into the meaning of a word shows what it is semantically differentiated from, we can see the disastrousness of this linguistic shift by considering the following: in Badiou's and Žižek's work, we understand the true nature of love by distinguishing it from charity.

---

7. See "Charitable Giving Statistics," National Philanthropic Trust, accessed 11 June 2016, http://www.nptrust.org/philanthropic-resources/charitable-giving-statistics.

8. See, for instance, Pullan (1994, 31–2) for the blurred lines between divine love, charity, and communion during the Counter-Reformation, as well as for the continuum between acts of love and acts of charity in medieval confraternities (183–4).

By contrast, for one early modern Christian thinker (Pascal; see more about him below), the primary binary opposite of charity was cupidity/covetousness (and its secondary binary opposite was reason). Charity as divine love could have been primarily opposed to (the emergent) spiritual callousness and/or atheism, but Pascal instead took the atheist as an interlocutor. By directly targeting cupidity,[9] Pascal communicated a very strong message that has been relatively neglected: charity, not only as love but simultaneously as care of the self and others, is the only way to reach the Divinity who has forsaken this earth. I thus argue that recognizing the historical kinship between agape and caritas would open new paths for emancipatory politics rather than undermine it, if charity is understood as the loving engagement with the less fortunate rather than pouring breadcrumbs upon them.

It is with Goldmann's foray into the Pauline "orthodoxy" of the Jansenists that we can start to restore charitable love's revolutionary potential. Even though this is not his intention, Goldmann teaches us that caring engagement with the wretched of the earth involves a love not simply of what they are but also of what they have the potential to become (as followers and leaders). Just like Lenin discovered in the Russian worker a potential interlocutor of the revolutionary intellectual (Lih 2011, 43–4), a reconstructed Goldmann would invite a wager for charitable love. Nevertheless, as will be discussed further below, a full rehabilitation of charity requires a discussion beyond Goldmann, whose Marxist incorporation of Christianity stops at the figure of Pascal. For this, we will have to engage with how Catholicism dealt with attacks against charity well after Pascal.

Goldmann's Hidden Theme

Illuminating insights regarding charity, though not any theorization of it, come from an unexpected figure. After (implicitly) recognizing the historical centrality of the attack against medieval charity early in his opus magnum, *The Hidden God*, Lucien Goldmann (renowned for his literary criticism rather than for theorizing charitable religion) buries generosity in between the lines. Yet we will see that the obliteration of medieval charity was the key to the making of a godless, individualist world (which is at the center of his theorization). Let's first walk through Goldmann's main arguments and then return later to our theme (with Pascal's help).

In his analysis of literature and its religious and philosophical roots, Goldmann emphasizes that the Cartesian understanding of the individual obliterates the need for (the Christian) God and transcendental values. Goldmann does not discuss charity in this context but quotes a paragraph from Descartes arguing that in a (deist) world where individuals took full responsibility for their actions there would be no need for charity. Descartes (quoted in Goldmann 1964, 28) has coolly stated that "God has so established the order of things and has joined men together in so

---

9. Saints Augustine and Thomas Aquinas also opposed caritas and cupidity, but for them the latter was *disorderly* love for earthly goods (Lindberg 2008, 106–7). Pascal's revolutionary break with this premodern theology lies in his recognition that the love of earthly goods constitutes an *order*, which in Pascal's language means a realm of being and acting with its specific ethics and system.

close a society, that even if every man were to be concerned only with himself, and to show no charity towards others, he would still, in the normal course of events, be working on their behalf in everything that lay within his power." The "hidden hand of the market" might have been explicitly theorized by Adam Smith, but it was clearly anticipated by earlier modern philosophy.

As Goldmann rightly points out, the consequences of the apotheosis of the responsible individual are momentous. If individuals *can* and *should* completely control their actions, then other human beings (along with the rest of nature) become mere objects for their responsible calculations. Even if the believer in such a position is still a Christian on paper, this becomes nominal Christianity: such a viewpoint recognizes no real authority beyond the individual (and therefore, no truly Christian God). This has epochal *social* consequences too. Individualists are hostile to the ignorant masses who fail to put reason at the center of their actions (Goldmann 1964, 28–34). Their rationalist God is pointedly elitist, Goldmann suggests: "The rationalists were all the more ready to accept the God who manifested himself through the rational order ... since, during the seventeenth and eighteenth centuries, He also came to perform a very useful service: that of controlling the 'irrational' and dangerous reactions of the 'ignorant masses' who could neither understand nor appreciate the value of the consistently selfish and rational activity of economic man and of his social and political creations" (32). It is indeed through mass action that any real authority beyond the individual remains after the eighteenth century: "If—in defiance of the God of enlightened rationalism—the ignorant masses have used political and trade-union action in order to impose some measure of control on the excesses of individualism in economic life, the absence of ethical forces capable of directing the use of scientific discoveries and of using them for the benefit of a genuine human community threatens to have unimaginable consequences" (32-3). God has left this earth. And the masses, Goldmann implies, have become a weak substitute for this absence (a quite different, and provocative, reading of the emergence of the proletariat when compared to those of Marx, Polanyi, and Draper). With Pascal, Western thought seeks to rediscover ethics in the absence of Church-sanctioned values. Pascal attempts this through "wagering" the existence of God: not a deist God that can be proven to exist through rational thinking (as for Descartes) but a God the existence of whom one can only "risk" and "hope."

Pascal's God is unlike the medieval Christian God too, since he is no longer immediately present. Still, his absence is starkly different from the removed, deist God, for he still expects certain actions and judges people. God is now "hidden": both present (as observer and judge) *and* absent (as supreme and effective authority). This is Goldman's reconstruction of Pascal, to whom we will return later in order to highlight the theme that Goldmann has downplayed (that of charity).

In Marxism, Goldmann (1964, 300-2) argues, this risky hope changes direction. Marx's wager is the proletariat and its historical mission to build the classless society: according to Goldmann's heterodox reading, Marx's singling out of the proletariat was a hope-driven act of the will (much like Pascal's wager) rather than solely a result of rational analysis.[10] The trajectory that connected Pascal to Marx and made them both essential to Goldmann's project was the unlikely duo's common objection to the liberal-rationalist belief that the pursuits of the utilitarian individual would ensure stability and happiness in a post-Christian world. Success and reason, Goldmann held, were poor replacements for good and evil. But only collectivities, not individuals, could resurrect good and evil. The tragedy of the modern condition was that it necessitated a "wager" in a scenario on which the individual had little impact. Goldmann's concept of the wager involved "risk"—the likelihood of "failure"—coupled with (somewhat illusory) "hope" (187–8, 302). Whereas the medieval Christian sought and found God and the modern individual has ceased seeking, the authentic Christian was bound to perpetually seek God, even after finding him (295).

Goldmann's ultimate heresy was not simply taking religion seriously (that would be forgivable for many Marxists today) but was also putting ethical creativity at the center of the Marxist emancipatory project. He oversimplified history, however, by attributing nihilism to the arc that connects Descartes to Ricardo and Smith. Rather than necessarily undoing transcendental values, being success oriented can actually foster its own ethics through a novel understanding of charity, as we shall see further below. In order to appreciate the complexity of this new development, we first need to unearth the theme that Goldmann has so carefully concealed.

From Goldmann Back to Pascal

It is symptomatic that charity is mentioned only a few times in *The Hidden God*, yet (through the discussion of several key quotes from others and in one of Goldmann's characteristically long footnotes) it turns out to be pivotal to the whole book. The "faculty of charity," as Goldmann (1964, 72–3n1) recognizes in a footnote only to never mention again, is indispensable for the believer's wager: "It is, in my view, obvious that this 'wholly pure light' [by which Pascal wishes to find goodness] can come only from Divine Grace, which reveals itself not to reason but to that faculty of charity which surpasses the intellect, and which is not an intellectual light but an illumination of the heart."

Moreover, charity's centrality to Divine Grace was not Pascal's invention but a recurrent theme in Jansenism. Pascal's contribution, according to Goldmann, was combining this absolute faith in charity with a deep dedication to reason. This Goldmann shows through discussing moderate and extremist Jansenism (the former a compromise between faith and reason, the latter a complete rejection of reason). According to Goldmann, Barcos (quoted in Goldmann 1964, 159) exemplifies extremist Jansenism, as demonstrated by one of his letters to Mother Angelique, another prominent Jansenist: "Thus, Reverend Mother, I like both the matter and the style of your letter, for the ease with which you allow your mind to wander from the laws of human reason, placing no other limits upon it but those of charity, which has no limits when it is perfect and yet too many when it is weak." Pascal also extensively polemicized

10. Today, it appears that the proletariat has left the earth (in the Pascalian sense). Whether it can come back is a faith question as much as an empirical one. This essay, however, would not be the right place to discuss whether the proletariat is still worthy of such quasi-theological "investment." Regarding Goldmann's own position on the topic, see Cohen (1994, chap. 8).

against reason, but he still spent a great deal of his life on scientific projects. In Pascal (quoted in Goldmann 1964, 200) we again see the centrality of charity to Jansenist antirationalism, followed again by Goldmann's silence on charity: "Jesus Christ and Saint Paul follow the order of charity and not that of the mind; for they wanted to stir men up, not to instruct them." Goldmann insists that the above is not an argument against reason. It is part of a larger argument in which reason cannot attain God/order: it needs help from the heart. Human existence is a quest for order, but reason cannot capture order; it can only construct fragments. The existence of order/God is a wager.

The belief in limitless charity struck home when Pascal's sister Jacqueline gave her wealth and life to charity and prayer, thus depriving Pascal of funds, which he intended to use for scientific research. For Goldmann, the discussion of Jacqueline's sacrifice serves the same purpose as his discussion of Barcos: to demonstrate that (in the Pascalian "tragic" vision) charity without calculation (i.e., pure submission to love) is not Christian enough. Goldmann defines the Pascalian tragic vision as a desire for a paradoxical unity between two apparently contradictory ideals (atomistic reason and totality), defying Badiou's (2003, 50) reading of Pascal as a thinker of balanced contradictions.[11] Pascalian Christianity aimed to unite total submission to charitable love *and* complete dedication to reason. Giving away everything to charity (even if the proceeds go to the religious sect on the correct path) would deter one from science and therefore from the dialectical tragedy so dear to Goldmann. A charitable way of life is potentially self-destructive, though it is also the only way to God.

We can further appreciate the place of charity in the tragic vision by directly consulting the *Pensées*. In Pascal's seminal work, charity is total devotion to God and everything that entails. It is used almost interchangeably with love and heart. Charity involves pity *and care* not only of others but also of oneself: "But as for those who live without knowing Him and without seeking Him, they judge themselves so little worthy of their own care, that they are not worthy of the care of others; and it needs all the charity of the religion which they despise, not to despise them even to the point of leaving them to their folly" (Pascal 2003, 58).

This is not at all surprising given the premodern, noncondescending usage of charity. Early Christians' use of the word caritas is complex and ambiguous. Saint Augustine's focus on caritas is as open to interpretation as Saint Paul's agape. While some commentators render Augustine's caritas as love of Christ, others see in it a call for love of fellow human beings and for the recognition of their dignity. Arguably, Saint Augustine paved the way for the later melding of benevolence and love (in the word charity) through his Christian rehabilitation of the classical Roman notion of self-sacrificing friendship with one's neighbor. In the Roman tradition, such friendship was based on common taste (and by implication, shared class status). Saint Augustine erected caring for one's neighbor on a new foundation: the love of God, who wanted to see the formation of tight human bonds (Augustine 1944, 48): "There is no true friendship unless You [God] weld it between souls that cleave together through that charity which is shed in our hearts by the Holy Spirit who is given to us." With this discursive move, caritas lost its class boundedness and became a name for the love of human

---

11. See Badiou (2005, 212–22) for a more sympathetic reading of Pascal.

beings in general. It is very clear, however, that Saint Augustine did not develop this thought in the direction of charitable giving in today's sense.

In medieval times, charity involved benevolent giving but went beyond it. Charity's meaning was more institutionalized and fixed. According to Thomas Aquinas, caritas was the Christian's closeness to God, which requires loving one's neighbor (as for Saint Augustine), the outward appearance of which is beneficence. A new formula crystallized with Aquinas's (1917, 262–372) writings: love of Christ and love of the poor are an indissoluble whole.[12] Aquinas's reconceptualization of charity also involved a defense of socioeconomic hierarchies against a few sects that had developed more egalitarian interpretations of caritas (Rubin 1987, 62–3, 95–6).

As Geremek (1994) shows, the centrality of charity marked not only high theology but also everyday practice. Medieval Christianity assumed that the rich and the poor mutually required each other's existence: the former needed the blessings and prayers of the latter to secure a place in heaven while the latter needed help from the former even to survive (living wages were not on the horizon for the crushing majority of society). Geremek also demonstrates that this explicit recognition of interdependence was part and parcel of a broader philosophy of interconnection.[13] The moral well-being of the good (well-to-do) Christian depended on a proper relation with the poor. Nevertheless, as the Middle Ages drew to a close and as marketization created immense wealth and misery, medieval charity proved to be highly inadequate in addressing the emergent problems (Dyer 2012). Moreover, despite growing uneasiness with the hierarchical assumptions of medieval charity and attempts to overhaul them (including those of the Franciscans), late medieval theology could not change donors' habitually condescending approach to the poor (Mollat 1986, 102–13, 156–7, 182–3). Under these economic and moral pressures, traditional charity would either be completely revamped or else marginalized by a rival ethic.

The defense came from Pascal. While building on the medieval notions discussed above, he developed a novel understanding of charity. He called charity an "order": a way of orienting oneself to existence.[14] Each order has a logic peculiar to itself, internalized by its practitioners (an idea that foreshadowed Bourdieu's concepts of

---

12. Some have argued, however, that a tradition that runs from Saint Paul to Saint Aquinas also posits a clear hierarchy between the love of God and the love of the poor. It is only with Saint Francis, according to these scholars, that the love of the poor becomes a good in itself (without hierarchical dependence on the love of God), though some precursors are observable in Eastern Christianity and in Old English homilies (Buhrer 2012).

13. Similar notions of interdependence marked class relations in the beginning of the modern era too. Kayatekin and Charusheela (2004) point out that sharecropping African Americans deployed notions of fairness, justness, reciprocity, and dignity to protest, to insult, and to make demands on landlords within the postbellum order. They did not base their claims on the independent, individual rights of black people but on the mutual obligations of interdependent sharecroppers and landlords. The landlords' assumptions about blacks' inferiority came with a set of obligations on their part to protect and care for sharecroppers, which enabled blacks' protests and demands. While in both the postbellum order and in medieval charity reciprocity and interdependence are based on essentially hierarchical assumptions, twentieth-century "solidarism" demonstrated how they could be wedded to relatively more egalitarian values and practices.

14. Others, including Aquinas, also called charity an order, but not with the same sociological overtones and insights.

field and habitus). Charity was, for Pascal, superior to the two other orders (of flesh and intellect, which have as their logic the accumulation of power/wealth and knowledge). It is not accidental that "during the last four years of his life Pascal's health grew steadily worse, and he also led an increasingly austere life, devoting much of his time, energy and money to caring for the poor" (Goldmann 1964, 410). Philosophical and sociological discussions of Pascal's "order" of charity usually omit discussion of care (e.g., Bourdieu 2000, 102, and see 97), but for this "post-Jansenist," love of God and of fellow human beings were inseparable. If caritas did not involve giving to the poor for the man who said that "the sole aim of the Scripture is charity," he would have spent his last years in silent contemplation of God. Instead, he sought the creator through "caring for the poor." With Pascal, charitable love became the solid linchpin (an "order") that connects theology and care. Nevertheless, whereas Aquinas's formulation of charity was in sync with his times, Pascal's was an untimely intervention.

Liberal Ethics

Pascal's clinging to charity as the fundamental "order" of Christianity came at dusk. During his lifetime, charity was already under debilitating attack, even from within Christianity itself. Pascal's pleas did not constitute an adequate shield. A fuller Christian reformulation would have to wait for liberation theology's discovery of charity's sworn enemy: political economy, along with its insider's critique.

As European markets expanded from the twelfth to the fourteenth centuries, so did cults of charity. Mendicant orders challenged the authority of the church. Cities became flooded with vagrants, posing both a moral and an administrative problem. From the fourteenth to the sixteenth centuries, Catholic charity went through considerable rationalization, which prepared the scene for the Reformation—despite common belief, Protestantism did not invent suspicion of the poor and of charity (Geremek 1994; Mollat 1986, 290–2). Moreover, the Protestant attack against medieval charitable ethics was not as harsh as the Malthusian one. The Elizabethan poor laws, the most institutionalized policy outcome of Protestantism, put the poor in their places but were not completely heartless. For instance, they punished (or imposed compulsory work on) the able-bodied vagrant but also dictated relief for the aged, the orphaned, and the disabled. Every Christian was guaranteed, in ideal conditions, a proper place in the community (Polanyi 2001, 91).

It was neither the bare functioning of the economy nor Protestantism but rather political economic thought that decisively swept away medieval protections of the poor. Ricardo, Malthus, Burke, and others reasoned that the best method of creating an efficient society was to starve those unwilling or unable to work (Polanyi 2001, chap. 10). These worthless creatures were artificially sustained by human laws; under natural circumstances, most of them would be eliminated. As a result of their influence, the negation of religious generosity reached its peak in the mid-nineteenth century. This was the height of the bourgeoisie's fight against all other existing classes and their cultures. The fight was eventually lost, and bourgeois ethics had to be tempered through the welfare state's caring for the poor.

One of the most dangerous tendencies of the ideas of Marx and Engels (and consequently of Marxism) is to inherit this ultrarationalist bourgeois attack against religious generosity. Here we need to recall Ernst Bloch's (2009) warning against the conflation of the Enlightenment as such with bourgeois hyperrationalism. Today's Marxist attacks against charity indeed reproduce bourgeois rationalism instead of creating a new ethos of generosity.

We should also seriously consider how the bourgeoisie itself needed to tone down its own hyperrationalist tendencies in order to become a hegemonic class. Right before the rise of the welfare state, the bourgeoisie experimented with a form of generosity that would be in line with the sway of the market. Even if many of the institutions that resulted died away by the end of the nineteenth century, one of them is with us today: the Salvation Army.

The 1870s and 1880s moved away from the initial heartlessness of early Victorianism and political economy. Reformers decided that the poor had a right to exist too. Yet sufficiently infused with merciless political economy, they could not go back to medieval charity or even to earlier forms of Protestant care. The charitable organizations springing up especially throughout the Anglo-Saxon world during these decades put an emphasis on *transforming* the poor. The right form of care would take the most wretched, seemingly most hopeless, most undeserving of the poor and create good workers out of them.

The Salvation Army's positive emphasis on the poor and their capacity for regeneration led Engels (2004, 24) to exalt the organization: "The Salvation Army ... revives the propaganda of early Christianity, appeals to the poor as the elect, fights capitalism in a religious way, and thus fosters an element of early Christian class antagonism, which one day may become troublesome to the well-to-do people who now find the ready money for it." Engels's misrepresentation of this new type of charity as a class war partially emanated from Marxism's kinship with liberalism. The moment Engels perceived initiative and independence on the part of subordinate strata, he glorified this initiative as class struggle. Any serious blow to interdependence was welcome.

Engels thus neglected a new style and era in the making of class power: the willing and active mobilization of subordinate strata for the sustenance and expansion of upper-class rule (which Gramsci would later conceptualize as "hegemonic" politics). Whereas the bourgeoisie built its hegemony mostly through political and economic concessions for a century or so, at the end of the twentieth century religion (and particularly charity) again moved to the core of active subaltern consent for capitalism. Religion no longer only puts to sleep—quite the contrary. It empowers, energizes, and mobilizes the poor. Caffeine has displaced opium.

There should be no surprise that the Salvation Army is today one of the biggest civic organizations in the United States. In 1993, it was the organization that Americans contributed to most (Allahyari 2000). Today, the organization not only shelters the poor but transforms them. The massive funds it receives are mobilized to build prison-like environments where the poor learn the virtues of sobriety and hard work through a strict regimentation of their lives.

The Catholic Wars over Caritas

If Badiou is *partially* right in stating that charity no longer means much, it is because of the centuries-long attack against its traditional pillars. Catholicism has been fighting a rearguard battle to retain charity's import. Until recently, this struggle rarely made headlines.[15] But the last two popes' efforts have pushed charity to the top of the agenda.[16]

Benedict's Way

While caritas might not mean much to "us," it found its way into the titles of the previous pope's two pathbreaking encyclicals. In these writings Pope Benedict XVI made two important interventions. First, and quite crucial for our purposes, he recentered Christian attention on the concept of caritas and sought to give it a new, more conservative, meaning. Even though the meanings of love and charity had been evolving in the Christian tradition for centuries, this was arguably the most major theological intervention since Pascal into the concept of caritas (a condensed term that captures both love and charity). Second, not only did he utilize this theological intervention to reinforce Pope John Paul II's disruption of Catholic social doctrine's shift to the left but he also attempted to swing it further to the right.

Pope Benedict XVI's first encyclical, *God is Love* (*Deus Caritas est*), issued in 2005, took its title from a phrase in the First Epistle of John. This encyclical attacked sex-centered modern (and ancient) culture and reminded moderns of Christian love's superiority to their flesh-bound version.[17] Having thus reinforced his conservative credentials (if they needed any beefing up),[18] Pope Benedict XVI moved on to claim the territory of the Christian Left.

In 2009, Benedict issued a third encyclical, *Love in Truth* (*Caritas in Veritate*), that directly addressed the issue of charity, playing on the ambiguity and double meaning of caritas. The second half of Benedict's (2005, sec. 26–7, 31) first encyclical had also focused on charity, evaluating the Marxist criticism thereof. These encyclicals (fulfilling all Marxist worries) offered charity as an alternative to collectivization and state property (though not to the state's support of social initiative), yet "chose" not to discuss the other dimension of the Marxist prescription: the self-organization of

15. Exceptions include Pius XII's calls to stop the Nazi threat through charitable love and Paul VI's speech during the last general meeting of the Second Vatican Council, in which he stated that "charity has been the principal religious feature of this council." See "Address of Pope Paul VI During the Last General Meeting of the Second Vatican Council," 7 December 1965, https://w2.vatican.va/content/paul-vi/en/speeches/1965/documents/hf_p-vi_spe_19651207_epilogo-concilio.html.

16. Certainly, these efforts had precursors in previous papal thinking (see especially Paul VI 1967, sec. 44, 67).

17. In actual modern practice, it may not be that easy to disentangle the two, since Christians may draw on more than one framework, and even among the most committed, it takes a lot of effort to align prescriptions with everyday activity (see Swidler 2001, 46–51, 60–6, 69).

18. See "From Hitler Youth to the Vatican," *Guardian*, 20 April 2005, http://www.theguardian.com/world/2005/apr/20/catholicism.religion3.

disadvantaged strata. The Christian "base communities," the spiritual leaders of which Cardinal Ratzinger had repressed, were also left out of the discussion.

In *Love in Truth*, Benedict shifted away from earlier, more structural church doctrine on poverty. The document boldly called for an economy based on gratuity and reciprocity (Benedict 2009, sec. 36, 38–9) in an apparently antiliberal (almost "Polanyian")[19] fashion. Nevertheless, the broader logic of the document insidiously (even if still partially) aligned caritas with liberalism. From 1891 onward, social encyclicals had targeted free-market economics and capitalism (not in order to abolish private property but to put it to social use through the moral guardianship of the church and the state). The word caritas came to capture both spiritual love and the care of others, especially the poor (O'Brien 2013, 576–7). These encyclicals not only criticized the unpleasant aspects of modernity but also openly named their root causes: liberal ideology and the capitalist economy (Laurent 2010).

Benedict's encyclical, in contrast, made no reference to liberalism or capitalism. Unlike his predecessors, he blamed the selfish individuals who abuse property (and occasionally backward and irresponsible countries) rather than liberalism and capitalism as such (Laurent 2010, 532–3; Benedict 2009, sec. 22, 33, 36). While avoiding open confrontation with (either economic or cultural) liberalism, the pope's first encyclical had targeted the obsession with eroticism. Caritas thus became the proper antidote to both cultural liberalism (as eros without divine love)[20] *and* poverty.

Benedict's encyclical provided ample documentation of liberalism's crushing consequences but did so without discussing the political and ideological causes, unlike even Jean Paul II, who is sometimes taken to be more favorable to capitalism than Benedict XVI (2009, sec. 22; Griffiths 2010, 113; Laurent 2010, 534–5). Benedict thus remained a critic of inequality, unemployment, and greed but sought solutions in the further encouragement of (individual and "social") "responsibility." To the extent that the encyclical called for redistribution, it highlighted that public assistance should promote individual responsibility and initiative, much in line with the Salvation Army's liberal charity (Benedict 2009, sec. 47; Laurent 2010, 542).

Jean Paul II had successfully aborted post-1960s leftist heresies within the Vatican (see Eagleton 2005), with ample help from Cardinal Ratzinger, yet the Catholic Church had apparently remained committed to an "option for the poor" in line with the heretics' teachings. The words "option for the poor" were first mentioned by a Jesuit leader in 1968 and were then systematized into a whole new way of thinking by the liberation theologian Gustavo Gutiérrez (1988), and "some devotees of Cardinal Ratzinger's early critiques of political theology were longing for a retrenchment from the Catholic Church's heavy involvement in social action, an engagement that, the suppression of Liberation Theology aside, had proceeded apace under his predecessor John Paul II" (Christiansen 2010, 4). But when Ratzinger was ordained as the Pope,

---

19. Benedict's language is reminiscent of Polanyi's critique of the liberal economy and creates the impression that he has read the author (or at least, those Polanyi has inspired). There are also close parallels between his arguments and Mauss's (1990). Nevertheless, he departs from both thinkers by ultimately subordinating reciprocity to markets and individuals.

20. See Benedict XVI (2005, sec. 5, 11). The other face of cultural liberalism on which Benedict (2009, sec. 26, 61) waged war was "relativism."

he embarked on a path of *taming* Gutiérrez's preference for the poor rather than *excluding* it.[21] He further fortified the doctrinal investment in caritas and accentuated the term's tight links to the care of the poor, but he laid a strong slant of individual responsibility onto this package. For liberation theologians, the "option for the poor" involved promoting the self-organization of the poor in "base communities"; for Benedict, it instead meant socially responsible business, a more caring (and church-promoting) state, and stronger international oversight (by mainstream organizations such as the United Nations).

Liberation Theology Travels to the Vatican

In glaring contrast to Benedict, his successor Pope Francis has incited Caritas Internationalis, a platform of 165 Catholic charitable organizations, to uphold the Christianity of the poor against the current world order (Roberts 2015). While Benedict banished Gutiérrez even when appropriating his words, Francis had Gutiérrez in his company when addressing Caritas.

Francis pursues the same line in his papal exhortations and encyclicals. He is not content with simply attacking capitalism and upholding charity (which he frequently does), but he also wages a war against self-centered, pleasure-seeking, consumerist charitable philistinism, suggesting that he has perhaps read and absorbed Marxist criticisms of charity (Francis 2013, sec. 180): "Nor should our loving response to God be seen simply as an accumulation of small personal gestures to individuals in need, a kind of 'charity à la carte,' or a series of acts aimed solely at easing our conscience ... Both Christian preaching and life ... are meant to have an impact on society."

What more could a pope say to urge Christians to avoid soothing their guilt with "a couple of cappuccinos" worth of dollars? In line with his approach to charity, Francis (2013, sec. 59, 188, 202, 218) also draws attention to economic "structures" that put poor people at a disadvantage, whereas Benedict (2009, sec. 17, 42) sought to reduce (though not dismiss) the centrality of this concept in Church doctrine. Francis also avoids begging the poor to become responsible; he instead calls for globally shared (and "differentiated") responsibility while pointing out that the poor usually suffer the most from society's (and power-holders') irresponsible practices (Francis 2013, sec. 54, 90, 206, 240; 2015, sec. 2, 26, 48–52, 95, 158). Conservative forces in the Church are highly suspicious of these pro-poor moves (see Gagliarducci 2015). They are also scandalized to see the Vatican's charitable arm, Caritas, join the World Social Forum, allegedly a crypto-communist organization (see Skojec 2014). The fight over caritas remains unresolved.[22]

21. Despite being solidly anti–liberation theology, Benedict (unsurprisingly) appropriated the phrase "option for the poor" by citing two encyclicals of Jean Paul II rather than the original coiners of the phrase (Cahill 2010, 304).

22. Just as Benedict claimed continuity with all post-1891 social encyclicals, Francis claims he follows those of Benedict XVI. See "Pope Francis: Charity in Truth Is the Basis for Peace," *Vatican* Radio, 10 February 2014, http://en.radiovaticana.va/news/2014/10/02/pope_francis_charity_in_truth_is_the_basis_for_peace/1107727.

The struggle over caritas frequently erupts between the lines rather than being fought openly. Benedict XVI's (2005, sec. 33) encyclicals sustained Ratzinger's witch hunt but did so without openly

The current pope's approach to charity is open to the usual misunderstandings, both of rightist and leftist varieties. Conservative criticism of liberation theology assumes that its proponents have moved away from charity to social justice (Lynch 1994). This assumption also shapes some left-wing criticism of Pope Francis: the pope emphasizes charity, so he has not really internalized liberation theology; he should emphasize social justice instead.[23] Neither the Left nor the Right completely understands liberation theology since they both tend to see it as Marxism in Christian clothing. Both positions misconstrue liberation theology's position on charity, which does not construct charitable love and structural transformation as binary opposites, no matter how ingrained the absolute belief in their mutual exclusivity might be in leftist thought.[24] Rather, as Gutiérrez points out, charity necessitates an investment in structural transformation.

In his recent 2015 address to the Caritas assembly, Gutiérrez plainly stated that theology "is not religious metaphysics, it is a *reflection on the practice of charity and justice*; it can provide inspiration to those who are engaged in the practice of charity and justice" when faced with "the biggest gap between rich and poor that humanity has ever witnessed."[25] Gutiérrez's ongoing commitment to charity is not random but is an essential part of liberation theology, as his classic book on the subject clarifies. His comments invalidate one kind of attack against the liberationist embrace of charity: "By preaching the Gospel message, by its sacraments, and by the charity of its members, the Church proclaims and shelters the gift of the Kingdom of God in the heart of human history. The Christian community professes a 'faith which works through charity.' It is—at least ought to be—real charity, action, and commitment to the service of others" (Gutiérrez 1988, 9, and see 6). Significantly, Gutiérrez supports this argument by a quote from Pascal (quoted in Gutiérrez 1988, 181n39): "All bodies together, and all minds together, and all their products, are not equal to the least feeling of charity ... From all bodies and minds, we cannot produce a feeling of true charity."

But as crucial as Pascal's incorporation into liberation theology is the sublation of his theorization. As mentioned above, Pascal's preliminary theorization of charity could not protect the term from the liberal-rationalist (and ultimately political-economic) onslaught. Gutiérrez (1988, 116) offers a much more comprehensive understanding of charity by sublating (the critique of) political economy too:

> It is also necessary to avoid the pitfalls of an individualistic charity. As it has been insisted in recent years, the neighbor is not only a person viewed individually. The term refers also to a person considered in the fabric of social relationships ... It likewise refers to the exploited social class, the dominated people, the marginated.

declaring war: "The personnel who carry out the Church's charitable activity on the practical level ... must not be inspired by ideologies aimed at improving the world, but should rather be guided by the faith which works through love." This was Benedict's way of advocating for the dismissal of those who believe that caritas involves radical change. Also see Francis (2015, sec. 231) for a critical appropriation of Benedict's emphasis on charity.

23. Even the title of an article is enough to demonstrate the binary nature of our thinking on this issue. See Eric Frith's (2014) "Charity or Justice? Pope Francis Revisits Liberation Theology."

24. For a recent example, see Snow (2015).

25. These quotes of Gutiérrez come from "Gustavo Gutierrez Introduces Caritas Assembly: The Church Is a Friend of the Poor," *Vatican Insider*, 12 May 2015, http://vaticaninsider.lastampa.it/en/the-vatican/detail/articolo/caritas-gutierrez-41032. The emphasis is added.

> The masses are also our neighbor ... Charity is today a "political charity" ... to offer food or drink in our day is a political action; it means the transformation of a society structured to benefit a few who appropriate to themselves the value of the work of others. This transformation ought to be directed toward a radical change in the foundation of society, that is, the private ownership of the means of production.

This reformulation of charity also goes to the heart of the overall Marxist attacks against it. If practiced in the correct way, with an intense eye on transforming the structures of ownership, charity would no longer obfuscate the true sources of wealth. Liberation theology shares with Marxism the idea that what is given to the poor through charity is already theirs to begin with (indeed, the very idea that what is given was at one point or another extracted from the poor themselves), but it departs from Marxism by revolutionizing charity rather than abandoning it.

In sum, the Vatican's simultaneous turn to caritas and liberation theology signals neither a surreptitious Marxism veiled by the Bible nor the emptying out of Gutiérrez's message. It rather expresses the necessity to integrate the critique of political economy with a transformed understanding of centuries of Christian thought, even if the integration is far from finalized. It is a reminder that political economy without a charitable heart is empty, and charitable love without a critique of exploitation is blind.

What has caused the Vatican's recent flirtation with the emancipatory vision of charity (after decades of repression and containment)? More than simply expressing the temperament of an individual pope, Francis's moves are indicative of a collective will within the Vatican to tilt the balance of forces in favor of the oppressed classes. It is no accident that the theme of the Caritas General Assembly in 2015 was "A Poor Church for the Poor." The increasing visibility of the Vatican's emancipatory wing might also be due to worldwide developments (such as the 2008 financial crisis and intensifying ecological problems). As the Vatican faces internal crises (financial corruption, child abuse) and growing competition from Protestantism and Islam in the developing world, it might be resorting to one of its unique resources (Catholic social doctrine) as a way to weather the storms. Only further research can reveal which of these dynamics are more decisive and whether the emancipatory version of caritas can make a lasting impact beyond the boundaries of Catholicism itself.

To See the Universe in a Raindrop ... and Transform It

What should militants do when they encounter a petty bourgeois who pours breadcrumbs on the tables of the poor? Should they scold or simply shrug and walk away? Or should they rather intervene in the situation by saying, "If you are going to love thy neighbor, do it in the proper way"? What tools has Marxism given them to transfigure the raindrop into a veritable weapon so that they can plunge into the ocean of suffering to reverse the tide? So far, close to none.

Marxism certainly cannot accept religious generosity (or for that matter, its secular, mostly antiradical counterparts) as it was traditionally practiced. But it can claim for itself benevolence, of which traditional giving is but one historical expression. It can approach charity with a spirit of rehabilitation, as did liberalism at the end of the nineteenth century (and as it does more aggressively today). Only then will the raindrops become essential parts of the poor's arsenal.

Such a novel approach to charity could only come with some change in Marxism's overall orientations to questions of social transformation. Most of twentieth-century Marxism focused on macro structures and therefore on big solutions.[26] Resolving poverty through taking over the state was at the center of its strategies. Integrating benevolence into the Left's arsenal will not necessarily repudiate all of this experience but will require the recognition of its insufficiency.

Detractors of any such change in Marxism will point out how state-socialist countries have rapidly reduced poverty. Indeed, if capitalism is the true cause of poverty, why look for other paths in its amelioration than the quick overthrow of that mode of production?

It is true that state socialisms have worked some miracles (given the constraints of the countries where they have been implemented)—a fact conveniently buried in the post–Cold War era. It is as obvious, however, that these miracles have come at the cost of a spiritless (at times brutal) rationalization. Moreover, they were not based on the consent of broad strata. These shortcomings have made state socialism quite unsustainable. Benevolence can be one (but is certainly not the only) way to fill the process of postcapitalist transformation with a spirit.

Charity, from the Marxist point of view, is a way of managing, legitimating, and maintaining capitalism. But this insistence on the one-dimensionality of charity contradicts with many actual practices. Pope Francis, for example, wants to give with a heart, but he also wants to give in a way that could undermine capitalism. In this regard he takes from both Marxism and varieties of traditionalism and conservatism. Such innovative benevolence can indeed help build a more willing, more sustainable, less statist, and more socially embedded socialism—if combined with other pertinent strategies. Melding processes of redistribution with processes of the heart, with charitable love (caritas), is meant to be no silver bullet but a necessary supplement (to class struggle, the self-organization of the oppressed, and state planning) in the combat against poverty and the subordination of the poor.

Acknowledgments

I would like to thank Michael Burawoy, Aynur Sadet, Ann Swidler, and the reviewers of Rethinking Marxism *for their contributions.*

References

Allahyari, R. A. 2000. *Visions of charity: Volunteer workers and moral community.* Berkeley: University of California Press.

Aquinas, St. T. 1917. Pt. 2 (2d pt.) of *The "Summa theologica."* London: R. & T. Washbourne.

Augustine, St. 1944. *Confessions.* London: A & C Black.

Badiou, A. 2003. *Saint Paul: The foundations of universalism.* Stanford: Stanford University Press.

———. 2005. *Being and event.* London: Continuum.

26. For a partial synopsis of remarkable exceptions, see Gardiner (2000). Also see Dhar (2015, 8–11), Chakrabarti and Dhar (2015), and Gibson-Graham (2006) along these lines.

Benedict XVI (pope). 2006. *God is love (Deus caritas est)*. Washington, D.C.: United States Conference of Catholic Bishops.

———. 2009. *Charity in truth (Caritas in veritate)*. Washington, D.C.: United States Conference of Catholic Bishops.

Bloch, E. 2009. *Atheism in Christianity: The religion of the Exodus and the Kingdom*. London: Verso.

Boer, R. 2007. *Criticism of Heaven: On Marxism and theology*. Leiden: Brill.

———. 2009. *Criticism of religion: On Marxism and theology II*. Leiden: Brill.

———. 2011. *Criticism of theology: On Marxism and theology III*. Leiden: Brill.

Bourdieu, P. 2000. *Pascalian meditations*. Stanford: Stanford University Press.

Buhrer, E. 2012. From *caritas* to charity: How loving God became giving alms. In *Poverty and prosperity in the Middle Ages and Renaissance*, ed. C. Kosso and A. Scott, 113–28. Turnhout, Belgium: Brepols.

Cahill, L. S. 2010. *Caritas in veritate*: Benedict's global reorientation. *Theological Studies* 71 (2): 291–319.

Chakrabarti, A., and A. Dhar. 2015. The question before the communist horizon. *Rethinking Marxism* 27 (3): 357–9.

Charities Aid Foundation. 2014. *World giving index 2014: A global view of giving trends*.

Christiansen, D., S.J. 2010. Metaphysics and society: A commentary on *Caritas in veritate*. *Theological Studies* 71 (1): 3–28.

Cohen, M. 1994. *The wager of Lucien Goldmann: Tragedy, dialectics, and a hidden god*. Princeton: Princeton University Press.

Collier, A. 2001. *Christianity and Marxism: A philosophical contribution to their reconciliation*. London: Routledge.

Dhar, A. 2015. Action research: Writing on righting wrongs? Paper presented at the Co-production of Knowledge in the Rural: Indian and Australian Perspectives Symposium, April, Delhi, India. Accessed 12 July 2016. https://www.researchgate.net/publication/278330150_Action_Research_writing_on_righting_wrongs.

Draper, H. 1971. The principle of self-emancipation in Marx and Engels. *Socialist Register*, no. 8: 81–109.

Dyer, C. 2012. Poverty and its relief in late medieval England. *Past and Present* 216 (1): 41–78.

Eagleton, T. 2005. The pope has blood on his hands. *Guardian*, 4 April. http://www.theguardian.com/world/2005/apr/04/catholicism.religion14.

Engels, F. 1987. *The condition of the working class in England*. London: Penguin.

———. 2001. *The condition of the working class in England*. London: Electric Book Company.

———. 2004. *Socialism: Utopian and scientific*. New York: International Publishers.

Francis (pope). 2013. *Evangelii gaudium*. http://w2.vatican.va/content/dam/francesco/pdf/apost_exhortations/documents/papa-francesco_esortazione-ap_20131124_evangelii-gaudium_en.pdf.

Francis (pope). 2015. *Laudato Si'*. http://w2.vatican.va/content/dam/francesco/pdf/encyclicals/documents/papa-francesco_20150524_enciclica-laudato-si_en.pdf.

Frith, E. 2014. Charity or justice? Pope Francis revisits liberation theology. *Dissent*, 24 September.

Gagliarducci, A. 2015. Pope Francis, charity in truth or truth in charity? *Monday Vatican*, 18 May. http://www.mondayvatican.com/vatican/pope-francis-charity-in-truth-or-truth-in-charity.

Gardiner, M. 2000. *Critiques of everyday life*. London: Routledge.

Geremek, B. 1994. *Poverty: A history*. Oxford: Blackwell.

Gibson-Graham, J. K. 2006. *A postcapitalist politics*. Minneapolis: University of Minnesota Press.

Goldmann, L. 1964. *The hidden God: A study of tragic vision in the "Pensées" of Pascal and the tragedies of Racine*. London: Routledge and Kegan Paul.

Gramsci, A. 1992. *Prison notebooks*. Vol. 1. New York: Columbia University Press.

Griffiths, B. 2010. *Caritas in veritate*: Pope Benedict's two cheers for globalization. *Faith & Economics* 56 (Fall): 111–24.

Gutiérrez, G. 1988. *A theology of liberation: History, politics, and salvation*. Maryknoll, N.Y.: Orbis Books.

Kautsky, K. 2001. *Foundations of Christianity*. London: Russell and Russell. https://www.marxists.org/archive/kautsky/1908/christ/index.htm.

Kayatekin, S., and S. Charusheela. 2004. Recovering feudal subjectivities. *Rethinking Marxism* 16 (4): 377–96.

Laurent, B. 2010. *Caritas in veritate* as a social encyclical: A modest challenge to economic, social, and political institutions. *Theological Studies* 71 (3): 515–44.

Lih, L. T. 2011. *Lenin*. London: Reaktion Books.

Lindberg, C. 2008. *Love: A brief history through Western Christianity*. Malden, Mass.: Blackwell.

Luxemburg, R. 2003. *Socialism and the churches*. https://www.marxists.org/archive/luxemburg/1905/misc/socialism-churches.htm.

Lynch, E. A. 1994. The retreat of liberation theology. *Homiletic & Pastoral Review*, February: 12–21.

Marx, Karl. 2008a. A contribution to the critique of Hegel's philosophy of right. In *On religion*, by K. Marx and F. Engels, 82–7. Mineola, N. Y.: Dover.

———. 2008b. The communism of the *Rheinischer Beobachter*. In *On religion*, by K. Marx and F. Engels, 41–58. Mineola, N. Y.: Dover.

Mauss, M. 1990. *The gift: The form and reason for exchange in archaic societies*. New York: W. W. Norton.

Mollat, M. 1986. *The poor in the Middle Ages: An essay in social history*. New Haven: Yale University Press.

O'Brien, T. 2013. A thematic analysis of "love" and "truth" in *Caritas in veritate*. *Political Theology* 14 (5): 573–88.

Pascal, B. 2003. *Pensées*. Mineola, N.Y.: Dover.

Paul VI (pope). 1967. *Populorum progressio*. http://w2.vatican.va/content/paul-vi/en/encyclicals/documents/hf_p-vi_enc_26031967_populorum.pdf.

Polanyi, K. 2001. *The great transformation: The political and economic origins of our time*. Boston: Beacon.

Pullan, B. S. 1994. *Poverty and charity: Europe, Italy, Venice, 1400–1700*. Aldershot, U.K.: Variorum.

Roberts, H. 2015. Pope to Caritas: You are witnessing to Christ, not just charity workers. *The Tablet*, 13 May. http://www.thetablet.co.uk/news/2063/0/pope-to-caritas-you-are-witnesses-to-christ-not-just-charity-workers.

Rodinson, M. 1972. *Marxisme et monde musulman*. Paris: Editions de Seuil.

Rubin, M. 1987. *Charity and community in medieval Cambridge*. Cambridge University Press.

Skojec, S. 2014. Why is the Church's largest charitable organization involved with communist, pro-abortion activism? *OnePeterFive*, 7 October. http://www.onepeterfive.com/why-is-the-churchs-largest-charitable-organization-involved-with-communist-pro-abortion-activism.

Snow, M. 2015. Against charity. *Jacobin*, 25 August. https://www.jacobinmag.com/2015/08/peter-singer-charity-effective-altruism.

Swidler, A. 2001. *Talk of love: How culture matters*. Chicago: University of Chicago Press.

Thompson, E. P. 1966. *The making of the English working class*. New York: Vintage.

Žižek, S. 2010. *Living in the end times*. London: Verso.

Gramsci's Concept of the "Simple": Religion, Common Sense, and the Philosophy of Praxis

Marcus E. Green

One of the minor yet recurring themes of Antonio Gramsci's Prison Notebooks *is his treatment of the "simple," a category he developed to examine the Catholic Church's paternalistic view of common people and peasants as "simple and sincere souls," in contrast to its superior view of cultured intellectuals. Throughout the* Notebooks, *he examines how the Church's condescending and fatalistic portrayal of the "simple" provides a basis for common sense, reinforcing the conditions of subalternity. Because of the uncritical nature of common sense and the simple's desire for change, he argues for the articulation of a "renewed common sense" containing critical and reflective philosophical foundations that transcend the passivity and paternalism of religion. Such a movement requires defining and disseminating new conceptions of philosophy and culture that are critically grounded and provide a basis of struggle in which the "simple" play the predominant role in the direction of their political lives and in the creation of a new hegemony.*

In the very first note in the *Prison Notebooks*, written in June 1929 and entitled "On Poverty, Catholicism and the Papacy," Gramsci reflected on the Catholic Church's position on poverty.[1] He recalled a passage from Arthur Roguenant's book *Patrons et ouvriers* in which the author asked a French Catholic worker to reconcile his professed principles of equality with the Gospels' claim that the rich and poor will always exist. In response, the worker said, "We will then leave at least two poor

1. For references to Gramsci's *Prison Notebooks*, I follow the international standard of citing the notebook number (Q), note number (§), year of publication, and page number. This standard follows the Italian critical edition of the *Quaderni del carcere*, edited by Valentino Gerratana (Einaudi, 1975). To date, Columbia University Press has published the first three of five volumes of Joseph A. Buttigieg's critical English translation of the *Prison Notebooks* (Gramsci 1992, 1996, 2007). For English translations that have not yet appeared in Buttigieg's critical edition, I refer to *Selections from the Prison Notebooks*, edited and translated by Quintin Hoare and Geoffrey Nowell Smith (International Publishers, 1971) and *Further Selections from the Prison Notebooks*, edited by Derek Boothman (University of Minnesota Press, 1995).

persons, so that Jesus Christ will not be proved wrong." The worker's sentiment
that according to the Gospels some level of inequality will always exist, Gramsci
explained, reflected Church doctrine that essentially justified the perpetual existence of poverty. As Gramsci wrote:

> This general question should be examined within the whole tradition and
> doctrine of the Catholic Church. The principal assertions made in the encyc-
> licals of the more recent popes, that is, the most important ones since the
> question assumed historical significance: 1) private property, especially
> "landed property," is a "natural right" which may not be violated, not even
> through high taxes (the programs of "Christian democratic" tendency for
> the redistribution—with indemnity—of land to poor peasants, as well as
> their financial doctrines are derived from these assertions); 2) the poor must
> accept their lot, since class distinctions and the distribution of wealth are or-
> dained by god and it would be impious to try to eliminate them; 3) alms-giving
> is a Christian duty and implies the existence of poverty; 4) the social question
> is primarily moral and religious, not economic, and it must be resolved
> through Christian charity, the dictates of morality, and the decree of religion.
> (See *Codice Sociale* and *Sillabo*). (Q1§1, Gramsci 1992, 100; 1975, 6)[2]

The Church's position in effect fostered a fatalistic view of poverty in that it
considered poverty a part of the order of things, not the result of historical
factors created by humans. According to the International Union of Social
Studies' *Codice Sociale* and Pope Pius IX's *Sillabo*, which Gramsci referenced at
the end of the note, the poor should resolve themselves to accept their conditions as natural.[3]

In early 1930, he returned to the theme in a note entitled "Father Bresciani's
Progeny. Catholic Art" (Q1§72, Gramsci 1992, 177-9). The note was prompted by
the summary of an article entitled "Domande su un'arte cattolica" (Questions on
Catholic art), written by Edoardo Fenu. In the article, Fenu (quoted in Gramsci
1992, 178; 1975, 80) criticized Catholic authors for adopting an apologetic tone in
their work, and he proceeded to explain that a writer, "just by virtue of being a
Catholic, is already endowed with that simple and deep spirit which, transfused
into the pages of a story or a poem, will make his art pure, serene, and not in
the least pedantic."[4] In response, Gramsci wrote that Fenu's article is filled with
"many contradictions and inaccuracies; but the conclusion is correct: religion is sterility for art, at least among the religious. In other words, there are no longer any

2. Gramsci eventually included this note in Q20, the "special notebook" titled "Catholic Action—
Catholic Integralists—Jesuits—Modernists."
3. While in prison, Gramsci possessed a book that contained Pius IX's encyclicals, including the *Il
Sillabo*, as well as a copy of the International Union of Social Studies' *Codice Sociale*. Both aimed to
propagate Catholic social teachings, and *Il Sillabo* contained in particular a "syllabus of errors"
pertaining to modern thought and liberalism. See Buttigieg's note in Gramsci (1992, 375-6).
4. Gramsci inserted a bracketed exclamation mark (!) between "his" and "art."

'simple and sincere souls' who are artists." Given its title, the note connects to the series of notes Gramsci labeled under the rubric "Father Bresciani's Progeny" to classify literary intellectuals who espoused antidemocratic and reactionary positions similar to those of conservative Jesuit novelist Antonio Bresciani.[5] However, in this note Gramsci also introduced the notion of "the simple" (*i semplici*), which he gradually developed into a category of analysis to examine the Church's treatment of common people as "simple and sincere souls."

In Notebook 1, §72, Gramsci explains that the Church since the time of the Counter-Reformation had maintained the existence of two unofficial religions: the religion of the "simple," composed of common people of humble circumstances, and the religion of intellectuals, composed of the "cultured" classes. This distinction, he writes, makes it "simultaneously very easy and very difficult" to be "Catholic." Common people are expected to believe and to respect the Church without having to strictly follow religious doctrine, such as denouncing pagan superstitions or religious deviations, in effect making the distinction between Catholic, Protestant, and Orthodox peasants only ecclesiastical and not religious. In contrast, Catholic intellectuals, he explains, are "expected to embrace a whole slew of notions on encyclicals, counter-encyclicals, papal briefs, apostolic letters, etc., and the historical deviations from the church's line have been so numerous and so subtle that it is extremely easy to fall into heresy or a semi-heresy or a quarter heresy" (Q1§72, Gramsci 1992, 81; 1975, 178).

Though it is not immediately apparent, the analysis Gramsci initiates in Notebook 1 becomes a minor yet recurring theme in the *Notebooks*, of how the Catholic Church's patronizing depiction of peasant life romanticizes, legitimizes, and in effect depoliticizes the impoverished conditions and suffering of common people —that is, the "simple." Following his treatment of the idea over time, the investigation of the "simple" connects to several of the major themes of the *Prison Notebooks*, including intellectuals, common sense, the philosophy of praxis, the critique of historical determinism, and subalternity. His investigation provides a particular example of the general conditions of subalternity and the ways in which sociopolitical subordination is produced and reproduced. The Church's depiction of the "simple" by itself does not create the conditions of subordination; in fact, the Church's portrayal confirms the already posited subordination of the masses that exists in society, but as the Church's representation of the "simple" is disseminated throughout the culture, it becomes an element of common sense and is internalized by the "simple" themselves, who accept their conditions as natural.

Throughout his early miscellaneous notebooks, there are a number of instances in which Gramsci documents how the Church treats intellectuals and common people differently. For instance, in Notebook 3, §76, he highlights the fact that the Church's use of Latin contributed to the historical "split between the people

---

5. On Brescianism, see Buttigieg (1992, 43–5) and Musitelli (2009).

and the intellectuals, between the people and culture," in that Latin functioned as an intellectual language and not as a spoken one. "(Even) religious books are written in Middle-Latin," he writes, "so that even religious discussion is inaccessible to the people, although religion is the dominant element of culture—the people *watch* the religious *rites* and *hear* the exhortatory sermons, but they cannot follow discussions and ideological developments which are the monopoly of a caste" (Q3§76, Gramsci 1996, 73; 1975, 353–4). In others words, due to linguistic inaccessibility, common people are unable to fully participate in religious life. Yet despite these dualisms, as he explains in Notebook 4, §3, the Church is able "to retain its ties with the people and at the same time to allow a certain aristocratic selection (Platonism and Aristotelianism in the Catholic religion)" among intellectuals (Gramsci 1996, 143; 1975, 424). In Gramsci's view, the Church's reinforcement of such class distinctions represents one of its deficiencies in providing a coherent and unitary worldview for the "simple" to understand the circumstances of their life, while also maintaining a paternalistic relationship with them.

Similarly, in Notebook 6, §48, he highlights how a popular Sicilian tale that appeared in Venetian prints utilized religious depictions to reinforce the subordinate position of peasants. In the prints, as he explains, "one sees God imparting the following orders from heaven: to the Pope: 'pray'; to the Emperor: 'protect;' to the peasant: 'and you toil.'" In response to these depictions, Gramsci writes that "the spirit of popular tales conveys the peasant's conception of himself and of his position in the world, a conception that he has resigned himself to absorbing from religion" (Gramsci 2007, 38; 1975, 722). With such divine commands, peasants are encouraged to accept both religious and political authority while also accepting their life of "toil." This produces multiple barriers for the "simple" to come to terms with their position. Given the condition of mass poverty and lack of access to political institutions, the masses often turn to superstition, faith, and the Church out of despair and hopelessness. However, Church doctrine and aspects of popular culture reinforce those very conditions. The Church praises the simple's faithfulness and humble circumstances but discourages their active political participation in the transformation of their conditions.

The "Simple" in Notebook 8: Religion and Common Sense

Gramsci's reflections on the "simple" initially emerge in the *Notebooks* as he works through a number of the "main topics" outlined in Notebook 1 that specifically connect to the analysis of religion, such as Catholic Action and, as we have already seen, Father Bresciani's "progeny." In March 1932, however, his discussion of the "simple" takes on new meaning as it becomes apparent that his observations also connect to his reflections on philosophy, one of the major research projects of the *Prison Notebooks*. In Notebook 4, Notebook 7, and Notebook 8, Gramsci composed a three-part series entitled "Notes on Philosophy. Materialism and Idealism" in which he aimed to respond to the materialist and idealist revisions of Marxism, as represented in the work of Nikolai Bukharin and Benedetto Croce.[6] He devoted specific attention to Bukharin's book *The Theory of Historical Materialism: A Popular Manual of Marxist Sociology*, which played a leading role in the international communist movement, as it was directed toward a mass audience and published in multiple languages.[7] One of Gramsci's major concerns was that Bukharin presented Marxism as a form of historical determinism that could be understood according to laws of social evolution, amounting to a form of teleological naturalism. In effect, Bukharin formulated a "materialist" conception of the world that closely resembled the Catholic Church's view. On this point, Gramsci writes that "the author [Bukharin] has no knowledge of the Catholic tradition and is unaware that religion, in fact, vigorously upholds this thesis against idealism; in this case, then, the Catholic religion would be 'materialist'" (Q7§47, Gramsci 2007, 194; 1975, 894). In the third series of "Notes on Philosophy. Materialism and Idealism," which appears in Notebook 8, §166–240, Gramsci composed a string of notes under the rubric "An Introduction to the Study of Philosophy" in which he sought to clarify his position in contrast to Bukharin's while also sketching preliminary details for writing an introduction to philosophy directed toward a mass audience. In the string of notes, he expands the examination of the "simple" by addressing the relationship between religion, philosophy, common sense, and the masses.

In Notebook 8, §204—the first note under the rubric "An Introduction to the Study of Philosophy"—he lays out a list of "preliminary principles" for approaching the topic. Through this exercise, he specifies what he means by "philosophy" and posits the idea that "all men are philosophers":

6. Gramsci initially conceived his investigation of philosophy as a study on the "theory of history and of historiography," which appears as the first entry in the list of "main topics" on the first page of Q1 (Gramsci 1992, 99; 1975, 5). In his letter to Tatiana Schucht of 25 March 1929, he specifies that he intends to focus on Bukharin, Marx, and Croce. Gramsci (1994, 1:257–8) writes:

> On the theory of history I would like to have a French book published recently: Bukharin—*Théorie du matérialisme historique* ... and *Oeuvres philosophiques de Marx* published by Alfred Costes—Paris: volume 1: *Contribution à la critique de la Philosophie du droit de Hegel*—volume 2: *Critique de la critique* against Bruno Bauer and company. I already have Benedetto Croce's most important books on this subject.

Over time he developed the project into the "notes on philosophy." On this point, see Frosini (2003, 48–54).

7. Nikolai Bukharin's book was first published in Russian in 1921. Gramsci frequently refers to it as the *Popular Manual*, and Buttigieg (1992, 520) suggests that "in all probability, Gramsci first read the book in the original Russian or in translation—it was widely available in German, French and English—during his stay in the Soviet Union in 1922–23." An authorized English translation of the third Russian edition was published in 1925 under the alternative title *Historical Materialism: A System of Sociology* (International Publishers, 1925).

> One must destroy the prejudice that philosophy is a difficult thing just because it is the specific activity of a particular category of learned people, of professional or systematic philosophers. It is, therefore, necessary to show that all men are philosophers, by defining the characteristics of this ["spontaneous"] philosophy that is "everyone's," namely, common sense and religion. Having shown that everyone, in his own way, is a philosopher, that no normal human being of sound mind exists who does not participate, even if unconsciously, in some particular conception of the world, since every "language" is a philosophy—having shown this, one moves on to the second stage, which is that of criticism and consciousness. (Q8§204, Gramsci 2007, 351–2; 1975, 1002; bracketed insertion in the original)

Gramsci is not suggesting here that "all men" are *professional* philosophers but rather that all individuals are philosophers in the sense that we participate in a conception of the world (or a "spontaneously philosophy") that is comprised of and represented in common sense, religion, and language. As he specifies in earlier notes, Gramsci conceives of "common sense" as common beliefs, modes of thought, opinions, and conceptions of the world that are held by the masses. He describes this "common sense" as a fragmentary collection of ideas and opinions drawn from religion, differing philosophies, ideologies, folklore, superstition, and scientific notions that have been absorbed into common usage (cf., Q1§65, Gramsci 1992, 173; 1975, 76). In Notebook 8, §173, which also appears in the third series of "Notes on Philosophy. Materialism and Idealism," he describes common sense as

> the "philosophy of non-philosophers"—in other words, the conception of the world *acritically* absorbed from the various social environments in which the moral individuality of the average person is developed. Common sense is not a single conception, identical in time and place. It is the "folklore" of philosophy and, like folklore, it appears in countless forms. The fundamental characteristic of common sense consists in its being a disjointed, incoherent, and inconsequential conception of the world that matches the character of the multitudes whose philosophy it is. Historically, the formation of a homogenous social group is accompanied by the development of a "homogenous"—that is, systematic—philosophy, in opposition to common sense. The main components of common sense are provided by religions—not only by the religion that happens to be dominant at a given time but also by previous religions, popular heretical movements, scientific concepts from the past, etc. "Realistic, materialistic" elements predominate in common sense, but this does not in any way contradict the religious element. (Q8§173, Gramsci 2007, 333–4; 1975, 1045).

Following from this, philosophy represents for Gramsci a "systematic" and "homogenous" conception of the world, whereas common sense represents a "disjointed, incoherent, and inconsequential conception of the world." Religion provides the "main components of common sense," and as he explains at the end of the passage, as well as in other notes, religious materialism predominates common sense in the form of predestination, providence, spiritualism, and superstition, which are "close to the people" in that people often believe that supernatural or external forces determine the conditions of their lives (Q4§3, Gramsci 1996, 143; 1975, 424; cf., Q4§48, Gramsci 1996, 198; 1975, 474). "Philosophy," in contrast, "is the critique of religion and of common sense, and it supersedes them. In this respect, philosophy coincides with 'good sense'" (Q8§204, Gramsci 2007, 352; 1975, 1063).

In Notebook 8, §213, the second note under the rubric "An Introduction to the Study of Philosophy," Gramsci (2007, 359–60; 1975, 1070–1) distinguishes three inter-related themes connected to the investigation of philosophy, introduced under successive subheadings: "I. The problem of 'the simple'"; "II. Christian religion'"; and "III. Philosophy and common sense or good sense." His arrangement of these seemingly disparate lines of inquiry reveals how his analysis of the "simple" directly connects to his study of philosophy. In the first section of the note ("The problem of 'the simple'"), he reflects on the Church's ability to maintain unity between the "simple" and intellectuals and to prevent the formation of two distinct religions:

> The strength of religions, and especially of Catholicism, resides in the fact that they feel very strongly the need for the unity of the whole mass of believers and do their utmost to forestall the detachment of the upper echelons from the lower strata. The Roman church is the most relentless in the struggle to prevent the "official" formation of two religions, one for the intellectuals and another for the "simple." This has had and continues to have serious drawbacks, but these "drawbacks" are connected with the historical process that totally transforms civic life and not with the rational relationship between the intellectuals and the "simple." The weakness of immanentist philosophies in general consists precisely in the fact that they have been unable to create an ideological unity between the bottom and the top, between the intellectuals and the mass (cf. the theme "Renaissance and Reformation").
> (Q8§213i, Gramsci 2007, 359; 1975, 1070)

This section of the note exemplifies Gramsci's critical analysis of the Church. He admires the Church's ability to maintain religious unity in light of the detached relationship between intellectuals and the "simple." As he documents in his earlier notes, the Church's distinct treatment of the "simple" and of intellectuals reinforces class differences, yet the Church is able to maintain a strong relationship with the "simple" so as to avoid the formation of two "official" religions. For the Church, according to Gramsci, the "drawback" hindering religious unity is not the relationship between intellectuals and the "simple" but the secularization of civil society as a "historical process" that is transforming life.

At the philosophical level, Gramsci questions the limits of the Church's ability to maintain unity. Similar to "immanentist philosophies" (in the transcendental sense), the Church is unable to create ideological unity between the masses and intellectuals, instead providing distinct philosophies restricted to specific social groups. His

parenthetical reference to "the theme 'Renaissance and Reformation'" at the end of
the passage alludes to his similar assessment of the Renaissance as a cultural movement that remained aristocratic and not popular—unlike the Reformation—in that
the Renaissance's influence did not extend beyond elite circles.[8] As he writes in
Notebook 8, §156: "In order for religion to have at least the appearance of being absolute and objectively universal, it would have been necessary for it to manifest itself
as monolithic or, at the very least, as intellectually uniform among all believers—
which is very far from reality (different doctrines, sects, tendencies, as well class differences: the simple and the cultured, etc.)" (Gramsci 2007, 323; 1975, 1035). The
Church, he later writes in Notebook 11, §13, retains a "'surface' unity" to avoid splin-
tering into different groups but "is in reality a multiplicity of distinct and often contradictory religions: there is one Catholicism for the peasants, one for the *petits-
bourgeois* and town workers, one for women, and one for intellectuals which is
itself variegated and disconnected" (Gramsci 1971, 420; 1975, 1397). In this sense, the
articulation of philosophy is not simply a theoretical question but a question of
how philosophy translates into practice. As he writes in Notebook 8, §213i:

> The question is this: should a movement be deemed philosophical just
> because it devotes itself to developing a specialized culture for a restricted
> group of intellectuals? Or is a movement philosophical only when, in the
> course of elaborating a superior and scientifically coherent form of thought,
> it never fails to remain in contact with the "simple," and even finds in such
> contacts the source of the issues that need to be studied and resolved? Only
> through this contact does a philosophy become "historical," cleanse itself of
> elements that are "individual" in origin, and turn itself into "life." (Gramsci
> 2007, 360; 1975, 1071)

Gramsci's idea of philosophy becoming "historical" and "turn[ing] itself into 'life'"
echoes Marx's notion of "thinking in practice," from his second thesis on Feuerbach, in that the significance of philosophy as a movement pertains to its level
of social diffusion and not simply to its adoption by intellectuals.[9] The implication
of this observation with respect to Catholicism is that the Church maintains a level

---

8. Cf. Q4§3 (Gramsci 1996, 141–2; 1975, 423); Q7§1 (Gramsci 2007, 153–5; 1975, 851–2); Q7§44 (Gramsci
2007, 193–4; 1975, 892–3).
9. In the second thesis, Marx (1976, 4) writes:

> The question whether objective truth can be attributed to human thinking is not a
> question of theory but is a *practical* question. Man must prove the truth, i.e., the
> reality and power, the this-worldliness of his thinking in practice. The dispute over
> the reality or non-reality of thinking which is isolated from practice is a purely *scholastic*
> question.

On the importance of Marx's second thesis on Feuerbach in Gramsci's thought, see Thomas
(2009, 307–83).

of contact with the "simple" but does not seek to resolve the contradictions of their existence. In fact, the Church reinforces their conditions. This relationship, as we shall see below, acts as a foil for Gramsci to envision the philosophy of praxis as a philosophy capable of transforming itself into "life" while yet needing to remain in contact with the "simple."

In the second part of Notebook 8, §213, Gramsci comments on an article entitled "Individualismo pagano e individualismo cristiano" (Pagan individualism and Christian individualism), published in the journal *La Civiltà Cattolica*. The article highlights how the Church's conception of life, which included elements of divine providence and immortality, underpinned the notion of Christian individualism. According to the article, "Faith in a secure future, in the immortality of the soul destined to beatitude, in the certainty of attaining eternal happiness, motivated the intense effort to achieve inner perfection and spiritual nobility."[10] Such a notion, as the article suggests, provided individuals with the security of knowing that their "struggle against evil" was supported by a "superior force." In response, Gramsci observes that such a conception provided the popular masses with a way of understanding and acting in the world. "In other words," he writes, "in a certain historical period and in certain specific historical conditions, Christianity was 'necessary' for progress; it was the specific form of the 'rationality of the world and of life,' and it provided the general framework for human practical activity" (Q8§213ii, Gramsci 2007, 360; 1975, 1071). Following the notion of translating philosophy into practice, Gramsci thus recognizes how Christianity functioned in specific cultural and historical conditions for making sense of life, yet he also recognizes the limits of such forms of religious materialism.

In the note's third part, Gramsci returns to the notion of common sense, distinguishing it from philosophy:

> Perhaps it is useful to make a "practical" distinction between philosophy and common sense in order to be better able to show what one is trying to arrive at. Philosophy means, rather specifically, a conception of the world with salient individual traits. Common sense is the conception of the world that is most widespread among the popular masses in a historical period. One wants to change common sense and create a "new common sense"—hence the need to take the "simple" into account. (Q8§213iii, Gramsci 2007, 360; 1975, 1071).

In addition to making a "practical" distinction between philosophy, as a coherent concept of the world, and common sense, as the popular mentality of the masses, Gramsci alludes to the radical implication of his investigation, which is the political and pedagogical project of changing common sense and creating a "new common

---

10. Quoted in Gramsci (2007, 360; 1975, 1071): "Individualismo pagano e individualismo cristiano." The passage is also quoted in Q11§12 (Gramsci 1975, 1389), from where it is translated in Gramsci (1971, 337).

sense." The process requires taking the "simple" into account in order to ascertain the "issues that need to be studied and resolved," as he mentioned in the first section of the note. As we shall see below, this requirement figures into his notion of the philosophy of praxis and into the relationship between intellectuals and the masses.

In the *Prison Notebooks*, Gramsci used the phrase "philosophy of praxis" partially out of the need to camouflage his references to Marxism, but more significantly it represents his own theoretical separation from Hegelian and Crocean notions of "philosophy of spirit," on the one hand, and the historical economism of mechanistic forms of Marxism, on the other.[11] In conceiving Marxism as a philosophy of praxis, Gramsci placed himself in a tradition of nondeterminist Marxist thought —as represented by the work of Antonio Labriola—that opposed idealist, positivist, naturalist, and universalist conceptions of history.[12] In the chronology of the *Prison Notebooks*, Gramsci used the phrase initially in Notebook 5 to describe the foundations of Machiavelli's conception of the world as a "'philosophy of praxis' or 'neo-humanism,' in that it does not recognize transcendental or immanent (in the metaphysical sense) elements but is based entirely on the concrete action of man, who out of historical necessity works and transforms reality" (Q5§127, Gramsci 1996, 378; 1975, 657). He also uses the phrase numerous times in Notebook 8, as we shall see below in his notes on religion, without fully articulating its meaning. However, in Notebook 11 he provides a definitive description of the notion, in a critique of Bukharin's conception of historical materialism: "It has been forgotten that in the case of a very common expression [historical materialism] one should put the accent on the first term—'historical'—and not on the second, which is of metaphysical origin. The philosophy of praxis is absolute 'historicism,' the absolute secularisation and earthliness of thought, an absolute humanism of history. It is along this line that one must trace the thread of the new conception of the world" (Q11§27, Gramsci 1971, 465; 1975, 1437; bracketed insertion added by Hoare and Smith). Though the object of Gramsci's critique is Bukharin in this passage, the thrust of his criticism also applies to religion and the formation of common sense.

In Notebook 8, §220, which is the third note under the rubric "An Introduction to the Study of Philosophy," Gramsci delineates the idea of the philosophy of praxis by distinguishing it in relation to "common sense" and the "simple." In this process, he further specifies what he means by the idea of wanting to "change common sense:"

> A philosophy of praxis must initially adopt a polemical stance, as superseding the existing mode of thinking. It must, therefore, present itself as a critique of "common sense" (but only after it has based itself on common sense in order

11. For discussions on these points, see Dainotto (2009), Green (2011), and Haug (2001).
12. See Q3§31 (Gramsci 1996, 30–1; 1975, 309–10), Q4§3 (Gramsci 1996, 140–1; 1975, 421–2), and Q8§198 (Gramsci 2007, 348; 1975, 1060). Cf., Dainotto (2009).

to show that "everyone" is a philosopher, and that the point is not to introduce a totally new form of knowledge into "everyone's" individual life, but to revitalize an already existing activity and make it "critical"). (Q8§220, Gramsci 2007, 369; 1975, 1080)

For Gramsci, the idea is not for the philosophy of praxis to replace common sense but to demonstrate that "everyone" is a philosopher and to criticize the existing elements of common sense in order to make it critical.

He proceeds in the same note to explain that the philosophy of praxis "must also present itself as a critique of the philosophy of the intellectuals, out of which the history of philosophy arises." The history of philosophy, in his view, "can be considered as the history of the 'high points' of the progress of 'common sense'—or, at least, of the common sense of the most culturally refined strata of the society." The point of such a critique is to "provide a synthesis of the 'problems' that arose in the course of the history of philosophy, in order to criticize them, demonstrate their real value (if they still have any) or their importance as links in a chain, and define the new problems of the present time" (Q8§220, Gramsci 2007, 369; 1975, 1080). In other words, he suggests that the critique of common sense includes the criticism of the history of philosophy itself, with the objective of ascertaining the relevance of particular modes of thought, their historical significance, and their relation to contemporary problems. As a critique of both common sense and the "high points" of philosophy that shape it, the philosophy of praxis aims to strengthen the critical elements of common sense in order to make it coherent.

In contrast, the Church, in Gramsci's view, attempts to preserve the status and worldview of the "simple" so as to avoid elevating them to a higher level of consciousness. The Church, he observes, is aware of the philosophical distinction between the religion of intellectuals and that of the "simple," but it wants to avoid the separation from becoming a political and organizational split:

> The fact that the Church finds itself facing a problem of the "simple" means that there has been a rupture within the community of the faithful, a rupture that cannot be healed by raising the simple to the level of the intellectuals (and the Church no longer plans to undertake such a task which is "economically" beyond its current means). The Church, instead, exercises an iron discipline to prevent the intellectuals from going beyond certain limits of "differentiation," lest they make the rupture catastrophic and irreparable. (Q8§220, Gramsci 2007, 369; 1975, 1080)

Historically, Gramsci observes, previous "ruptures" among the community of the faithful prompted the formation of new religious orders, such as the Dominican and Franciscan orders and the Society of Jesus, so as to "'discipline' the masses of the 'simple'" and preserve the prevailing relations (Q8§220, Gramsci 2007, 370; 1975, 1080–1). Although the Church maintained unity—by preventing the formation of two official religions—the Catholicism of the intellectuals remained restricted to a narrow segment of the population, as the intellectuals did not align themselves with the masses so as to address their interests and raise them to a higher level of cultural understanding. As Gramsci writes later, "The Church does not even envisage such a task" (Q11§12, Gramsci 1971, 331; 1975, 1383). Thus, by not aligning itself with the masses, the Church reinforced the common sense of the "simple," who drew upon it to understand and ameliorate their conditions.

Prior to the notes devoted to "An Introduction to the Study of Philosophy" in Notebook 8, Gramsci's discussions of the "simple," of common sense, and of philosophy appear as distinct lines of inquiry in the *Prison Notebooks*. The three notes create a nexus that reveals how the separate investigations intersect and illuminate one another. These notes reveal how his previous notes documenting the Church's paternalistic view of the "simple" in effect pertain to the formation of popular knowledge, common sense, and the ways in which the masses conceive themselves and the world. It is along these lines that the Catholic Church can be understood as a "collective intellectual," as Tommaso La Rocca (1991, 87; 2009) has argued. As an organization, it established and maintained historical relationships with the "simple" while also promoting patronizing depictions of peasant life and praising common people's humble and poor circumstances. Such depictions, as Gramsci documents, are manifest in encyclicals, papal briefs, literature, art, and folktales. Such representations reinforce the conditions of the "simple" and provide a basis for political and intellectual passivity, as the poor view their social position as natural or as a result of God's will. Gramsci's concern is that such views are absorbed into common sense and become an active part of culture, which in turn reinforces the status quo. In addition to echoing Marx's notion of "thinking in practice," this aspect of Gramsci's analysis, as Derek Boothman (1995, xx) has pointed out, also draws from Marx's *Contribution to the Critique of Hegel's "Philosophy of Right"* in that Gramsci conceives religious ideology as a "material force" when it is gripped by the masses.[13] In other words, Gramsci is interested in how religious ideology becomes an element of common sense and in turn affects modes of thought, political participation, and the organization of society. It is in this sense that religion is absorbed by common sense and "turn[s] itself into 'life'" (Q8§213i, Gramsci 2007, 360; 1975, 1071).

The "Simple" in Notebook 11: The Philosophy of Praxis and "Renewed Common Sense"

Soon after completing Notebook 8, Gramsci devoted two thematically organized "special" notebooks to the topic of philosophy: Notebook 10 ("The Philosophy of

13. In a "Contribution to the Critique of Hegel's "Philosophy of Right," Marx (1975 [1844], 182) writes: "The weapon of criticism cannot, of course, replace criticism by weapons, material force must be overthrown by material force; but theory also becomes a material force as soon as it has gripped the masses."

Benedetto Croce") and Notebook 11 ("Notes for an Introduction and Starting Point for the Study of Philosophy and the History of Culture").[14] He organized and re-drafted the three-part series of "Notes on Philosophy. Materialism and Idealism" from Notebook 4, Notebook 7, and Notebook 8, devoting Notebook 10 largely to the critique of idealism and Notebook 11 to materialism. In the first entry of Note-book 11—which he entitled "Some Preliminary Points of Reference" and which appears as Notebook 11, §12, in the Gerratana edition[15]—he synthesized his earlier ideas on philosophy, the "simple," and common sense. In effect, he com-bined, rewrote, and expanded six notes from Notebook 8, including the three notes on "An Introduction to the Study of Philosophy" discussed above, and one note from Notebook 10. In his explication of these themes, he approached the study of philosophy from the perspective of presenting it to a mass audience while also posing the philosophy of praxis as an independent and self-sufficient philosophy.

Gramsci opens Notebook 11, §12, by reaffirming that it must be shown that "all men are 'philosophers.'" He explains that everyone is a philosopher because each one's intellectual activity is a manifestation of a conception of the world that is posited in language, common sense, good sense, and popular religion, which includes "the entire system of beliefs, superstitions, ways of seeing things and of acting" (Q11§12, Gramsci 1971, 323; 1975, 1375). In other words, all humans engage in philosophical and intellectual activity at various levels of life activity. The content of that philosophy—for instance, the Church's portrayal of the "simple"—is what Gramsci wants to examine and question. After demonstrating that "everyone is a philosopher," he explains, "one moves on to the second level, which is of awareness and criticism":

> That is to say, one proceeds to the question—is it better to "think," without having a critical awareness, in a disjointed and episodic way? In other words, is it better to take part in a conception of the world mechanically imposed by the external environment, i.e. by one of the many social groups in which everyone is automatically involved from the moment of his entry into the conscious world (and this can be one's village or province; it can have its origins in the parish and the "intellectual activity" of the local priest or ageing patriarch whose wisdom is law, or in the little old woman

---

14. Gramsci entered the title of Q11 ("Notes for an Introduction and Starting Point for the Study of Philosophy and the History of Culture") on page 11 of his notebook, which was untypical of his usual practice of entering a title on the first page of his "special" notebooks. However, in Q10II§60 he refers to Q11 as "the notebook on the 'Introduction to the Study of Philosophy'" (Gramsci 1995, 319; 1975, 1357). On these points, see Francioni and Frosini (2009a, 3).

15. Although "Some Preliminary Points of Reference" appears as the twelfth entry in Q11, evi-dence suggests that it is likely the first note Gramsci entered in the notebook. As Gianni Francioni has documented, Gramsci reserved the first ten pages of some of his "special" notebooks for later-planned introductions, meaning that the first notes he entered appear on page 11. Along with Q11, Q19–22 and Q25 follow this pattern. See Francioni (2009, 31) and Francioni and Frosini (2009a, 3).

who has inherited the lore of the witches or the minor intellectual soured by
his own stupidity and inability to act)? Or, on the other hand, is it better to
work out consciously and critically one's own conception of the world and
thus, in connection with the labours of one's own brain, choose one's
sphere of activity, take an active part in the creation of the history of the
world, be one's own guide, refusing to accept passively and supinely from
outside the moulding of one's personality? (QII§12, Gramsci 1971, 323–34;
1975, 1375–6).

As these rhetorical questions suggest, the idea of living according to one's own intellect and will presents an opening to question common sense and to formulate a
systematic conception of the world. The point is to become critically self-aware of
one's conception of the world, to think independently, and to be cognizant of the
mental and practical activities one adopts as one's own. Whether one is aware of it
or not, one's conception of the world is mediated through the social environment
of which one is a part and by "the many social groups in which everyone is auto-
matically involved" from the moment of consciously engaging with the world.
One's intellectual orientation, as Gramsci illustrates, can range from that of the
local priest or the lore of witches to that of an intellectual. In other words, one's
socialization and formation of consciousness is subject to one's social position, cultural environment, and interaction with others.

However, Gramsci argues that it is preferable to develop one's consciousness
critically with respect to externally imposed elements, and this requires consciously developing one's conception of the world as opposed to uncritically or passively
accepting elements of thought that may contradict one's own activity. Such an undertaking includes understanding one's self in relation to the historical processes
of which one is a part: "The starting-point of critical elaboration is the consciousness of what one really is, and is 'knowing thyself' as a product of the historical
process to date which has deposited in you an infinity of traces, without the
benefit of leaving an inventory. At the outset, it is necessary for one to compile
such an inventory" (QII§12, Gramsci 1971, 324; 1975, 1376; translation slightly modified). As this suggests, our consciousness is always situated within historical processes, and those processes deposit "an infinity of traces" in our consciousness
without "leaving an inventory." To know one's self critically requires compiling
such an inventory, to be self conscious of the composition of one's consciousness.
This process itself involves understanding one's material situation and social position historically and within the ensemble of one's social relations.

Gramsci's reference to the idea of "knowing thyself" in Notebook II echoes a
similar idea he developed sixteen years earlier in an article entitled "Socialism
and Culture," which appeared in the newspaper *Il Grido del Popolo* in 1916. In
that context, Gramsci's concern was similar to his focus of Notebook II: namely,
providing a critique and alternative to determinist conceptions of history and
culture. Expounding on the idea of critical self-awareness, he paraphrased

passages from Vico's *New Science*, in which Vico provided a political interpretation of Solon's dictum to "know thyself," which Socrates later adopted as his own:

> Vico maintains that in this dictum Solon wished to admonish the plebeians, who believed themselves to be of *bestial origin* and the nobility to be of *divine origin*, to reflect on themselves and see that they had the *same human nature as the nobles* and hence should claim to be *their equals in civil law*. Vico then points to this consciousness of human equality between plebeians and nobles as the basis and historical reason for the rise of the democratic republics of antiquity. (Gramsci 1977 [1916], 10)

Gramsci draws into focus the point that Solon prompted the plebeians to question their own conception of themselves as bestial in origin. Such an overturning of their internalized notions of themselves was necessary for their struggle for equality to advance. In this sense, the notion of "knowing thyself" has radical political implications. The point is not simply to know one's individual self but to understand one's historical self, as in one's social position within the larger historical trajectory—that is, to understand oneself in relation to the philosophical foundations of one's political context and to question the dominant discourses that structure the formation of one's existence, especially those discourses that reinforce the subordination of one social group to another. With respect to the "simple," their position is comparable to the plebeians of ancient Athens in that they have internalized a religious conception of themselves that has justified their subordinate social position. Yet, in reality, their conditions were not the creation of God but of humans.

The process of "knowing thyself" in the formation of a historical consciousness requires a critical analysis of the context and origins of one's beliefs, to be aware of the elements of one's thought, even the elements that have become uncritically absorbed from popular philosophy, religion, and common sense. However, this is a difficult process due to the contradictory nature of the ensemble of social relations and the varying elements of historical consciousness among different social groups. "Among subaltern groups," Gramsci writes in Notebook 8, "given the lack of historical initiative, the fragmentation is greater; they face a harder struggle to liberate themselves from imposed (rather than freely propounded) principles in order to arrive at an autonomous historical consciousness" (Q8§153, Gramsci 2007, 321; 1975, 1033). The idea of arriving at "an autonomous historical consciousness" suggests that the point is not for intellectuals to impose a new philosophy or set of beliefs on the "simple" but to address the concerns of the "simple" from where they are at—from their common sense—so as to confront the practical necessity of giving conscious direction to their activity. There are a number of historical examples, as Gramsci points out, such as the rise of popular universities and other movements in Italy, that demonstrate the simple's "genuine enthusiasm and a strong determination to attain a higher cultural level and a higher conception of the world" (Q11§12, Gramsci 1971, 330; 1975, 1382).

Attaining a higher level of culture presents a moment of transformation in which one questions the coherence of one's conception of the world in order to provide "conscious direction to one's activity." Gramsci describes this process as the formation of "good sense," defined as "the healthy nucleus that exists in 'common sense' ... which deserves to be made more unitary and coherent," and also as a "renewed common sense" that possesses coherence (QII§12, Gramsci 1971, 328; 1975, 1380). In his words:

> A philosophy of praxis cannot but present itself at the outset in a polemical and critical guise, as superseding the existing mode of thinking and existing concrete thought (the existing cultural world). First of all, therefore, it must be a criticism of "common sense," basing itself initially, however, on common sense in order to demonstrate that "everyone" is a philosopher and that it is not a question of introducing from scratch a scientific form of thought into everyone's individual life, but of renovating and making "critical" an already existing activity. (QII§12, Gramsci 1971, 330–1; 1975, 1383)

"But," he argues, "this can only happen if the demands of cultural contact with the 'simple' are continually felt" (QII§12, Gramsci 1971, 330; 1975, 1382–3). Unlike the relationship with the Church, this requires "a dialectic between the intellectuals and the masses" in which "the intellectual stratum is tied to an analogous movement on the part of the mass of the 'simple,' who raise themselves to higher levels of culture and at the same time extend their circle of influence towards the stratum of specialised intellectuals" (QII§12, Gramsci 1971, 334; 1975, 1386).

This makes the philosophy of praxis distinct from Catholicism:

> The position of the philosophy of praxis is the antithesis of the Catholic. The philosophy of praxis does not tend to leave the "simple" in their primitive philosophy of common sense, but rather to lead them to a higher conception of life. If it affirms the need for contact between intellectuals and simple it is not in order to restrict scientific activity and preserve unity at the low level of the masses, but precisely in order to construct an intellectual-moral bloc which can make politically possible the intellectual progress of the mass and not only of small intellectual groups. (QII§12, Gramsci 1971, 332–3; 1975, 1384–5)

In this sense, unlike the Catholic Church, the task of the philosophy of praxis is to remain in contact with the "simple" so as to develop a higher level of culture. As Gramsci noted earlier, the Church could not conceive of raising the "simple" to the level of the intellectuals so as to heal the rupture among the faithful. A "dialectic between the intellectuals and the masses" presents the conditions for the diffusion of a higher conception of the world to expand beyond the confines of narrow intellectual groups and to transform the greater culture.

The process of defining a critical conception of the world and formulating a decisive will includes confronting traditional ways of thinking. It is on this point that

Gramsci's criticisms of religion and mechanistic notions of Marxism intersect. The Church presents a deterministic conception of the world in which the "simple" are portrayed as an object, without freedom or agency, whose conditions have been created by God. Determinist conceptions of Marxism, such as the one Bukharin presents in the *Popular Manual*, amount to a similar form of fatalism, in Gramsci's view, in that social conditions are conceived as constructions of objective historical laws. "It should be noted," he writes, "how the deterministic, fatalistic and mechanistic element has been a direct ideological 'aroma' emanating from the philosophy of praxis, rather like religion or drugs (in their stupefying effect)." Such a conception, he argues, was "made necessary and justified historically by the 'subaltern' character of certain social strata," providing a general framework to understand life and the world (QII§12, Gramsci 1971, 336; 1975, 1387–8). Both views amount to mechanistic conceptions of history in that the conditions of the "simple" are posited as the consequence of extrahuman causes. It was along these lines, Gramsci suggests, that Bukharin reproduced a Catholic conception of the world, albeit without having knowledge of its tradition.[16]

The "mechanicist conception" of the world, Gramsci writes, "has been a religion of the subaltern [which] is shown by an analysis of the development of the Christian religion" (QII§12, Gramsci 1971, 337; 1975, 1389). Such a conception, he continues, provides the popular masses not only with "a specific way of rationalising the world" and a "general framework for real practical activity" but also with justifications for historical defeats and faith in an indeterminate future:

> When you don't have the initiative in the struggle and the struggle itself comes eventually to be identified with a series of defeats, mechanical determinism becomes a tremendous force of moral resistance, of cohesion and of patient and obstinate perseverance. "I have been defeated for the moment, but the tide of history is working for me in the long term." Real will takes on the garments of an act of faith in a certain rationality of history and in a primitive and empirical form of impassioned finalism which appears in the role of a substitute for the Predestination or Providence of confessional religions. (QII§12, Gramsci 1971, 336; 1975, 1388)

In this instance, historical determinism functions similar to religion, but religion in a new guise. Religious providence is replaced with historical providence, religious salvation with historical salvation. In both instances, the conditions of the "simple" are understood as being determined by an external force and their resolution as occurring in the next world or in an unknown future. In this sense, Gramsci's criticism of religious materialism functions along the same lines as his criticism of vulgar forms of historical materialism.

---

16. See Q7§47 (Gramsci 2007, 194–5; 1975, 894), Q8§215 (Gramsci 2007, 364–5; 1975, 1075–6); QII§17 (Gramsci 1971, 440–6; 1975, 1411–16).

A critical turning point, as discussed above, emerges when subaltern groups confront their mechanistic conception of the world through the practical necessity of
giving conscious direction to their will and activity:

> But when the "subaltern" becomes directive and responsible for the economic
> activity of the masses, mechanicism at a certain point becomes an imminent
> danger and a revision must take place in modes of thinking because a change
> has taken place in the social mode of existence. The boundaries and the
> dominion of the "force of circumstance" have become restricted. But why?
> Because, basically, if yesterday the subaltern element was a thing, today it
> is no longer a thing but an historical person, a protagonist; if yesterday it
> was not responsible, because "resisting" a will external to itself, now it feels
> itself to be responsible because it is no longer resisting but an agent, necessar-
> ily active and taking the initiative. (QII§12, Gramsci 1971, 336–7; 1975, 1388)

Here Gramsci describes how one's mode of thinking is transformed from a determinist to an absolute historicist conception of the world. It is in this moment that
the "subaltern element"—which Gramsci uncharacteristically uses in the singular
in this passage—no longer sees itself as a "thing," as a determined artifact produced by the immutable laws of history or God, but as a "historical person, a protagonist," transformed by a critical understanding of one's situation through the
process of self-liberation. In effect, liberation begins with critical thinking and
the formulation of critical consciousness (Buttigieg 2011).

After "Some Preliminary Points of Reference" in Notebook 11, Gramsci devotes a
section of the notebook to an analysis of Bukharin's *Popular Manual* under the title
"Critical Observations and Notes on an Attempt at a *Popular Manual of Sociology*."[17]
In the first note of the section, he returns to the question of how one should
approach writing a book on philosophy directed toward a mass audience, and
he argues that "a work like the *Popular Manual*, which is essentially destined for
a community of readers who are not professional intellectuals, should have
taken as its starting point a critical analysis of the philosophy of common sense"
(QII§13, Gramsci 1971, 419; 1975, 1396). Because the religious and materialistic elements that predominate common sense are based upon "'superstitious' and acritical" foundations, one of the dangers of Bukharin's *Popular Manual* is that it "often
reinforces, instead of scientifically criticising, these acritical elements which have
caused common sense to remain Ptolemaic, anthropomorphic and anthropocentric" (QII§13, Gramsci 1971, 420; 1975, 1397). The critical analysis of common sense,
following Gramsci's approach, entails addressing it in a way similar to the analysis
of philosophy or of a conception of the world, but with the intent of ascertaining
what the masses think. The point of such an approach is to go beyond common

---

17. See QII§13–35, Gramsci (1975, 1396–1450). Also see Gramsci (1971, 419–72), although appearing in
a different order.

sense and to present an opening for the articulation of a new philosophy and "to create a 'new' good sense" (QII§13, Gramsci 1971, 423; 1975, 1400).

Conclusion

Gramsci's observations on the "simple" and the Catholic Church's paternalistic portrayal of common people that initially appear in Notebook 1 present an entry point into several intersecting lines of inquiry in which he examines how religious, philosophical, and cultural currents become elements of common sense and affect modes of thinking, political participation, and the organization of society. He was motivated by the idea of examining the relationship between intellectuals and the people in the formation of common ways of thinking and modes of life.[18] Given the Catholic Church's influential position in the formation of the Italian state and culture, it functioned as a collective intellectual. It actively disseminated a philosophy and worldview that reinforced the impoverished conditions of common people with religious and divine explanations that in effect depoliticized class inequality and circumvented its resolution. As the "simple" had internalized a conception of the world that justified their own subalternity, Gramsci believed it was necessary to develop a mode of thinking that addressed the complexities of modern society.

Because of the uncritical nature of common sense, Gramsci argues that it is necessary for the "simple" to develop a "new common sense, " or a "renewed common sense," that contains critical and reflective philosophical foundations that transcend the passivity and paternalism of religion and dominant ideologies. In his view, deterministic and positivist forms of Marxism provide inadequate responses to religion because they are founded upon a similarly fatalistic worldview. The philosophy of praxis, as complete and autonomous, provides, he contends, the basis for a new common sense based upon critical consciousness. The philosophy of praxis, in his view, presents a superior conception of the world when compared to common sense and other ideologies, including religion, because it is founded upon an "absolute secularisation and earthliness of thought" and upon a practical understanding of human existence that aims to empower subaltern groups in their struggle for intellectual and political hegemony (QII§27, Gramsci 1971, 465; 1975, 1437).[19] He writes in Notebook 10: "For the philosophy of praxis, ideologies are anything but arbitrary; they are real historical facts which must be combated and their nature as instruments of domination revealed, not for reasons of morality and so on, but precisely for reasons of political struggle so as to make the governed intellectually independent of the

18. On this point, see Gramsci to Tatiana Schucht, 19 March 1927 (Gramsci 1994, 1:84); and Gramsci to Tatiana Schucht, 3 August 1931 (Gramsci 1994, 2:52).
19. On this point, see Green and Ives (2009) and Wainwright (2010).

governors, in order to destroy one hegemony and create another as a necessary moment in the overturning of praxis" (Q10II§41xii, Gramsci 1995, 395; 1975, 1319). The development of a "new common sense" is therefore necessary for the "simple" to become "intellectually independent" in the struggle to transform their social conditions and lives.

Gramsci's critique of common sense illustrates the radically democratic and critical focus of his analysis of the "simple" in that he identifies the limitations of their conception of the world and modes of thought in order to improve and strengthen their intellectual capacities and in turn the effectiveness of their political activity. In viewing the philosophy of praxis as the basis for a renewed common sense, he sought to demonstrate that the conditions of the "simple" are neither divine nor natural and that prayer, predestination, and what he calls "superstition" will not transform their circumstances. Producing a higher conception of culture requires a philosophical movement that does not remain restricted among intellectuals, that "never forgets to remain in contact with the 'simple' and indeed finds in this contact the source of the problems it sets out to study and to resolve" (Q11§12, Gramsci 1971, 330; 1975, 1382). Such a movement requires articulating and disseminating a new conception of philosophy and culture as critically grounded while providing a basis of struggle. This essentially constitutes the foundation for a radical form of democracy in which the "simple" play the predominant role in the direction of their political lives and in the creation of a new hegemony.

Acknowledgments

I wish to thank Joseph A. Buttigieg and Cosimo Zene for reflections on earlier versions of this article.

References

Boothman, D. 1995. Introduction to *Further selections from the "Prison Notebooks,"* by A. Gramsci, xiii–lxxxvii. Minneapolis: University of Minnesota Press.

Bukharin, N. I. 1925. *Historical materialism: A system of sociology.* New York: International Publishers.

Buttigieg, J. A. 1992. Introduction to vol. 1 of *Prison notebooks,* by A. Gramsci, ed. J. A. Buttigieg, 1–64. New York: Columbia University Press.

———. 2011. Antonio Gramsci: Liberation begins with critical thinking. In *Political philosophy in the twentieth century: Authors and arguments,* ed. C. H. Zuckert, 44–57. Cambridge: Cambridge University Press.

Dainotto, R. M. 2009. Gramsci and Labriola: Philology, philosophy of praxis. In *Perspectives on Gramsci: Politics, culture and social theory,* ed. J. Francese, 50–68. New York: Routledge.

Francioni, G. 2009. Come lavorava Gramsci. In *Quaderni del carcere: Edizione anastatica dei manoscritti*, by A. Gramsci, ed. G. Francioni, 1:21–60. Rome: Istituto della Enciclopedia Italiana-L'Unione Sarda.

Francioni, G., and F. Frosini. 2009. Quaderno 11 (1932): Nota introduttiva. In *Quaderni del carcere: Edizione anastatica dei manoscritti*, by A. Gramsci, ed. G. Francioni, 15:1–22. Rome: Istituto della Enciclopedia Italiana-L'Unione Sarda.

Frosini, F. 2003. *Gramsci e la filosofia: Saggio sui Quaderni del carcere*. Rome: Carocci.

Gramsci, A. 1971. *Selections from the "Prison notebooks."* Ed. and trans. Q. Hoare and G. N. Smith. New York: International Publishers.

———. 1975. *Quaderni del carcere*. 4 vols. Ed. V. Gerratana. Turin: Einaudi.

———. 1977. *Selections from political writings, 1910–1920*. Ed. Q. Hoare. Minneapolis: University of Minnesota Press.

———. 1992. *Prison notebooks*. Vol. 1. Ed. J. A. Buttigieg. Trans. J. A. Buttigieg and A. Callari. New York: Columbia University Press.

———. 1994. *Letters from prison*. 2 vols. Ed. F. Rosengarten. Trans. R. Rosenthal. New York: Columbia University Press.

———. 1996. *Prison notebooks*. Vol. 2. Ed. and trans. J. A. Buttigieg. New York: Columbia University Press.

———. 2007. *Prison notebooks*. Vol. 3. Ed. and trans. J. A. Buttigieg. New York: Columbia University Press.

Green, M. E. 2011. Rethinking the subaltern and the question of censorship in Gramsci's *Prison notebooks*. *Postcolonial Studies* 14 (4): 387–404.

Green, M. E., and P. Ives. 2009. Subalternity and language: Overcoming the fragmentation of common sense. *Historical Materialism* 17 (1): 3–30.

Haug, W. F. 2001. From Marx to Gramsci, from Gramsci to Marx: Historical materialism and the philosophy of praxis. *Rethinking Marxism* 13 (1): 69–82.

La Rocca, T. 1991. *Gramsci e la religione*. Brescia, Ital.: Queriniana.

———. 2009. Chiesa cattolica. In *Dizionario gramsciano 1926–1937*, ed. G. Liguori and P. Voza, 126–9. Rome: Carocci.

Marx, K. 1975. A contribution to the critique of Hegel's "Philosophy of right." In vol. 3 of *Collected works*, by K. Marx and F. Engels. New York: International Publishers.

———. 1976. Theses on Feuerbach. In vol. 5 of *Collected works*, by K. Marx and F. Engels. New York: International Publishers.

Musitelli, M. P. 2009. Brescianesimo. In *Dizionario gramsciano 1926–1937*, ed. G. Liguori and P. Voza, 80–3. Rome: Carocci.

Thomas, P. D. 2009. *The Gramscian moment: Philosophy, hegemony and Marxism*. Boston: Brill.

Wainwright, J. 2010. On Gramsci's "conceptions of the world." *Transactions of the Institute of British Geographers* 35 (4): 507–21.

Subalterns, Religion, and the Philosophy of Praxis in Gramsci's *Prison Notebooks*

Fabio Frosini

Translated by Derek Boothman

The purpose of this essay is to reconstruct the relationship between subalterns, religion, and philosophy in Antonio Gramsci's Prison Notebooks. *With the birth of mass society—that is, with the entry onto the political scene of the popular masses, and above all of the peasantry—politics entered directly into relation with irrational passions bound up with the religious mentality, and hegemony was constructed not thanks to the institution of a "filter" for the passions (as was the parliament of "notables") but through the mastering of those "passions" using forms of Caesarist and charismatic democracy. In Gramsci's view, the political action of the subaltern classes had to confront this new form of hegemony by recognizing the value of the profound content of religious ideas (which always indicate the need for a unification of theory and practice) and by working on a "translation" of those ideas into the forms of self-organization and self-emancipation.*

In this contribution I want to propose a reconstruction of the relationship between "subalterns" and the "state" in Gramsci's *Prison Notebooks* from the point of view of the concept of "religion." As we shall see, the concept of religion is interpreted by Gramsci in an original way. In fact, for him religion lies at the root of all political activity and at the same time is the content that mainly characterizes Marxism as a "philosophy of praxis." To unravel these nexuses, I want first (section 1) to reconstruct the way in which Gramsci presents the relationship between subaltern classes and the modern state—in particular, the situation that began to be created in Europe after the Great War. The drive by subaltern classes to give themselves forms of autonomous organization was challenged by an equivalent intervention by the state, which "entered" into society to prevent the masses from organizing themselves autonomously and thereby mounting a hegemonic challenge. Following from this, I will then (section 2) show how, according to Gramsci, fascism's "occupation" of society and its reorganization of society on a corporative basis was not an abnormal exception but became the European model for restructuring bourgeois hegemony. Through the categories of "intellectuals" and—linked to this—of "bureaucracy," Gramsci tried to think through the fundamental traits of the new politics during the crisis of parliamentarism and as politics shifted to the articulation of society. In order to be able to think through this new form of politics, in section 3 I see Gramsci as having recourse to the category of "religion"—derived from Benedetto Croce—as the equivalent of any conception of the world having "a conformant ethic."[1] The use of this category allows him to consider simultaneously two distinct but connected moments: the irruption of the masses into political life, with the irrational and impassioned aspects that this involved, and the impassioned nature of philosophy at the moment when it ceases to be simple *individual* speculation and becomes a historical fact, a *collective* mentality. The final two sections are dedicated to exploring the implications of the use of this wider concept of religion. On the one hand (section 4), I show how Benedetto Croce made this concept of religion functional to a recovery of bourgeois hegemony in the presence of the broad, politically active popular masses, insofar as religion allows a connection between philosophy and common sense, rationality, and irrationality in a renewed form of national unity. On the other hand (section 5), I reconstruct the way in which, in the *Prison Notebooks*, Gramsci frees himself from his youthful ideological subalternity to Croce and redefines religion, inasmuch as it is a conception of the world, in the terms of a Sorelian-style "myth." In this way, on the one hand he subtracts myth from irrationalism, and on the other he breaks asunder the Crocean representation of a "religious" type of national unity. Redefining religion as a political myth makes it possible to shift the whole discourse onto a practical level, and in this way subaltern classes are able to recover a space in which they can conceive their own autonomous organization.

A Reciprocal Siege

In a text written in June 1930[2] and entitled "History of the Subaltern Classes," Gramsci focuses on the notion of the "modern State" in relation to subaltern classes.[3] In Gramsci's view, the modern state is characterized by the fact of *including* subaltern classes within a unitary political space. Gramsci contrasts this modern state to ancient and medieval polycentrism, with its coexistence of a plurality of juridical ordinances and social statuses, its juxtaposition of "different races," and its superposition and stratification of jurisdictions, competences, and prerogatives. The "territorial and social centralization (the one is but a function of the other)" of the modern political space is comparatively homogeneous and of univocal nature (Q3§18, Gramsci 1975, 302–3; 1996, 24). In this notion of the state as Gramsci outlines it, there is an evident convergence between

---

1. See Gramsci (1995, 390) and also Gramsci's point of reference—i.e., Croce (1932, 21; 1933, 18): "Now he who gathers together and considers all these characteristics of the liberal ideal does not hesitate to call it what it was: a 'religion.' He calls it so, of course, because he looks for what is essential and intrinsic in every religion, which always lies in the concept of reality and an ethics that conforms to this concept. It excludes the mythological element, which constitutes only a secondary differentiation between religion and philosophy."

Note that citations of content from the *Prison Notebooks* in this essay generally list the critical edition (Gramsci 1975) of the Istituto Gramsci, by notebook and section number, and then one of the various English translations from which the English quotations are taken. Any alterations from the English translations are noted. Citations of the works of Croce and others likewise often list first the original source and then an English translation.

2. For the dating of texts in the *Prison Notebooks* (*Quaderni del carcere*), see Cospito (2011, 896–904).

3. For an analysis of the concept of the subaltern in the *Prison Notebooks*, see Francioni and Frosini (2009), Green (2011), Zene (2011), and Liguori (2015a, 2015b).

modern monarchical absolutism and the process that culminated in the French Revolution (and then in Napoleon), seen together as moments of a homogeneous dynamic
process—the bourgeoisie's assertion of itself as the dominant class.

But the inclusion of subalterns in the state is ambivalent. If the modern state abolishes the "State as a federation of classes" (Q3§18, Gramsci 1975, 303; 1996, 25) by sup-
pressing the autonomous statuses of subaltern groups and subjugating them to the
same juridical discipline, thereby making possible the development of the bourgeoisie
as the dominant class, at the same time this unification makes it possible for subaltern
groups to undertake political action since now the processes of corporative and trade-
union self-organization, followed by the politics of subaltern groups, are no longer
limited within defined spaces. Instead, they potentially involve the entire national
society: "Certain forms of the internal life of the subaltern classes are reborn as
parties, trade unions, cultural associations." And it is for this reason that, as Gramsci
observes, the politics of inclusion must, at the same time, always and also be one of neutralization. Gramsci ends this section with a reference to fascism ("the modern dictatorship"), which "abolishes these forms of class autonomy as well, and tries hard to
incorporate them into the activity of the State: in other words, the centralization of
the whole life of the nation in the hands of the ruling class becomes frenetic and all-
consuming."[4]

With fascism, then, the modern intertwining of inclusion and neutralization underwent no *essential* change as compared with previous history but was intensified and
became more dramatic as a direct reflection of the degree of self-organization
reached by subaltern classes. Gramsci clarified this point of view in a text dating to
August 1931 in which the current situation was described as an organic connection
between a "war of position" and "hegemony." In other words, in the twentieth
century—and especially after 1917 and the war—thanks to the coupling of "inclusion
+ neutralization," the state's policy of exercising hegemony had to take on the form
of a "war of position": namely, a struggle that ranged over all locations in society.
The government of the masses—that is, the organization of all aspects of the life of
the entire population—became one of the essential tasks of the state, which thus
"entered" into society, thereby redefining the distinction between "public" and
"private."[5]

The birth of "mass society" was interpreted by Gramsci (Q6§138, 1975, 802; 2007, 109)
as the advent of a partially new form of hegemony, a hegemony that possessed a pervasive and wide-ranging character: "The war of position," he wrote, "calls on enormous
masses of people to make huge sacrifices; that is why an unprecedented concentration
of hegemony is required and hence a more 'interventionist' kind of government that
will engage more openly in the offensive against the opponents and ensure, once
and for all, the 'impossibility' of internal disintegration by putting in place controls
of all kinds—political, administrative, etc." This massive process of organizing the
whole of society, insofar as it is a form of "attack" on the popular masses, takes the

---

4. For a comment on this text see Frosini (2012c, 71–2). In the second draft of this text (Q25§4, Gramsci
1975, 2287), written in 1934, "all-consuming" is replaced by "totalitarian," which Gramsci places in inverted commas in order to emphasize the technical nature of the word.
5. See De Felice (1977) and Portantiero (1981, 10–22, 42–59, 161–71).

form of a "war of siege [*assedio*]," which in this passage Gramsci contrasts with a "war of maneuver." The masses are "besieged," but this takes place precisely because of the degree of self-organization attained by the masses themselves, for whom "the siege is reciprocal, whatever the appearances; the mere fact that the ruling power has to parade all its resources reveals its estimate of the adversary."[6] Expressing this in other terms, the state has to besiege the masses because the masses are besieging the state. Not only is there a process of the "statalization" of society—in the sense of its becoming bureaucratically more rigid—but also intertwined with this is a process of the socialization of politics: that is, of the internalization of the contradictions of society inside the public structures of the state, which in consequence becomes in part "a house divided against itself" and pluralized through the presence within it of huge politicized and mobilized masses.[7]

The attempted absorption of the forms of class autonomy within the state therefore has the consequence of annulling the "autonomous" character of these forms of organization but does not change the fact that the masses are "organized." In short, the expansion of the state changes the nature of both public and private spheres, and the borderline between state and civil society, which had previously seemed to be annulled, returns to constitute itself in a fragmentary way inside the articulations of the totalitarian state (which is in fact a state-society in the double sense that it "invades" society but is also modified by it). In this way, throughout the whole fascist organization of social life, just as in the totalitarian party, different currents are reformed and class conflict is reproduced.[8]

Fascism, Bureaucracy, and the "Intellectuals"

In Gramsci's view, fascism provided the "model" for reorganizing bourgeois hegemony in Europe.[9] This point is obvious in the above quoted text on the nexus between the war of position and hegemony, written in August 1931, and it was made explicit later, in April 1932, when Gramsci (Q8§236, 1975, 1089; 2007, 378) wondered whether fascism was "the form of 'passive revolution' specific to the 20th century just as liberalism was the form of 'passive revolution' specific to the 19th century." Far from considering it a terrorist dictatorship, this regime was for Gramsci the source of

6. In two texts written in May–June 1933, Gramsci (Q15§47, 1975, 1807–8; Q15§59, 1975, 1822–4; 1971b, 104–6) went as far as defining the "trade-union phenomenon" (i.e., the complex processes of the self-organization of subaltern classes) as the origin of the crisis of bourgeois hegemony that broke out after the war, a crisis expressed on the one hand in the decadence of parliamentarism and on the other in the more general economic crisis.
7. See Portantiero (1981, 22).
8. See Rossi and Vacca (2007, 108–9). Gramsci (1971a, 486; 1978, 331) and Togliatti had already formulated this idea in the intervention of the political commission of the Lyon Congress in 1926: "It is necessary to examine the stratifications of fascism itself: for given the totalitarian system which fascism tends to install, it will be within fascism itself that the conflicts which cannot express themselves in other ways will tend to re-emerge."
9. On this assessment of Gramsci's, see De Felice (1977), Mangoni (1977), and Frosini (2012a). In general, see also Maier (1975) and De Felice (2007).

inspiration for all the types of regimes that in Europe, with different and even opposed modalities, posed the question of the reorganization of bourgeois hegemony.

"Passive revolution"[10] consists in the capacity to repropose *in a new form* that intertwining of inclusion and neutralization that in the nineteenth century was realized by the liberal state. In the era of liberalism, the goal of including and neutralizing the masses was reached in Gramsci's (Q1§47, 1975, 56–7; 1992, 153–4) view through the extremely broad development of organizations in civil society, promoted in the private form by the bourgeois class. In the presence of a massive movement of self-organization by the popular classes (a "trade-union phenomenon"),[11] this policy could no longer prove effective. The fascist response consisted, as we have seen, in what Gramsci called a "more 'interventionist' form of government" united in an "unprecedented concentration of hegemony." The situation of "siege" is precisely what comes from a greater aggressiveness and dynamism combined with an increased concentration of hegemonic politics, with a progressive superposition between the activity of the state and private intervention.[12]

The whole of society is now "organized"—in other words, articulated in hegemonic institutions: "Nobody is unorganized and without a party, provided that organization and party are understood broadly, in a nonformal sense" (Q6§36, Gramsci 1975, 800; 2007, 107). This self-organization, which subaltern classes had attempted to realize from the end of feudalism onward, is now brought to its completion by the adversary.[13] We are undoubtedly dealing here with a "revolution" whose "passive" character lies in the heteronomous nature of its realization. In fact, the bourgeoisie appropriates to itself some of the basic demands of the working classes, such as the need to overcome the anarchy of market society, and realizes this in its own way by maintaining the division of society into classes:

> A passive revolution takes place when, through a "reform" process, the economic structure is transformed from an individualistic one to a planned economy (economia diretta) and when the emergence of an "intermediate economy"—i.e., an economy in the space between the purely individualistic one and the one that is comprehensively planned—enables the transition to more advanced political and cultural forms without the kind of radical and destructive cataclysms that are utterly devastating. "Corporativism" could be—or, as it grows, could become —this form of intermediate economy that has a "passive" character. (Q8§236, Gramsci 1975, 1089; 2007, 378)[14]

10. On this category see Kanoussi (2000, 66–81), Voza (2004), and Thomas (2006).

11. See note 6 above.

12. Not by chance was it only after August 1931 (when he wrote Notebook 6, §138, on the "reciprocal siege") that Gramsci began to append explanatory adverbs to the adjective "private" when referring to the organisms of civil society (specifications such as "so-called" or "commonly called"), which emphasize civil society's real character of being "public-State." See Gramsci and Schucht (1997, 791; and see Q8§179, Gramsci 1975, 1049; 2007, 338; Q12§1, Gramsci 1975, 1518–9; 1971b, 12).

13. See Gramsci (Q1§43, 1975, 35–6; 1992, 131): "The current corporativism, with its consequent diffusion of this social type [namely, "the factory 'technician'" and the "trade-union organizer"] on a nation scale in a more systematic and consistent way than the old trade unionism could have achieved, is in a certain sense an instrument of moral and political unity."

14. For the first of these expressions ("economia secondo un piano") I adopt the translation by David Forgacs, "planned economy" (see Gramsci 2000, 265), and not "economy according to a plan," proposed

In order to "organize" society on a mass scale, fascism has to develop its own bureaucratic apparatus, enormously. For Gramsci, however, this proliferation of the bureaucratic structure is not an abnormal characteristic of the Italian state. It reflects a long-term trend in bourgeois society in general, which after the Great War underwent a strong acceleration in all countries. On this subject Gramsci drew from a number of Max Weber's reflections[15] regarding the situation in which Germany found itself at the end of the war, and Gramsci transferred these to the case of Italy.[16]

According to Weber (1919, 23; 1994, 220), the increase in the organization of society corresponds both to a growth in the extension and degree of autonomy of the bureaucracy as a specialized administrative stratum (ceto)[17] and also to the entrance en masse of the masses into political activity. The consequence of this dual process of the bureaucratization and massification of politics is the crisis of the centrality of parliament. The parliamentary mediation of social interests is replaced by processes of a "Caesaristic" nature: that is, the direct investiture of a "chief" by the "masses." Different from the case of democracy of a liberal type, in which it was just a few "notables" gathered together in parliament who chose a political leader, now there is a direct passage, through acclamation or plebiscite, from the "masses" to the "chief" (Weber 1919, 124–5; 1994, 220–1).

For this reason, bureaucracy as a politically "non-responsible" power and Caesaristic democracy as an antiparliamentary and "plebeian" power (Weber 1919, 124; 1994, 220), by bringing about a crisis of parliament, favor the advent of a process of political selection no longer based on a rational assessment but on "faith" and on the "purely emotional and irrational" nature of the masses (Weber 1919, 139; 1994, 230; see also Portantiero 1981, 11–9).

These reflections of Weber's started from the standpoint of a reorganization and reform of the power of parliament vis-à-vis the bureaucracy (and therefore also the government) and the masses of the ruled. The importance of these reflections, from Gramsci's point of view, is to have clearly shown the nexus between the processes of the socialization of politics, the massification of society, and the growth of the bureaucratic apparatus. Gramsci's perspective, however, goes much wider. The phenomenon of bureaucracy cannot be isolated from the overall reorganization of the bourgeois hegemonic model. As we have seen, the decadence of parliament does not in fact imply for Gramsci an irreversible crisis of bourgeois hegemony, and neither is this decadence due to the growth of the bureaucracy. Rather, the reason for the crisis of the parliamentary institution lies in the fact that political mediation has been shifted elsewhere.

The category of "intellectuals"—which Gramsci (Q4§49, 1975, 476; 1996, 200) redefines as the ensemble of those who in a given society have an "'organizational' or

---

by Joseph A. Buttigieg (see Gramsci 2007, 378), because in the latter the allusion to contemporary debates becomes less visible. I prefer to leave the second expression, "economia diretta," in Italian since it is the Italian translation of the French "économie dirigée" and of the English "planned economy." Forgacs's ("command economy") and Buttigieg's ("administered economy") translations tend to hide this fact. See the unsigned article "Economia diretta" (1932; a report of the World Social Economic Congress held in Amsterdam in August 1931), which is the source for Gramsci's statement in Notebook 8, §236.

15. Beside the English translation (Weber 1994), I also make reference to an Italian translation of Weber's (1919) *Parlament und Regierung im neugeordneten Deutschland* since it is the one used by Gramsci.

16. See Gramsci (Q3§319, 1975, 388; 1996, 105–6; 1971b, 227–8).

17. See Weber (1919, 21–63; 1994, 145–77).

connective" function, both in the public sphere (as bureaucracy) and in the private one (as promoters of activity in civil society)—helps us interpret this shift in the locus of "politics."[18] This is because intellectuals, different from the Weberian bureaucracy, are not independent of politics, while on the other hand neither do they come into classic parliamentary politics. Only if we reduce politics to parliamentary mediation will it be possible for bureaucratic activity to appear as something completely antithetic to political activity in the real sense, and only then will the growth in the powers of the "administration" turn out to favor the unleashing of demagogic processes. In actual fact, from the Gramscian point of view, between bureaucracy in the strict sense and professional politicians (in the Weberian sense of *Beruf*), there is indeed no antithesis. Rather, they connect up organically on the level of the new type of politics inaugurated after the First World War.

Masses, Religion, and "Orthodoxy"

A consequence of great importance for the institution of a new relationship between the masses and politics is, as we have seen through the reading of Weber, the fact that *faith* and *irrational passions* become determining elements of political life. This problematic is taken up again in the *Prison Notebooks*, but from a standpoint opposed to that of Weber. If it is true that the presence of the masses in public life implies the end of the filtering role played by the parliament of "notables," then what one must rely on in Gramsci's view is not, as Weber (1919, ch. 3) asks, a parliament that has been renewed and is therefore capable of reestablishing that filter in the new situation. The presence of the masses within politics does however represent *progress* as compared with the previous situation, even if this presence opens the path to Caesarist processes and produces a constant oscillation between "democracy" and "demagogy" (see Q6§97, Gramsci 1975, 771–2; 2007, 81–3). What one has to rely on, according to Gramsci, are the new forms of representation that the masses of subalterns incessantly try to build, a process that now happens *inside* the hegemonic apparatuses of the post-liberal state.[19]

In essence, while Weber puts us on our guard against the dominion of irrational passions—since the perspective that he adopts is that of the dominant class, which asks itself the question of how to neutralize the political action of the popular masses— Gramsci's interests go to the possibilities opened by this new fact in the history of the modern state. The question of interest to him is how it may be possible to "translate" those irrational passions into organized political action—in other words, how to overthrow bourgeois hegemony. In consequence, as well as the relation between religion and *politics*—which is also present in Weber's thought[20]—in Gramsci's work one finds something missing in Weber's: that is to say, the relation between religion and *philosophy* (i.e., between the irrational and reason).

18. See Portantiero (1981, 47–59).
19. Relevant here are Gramsci's reflections on the relation between "self-government" and bureaucracy. See Gramsci (Q8§55, 1975, 974; 2007, 268; Q13§36, 1975, 1632–5; 1971b, 185–90).
20. In prison Gramsci read with interest Weber's (1931–2) *Protestant Ethic and the Spirit of Capitalism.*

It is in this perspective, which one may define as "historical-political," that we must insert Gramsci's interest in religion.[21] This interest can be traced back to his Turin period. For Gramsci, religion is in fact and above all that which orders the way of thinking, and thus of acting, of the broadest popular masses: to a great extent peasants, who in that period—and not only in Italy—constituted the great majority of the population. The growth of the importance of religion in public life went hand in hand with the appearance on the historical scene of the masses of the "uneducated" and with the concomitant increasing loss of control over them by the Catholic Church.[22] It is because the peasant masses became politically active that the liberal compromise entered into crisis. That compromise consisted (in Italy, but also in part this was the situation in other European countries) in a clear division of society between a small minority of active citizens, who constituted the lay and liberal ruling class, and the majority of the population left to the hegemony of the Catholic Church and immersed in a culture that was still "medieval."[23]

Right from the war years, the idea is clear in Gramsci's thought that the religious history of modern Europe is a secular dispute for ideological control over the peasant masses—that is, over the nation. In an article of 1916, "The Syllabus and Hegel," he singles out the Protestant heresy as having set off the process of secularization that—beginning with Luther and passing through Hegel, with thanks to the ferocious lesson of mass Realpolitik given by the experience of the First World War— would become part of the common heritage of the whole of Europe (Gramsci 1980a [1916], 70–1). The process of secularization is, however, not interpreted by Gramsci as the disappearance of religion but as its substitution in favor of a secular *Weltanschauung* that he defines as "faith:" "In reality, every man has his religion, his faith, that fills his life and makes it worthy of being lived" (71).

As may be seen, Gramsci, in taking over a proposal of Benedetto Croce,[24] here broadens the meaning of the terms "religion" and "faith," transforming them into the synonyms of (respectively) a conception of the world and a system of convictions that drive to action and that are impervious to rational critique. In so doing, the critical analysis of religion changes guise: it is not of interest to give formal or theological definitions of what religion is.[25] Religions are nothing other than the attempt to attribute a certain "form" to this universal experience that is the search for coherence of thought and action, for unity of theory and practice.

21. See Portelli (1974), Luporini (1979), Fulton (1987), and Adamson (2013). See also Lombardi Satriani (1970), Cristofolini (1976), Sobrero (1976), Frosini (2003, 168–82), Boninelli (2007), and Liguori (2009).
22. See, for example, Gramsci (1982 [1918]).
23. See Gramsci (Q4§3, 1975, 472; 1996, 141): "Marxism had two tasks: to combat modern ideologies in their most refined forms; and to enlighten the minds of the popular masses, whose culture was medieval."
24. See Croce (1931, 23–5, 45, 102–4) on "faith" as thought that becomes "action"; Croce (1931, 283; 1945, 110) on religion as "every mental system ... every concept of reality, which, transformed into faith, has become the basis for action and also the light of moral life"; and Croce (1932, 21; 1933, 18) on religion as "the concept of reality and an ethics that conforms to this concept." As Croce states, the idea stems from Goethe.
25. "Formal definitions of religion are of little significance for Gramsci. Religions for him are not fixed entities but dynamic forces that are constantly changing as they both shape and respond to a wide complex of historical events and processes" (Adamson 2013, 471).

From this set of assumptions Gramsci develops an extremely original Marxist approach to the religious factor[26]—so original that Marxism itself falls under the concept of "religion" in that it is a "philosophy" (i.e., a "conception of the world") and not a "science." The Marxist critique of religion is always therefore for Gramsci also a self-critique of Marxism itself. Insofar as Marxism is a "religion," it takes part by full right in the religious conflict that runs through modernity in the sense that Marxism, like traditional religions, addresses itself to the masses and tries to give an answer to their demand for coherence between thought and action. But the response given by Marxism has not only to be different and original but also collocated on a completely new plane. In fact, all religions have given a confessional answer to that need for coherence (i.e., a response that is theoretical), which is succinctly expounded within some type of orthodoxy. In doing so, these religions have "blocked" the energy that comes from the demand for coherence, reducing it to a given cultural form.

If, as one reads in the *Prison Notebooks*, Marxism is not solely a new philosophy but a philosophy that renews from head to toe the *mode itself* of doing philosophy—since it puts itself forward as a mass philosophy that is not only an individual elaboration but also a collective praxis, an organized political will (in a single expression: a "philosophy of praxis")[27]—then it cannot be proposed as a new orthodoxy that simply substitutes itself for the old religious beliefs. Quite the contrary, Marxism has to make its constant reference point the lack of an *already written* orthodoxy.[28] Orthodoxy must be redefined as the coherence of Marxism with itself: that is, with the need to be autonomous and independent of any other conception of the world. This coherence with itself can be found solely if the identity of Marxism is not sought in some type of theory but precisely in that unity of theory and practice that lies at the basis of all "religions." This is the sole guarantee of not falling back into some form of revisionism, which for Gramsci is the signal of the fact that the movement of the emancipation of subalterns has come to a stop and handed over its own leadership to the bourgeoisie.[29]

In the critique of religion, then, Marxism must simultaneously criticize the orthodoxy of others and also put a brake on the temptation, inside itself, to give itself an orthodoxy: the two movements, criticism and self-criticism, are conditioned in the sense that only if Marxism succeeds in keeping the perspective of the unity of theory and practice open inside itself will it also be able to convincingly propose itself to the popular masses saturated in a religious mentality.

"Faith" and "Good Sense" in Croce's Thought

We have said that in 1916 Gramsci took Benedetto Croce's proposed definition of religion—namely, a "conception of the world." For Croce, then, there was no qualitative difference in a proper sense between philosophy and religion. There remained,

26. See, in general, La Rocca (1996).
27. See Gramsci (Q4§11, 1975; 1996, 152–3); see also Thomas (2009, 244–306) and Frosini (2010, 50–111).
28. See Gramsci (Q4§14, 1975, 435–6; 1996, 155–6). And see, in its rewritten form in translation, Gramsci (1971b, 462–3).
29. See Gramsci (Q4§3, 1975, 421–5; 1996, 141–5).

however, the politically important fact that the supersession of mythological religion in the direction of philosophical religion could come about, in his opinion, only for restricted circles of the population. For the popular masses, the "mythological" conceptions continued to exercise their "role of protecting civilization," for which religion was "necessary for the people" (Desidera 2005, 34).

Taking over this conception, the young Gramsci limited himself, so to speak, to not sharing the consequence, and he hoped for a sort of extension of philosophy among the people and therefore for a mass supersession of religion (the above-mentioned article, "The Syllabus and Hegel," goes in this direction). There remained in his thought, however, the idea—of Crocean origin—that the mass of people is an "amorphous mass that eternally floats outside any spiritual organization" and for this reason "is good prey to all: to the witch doctors when mystery descends, to the socialists when effects demonstrate the organic sterility of war. It is the human material necessary for creating history, *material to be precise and not consciousness*, which in itself creates nothing, if the spark of intelligence does not bring it to life and ignite it" (Gramsci 1980b [1916], 175; emphasis added).

The idea of a basic passivity in the popular masses—an idea that connects to that of their basic "irrationality"—and of religion as their "mentality" is not new. Gramsci finds it in Croce's thought, and it is present as we have seen in Weber's, who claimed that the popular mass is characterized by an extreme fluidity of opinions and by the inability to think beyond the narrow space of the present.[30] But this negative image of the popular mass as passive and irrational is a commonplace—with few exceptions—of modern political thought. In this thought the popular mass (*vulgus, plebs, multitudo, populace*) is internally divided into many different opinions that the mass follows on the basis of their attractiveness and not their credibility; it is attracted by novelty; it is always on the lookout for a "chief," whom it is ready to abandon when faced with the first difficulty. Furthermore, the mass is often compared to the sea in a storm or to a chameleon, and its mode of being is defined by the lack of any firmness and coherence.[31] Just through this internal incoherence and irrationality, only a "myth," such as religion, is able to give form to the *multitudo*, reducing this multiheaded hydra to obedience.

Against this background, by coining the category of "faith," Benedetto Croce showed that he had understood perfectly—as Weber had done, moreover—the new political centrality of the popular masses in the world that had emerged from the war. But different from Weber, who markedly opposed the rationality of philosophy to the irrational religious passions of the world of the people, with "faith" Croce instituted an intermediate term between reason and the passions, between philosophy and religion. If faith is the result of philosophy, the hardening of philosophy into a "prejudice" that pushes people into action, then the result is that between philosophical thought and faith (and therefore between philosophers who think critically and the people who

30. See Weber (1919, 139–40; 1994, 230–1): "The *danger* which mass democracy presents to national politics consists principally in the possibility that *emotional* elements will become predominant in politics. The 'mass' as such (no matter which social strata it happens to be composed of) 'thinks only as far as the day after tomorrow.' As we know from experience, the mass is always exposed to momentary, purely emotional and irrational influences ... as far as national politics are concerned, the *un*organised mass, the democracy of the street, is wholly irrational."

31. See Villari (1987, 1–48).

act fanatically) there is no *qualitative* gap. Consequently, truth is not something aristo-cratic; it is not "something extraneous to the human multitude," which therefore cannot be considered as an "irredeemable and almost animal-like vulgus" (Croce 1926, 210).

Philosophy must therefore not propose for itself the task either of rejecting common sense or of transforming common sense to make it critical. The task of philosophy must instead consist in finding once more the "agreement" between what philosophy discov-ers through its means and the results of popular wisdom. These "agreements" between philosophical propositions and the popular wisdom deposited "in proverbs and common sayings"[32] are not for Croce the point of departure for a labor of reforming the masses' way of thinking; on the contrary, they are the point of arrival: the demon-stration that *social unity* is guaranteed by this universal circulation of truth.

"Faith," as an intermediate category between philosophy and religion, and the agree-ment between philosophy and popular proverbs are the two pillars that support social unity. The latter of these describes the universal circulation of truth, which thus can be one and only one, independent of class points of view, while the former states a guar-antee of the fact that the fanatical and impassioned action of the masses is not some-thing extraneous as regards that sole philosophical truth but may rather be absorbed within it. But Croce knew well that this absorption does not come about spontaneously. A further category has therefore to be "invented," able to explain the way in which the unique truth in reality imposes itself in practice. This category is "good sense,"[33] under-stood by Croce as "the *trait d'union* between theory and practice" (Escher Di Stefano 2003, 218). Good sense is the result of the coherent elaboration of common sense so that it becomes assimilable by philosophy, and vice versa, so that it may assimilate the teachings of philosophy.

This architecture of categories has an equivalent in political terms. At the political level, the intertwining of "faith" and "good sense" means that the role of "filter," the disappearance of which had been given attention by Weber with the end of the parlia-ment of "notables," has now to be handed over to the intermediate category "good sense." The "man of good sense," Croce claims, is a figure that stands between the man of the people, who acts as prey to the passions, and the philosopher; this person in a nutshell is the good bourgeois, the respectable person, the representative of the moderate middle class.[34] The category of faith is not therefore pure irrationality. Within itself, it mediates passion and reason since the prejudice that faith represents has already been mediated through the moderating activity of the man of good sense. The filter, which is no longer in parliament, now finds itself assigned to this figure who is active in society. Croce's whole discourse is directed toward the bourgeoi-sie as a class capable of the ideological leadership of society. Independently of the po-litical regime—whether the liberal state or the fascist one—Croce was engaged in

---

32. "One derives great satisfaction (or at least I derive such) in being able to recognize the substantial agreement of proverbs and common sayings with the highest and most difficult philosophical proposi-tions" (Croce 1926, 210).
33. There is "no greater satisfaction for the philosopher than to find his philosophemes in the sayings of good sense" (Croce 1926, 211).
34. See Croce (1931, 195–6).

constructing the premises for the possibility of bourgeois hegemony to be exercised once again over the popular masses after the post–First World War crisis.

It is important to note, however, that Croce firmly denies that this directive element, this "man of good sense," is the "good bourgeois." It is the self-same category of "bourgeoisie" that Croce, in a 1928 essay, argues is an "ill-defined historical concept." For if we attempt to identify the "bourgeois," at the end what we find before us is an element that "mediates" conflicts, and the mediation of a conflict cannot belong to the sphere in which the conflict arises. Thus, the element that directs the economic sphere—the world of labor—must carry out this mediation on the basis of moving within the sphere of ethics. "Therefore, the 'middle class,' of which we are speaking here is a 'class not a class,' similar to that 'general class,' to that *allgemeine Stand*, to which Hegel granted the 'general interests,' *die allgemeine* [sic] *Interessen* as a sphere of activity belonging to it and as its own business" (Croce 1931, 338; 1945, 180). But, Croce (1931, 338; 1945, 180–1) adds, "I say 'similar' and not completely 'identical' because Hegel, letting himself be influenced, as elsewhere, by the conditions of the Germany of his time, attributed economic stability to that class in the comforts granted to it by fortune or by the stipends furnished by the State, and he assigned it solely to the 'service of the government' (*dem Dienst der Regierung*)."

Croce here brings to its conclusion a dual operation. On the one hand, he frees "bourgeois" from where it belongs socially. In denying that the bourgeoisie is a class and claiming that it is nothing other than the ensemble of men of "good sense," he denies that the ideological and organizational labor carried out by the bourgeoisie in civil society responds to the interest of one side: it is instead carried out in the name of the universal (or better, in the name of social unity). On the other hand, Croce distinguishes within ideological and organizational activity the labor undertaken by the state bureaucracy in the strict sense from that undertaken by a wider "informal bureaucracy." There therefore exists, he claims, a ruling class that is not a social class, which acts in the name of universal interests and which exerts its political action not only inside the bureaucracy but also outside it.

From "Religion" to "Myth"

From the above, not only does it emerge that there is a close relationship between Croce's reflection regarding religion, faith, and myth on the one hand and his reflection on the state and on the informal bureaucracy on the other; it also emerges that all these aspects of his thought belong to the problematic space opened up by the war, with the unheralded protagonism of the masses and the "double siege" situation, described already in section 1. Confronting fascism, Croce developed a renewed liberal proposal, which attempted to suggest a complementarity between the bureaucracy in the strict sense and that sort of informal bureaucracy constituted by the ensemble of men of good sense, who are active in all realms of society, with the aim of reducing the "irrational" activity of the popular masses to the common measure of bourgeois "reason." In other words, the main proposition he put forward was not the problem of an alternative to the fascist regime. His main preoccupation was rather the one which he *shared* with fascism, that of finding a new method of government, appropriate to the situation created after the war, in order to contain and repel the siege of state power by the popular masses. To this end is addressed his analysis of religion as the matrix of social unity and of the role of the "general class" in society—in short, his theorization of a new intertwining of "public" and "private," typical of the new political situation.

It is for this reason that in the *Prison Notebooks* Gramsci decided to reconstruct and make a careful critique of Croce's thought, since Croce was the liberal philosopher who in his eyes offered the strongest and most solid guarantee of the continuity of bourgeois power in Italy. Croce had begun his activity as a theorist with a series of essays, published at the end of the nineteenth century, that constituted his critique of Marxism and that were among the main contributions—together with those of Bernstein and Sorel—to the revisionist movement in Marxism.[35] In Gramsci's view, he never in actual fact ceased to be a "revisionist" (in a very broad sense) since in every phase of his intellectual activity he posed the problem of how to realize the passive absorption of the demands of the popular masses in order to avoid their being able to become a hegemonic force.[36]

With the First World War, all became more difficult. Croce responded to the new situation with the development of a historiographical conception—"ethico-political history"—that implied a conception of philosophy that in part was new and more attentive to the problem of the unity of "the concept of reality and an ethics that conforms to this concept"[37] and to which, to be exact, he gave the name "religion." For this reason, when in 1932 Croce published his *History of Europe in the Nineteenth Century*,[38] Gramsci judged it to be "a tract of passive revolutions" since it demonstrated how Jacobinism had been absorbed and metabolized by liberalism. What value can this presentation have in today's world? Fascism, Gramsci (Q8§236, 1975, 1088–9; 2007, 378) observes, in effect presents itself as the position whose purpose is that of saving the old world by absorbing the novelties proposed by the popular classes, by the new Jacobinism. It is "the form of 'passive revolution' specific to the 20th century." Croce's *History of Europe* could, in consequence, function as a "model" for the possible developments of fascism.

Beyond any doubt Croce's book, which celebrated nineteenth-century liberalism as the "religion of liberty," was welcomed in numerous critical reviews by fascist intellectuals. Gramsci (Q10II§2, 1975, 1261; 1995, 468) notes, however: "But one would have to see whether Croce is not setting himself this very task in order to get a reformistic activity from above that would weaken the antitheses and reconcile them in a new, 'transformistically' obtained legality." In this way, Croce would contribute to "strengthening fascism by indirectly providing it with an intellectual justification after having helped to purge it of a number of secondary characteristics" (Q10I§9, Gramsci 1975, 1228; 1995, 349–50) and would thereby act as the "channel between the stabilization of capitalism, to which social democracy tended in Europe as from the immediate post-war period, and the stabilization put into operation in Italy by fascism" (Rossi and Vacca 2007, 53).

35. See Croce (1921; the first edition dates to 1900).

36. See Gramsci (Q10§3, 1975, 1214–5; 1995, 335–6).

37. Summarizing his previous reflections, this is the definition of religion given by Croce in 1932 in his *History of Europe* (see notes 1 and 24 above).

38. Of this work Gramsci was able to read only the first three chapters. See Frosini (2012b, 65).

This judgment finds its conclusion in the letter of 6 June 1932 that Gramsci wrote to his sister-in-law Tat'jana (Tatiana) Schucht: "Placed in a historical perspective, of Italian history naturally, Croce's efforts appear to be the most powerful machinery for 'adjusting' the new forces to their vital interests (not only immediate but long-range as well) that the dominant group now possesses and that I believe it properly appreciates despite some superficial appearances" (Gramsci and Schucht 1997, 1023; Gramsci 1994, 182; translation slightly modified). In essence, Gramsci was maintaining that Croce was—from the point of view of the subaltern classes in Italy, and despite his pompous self-definition as the leader of antifascism—the main obstacle to oppose in the struggle for hegemony in Italy since the "revisionist" role that he fulfilled succeeded in inserting into the bourgeois power bloc those new social forces that had been brought into life by the experience of the war and (above all) the economic transformations of the postwar period. To tear these forces away from that power of attraction was an essential task to be achieved in the context of any hypothesis of struggle against the fascist regime.

For the reasons that we have expounded in this section, Gramsci maintained that a central point of attack in order to neutralize Croce's revisionist intervention was in fact religion. This interest of Gramsci's emerges clearly in a passage of the *Prison Notebooks* written between February and November 1931. Gramsci (Q7§39, 1975, 888; 2007, 189) here observes that the "myth," according to Sorel's formulation, "is nothing other than the [Crocean] 'theory of passions' articulated in less precise and formally coherent language." And rewriting this after a time lapse of a year and rethinking his thesis, Gramsci (Q10II§41, 1975, 1308; 1995, 390) defines the Sorelian theory of the myth as "Croce's 'passion' studied in a more concrete manner, it is what Croce calls 'religion,' i.e. a conception of the world with a conformant ethic, it is an attempt to reduce the conception of ideologies in the philosophy of praxis, exactly as seen through the eyes of Crocean revisionism, to scientific language."

As one can see, there is a very marked shift in position that took place over the course of 1932, the year in which Gramsci began the Notebook on "The Philosophy of Benedetto Croce." From this vantage point, it comes out clearly to Gramsci that Croce has "reduced" Marx's theory of ideology to just its critical-destructive aspect, bringing politics down to a "passion." Indeed, for Croce the whole of public political life does not belong to the sphere of ethics but to that of economics: that is, to the terrain on which the struggle takes place for the attainment of the "useful." Faced with this restrictive definition of politics, Sorel, while setting off from Croce's revisionism, took back some aspects of the concreteness of ideology, renewing the nexus between passion, polemical representations, and collective political will, but he stopped short of an understanding of the role of the political party.[39] Only if "the political parties" are understood as "the crucible where the unification of theory and practice, understood as a real historical process" (Q11§12, Gramsci 1975, 1387; 1971b, 335), takes place—only then will it even be possible to subtract politics from being confined within "passion," and only then will the process become possible whereby "reason" itself (and therefore "history") will *emerge from* struggles rather than being the premise of those struggles.

39. See Gramsci (Q13§1, 1975, 1556–7; 1971b, 127–9).

In other words, only then will the process of the autonomous constitution of subaltern classes in hegemonic classes become possible.[40]

The "myth" becomes for Gramsci the true incarnation of what Croce calls "religion." The myth is its true incarnation because, different from religion, it finds its place explicitly within politics. One might say that while religion expresses (in Crocean language) the directive function of the bourgeoisie as "universal class," and while politics reduced to "passion" expresses the dominated classes' impossibility for self-emancipation, in the myth Sorel has in some way fused together these two moments. But Sorel considered the myth an irrational fact,[41] and this is linked up with his refusal of the political party and of the role of intellectuals. Against this, for Gramsci the myth can grow and develop only within a political organism that is capable of organizing itself in a democratic manner.

This helps explain why the myth in Gramsci's thought, different from Sorel, is not an irrational fact. It is inside the political party that the "fanaticism" of action is mediated with "reflection" in a concrete hegemonic practice of mass training for the role of leadership, and this finds its verbal expression in the concept of "intellectual and moral reform," which—Gramsci (Q8§21, 1975, 953; 2007, 248) goes on to make explicit—is the "terrain for a subsequent development of the national popular collective will rooted in a complete and accomplished form of modern civilization." And that is to say that the party is the place in which the collective will, stimulated by the myth, organizes *itself* and takes on a critical form, without however ceasing to be religious. However paradoxical this may seem, the only true response to the masses' demand for religion lies in an active participation in this process of the self-organization and self-education of subalterns in the art of government.

References

Adamson, W. L. 2013. Gramsci, Catholicism and secular religion. *Politics, Religion & Ideology* 14 (4): 468–84.

Boninelli, G. M. 2007. *Frammenti indigesti: Temi folclorici negli scritti di Antonio Gramsci*. Rome: Carocci.

Cospito, G. 2011. Verso l'edizione critica e integrale dei "Quaderni del carcere." *Studi Storici* 52 (4): 881–904.

Cristofolini, P. 1976. Gramsci e il diritto naturale. *Critica Marxista* 14 (3–4): 105–16.

Croce, B. 1915. Religione e serenità. *La Critica* 13 (2): 153–5.

———. 1921. *Materialismo storico ed economia marxistica*. 4th ed. Bari, It.: Laterza.

———. 1926. *Cultura e vita morale: Intermezzi polemici*. 2d ed. Bari, It.: Laterza.

———. 1931. *Etica e politica: Aggiuntovi il "Contributo alla critica di me stesso."* Bari, It.: Laterza.

———. 1932. *Storia d'Europa nel secolo decimonono*. Bari, It.: Laterza.

———. 1933. *History of Europe in the nineteenth century*. Ed. H. Furst. New York: Harcourt, Brace.

40. Croce, according to Gramsci, reduces politics to "passion" insofar as he intends to make impossible even the thought that the subaltern classes, whose action is "impassioned" because it is of a "defensive" nature, may ever come out of this state. "In consequence, one can say that, in Croce, the term 'passion' is a pseudonym for social struggle" (Q10§56, 1975, 1350; 1995, 392).

41. See Sorel (1999, 113).

————. 1942. Perché non possiamo non dirci cristiani. *La Critica* 40 (6): 289–97.

————. 1945. *Politics and morals.* Ed. S. J. Castiglione. New York: F. Hubner.

————. 1949. *My philosophy and other essays on the moral and political problems of our time.* Ed. R. Klibansky and E. F. Carritt. London: Allen and Unwin.

De Felice, F. 1977. Rivoluzione passiva, fascismo, americanismo in Gramsci. In *Politica e storia in Gramsci*, vol. I, ed. F. Ferri, 161–220. Rome: Editori Riuniti-Istituto Gramsci.

————. 2007. *Alle origini del welfare contemporaneo: L'Organizzazione internazionale del lavoro tra le due guerre (1919–1939).* Rome: Istituto della Enciclopedia Italiana.

Desidera, B. 2005. *La lotta delle egemonie: Movimento cattolico e Partito Popolare nei Quaderni di Gramsci.* Padua, It.: Il Poligrafo.

Economia diretta. 1932. *La Nuova Italia* 3 (3): 85–8.

Escher Di Stefano, A. 2003. Croce e Gramsci: La sopravvalutazione di un'appartenenza. In *Croce filosofo*, vol. I, ed. G. Cacciatore, G. Cotroneo, and R. Viti Cavaliere, 291–320. Soveria Mannelli, It.: Rubbettino.

Francioni, G., and F. Frosini. 2009. Nota introduttiva al quaderno 25. In *Quaderni del carcere: Edizione anastatica dei manoscritti*, vol. 18, ed. A. Gramsci, 203–11. Rome: Istituto della Enciclopedia Italiana.

Frosini, F. 2003. *Gramsci e la filosofia: Saggio sui "Quaderni del carcere."* Rome: Carocci.

————. 2010. *La religione dell'uomo moderno: Politica e verità nei "Quaderni del carcere" di Antonio Gramsci.* Rome: Carocci.

————. 2012a. Croce, fascismo, comunismo. *Il Cannocchiale: Rivista di Studi Filosofici* 48 (3): 141–62.

————. 2012b. I "Quaderni" tra Mussolini e Croce. *Critica Marxista* 53 (4): 60–8.

————. 2012c. Reformation, renaissance and the state: The hegemonic fabric of modern sovereignty. *Journal of Romance Studies* 12 (3): 63–77.

Fulton, J. 1987. Religion and politics in Gramsci: An introduction. *Sociological Analysis* 48 (3): 197–216.

Gramsci, A. 1971a. *La costruzione del Partito Comunista: 1924–1926.* Ed. E. Fubini. Turin: Einaudi.

————. 1971b. *Selections from the "Prison notebooks."* Ed. Q. Hoare and G. N. Smith. London: Lawrence and Wishart.

————. 1975. *Quaderni del carcere.* Ed. V. Gerratana. Turin: Einaudi.

————. 1978. *Selections from political writings, 1921–1926.* Ed. Q. Hoare. London: Lawrence and Wishart.

————. 1980a (1916). Il sillabo ed Hegel. In *Cronache torinesi: 1913–1917*, ed. S. Caprioglio, 69–72. Turin: Einaudi.

————. 1980b (1916). Stregoneria. In *Cronache torinesi: 1913–1917*, ed. S. Caprioglio, 174–5. Turin: Einaudi.

————. 1982 (1918). Azione sociale. In *La città futura: 1917–1918*, ed. S. Caprioglio, 822–3. Turin: Einaudi.

————. 1992. *Prison notebooks.* Vol. 1. Ed. J. A. Buttigieg. New York: Columbia University Press.

————. 1994. *Letters from prison.* Vol 2. Ed. F. Rosengarten. New York: Columbia University Press.

————. 1995. *Further selections from the "Prison notebooks."* Ed. D. Boothman. London: Lawrence and Wishart.

————. 1996. *Prison notebooks.* Vol. 2. Ed. J. A. Buttigieg. New York: Columbia University Press.

————. 2000. *The Gramsci reader: Selected writings 1916–1935.* Ed. D. Forgacs. New York: New York University Press.

———. 2007. *Prison notebooks*. Vol. 3. Ed. J. A. Buttigieg. New York: Columbia University Press.

Gramsci, A., and T. Schucht. 1997. *Lettere 1926–1935*. Ed. A. Natoli and C. Daniele. Turin: Einaudi.

Green, M. 2011. Rethinking the subaltern and the question of censorship in Gramsci's *Prison Notebooks*. *Postcolonial Studies* 14 (4): 387–404.

Kanoussi, D. 2000. *Una introducción a "Los cuadernos de la cárcel" de Antonio Gramsci*. Mexico City: Plaza y Valdés.

La Rocca, T. 1996. *La critica marxista della religione*. Ferrara, It.: Corso Editore.

Liguori, G. 2009. Common sense in Gramsci. In *Perspectives on Gramsci: Politics, culture and social theory*, ed. J. Francese, 122–33. London: Routledge.

———. 2015a. Conceptions of subalternity in Gramsci. In *Antonio Gramsci*, ed. M. McNally, 118–33. Basingstoke: Palgrave Macmillan.

———. 2015b. "Classi subalterne" marginali e "classi subalterne" fondamentali in Gramsci. *Critica Marxista* 56 (4): 41–8.

Lombardi Satriani, L. M. 1970. Gramsci e il folclore: Dal pittoresco alla contestazione. In *Gramsci e la cultura contemporanea*, vol. 2, ed. P. Rossi, 329–38. Rome: Editori Riuniti-Istituto Gramsci.

Luporini, C. 1979. Gramsci e la religione. *Critica Marxista* 17 (1): 71–85.

Maier, C. S. 1975. *Recasting bourgeois Europe: Stabilization in France, Germany, and Italy in the decade after World War I*. Princeton, N.J.: Princeton University Press.

Mangoni, L. 1977. Il problema del fascismo nei *Quaderni del carcere*. In *Politica e storia in Gramsci*, vol. 1, ed. F. Ferri, 391–438. Rome: Editori Riuniti-Istituto Gramsci.

Portantiero, J. C. 1981. *Los usos de Gramsci*. Mexico City: Folios.

Portelli, H. 1974. *Gramsci et la question religieuse*. Paris: Anthropos.

Rossi, A., and G. Vacca. 2007. *Gramsci tra Mussolini e Stalin*. Rome: Fazi.

Sobrero, A. 1976. Folklore e senso comune in Gramsci. *Etnologia, Antropologia Culturale* 3 (4): 70–85.

Sorel, G. 1999. *Reflections on violence*. Ed. J. Jennings. Cambridge: Cambridge University Press.

Thomas, P. D. 2006. Modernity as "passive revolution": Gramsci and the fundamental concepts of historical materialism. *Journal of the Canadian Historical Association* 17 (2): 61–78.

———. 2009. *The Gramscian moment: Philosophy, hegemony and Marxism*. Leiden: Brill.

Villari, R. 1987. *Elogio della dissimulazione: La lotta politica nel Seicento*. Rome: Laterza.

Voza, P. 2004. Rivoluzione passiva. In *Le parole di Gramsci: Per un lessico dei "Quaderni del carcere,"* ed. F. Frosini and G. Liguori, 189–207. Rome: Carocci.

Weber, M. 1919. *Parlamento e governo nel nuovo ordinamento della Germania: Critica politica della burocrazia e della vita dei partiti*. Ed. E. Ruta. Bari: Laterza.

———. 1931–2. L'etica protestante e lo spirito del capitalismo. Pts. 1–5. Trans. P. Burresi. *Nuovi Studi di Diritto, Economia e Politica* 4 (3–4): 176–223; 4 (5): 284–311; 4 (6) 369–96; 5 (1): 58–72; 5 (3–5): 179–231.

———. 1994. *Political writings*. Ed. P. Lassman and R. Speirs. Cambridge: Cambridge University Press.

Zene, C. 2011. Self-consciousness of the Dalits as "subalterns": Reflections on Gramsci in South Asia. In *Rethinking Gramsci*, ed. M. E. Green, 90–104. London: Routledge.

Marxism as *Asketic,* Spirituality as *Phronetic*: Rethinking Praxis

Anup Dhar and Anjan Chakrabarti

This paper departs from the hegemonic notion of truth—the cognitive notion of truth—and arrives at four other notions of truth in Marx, Gandhi, Heidegger, and Foucault. It puts the four to a possible dialogue. It argues that one can get a glimpse of the cusp of Marxism and spirituality in the dialogue among the four. The work at the cusp, in turn, renders Marxism asketic and the spiritual phronetic. Thinking at the cusp also inaugurates the possibility of an anti-Oedipal future for Marxism and a this-worldly present for spirituality.

> Whereas the political organization of all pre-modern societies was in some way connected to, based on, guaranteed by some faith in, or adherence to God, or some notion of ultimate reality, the modern Western state is free[1] from this connection.
>
> —Charles Taylor, *A Secular Age*

This essay is on the uneasy *and* that connects Marxian questions and spiritual quests. Conventionally, Marx and Marxism have been associated with materialism, and spirituality has been ascribed to, at times, things that are somewhat transcendental, somewhat akin to what Marx and Engels call "speculative idealism" in *The Holy Family* (Marx and Engels 1956). Critiques of Marxism have targeted materialism for its

---

1. The essay asks two questions. One, is it desirable to be totally and unconditionally free of "some faith"? Is such freedom from faith at the root of the problems of the modern proclivity and the current political imagination? Is "spiritual deficit" one of the fundamental problems of Marxism? Two, is it indeed free? Building on Lacan's *Seminar XX*, Braungardt (1999) shows how "a central event in the development of Western philosophy and theology was the merger between Christian theology and Greek philosophy [Lacan shows how the Jewish response to human fragility, however, was theological, and not philosophical] ... The philosopher who created a synthesis on the basis of a theism, which lasted for almost nine centuries, is Thomas Aquinas. What would we call this? Christianization of (Greek) philosophy? Or the turning Hellenic of Christianity? Does Marx's dual critique—critique of both philosophy and theology—stem from an appreciation of this "merger" by Thomas Aquinas? Does this Marxian double critique—doubled-up critique, one critique folded into the other —then get split into (1) the Foucauldian critique of Christianization and (2) the Derridean critique of the metaphysics of presence?

mechanomorphic nature, and the hardheartedness it may precipitate (in, say, actual practices of Marxian statecraft). Critiques of spirituality have targeted its focus on individual *moksha* (liberation), its asociality (Marx argues that the "religious sentiment" is itself a social product), its proximity to capital-logic, and its rather "pop" nature in the Western world or among the elite in erstwhile colonies. Making sense of Marx beyond simple materialism and making sense of spirituality beyond simple transcendentalism is hence the focus of this essay. The connection between Marxism and spirituality is not a connection between materialism and idealism/transcendentalism but a connection between the two "beyonds"—the beyond of Marxian materialism and that of spiritual transcendentalism—which, in other words, is a rethought materialism and a rethought spiritualism: a materialism that is overdetermined by "ideas" and a spiritualism that is less transcendent; a materialism that is overdetermined by what Foucault calls the *asketic* (where "truth" is tied to the question of "being-becoming" and where "self-transformation" is the context and condition of "truth") and a spiritualism overdetermined by what Heidegger calls *phronesis* (where "truth" is "practical" and "social" and is contingent upon "praxis" and "this-worldliness"). The curious byproduct of the spiritualization of Marxism or the Marxianization of spirituality is a somewhat secret communion that gets set up with psychoanalysis, rethought as asketic and phronetic.[2]

The Question of Interlocutors

We begin this section by looking closely at the possible set of interlocutors that could exist between Marxism and spirituality; one can make sense of the uneasy *and* between Marxism and spirituality only in terms of their interlocutors, by resetting or remapping the relationships between them. First is liberalism and Marxism as somewhat antagonistic interlocutors to each other; however, the "crisis" of "liberal democracies in today's world," as well as the crisis of statist Marxism, is not letting us choose between the two anymore, which was possible before; this crisis is instead demanding from us a "re-investigation of the notion of the political" (and not just liberal or Marxist politics), including importantly the "secularization of historical reason," primarily because the dual or simultaneous crisis of liberalism and Marxism is coming with a simultaneous "exhaustion of the notion of 'secularization'" (Das 2014, 13). Second is theology as antagonistic interlocutor to enlightened secular liberalism. Third is religion as antagonistic interlocutor to secularism (see Anzi 2014, 152–63), but secularism as a curious accompaniment of both Marxism and liberalism, and hence religion by default becomes the antagonistic interlocutor to both Marxism and liberalism. Fourth is science as another apposite interlocutor to both Marxism and liberalism, but scientific rationalism (or the scientific search for truth) is also the antagonistic

2. The specter of a thinker, Freud, who purportedly had nothing to do with the political but had lots to do with the noncoercive, the nonjudgmental, and with patient reorganization of desire, haunts this exchange between Marxism and spirituality: "Psychoanalysis offers a method of intervening non-violently between our overbearing conscience and our raging affects, thus forcing our moral and our 'animal' natures to enter into respectful reconciliation" (Erikson 1969, 439).

interlocutor to theological thinking and religion. Idealism is antagonistic interlocutor to Marxian materialism; thus, "matter" and "spirit" are becoming opposed as interlocutors. The modern is an opposed interlocutor to tradition, and reason/rationality are opposed interlocutors to irrationality/superstition. Finally, flesh and corporeality are antagonistic interlocutors to the spiritual. The contesting cosmology of the interlocutors, as enunciated above, takes the form of a polylog among four contending notions of "truth"—of Marx, Gandhi, Heidegger, and Foucault—in this essay. It argues that the polylog among the four contending but related notions of "truth" could in turn be the ground for a possible dialog between Marxism and spirituality.

It would not be out of context to take note of Marx and Engels' anguish with respect to the spiritual in *The Holy Family*. The nature of this anguish also shows how antagonistic interlocutors (for example, "self-consciousness" and "spirit" on the one hand and "real humanism," "flesh," and "corporeal" on the other) are taking form in Marx (ism): "Real humanism has no more dangerous enemy in [Christian] Germany than spiritualism or speculative idealism, which substitutes 'self-consciousness' or the 'spirit'[3] for the real individual man ... 'It is the spirit that quickeneth; the flesh profiteth nothing.' Needless to say, this incorporeal spirit is spiritual only in its imagination" (Marx and Engels 1956). Marx's attack on (speculative) idealism takes further form in *The German Ideology*. Marx (1932) wants to "liberate" men "from the chimeras, the ideas, dogmas, imaginary beings under the yoke of which they [i.e., the masses] are pining away": "Once upon a time a valiant fellow [in Germany] had the idea that men were drowned in water only because they were possessed with the idea of gravity. If they were to knock this notion out of their heads, say by stating it to be a superstition, a religious concept, they would be sublimely proof against any danger from water."[4]

The question of Marxism and spirituality thus takes many forms: liberal and religious, secular and religious, secular and theological, scientific and theological, of matter and of spirit, of flesh/corporeality and of spirit, modern and traditional. Two clusters thus come face to face: liberalism, secularism, science, the modern, flesh/the corporeal, and materialism on the one hand come face to face with theology, religion, idealism, spirit, and the traditional on the other. Though the genealogy of each division is different, the question of the unease between Marxism and spirituality remains haunted by the interconnected genealogy of each division/binary. The argument this essay makes is that to rethink this relationship, as well as to rethink the uneasy *and* between Marxism and spirituality, one will first have to make sense of the set of interlocutors[5] and the genealogy of the divisions/binaries, and second, one will have to rethink the architecture/map of the interlocutor concepts in order to also redraw the

---

3. Derrida (1991, 99) shows how "we have a trio of languages: Greek (*pneuma*), Latin (*spiritus*), German (*Geist*)" and how "Heidegger does not disqualify the immense semantics of breathing, of inspiration or respiration, imprinted in Greek or Latin. He simply says they are less originary." Marx, however, is responding to the German, to Geist. Building on Derrida's reading of Geist in Heidegger, this essay explores which understanding of Geist Marx is responding to: would Marxism's relationship with spirituality change, get displaced, if the understanding of Geist changes, gets displaced? The last part of the section titled "The Other Spiritual" is a reflection on three other conceptualizations of Geist (in Heidegger), conceptualizations that would render Marxism and spirituality apposite.
4. See the preface to *The German Ideology* (Marx 1932).

relationships between the interlocutors.[6] This architecture/map of interlocutor concepts will be approached—perhaps translated—in this essay in terms of the architecture/map of four related notions of "truth," in the thought of Marx, Gandhi, Heidegger, and Foucault. Such a remapping of interlocutors in terms of (rethought or redrawn) conceptions of "truth" will in turn help redraw the relationship between the interlocutors. More specifically, it will throw some light on the space of the uneasy *and* between Marxism and spirituality.

The Marxian Conception of "Truth"

Marx (2016 [1845]) begins "Theses on Feuerbach" with the question of the "chief defect of all hitherto existing materialism" (he does not begin with the chief defect of idealism!). And what is the defect? The defect is that the "thing, reality, sensuousness" is conceived only in the form of either "the object" or "of intuition" but not as "human sensuous activity, practice."

Defect two: Feuerbach wants "sensuous objects" to be distinct from "objects of thought," and Marx looks to be fine with this division, but "he does not conceive human activity itself as objective activity."

Defect three: In *The Essence of Christianity*, "Practice is conceived and fixed [by Feuerbach] only in its dirty Jewish manifestation" (Marx 2016). Why is practice Jewish? Why is practice dirty? Here Marx makes an interesting distinction—a distinction that looks to have been missed in the hypersecular rhetoric of most Marxists—between the Christian discourse on creation and the Judaic discourse on creation: "'Dirty Jewish'—according to Marshall Berman, this is an allusion to the Jewish God of the Old Testament, who had to 'get his hands dirty' while making the world, and is tied up with a symbolic contrast between the Christian God of the Word, and the God of the Deed, symbolizing practical life" (Marx 2016, note 1). This distinct marking of the Deed as against the "dead" (i.e., dead or inert matter), in sharp contradistinction to Feuerbach, is key to the Marxian perspective on materialism. Marx is thus marking a distinction not just between the "real" and the "speculative," between matter and idea, materialism and idealism, but also between the mere Word and the Deed and the distinction (or more specifically the relationship) between a rethought Word and a rethought Deed, which could be a way to rethink the relationship between Marxism and spirituality beyond the paradigmatic distinction in the Western/Occidental tradition—that of "real/speculative," "matter/idea"—which is why Marx (2016) feels that the "dispute over the reality or unreality of thinking" is a "practical question" and "it is in practice [in Deed, indeed] that man must prove the truth."

5. Including the ghosts/specters of interlocutors "flapping in the wings" of the nineteenth-century "alchemical theatre" in which "one of the most obsessing ghosts among the philosophers of this alchemy would ... be Hegel who ... situated the passage from the 'philosophy of nature' to the 'philosophy of spirit'" (Derrida 1991, 99).
6. One note of caution: the above is put to crisis by Foucault when he brings to a troubled apposition the secular and the theological in his description of European enlightened modernity as a "secular theology" or a kind of "theological secularism."

Defect four: "The materialist doctrine" that one is a product of "circumstances and upbringing"—in a word, of "history"—is standing on one leg (Marx 2016). It misses out on the overdetermined other side, the other leg: that one also transforms circumstances, through what Marx calls a revolutionizing of practice.[7]

Defect five: Feuerbach's materialist turn embodies "the dissolution of the religious world into its secular basis." But Feuerbach overlooks the fact that after completing this work, the chief thing still remains to be done. What then is the chief thing that still needs to be done? Marx's answer: a critique of the secular (and not just a secular critique of religion). Here Marx (2016) radically departs from liberal understandings of, and peace with, the assertion of the secular, the secular as given:

> For the fact that the secular foundation detaches itself from itself and establishes itself in the clouds as an independent realm is precisely only to be explained by the very self-dismemberment and self-contradictoriness of this secular basis. The latter itself must, therefore, first be understood in its contradiction and then revolutionized in practice by the elimination of the contradiction. Thus, for instance, once the earthly family is discovered to be the secret of the holy family, the former must then itself be criticized in theory and revolutionized in practice.

Marx wishes to criticize in theory and revolutionize in practice the "secular" as well as the "earthly family."

Defect six: It is not that the religious essence is social[8]; rather, the human essence, as critique of religious essence, is also social: the apparent abstraction inherent in each individual human is in reality an ensemble of social relations (spiritualism misses this ensemble of "social relations" in its conceptualization of the individual human). What is hence at stake is not civil society but human society or "socialized humanity."

Defect seven: The social (life) is essentially practical. Even "sensuous intuition" is practical. The problem for Marx is not just that "spiritualism" or "speculative idealism" have presupposed that things take place only in "the realm of pure thought," premised in turn on what Marx (1932) calls "unfalsified Hegelian categories" such as "substance" and "self-consciousness." The added problem is that (old) materialism has neither turned social nor turned practical in its turning away from either spiritualism or idealism. The problem is not that the dominance of religion was being taken for granted. It is that the "secular critique of religion" requires "critique of the secular."

---

7. See the last section of this essay, "'An Ethical Guide for Transforming Our Communities,'" for a discussion on noncoercive yet Marxian transformation.

8. Religion has conventionally been seen as personal salvation/*moksha*. Ambedkar, like Marx, saw religion or *dhamma* as social. From the 1930s, Ambedkar's lifework was to delineate two strategies for emancipation for the Dalits in India. The first was a strategy of critical legal constitutionalism. The other was a turning away from Hinduism in particular and religion in general, not to land in secularism but to arrive at a form of Buddhism that official Buddhism cannot host, and hence a new *yana*—Navayana as against Hinayana, Mahayana, and Vajrayana. It is as if Ambedkar was looking for a third way—an in-between that puts under erasure the two poles of liberal discourse and theological discourse; the two poles of the theologizing of liberal political views and the politicizing of Buddha's views; the two poles of an ab-Original Enlightenment and an ab-Original religion. This is religion as social, which runs counter to the Orientalism of Buddhist studies and to the commodified discourse of "pop" Buddhism.

The Gandhian Conception of Truth

It would not be out of context to foreground for a moment that while Marx generates critical reflection on the "secular," Gandhi generates critical reflection on "religion." As Marx generates critical reflection on the secular not to discard it but to rethink the secular, Gandhi also develops critical reflection on religion not to discard it but to rethink religion. Further, while Marx has a "diagnostic relation"[9] with religion (Marx is focused on what religion is[10]), Gandhi has a more etho-poetic relationship with lived religion (Gandhi is focused on what it is to live religion).

Parekh (2001, 37–8) shows how Gandhi's conception of "cosmic spirit" (*shakti*) needs to be contrasted with the standard Christian view of God.[11] In the standard view, God is extracosmic. God preexists the universe. God creates and imposes laws on the universe, and God, though loving, is also powerful and at times punitive. For Gandhi, the universe was eternal and a priori. The cosmic spirit was not a creator but a "principle of order," regulating the universe from within. The "mysterious" yet "benevolent" cosmic spirit was internal and inspired love and intimacy rather than fear and awe. The cosmos for Gandhi was "not a pyramid of which the material world was the base and human beings the apex, but a series of ever-widening circles encompassing humankind, the sentient world, the material world, and the all including cosmos. Since the cosmic spirit pervaded or infused the universe and was not outside it, the so-called natural world was not natural or material but spiritual" (50). Unlike many believers, Gandhi did not advance the familiar thesis of an omnipotent God who created the universe but instead a much weaker one that entailed there being "some" spiritual power who "gently" guided the universe. Gandhi's religion thus transcended codified texts and ritualism and involved nothing more than faith in the cosmic spirit and the commitment to realize it in one's life and action.

For Gandhi, religion was concerned with "how" one lived, not "what" one believed; it was a lived and living faith, not the "dead bone of dogmas." It had nothing much to do with theology, which overintellectualizes religion and privileges belief over conduct. For Gandhi, not theology but morality was the core of religion, and the latter was not to be judged by the philosophical coherence and subtlety of its system of beliefs. Parekh (2001) argues, "Since one lived out one's religious beliefs in all areas of life including the political, 'those who say that religion has nothing to do with politics do not know what religion means.'"

---

9. Lacan also has a "diagnostic relation" with theology: "God can either be a face of the Other, and then he becomes a Father-God, author of the Law. Or he is the dark God of jouissance, the God of the mystics: this God is unconscious" (Braungardt 1999). But Lacan also moves toward a radical displacement of theology—Braungardt diagnoses it as "the endpoint of a two-century long project of secularization"—into a "theory of the subject," recreating the tension between immanence and transcendence within the subject itself.

10. For Marx (1970), religion is "the expression of real distress," a "protest against real distress," "the sigh of the oppressed creature," the "heart of a heartless world," the "spirit of spiritless conditions," etc. See the introduction to Marx's *Critique of Hegel's Philosophy Of Right*.

11. Alternative views of Christianity have been proposed by scholars such as Bloch, Derrida, Agamben, Negri, and Žižek.

Religion, for Gandhi, was a spiritual resource from which one freely borrowed what-ever one found persuasive. It was a body of insights to be interpreted in the way one thought proper. His approach to religion was therefore profoundly anti-traditionalist —in a word, antireligious. Gandhi's view placed the human (and not God) at the center of religion and encouraged fresh readings of scriptures. Gandhi also retained the polysemic term *dharma*, which signified nature, [moral] right, and duty (and not re-ligion; see Parekh 2001, 63).

Parekh (2001, 35) also shows how Gandhi moved in 1926 from an earlier formulation that "God is Truth" or "God is the ultimate truth" to "Truth [*sat*] is God"; this move cul-minates in Gandhi's psychoanalytic autobiography *The Story of My Experiments with Truth*.[12] Here Gandhi is not conducting experiments to reach the truth, which is usual in the science lab, but is experimenting with truth, with truth itself, with the truth of truth. For Gandhi (2011, 287), truth is a moral notion: "*sat* is employed in the sense of 'real' and 'good' ... *sat* is also applied to beautiful deeds." *Sat* is thus trifurcated into the really real, the good/moral deed, and the beautiful/aesthetic act. While Enlight-enment science focuses on *sat* as the repository of the really real, Gandhi focuses on *sat* as the register of the moral deed. Tagore (2004) focuses, on the other hand, on *sat* as the register of the aesthetic (truth as "sundarer shadhana," as the "devoted praxis of the aesthetic"). Bilgrami (2003, 4164) shows that, for Gandhi, truth "is not a cognitive notion at all. It is an experiential notion. It is not propositions purporting to describe the world of which truth is predicated, it is only our own moral experience which is capable of being true."

The connection we wish to make between Marx's and Gandhi's notion of truth becomes clearer now. Marx is also, as we have seen above, in search of a notion of truth that is not merely cognitive. Marx hence inaugurates in thinking an attention to the overdetermined triad: (1) materiality—both human and the world; (2) the irreduc-ibly social nature of materiality; and (3) praxis as transformative of social materiality and also as birthing truth. If for Gandhi truth is predicated on our own moral experi-ence, for Marx truth is predicated on the ethic of transformative praxis in the material social. Consistent with Marx's dictum, "The philosophers have only interpreted the world in various ways; the point however is to change it," Gandhi literally produced a philosophy of praxis "in the form of example [the *satyagrahi* as the living moral ex-emplar] rather than [abstract] principles" (Bilgrami 2003, 4163).

Marxism and Gandhian spirituality are both apposite in their respective yet related departures from post-Enlightenment (and scientific) notions of truth, which are largely abstract and cognitive. Both, however, require handholding from the other. Marxism requires handholding from spirituality on the question of self-transformation (more on this in the section on "askesis") and on questions of "being-the-embodied-moral-ex-emplar" (and not the vanguard of scientific socialism or historical-materialist thesis).

12. We see a connection at the level of spiritual exegesis between *The Story of My Experiments with Truth* and the *Meditations* of Marcus Aurelius. Hadot (2001, 11, and 10, 179–205) sees the *Meditations* of Marcus Aurelius (a better translation of the Greek title would be "Exhortations to Himself") as "spiritual exer-cises, practiced according to a certain method ... The key to this method, and thus to the *Meditations*, is to be found in the three philosophical *topoi* distinguished by Epictetus ... judgment, desire, and inclination or impulsion ... each of these activities corresponds to a spiritual exercise, a discipline of representation and judgment, a discipline of desire, and a discipline of inclinations or impulses to action."

This, of course, requires a rethinking of religion and spiritualism, and Gandhi (2011, 277) was attempting such a rethinking in his translation and rereading of the Book of Life, the Bhagavad Gita,[13] which he held to be the "guide in life," the book "unrivalled for its spiritual merit": "The teachings of the Gita are not meant to be merely preserved in a book; they are meant to be translated into action ... to put into practice."

> It has [hence] been my endeavor ... to reduce to practice the teaching of the Gita as I have understood it. The Gita has become for us a spiritual reference book. Even in 1888–89, when I first became acquainted with the Gita, I felt that it was not a historical work, but that, under the guise of physical warfare, it described the [psychological] duel that perpetually went on in the hearts of mankind, and that physical warfare was brought in merely to make the description of the internal duel more alluring ... The author ... has not established the necessity of physical warfare; on the contrary, he has proved its futility. (Gandhi 2011[1980], 12–14)

In the process, the Bhagavad Gita has shown that truth—truth as a moral notion, as ground for moral deeds—is not in violence. Truth is elsewhere. Gandhi's Bhagavad Gita as guide to moral action, to Gandhi's moral action (where the Bhagavad Gita is not a book *on* ethics but *of* ethics), is radically different from the conventional guides to violent action wrenched out of the same text through rather conventional and predictable readings (more on the legitimating of violence in Marxian praxis in the last section of the essay).

Spiritualism, however, still requires handholding from Marxism on the question of social transformation (more on this in the section on "phronesis") and on questions of "being-the-transformative medium-in-the-material social" (and not the one obsessed with individual *moksha*). This of course requires a rethinking of materialism, and Marx is doing exactly that in his "Theses on Feuerbach." We will see in subsequent sections how the turn to askesis a la Foucault (and Gandhi) and the turn to phronesis a la Heidegger (and Marx) will require two more departures from abstract and cognitive notions of truth. The uneasy *and* between Marxism and spirituality begins to make sense after this fourfold departure in our relations with truth.

The Other Spiritual

Just like the relationship of spirituality to Marxism emerges as interesting once one begins to see materialism as social and practical enouncements and not as facile, dead, or mechanical invocations of the really real; and just like the relationship of Marxism to religion materializes as meaningful once one begins to see religion as lived moral poesies in relation to a personalized God/Truth/*dharma* (and not as blind allegiance to a quasi-dogmatic belief system), as Gandhi did; or religion as ground and spirit for social *moksha*, as Ambedkar did; or religion as unworldly[14] (and not

13. *The Bhagavad Gita According to Gandhi* is based on talks given by the Mahatma at the Sabarmati Ashram, Ahmedabad, over a nine-month period between 24 February and 27 November 1926.
14. "As de-legitimization of all worldly sovereign powers, the scandal of religion keeps alive the other absolute demand of mankind for unconditional happiness or justice. It is thus an absolute hope

"otherworldly"), as Das (2014, 19) suggests; just so, the relationship of Marxism to spirituality also becomes evocative when one begins to see spirit (*Geist*) or spiritualism not as "speculative idealism"—not as one arm of the real/speculative, matter/spirit binary, as Marx did (where spiritualism substitutes "self-consciousness" or the "spirit" for the real individual man)—but as:

1. A movement, a quasi-poetic trajectory of "turning and returning" (*en revenant*, returning as ghost, and not as full presence)—"returning home," but a returning that is "still to come," to a home that is unhomely; where the invitation, "to come," is a deferral of a final unveiling of meaning (as against the secure Hegelian return, the "unification" and "gathering function" in Hegel belonging to the metaphysics of the Absolute Spirit as self-thinking thought or self-knowing presence that comes to be "at home," securely at home); Geist then as the restlessness of "never being at home" (à la Derrida's reading of Heidegger's reading of Holderlin).
2. Spirit-in-flames (*der Geist is das Flammende*) or "spirit is flame" (*Der Geist ist Flamme*).
3. *Pneuma* understood as the breathing of "sighing and longing" and "not the breath of a self-imposing [Cartesian] voice."

Derrida (1991, 1) asks in *Of Spirit*, "What is spirit?": "What might he [i.e., Heidegger] have meant when it comes to 'spirit' or the 'spiritual'?" In fact, "not spirit or the spiritual but *Geist, geistig, geistlich*." For the question of spirit or the spiritual will be the question of the *Geist, geistig*, and *geistlich*. The question will have to be approached, according to Derrida, "through and through, [as] that of language" because "these German words"[15] do not "allow themselves to be translated."

> *Sein und Zeit* (1927): what does Heidegger say at that time? ... He *warns* [*avertit*]: a certain number of terms will have to be avoided (*vermeiden*). Among them, spirit (*Geist*). In 1953, more than twenty-five years later ... in the great text devoted to [the Austrian poet Georg] Trakl [1887–1914], Heidegger notes that Trakl always took care to avoid (*vermeiden* again) the word *geistig*. And, visibly, Heidegger approves him in this, he thinks the same. But this time, it is not *Geist* nor even *geistlich* which is to be avoided, but *geistig*.

> How are we to delimit the difference, and what has happened? What of this meantime? How are we to explain that in twenty-five years, between these two *warning* signals ("avoid," "avoid using") Heidegger made a frequent, regular, marked (if not remarked) use of all this vocabulary, including the adjective *geistig*? And that he

---

contra all hopelessness of the world. But this hope against all worldly hopelessness is not in turn the 'other' world of hope against 'this' world of hopelessness, but otherwise than the world at all. Religion is 'un-worldly' in that sense and not 'other-worldly'; happiness is not realized in this 'worldly' world, nor in that another world beyond, but which, in its arrival, calls into question each worldly world in the name of the world to come" (Das 2014, 18–9).

15. "*De l'esprit* is a thoroughly French title, much too French to give the sense of the *geistig* or *geistliche* of *Geist* ... This motif of spirit or of the spiritual acquires an extraordinary authority in its German language" (Derrida 1991, 4–5). Did Marx then reduce the pluripotency of *Geist* in the German to the simple matrix "matter/idea"?

often spoke not only of the word "spirit" but, sometimes yielding to the emphatic
mode, in the name of spirit? (1–2)

Everything suggests that, from as early as 1933, the date at which, lifting at last the quo-
tation marks, he begins to talk of spirit and in the name of spirit, Heidegger never
stopped interrogating the Being of Geist. "What is spirit? Final reply, in 1953: fire,
flame, burning, conflagration. Twenty years later" (83).

Is then the spirit that which inflames? No. The spirit is "what inflames itself, setting
itself on fire, setting fire to itself ... Spirit is flame. A flame which inflames, or which inflames itself" (Derrida 1991, 84). Spirit in flames, spirit is flame, and spirit as flame stresses the ambivalent or ambiguous duplicity of spirit; spirit can "light up," spirit can "give
light"; spirit can also burn, consume, and destroy. Derrida hence reads spirit as flame,
as a mode of burning oneself to virtually "nothing"; also as ashes, ashes as the
rem(a)inder of fire, of burning, of consuming, a remainder that reminds us of the
fact that consuming or consumption is never ever full; and as ghost (revenant) or
return. Such a reading of the spirit/spiritual resets Marxism's relation with the spirit/
spiritual as speculation/idealism.

The concept of spirit has been conventionally constructed in Western philosophy
(and also by Marx at times) in terms of a binary opposition to corporeality/materiality
(i.e., in opposition to the sensible, the physical, the bodily). Spirit as one of the core or
key principles of Western metaphysics has in turn been associated largely with transcendence and has been elevated to an absolute according to which pure spirit
resides in the Idea, or God; the physical world on the other hand has been perceived
as an "aberrant manifestation of impurity and imperfection" (Gritzner 2011, 86).
Derrida, however, building on Heidegger's reading of Holderlin and Trakl, sees
spirit not just as flame but in contrast as ashes and ghosts. For "flame is something
which burns while material is present, but in contrast ashes and ghosts are what is
still there after material has been reduced to its furthest limit, after the metaphorical
fire is extinguished" (Gritzner 2011, 91). For Derrida spirit thus becomes "an uncanny
supplement" (88): a revenant (ghost, apparition, but literally "that which returns"); a
rem(a)inder of the burnt out, the consumed, the expired, lending in turn to a deferred
transcendence. A ghost or revenant would be the trace of the subject that has not as-
cended to the metaphysical world of pure spirit; its transient "return" thus problema-
tizes the secured opposition between matter and spirit, presence and absence. The
Derridean turn to thinking anew around questions of the spirit (and the turn to spirituality) offers us a way to think beyond simple materialism and simple spiritualism.

Spiritual as Phronetic

Dasein, as acting in each case now, is determined by its situation in the largest
sense. This situation is in every case different. The circumstances, the givens,
the times and the people vary. The meaning of the action itself, i.e. precisely
what I want to do, varies as well ... It is precisely the achievement of *phronesis* to
disclose the respective Dasein as acting now in the full situation within which it
acts and in which it is in each case different .... .

... In *phronesis* ... in a momentary glance [*Augenblick*] I survey the concrete situation
of action, out of which and in favor of which I resolve [*Entschliesse*] myself.
                                                    —Martin Heidegger, *Plato's "Sophist"*

In 1923 at the University of Freiburg, Heidegger delivered a seminar on the Aristotelian
concept (invoked in book 4 of the *Nichomachean Ethics*) of phronesis—phronesis as distinct from *"sophia"* and *"episteme"*[16]; phronesis as the "other reason" or the other (way to)
truth; phronesis as pointing to "the possibility of developing a critically self-reflective
model of ontological knowledge firmly embedded in the finite world" (Long 2002,
36)[17]; phronesis as being-related to the with-which.

   This seminar serves as a dual critique of the forgetting of being in the Occidental tradition and of Enlightenment modernity, which in turn is a critique of abstract and cold
Reason. What is phronesis? In one sense, practical reason, as distinct from theoretical
reason. In another sense, it is reasoning based on concrete action, as distinct from speculative reason. In yet another but related sense, it is reason based on experience as distinct from abstract deductions; phronesis is thus "a form of knowledge capable of
critically considering [i.e., reflecting upon] the conditions of its own operation" (Long
2002, 36). Where sophia seeks "eternal certainty," phronesis settles for the "contingent
existence of human beings" and works with "dynamic, contingent principles endemic
to ethics" (37); where sophia posits the absolute authority of "first principles," phronesis
identifies the concrete encounter with the other qua other as the ultimate ground for
truth; where sophia demeans "being-related to the with-which,"phronesis affirms its
fundamental significance as a determining condition for truth. Phronesis recognizes
that truth lies not in ultimates but rather in the give and take between actually existing
beings, between self and other, as well as in action, in practice. An ontology directed by
phronesis rather than sophia would not seek refuge in the realm of "universal knowledge" but would recognize its own inherent embeddedness in the world and would
thus be capable of critically considering the historico-ethico-political conditions
under which it is deployed.

   Long (2002) posits two basic features of sophia:

1. It attempts to transcend its own embedded contingency by looking toward the
    eternal.
2. "Philosophical autarky" renders it monological in nature against the two basic fea-
    tures of phronesis, as follows.
    a. Phronesis is firmly situated in and directed toward the world of human turbid
        finitude, as well as human action or practice.

16. Or circumspection as distinct from religious dogma: phronesis is attentive to "totality constantly
sighted beforehand in circumspection," but it is with this totality, however, that "the world announces
itself" (Heidegger 1985 [1962], 105).
17. Not just the seminar on phronesis but even "an essay like 'The Origin of the Work of Art' ... offers a
number of important insights to a contemporary Marxist criticism wishing to engage with art as a 'construction' and an 'event' of truth rather than a simple 'document' of social reality ... Heidegger's notion
of the philosopher or artist as a figure who uses words and images as 'tools' for engaging with his or her
environment, as a precondition for *transforming* the world, is surely of continuing relevance if Marxism
is to continue functioning as a philosophy of 'praxis'" (Pawling 2010, 603).

b. It is "ethically autarkic" and thus dialogical in nature, with both experience and praxis.

Phronesis would thus work to mitigate violence—a mitigation important to Marxism —by attending to the with-which of the other being with which it is concerned/related. It would recognize this encounter with the other as the site from which both self-critique and critique first become possible and to which it must remain responsible. Its goal would not be the abstract causes of all things but the finite truth that emerges out of mediated encounters—that is, praxis between existing/relating beings.

The phronetic turn also renders truth practical (i.e., as praxis or as action oriented), finite, particular, and in relation with the with-which or the world. Phronesis—which is concerned with things human (*anthropina*) and which arises out of lived experience and what Long (2002) calls "situated empiricism"—thus renders the transcendental and totalizing imagination of the spiritual this-worldly as well as praxis-oriented. The phronetic rewriting of truth—truth that is not born out of the annihilation of the uncertainty endemic to truth, truth that is born out of each particular and practical encounter with the other and the world in which one is embedded—is different from the modern incarnation of sophia, the Enlightenment notion of (scientific) universals. The phronetic rewriting of truth, truth emanating out of one's be-ing in the world's irreducible sociality and practicality offers the classical spiritual imagination a way (i.e., a path) to be apposite to Marx's concerns regarding truth: truth as not just social and practical but also as tied to "conscientious apprehension" and "fairness." The turn to phronesis —as both a register of truth and a mode of being—could take the spiritual closer to Marxism.

The phronetic turn inaugurates the need for the missing perspective of (Marxian) praxis and social action in a rather individualized, at times self-obsessed framework of the spiritual. But if the spiritual lacks the material, social, and transformative social praxis as a ground for truth, then the Marxian attitude lacks self-reflection: reflection on one's own fascism (see the section titled "Being Anti-Oedipal") as a ground for one's search for truth. In a word, if the spiritual lacks action, Marxism lacks reflection. If the spiritual is self-obsessed, Marxism is tragically stripped of the self. The turn to Foucault and to askesis is an attempt to inaugurate the question of the (transformation of) self in Marxism, as well as to undo the utter neglect of the question of the self in much of the Marxian tradition—a question that has traditionally been seen as the exclusive domain of the spiritual tradition.

Marxism as Asketic

Foucault makes an interesting move while foregrounding the spiritual: he does not invoke matter as interlocutor to spirit. His interlocutor is philosophy. In the process, Foucault sees the spiritual as the praxis of self-transformation.[18] Foucault (2005, 15)

18. This calls for a move from "transition" to "transformation": the imagination of the political has hitherto been colonized by the concept of transition; it is time to envision the political in terms of transformation—that of self (à la askesis) and of the social. Because of this obsession with transition, much of

calls "philosophy" the form of thought that asks what determines truth and falsehood and whether or not we can separate the true from the false, including what it is "that enables the subject to have access to the truth" and that "attempts to determine the conditions and limits of the subject's access to the truth." The debate on false and "true-hence-revolutionary" or "revolutionary-hence-true" consciousness in scientific/scientistic Marxism stems from this kind of obsession with one kind of truth, the cognitive kind. Foucault calls spirituality "the search, practice, and experience through which the subject carries out the necessary transformations on himself in order to have access to the truth" (13). Spirituality for Foucault is then "the set of these researches, practices, and experiences, which may be purifications, ascetic exercises, renunciations, conversions of looking, modifications of existence, etc., which are, not for knowledge but for the subject, for the subject's very being, the price to be paid for access to the truth" (15–6). The Foucauldian understanding of spirituality postulates that truth is never given to the subject by the simple act of knowledge (*connaissance*); for the subject to have right of access to the truth, the subject must be transformed, and this we see as another radical rereading of truth, after the Marxian, Gandhian, and Heideggerian rereadings of truth. The question is therefore not reducible to the what or the whether of truth but to the how of truth, a question Foucault brings alive in his preface to *Anti-Oedipus* (more on this in the next two sections).

Truth is thus only given to the subject at a price that brings the subject's being into play; there can be no truth without a transformation of the subject, without (what Foucault calls) the long labor of askesis. Foucault's philosophical praxis appears then to be both a sort of retrieval of a forgotten moment—the moment of the coming together of self-transformation and truth—from a philosophical past and also a problematization of our philosophical present as marked by only one kind of truth—the cognitive notion of truth. By excavating this ancient practice of philosophy (which is also a "philosophy of practice"), Foucault forces contemporary philosophy to come face-to-face with what it has "neglected" hitherto: the self and the politically indispensable task of constituting a praxis-based (and not a theoretical) ethic of the self. Foucault (2005, 29) also argues that, in both Marxism and psychoanalysis (Lacanian psychoanalysis to be precise) there is:

> For completely different reasons but with relatively homologous effects, the problem of what is at stake in the subject's being (of what the subject's being must be for the subject to have access to truth) and, in return, the question of what aspects of the subject may be transformed by virtue of his access to the truth, well, these two questions, which are once again absolutely typical of spirituality, are found again at the very heart of, or anyway, at the source and outcome of both these knowledges. I am not at all saying that these are forms of spirituality. What I mean is that, taking a historical view over some, or at least one or two millennia, you find again in these forms of knowledge the questions, interrogations, and requirements which, it seems to me, are the very old and

Marxism's passion and energy has gone into historical materialism. Gandhi and Tagore, on the other hand, are philosophers of transformation, which is why their vision of the political looks a little strange (and also estranged) when evaluated from standard frameworks of transition, either liberal or Marxian.

fundamental questions of the *epimeleia heautou*,[19] and so of spirituality as a condition of access to the truth. What has happened, of course, is that neither of these two forms of knowledge has openly considered this point of view clearly and willingly. There has been an attempt to conceal the conditions of spirituality specific to these forms of knowledge within a number of social forms.

The distinction Foucault marks between philosophy and spirituality, between asceticism and askesis, helps us rethink not just the relationships between Marxism and truth and Marxism and spirituality but between Marxism as an academic discipline and Marxism as a "way of living"—a way of living counter to all forms of (inner) fascism. Can such ways of living Marxism (like living religion for Gandhi)—living like a Marxist, being Marxist as against speaking or writing Marxism—be seen as a way of becoming (postcapitalist), as Gibson-Graham, Cameron, and Healy (2013) have shown in their efforts at taking back the economy? Can Marxism then be seen as an everyday exercise and not just an analysis (say, class analysis) or thought, where the purpose of the exercise is not just to transform the world but to also transform oneself, an exercise classically handed over to the spiritual tradition? Marxism has largely become "the way one sees," or "to regard otherwise the same things," but it has not been the way one transforms oneself. "Marxism as asketic" or "asketic Marxism" is then not just a form of accumulating knowledge about labor but is about labor itself, is about laboring: laboring in the household, as Fraad, Resnick, and Wolff (1994) show; laboring to labor; in a word, laboring as a kind of (postcapitalist) praxis a la Gibson-Graham (2006), where postcapitalist praxis is not necessarily the practice of self-denial.

Being Anti-Oedipal

Foucault sees *Anti-Oedipus* as a book of (and not "on") ethics: a book of ethical action and living; a book that, like the Bhagavad Gita, is not *on* ethics (which is usual in philosophy) but that is a book *of* ethics, a book that itself, in itself, exudes ethics. But how can a book be ethical? Being anti-Oedipal, becoming anti-Oedipal, is for Foucault—who stands at the threshold of foregrounding concepts like Greek askesis (as against Christian asceticism)—a way not just of thinking (the ethical) but of living (the ethical). In that sense, the anti-Oedipal impulse displaces the ethical, first from the cognitive to the practical and then from the phronetic to the asketic. The question of *Anti-Oedipus*, or the "anti-Oedipal question," is: "How does one keep from being fascist, even (especially) when one believes oneself to be a revolutionary militant? ... The Christian moralists sought out the traces of the flesh lodged deep within the soul. Deleuze and Guattari, for their part, pursue the slightest traces of fascism in the body" (Foucault 2000, xv).

19. *Epimeleia heautou* or "care of oneself is a sort of thorn which must be stuck in men's flesh, driven into their existence ... *epimeleia heautou* is an attitude towards the self, others, and the world ... *epimeleia heautou* is also a certain form of attention, of looking. Being concerned about oneself implies that we look away from the outside ... we must convert our looking from the outside, from others and the world etc., towards 'oneself.' The *epimeleia* also always designates a number of actions exercised on the self by the self, actions by which one takes responsibility for oneself and by which one changes, purifies, transforms, and transfigures oneself" (Foucault 2005, 8–11).

Foucault thus marks a sharp distinction between *Anti-Oedipus* the book and "anti-Oedipus" the subject, between *Anti-Oedipus* the written text and "anti-Oedipus" the being—that is, being anti-Oedipal, the process of becoming, the praxis, the art, but not art as an object; rather, art as artisanal, art as the art of, the art of doing-living-being. In other words, Foucault renders anti-Oedipus, or the anti-Oedipal (as against the Oedipal), asketic. He thus replaces the cognitive notion of ethics with the practical and the self-transformative perspective.

Thus, while the Oedipal subject is a hopelessly melancholic victim-subject of the foundational asceticism of being-in-the-family, and while the Oedipal is a product of the "multiplicity of desire" being subjugated to the "twofold law of structure and lack" (i.e., to the totem and the taboo) in psychoanalysis, the anti-Oedipal is an art of living—that is, living desire. Thus, while the Oedipal is about a tragic "subject of asceticism," the anti-Oedipal is about the asketic praxis of necessary transformations of the self, a praxis that keeps eros alive (here Foucault sharply distinguishes between Christian asceticism and Greek askesis; see Foucault 2005, 10). There is thus a connection between *Anti-Oedipus* by Deleuze and Guattari—published in 1972—and *Hermeneutics of the Subject* by Foucault, lectures delivered in 1982. The anti-Oedipal is thus for Foucault (2000, xiv) a "tracking down of all varieties of fascism, from the enormous ones that surround and crush us to the petty ones that constitute the tyrannical bitterness of our everyday lives."

The history of Marxism (and the history of religion) has been a history of violence. Can Marxism (and religion) track down its own fascism? Does the spiritual deficit in Marxism stem from the inability to set up a relationship with violence (as Gandhi did)? Does the inability to set up a relationship with violence lead to the spiritual deficit? Marxists have stood for social change, but the labor of change was made to fit the framework of historical materialism, a framework that offered legitimating ground to the colonization of Tibet by the Peoples Republic of China—legitimating in the name of progress, growth, developmentalism, scientism and secularization, and also liberation from what Chinese secular orthodoxy saw as recalcitrant religious orthodoxy "out in left field" (Spivak 1994, 46).[20] That change was also instituted in haste. It was done without the kind of "work on the self" that (Freud foregrounds and) Foucault talks of in *Hermeneutics of the Subject*. The dream of Marxian social transformation without a (pre)cursor of self-transformation becomes a nightmare. The praxis of self-

---

20. "Out in left field," Ama Adhe—an eighty-six-year-old Tibetan woman—spent twenty-seven years of her life (1958–85) in a Chinese prison. She now lives in exile in India. Her crimes: she retained faith in a kind of Buddhism torn in turn between a pre-Buddhist paganism of nature Gods and a Tantric sublime; she maintained obeisance toward a spiritual healer, the 14th Dalai Lama; her life perspectives and personal standpoints were not in tune with "Chinese Marxism," which in turn was a shorthand for "Han nationalism," "modern statecraft," "democratic centralism" (with little attention to the "democratic"), the "rule of Party priests" in the name of the "dictatorship of the proletariat," etc., and what could be called "secular theologisms" or "theological secularisms" (see Tapontsang 1997). What would contemporary efforts at rethinking Marxism make of the story of this woman? How would it reflect or fold back on the given idioms of Marxism? Would it? Let us also not forget, in the process, the story of the other left field, Sri Lankan Theravada Buddhism, which corners, pulverizes, and violates the rights of countless Tamilians, both Hindu and Muslim.

transformation without an antecedent or a parallel praxis of social liberation becomes individualized forms of self-liberation and, hence, alienation from the world.

"An Ethical Guide for Transforming Our Communities"[21]

How would Marxism (and spirituality) conceptualize and bring to everyday practice—make, in other words, a "way of living"—the difficult dialectic of social transformation and self-transformation, as well as the dialectic of phronesis and askesis? How would Marxists remain aware and infinitely reflexive about all the varieties of fascism, from the "enormous ones ... that crush us to the petty ones that constitute the tyrannical bitterness of our everyday lives" (Foucault 2000, xiv), as well as our everyday praxis? What would be the relationships between transformative class praxis, violence, and postcapitalist futures?

Cohen (1986, 227) summed up historical materialism as revolutionary by suggesting that it places "growth of human powers at the center of the historical process ... and it predicts large-scale social transformations, and it claims that their course is violent." Cohen thus justifies violence and makes the philosophy, vision, and praxis of Marxian social transformation indissolubly and inalienably tied to (proletarian) counter violence against the ruling class. Much of the history of proletarian statecraft stands as testimony to Cohen's argument for violence. Much of the history of Marxist praxis has rendered the manner of social transformation and its leftovers rather unpalatable; they certainly have not represented much of a move toward creating a social humanity or a human sociality, as Marx suggested. Is there any other path to social transformation?

We believe there is. But for that, Marxian thinking had to be displaced—precisely the contribution of Resnick and Wolff (1987, 2002, 2006), who argued for abandoning the classical understanding of class in terms of the ownership/nonownership of property/power in favor of an understanding of class as process pertaining to surplus labor. Resnick and Wolff of course did not address the question of spirituality but shifted Marxism onto a softer ground (from its extant hard, rock-like existence where nothing more can be written and no guests are allowed). In the classical understanding of "class as noun," classes are divided into two antagonistic groups that struggle against one another. Class struggle is hence, à la Cohen, a struggle between antagonistic human groups, entities, and identities so as to either annihilate each other or expropriate one another. The violent annihilation of capitalists—in their real and embodied forms—becomes the natural fallout of expropriating the expropriators through the socialization of property, as it happened in the Soviet Union and in China. Therefore, whatever maybe the context and content of the struggle against extant oppressions and its success/failure, the primacy of violence remained embodied in the structure of Marxian struggle, in the institutions it shaped, and in its very exercises, including those conducted on itself (purges, prison/labor/rectification camps, etc.). At times, the violence projected onto capitalists was tragically directed at and inflicted upon

21. See Gibson-Graham, Cameron, and Healy (2013).

others: minorities, ethnic communities, religious sects, precapitalist relics, and so on, as in the case of Tibet.

In contrast, Resnick and Wolff understood class not as a noun, not as a group of people, but as a process of (the performance, appropriation, distribution, and receipt of) surplus labor, and they understood class struggle as a struggle over processes of surplus performance and appropriation that takes place between contingently placed subjects. The fundamental praxis of Marxian struggle, post–Resnick and Wolff, is to transform the extant organizations of surplus from exploitative to nonexploitative, and the essential site of social transformation is the processes (of surplus labor) pertaining to appropriation (see Cullenberg 1992). The struggle for social transformation does not necessitate violence because the struggle is not against capitalists as embodied entities per se but is in class processes, a subtle but decisive and fundamental difference. The annihilation of capitalists without eliminating exploitation (as happened in the erstwhile Soviet Union) would hardly be considered an appropriate political transformation in Marx's terms; it would only replace (as in the Soviet Union) private capitalists with state capitalists by virtue of the fact that the surplus is now appropriated from the workers by bureaucrats connected to the state (see Resnick and Wolff 2002). The focus of Marxian social transformation is hence not the annihilation of a class of people, capitalists, but the annihilation of exploitative class processes (just as the "annihilation of caste" for Ambedkar did not mean the annihilation of a class of people, Brahmins, but the annihilation of processes of caste oppression and caste-based humiliation embedded, in turn, in extant casts of mind). The end of capitalism hence need not be altogether inconsistent with "nonviolence."

This brings us to the question of the self, one's inner seeds of fascism, and self-transformation (as invoked in the section, "Marxism as Asketic"). Resnick and Wolff's analysis of class as a contingent process of performance and appropriation (and also distribution and receipt) of surplus labor entails that the "classed subject" can occupy, at one and the same time, multiple and contradictory class positions; thus, the subject exploited at the office/factory could be an exploiter at home. The question of exploitation hence moves from the capitalist "enemy" to be liquidated and returns all the way back home, to the self. It renders explicit that exploitation embodied by/in the self; such subtle complicity in exploitation points to the secret and disavowed seeds of fascist content in our subjectivities. Marxism, after the turn to class as process, remains reflexive about these multiple instances of exploitation as containers for and sources of deep-rooted fascism.

Class struggle or social transformation is thus not just that which occurs with respect to processes in which others are persecutors who hence need to be counterpersecuted, but it occurs with respect to processes in which the self can be the persecutor. It is then a "movement," "a quasi-poetic trajectory" of turning toward one's own violence,[22] one's own fascism, or a return to the truth and the self-realization of how one is also an appropriator of surplus and not just a performer—that is, how one is also an exploiter, even if minimally, even when one is exploited—exploitation coming to finally haunt oneself. Geist here is the restlessness of "never being at home," either as bourgeoisie

---

22. As Derrida suggests in his rereading of Geist—Geist not as speculation or idealism. And it is this returning that makes Marxism apposite to the spiritual.

or as proletariat; one is always already unhomely. Marxism, after Resnick and Wolff, thus becomes a critically self-reflective model of ontological knowledge firmly embedded in the finite world; it is a process of being reflexively related to the with-which of class processes and classed subject positions. Class as process is thus the *Grundrisse* to the kind of asketic work Foucault talks of. It also shows to the self the importance of "self-conversion" rather than "exteriorized coercion."

Further, phronesis as a turning to the not-too-easily-assailable other puts to question the convention of the distinction—which is also the conventional distinction—between "left" and "right" in much of Marxism. It also puts to question the time-space curvature of the political. The given distinction between the Left and the Right come to occupy different meanings after the phronetic turn: "left" comes to mean, at the very least, that the political as such is receptive to what is at stake in the community. On the other hand, "right" comes to mean that the political is merely in charge of order and administration (Nancy 1991). In this sense the political is indissociable from something that the word "communism" has expressed all too poorly, even as it remains the only word to point toward it. The political after the phronetic turn is the place where the community-as-Other is brought into play; the political is the place of the community-as-Other; the place of a specific existence, the existence of being-in-common, which gives rise to the existence of being-self. The phronetic turn—say, as embodied in the Community Economies work of Gibson-Graham et al.—adds substance and flesh to Marx's stress on the irreducible and inescapably social nature of all humanity in the "Theses on Feuerbach."

This is not to ignore or demote the praxis of transformation in two other possible forms: "mass movements" or even "social revolution." Rather, the point is to argue that "self-transformation," "social transformation," and "political transformation" (see Chakrabarti and Dhar 2015) must proceed in tandem and along overdetermined axes, and for that to happen, different routes are available, the above being an example of one possible route. A slightly different route is the Gandhian idea of "social revolution" that, after our working through the "four other notions of truth," can be construed as based on a philosophy of transformation that works toward a displacement of the self, social, and political axes at the micro level, accompanied by a movement for *janajagaran* (mass awakening)—but mass awakening way beyond "identitarian nationalisms" (as of extant right-wing practices; see Chakrabarti and Dhar 2012) and "secular universalism" (as of extant left-wing ideologues).[23] The elements of

23. Pyarelal (1951, 160), a close associate of Gandhi, observed that the ruling principle of Gandhi's Ashram life was "to each according to his need, from each according to his capacity." This is a communist principle. In this regard, "His Ashrams are thus themselves experiments in Communism based on non-violence and Indian village conditions." Gandhi (1951, 152) confronted the Indian Communists thus: "You claim to be Communists, but you do not seem to live the life of Communism. I may tell you that I am trying my best to live up to the ideal of Communism in the best sense of the term." Finally, Gandhi argued against the Communists by insisting on the importance of self-social transformation: "Socialism is a beautiful word ... In order to reach this state we may not look on things philosophically and say that we need not make a move until all are converted to socialism. Without changing our life we may go on giving addresses, forming parties and hawk-like seize the game when it comes our way. This is no socialism. The more we treat it as game to be seized, the farther it must recede from us. Socialism begins with the first convert. If there is one such, you can add zeros to the one and the first zero will account for ten and every addition will account for ten times the previous number. If, however, the beginner is a zero, in

Gandhi's "phronetic turn" through practices of rural Swaraj (imperfectly translated as "self-rule"), in reshaping the construction of the self (i.e., our moral compass of truth and freedom), and in community/"nation" building (his work in Ashrams, abodes of moral collectivities), accompanied by mass movements such as in the form of the Quit India Movement, had to be in sync with one another. There was no freedom outside of their mutually constitutive complexity: "If we become free, India is free" (Gandhi 2010, 59)—the idea and existence of self and collective cannot be detached, except by paying a heavy price.

As we understand, it was only in the overdetermination of the three axes that the truth and freedom he sought would be achieved and unalienated life—as Marx (1987) also longed for—reclaimed. At the least then, without recovering our anti-Oedipal moral compass through the asketic and the phronetic turn of self-realization, action, and construction, including self-transformation and social transformation, un-alienated life will remain a distant dream and mass awakening/movements will collapse into dystopias (as in the Soviet Union and China). To truly live up to what Marxism says and to what it seeks, as well as what it ought to practice (in which it has failed time and again), the phronesis of social revolution needs to be singed in askesis—that is, in the unending spiritual stream of self-transformation.

Acknowledgments

This paper is a "gift" to Serap Kayatekin, whose constant urging inspired us to embark on this not-so-usual journey of bringing to dialog Marxism and spirituality. Special thanks to her and Stephen Healy for reviewing and commenting on the essay. Parts of what is covered here were discussed in classrooms, seminars, and summer schools on Marxism. The political theology study group at Jawaharlal Nehru University—especially Satya Brata Das, Soumyabrata Choudhury, Franson Manjali, Babu Thaliath, Soumick De, and Achia Anzi—has contributed to this paper in mostly noncited ways. The usual disclaimer applies.

References

Ambedkar, B. R. 2010. *Words of freedom: Ideas of nation.* New Delhi: Penguin.
———. 2014. *Annihilation of caste.* Ed. S. Anand. New Delhi: Navayana.
Anzi, A. 2014. Politics, secularism, religion and the order of things. In *Politics and religion,* ed. S. B. Das, 152–63. Delhi: Aakar Books.
Bilgrami, A. 2003. Gandhi, the philosopher. *Economic and Political Weekly,* 27 September: 4159–65.
Braungardt, J. 1999. Theology after Lacan? A psychoanalytic approach to theological discourse. *Other Voices* 1 (3). http://www.othervoices.org/1.3/jbraungardt/theology.php.
Chakrabarti, A., and A. Dhar. 2012. Gravel in the shoe: Nationalism and world of the third. *Rethinking Marxism* 24 (1): 106–23.
———. 2015. The question before the communist horizon. *Rethinking Marxism* 27 (3): 357–9.

other words, no one makes the beginning, multiplicity of zeros will also produce zero value. Time and paper occupied in writing zeroes will be so much waste" (9–10).

Cohen, G.A. 1986. Marxism and functional explanation. In *Analytical Marxism*, ed. J.E. Roemer, 221–34. Cambridge: Cambridge University Press.

Cullenberg, S. 1992. Socialism's burden: Toward a "thin" definition of socialism. *Rethinking Marxism* 5 (2): 64–83.

Das, S. B. 2014. *Politics and religion*. Delhi: Aakar Books.

Derrida, J. 1991. *Of spirit: Heidegger and the question*. Trans. G. Bennington and R. Bowlby. Chicago: University of Chicago Press.

Dreyfus, H. L. 1999. Could anything be more intelligible than everyday intelligibility? Reinterpreting Division I of *Being and time* in the light of Division II. Paper presented at the inaugural Meeting of the International Society for Phenomenological Studies, Asilomar, California, 19–23 July.

Erikson, E. 1969. *Gandhi's truth: On the origins of militant nonviolence*. New York: W. W. Norton.

Foucault, M. 2000. Preface to *Anti-Oedipus: Capitalism and schizophrenia*, by G. Deleuze and F. Guattari, xi–xiv. Trans. R. Hurley, M. Seem, and H. R. Lane. Minneapolis: University of Minnesota Press.

———. 2005. *The hermeneutics of the subject: Lectures at the Collège de France 1981–1982*. Trans. G. Burchell. London: Palgrave Macmillan.

Fraad, H., S. A. Resnick, and R. D. Wolff. 1994. *Bringing it all back home: Class, gender & power in the modern household*. London: Pluto.

Gandhi, M. K. 1951. *Towards non-violent socialism*. Ed. B. Kumarappa. Ahmedabad, India: Navajivan Publishing House.

———. 2010. *Hind swaraj*. Ed. S. Sharma and T. Suhrud. Delhi: Orient Blackswan.

———. 2011 (1980). *The Bhagavad Gita according to Gandhi*. Delhi: Orient Publishing.

Gibson-Graham, J. K. 1996. *The end of capitalism (as we knew it): A feminist critique of political economy*. Oxford, U.K.: Blackwell.

———. 2003. An ethics of the local. *Rethinking Marxism* 15 (1): 49–74.

Gibson-Graham, J. K., J. Cameron, and S. Healy. 2013. *Take back the economy: An ethical guide for transforming our communities*. Minneapolis: University of Minnesota Press.

Gritzner, K. 2011. Spirit to ashes, performance to dust: Derrida, Théâtre de Complicité, and the question of a "holy theatre." *Performance and Spirituality* 2 (1): 85–110.

Hadot, P. 2001. *Philosophy as a way of life: Spiritual exercises from Socrates to Foucault*. Ed. A. I. Davidson. Malden, Mass.: Wiley-Blackwell.

Healy, S. 2015. Communism as a mode of life. *Rethinking Marxism* 27 (3): 343–56.

Heidegger, M. 1985 [1962]. *Being and time*. Trans. J. Macquarrie and E. Robinson. Oxford: Basil Blackwell.

———. 1997. *Plato's sophist*. Bloomington: Indiana University Press.

Hunter, I. 2009. Spirituality and philosophy in post-structuralist theory. *History of European Ideas* 35 (2): 265–75. doi: 10.1016/j.histeuroideas.2008.11.002.

Long, C. P. 2002. The ontological reappropriation of phronesis. *Continental Philosophy Review* 35 (1): 35–60.

Marx, K. 1932. *The German ideology*. In *Marx-Engels Collected Works*, vol. 5, by K. Marx and F. Engels. Moscow: Progress Publishers. https://www.marxists.org/archive/marx/works/1845/german-ideology/preface.htm.

———. 1970. *Critique of Hegel's philosophy of right*. Trans. A. Jolin and J. O'Malley, ed. J. O'Malley. Cambridge: Cambridge University Press. https://www.marxists.org/archive/marx/works/1843/critique-hpr.

———. 1987. *Capital*. Vol. 1. Moscow: Progress Publishers.

———. 2016. Theses on Feuerbach. Trans. C. Smith (2002). Marxists Internet Archive. Accessed 7 September. https://www.marxists.org/archive/marx/works/1845/theses/.

Marx, K., and F. Engels. 1956. *The holy family, or Critique of critical criticism: Against Bruno Bauer and company*. Moscow: Foreign Languages Publishing House. https://www.marxists.org/archive/marx/works/1845/holy-family/index.htm.

Nancy, J.-L. 1991. *The inoperative community*. Minneapolis: University of Minnesota Press.

Resnick, S. A., and R. D. Wolff. 1987. *Knowledge and class*. Chicago: University of Chicago Press.

———. 2002. *Class theory and history: Capitalism and communism in the USSR*. New York: Routledge.

———, eds. 2006. *New departures in Marxian theory*. New York: Routledge.

Parekh, B. 2001. *Gandhi: A very short introduction*. New Delhi: Oxford University Press.

Pawling, C. 2010. Rethinking Heideggerian Marxism. *Rethinking Marxism* 22 (4): 590–604.

Pyarelal. 1951. Gandhiji's communism. In *Towards non-violent socialism*. Ed. B. Kumarappa. Ahmedabad, India: Navajivan Publishing House. Originally published in *Harijan*, 31 March 1946.

Spivak, G. C. 1994. Psychoanalysis in left field and fieldworking: Examples to fit the title. In *Speculations after Freud: Psychoanalysis, philosophy and culture*, ed. S. Shamdasani and M. Munchow, 41–75. New York: Routledge.

Tagore, R. 2004. *Selected essays*. New Delhi: Rupa.

Tapontsang, A. 1997. *The voice that remembers: One woman's historic fight to free Tibet*. Boston: Wisdom Publications.

Religion in Russian Marxism

Ross Wolfe

Of all the past efforts to reconcile Marxism and religiosity, the "god-building" episode within the Russian Social Democratic Labor Party (RSDLP) is especially fascinating. Situating god building in its historical context, amidst the reaction that followed the revolutionary defeat of 1905, this essay reconstructs the intellectual drama which subsequently ensued. Maksim Gorkii and Anatolii Lunacharskii emerge as the progenitors and main protagonists of the god-building current, in debate with more orthodox Marxists like Plekhanov and Lenin. God building was articulated in a number of different literary forms, from poems and letters to novels, articles, and even philosophical treatises. Ultimately, the objections raised by Lenin and others are found to be more in line with the views of Marx and Engels, though god building does pose important questions about the redeemable content of religious belief.

The question of Marxism's compatibility with religion has been raised at various points over the years. Despite the unapologetic atheism of its founders and leading exponents, frequent attempts have been made to incorporate spiritual themes into the materialist conception of history. Some feel that Marx and his successors neglected the role played by religious belief in social life, treating ritual and faith as mere epiphenomena—surface effects of underlying causes—without any force of their own. One result of this narrow focus on class struggle, critics maintain, is an "ethical deficit" or "lack of spirituality" (*безду́ховность*) in theory and in practice (see, respectively, Callinicos 2006, 220; Kuznetsov 2004), which must be corrected if Marxists ever hope to again change the world. Most recently, scholars such as Terry Eagleton, Jan Rehmann, Alberto Toscano, and Roland Boer have revisited this question in light of widespread desecularization, alongside "the turbulent rise of explicitly religious forms of political subjectivity" (Toscano 2010, 173). Eagleton (2009a, 90; 2009b) insists that "religion must be patiently deciphered, not arrogantly repudiated" and urges radicals to "read the Bible." Rehmann (2011, 145), for his part, doubts if revolutionaries can ultimately do away with religion "since it constitutes a major form in which protest against real misery and suffering is articulated." Finally, Boer (2013, 100), who has done more than any other to reconcile Marxism and theology, seeks to recover "the emotional, enthusiastic, ethical dimension of socialism" against the cold rationalism of its economic critique.

It should come as no surprise to learn that these authors are interested in earlier efforts to answer this question. Precedent provides a sense of rootedness in the past as well as an opportunity for reflection. Cases that appear to challenge "the old antithesis between spiritualism and materialism" (Marx and Engels 1975b, 94) are thus drawn from the Marxist tradition, ranging from Muslim national communism in central Asia following the October Revolution (Renault 2015) to Catholic liberation theology in Latin America following the Medellín Conference (Löwy 1996, 137). Boer's latest study, *Lenin, Religion, and Theology*, proceeds in much the same spirit. It explores the always-fascinating "god-building" tendency in the Bolshevik party prior to the outbreak of European war in 1914, led by Maksim Gorkii and Anatolii Lunacharskii. The treatment this tendency receives from Boer serves as the point of departure for this essay.

God building has long been a favorite topic of inquiry for those aiming at a rapprochement between Marxism and religion, both because of the historical personalities involved and the oddness of Marxism's approach to the question. Since it met with such harsh censure in Lenin's polemics after 1908, the god-builders' synthesis has come to be regarded as a promising "path not taken" (Boer 2013, 86–7). Yet it would be a mistake to exaggerate its significance: god building was never really a movement per se. At most it was an intellectual current within the Vperëdist wing of prewar Bolshevism (Stites 1989, 103). Juxtaposed against the later League of the Militant Godless, an atheist agitprop organization formed in 1927, its number of adherents was relatively small (Peris 1998, 2). Nevertheless, though Lenin was no doubt right to take issue with the god builders for their mysticism, the notion that socialists might overcome religion by realizing its ideals contains a kernel of truth. In order to extract this kernel, one must step back from the specifics of the debate from more than a century ago. Forgetting the internecine squabbles of rival factions at the school established by the Bolsheviks on the Isle of Capri, the broader role of religion in the development of modern society may be ascertained.

Like other forms of social consciousness—for example, philosophy and art—religious ideology corresponds to definite historical relations that are obscure to it, despite furnishing its basis. Religion thus addresses antagonisms that it is powerless to resolve, offering allegories or images of redemption in its holy texts but little else. These quasi-pictorial representations of redeemed humanity, of sovereign spirit removed from natural constraint (Hegel 1971, 299), persist well after enlightenment has pierced the veil of the ancient myths (Horkheimer and Adorno 2002, 1–34). Of course, none of this should be seen to vindicate the positions of either Gorkii or Lunacharskii. Quite the opposite, as the desiderata left by religion can be fulfilled only through a secular transformation—a revolution in this world, not the next. By erecting a new mythology, Lenin (1973c, 122) argued in a letter to Gorkii, the god builders simply swapped one "ideological necrophily" for another.

"Mankind loses religion as it moves through history, but the loss leaves its mark behind," the critical theorist Max Horkheimer (1972, 131) wrote in a 1935 text. "Part of the drives and desires which religious belief preserved and kept alive are detached from their inhibiting mythical form and become productive forces in social practice ... It keeps society from indulging in thoughtless optimism, an inflation of its own knowledge into another religion."

Even if this conclusion was not apparent to either side of the dispute, falling just beyond its historic purview, the god-building episode in Russian Marxism remains instructive for any survey of socialism and spirituality. Because the controversy took place during a moment of heightened class conflict, at least relative to the present, the question acquired an urgency it otherwise lacks. Such moments allow greater insight into the truth. Whatever currency may be claimed for god building today is owed to the fact that the stakes were much higher then. Consequently, its obvious errors still shed more light on the dichotomy of spirit and matter than the subtle prevarications of recent memory. This essay therefore examines the Marxist theory of religion as a whole through the prism of a particular instance.

Between *Vekhi* and *Vperëd*: Machists and God Seekers

Very few histories written in English deal with god building directly. Occasionally, essays will appear devoted to the subject, sometimes chapters in books. Most of the time, however, it is mentioned only in the context of Lenin's quarrel with his onetime lieutenant, an engineer by the name of Aleksandr Bogdanov (Sochor 1988, 153). Along with Lunacharskii and Gorkii, Bogdanov was a regular contributor to the Bolshevik periodical *Vperëd* (Forward). In the lull that followed the revolutionary upsurge of 1905, the journal became a flashpoint in the leadership crisis afflicting the party. Bogdanov, who had worked closely with Lenin to procure funds while in Finnish exile (Nikolaevskii 1995, 29), now vied with Lenin for the future of Bolshevism.

Here it is necessary to clear up some of the confusion that often surrounds the topic of god building. Gorkii and Lunacharskii first advanced their idea of a proletarian religion in standalone novels and treatises, and they later defended it in the pages of *Vperëd*. Unsurprisingly, god building came to be identified with the other political and philosophical viewpoints published therein (Lenin 1977a, 124). Due to this association with "Vperëdism"—itself a highly complex phenomenon, combining multiple strands—god building's peculiar qualities tend to get lost. This is not to suggest that there was no affinity between the various groups under the Vperëdist heading, of course. For the most part, though, the cluster of ideologies known as Vperëdism can be disaggregated according to political and philosophical elements. John Eric Marot (2012, 193) wisely cautions against equating these two registers or positing a parallelism between them. "Political divisions [did not] coincide with philosophical divisions," he writes. "The Vperëdists were a heterogenous lot," and they "disagreed among themselves about philosophy. Some were orthodox materialists, some 'God-builders,' some neo-Kantian 'Machists.' Many who parted from Lenin politically in 1909 did not care for either Bogdanov's empirio-monistic philosophy or for Lunacharskii's 'religious' atheism."

Initially, the editorial staff of *Vperëd* favored maintaining the Bolsheviks' boycott of Duma elections, a policy initiated in 1905 amid violent riots, street clashes, and strikes (Lunacharskii 1926, 110). At the time, the hope was that the workers' militancy would continue to intensify. Lenin reckoned that this window of possibility had closed by April 1906, however, and he reversed his stance in light of this judgment (Krausz 2015, 127–8). He managed to bring Bogdanov around to this assessment of the situation, and together they eventually convinced the ultimatumists and "otzovists" to abide by the decisions of the majority (Yassour 1981, 9). Before 1909, therefore, Lenin was happy to overlook Bogdanov's syncretism and penchant for baroque theoretical speculations, upholding an unofficial line of "philosophic neutrality" so long as their political agreement held (Joravsky 2009, 24–43). Once they finally did split that year at Capri, Bogdanov (1995, 92) accused Lenin of class collaboration (*классового сотрудничества*) for working with Menshevik spokespersons such as Georgii Plekhanov and Liubov Akselrod, forgetting that his fellow Vperëdist, Pavel Iushkevich, was a Menshevik as well.

Where did god building fit into all this? Remarking at a symposium just a few years later, Lenin (1977c, 266) lumped it rather indiscriminately with the other facets of Vperëdism: "The spring of 1909 saw a final break between the Bolsheviks and the so-called Vperëdists, who accepted otzovism or considered it a 'legitimate trend' and defended 'god-building' and the reactionary philosophy of Machism." Evidently, Lenin felt god building flowed from the same faulty premises as empirio-omonism—namely, from the premises of Mach's epistemology. Since it failed to distinguish between idealism and materialism, Lenin (1977g, 291) contended that "Machist science has no right to deny theology." Furthermore, empiriocriticism's agnostic attitude toward objective reality collapsed knowledge into faith, leading to a kind of fideism that sanctioned religious superstition. God building was just the most extreme expression of this viewpoint, as Lenin made clear: "Supported by these purportedly recent doctrines, our destroyers of dialectical materialism proceed fearlessly to downright fideism. This is clearest in the case of Lunacharskii, but by no means in his case alone!" (19).

Boer (2013, 94) has good reason to reject Lenin's inference. Doubt of the external world does not necessarily entail belief in God. Lunacharskii wrote a popular guide to the *Critique of Pure Experience* by Avenarius in 1905, but none of the major tenets of what would later become god building showed up in this earlier book. Moreover, while Bogdanov (1995, 160) objected to the "unfairly polemical methods" employed against the god builders, he never found himself attracted to their brand of socialist spirituality. Perhaps Lenin can be forgiven some sloppiness, however, given the more strategic concerns of *Materialism and Empiriocriticism* and his pamphlet "On the Faction of Supporters of Otzovism and God-Building." Nuance was sacrificed for the sake of expediency. His instincts were not too far off, in any event, given Lunacharskii's (1908a, 153) claim, in his 1908 diatribe against the renowned biologist and outspoken atheist Félix Le-Dantec, that "the ideas of 'Machism' stand in perfect accord with those of scientific socialism." Years later, Lunacharskii (1972, 438) sheepishly reminisced: "Though I did not subscribe to Bogdanov's empiriomonist philosophy, I nonetheless came close to it. At any rate, I stood no closer to the party than he did in a philosophical sense, insofar as I sought to introduce altogether alien elements such as empiriocriticism into Marxism." Self-criticism (самокритика) of this sort ought to be taken with a grain of salt, to be sure, since public recantation of previously held beliefs was something of a ritual performance already by the late twenties. In this particular instance, the testimony Lunacharskii (1911, 371) gave in 1928 in fact understated the sympathy he once felt for empiriomonism, describing Bogdanov as "the only Marxist philosopher carrying on the unsullied philosophical tradition of Marx," without Plekhanovesque adulteration.

One may grant to Boer, then, that god building is not exhausted by its source in Mach or any other single figure, and one may concede that "Vperëdism" elides several separate tendencies, yet one may still find components missing from his account. Boer omits a crucial piece of the puzzle in his spirited defense of Lunacharskii: *Vekhi* (Landmarks), a collection of essays written by former Marxists on the Russian intelligentsia. This omission is all the more puzzling in view of Boer's tendency to highlight points of contact between religion and revolution. *Vekhi* served as an outlet for many erstwhile members of the Russian Social Democratic Labor Party (RSDLP)—such as Sergei Bulgakov, Nikolai Berdiaev, and Semën Frank—in which they could theorize the so-called spiritual dimensions of social strife. Lenin was predictably dismissive, condemning the volume tout court as "a veritable torrent of reactionary mud poured on the head of democracy" (1977b, 129). Following the upheaval of 1905, intellectuals in Russia suddenly began thinking along these same lines. Gorkii and Lunacharskii had little patience with the liberalism of *Vekhi*'s authors, and the latter was almost surely nonplussed by Berdiaev's contribution to the anthology. "All sorts of mysticism was concealed beneath the word 'god-seeking' in those times, which did not yet wish to be compromised through a connection to this determinate God or that official religion," Lunacharskii (1972, 439) recalled. Both were far more receptive to its contents than Lenin, however. Bulgakov, Berdiaev, and Frank all blamed the intelligentsia for the defeat of the 1905 Revolution, arguing that its resolute atheism isolated the masses. Young radicals had been led astray by a quasi-religious faith in "Enlightenment, materialism, and socialism" (Bulgakov 1994, 25). Corrupted by ideological imports from the West, they soon succumbed to "spiritual decay" (36–7). Emancipation was impossible, Bulgakov concluded, on the impoverished foundations of atheistic spirituality.

So how would liberation occur for the god seekers? "Ultimate liberation is possible only by God-manhood," asserted Berdiaev (1994), in a 1907 essay reprinted in *The Spiritual Crisis of the Intelligentsia*. "And ultimate joy is possible only in God." Here the esoteric concept of God-manhood is invoked, devised by the Russian religious philosopher Vladimir Soloviev (2008, 28), for whom the highest symbol of human freedom was Christ as God-incarnate, the image of divine humanity. For the god builders, on the contrary, god was not something preexisting that must be sought. Kline (1968, 105) explained in his study of *Religious and Antireligious Thought in Russia* that "Gorkii and Lunacharskii preached not the ideal *in* man, with the ethicists and humanists, or the ideal *above* man, with the theists, but the ideal *ahead* of man in history." In other words, God was not *transcendent to* but rather *immanent in* humanity, a latent potential manifesting itself down through the ages. Lunacharskii had no qualms with the mystical language of God-manhood used by Berdiaev and the god seekers; the trick was to invert this language by giving it a future aspect: ennobled by the pursuit of its endeavor, striving for self-knowledge, humanity would finally attain the level of "God-man" (*богочеловеком*).

Quite in keeping with this constructive metaphor, Lunacharskii (1911, 12) declared at the outset of the second volume of *Religion and Socialism* that God is "given to the world through man's triumph over nature." Vladimir Bazarov, the third-leading god builder beside Gorkii and Lunacharskii, counterposed god building to god seeking even more emphatically: "The main content of 'god-building' is composed not in the form of a simple protest against God," asserted Bazarov (1909, 355), "but precisely in the form of a creative overcoming of God. God-building is diametrically opposed to god-seeking. In spirit, the former is much more hostile to the latter than the so-called scientific worldview. Even more than dogmatic materialism, for example." Bazarov turned the tables on Soloviev's "divine materialism" (*богоматериализм*) in his subsequent anthology *On Two Fronts*. While praising the courage and ingenuity Soloviev exhibited in this undertaking, Bazarov (1910, vii) felt he had gone about it the wrong way. Soloviev had been right, he felt, to suppose that "spiritualism and materialism are equally untenable taken on their own" and must therefore "dialectically complement" one another in their thirst for completion, each being "imbued with the spirit of absolutism" (vi). As Bazarov saw it, however, Soloviev's proposed solution set out from the wrong side:

> Proceeding from God, it is impossible to grasp the meaning and necessity of creation ... For Soloviev the self-developing Hegelian concept, which creates itself out of "nothing" [*creatio ex nihilo*] in a process of dialectical development, achieves fullness and perfection only in a future theanthropic, divinely material apotheosis ... Yet clearly there is no God to raise man up to Himself. Rather the reverse: man raises himself up by degrees, and passes into God.

Or, what is perfectly the same, he realizes in the world the perennial idea of godlike perfection, without which man would be "nothing." (xv–xvi)

However, Soloviev could not countenance this argument, for the resulting "man-godhood" (человекобожество) would not be Christ but, in true Nietzschean fashion, the Antichrist (xvi).

Now that god building has been situated at the crossroads of *Vekhi* and *Vperëd*, its own positive attributes can be readily supplied. In order to trace out the logic of this idea, it is essential to go to the root of the matter. This requires an investigation of origins. After all, as Bazarov indicated, it was Gorkii who originally coined the term. What was this neologism meant to signify? Out of what material conditions did it arise? Disappointingly, despite being at the forefront of recent scholarship on god building, Boer has not engaged at much length with the great novelist's writings, preferring to concentrate on Lunacharskii's systematization instead. Gorkii's early writings on religion form the focus of the next section.

Gorkii and the Genesis of God Building

Most interpretations of god building written in the past several decades start by outlining its philosophical antecedents. These are doubtless important. But in the case of Maksim Gorkii, figures like Feuerbach and Dietzgen—usually cited as precursors—did not enter into the concept's formulation (Yedlin 1999, 28–9). Nietzsche was probably somewhere in the back of Gorkii's mind as he sat down to write the dialogue for *Confession*, though the German thinker is never mentioned by name and would later be publicly disavowed by Gorkii (38). Some specialists surmise that William James may have exerted an influence, as Gorkii met the American pragmatist twice during a lecture tour in 1906 and praised his landmark study, *The Varieties of Religious Experience* (Scherr 2003, 189–91). To assume that Gorkii was a disciple of Lunacharskii or Bogdanov would likewise be too hasty. Lunacharskii was in his estimation a "very talented man," of course, destined for greatness as a "philosopher-publicist" (Gorkii 1954b, 49), but his admiration for Bogdanov was even stronger: "Bogdanov is the most sound [здоровый] and original philosopher today," Gorkii (1966, 411) affirmed.

Raimund Sesterhenn (1982, 135–61), whose untranslated dissertation on god building remains the most thorough inquiry into the subject to date, persuasively argues that Gorkii's ideas about religion were already in place before he even read the work of Bogdanov or Lunacharskii. Gorkii's correspondence from roughly 1898 up through 1904 amply demonstrates this point, as religious rumination recurs throughout. For instance, in his 1902 letter to the author Leonid Andreev, he proclaimed, "There is no God, Leonidushka; there is a dream about Him, there is an eternal and unsatisfied drive to explain life to ourselves in some way or other. God is a convenient explanation for everything happening around us, but that only.

We'll make for ourselves a great, wonderful, joyful God" (Gorkii 1965, 129). All of this was an extension of Gorkii's (1954a, 101) profound humanism, which he cultivated while living in Nizhnii Novgorod at the turn of the century: "I know of nothing greater, more interesting or complex, than man," he wrote to the realist painter Il'ia Repin in 1899. "Man is everything—he even created God. Humanity's capacity for perfection is limitless." Unconsciously or not, a resemblance may be seen between this sentiment and the truism voiced by the young Marx (1975a, 175): that man made God in his own image, and not the other way around. Gorkii (1950c, 170) reprised this idea in his play *The Lower Depths*, just three years later, in the final speech by the character Satin: "Everything is in man, and everything is for man! Only man exists, and the rest is the doing of his hands and his brain."

By the time he penned the prose poem "Man" in 1904, where the previous line appears again verbatim, Gorkii (1950a, 367) was already well on his way to god building: "Come the day, the sensuous world will merge with immortal thought into one great, creative flame burning in my breast. And with that flame, I will incinerate all that is dark, cruel, and evil from my soul, and will be like the gods." Sesterhenn (1982, 214–15) analyzes such scattered statements across Gorkii's oeuvre as his "pathos of man" (*Pathos des Menschen*), an emotional side that runs throughout these early texts. Their protagonist is universal humanity; only the mouthpiece, the particular persona, varies. Echoes of Feuerbach resound, as his lesson—that nothing exists beside nature and man and that the higher beings created by his fantasy are merely the fantastic reflections of his own essence— was learned by Gorkii independently (Engels 1990a, 364). Vitalii Pimenov (2012, 172; translation from Russian by author), a contemporary commentator on the philosophy of god building, also detects an "anthropocentric theology [богословие] of power and pathos [пафос]" at work in "Man."

Indeed, "pathos" was a word Gorkii used repeatedly in his response to an international questionnaire (*enquête internationale*) put out by the symbolist literary magazine *Mercure de France* in 1907. This call for papers garnered submissions from well over a hundred eminent intellectuals, thirty-three of which were published, including a piece by Plekhanov (1976, 98–9). Frédéric Charpin (1907, 578) posed the question to readers: "Are we witnessing a dissolution or an evolution of the religious idea and religious feeling?" Never much of a believer himself, Gorkii had been skeptical a few years earlier when his comrade Posse (1950d, 169–70), who edited a socialist paper, privately remarked that it is impossible to live without religion. Gorkii's (1907, 595) essay for the *Mercure de France* took a seemingly similar tack, however, albeit with qualifications: "Religious feeling, as I understand it," he specified, "must exist, develop, and render man perfect." Obviously, a great deal hinges on the rather expansive definition of religious feeling that Gorkii provided in the body of his response. Here he defined it as that feeling which results from "recognition [conscience] of a harmonious link uniting man with the universe." With regard to its genesis, he hypothesized:

This feeling is born of the aspiration toward synthesis inherent in every individual, nourished by experience. It first manifests itself in man's consciousness of his role and place within the countless successions of phenomena in life, and from there is transformed into "pathos" by the *joyous* sensation of inner freedom that awakens in man. "Pathos" is religious. The infinite variety of facts of life, the beauty of the human endeavor that tends to fathom its mysteries; the creative force of our desire for freedom, truth, and justice; the slow but sure ascent of humanity toward perfection—these are the sources from which man draws "pathos." (593–4)

Many who had followed Gorkii's career were caught off guard by his column in the *Mercure de France*. Critical reaction was mixed. Lenin (1977d, 393) was undeniably displeased by all this pious talk and told Gorkii in a letter dated April 1908 that he would not abide anyone "preaching the union of scientific socialism with religion." For the moment, however, Lenin refrained from publicly admonishing his friend, possibly because this would jeopardize further donations to the party (Yedlin 1999, 87). Writing in the British monthly *The Social-Democrat*, S. N. Preeve (1907, 616) was much more appreciative. He hailed Gorkii's speculative argument as "easily the most interesting answer" to Charpin's question. But the most significant analysis by far came from Lunacharskii.

Lunacharskii's Religion of Labor

Lunacharskii welcomed the "religious turn" in socialist discourse. When the special issue on "la question religieuse" came out, he was just completing his preparatory notes for *Religion and Socialism*. A review of the French journal's contents would permit him to summarize some of his own findings. "The Future of Religion" was released in two parts—spaced out over the October and November editions of *Obrazovanie* (Education)—and addressed the *Mercure de France* entries most germane to Lunacharskii's purposes: the entries of Plekhanov and Gorkii, respectively. Contrasting the replies of his fellow countrymen, Lunacharskii (1907a, 30) deemed "the answer of Gorkii more momentous, vibrant, and profound than the answer of Plekhanov." In the first installment of the essay, he disparaged the latter for supposedly "adhering to the metaphysical materialism of the eighteenth century." Plekhanov was closer to Helvétius and d'Holbach than to Marx, Lunacharskii (1907b, 3) alleged, perpetuating an error committed by Engels in the mid 1870s. Engels (1985, 15–16) advised revolutionaries to distribute "the splendid French materialist literature of the last century" without bothering to explain the sociological basis of religious ideology. "Regardless of what Engels says about their depth and brilliance, historical merits notwithstanding ... Voltaire, Diderot, et alia suffered from the same shallow understanding of religion" (Lunacharskii 1907b, 13). Insofar as Plekhanov espoused views similar to the philosophes, he regressed to a pre-Marxist form of materialism. Feuerbach was superior, at least in this respect, to Marxists like Joseph Dietzgen, Friedrich Stampfer, and Anton Pannekoek (9–15).

Gorkii did not escape "The Future of Religion" entirely unscathed, however. Though for the most part the essay lauded his efforts, it featured a couple of gentle criticisms as well. Even then, Lunacharskii (1907a, 42) usually looked to soften the blow. Underscoring his reluctance, he wrote: "I do not want to polemicize with Gorkii. His reply [to the *Mercure de France* questionnaire] was for me the most satisfactory, the one closest to my heart." Nevertheless, Lunacharskii believed that Gorkii's answer consisted of two distinct "elements" that it mistakenly treated as equivalent: cosmism and humanism. Both of these elements represent self-contained and all-encompassing systems (31). Cosmism takes for its starting point the cosmos, or the substantial totality of nature, while humanism takes for its starting point humanity, or the spiritual totality of history (Young 2012, 180–2). For Lunacharskii (1907a, 36), cosmism was a sort of grandiose paganism, "the highest form of naturalistic religion," worshipping the harmony of natural forces. One could look to the *natura naturans* of Spinoza, Goethean pantheism, or Nietzsche's affirmative philosophy of life [*Lebensphilosophie*] for modern examples of this system (32–3), and to Hellenism or Brahmanism for their ancient forerunners. In Lunacharskii's perspective, the return of cosmist sympathies toward the beginning of the modern period owed to the rapid disintegration of the feudal order. With the breakdown of the "great chain of being," the naturalism of *Sturm und Drang* and Rousseau stood in stark contrast to the artificial world of commodities, which is why it so disturbed later apologists of bourgeois society. Long after Romanticism grew old and slid into reaction, Engels (1987, 49) saw in Jean-Jacques the roots of scientific socialism.

Turning his gaze to humanism, Lunacharskii (1907a, 38) identified several layers of possible meaning. Historically, this religion of humanity derived more from monotheistic spiritualism than from polytheistic naturalism. Spiritualism, historicism, anthropologism, and economism were just different ways of expressing the same content. And "economism," here in Lenin's (1974b, 408) sense, was the assumption that purely economic struggle will lead straightaway to the emancipation of the proletariat. Religious consciousness, Lunacharskii wrote, must be completely cleansed of theology. By theology, he seems to have meant teleology (almost homophonous in Russian: *телеология*). Humanity must accept that historical progress is not providentially ordained—not handed down from on high—but that it must instead be won without guarantee (*без гарантии*) of redemption:

> Does the religion of labor, as we have called it, not presuppose some assurance of victory, or everlasting progress? The great idealists spoke of humanity as a burgeoning deity, but regarded its advance as if it were an immanent law of nature or spirit ... Obviously we cannot recognize such a law, for it is obvious theology! We realists cannot stoop to this stupefying faith in divine patronage; we know that humanity is given only to itself. Is it headed

toward apotheosis, toward everlasting progress? Perhaps it waits in the
corner, with an idiotic smile, ready for the chance to snatch world-history
out of the rubbish heap of worlds? (Lunacharskii 1907a, 43)

Victory is thus not assured, and no preestablished harmony exists between man
and nature. However, by raising this objection to Gorkii's schema, Lunacharskii
was hardly looking to set up a rigid barrier to divide them. As a Marxist, he rejected
every imaginable dualism (40). From classical German philosophy, Marxism had
inherited a number of antinomies, or conceptual pairs arrayed against one
another: form/content, subject/object, spirit/matter, freedom/necessity (Engels
1990a, 362). Cosmism and humanism are each elaborations of the antinomy of humanity and nature, wherein the opposite term is subordinated. The problem for
Marxists has always been to determine how such relationships are mediated. Humanity has since time immemorial participated in a "metabolic interaction" with
nature, primarily through labor (Marx 1982, 283). Humanity is not somehow
outside of or otherwise apart from nature. Elisée Reclus (quoted in Serge 2012,
39) put it well: "Man is nature become conscious of itself." Yet the integral whole
to which nature and culture both belong is not a seamless equilibrium; it is
riven through and through.

   Religious ideology depends in no small part on humanity's shifting relationship to nature, and this in turn depends on humanity's own shifting forms of
social organization. Before the dawn of industrial capitalism in Europe, the
human bond with nature was fairly immediate, as life was still governed by
natural tempos (daily rhythms of sunup and sundown, seasonal patterns of
seedtime and harvest) that stretched back into the mists of prehistory. Production and consumption were circumscribed within more or less narrow geographic boundaries. Following Feuerbach, Marx and Engels concurred that
primitive religions tend to worship phenomena of nature taken from their surroundings—sun gods and fertility goddesses, animal totems, and so on (Engels
1982, 76). With the arrival of a society governed by the prerogatives of commodity production, based on the principle of exchange, the hierarchical *scala naturae*
of precapitalist times gave way to formal equality. A kind of human-made
"second nature" that seemed to possess the same inexorability as the first gradually built up around humanity (Lukács 1971, 128). Social antagonisms replaced
natural antagonisms as the wellspring of religious ideas since "religion … is
nothing but the fantastic reflection in men's minds of external forces which
control their daily life, in which terrestrial forces assume the form of celestial
forces. In the beginnings of history," Engels (1987, 300–1) continued, "it was
the forces of nature which were first so reflected … but it is not long before
social forces begin to be active which confront man as equally alien and inexplicable, dominating him with the same apparent necessity as the forces of
nature themselves." To Marxists, mastery of the first nature is contingent
upon mastery of the second (270).

Until mankind achieves this self-mastery, then, and thereby mastery over nature, religion will endure. Or as Marx (1982, 173) argued in *Capital*, "The religious reflections of the real world can vanish only when the practical relations of everyday life between man and man, as well as man and nature, present themselves in a transparent and rational form." Leon Trotsky (1973, 309–13), among the more hardline atheists within Russian Marxism—and who led the original Soviet atheist commission in 1920—pithily summed up the rationale for this in 1924: "Religious fiction has two sources, the weakness of man before nature, and the incoherence of social relations. The total abolition of religion will be achieved only when there is a fully developed socialist system, a technology that frees man from any degrading dependence upon nature." Externality is perhaps the decisive category here, since this is what gives both natural and historical necessity their heteronomous character (i.e., as a power "outside," compelling humanity to foreign ends). "It is clear that with every great upheaval, the outlooks and ideas of men are revolutionized, and thus their religious ideas as well," argued Marx (1976, 244), adding that "the difference between the present upheaval and all earlier ones lies in the fact that man has at last found out the secret of this [tumultuous] process ... and hence, instead of again exalting this practical, 'external,' process in the rapturous form of a new religion, he divests himself of all religion."

Lunacharskii deployed a variation of this same argument in "The Future of Religion," but with a key difference. He felt the conciliation of man and nature would signal the fulfillment, not the repudiation, of humanity's spiritual impulses. "When we think in terms of economic materialism proceeding from *labor* as the primary fact," Lunacharskii (1907a, 62) maintained, "then we must determine nature not epistemologically [*гносеологически*], but rather *economically*, not theoretically, but rather *practically*. Nature, the environment, shapes man, but once shaped, man overcomes the difficulties that nature places before him, little by little becoming lord of his own productive forces and thereby those of nature." This was not pure innovation on of Lunacharskii's part. Dietzgen also painted a Promethean picture of historical development in his six sermons on "The Religion of Social Democracy," delivered between 1870 and 1875. Acknowledging the *Urgrund* of religion in humanity's sense of primeval helplessness (Dietzgen 1906, 93), he unhesitatingly affirmed that "all exertion and struggle in human history, all aspirations and researches of science find their common goal in the *freedom of man*, or the subjection of nature under the sway of his mind" (96). For Dietzgen, as for Lunacharskii, this subjection would bring about the deification of man. "Civilized human society is the supreme being in which we believe; on its transformation to socialism we build our hope" (109). Robespierre's revolutionary Cult of the Supreme Being [*Culte de l'Être suprême*] is tacitly alluded to in this passage, though with the difference that humanity would bring nature under its fold rather than realign itself with *droit naturel* (Jaurès 2015, 231–5). In Lunacharskii's (1908c, 186–7) view, both Dietzgen and the deists overestimated natural science's ability to supplant religious feeling or serve as a surrogate. Such conceptions were still far too cold, too rationalistic; socialism requires good citizens, not scientists (36).

By placing labor at the center of his analysis of religion, Lunacharskii believed that he had critically grounded the discourse of Gorkii and Plekhanov in the terra firma of Marxist theory. Plekhanov was outraged by the polemical tenor of the essay, however, and thus unleashed a scathing riposte, "On the So-Called Religious Seekings in Russia." Gorkii, conversely, took Lunacharskii's criticisms more to heart. Their imprint can be seen in the celebrated passages on god building in his *Confession*, covered in the next section.

Confession, Commentary, Critique

Maksim Gorkii's novel *Confession* was met with great fanfare upon its release, both at home and abroad. Dmitrii Filosofov (1997, 62), who just a year earlier had dismissed Gorkii as a "finished" author, heralded this new book as proof of his intellectual maturity. Véra Starkoff (1909, 104), an émigré critic and playwright who wrote for *La Revue*, pronounced it a success: "Gorkii has discovered in the philosophy of socialism a God that responds to his aspirations." Aleksandr Blok came to Gorkii's defense against allegations of "demotheism" (демотеизм) leveled by German Baranov, a conservative member of the Religious-Philosophical Society in Saint Petersburg for whom the deification of man proposed by the novel was sheer idolatry. "If Gorkii ends his *Confession* with a prayer to some sort of a 'people' [народ], then the pathos of his story lies much deeper," Blok (2010, 71) opined. Blok even claimed that this was Gorkii's first truly literary work, or the first to reach beyond journalism toward art (72). The next portion of this essay thus assesses the presentation of god building in *Confession* as well as its reception by four prominent Russian Marxists: L'vov-Rogachevskii, Lunacharskii, Plekhanov, and Voronsky.

Without having to reconstruct its entire plot, one can still get the gist of god building in *Confession* by examining a few snippets of dialogue from the book's hero, Matvei, who narrates the story mainly in the first person. Matvei is in many respects a fictionalized version of Gorkii himself. He is orphaned from the provinces, tormented by questions of faith, spirituality, and the death of God, wandering from factory to factory amid scenes of desperate class struggle. And to the extent that Matvei's journey mirrors that of the author, *Confession* may be read as semiautobiographical—or even as a confession, as its title suggests. In conversation with Matvei, the old man Iona (formerly a priest, now turned beggar and holy fool) sermonizes about his idea of the divine:

> People did not create God out of weakness, no, but from an overflow of strength. And He does not live outside us, my brother, but rather within us. We ripped God out of our very selves, in our terror before the problems of

the soul. We placed Him above us, wishing to temper our pride—which bristles at any such limitation. I say that we turned strength into weakness, constraining our growth by force! By hurriedly imagining perfection, this became a detriment and burden to us. However, men are divided into two tribes. The first are the eternal god-builders; the second are slaves, forever captive to the ambition to rule over the first and thus the whole earth. [The second] seized this power, and claimed that God exists outside of Man; that God is everyone's enemy, lord and judge of the earth. (Gorkii 1950b, 330–1)

Asked to specify who were the builders of God, Iona tells Matvei that "the god-builders are the people [*народушко*], the great martyrs—greater than all those the church celebrates! They are God, creators of miracles." He proceeds in his old-fashioned dialect to confess his faith: "The people are immortal … they are the only unquestionable source of life, the father of all the gods that have been and will be" (331). In these pages the terms "god-building" and "god-builders" made their premiere. Still, the terms Gorkii was relying on, speaking through Iona, retained populist (or, more properly, Narodnik) resonances; it was unclear whom he meant. What classes comprised "the people"? Did he mean the rural peasants? Perhaps he had the urban workers in mind? Gorkii thus had Matvei press Iona harder on this issue. "Yes," replies Iona, "I mean the whole working people of the earth, all their strength—the eternal fount of God's creation [*богот-ворчества*]! In this awakens the will of the people, that great mass forcibly disunited, which shall unite" (332).

Lunacharskii's intervention into the *Mercure de France* debate on religion, stressing labor, can be seen most clearly in this back-and-forth. At the time, importantly, the Bolsheviks' line on revolutionary governance was such that a joint democratic dictatorship of the proletariat and the peasantry ought to be constituted in the event of a seizure of power, given Russia's class composition (Lenin 1962, 293–303). Hence, in Gorkii's *Confession*, both proletarians and peasants fell under the rubric of "working people." Matvei describes as god builders a gathering of coarsened peasants that he meets on the road to the Isetskii plant (Gorkii 1950b, 338). Once Matvei arrives at the plant, the scene of metalworkers coated in soot prompts him to privately exclaim: "God-builders!" (339). Contemplating his new-found theanthropic creed, Matvei wonders: "Does the Lord descend from heaven to earth, or does He ascend from earth to heaven, lifted up by the strength of the people? And here kindled the idea of god-building as the eternal doing of the entire people" (360). Near the end of the novel, though Matvei's faith has been tested along the way, he solemnly prays before the toiling masses:

I saw [the earth], my mother, in space between the stars. How proudly she gazed out, with her oceanic eyes, into the distance and the deep. Like a chalice full of bright red, relentlessly seething human blood. And I saw her master: the omnipotent, immortal people. "Thou art my God, creator of all gods, whom thou weaves out of the beauty of thy spirit, in the labor of thy pursuit. Yes, there shall be no God, save thou. For thou art the only God, performing miracles." This I believe and confess ... [in] the great cause of universal god-building. (378)

Gorkii bolstered his god building narrative by embedding in *Confession* a series of interpretive claims about the hypertrophied individualism of modern times. Just a few months prior, he had sketched a long conjectural history on "The Disintegration of Personality." Yet again, Gorkii (1978, 89) had identified the people as the "exclusive and inexhaustible source of spiritual values." He had detailed the *principium individuationis* from its inception in early hero cults, chieftains, and god-kings up to the enshrinement of the one true God, the spread of private property, and the concomitant atomization of society. "Contemporary individualism is trying to revive God, so as to use His authority to refortify the spent forces of the 'I,' which has lost touch with the collective, the source of all living creative forces," he had asserted (95).

In *Confession*, Gorkii ventriloquized this argument in a condensed form, placing it in the mouth of Mikhail, son of the old beggar Iona. Vasilii L'vov-Rogachevskii, a Marxian litterateur and longtime friend of Gorkii, read Gorkii's *Confession* as a response to Tolstoi's 1880 *Confession*. L'vov-Rogachevskii (1908, 20–1) observed that this earlier book by the same name opened with the first-person singular ("I"), whereas Gorkii's version opened with the first-person plural ("we"), illustrating their divergent subjectivities. Although he drew attention to some populist slippages in which Gorkii sounded more like a socialist revolutionary anarchist than a Marxist social democrat (Lunacharskii 1908b, 92), L'vov-Rogachevskii (1908, 28) nevertheless lauded *Confession* as a "valuable supplement" to Lunacharskii's *Religion and Socialism*, presaging a new spirit in the party. "God is dead, long live God!" quipped L'vov-Rogachevskii, suggesting this serve as the slogan of god building (25). But no one gave Gorkii higher marks than Lunacharskii. His rave review of *Confession* appeared in *Literaturnyi raspad* (Literary disintegration) in August 1908. "The ideal power and absolute novelty of Gorkii's novella," wrote Lunacharskii (1908b, 91), "consists in the grandiose image of a weary people in the features of its wanderer ... brushing up against the 'new faith,' face to face with the truth the proletariat has shown the world." Most of Lunacharskii's piece was devoted to exegesis, clarifying what he believed were the core messages, beyond any ambiguity and equivocation. Regarding the speech by Iona excerpted above, for instance, "The God about whom the old man spoke is ... socialist humanity; this is the sole divinity available to us. And who built God? Obviously the proletariat" (94).

Even staunch critics of god building like Plekhanov (1974, 370) were grateful for the commentary by Lunacharskii, if only for the fact that he rendered Gorkii's novel more consistent. But one ought not conflate the god building of Lunacharskii with the god building of Gorkii. Though they consulted each other often, both by letter and in person, Lunacharskii (1908b, 97) was undoubtedly eager to pass off his

views as consonant, or at least complementary: Iona's testimony "is that living, concrete feeling of collective unity, just as necessary a part of genuine proletarian
socialism as the stern 'cold' formulae that many perceive as the alpha and
omega of Marxist orthodoxy." *Confession* was, in Lunacharskii's appraisal, an artistic "symbol of the future" (99), the same future he had written about in *Religion and
Socialism* in a more philosophical idiom. Though Plekhanov (1974, 367) took their
positions to be identical, he suspected it was Lunacharskii who put Gorkii up to
this god-building mischief in the first place. For the esteemed Menshevik, their
common fallacy was to "give the name of *religion* to every *social* feeling" (368). Lunacharskii (1907a, 30) had already drawn a favorable comparison between Gorkii and
the French sociologist Émile Durkheim. Durkheim (1995, 201) would later famously
define religion as "society worshiping itself," vaguely reminiscent of god-building
conceptions (Gofman 2013, 101–24). So there was some truth to Plekhanov's accusation. But the most incisive line of Marxist criticism came from a young Bolshevik
editor and ex-seminarian from Saint Petersburg, Aleksandr Voronsky.

Voronsky's "Polemical Remarks on Gorkii" appeared in 1911, by which time the
uproar over *Confession* had mostly subsided. His essay approached the text from a
different angle than Plekhanov had chosen. Rather than attack Gorkii's mystification of historical processes, Voronsky (1998, 6) took aim at his undialectical exposition of the antinomy of society versus the individual: "In *Confession* Gorkii states
that unhappiness and evil in life began the moment when the pitiful little lump
called 'I' broke away from the human whole and became conscious of its own individuality." Marx and Engels did not moralize about egocentrism, after all. Even
in their tirades against Stirner, they did not prescribe selflessness or tell people to
"love one another" (Marx 1975e, 247). Just the opposite: in the *Manifesto* they stated
that "the freedom of each" is the prerequisite for "the freedom of all" (Marx and
Engels 1975c, 506). "Theoretically and practically we must say [that] the problem
of the individual and society is resolved in Gorkii's god-building ... by removing
one of the opposed elements," asserted Voronsky (1998, 8). "Both ways are
equally wrong: to dismiss the individual for the sake of society, or society for the
sake of the individual. Our 'I' must grow and develop, and its task with regard
to society must be to insert the self into social life; only in this way can society
develop." Alienation cannot be overcome by drowning one's sense of self in a
sea of common humanity.

Like Lenin, Voronsky saw the god builders' desire to found a positive "religion of
labor" as symptomatic of setbacks suffered after 1905. "Gorkii's god-building has
been inundated by the squall of inner reaction, which we have been living
through in recent years," Voronsky (1998, 9) remarked. This was how Lunacharskii
(1972, 438) would himself remember the counterrevolutionary circumstances in
which god building was first theorized: "During the interval after the defeat of
the revolutionary movement of 1905, I bore witness to [a surge of] religious striv-
ings and sentiments ... My misstep then was to invent a kind of philosophical
theory, that of so-called 'god-building.'" He thought socialists might gain from

an appeal to the spiritual sensibilities of the masses since "certain circles (especially peasant circles) often ... arrive at the truth of socialism more easily through religio-philosophical thinking than by any other path" (439).

In this essay's penultimate section, Lunacharskii's massive two-volume tome on *Religion and Socialism* will be addressed along with critiques written by Martov, Plekhanov, and Kamenev.

Religion and Socialism and After

Volume 1 of Lunacharskii's *Religion and Socialism* hit the shelves in 1908, the same month as *Confession*. A flurry of criticism ensued. However, when the second volume was published in 1911, the storm had already passed. No one seemed to take much notice. By that time, of course, Lunacharskii had been expelled from the Bolshevik faction along with the rest of the Vperëdists, his doctrine of god building officially denounced (Lenin 1973a, 450). Since then, despite a translation into Yiddish in 1921 and Italian in 1973, copies of the Russian original have been exceedingly difficult to come by (Boer 2014, 189).

It is perhaps noteworthy that the word god building does not occur in either volume of *Religion and Socialism*. Of course, it did figure into Lunacharskii's essays on Gorkii. The term was mentioned in passing in a 1908 piece on "Socialism and Art," dashed off without much argumentation. Lunacharskii baldly asserted, for example, that "socialism *as a doctrine* is the true religion of humanity stripped of the mythological garments worn during its youth, in the thoughts and feelings of our fathers." Humanity's historic mission, which only the proletariat could carry out, was thus "to become a living god, blessed and all-powerful." The Bolshevik philosopher announced: "We will build Him!" (Lunacharskii 1908d, 26). Again, this was of a piece with Mikhail's idea in *Confession* that "God has not yet been created" (Gorkii 1950b, 350). Regarding the secondary claim it made, about the progressive disrobing of revealed religion, Lunacharskii had a more difficult go of it, as he was torn between competing poles. Demythologization was always tempered for him by the perception that revolutionaries required a new social mythology to buoy the hopes of the masses and spur them to great acts.

Mythology for Lunacharskii (1908c, 38) was not an assortment of traditional stories or tribal tales but rather a form of "primitive poetic knowledge [наука]" clarifying human nature (like modern science) while at the same time giving vent to the imagination (like modern art). Putting it a bit differently, one may say that myth for him was less the product of humanity's primal curiosity or insatiable appetite for fantasy (*Lust zu fabulieren*) than it was a "practical necessity." Nor was its work finished, according to Lunacharskii. Far from having outlived its usefulness, myth must be seized upon by a movement capable of making good on all the unkept promises of the historic religions. "The old myths, the old hopes stretch their hands out to the new," he wrote. "Come, poets of the great movement and artists of tomorrow, breathe new life into the worn-out myths and create new ones. Show man his own clarified, enlightened reflection in the ecstatic spirit of sublime, engrossing symbols; come promote the growth of sympathy and solidarity throughout all mankind" (102). Lunacharskii called for a "mythology of labor" that would galvanize workers to revolt and build a new society upon the ashes of the old (95–104). Boer (2014, 197) particularly appreciates this facet of *Religion and Socialism*, having fought for some time now to rehabilitate mythology. Indeed, the temptation to conjoin myth and revolution, as propaganda for "the heroic deed," is as strong today as ever (Greene 2015).

Around the time *Religion and Socialism* was published, the question of Marxism and myth (as well as religion) was a topic of international dispute. Georges Sorel's (2004, 118) *Reflections on Violence* was also published in 1908, wherein he described the general strike—a coordinated work stoppage across vital sectors of the economy—as "the myth in which socialism is wholly comprised, i.e., a body of images capable of evoking instinctively all the sentiments [of the revolutionary proletariat]." One of the earliest engagements with this text, outside of France, appeared near the end of Lunacharskii's contribution to *Studies in the Philosophy of Marxism*, a compendium anathematized by Lenin (1977f, 33–4). While Lunacharskii (1911, 311) considered Sorel's syndicalism too fatalistic and recoiled from the cynical imposture of an impossible-but-necessary *grève générale*, he believed the concept of "social myth" might be salvaged within a more Marxian framework since Marx had so decisively demonstrated that the future belongs to socialism. He continued: "The [Sorelian] theory of social myth could never pertain to the new religious consciousness of the proletariat ... For God—qua omniscient, omnibenevolent, omnipotent, omnipresent, eternal life—is, in effect, what is human in its highest potential. So then, we also say, God is humanity in its highest potential. But does humanity in its highest potential not exist?" (Lunacharskii 1908a, 159). Iurii Martov (1909, 35), the Menshevik leader, was unimpressed by this reasoning and derided as ideological "demagoguery" Lunacharskii's effort to extract a moral imperative from scientific socialism. Materialism required no such spiritual supplement.

Elsewhere, Lunacharskii's lyrical flights of fancy were even more egregiously overwrought. Karl Marx was not merely an insightful critic of bourgeois society but the last great Hebrew prophet, founder of the fifth and final religion of mankind. Revising the definition offered by the acclaimed French orientalist and antiquarian James Darmesteter (1895, 24), Lunacharskii (1908c, 71–2) proposed:

> Prophets are journalists, teachers, and revolutionaries who emerged from a milieu opposed to the official priesthood. They are popular, democratic bearers of [new] truths ... From our prophets we demand not only passion, energy, loving warmth, poetic imagery, and a knack for creating slogans, but also the cool reflection and restraint of an objective researcher. Can these be brought together in one person who can do both? Yes, for we witnessed just such a miracle: we were taught by the greatest prophet of peace, Marx.

Later on, Lunacharskii allegorized Bakunin, Owen, and Marx as the three wise men of the nineteenth century, all of whom knelt before Labor, their messiah, and thus "bowed deeply to the manger-born proletariat" (101). Kamenev (1923, 262, 265) made endless fun of Lunacharskii for such "pseudo-peasant" (*полу-крестьянский*) prattle, calling his desire to make socialism more palatable to non-proletarian strata a bad joke. "And so comrade Lunacharskii has unwittingly found himself on the other side of the barricades. On this side, for which scientific social-ism is fighting, lies the complete liberation of mankind from all oppression, includ-ing from the oppression of religious fetishes, among other things."

However, the most devastating blows to Lunacharskii's intellectual enterprise in *Religion and Socialism* would be dealt by Plekhanov. Marshaling a host of docu-ments from the combined corpus of Marx and Engels—he pointed out how the latter had reproached Feuerbach's idealism: "Feuerbach by no means wishes to abolish religion; he wants to perfect it" (Engels 1990a, 374)—the stately Menshevik philosopher then scolded Lunacharskii for forgetting the blistering circular the duo had written in response to Kriege in 1846. Against such flirtations with religion, the young firebrands remarked, "Kriege's amorous slobberings and his opposition to selfishness are no more than the inflated utterances of a mind utterly and completely absorbed by religion. In Europe, Kriege always claimed to be an atheist, but here he seeks to foist off the infamies of Christianity under the sign-board of communism and ends, perfectly logically, with *man's self-desecration*" (Marx and Engels 1975a, 46). Plekhanov provided several further examples. He asked with bitter irony "why Lunacharskii is more and more at variance with the founders of scientific socialism, and more and more in agreement with the Apostle Paul" (Plekhanov 1974, 355). Lunacharskii (1911, 397) eventually addressed these criticisms in the second volume of *Religion and Socialism*, after having been denied the chance to respond in the journal that printed Plekhanov's piece, but his answer was evasive. In the end, Plekhanov was supposedly "blinded by polem-ical rage."

Pavel Iushkevich (1910, 109, 176) tried to establish a middle ground between the rationalist reductionism of Plekhanov and the emotionalist emergentism of Luna-charskii, criticizing the former for being too narrow and the latter for being too broad. "When Lunacharskii speaks of religion or god-building, he naturally means that religion is a mood," wrote Iushkevich in a chapter on socialist religios-ity. "Socialism, in his thought, not only does not extinguish celebratory, supra-in-dividual, enthusiastic emotions, but on the contrary will bring about a sumptuous flowering of such 'religious' feelings" (127-8). According to Iushkevich (115), these views approximated those of the late French poet-philosopher Jean-Marie Guyau, who in 1887 described divinity *sub specie societatis*:

> [God] became the personification of the moral law and the moral sanction, the sovereign legislator and judge, in a word, the living law of universal society ... Today God tends to be identified with human consciousness purified *ad*

infinitum, and adequate to the universe. One may see in this evolution of religious ideas the gradual triumph of sociomorphism, since it is characterized
by an extension to the universe at large of social relations which are incessantly progressing toward perfection among men. (Guyau 1962, 116)

Lunacharskii (1911, 364) seemed to take Iushkevich's recommendations seriously, as
the second volume of *Religion and Socialism* borrowed this sociomorphic
(*социоморфное*) conception, quoting with approval "the profound expression of
Guyau." He was decidedly less flattered by repeated comparisons to Comte's positivist "religion of humanity" (Wernick 2001). Both Filosofov and Iushkevich observed this overlap. Much like Weber, Iushkevich (1910, 173) noted that the
scientific disenchantment of the world in the eighteenth and nineteenth centuries
had upset earlier modes of apprehending natural and social phenomena. Responding to this pervasive loss of meaning and its resulting "spiritual anarchy" (*анархия
духа*) were numerous "religious reformers, renovators of spiritual life … creators of
'atheistic' religions like Auguste Comte, Nietzsche, our Russian 'god-builders.'"
Filosofov (1909, 146) likewise wrote that "the god-builders, like Comte, were not
born into the old Christian era, but rather the new [post 1789]." God building
was merely a continuation of Condorcet's vision of progress and Robespierre's
deism (142).

Near the end of volume 2 of *Religion and Socialism*, Lunacharskii (1911, 364) was
therefore obliged to differentiate himself from Comte. At first, he acknowledged
their apparent closeness: "In the press whispers have already been heard as to
the proximity of our ideas to the religious philosophy of the father of positivism.
Being the disciple of Feuerbach and Marx in the realm of religious philosophy,
one of course finds oneself at some points a neighbor of Comte." Unlike Comte,
however, whose secularized religion Lunacharskii considered too "Catholic," god
building was expressly proletarian in scope and outlook. It could not be recon-
ciled with Comte's arch-bourgeois socialism, which was more akin to John
Stuart Mill's (Lunacharskii 1907a, 45). Class divisions are hardly abolished in
this "absurd utopia" but are instead just suspended indefinitely: "Sociocracy con-
solidates bourgeois structures once and for all … The religion of humanity was
perverted by Comte" (Lunacharskii 1911, 390–1). Feuerbach was absolved of
this sin, Lunacharskii felt, since "recognition of the proletariat as bearers of a
higher form of society was not given to him to make" (268). Lunacharskii
(1911, 392) then cited a critique of Comteanism leveled by the contemporary
Danish theologian Harald Høffding (1914, 283), suggesting that Comteanism
ignored the issue of man's relationship with nature and extending this
reproof to Guyau as well. While Feuerbach could be a bit romantic at times
in his contemplation of nature, Lunacharskii (1911, 300) believed that Marx
and Engels were often too hard on him. Engels, the stubborn rationalist, was
especially insensitive to Feuerbach's emotional outpourings, having no time
for such ebullience (304).

Of all the social democrats, Lunacharskii (1911, 378) appealed to the spiritual authority of "the Marxist pope," Karl Kautsky, a figure to whom he felt substantially closer than many others discussed in *Religion and Socialism*. He regarded Kautsky's 1908 *Foundations of Christianity* as a methodological masterpiece, even if Kautsky sometimes got wrapped up in economic details (17–18, 27–30, 34, 63, 115–22). The German socialist David Koigen, who hailed originally from Ukraine, also received Lunacharskii's warm commendation for his book *The Worldview of Socialism* (385–7). Despite what Toscano (2010, 176–7) has called Marx's "awesome arsenal of antireligious invective," as well as his self-professed atheism (see Marx 1986, 605), Lunacharskii (1911, 347) steadfastly asserted that there was a clandestine spirituality to his thought: "An understanding of the value of individual [личной] life only in connection with the grand sweep of collective life—that is, the religious feeling of Marx." More controversially still, he held that the materialism of Marx was not identical to the materialism of Engels. Possibly taking his cue from the Marxian philosopher Stanisław Brzozowski, Lunacharskii (1907a, 61–6) maintained that "the materialism of Engels is slightly different from the materialism of Marx, as the ultimate reality for Marx is social reality ... while for Engels it is cosmic [космическое]." This attempt to drive a wedge between the lifelong collaborators and founders of scientific socialism was met with resistance from orthodox Marxists —not least of all, from Lenin.

Atheism and the Workers Party

Even more so than his 1905 piece on "Socialism and Religion," Lenin's 1909 essay addressing "The Attitude of the Workers Party toward Religion" is the most programmatic statement he ever made on the subject. Together with his letters to Gorkii between 1911 and 1913, it represents a pinnacle of Marxian thought, one of the highest achievements of this period. If Marx's oft-quoted remark that "religion is the opiate of the masses" has been misunderstood, taken out of context, and turned into a cliché, then observation of this fact today has become just as hackneyed and repetitious. Kahl and Rehmann's (2013, 46) reminder to read the passage in full, with special attention to the lines about how religion is also the "heart of a heartless world" and "sigh of the oppressed creature," simply restates Bloch's (2009, 50–1) injunction of fifty years prior. John Molyneux's (2008) insistence that religion is "more than opium" and Phil Gasper's (2009) claim that focusing on this quote "diverts ... from the deeper point Marx was making" is that much odder given that both authors see themselves as defenders of Lenin's legacy. Yet it was Lenin (1977h, 402–3) who wrote, "Religion is the opium of the people—this dictum by Marx is the cornerstone of the whole Marxist outlook on religion."

Lenin used this metaphor quite liberally, introducing several spinoffs of his own. "Religion is a sort of spiritual booze," he maintained, playing up its soporific effects, "in which the slaves of capital drown their human image, their demand for a life more or less worthy of man" (Lenin 1978, 83). It is a kind of "fog" that must be dispelled (84), a "medieval mildew" that must be cleansed (87). He therefore urged Marxists to wage "a struggle against every religious bamboozling of the workers" (86). Several years later, Lenin (1977h, 403) was no less categorical: "Marxism has always regarded all modern religions and churches, and each and every religious organization, as instruments of bourgeois reaction that serve to defend exploitation and to befuddle the working class." Although Boer (2013, 128) suggests that Lenin (1973e, 229) moderated these views after completing his close study of Hegel in 1914, it was precisely in connection with Hegelian dialectics that the architect of the Soviet state advocated "militant atheism." Thus, in 1922, Lenin (1971, 570) wrote to Ivan Skvortsov-Stepanov, Commissar of Finance, imploring him to "write ... another little book on the history of religion *and against all* religion, along with a survey of material on the history of atheism." While Lenin (1976b, 119) warned communists not to needlessly antagonize or gratuitously offend the faithful, this had nothing to do with religious views being held sacrosanct and everything to do with the fact that such behavior was "tactless" and might prove counterproductive to their actual eradication. Engels (1988, 608) had already pointed out in 1873 that "religion is not destroyed by ridicule and invective alone; it also needs to be overcome scientifically, i.e., explained historically, which is beyond even the natural sciences."

Unlike Lunacharskii, however, who scoffed at Engels's proposal to republish old anticlerical tracts from the heroic age of bourgeois revolution, Lenin (1978, 86) considered it valid more than four decades later: "We now probably have to follow the advice Engels once gave ... to translate and widely disseminate the literature of the eighteenth-century enlighteners and atheists," he declared in 1905. Like Marx, he saw proletarian socialism as the sole legitimate heir to the radicalism of the nascent bourgeoisie. Beyond Marx and Engels's (1975b, 124–34) paean to French and British materialism in their 1845 *Holy Family*, which Lenin (1976a, 19–59) studied in detail while staying abroad in 1895, Marx defended secular Enlightenment against the pompous piety of socialist movements during the 1840s. Indeed, the only thing Marx (1985b, 32) seemed to embrace wholeheartedly in Proudhon—more so than his economics or philosophy—was his atheism: "Proudhon's attacks on religion, the church, etc., were of great merit locally at a time when French socialists thought to show by their religiosity how superior they were to bourgeois Voltairianism of the eighteenth century and German godlessness of the nineteenth." Marx and Engels (1975c, 508) had already indicated in their *Manifesto* that "nothing is easier than to give Christian asceticism a Socialist tinge." Engels (1989b, 285) added to this in his 1880 *Socialism: Utopian and Scientific* in which he eulogized "the great men [Rousseau, Diderot, etc.] who in France prepared men's minds for the coming revolution, themselves extreme revolutionists."

The historian of ideas Louis Menand (2003, xvi) has argued that Marx and Engels were initiators of a sort of "second Enlightenment," consciously taking over the emancipatory project of the first. Lenin would have no doubt endorsed this characterization: "The philosophical basis of Marxism has fully taken over the historical traditions of eighteenth-century materialism in France and of Feuerbach in Germany, a materialism that is absolutely atheistic and positively hostile to all religion" (Lenin 1977h, 402). "Marxism is materialism," Lenin declared in 1909, without mincing words. "As such, it is as relentlessly hostile to religion as the materialism of the eighteenth-century Encyclopedists or ... of Feuerbach" (405). He had the old objections voiced by Lunacharskii in mind when he wrote "On the Significance of Militant Materialism" in 1922. Now in power, near the end of his life, Lenin urgently repeated Engels's 1874 demand:

> Engels long ago advised the contemporary leaders of the proletariat to trans-
> late the militant atheist literature of the late eighteenth century for mass dis-
> tribution among the people. We have not done this up to the present, to our
> shame be it said (this is one of the numerous proofs that it is much easier to
> seize power in a revolutionary epoch than to know how to use this power
> properly). Our apathy, inactivity, and incompetence are sometimes excused
> on all sorts of "lofty" grounds, as for example that the old atheist literature
> of the eighteenth century is antiquated, unscientific, naïve. There is nothing
> worse than such pseudo-scientific sophistry, which serves as a screen either
> for pedantry or for a complete misunderstanding of Marxism. There is, of
> course, much that is unscientific and naïve in the atheist writings of the eigh-
> teenth-century revolutionaries. But nobody prevents the publishers of these
> writings from abridging them and providing them with brief postscripts
> pointing out the progress made by mankind in the scientific criticism of reli-
> gions since, mentioning the latest writings on the subject, and so forth. It
> would be the ... most grievous mistake a Marxist could make to think that mil-
> lions of people (especially peasants and artisans) who have been condemned
> by all modern society to darkness, ignorance, and superstitions—can extricate
> themselves from this darkness only along the straight line of a purely Marxist
> education ... The keen, talented, and vivacious writings of the old eighteenth-
> century atheists wittily and openly attacked the prevailing clericalism and ...
> often prove a thousand times more suitable for arousing people from their
> religious torpor than the dry, dull paraphrases which predominate our liter-
> ature and distort Marxism. We have translations of all the major works of
> Marx and Engels, and so there are no grounds for fearing that the old mate-
> rialism will remain unsupplemented by the corrections introduced by Marx
> and Engels. (Lenin 1973e, 229–30)

Organizationally, as well, Lenin adopted a much harder stance toward religious affairs when it came to the party than his German comrades. Engels (1989a, 184–5) had of course unequivocally rejected every alliance between socialist and "faith-based" groups and explained this to Carlo Cafiero in an 1871 letter: "As for the religious question," he wrote, "we cannot speak about it officially, except when priests provoke us, but you'll detect the spirit of atheism in all our publications. Moreover, we do not admit any society [to the International] which has the slightest hint of religious allusion in its statutes." The critical notes Marx left on the Gotha Program's lines about religion were also of paramount importance for Lenin, especially regarding "freedom of conscience." While everyone ought to be free to worship as he pleases, socialists cannot simply parrot the liberals:

> "*Freedom of conscience!*" If one desired at this time of the *Kulturkampf* to remind liberalism of its old catchwords, it surely could have been done only in the following form: Everyone should be able to attend to his religious as well as his bodily needs without the police sticking their noses in. But the workers' party ought at any rate ... to have expressed its awareness of the fact that bourgeois "freedom of conscience" is nothing but the toleration of all possible kinds of *religious unfreedom of conscience*, and that for its part it endeavors rather to liberate conscience from the witchery of religion. (Marx 1985a, 98)

Lenin (1977e, 94) seized on this passage fairly early in his revolutionary career, writing to Plekhanov with the inquiry: "Regarding religion, in a letter of Karl Marx on the Gotha Program I read a sharp criticism of the demand for *Gewissensfreiheit* [freedom of conscience] and a statement that Social-Democrats ought to speak out plainly about their fight against *religiösem Spuk* [religious spookery]. Do you consider such a thing possible and in what form?" He observed not only Engels's (2002a, 103) regret that Kautsky could not include Marx's "excellent passage on religious needs" in the *Gothakritik*'s official publication but also his entreaty to at least allude to its absence by way of ellipsis (Engels 2002b, 107). Taking up Engels's (1990b, 185) specification, from his 1891 preface to *The Civil War in France*, "that *in relation to the state*, religion is a purely private matter," Lenin (1977h, 404) emphasized that the proletarian party could not be neutral. "We demand that religion be held a private affair so far as the state is concerned," he explained, "but by no means can we consider religion a private affair so far as our party is concerned" (Lenin 1978, 84). In 1916, in the margins of a statement by Kautsky reaffirming freedom of conscience, Lenin (1974a, 590) exclaimed: "Vulgarian!" Writing in a telegram to the Central Committee in 1919, Lenin (1975, 239) indicated that he was "for expulsion from the party of people who take part in religious ceremonies."

The Showdown with Lenin

But why would Lenin so adamantly oppose the theory of god building? It should be stressed, after all, that its proponents did not envision their new faith as just another system of deity worship. Pressed about it, the god builders would explain that theirs was a kind of "religious atheism" (*религиозный атеизм*) or a "religion without God," as Lunacharskii (1908a, 156; 1908c, 29, 45, 49, 88; 1911, 396–7) phrased it. Gorkii (1907, 593) was in no sense hostile to disbelief: "Atheism, as a denial of belief in the existence of a personal God, appears to me desirable, because it delivers humanity from a dangerous error." Vladimir Bazarov, by far the most blasphemous of the bunch, invited Dmitrii Merezhkovskii's comparison (stolen from Dostoevskii) of modern socialism to the prideful attempt of mankind to build a tower that would reach heaven. "We [the socialist god-builders] assume ... that the *ideal* of culture is to solve once and for all the mysteries of the world, thereby eliminating any possibility that new problems might arise," announced Bazarov (1910, 172). "The ultimate aim of godless progress is to *finish* building the Tower of Babel." Later on, in 1928, Lunacharskii (1972, 440) recounted that "in my books I meticulously maintained that socialism was a religion without God, without mysticism. My definition of socialism and my expression 'god-building' by no means deprived my thought of its consistently atheistic character."

Incidentally, this was how Nikolai Berdiaev understood god building, as purely atheistic yet still somehow heretical to Lenin's strict orthodoxy. For Berdiaev (1972, 119), this paradoxically confirmed the cryptoreligious character of Bolshevism itself; confronted with this heresy, Lenin had no choice but to "excommunicate" Lunacharskii. René Fülöp-Miller, the Hungarian philosopher whose 1926 exposé *The Mind and Face of Bolshevism* became an instant success, likewise suspected that the Bolshevik leader's antipathy to religion was a cipher for his own repressed religiosity. "Whenever Lenin spoke or wrote on things of faith," declared Fülöp-Miller (1965, 72–3), "it was nothing other than the denunciations of a man quivering with rage. His sectarian intransigence against any heterodox movement, however subtle, emerges most clearly from Lenin's letters to his friend and comrade Maksim Gorkii, who entirely shared his sociopolitical views and his antagonism to religion, but in one novel [*Confession*] allowed for 'god-building' to spring from man's inner nature. Seized with boundless wrath at this 'underhanded religiousness' ... Lenin wrote to Gorki that he saw that he would be opposed to 'god-seeking' only for 'a time,' and that only because he aimed at replacing it by a 'god-building.'"

One of the oldest rebukes hurled at Marxist revolutionaries, whose project of universal emancipation placed them at odds with every form of religious ideology, is that Marxism too is merely a form of secular religion. "Marxism played the part of a religion for the intelligentsia," wrote the embittered Polish ex-communist Leszek Kołakowski (1978, 94–5). By then, Kołakowski was halfway back to the Catholic Church. Anticommunists like Raymond Aron and Simone Weil wrote off Marxism as "the opiate of the intellectuals": "Undoubtedly a religion, in the lowest sense of the word" (Aron 1962, vii). To be sure, Marxists have cribbed a fair number of religious terms (e.g., "orthodox," "sectarian," "dogmatic") in articulating their own discourses.

It does not end there, however. Even further, Marxists have explicitly emulated rites and rituals associated with religion, perhaps nowhere more so than in Lenin's mummification, against his own stated wishes and against the fervent protestations of Trotsky, Krupskaia, and remaining family members. Krasin, one of the lesser god builders and Vperëdists, assembled the so-called Immortalization Commission charged with the morbid task of preserving Lenin's body against decay (Gray 2011,

104–204). Venerating Lenin in this fashion was far from unanimously agreed upon, although Boer (2013, 177) prefers to see it in a more positive light, as a literal sepulchral monument built to commemorate god building after the fact: "Lenin's veneration became a necessary feature of a new form of compulsion for people to engage, with revolutionary fervor, in constructing a new socioeconomic system." Many who had been close to Lenin begged to differ, even if they eventually acceded to the corpse's beatific display (Krausz 2015, 74). But some, such as Trotsky (1972, 190), warned against the potentially baleful effects of this cult:

> From the very beginning I was a determined opponent of the embalming, the mausoleum, and the rest, as was also Lenin's widow, Krupskaia. There is no doubt whatever that if Lenin on his sickbed had thought for one moment that they would treat his corpse like that of a pharaoh, he would have appealed in advance, with indignation, to the party. I brought this objection forward as my main argument but also pointed to the fact that the "incorruptibility" of the embalmed corpse of Lenin might nourish religious superstitions. Krasin, who defended and apparently initiated the idea of the embalming, objected: "On the contrary, what was a matter of miracle with the priests will become a matter of technology in our hands. Millions of people will have an idea of how the man looked who brought such great changes into the life of our country. With the help of science, we will satisfy this justifiable interest of the masses and at the same time explain to them the mystery of incorruptibility." Still, the body of Lenin must not be used against the spirit of Lenin.

No wonder Lenin worried about the necrophiliac dimension of god building, and indeed of all religion. He first issued this bon mot in response to a letter Gorkii sent trying to explain the difference between god seeking and god building. Lenin's (1973c, 121) reply was icy: "God-seeking differs from god-building no more than a yellow devil differs from a blue devil," he told the novelist. "To talk about god-seeking, not in order to declare against *all* devils and gods, against every ideological necrophily (all worship of divinity is necrophily; be it the cleanest, most ideal, not sought-out but built-up divinity, it is all the same), but to prefer a blue devil to a yellow one is a hundred times worse than saying nothing about it at all." In a subsequent letter, Lenin (1973d, 128) further clarified this line about "necrophily," explaining that "the idea of God has *always* put to sleep and blunted 'social feelings,' replacing the living by the dead." As with capitalism in general, the old is reproduced alongside the semblance of the new. Dead labor rules over living labor under capitalism; the present serves the past. "We suffer not only from the living, but from the dead," Marx (1982, 91) wrote. "Le mort saisit le vif!"

Reading these lines, Boer's (2013, 89) claim that Ernst Bloch was a god builder without knowing it is all the more tenuous: "Bloch too ... was a God-builder, carrying on the tradition and enriching it, even if he may not have been aware of Lunacharsky's [*Religion and Socialism*]." Whether or not he knew of god building as it was conceived by Lunacharskii, Bloch certainly knew of god building as it was conceived by Gorkii. In a 1966 essay, Bloch (1970, 164) commented on the foregoing exchange between Lenin and the novelist: "Rilke, Bergson, and even the early Gorkii have variously failed to achieve distinction by such god-making, and Lenin rightly described efforts of the sort as 'necrophilia.' An atheist who knows what the word means will not try a poor imitation of the founders by going back to god-making [Gottmacherei]." Two years later, in Atheism in Christianity, Bloch (2009, 221) repeated that "Lenin was certainly right when he attacked the semi-disillusioned [in 'The Attitude of the Proletarian Party toward Religion'], not to mention the smugglers of reactionary contraband." He then went on to quote from Lenin's brilliant reversal of the analogy of "socialism as religion," distinguishing between those, like Dietzgen, who draw such analogies in order to explain a point and those, like Lunacharskii, who draw such analogies in order to demonstrate their own cleverness. "For some," Lenin (1977h, 409) wrote, "the statement 'socialism is a religion' is a form of transition from religion to socialism; for others, it is a form of transition *from* socialism to religion." The Marxist writer Walter Benjamin (1972, 52–3), in his review of the German publication of Lenin's correspondence with Gorkii at Capri, noted Lenin's "vehement attacks against the social-religious movement, propagated by Lunacharskii, that fell under the name god-creation [Gotterschaffung] in Russia." Nevertheless, Benjamin believed that Lenin had acted responsibly in sharing such criticisms and reservations with his friend, a testament to his great stature.

Lenin (1973b, 70) reached out to Gorkii again via mail in 1913, inviting the Vperëdists to rejoin so long as "Machism, god-building, and such nonsense has been dumped forever." Gorkii and Lunacharskii had in the meantime parted ways, as had Bogdanov from both, the group having been estranged after 1911. Though Lenin's stipulation would likely have proved too much to accept even at such a date, Lunacharskii in any case later drifted back into Lenin's orbit, pulled in by the gravity of revolution. Yet this should not be seen to imply that either was won over to the other's position, as Boer (2013, 110) seems to think.

There is no definitive evidence that Lenin changed his mind about god building or religion after reading Hegel. But neither should one think that Lunacharskii cut a deal with the devil in returning to the party, or that Lenin played the Mephistopheles to Lunacharskii's Faust. (Mikhail Lifshits (1988, 189), the great Soviet literary critic and protégé of Lukács, affectionately referred to Lunacharskii as the "revolutionary Faust"—Lunacharskii had composed a sequel to Goethe's play in 1921 entitled Faust and the City.) For above all, it was the empiriocriticism of the Vperëdists that Lenin found so objectionable; the Nietzschean influence on the group never came up. When October finally came, it was Nietzsche—not Avenarius, not Mach—whose line Lunacharskii (1919, 31) quoted in The Great Upheaval: "The world has no meaning, but we must give it a meaning."

Conclusion

Strangely, the god builders may have been onto something with their notion that the wish-images passed down by historical religions can only be fulfilled by socialist revolution. Not in the way they imagined, however. Their theories were far too speculative and positivistic to ever have been meaningfully put into practice. Roberto Mangabeira Unger, a contemporary Brazilian philosopher, neatly reformulates their thesis in his 2014 book *The Future of Religion*, without knowing either the god builders or the Lunacharskii essay of the same title. Unger (2014, 116) draws upon Feuerbach in order to say that humanity "becomes more human by becoming more godlike." Dupont (2016) prefers an apophatic approach, writing that "the misconceptions of religion more accurately convey the contents of human perversity than do the findings of science." In its resolute negativity, this last statement is the one nearest to the thought of Marx and Engels.

Early in their careers, Marx and Engels arrived at the conclusion that philosophy was for the most part over, having culminated in Hegel's system—given perfect form and thereby effectively ended. All that remained was to translate into reality the ideals that it already expressed. Marx (1975c, 85) thus postulated that the final goal of communism was to make the world philosophical, but not by drawing up some sort of blueprint or fully worked-out vision of how the world should look. "It must be admitted that no one has an exact idea what the future ought to be," asserted Marx (1975b, 142). "We do not dogmatically anticipate the world, but only want to find the new world through criticism of the old one. Hitherto philosophers have had the solution to every riddle lying in their writing-desks. But now that philosophy has become mundane ... it is all the more clear what we have to accomplish at present: *the ruthless criticism of everything that exists*." Rather than fixate on the speculative (positive) moment, Marx (1975e, 49; and see Hegel 1991, 125) dwelled on the dialectical (negative) moment: "Communism is not a *state of affairs* which is to be established, an *ideal* to which reality will have to adjust itself but the *real* movement that abolishes the present state of things." Or as Marx (1975d, 296–7) put it elsewhere, "Communism is the riddle of history solved, and it knows itself to be this solution."

Karl Korsch (2008, 97) closed his 1923 essay on "Marxism and Philosophy" with the observation that "philosophy cannot be abolished without being realized." The failed world revolution inaugurated in October 1917 in Russia was to provide this realization. Four decades on, the critical theorist Theodor Adorno (1973, 3) added, "Philosophy, which once seemed obsolete, lives on because the moment to realize it was missed." Something similar might be said of religion and spirituality today. Along with art, religion was for Hegel one of the two nonphilosophical routes by which spirit could approach the absolute. Whereas in art the absolute is intuited immediately via the senses and in philosophy it is cognized through a process of mediation with concepts, in religion the absolute is represented by means of metaphors, parables, and myths. Insofar as Marx inverted Hegel's system of absolute idealism and applied his negative-dialectical method with even greater rigor, the advent of a truly socialist society would mean the consummation of religion, philosophy, and art. But to posit this explicitly as a goal would be to foreclose its possibility since "Marx and Engels were enemies of utopia for the sake of its realization," as Adorno recognized (322). Religious, philosophical, and aesthetic utopias must be rejected if they are to have any chance of ever being realized. Marxists must be enemies of God, of metaphysics, and of aesthetics if the spiritual potential these contained is to someday materialize. Dietzgen (1906, 118) was basically correct that "*the progress or development of religion* [today] *consists in its gradual dissolution.*"

Of course, philosophy occupied a privileged place within the Hegelian system. So it would be folly to try and artificially elevate religion or art to its level in order to weigh them more heavily once Marx has turned this system upside down. Furthermore, even if Toscano is right that all the hullabaloo about the "return of the religious" discussed by Derrida (2002, 65–89), Vattimo, and Badiou —or of "the political" or "the aesthetic"; pick your hypostasis—is "more a byproduct of the drastic setbacks to emancipatory projects and ideals than the reemergence of something 'repressed' by a secular 'age of extremes'" (Toscano 2011, 11), it does not at all follow that revolutionaries ought to opportunistically throw their support behind reactionary forces of religion that stir the hearts of the oppressed. Better to follow Lenin's advice to say nothing at all than to seek in vain the germ of rationality buried inside; otherwise, simply state communism's opposition to religion forthrightly. Religious sentiment diminishes in precise proportion to the increased likelihood of historical emancipation. Its return in modern times, unmoored from the foundation of ethical objectivity (*Sittlichkeit*) that existed in former ages, long after it should have been superseded, is that of a phantom— though it is hardly less frightening for being so. "The new religious attitude is that of the convert, even among those who do not formally convert or who simply support emphatically whatever is sanctioned as the 'religion of the fathers' [*religio perennis*] as well as what with fatherly authority since time immemorial has helped to suppress through intimidation rising doubt" (Adorno 2005, 137). Political realism does not mean one ought to accommodate those conditions that happen to presently obtain; it means to transform them by critically engaging the possibilities that still lie dormant within them.

References

Adorno, T. 1973. *Negative Dialectics*. Trans. E. B. Ashton. New York: Continuum.
———. 2005. *Critical Models: Interventions and Catchwords*. Trans. H. W. Pickford. New York: Columbia University Press.
Aron, R. 1962. *The Opium of the Intellectuals*. Trans. T. Kilmartin. New York: W. W. Norton.
Bazarov, V. 1909. *Vershiny: Literaturno-kritiheskie i filosofsko-publitsisticheskie sborniki*. Moscow: Prometei SPB.

————. 1910. *Na dva fronta*. Moscow: Prometei SPB.

Benjamin, W. 1972. "Rezension: *Lenin, Briefe an Maxim Gorki 1908–1913: Mit Einleitung und Anmerkungen von L. Kamenew*." In vol. 3 of *Gesammelte Schriften*, 51–3. Frankfurt: Suhrkamp Verlag.

Berdiaev (Berdyaev), N. 1972. *The Origin of Russian Communism*. Trans. R. M. French. Ann Arbor: University of Michigan Press.

————. 1994. "Philosophical Verity and Intelligentsia Truth." In *Vekhi (Landmarks): A Collection of Articles about the Russian Intelligentsia*, trans. and ed. M. Shatz and J. Zimmerman, 1–16. Armonk, N.Y.: M. E. Sharpe.

Bloch, E. 1970. "Man's Increasing Entry into Religious Mysticism." In *Man on His Own: Essays in the Philosophy of Religion*, 147–240. Trans. E. B. Ashton. New York: Seabury.

————. 2009. *Atheism in Christianity: The Religion of the Exodus and the Kingdom*. Trans. J. T. Swann. New York: Verso.

Blok, A. 2010. "Narod i intelligentsiia." In *Polnoe sobranie sochinenii i pisem*, 8:70–6. Moscow: Izdatel'stvo "Nauka."

Boer, R. 2013. *Lenin, Religion, and Theology*. New York: Palgrave Macmillan.

————. 2014. "Religion and Socialism: A. V. Lunacharskii and the God-Builders." *Political Theology* 15 (2): 188–209.

Bogdanov, A. 1995. *A. Bogdanov i gruppa RSDRP "Vpered," 1908–1914 gg*. Vol. 2 of *Neizvestnyi Bogdanov*. Moscow: AIRO XX.

Bulgakov, S. 1994. "Heroism and Asceticism: Reflections on the Religious Nature of the Russian Intelligentsia." In *Vekhi (Landmarks): A Collection of Articles about the Russian Intelligentsia*, trans. and ed. M. Shatz and J. Zimmerman, 17–49. Armonk, N.Y.: M.E. Sharpe.

Callinicos, A. 2006. *The Resources of Critique*. Malden, Mass.: Polity.

Charpin, F. 1907. "La Question religieuse: Enquête internationale." *Mercure de France* 17 (236): 577–623.

Darmesteter, J. 1895. "The Prophets of Israel." In *Selected Essays*, 16–104. Trans. H. Jastrow. New York: Houghton Mifflin.

Derrida, J. 2002. "Faith and Knowledge: The Two Sources of 'Religion' at the Limits of Reason Alone." In *Acts of Religion*, 40–101. Trans. G. Anidjar. New York: Routledge.

Dietzgen, J. 1906. "The Religion of Social Democracy." In *Philosophical Essays*, trans. M. Beer and T. Rothstein, 90–154. Chicago: Charles H. Kerr.

Dupont, M. 2016. "Tinned Chunks." *Insipidities*, 16 January. https://insipidities.blogspot.com/2014/11/tinned-chunks-introduction-to-rejection.html

Durkheim, É. 1995. *The Elementary Forms of Religious Life*. Trans. K. Fields. New York: Free Press.

Eagleton, T. 2009a. *Reason, Faith, and Revolution: Reflections on the God Debate*. New Haven, Conn.: Yale University Press.

————. 2009b. "Religion for Radicals." *Immanent Frame*, 17 September. https://tif.ssrc.org/2009/09/17/religion-for-radicals-an-interview-with-terry-eagleton.

Engels, F. 1982. "Letter to Marx, 18 October 1846." In *Collected Works*, by K. Marx and F. Engels, 38:75–81. Trans. P. Ross and B. Ross. New York: International Publishers.

————. 1985. "Program of the Blanquist Refugees." In *Collected Works*, by K. Marx and F. Engels, 24:12–18. Trans. B. Selman. New York: International Publishers.

————. 1987. *Anti-Dühring: Herr Eugen Dühring's Revolution in Science*. In *Collected Works*, by K. Marx and F. Engels, 25:5–311. Trans. E. Burns. New York: International Publishers.

————. 1988. "Varia on Germany, 1789–1873." In *Collected Works*, by K. Marx and F. Engels, 23:599–610. Trans. D. Forgacs. New York: International Publishers.

————. 1989a. "Letter to Cafiero, 28 July 1871." In *Collected Works*, by K. Marx and F. Engels, 44:180–8. Trans. R. Livingstone. New York: International Publishers.

————. 1989b. *Socialism: Utopian and Scientific*. In *Collected Works*, by K. Marx and F. Engels, 24:281–325. Trans. E. Aveling. New York: International Publishers.

————. 1990a. *Ludwig Feuerbach and the End of Classical German Philosophy*. In *Collected Works*, by K. Marx and F. Engels, 26:353–98. New York: International Publishers.

————. 1990b. Introduction to *The Civil War in France*. In *Collected Works*, by K. Marx and F. Engels, 27:179–91. Trans. B. Selman. New York: International Publishers.

————. 2002a. "Letter to Kautsky, 7 January 1891." In *Collected Works*, by K. Marx and F. Engels, 49:103–4. Trans. P. Ross and B. Ross. New York: International Publishers.

————. 2002b. "Letter to Kautsky, 15 January 1891." In *Collected Works*, by K. Marx and F. Engels, 49:107–8. Trans. P. Ross and B. Ross. New York: International Publishers.

Filosofov, D. 1909. "Druz'ia ili vragi?" *Russkaia mysl'*, no. 8: 120–47.

————. 1997. "Evsei i Matvei." In *Maksim Gorkii, Pro et Contra: Lichnost' i tvorchestvo Maksima Gor'kogo v otsenke russkikh myslitelei i issledovatelei, 1890–1910* gg.:817–23. Saint Petersburg: Izdatel'stvo Russkogo Khristianskogo Gumanitarnogo Instituta.

Fülöp-Miller, R. 1965. *The Mind and Face of Bolshevism: An Examination of Cultural Life in the Soviet Union*. Trans. F. S. Flint and D. F. Tait. New York: Harper and Row.

Gasper, P. 2009. "Marxism and Religion." *International Socialist Review*, no. 63. https://isreview.org/issue/63/marxism-and-religion.

Gofman, A. 2013. "The Russian Career of Durkheim's Sociology of Religion and *Les Formes Élémentaires*: Contribution to a Study." *Durkheimian Studies*, n.s., no. 19: 101–24.

Gorkii (Gorky), M. 1907. "Untitled Response to Questionnaire." *Mercure de France* 17 (236): 592–5.

————. 1950a. "Chelovek." In *Polnoe sobranie sochinenii*, 5:362–8. Moscow: Goslitizdat.

————. 1950b. "Ispoved'." In *Polnoe sobranie sochinenii*, 8:211–378. Moscow: Goslitizdat.

————. 1950c. "Na dne." In *Polnoe sobranie sochinenii*, 6:103–76. Moscow: Goslitizdat.

————. 1950d. "Pis'mo Posse, 23 avgusta 1901g." In *Polnoe sobranie sochinenii*, 28:169–71. Moscow: Goslitizdat.

————. 1954a. "Pis'mo I. E. Repinu, 5 dekabria 1899g." In *Polnoe sobranie sochinenii*, 28:100–2. Moscow: Goslitizdat.

————. 1954b. "Pis'mo K. P. Piatnitskomu: 27 ianvaria 1908g." In *Polnoe sobranie sochinenii*, 29:100–2. Moscow: Goslitizdat.

————. 1965. "Pis'mo Andreevu, 9 ianvaria 1902g." In *Gorkii i Leonid Andreev, Neizdannaia perepiska*, 128–9. Moscow: Goslitizdat.

————. 1966. "Pis'mo E.P. Peshkovoi: Fevralia 1908g." In *Arkhiv A. M. Gor'kogo: Pis'ma k E. P. Peshkovoi, 1906–1932*. Moscow: Khudozhestvennaia Literatura.

————. 1978. "The Disintegration of Personality." In *Collected Works*, 10:89–150. Trans. J. Katzer. Moscow: Progress Publishers.

Gray, J. 2011. *The Immortalization Commission: The Strange Quest to Cheat Death*. New York: Farrar, Strauss, and Giroux.

Greene, D. E. 2015. "The Heroic Deed: Myth and Revolution." *Red Wedge*, 6 August. http://www.redwedgemagazine.com/essays/heroic-deed-myth-revolution.

Guyau, J.-M. 1962. *The Non-Religion of the Future: A Sociological Study*. Trans. N. Glatzer. New York: Schocken.

Hegel, G. W. F. 1971. *The Philosophy of Mind*. Vol. 3 of *Encyclopedia of the Philosophical Sciences*. Trans. W. Wallace. New York: Oxford University Press.

————. 1991. *Logic*. Vol. 1 of the *Encyclopedia of the Philosophical Sciences*. Trans. T. F. Geraets, W. A. Suchting, and H. S. Harris. Indianapolis: Hackett.

Høffding, H. 1914. *The Philosophy of Religion*. Trans. B. E. Meyer. London: MacMillan.

Horkheimer, M. 1972. "Thoughts on Religion." *Critical Theory: Selected Essays*, 129–31. Trans. M. O'Connell. New York: Continuum.

Horkheimer, M., and T. Adorno. 2002. *Dialectic of Enlightenment: Philosophical Fragments*. Trans. E. Jephcott. Stanford, Calif.: Stanford University Press.

Iushkevich, P. 1910. *Novye veianiia: Ocherki sovremennykh religioznykh iskanii*. Saint Petersburg: Tipografiia t-va "Obshchestvennaia Pol'za."

Jaurès, J. 2015. *A Socialist History of the French Revolution*. Trans. M. Abidor. New York: Pluto.

Joravsky, D. 2009. *Soviet Marxism and Natural Science, 1917–1932*. New York: Routledge.

Kamenev, L. 1923. "Ne po doroge." In *Mezhdu dvumia revoliutsiiami: Sbornik statei*. Moskva: Novaia Moskva.

Kline, G. 1968. *Religious and Antireligious Thought in Russia*. Chicago: University of Chicago Press.

Kołakowski, L. 1978. *The Golden Age*. Vol. 2 of *The Main Currents of Marxism*. Trans. P. S. Falla. New York: Oxford University Press.

Korsch, K. 2008. *Marxism and Philosophy*. Trans. F. Halliday. New York: Monthly Review Press.

Krausz, T. 2015. *Lenin Reconstructed: An Intellectual Biography*. Trans. B. Bethlenfalvy and M. Fenyo. New York: Monthly Review.

Kuznetsov, F. 2004. "Khraniteli dukhovnogo ognia." *Pravoslavie*, 12 July. http://pravoslavie.ru/4575.html.

L'vov-Rogachevskii, V. 1908. "Novaia vera." *Obrazovanie* 7 (7): 19–38.

Lenin, V. 1962. "The Revolutionary-Democratic Dictatorship of the Proletariat and the Peasantry." In *Collected Works*, 8:293–303. Trans. B. Isaacs. Moscow: Progress Publishers.

———. 1971. "Letter to Skvortsov-Stepanov, 19 March 1922." In *Collected Works*, 36:570. Trans. A. Rothstein. Moscow: Progress Publishers.

———. 1973a. "Conference of the Extended Editorial Board of *Proletarii* (June 8-17, 1909)." In *Collected Works*, 15:425–51. Trans. A. Rothstein. Moscow: Progress Publishers.

———. 1973b. "Letter to Gorkii, 8 January 1913." In *Collected Works*, 35:69–72. Trans. A. Rothstein. Moscow: Progress Publishers.

———. 1973c. "Letter to Gorkii, 14 November 1913." In *Collected Works*, 35:121–4. Trans. A. Rothstein. Moscow: Progress Publishers.

———. 1973d. "Letter to Gorkii, late November 1913." In *Collected Works*, 35:127–9. Trans. A. Rothstein. Moscow: Progress Publishers.

———. 1973e. "On the Significance of Militant Materialism." In *Collected Works*, 33:227–36. Trans. D. Skvirsky. Moscow: Progress Publishers.

———. 1974a. "Kautsky on Religion." In *Collected Works*, 39:590. Trans. C. Dutt. Moscow: Progress Publishers.

———. 1974b. *What is to be Done? Burning Questions of Our Movement*. In *Collected Works*, 5:347–529. Trans. J. Fineberg. Moscow: Progress Publishers.

———. 1975. "To the Organizing Bureau of the Central Committee." In *Collected Works*, 44:239. Trans. C. Dutt. Moscow: Progress Publishers.

———. 1976a. "Conspectus of *The Holy Family* by Marx and Engels." In *Collected Works*, 38:19–51. Trans. C. Dutt. Moscow: Progress Publishers.

———. 1976b. "Letter to Molotov, 19 April 1921." In *Collected Works*, 45:119–20. Trans. Y. Sdobnikov. Moscow: Progress Publishers.

———. 1977a. "Concerning A. Bogdanov." In *Collected Works*, 20:121–4. Trans. B. Isaacs. Moscow: Progress Publishers.

————. 1977b. "Concerning *Vekhi* (Dec. 13, 1909)." In *Collected Works*, 16:123–31. Trans. C. Dutt. Moscow: Progress Publishers.

————. 1977c. "Concluding Remarks to the Symposium 'Marxism and Liquidationism.'" In *Collected Works*, 20:265–73. Trans. B. Isaacs. Moscow: Progress Publishers.

————. 1977d. "Letter to Gorkii, 16 April 1908." In *Collected Works*, 34:393. Trans. C. Dutt. Moscow: Progress Publishers.

————. 1977e. "Letter to Plekhanov, 7 February 1902." In *Collected Works*, 34:94–5. Trans. C. Dutt. Moscow: Progress Publishers.

————. 1977f. "Marxism and Revisionism." In *Collected Works*, 15:29–39. Trans. A. Rothstein. Moscow: Progress Publishers.

————. 1977g. *Materialism and Empiriomonism: Critical Comments on a Reactionary Philosophy.* In *Collected Works*, 14:17–361. Trans. A. Fineberg. Moscow: Progress Publishers.

————. 1977h. "The Attitude of the Workers' Party Toward Religion." In *Collected Works*, 15:402–13. Trans. A. Rothstein. Moscow: Progress Publishers.

————. 1978. "Socialism and Religion." In *Collected Works*, 10:83–7. Trans. A. Rothstein. Moscow: Progress Publishers.

Lifshits, M. 1988. "A. V. Luncharskii." In *Sobranie sochinenii*, 3:188–212. Moscow: Iskusstvo.

Löwy, M. 1996. *The War of Gods: Politics and Religion in Latin America.* New York: Verso.

Lukács, G. 1971. *History and Class Consciousness: Studies in Marxist Dialectics.* Trans. R. Livingstone. Cambridge, Mass.: MIT Press.

Lunacharskii (Lunacharsky), A. 1905. *Kritika chistogo opyta v populiarnom izlozhenii s dopolneniem: Novaia teoriia pozitivnogo idealizma (Holzapfel: Panideal); Kriticheskoe izlozheniia.* Saint Petersburg: Izdatel'stvo S. Dorvatovskogo i A. Charushnikova.

————. 1907a. "Budushchee religii (okonchanie)." *Obrazovanie.* 6 (11): 30–67.

————. 1907b. "Budushchee religii (prodolzhenie)." *Obrazovanie* 6 (10): 1–25.

————. 1908a. "Ateisty." In *Ocherki po filosofii marksizma.* Moscow: SPB.

————. 1908b. "Dvadtsat' tretii sbornik *Znaniia*." In *Literaturnyi raspad: Kriticheskii sbornik*, 1:148–72. Saint Petersburg: T-va Izdatel'skoe Biuro.

————. 1908c. *Religiia i sotsializm.* Vol. 1. Saint Petersburg: Shipovnik.

————. 1908d. "Sotsializm i iskusstvo." *Teatr: Knigi o novom teatre.* Saint Petersburg: Shipovnik.

————. 1911. *Religiia i sotsializm.* Vol. 2. Saint Petersburg: Shipovnik.

————. 1919. *Velikii perevorot.* Saint Petersburg: Grzhebin.

————. 1926. "Partiinaia shkola v Bolon'e." *Proletarskaia Revoliutsiia* 6 (3): 109–44.

————. 1972. "K voprosu o filosofskoi diskussii, 1908–1910." In *Ob ateizme i religii.* Moscow: Izadatel'stvo "Mysl'.

Marot, J. E. 2012. "Aleksandr Bogdanov, *Vperëd*, and the Role of the Intellectual in the Workers' Movement." *The October Revolution in Prospect and Retrospect: Interventions in Russian and Soviet History*, 187–210. Boston: Brill.

Martov, I. (Julius). 1909. "Religiia i marksizm." In *Na rubezh: Kritisheskii sbornik.* Moscow: Nashe Vremia SPB.

Marx, K., and F. Engels. 1975a. "Circular against Kriege." In *Collected Works*, by K. Marx and F. Engels, 6:35–51. Trans. C. Upward. New York: International Publishers.

————. 1975b. *The Holy Family; or, Critique of Critical Criticism.* In *Collected Works*, by K. Marx and F. Engels, 4:5–211. Trans. R. Dixon and C. Dutt. New York: International Publishers.

————. 1975c. *Manifesto of the Communist Party.* In *Collected Works*, by K. Marx and F. Engels, 6:477–519. Trans. S. Moore. New York: International Publishers.

Marx, K. 1975a. Introduction to *A Contribution to the Critique of Hegel's Philosophy of Law*. In *Collected Works*, by K. Marx and F. Engels, 3:175–88. Trans. J. Cohen. New York: International Publishers.

———. 1975b. "Letters from the *Deutsch-Französische Jahrbücher*: Marx to Ruge, September 1843." In *Collected Works*, by K. Marx and F. Engels, 3:133–45. Trans. C. Dutt. New York: International Publishers.

———. 1975c. "The Difference between the Democritean and Epicurean Philosophy of Nature." In *Collected Works*, by K. Marx and F. Engels, 1:25–108. Trans. D. Struik and S. Struik. New York: International Publishers.

———. 1975d. *Economic and Philosophic Manuscripts of 1844*. In *Collected Works*, by K. Marx and F. Engels, 3:229-346. Trans. M. Milligan and D. J. Struik. New York: International Publishers.

———. 1975e. *The German Ideology*. Vol. 5 of *Collected Works*, by K. Marx and F. Engels. Trans. C. Dutt. New York: International Publishers.

———. 1976. "Review of Daumer, *Die Religion des Neuen Weltalters*." In *Collected Works*, by K. Marx and F. Engels, 10:241–47. Trans. H. Rodwell. New York: International Publishers.

———. 1982. *Capital*. Vol. 1. Trans. B. Fowkes. New York: Penguin.

———. 1985a. "Critique of the Gotha Program." In *Collected Works*, by K. Marx and F. Engels, 24:75–99. Trans. P. Ross. New York: International Publishers.

———. 1985b. "On Proudhon." In *Collected Works*, by K. Marx and F. Engels, 20:26–33. Trans. C. Carlyle. New York: International Publishers.

———. 1986. "Interview with *The World*." *Collected Works*, by K. Marx and F. Engels, 22:600–6. New York: International Publishers.

Menand, L. 2003. Foreword to *To the Finland Station*, by E. Wilson. New York: NYRB Classics.

Molyneux, J. 2008. "More than Opium: Marxism and Religion." *International Socialist Journal*, no. 119. http://isj.org.uk/more-than-opium-marxism-and-religion.

Nikolaevskii, B. 1995. "K istorii 'bol'shevistskogo tsentra.'" In *Tainye stranitsy istroii*. Moskva: Izdatel'stvo Gumanitarnoi Literatury.

Peris, D. 1998. *Storming the Heavens: The Soviet League of the Militant Godless*. Ithaca, N.Y.: Cornell University Press.

Pimenov, V. 2012. "*Ispoved'* M. Gorkogo kak manifest bogostroitel'stva." *Izdatel'stvo "Gramota"* 2 (16):169–74. http://scjournal.ru/articles/issn_1997-292X_2012_2-2_47.pdf.

Plekhanov, G. 1974. "On the So-Called Religious Seekings in Russia." In *Selected Philosophical Works*, 3:306–413. Trans. R. Dixon. Moscow: Progress Publishers.

———. 1976. "Reply to Questionnaire from the Journal *Mercure de France* on the Future of Religion." In *Selected Philosophical Works*, 3:98–9. Moscow: Progress Publishers.

Preeve, S. N. 1907. "Maxim Gorky on Religion and Socialism." *Social-Democrat* 11 (10): 616–17.

Rehmann, J. 2011. "Can Marx's Critique of Religion Be Freed from Its Fetters?" *Rethinking Marxism* 23 (1): 144–53.

Rehmann, J., and B. Kahl. 2013. "A Spirituality of the Commons: Where Religion and Marxism Meet." *Tikkun* 28 (1). https://doi.org/10.1215/08879982-1957495.

Renault, M. 2015. "The Idea of Muslim National Communism: On Mirsaid Sultan-Galiev." Trans. P. King. *Viewpoint*, 23 March. https://www.viewpointmag.com/2015/03/23/the-idea-of-muslim-national-communism-on-mirsaid-sultan-galiev.

Scherr, B. P. 2003. "Gorkii and God-Building." In *William James in Russian Culture*, ed. J. D. Grossman and R. Rischin, 189–210. New York: Lexington Books.

Serge, V. 2012. *Memoirs of a Revolutionary*. Trans. P. Sedgwick and G. Paizis. New York: New York Review Books.

Sesterhenn, R. 1982. *Das Bogostroitel'stvo bei Gor'kij und Lunatscharskij bis 1909: Zur ideologischen und literarischen Vorgeschichte der Parteischule von Capri*. Munich: Verlag Otto Sagner.

Sochor, Z. 1988. *Revolution and Culture: The Bogdanov-Lenin Controversy*. Ithaca, N.Y.: Cornell University Press.

Soloviev, V. S. 2008. "On the Christian State and Society." In *Essays on Politics, Law, and Morality*, 20–31. Trans. and ed. V. Wozniuk. New Haven, Conn.: Yale University Press.

Sorel, G. 2004. *Reflections on Violence*. Trans. T. E. Hulme and J. Jennings. New York: Cambridge University Press.

Starkoff, V. 1909. "Le renouveau mystique dans la Littérature russe." *La Revue*, no. 78.

Stites, R. 1989. *Revolutionary Dreams: Utopian Vision and Experimental Life in the Russian Revolution*. New York: Oxford University Press.

Toscano, A. 2010. *Fanaticism: On the Uses of an Idea*. New York: Verso.

———. 2011. "Interview with Alberto Toscano." *Shift Magazine*, no. 11: 10–12. http://libcom.org/files/Issue%2011_Shift%20magazine.pdf.

Trotsky, L. 1972. *Writings of Leon Trotsky (1932)*. Trans. I. Fraser. New York: Pathfinder Press.

———. 1973. "Leninism and the Workers Clubs." In *Problems of Everyday Life and Other Writings on Culture and Science*, 288–319. Trans. G. Saunders. New York: Pathfinder.

Unger, R. M. 2014. *The Religion of the Future*. Cambridge, Mass.: Harvard University Press.

Voronsky, A. 1998. *Art as the Cognition of Life, Selected Writings: 1911–1936*. Trans. and ed. F. S. Choate. Oak Park, Mich.: Mehring Books.

Wernick, A. *Auguste Comte and the Religion of Humanity: The Post-Theistic Program of French Social Theory*. New York: Cambridge University Press.

Yassour, A. 1981. "Lenin and Bogdanov: Protagonists of the 'Bolshevik Center.'" *Studies in Soviet Thought* 22 (1): 1–32.

Yedlin, T. 1999. *Maksim Gorkii: A Political Biography*. Westport, Conn.: Praeger.

Young, G. 2012. *The Russian Cosmists: The Esoteric Futurism of Nikolai Fëdorov and His Followers*. New York: Oxford University Press.

Serving the Sighs of the Working Class in South Africa with Marxist Analysis of the Bible as a Site of Struggle

Gerald O. West

In 1987 the South African biblical scholar Itumeleng Mosala was the first black theologian from either the United States or South Africa to argue that the Bible was intrinsically a site of class struggle. Mosala's argument recognized the value of redaction criticism, which Mosala extended to include an ideological recognition of the class sectors engaged in ideological contestation, providing him an entry point into the ideological contestation inherent within the biblical text. Likewise, Marxist sociological categories, particularly notions around mode of production, gave Mosala resources with which to assign a particular class identity to a particular redacted "voice." This essay reflects on Mosala's contribution and its significance thirty years later, particularly in the South African context, and considers Mosala's use of Marxist concepts such as "mode of production," his understanding of the relationship between biblical text and interpretive context, and his "prophetic" warnings about working with an ideologically uncontested Bible.

South African black theology of the 1970s assumed or argued for a Bible that was ideologically aligned with the race-and-class/race-as-class struggle in South Africa (West 2016, 326–8). Sharing the perspective of Latin American liberation theology, this first phase of South African black theology worked with the conviction that the ideological trajectory or "semantic axis" of the Bible was on the side of "God's project" of liberation (see Croatto 1987; Mesters, n.d.). However, in the 1980s an overlapping but hermeneutically second phase of South African black theology argued for a Bible that was itself, inherently and intrinsically, a site of ideological contestation, a "site of struggle" (West 2016, 328–39). Marxist analysis, though evident even in the first phase (Tutu 1979a), was a distinctive component of the second phase in making the argument of the Bible as a site of struggle.

Indeed, there was an argument within the second phase of South African black theology that the Bible should be replaced by Marxism. Takatso Mofokeng (1988)—in a seminal essay presented to the Ecumenical Association of African Theologians (EATWOT) in Cairo in August 1987 and published in the *Journal of Black Theology* in 1988—outlined why South African black theology reluctantly continues to work with the Bible. The Bible's complicity with missionary colonialism and apartheid makes it clear, Mofokeng argued, even to black Christian South Africans, "that the Bible itself is indeed a serious problem to people who want to be free" (37). Mofokeng then went on to analyze black Christian attempts "to locate and solve this problem of the Bible" (37), and in so doing established a dialectic between the Bible and Marxism.

"The most commonly held approach," Mofokeng (1988, 37) argued, "has been to accuse oppressor preachers of *misusing* the Bible for their oppressive purposes and objectives. This misuse is based, it is argued, on misinterpretations of biblical texts to support or promote oppressive intentions." In responding to this approach, Mofokeng introduced the key conceptual difference between first-phase and second-phase South African black theology: "It is clear that this critique is based on the assumption that the Bible is essentially a book of liberation. This assumption is held in spite of the obvious presence in the Bible of texts, stories and books which can only serve an oppressive cause" (37). Over against the first-phase assumption that the Bible "is essentially a book of liberation," Mofokeng clearly put the second phase's position: "We contend that there are stories and texts which are basically oppressive and whose interpretation (not misinterpretation) only serves the cause of oppression. On the contrary it is (in fact) their interpretation and use for liberation that would constitute misinterpretation and misuse" (37). Black theologians, argued Mofokeng, must therefore "abandon the ideologically motivated concept of the unity of the Bible as well as the assumption that it is a book of liberation per se" and in so doing "join those grassroot Christians who made the necessary distinctions long ago and identified their texts and used them to the exclusion of others" (37–8).

Formally trained black biblical scholars and theologians are part of the problem, argued Mofokeng (1988, 37), for they "have been brought into the ideological universe of the dominant and oppressive Christian world and accepted it," and so they attempt to "save" or "co-opt" inherently oppressive biblical texts (38). Such attempts to use "oppressive texts for the oppressed only serve the interests of the oppressors who desire to have the oppressed under the same cultural, spiritual and ideological universe as themselves because they are in control of it" (38).

Another approach to the problem of the Bible, Mofokeng (1988, 40) continued, has been led by black youth who "have gone further than Steve Biko who asked rhetorically whether the decolonization process should not be accompanied by a process of the de-christianization of Africa—a process which if successfully accomplished, would remove the Bible from Africa. Young blacks," Mofokeng argued, "have categorically identified the Bible as an oppressive document by its very nature and to its very core ... They have zealously campaigned for its expulsion from the oppressed Black community but with little success." This failure "to disavow the Christian faith and consequently be rid of the obnoxious Bible" led Mofokeng to an analysis of how Marxism might offer resources in dealing with the problem of the Bible.

African Traditional Religion, the Bible, and Marxism

Mofokeng's (1988, 40) analysis of the situation in 1980s South Africa was that the failure of this black youth's project to be rid of the Bible "is largely due to the fact that no easily accessible ideological silo or storeroom is being offered to the social classes of our people that are desperately in need of liberation." He then identified the other available options, including Marxism: "African traditional religions are too far behind most blacks while Marxism, is [sic] to my mind, far ahead of many blacks, especially adult people. In the absence of a better storeroom of ideological and spiritual food, the Christian religion and the Bible will continue for an undeterminable period of time to be the haven of the Black masses par excellence."[1] Mofokeng located the Bible within a dialectic that involves an anticipated movement from African (traditional) religions, via the Bible, to Marxism. Marxism had the capacity, Mofokeng implied, to provide the masses with the resources they required for the struggle against apartheid settler-colonial capitalism.[2] For Mofokeng and many others in the struggle against apartheid, Marxist analysis on 1970s–80s South Africa "offered important insights into the character of the apartheid state" (Helliker and Vale 2013, 25). Both first- and second-phase South African black theology drew deeply from this Marxist analysis (Govender 1987). Indeed, it was the uncompromising commitment to Marxism of South African black theology and Tanzanian Ujamaa theology that generated tensions between these two African "liberation" theologies and other "African" theologies (Mbiti 1979, 88–90; Tutu 1979b, 1979a; Frostin 1988, 34–45, 181–4).

But, as Mofokeng (1988, 40) lamented, Marxism as an ideological silo (independent of the Bible) was not yet, in the 1980s, a reality: "In this situation of very limited ideological options, Black theologians who are committed to the struggle for liberation and are organically connected to the struggling Christian people, have chosen to honestly do their best to shape the Bible into a formidable weapon in the hands of the oppressed instead of just leaving it to confuse, frustrate or even destroy our people." Mofokeng called on "formally-trained" black biblical scholars and theologians to align themselves with the "hermeneutical approach of lay Christians" in which "untrained Black hermeneutists" brought their social context "into a dynamic and fruitful interaction with the Bible" so that "the progressive elements of the Black life experience, history and culture interact with the progressive life experience, histories and cultures of some biblical communities" (39–41). Black biblical scholars and theologians "who are organically connected to the above Christian hermeneutical communities but who also stand with both feet in the liberation struggle do not frown on this hermeneutical approach

1. David Jobling (2005) offers an incisive non–South African biblical scholar's reflection on Mofokeng's analysis.
2. For a detailed analysis of the "history of inequality" that has shaped postcolonial South Africa, see Terreblanche (2002).

of lay Christians," insisted Mofokeng, but "on the contrary they lift the above hermeneutical exercise to a higher formal level" (41), joining with the black masses "to
assert their claim on the Bible as a weapon of ideological and spiritual struggle for
liberation. As they assert this claim," Mofokeng continued, "a new kind of struggle
ensues, namely, the struggle for the Bible or, to be more precise, the struggle for
control of the Bible" (39).

Mofokeng did not develop how he understood the task of lifting lay hermeneutical practice to a higher level, but his comrade and dialogue partner, Itumeleng
Mosala, did. Mosala (1989a) took up the hermeneutical task where Mofokeng left
off, using Marxist theory and method to construct a historical-materialist biblical
hermeneutics of liberation. Mofokeng was clear, however, that the "analytical
tools" forged by black theology in collaboration with the masses of lay black Christians must serve what Marx (2010, 175) referred to as "the sigh of the oppressed" and
what Mofokeng (1988, 41) referred to as the "story of pain, fears, and hopes" told by
"the downtrodden of this world":

> Using these analytical tools as members of a silenced, marginalized and some-
> times ignored race, they discover the silenced, ignored and marginalized
> people in the Bible and develop an affinity with them. They also discover
> the text behind the text of the Bible—a text that has been silenced but one
> that speaks through this silence about the struggles of the silenced and mar-
> ginalized people of the Bible. As members of a people whose story of pain,
> fears and hopes has been suppressed, they are enabled, by their physical
> and psychological scars, together with the analytical tools they have chosen,
> to discover the suppressed and forgotten stories of the weak and the poor
> of the Bible. These seem, according to them, to be the stories wherein God
> is identifying with the forgotten and the weak and is actively retrieving
> them from the margins of the social world. It is through these stories that
> God the creator of humans is manifested as the God of the oppressed and ac-
> cepted as such. This creator God acts incarnately in Jesus to end the rampant
> enmity in creation and restore real humanity to people. Only the reading of
> these stories of the downtrodden God among the downtrodden of this
> world strengthens the tormented faith of the oppressed of our time, as well
> as enhancing the quality of their commitment to the physical struggle for lib-
> eration. This discovery constitutes the liberation of the Bible from the clutches
> of the dominant in the Christian fold who impose the stories that justify their
> victories onto the oppressed. (41)

Mofokeng recognized and offered a theological shape to the sigh of the oppressed.
Mosala would provide Marxist methodological and analytical tools to serve this
sigh with an appropriate biblical hermeneutics of liberation. I invoke Marx's
notion of "the sigh of the oppressed" because I think it a significant component
in the dialectic of African forms of Marxism. So before we come to Mosala's
Marxist hermeneutical contribution, I want to pause and reflect further on the

continuum or dialectic invoked by Mofokeng's argument that African traditional religions were "too far behind most blacks while Marxism," he thought, was "far ahead of many blacks" (40). Mofokeng's formulation is suggestive, constructing a tensive dialectic between the Bible and African traditional religion (in the past) and Marxism (in the future). Though Mofokeng did not opt for a Marxist framing of the dialectic, we might rephrase this threefold dialectic as a dialectic between the sigh of the oppressed, the opium of the people, and Marxism.

My formulation is provocative but captures some of the contestations within African—and specifically South African—black theology's appropriations of "classical" Marxism. As Per Frostin (1988, 182) argued, there are a number of differences between African liberation theologies (specifically Ujamaa theology and South African black theology) and what he referred to as "classical Marxism." Of particular relevance to my argument here are two of the four differences Frostin identified in his careful analysis of "Third World"—and specifically African—forms of liberation theology: namely, "the cultural dimension of oppression" and "the creativity of the oppressed" (182). Frostin cited Cornel West's incisive analysis, intersecting as it does with the cultural realities and creative capacities of oppressed peoples:

> Though Marxists have sometimes viewed oppressed people as political or economic agents, they have rarely viewed them as cultural agents. Yet without such a view there can be no adequate conception of the capacity of oppressed people—the capacity to change the world and sustain the change in an emancipatory manner. And without a conception of such capacity, it is impossible to envision, let alone create, a socialist society of freedom and democracy. It is, in part, the European Enlightenment legacy—the inability to believe in the capacities of oppressed people to create cultural products of value and oppositional groups of value—which stands between contemporary Marxism and oppressed people. (183)[3]

South African black theology in the 1980s wrestled with the relationship between Marxist forms of economic analysis and African forms of cultural analysis (Tlhagale 1985; Chikane 1985), particularly as "race" was a distinctive feature of both class and culture in apartheid South Africa. African (traditional) religion, along with its "Christian" forms, particularly evident in African Independent Churches, was an integral component of the analytical struggle, given that African Independent Churches were the primary sites of the black working class (Mosala 1985, 1986a). These sites, Mosala (1996, 54; first written in 1989) argued, were not only "black working class churches par excellence" but also sites of what Mosala referred to as a "hermeneutics of mystification" (57)—or what I prefer, following Marx (and the analysis of Jan Rehman): sites of the sigh of the oppressed.

---

3. See West (1984, 17).

The Sigh of the Oppressed

Hail, holy Queen, Mother of Mercy,
Our life, our sweetness and our hope.
To thee do we cry,
Poor banished children of Eve;
To thee do we send up our sighs,
Mourning and weeping in this vale of tears.
Turn then, most gracious advocate,
Thine eyes of mercy toward us;
And after this our exile,
Show unto us the blessed fruit of thy womb, Jesus.
O clement, O loving,
O sweet Virgin Mary.

—"Hail, Holy Queen"

The Marian prayer "Hail, Holy Queen," known in its Latin version as "Salve Regina," is usually recited after compline and is therefore especially an anthem of the night. It dates from at least the twelfth century and so considerably predates Karl Marx. Indeed, this prayer, as I will argue, may well have been one of his intertexts.

Catholics, and in particular women of the Catholic faith, had been reciting this prayer for centuries before Marx spoke of "the sigh of the oppressed creature." I have been unable to find anyone who argues for a direct link or allusion between Marx's "Seufzer der bedrängten Kreatur" and the German version of "Hail, Holy Queen" ("Zu dir rufen wir verbannte Kinder Evas; zu dir seufzen wir trauernd und weinend in diesem Tal der Tränen"), but there is a biblical connection. In an insightful analysis of Marx's critique of religion, the Marxian scholar Jan Rehmann interrogates much of the reception history of the oft-cited slogan that religion "is the *opium* of the people." By considering the sentence's textual context, Rehmann argues, "the picture changes considerably." Rehmann (2013, 6; quoting Marx 2010) sets this sentence in its literary context within Marx's early work, focusing specifically on "the two sentences that precede it" in Marx's introduction to *Contribution to the Critique of Hegel's Philosophy of Law*: "Religious distress [das religiöse Elend] is at the same time the *expression* of real distress and also the *protest* against real distress. Religion is the sigh of the oppressed creature [Seufzer der bedrängten Kreatur], the heart of a heartless world, just as it is the spirit of spiritless conditions."

Rehmann (2013, 6) goes on to ask a series of rhetorical questions: "Isn't the 'sigh' of the oppressed a precondition and the very foundation of the resistance of exploited and marginalized classes? Can Marxists do away with religion when it actually constitutes a major form in which protest against real misery and suffering is articulated? Wouldn't that mean that Marxism cuts itself off from popular protest movements in society?" "It is furthermore very likely," Rehmann continues, "that the expression 'sigh of the oppressed creature' has biblical origin." The phrase "can be traced back," he argues, "through Ludwig Feuerbach's *Essence of Christianity* and the German mystic Sebastian Frank" to the biblical text of the letter to the Romans in which Paul "describes how the entire creation 'has been groaning in travail together until now' and also that we 'groan inwardly as we wait for ... the redemption of our bodies.'"

Elaborating on his understanding of Marx's argument here, Rehmann (2013, 7) points out that "there is no marker in the text that indicates a linguistic opposition between the 'sigh' and the 'opium.'" The import is that "even if Marx never makes this explicit, it contains the conclusion that the 'sigh of the oppressed creature,' *because* of its immediacy and distance from a 'determinate negation,' is to be connected with a critical analysis of exploitation and oppression, and a rational strategy to overcome the structural causes of misery and suffering."

This understanding that "the sigh of the oppressed" requires a critical analysis of exploitation and oppression—precisely to prevent religion becoming merely "the opium of the people"—becomes more readily apparent within the wider discursive context of Marx's essay, which is not strictly speaking an essay on religion but, Rehmann (2013, 7) argues, an appeal to Hegelian philosophers "to give up their fixation on religion, the obsessive limitation of their criticism to the domain of religion":

> Marx calls upon the critical philosophers to stop their obsession with pulling apart the "holy form of human self-estrangement" and to transition to a critique of the "*vale of tears*, the *halo* of which is religion," to unmask human self-alienation no more in its sacred forms, but in its secular forms: the "criticism of heaven" is to be turned into the "criticism of earth," the criticism of religion into the "criticism of law," the criticism of theology into the "criticism of politics." (7–8)[4]

But having invoked religion, says Rehmann, Marx calls for a shift, following the fourth thesis on Feuerbach, "to analyze 'the inner strife and intrinsic contradictoriness' of the real world, its 'secular basis'"—or, as Marx would put it in *Capital*, to analyze "the earthly kernel of the misty creations of religion" (7–8). According to Rehmann, Marx moves away from a critique of religion but "takes up the pattern of a critique of religious alienation and applies it to the secular forms of ideology," particularly "the critique of the 'fetishized' capitalist market and its underlying relations of production" (8).

As Rehmann (2013, 8) notes, in the *Economic and Philosophic Manuscripts*, "Marx argues that the product of labor gets alienated from the workers and confronts them as a foreign power, like in religion. The real God of bourgeois society is

---

4. Marx's "vale of tears" metaphor is another allusion, it would seem, to the Marian prayer "Hail, Holy Queen."

money, he observes; it rules over the human beings, who bow to it, and degrades the traditional gods by turning them into commodities." In *Capital*, notes Rehmann, Marx again turns to the Bible,[5] illustrating the omnipotence of money with a reference, in Latin, to the book of Revelation (combining 17:13 and 13:17) and arguing that bourgeois society has handed over its power and authority to the "beast."

Itumeleng Mosala also turned to the Bible, in order to turn away from it to the systemic economic struggles that undergird it, that reside within its redactional construction, and that, unless unmasked with Marxist methodological resources, render the sigh of the oppressed an opiate instead of the resilient and resisting hermeneutic that it might be.

African Independent Churches as Sites of Interpretive Struggle

> The Bible plays a crucial role in the lives of black working class people in South Africa. It has a such a grip on the minds and hearts of the majority of them that often they do not have the luxury, as do members of other classes and races, of choosing to be or not to be Christian ... This situation obtains with even greater force among members of the African Independent Churches. It may be somewhat natural that it should be so with these churches as they are made up of predominantly the under-classes of the black working class people.
>
> —Itumeleng Mosala, "Race, Class, and Gender as Hermeneutical Factors in the African Independent Churches' Appropriation of the Bible"[6]

Drawing deeply on the Marxist-orientated "cultural studies" work of the Centre for Contemporary Cultural Studies (CCCS) at Birmingham University in England (Schulman 1993), Mosala (1996, 45) analyzed the biblical hermeneutics of African Independent Churches (AICs) within a historical-materialist conception of cultural studies as "a cultural configuration in articulation with other wider social configurations." For Mosala (1996, 45; citing Johnson, Critcher, and Clarke 1980), following the formulation of the CCCS, "Culture is the way, the forms, in which groups 'handle' the raw materials of their social and material existence." And the AICs "can be understood as a sub-culture ... related to, and distinct from, both black working class culture and the dominant [white settler-apartheid] culture" (46).

I invoke Mosala's (1996, 47) analysis of AICs because he went on to ask whether there is "a particular form of appropriation of the Bible which reflects this sub-culturally distinctive way of 'handling' the raw material of its existence?" The

---

5. For a detailed analysis of how Marx and Marxism have engaged the Bible, see Roland Boer's (2003, 2005, 2007a, 2007c) ongoing work.
6. See Mosala (1996, 43).

need to probe this question, Mosala insisted, is underscored by the theoretical an-
alytics of the CCCS:

> Negotiation, resistance, struggle: the relations between a subordinate and a
> dominant culture, wherever they fall within this spectrum, are always intense-
> ly active, always oppositional, in a structural sense ... Their outcome is not
> given but *made*. The subordinate class brings to this "theatre of struggle" a
> repertoire of strategies and responses—ways of coping as well as of resisting.
> Each strategy in the repertoire mobilises certain real material and social ele-
> ments: it constructs these into the supports for the different ways the class
> lives and resists its continuing subordination. (47)

Mosala's "preliminary research," requiring "a fuller and more detailed study," as he
acknowledged, refers to the biblical hermeneutics of AICs as "the hermeneutics of
mystification" (55, 57). AICs, lacking "a literate knowledge of the Bible," derive their
knowledge of the Bible "not from the biblical texts themselves" but instead "have
an oral knowledge of the Bible," most of which "comes from socialisation in the
churches themselves as they listen to prayers and sermons," appropriating the
Bible "in terms of what it stands for—a canonical authority" (55).

Mosala (1996, 55) recognized that sectors of black working-class culture—such as
the Madodana (men's guilds) and Manyano (women's guilds) movements within
the historically missionary/settler-initiated churches (including his own Methodist
Church), which "appropriate the Bible in terms of its contents"—had been "assimilated into a reading culture of the Bible." Literacy increases the capacity to
"address the contradiction of class" in the biblical text, drawing "weapons
largely from the work place experiences." Though it is not precisely clear what
Mosala was arguing here, it seems that the capacity to read the Bible as text
enables the "struggle" in the workplace to engage with the "struggle" in "the biblical texts themselves." An "unread Bible" is the problem for AICs: the "mystifica-
tions generated by the authoritative status of an unread Bible," while "it does
enable them to negotiate their reality and even to resist the forces of brutalisation
with which the whole class is faced," does not facilitate accessing "hermeneutical
weapons ... from the concrete experiences of the work place." Instead of the workplace struggle engaging with the struggle within biblical texts, AICs—unlike their
more literate working-class cousins—use the "African symbols and [traditional]
discourses" that characterize their AIC faith to engage with "the mysteries of the
Bible."

While Mosala (1996, 55) is clear that the literate faith-based movements of South
African Christianity, specifically the Madodana and Manyano movements, represent "a better chance of enabling its bearers to find a resolution to the problematic
of the entire class of which they are members," still other "tools" or "hermeneutical
weapons" are required, "located externally in the parent culture of the black
working class" before "transformation can be hoped for." What Mosala is

looking for but not finding within AICs is a hermeneutical "deliberateness in the movement's manner of appropriating the Bible from the perspective of a dominated race" (56).

Mosala would go on in his primary work to forge the required "hermeneutical weapons" as a contribution by black theologians who are themselves organic intellectuals of the black working class. But before we turn to this contribution, it is important to recognize the epistemological privilege Mosala afforded to the AICs. While Mosala (1996, 55) was worried by the largely "symbolic" engagement between the AIC working-class sociocultural context and an iconic-semiotic Bible, lamenting their lack of capacity to engage with the detail of the biblical text, he affirmed their reality as the primary site/text of the sigh of the oppressed: "Should we not," asked Mosala, "when looking at the biblical hermeneutics of the AICs, broaden our concept of text to include the historical text of the lives of the members themselves?" (57) The embodied sigh of the oppressed is the "first text," the Bible is the "second text."[7]

In this seminal work on developing a black biblical hermeneutics of liberation, Mosala positioned the historical text of the lives of the black working class—represented par excellence by AIC subculture[8]—as the hermeneutic starting point of a black biblical hermeneutics of liberation. Those committed to the struggles of oppressed and exploited black people "cannot ignore," insists Mosala (1986b, 197), "the history, culture, and ideologies of the dominated black people as their primary hermeneutical starting point." However, for the Bible to become a "weapon" of struggle in the hands of the black working class, the Bible cannot be understood "as an innocent and transparent container of a message or messages" (Mosala 1989a, 40, 41, 193; and see Mofokeng 1988, 40). Indeed, as Mosala (1989a, 41) argues at length, it is precisely such a nonideological understanding of the Bible "that has caused black and liberation theologians not to be aware of—or, more correctly, to appropriate as otherwise—the presence and significance of oppression and oppressors, exploitation and exploiters in the signified practices that the biblical texts really are."

Serving the sigh of the black working class—embodied most clearly in the AICs' hermeneutics of mystification—requires, Mosala (1989a, 32) argues, the Marxist resources of "a revolutionary cultural worker." Furthermore, "My fundamental objection to the biblical hermeneutics of black theology" (in its first phase), states Mosala, "is that not only does it suffer from an 'unstructural understanding of the Bible' [see Gottwald 1985, 5], but—both as a consequence and as a reason—it also suffers from an unstructural understanding of the black experience and struggle." Black theology to date has failed, argues Mosala, in what Terry Eagleton (1981, 113) has called "the threefold task of a revolutionary cultural worker":

---

7. A maxim of liberation theologies holds theology as critical reflection (the second text) on the praxis of life (the first text). See Gutiérrez (1973, 6) and Bonino (1975, 61).
8. Mosala (1986a, 98–9) makes a similar argument with respect to "African traditional religions."

According to Eagleton, a revolutionary cultural worker must (1) participate in the production of works and events, thereby intending those effects commensurate with the victory of socialism; (2) function as a critic, exposing the rhetorical structures of works and combatting whatever deceptions are intended through them; (3) interpret works and events "against the grain." Presumably, in making this last point Eagleton seeks to remind us that the appropriation of works and events is always a contradictory process that embodies some form of a "struggle." (Mosala 1989a, 32)

Black theologians, formally trained in the critical discipline of biblical studies, have no excuse, argues Mosala, yet they have failed to recognize that the three tasks of a revolutionary cultural worker—"projective, polemical, and appropriative" (Eagleton 1981, 97)—are interrelated:

The interrelatedness of the tasks of a revolutionary cultural worker can scarcely be overemphasized. There is no doubt that black theology is "projective" and "appropriative," albeit vaguely and loosely, in its use of the Bible. It is certainly *not* polemical—in the sense of being critical—in its biblical hermeneutics. Rather, it lifts and appropriates themes from the Exodus, the prophetic, and the Jesus traditions into the service of a liberation project. It uncritically enlists the rhetorical structures that inhere in and circumscribe those themes—and which have an inbuilt proclivity to produce politically undesirable effects—on the side of the struggle for liberation of the oppressed. And it fails to detect oppression and oppressors, exploitation and exploiter in the text of the Bible. Nothing, of course, could be more subversive to the struggle for liberation than enlisting the oppressors and exploiters as comrades in arms. (Mosala 1989a, 33)

It is the recognition that biblical texts are ideologically inscribed products of class struggle that leads Mosala to insist "that this struggle is a key category in developing a biblical hermeneutics of liberation. The struggle is, depending on the class forces involved, either to harmonize the contradictions inherent in the works and events or to highlight them with a view toward allowing social class choices in their appropriation" (32).

Mosala's Marxist Method

A significant contribution of biblical studies to contemporary appropriations of biblical texts, Mosala (1989a, 101) maintained, is that it has "always been aware of the tendency in biblical literature for older traditions to be reused to address the needs of new situations." Within biblical studies this is known as "redaction criticism." What Mosala (1989a, 125) wanted to add to the usual understandings of redaction criticism—see Römer (2013)—is that such understandings reuse "what has thus far [in the 1980s] been an elusive trait of scriptural texts: their class and ideological nature." While Mosala drew on the work of the few biblical scholars who have analyzed "the class nature and commitments of the various editions or recompositions" of biblical texts (see Coote 1981), their work "falls short," argued Mosala (1989a, 125), "of providing an adequate hermeneutical *appropriation* of these texts in class and ideological terms." Mosala was looking for a recognition of "the question of 'struggle' as a fundamental hermeneutical factor in the text, as indeed in the communities behind the text and those appropriating the text presently."

Mosala was quick to reject a redactional approach that recognizes and valorizes "an original [biblical] prophet surrounded by secondary additions" (Mosala 1989a, 125). For Mosala, each redactional edition has its value, for it represents the contestation within a particular moment of sociohistorical struggle. So redactional recognition "has as its purpose not the selection of one edition and the dismissal of others. On the contrary, the aim is to resurrect and identify the forces of struggle inherent and dominant in each edition" (125–6). "Put simply," he said, ideological redactional analysis "acknowledges the value of all the editions of the texts." But, he insisted with respect to contemporary appropriation, "such value is variable: it could be positive or negative. It is fundamentally framed by the nature of the social and ideological struggles in the text as well as of similar struggles in the life of the readers" (126). And while Mosala accepted the final canonical form of the Bible and its various biblical books as a starting point for ideological-redaction critical work, he recognized that the final form "cannot provide inspiration to oppressed peoples because it is inherently a theology of domination and control" (134).

Key to Mosala's (1989a, 148–9) understanding of the redactional task is the recognition that the voice of the biblical prophet—in this case the prophet Micah, a prophet who stands and speaks, primarily, against local city-temple-states and, secondarily, against the imperial powers that struggle to exert their control over such local "Israelite" or "Judahite" city-temple-states—"re-presents" the voice of the exploited classes. The voices of the exploited classes are almost entirely redacted in the final form, except in their fragmentary *re*-presentation and in the reverberations of their struggles in more dominant discourses.

These are thus the two ends of an ideological orientation toward redactional criticism. At the one end are the voices of the exploited classes; at the other end is the final form of the text. In between are layers of redaction. However, as we have seen, Mosala did not deny that there are traces of even the most marginalized voices in the final canonical literary layer. I concur, arguing for more of a presence than Mosala acknowledges, drawing as I do on thinner notions of hegemony than Mosala's, as well as on poststructuralist notions of presence/absence. Marginalized voices are always present in some form (West 2009; see also Wittenberg 2007). The purpose of an ideologically determined (in both senses of the English word) redaction criticism is precisely to delve for each and every voice, no matter how co-opted and "redacted."

The substantive contribution of Mosala with respect to redaction criticism was his elaboration of Robert Coote's recognition of the ideological dimension of redactional recomposition. Mosala's own work on Micah followed the contours of Coote's work on Amos. However, it is important to note that Coote's (1981, 2) work was focused on "the process by which the book of Amos came to be," so he offered an accurate but simplified analysis of the process of redactional composition, limiting his analysis to "a three-stage process" of redaction (3). This enabled Coote to identify three significant redactional editions in Amos: the oracles of the prophet Amos himself, stage A (11–45); a scribal recomposition of the oral oracles as they were "reactualized in the seventh century," stage B (47, 46–109); and an "updated" edition of a "resourceful, imaginative scribe who picked up and read the B stage of Amos sometime in the last third of the sixth century BC," stage C (110–11, 110–34).

Mosala (1989a, 126) adopted Coote's three-stage process for his redactional analysis of Micah, though he did not argue, as Coote did, that a three-stage process is in line with the redactional scholarship on Micah. Coote was aware with respect to Amos that redactional scholarship had made an argument for more than one stage-B edition, between the original oracles and the final form. He was clear that "to reduce the composition of the book of Amos to a three-stage process is an oversimplification" (Coote 1981, 8), and he only posited a three-stage redaction in order to illustrate the redactional *process*. He recognized that "the analysis of stages of composition has to be done separately for each prophetic book" (9). Coote was overt about his oversimplification; Mosala was not.

Coote's (1981, 5) oversimplification allowed him to demonstrate the ideological moves the redactional process makes and, specifically with respect to Amos, how the "Bethel editor" (stage B) collected some of the oracles of the prophet Amos (stage A), combining them together in a written recomposition with his own compositions, and how the stage-C editor "rewrote this work with the addition of an opening and closing." Coote described this three-stage process carefully, acknowledging throughout that the redactional detail could be elaborated. Coote wanted us to understand that the redactional process of collection and recomposition "involves [ideological] selection, retelling, organizing" (4).

Mosala's emphasis was not so much the redactional process as it was the identification of the ideological voices within each redaction. Mosala worked backward toward the prophet and the exploited classes the prophet represents, tracing the various redactional voices from the final form back in historical time and its sociological setting toward the voice of the prophet and the exploited classes represented by the prophet. Working backward in Mosala-like fashion from the final redactional form that is the Bible as we have it in its canonical form(s), we may posit the most prevalent voice of the final edition as the voice of the dominant ideology, with hegemonic aspirations, for "the perspective of these texts frames the various other layers of meaning of the discourse in such a way as to relegate these layers of meaning to a secondary position" (Mosala 1989a, 131). This final redaction, Coote's stage C, derives from ruling-class groups, including Israelite and Judahite royal houses, temple-city-aligned priests, and temple-city-based landowners and merchants.

The final redactor takes up, redacting and therefore partially co-opting—for hegemonic appropriations are never complete in their attempts to recodify the voices they subsume (Scott 1990)—the professional or scribal, economically "middle layer" (Mosala 1989a, 117), the stage-B (in Coote's terms) re-presentations of the prophet's oral or written text, depending on the prophet. This scribal voice tends to accommodate its re-presentation to the ruling class it serves and subsists on (141), using a form of "negotiated code" (42, 138), but with an emphasis on the "adaptive" rather than the "oppositional" elements of this code (141).[9] This redactional voice, Mosala argues, tends to be "shot through with contradictions," arising from, in Stuart Hall's (quoted in Mosala 1989a, 138) words, "the differential position of those who occupy this position in the spectrum, and from their differential and unequal relation to power."

The voice redacted by the scribal voice is that of the prophet, though Coote (1981, 7) admits that "it is doubtful that the first recorder of Amos's words in writing was Amos himself." Like so many Old Testament/Hebrew Bible redactional scholars, Coote cannot imagine an oral-aural "composition." As envisaged by both Coote and Mosala, the prophet is a socially engaged intellectual, either organic to or in solidarity with the exploited classes, those excluded from the discourses of the city-temple-state and the encompassing economic systems of empire, re-presenting them as the prophet speaks to the dominant power structures. Though Mosala is not explicit about the voices of the exploited classes (re-presented by the prophet Micah), here too we can posit the use of a form of negotiated code, except the use of oppositional elements is more pronounced. Yet even here adaptive elements are included in order to have the oppositional elements heard in the struggle with ruling-class power. Among the exploited classes, if we follow the astute ideological analysis of James Scott (1990), is both a public and a hidden "transcript," with the hidden transcript reserved for talk among the exploited classes themselves and the public transcript being shared with the prophetic sectors in solidarity with them. The prophet would then "re-member" the public components (West 2016, 363–5), reconfiguring them in both a strategic and substantive form within the prophet's oral-aural performances—*strategically*, to secure access to state power, and *substantially*, to talk back to state power.

Which then brings us to the voices of the exploited classes themselves, for as Mosala (1989a, 153) reiterates, "The task of a biblical hermeneutics of liberation is to go behind the dominant discourses to the discourses of oppressed communities in order to link up with kindred struggles." However, somewhat strangely, neither Coote nor Mosala postulate a distinctive "textual" layer for the exploited classes. They are always only re-presented. But if we use redactional notions from New

9. Mosala is here drawing on the Marxist analytical work of Stuart Hall (1980).

Testament gospel research, we can posit an oral "textual" layer whose public tran-script the prophet has access to.[10] As Scott (1990, xi) so carefully argues,[11] the ex-ploited classes are not silent, for they "create and defend a social space in which offstage dissent to the official transcript of power relations may be voiced." And when they do venture to speak in the public realm, their speech takes on "a dialogic form in which the language of the dialogue will invariably borrow heavily from the terms of the dominant ideology prevailing in the public transcript" (102). The dom-inant discourse then becomes "a plastic idiom or dialect that is capable of carrying an enormous variety of meanings, including those that are subversive of their use as intended by the dominant," for in most contexts of domination "the terrain of dominant discourse is the only plausible arena of struggle" (102–3). So by recogniz-ing that adopting and adapting the dominant discourse is a guise induced by power relations that is necessary outside of the safety of the hidden transcript, and by learning to read the dialects and codes generated by the techniques and arts of re-sistance, we can discern a dialogue with power in the public transcript (101–5, 138). The voices of the exploited classes are a real presence, even in redaction. Ideolog-ical analysis along the lines of Scott's is required to enable us to recognize this real presence.

Though not always as nuanced as he could be in his analysis of the book of Micah, Mosala insists that there are distinguishable voices and that they are engaged in a "class" struggle across a biblical text's redactional history. Recogniz-ing and recovering these contending voices is so difficult because of the reality of redactional work, that it is not additive, with one voice being added on top of another voice. As Coote (1981, 5) argued with respect to Amos, redactional work is about revision and rewriting rather than addition or accretion. Redaction is a process of "gradual combination and recomposition" (3). The redactional process "entangles" voices and time,[12] collecting and combining/composing and then re-collecting and recombining/recomposing, over and over again. Disentangling com-posite redacted texts in order to discern different ideological voices is difficult but necessary for a Marxist reading of the Bible.

For Mosala, each redactional edition is a site of ideological contestation, a signi-fied practice representing actual socioeconomic contestation in particular sociohis-torical sites of struggle within what Roland Boer (2007b) refers to as "the sacred economy of ancient 'Israel.'" Boer draws extensively on "Soviet Ancient Near Eastern scholarship" (30), and he uses these relatively unknown (within Euro-American biblical studies) Marxian-informed biblical studies resources to trace "the emergence of the state in response to the conflict between the village

10. Though Mosala (1989a, 154–72) did analyze Luke 1–2, he did not delve into gospel redaction criticism. Indeed, in his work on Luke, Mosala took up more of a literary approach than a redac-tional approach (161). Like so many scholars, Mosala was trapped by the scholarly conventions of his testament.
11. For a fuller discussion, see West (2004, 2011).
12. Achille Mbembe (2001, 16) uses this term to speak of "African time."

commune and the city-temple complex" (30). Insisting on "the necessary centrality of economic analysis in any historiography of the Ancient Near East" (29), Boer focuses on the constituent elements of the ancient "system of *theo-economics*, and its constituent *regimes of allocation* and *regimes of extraction*" (30). Though the emphasis in Boer's analysis is regimes of allocation, he recognises with a number of Marxist orientated biblical scholars, including Mosala, that it is through regimes of extraction that "the main tension of the sacred economy shows up" (Boer 2007b, 41).

The primary regime of extraction in the ancient sacred economy is a tribute regime of extraction, conceptualised in the late 1970s by the biblical scholar Norman Gottwald (one of Mosala's primary sources) as the tributary mode of production. Gottwald reconceptualised biblical studies by shifting the orientation from historical reconstruction to sociological reconstruction, using Marxian notions of socioeconomic analysis. In particular, Gottwald offers biblical studies Marx's conceptualization of "mode of production" (Gottwald 1999, 631, citing Marx and Engels 1970, 42). Many years later, David Jobling is able to claim that in his opinion, "The greatest theoretical debt which Biblical Studies owes to Marxism ... is the understanding of historical modes of production (MPs)" (Jobling 2005, 192).

Mosala's work, cut short by his commitments to active political involvement within the Azanian People's Organisation (AZAPO) in the early 1990s, attempts to locate the contending classes within a particular sociohistorical context in the ancient world that produced particular biblical texts within the tributary regime of extraction. Briefly,[13] rereading the biblical book of Micah backwards, Mosala identifies the final canonical form as arising "out of the tributary mode of production represented by the Israelite monarchy" (Mosala 1989a, 118). The most "fundamental means of production" in ancient Palestine "was the land" (Mosala 1989a, 103), which was gradually controlled by an emerging monarchic sacred economy, whereby "the incipient [monarchic] kingdom required a system of surplus extraction whose presupposition is *unrewarded* human labor" (Mosala 1989a, 107), constructing a "class structure" that was characterised by "a social division of labor resulting in antagonistic social relations of production, exchange, and distribution" (Mosala 1989a, 115). The final redactional form of Micah "frames" the various other class voices in such a way, argues Mosala, as to "relegate" these voices "to a secondary position" (Mosala 1989a, 131). The scribe who re-presents the voice of the prophet Micah occupies a class position within the retainer middle layer of ancient "Israel," serving the ruling-class groups (including the royal house, city-temple priests, imperial representatives, and latifundaries) and subsisting on their patronage (Mosala 1989a, 117). The scribal re-presentation of the oral voice

13. Mosala (1989b, 103–22) offers extensive analysis of "the material conditions" of the book of Micah.

of the prophet Micah negotiates with but adapts itself to the ruling class, which "made up 2 percent or less of the population yet controlled half or more of the total goods and services produced in the society" (Mosala 1989a, 116). The oral voices of the "exploited classes," whether the voice of peasants with land tenure, peasants who had lost their land through debt and worked as tenant farmers on the estates of latifundaries, or landless peasants (Mosala 1989a, 117), find oral re-presentation in the voice of the prophet Micah, again in negotiated terms, though with an oppositional, ideological orientation.

Again, though oversimplified, the process is clear. Turning to Marx once again, Mosala is explicit about both the redactional process and why Marxist method is required to serve "those who lack the means of mental production":

> The ideas of the ruling class are in every epoch the ruling ideas, i.e. the class which is the ruling material force of society, is at the same time its ruling intellectual force. The class which has the means of material production at its disposal, has control at the same time over the means of mental production, so that thereby, generally speaking, the ideas of those who lack the means of mental production are subject to it. (Mosala 1989a, 153; citing Marx and Engels 1970, 64)

Particularly significant about Mosala's contribution to South African black theology is his emphasis on the use of Marxist method both for an analysis of the socio-history of the Bible's production and for an analysis of black South African contemporary contexts. In my early reflections on Mosala's argument, I referred to this as an "analogy of method" (West 1995, 74–5). Mosala wants South African black theology to use Marxist categories for an analysis of both the ancient biblical sites of class contestation and the contemporary South African sites of class-and-race/class-as-race contestation. "The task," said Mosala (1989a, 153), "of a biblical hermeneutics of liberation is to go behind the dominant discourses [of the Bible] to the discourses of oppressed communities in order to link up with kindred [contemporary] struggles." Mosala then offered his own take on a popular anecdote:

> In South Africa a common mythological expression of the role of biblical discourses in the dispossession of blacks runs like this: "When the white man came to our country, he had a Bible and we had the land. The white man said to the black man, 'Let us pray.' After the prayer, the white man had the land and the black man had the Bible." The task now facing a black theology of liberation is to enable black people to use the Bible to get the land back and to get the land back without losing the Bible. In order for this to happen, black theology must employ the progressive aspects of black history and culture to liberate the Bible so that the Bible may liberate black people. That is the hermeneutical dialectic. (153)

Mosala was clear that, in order for this to happen, "a theoretically sound and an ideologically clear approach to the text of the Bible is a prerequisite" (153). Marxist analysis as conceptualized in Mosala's "materialist" method (103) offers the focal concept "mode of production" to South African black theology. Mosala used an analogy of method to bring African modes of production (the communal, tributary, and capitalist modes of production) into dialogue with ancient biblical modes of production (the agricultural and tributary modes of production; 69–99, 103–21). Mosala's answer to Terry Eagleton's (1978, 11) question about how we are to facilitate "the troubled passage between text and reader" involves unleashing "the forces of struggle that each brings in the encounter with the other," with the "social-ideological location and commitment of the reader" being "accorded the *methodological* priority" (Mosala 1989a, 123, 124).

The category of "the black struggle" is Mosala's (1989a, 123) hermeneutical starting point, even if the black masses (and their companion black theologians) often have an "unstructural" or "nonsystematic" understanding of their struggle (32, 191). By using Marxist methods in their biblical interpretation, recognizing that biblical texts are "*signified practices*" representing "particular *productions*" of sociohistorical struggle (124), both the working-class masses and their middle-class theologian compatriots may be empowered to understand the black struggle "more *systematically* and *critically*" within "an ideological and theoretical framework that is capable of bringing about the material liberation of black working-class people" (192).

In summary, at the methodological level, Mosala's (1989a, 185) biblical hermeneutics drew on Marxist analysis in order to offer insight and access into the ideological redactional history of the Bible. His historical-materialist analysis "laid bare," he argued, "the class character and ideological commitments of" a particular redactional layer of the text, enabling contemporary working-class black South Africans to recognize four things: First, Mosala's method offered a way of analyzing both biblical text and contemporary sociohistorical context; the method was useful for each of these terrains of struggle, whether the ancient sites of struggle that produced the biblical texts or the contemporary sites of struggle that generated a black working class (4, 192). Second, Mosala's method offered black working-class Christians a way of connecting "kin struggles" across (sacred) time and space (188), identifying and foregrounding the economic and ideological connections between biblical text and contemporary context (4–5). Third, Mosala's method, by identifying the ideological and economic agenda of a particular (layer of) text, enabled black working-class Christians to recognize when they must interpret with or against the ideo-economic grain of a particular (layer of) text (32, 41, 123–53, 173–89). And fourth, Mosala's method was meant to demonstrate the reality of ideological co-optation, both within the Bible and in our contemporary contexts; again, biblical methodology offers ideological shape to contemporary methodology; Marxist resources offer significant modes of analysis for both, and particularly the recognition that biblical text and contemporary context are ideologically contested with respect to modes of production.

Mosala's Method at Work

Mosala's insistence on a contestation within the biblical text (not only between different biblical books but also within a single biblical book)[14] has been taken up by other biblical scholars, including a new generation of black South African biblical scholars (Nzimande 2008; Ramantswana 2016, 2017). Mosala's work has also been taken up by others who understand the significance of building ethical and theological resources on the realistic recognition of the Bible as a site of ideo-theological contestation. David Pleins (2001, vii) has offered a readily accessible appropriation of Mosala's method in his own quest for a "social vision" based on the Bible's social ethics.

Focusing on the social ethic of the biblical prophets, Pleins's (2001, 224) work on the prophet Isaiah takes as its starting point "the competing theological trajectories of the text." His approach, which combines literary and redactional analysis, enables him to identify contending notions of "the poor" ('anî/'ănāwîm) within the different redactional editions of Isaiah. "The early chapters of Isaiah [those deriving from the prophet] depict the members of the urban establishment as exhausting the produce of the vineyard, God's people, and taking the property of the 'ani (3:13–14). The driving concern of the decadent upper classes is depicted as enhancing pleasure and increasing material prosperity ... (5:22–23; cf. 5:18–21)" (254). Furthermore, continues Pleins, "The prophet specifies the mode of exploitation adopted by the rich: 'Ah [woe to] those who add house to house and join field to field, till there is room for none but you to dwell in the land' (5:8)" (254). In sum, argues Pleins, "The prophetic critique is clear: The prosperity of the wealthy is directly linked to injustices against other members of Israelite society" (254). Poverty and wealth are directly and systemically related; the poor are poor *because* the wealthy have exploited them (254–9).

However, "the poor" were reframed in subsequent redactions, as the voices of the poor and their prophet were redacted by elite-aligned scribal voices. Though this recomposition of "the poor" is evident in chapters 40–66, it is particularly prevalent in 55–66, argues Pleins (2001, 264), where the terms 'anî/'ănāwîm were used to "reconceptualize the experience of Israel's dislocated elite." Even chapters 1–39, which reflect a substantial presence of the voice of the prophet (and the exploited classes he re-presents), were recomposed when chapters 40–55 and then 56–66 were added at a later time.[15] Later redactions co-opted and ideologically reframed the voice of the prophet (and the exploited classes he re-presents), constructing, in Mosala's (1989a, 118–19) words, "a harmonization of contradictions in such a way that the class interests of one group are universalized." For example, referring to Isaiah 26:1–7, Pleins (2001, 251) states:

---

14. For a detailed example of ideological contestation between biblical books see West (2019).
15. Once again, this summary of the redaction of Isaiah is an oversimplification.

Presumably here the "poor and needy" are the returning exiles who will lay claim to the seats of power. One does not imagine here a proletarian revolution of the Marxist variety. As will become clear in our discussion of chaps. 40–66, the exile has brought about an adaptation of the ancient prophetic call for justice for the poor. Where once this language may indeed have been spoken in relation to the concrete needs of Israel's oppressed, this language has, with the exile, been amalgamated, via prophetic recasting, into the political program of the displaced *elite* in ancient Israel.

Materials in Isaiah 1–39 that may have their social location in ideological codes connected to the poor of Palestine "have been grossly recast to follow the theological project of the postexilic author(s)" (264). The voices of the poor have been co-opted; the problem is no longer systemic economic oppression but sin in a more general moral sense (Isaiah 50:1, 59:1–4; Pleins 2001, 265). Referring directly to Mosala's work, Pleins concludes: "Such a shift would appear to mimic that identified by Mosala for Micah, wherein an original prophetic critique of social injustice is later toned down into a message about abstract 'justice,' only to finally be commandeered by the elite as a message about its own predicament of judgement" (267).

If contemporary appropriations of the Bible by communities of faith are looking for an economic ethic, the worry for both Pleins and Mosala is that they will embrace the ethic of the elite, given that their economic ethic reshapes the economic ethic of other voices through redactional power and so represents itself as the "final" and "sacred" ethic. Mosala (1989a, 28) argued that South African black theology, unless it embraced Marxist analysis, would find itself succumbing "to precisely this danger, the danger of collaborating with the Bible's dominant ruling class ideologies." In so doing, he insisted, they would be engaging in a "useless sparring with the ghost of the oppressor, whom ... [they] have already embraced in the oppressor's most dangerous form, the [final] ideological form of the [biblical] text."

Ideological Co-optation after Liberation

Mosala's call in the late 1980s for the black working class to liberate the Bible so that it might liberate them has taken on a particular poignancy in the South Africa of today, twenty-five years after political liberation. I say "political liberation" advisedly. The long struggle for liberation has achieved substantial political and legal gains. And 1994 did usher in a new era and a "new" South Africa that is— politically and legally—systemically different from apartheid South Africa. Apartheid, a race-based social construct established by the British and refined by white Afrikaner Nationalist rule, has been systemically dismantled, politically and legally. What has not changed sufficiently is racial capitalism, the economic system of apartheid (Terreblanche 2002, 15).

Mosala's Marxist methodological warning about the struggles of working-class and other marginalized sectors being co-opted by dominant ideologies, a process he found in the production of biblical texts, has until recently not been heeded. By not recognizing that the Bible was itself a site of struggle, the bulk of practitioners of 1980s and 1990s South African black theology failed to equip postapartheid forms of liberation theology with the capacity to resist the co-optation of the Bible by the postliberation state and church.

As South Africa entered the militant period of "rolling mass action" in the early 1990s, what *The Kairos Document* referred to as "State Theology" (the "law and order" theology of the apartheid state) and "Church Theology" (the "personal piety" theology of the churches under apartheid) were on the retreat, and "Prophetic Theology" (the theology of "the struggle" against apartheid) was in control of the theological terrain (Kairos Theologians 1985). It could be argued, and was argued by apartheid state propaganda, that prophetic theology was "the ANC [African National Congress] at prayer." Though a catchy way of representing solidarity within "the struggle" between the theological wing and the political wing of the struggle, respectively, it would be more accurate to represent the relationship of black theology with the Tripartite Alliance of the ANC, the Congress of South African Trade Unions (COSATU), and the South African Communist Party (SACP) as one of "critical solidarity," though precisely how this concept was to be understood and practiced was contested (Vellem 2013).

Notions of "critical solidarity" implied an engaged and relational dimension between the postliberation South African state and liberation theologians. Some of these theologians were drafted into government or parastatals (state-owned enterprises) while others retained their leadership in the South African Council of Churches (SACC) and other faith-based NGOs. So it was somewhat unexpected when President Thabo Mbeki, Nelson Mandela's successor, began to use the Bible in church-theology ways, effectively aligning what might be considered a "new" state theology with church theology.

Thabo Mbeki used the Bible, I have demonstrated (West 2016, 445–542), to deflect the critical engagement of Marxist forms of prophetic theology with the post-1996 macroeconomic policies of the South African state. Having abandoned the pro-poor and socialist-inclined Reconstruction and Development Programme (RDP) with which it came to power in 1994, the South African state sought to disrupt and deflect the critique of South Africa's liberation theologies as it replaced the RDP with a procapitalist macroeconomic policy, GEAR (Growth, Employment and Redistribution). Mbeki used the Bible in church-theology ways in order to assert that liberation theologies ought to focus on the personal and moral dimensions of South African life and leave the structural and economic dimensions to the state.

That Mbeki used the Bible at all probably reflects his understanding of the importance of what Gillian Hart calls "re-nationalisation," a process that "engages ... crucial questions about how the post-apartheid 'nation' came to be produced, as well as the ongoing importance of articulations of the 'nation' to the ANC's hegemonic project" (Hart 2013, 156–7). The Bible, Mbeki came to recognize (like Mofokeng), was a symbolic silo from which a diverse range of South Africans could find sustenance in church-theology terms. The Bible would nourish their collective "souls." Indeed, borrowing the phrase from Nelson Mandela, Mbeki made an extended argument, using the Bible, for an "RDP of the soul" (West 2016, 498–512), effectively severing the notion of "reconstruction and development" from the economic terrain and attaching it (or redeploying it) to the religious terrain.

Church theology has become state theology, for the trajectory that Mbeki has established of how the Bible ought to be used in the public realm has been mimicked by his party, the ANC, by his successor, Jacob Zuma, and recently by Cyril Rhamaphosa, our new president (West 2016, 512–42). This co-optation has been possible precisely because the Bible has not been understood as a site of struggle by the remnant of prophetic theology. The redactional layers of the Bible that lend themselves to church theology, found in the final canonical form of the Bible, have been taken up in the public realm, by both the state and the churches, as if they represent "the" theological trajectory of "the Bible."

Both the South African state and the South African churches have settled for a church-theology Bible, with an emphasis on the personal and the moral. With respect to the economic, the emphasis has been on individual personal moral corruption. And while we can forgive the politicians for failing to grasp Mosala's analysis of the exploitative economic systems that partially constitute the biblical text, the churches have no excuse, for Mosala's analysis is part of their inheritance. Yet they too have failed to engage with the class and economic systems of exploitation that characterize the sacred economy of the dominant sectors of biblical societies. "Bewitched" by the final form of the biblical text, our South African churches are unable to delve beneath the ruling-class ideologies that characterize the final (canonical) form of the Bible.

Fortunately, the resources Mosala's Marxist analysis offers to the sigh of the oppressed remain available to us. Working with a Bible that is a site of struggle has significant potential for a truly prophetic theology, postliberation, as we struggle for "economic freedom in our lifetime."[16]

Conclusion

Mofokeng (1988, 38) argues that there is a long history within the church of "the weakest, neglected, poor and marginalised people," recognizing "the usefulness of the Bible as a book with a message of survival, resistance and hope," giving them "a reason for hoping for a different future and believing in their right to a decent human existence." What their sigh offers us, Mofokeng recognizes, is a historical praxis that is "a new kind of struggle ... namely, the struggle for the Bible or, to be more precise, the struggle for control of the Bible" (39). While Mofokeng

---

16. The slogan "economic freedom in our lifetime" has been used by both the ANC Youth League and the more recently formed Economic Freedom Fighters (EFF) political party.

identifies this "new kind of struggle," Mosala (1989a, 192) offers the Marxist tools with which to analyze how to read the Bible "backwards," recognizing the final form of the Bible as the oppressor's form (28), representing the ideology of the dominant socioeconomic sectors within a particular historical mode of production.

The religious sigh of working-class black South Africans embodies their struggle and is the starting point for a black biblical hermeneutics of liberation. While the Bible cannot be the primary starting point for black theology, Mosala (1986b, 196) concedes that "there are enough contradictions" within biblical texts "to enable eyes [and sighs] that are hermeneutically trained in the struggle for liberation today to observe the kin struggles of the oppressed and exploited of the biblical communities in the very absences of those struggles in the text." The contradictions are present within the text because the Bible is itself "a product and a record of class struggles" (196). Black theologians who are committed to liberation theology's project "to emancipate the poor and exploited of the world" (Mosala 1989a, 193) must align themselves with the sigh of the most marginalized of the working class and serve their sigh with Marxist analysis, so that they are hermeneutically capacitated to move beyond the Bible as opiate. The Bible is a site of struggle, and Marxist analysis enables the sighs of the masses to move beyond the mere recognition of "glimpses of liberation" (40) in the Bible and toward an understanding and appropriation of what liberation is and how liberation is struggled for, both within biblical texts and contemporary contexts.

References

Boer, R. 2003. *Marxist Criticism of the Bible*. London: T&T Clark.
———. 2005. "Marx, Postcolonialism, and the Bible." In *Postcolonial Biblical Criticism: Interdisciplinary Intersections*, ed. S. D. Moore and F. F. Segovia, 166–83. London: T&T Clark.
———. 2007a. *Criticism of Heaven: On Marxism and Theology*. Leiden: Brill.
———. 2007b. "The Sacred Economy of Ancient 'Israel.'" *Scandinavian Journal of the Old Testament: An International Journal of Nordic Theology* 21 (1): 29–48.
———. 2007c. "Twenty-Five Years of Marxist Biblical Criticism." *Currents in Research* 5 (3): 298–321. https://doi.org/10.1177/1476993x07077963.
Bonino, J. M. 1975. *Doing Theology in a Revolutionary Situation*. Philadelphia: Fortress.
Chikane, F. 1985. "The Incarnation in the Life of the People in Southern Africa." *Journal of Theology for Southern Africa*, no. 51: 37–50.
Coote, R. B. 1981. *Amos among the Prophets: Composition and Theology*. Eugene, Ore.: Wipf and Stock.
Croatto, J. S. 1987. *Biblical Hermeneutics: Toward a Theory of Reading as the Production of Meaning*. Maryknoll, N.Y.: Orbis.
Eagleton, T. 1978. *Criticism and Ideology: A Study in Marxist Literary Theory*. London: Verso.
———. 1981. *Walter Benjamin; or, Towards a Revolutionary Criticism*. London: Verso.
Frostin, P. 1988. *Liberation Theology in Tanzania and South Africa: A First World Interpretation*. Lund: Lund University Press.
Gottwald, N. K. 1985. *The Hebrew Bible: A Socio-Literary Introduction*. Philadelphia: Fortress.

————. 1999. *The Tribes of Yahweh: A Sociology of the Religion of Liberated Israel, 1250–1050 BCE.* Sheffield: Sheffield Academic Press.

Govender, S. 1987. *In Search of Tomorrow: The Dialogue between Black Theology and Marxism in South Africa.* Kampen, Neth.: J. H. Kok.

Gutiérrez, G. 1973. *A Theology of Liberation: History, Politics and Salvation.* Maryknoll, N.Y.: Orbis.

Hall, S. 1980. "Encoding/Decoding." In *Culture, Media and Language: Working Papers in Cultural Studies, 1972–79*, ed. S. Hall. London: Routledge.

Hart, G. 2013. *Rethinking the South African Crisis: Nationalism, Populism, Hegemony.* Pietermaritzburg, S. Afr.: University of KwaZulu-Natal.

Helliker, K., and P. Vale. 2013. "Marxisms Past and Present." *Thesis Eleven* 115 (1): 25–42. https://doi.org/10.1177/0725513612470532.

Jobling, D. 2005. "'Very Limited Ideological Options': Marxism and Biblical Studies in Postcolonial Scenes." In *Postcolonial Biblical Criticism: Interdisciplinary Intersections*, ed. S. D. Moore and F. F. Segovia, 184–201. London: T&T Clark.

Johnson, R., C. Critcher, and J. Clarke. 1980. *Working-Class Culture: Studies in History and Theory.* London: Hutchinson.

Kairos Theologians. 1985. *The Kairos Document: Challenge to the Church; A Theological Comment on the Political Crisis in South Africa.* Braamfontein, S. Afr.: The Kairos Theologians.

Marx, K. 2010. Introduction to *Contribution to the Critique of Hegel's Philosophy of Law.* In vol. 3 of *Collected Works*, by K. Marx and F. Engels, 175–87. London: Lawrence and Wishart.

Marx, K., and F. Engels. 1970. *The German Ideology.* London: Lawrence and Wishart.

Mbembe, A. 2001. *On the Postcolony.* Berkeley: University of California Press.

Mbiti, J. S. 1979. "The Biblical Basis for Present Trends in African Theology." In *African Theology en Route: Papers from the Pan-African Conference of Third World Theologians*, ed. K. Appiah-Kubi and S. Torres, 83–94. Maryknoll, N.Y.: Orbis.

Mesters, C. n.d. *God's Project.* Cape Town: Theology Exchange Programme.

Mofokeng, T. 1988. "Black Christians, the Bible and Liberation." *Journal of Black Theology* 2 (1): 34–42.

Mosala, I. J. 1985. "African Independent Churches: A Study in Socio-theological Protest." In *Resistance and Hope: South African Essays in Honour of Beyers Naude*, ed. C. Villa-Vicencio and J. W. De Gruchy, 103–11. Cape Town: David Philips.

————. 1986a. "The Relevance of African Traditional Religions and Their Challenge to Black Theology." In *The Unquestionable Right to Be Free: Essays in Black Theology*, ed. I. J. Mosala and B. Tlhagale, 91–100. Johannesburg: Skotaville.

————. 1986b. "The Use of the Bible in Black Theology." In *The Unquestionable Right to Be Free: Essays in Black Theology*, ed. I. J. Mosala and B. Tlhagale, 175–99. Johannesburg: Skotaville.

————. 1989a. *Biblical Hermeneutics and Black Theology in South Africa.* Grand Rapids, Mich.: Eerdmans.

————. 1989b. "Race, Class, and Gender as Hermeneutical Factors in the African Independent Churches." Unpublished report to the Human Sciences Research Council.

————. 1996. "Race, Class, and Gender as Hermeneutical Factors in the African Independent Churches' Appropriation of the Bible." *Semeia*, no. 73: 43–57.

Nzimande, M. K. 2008. "Reconfiguring Jezebel: A Postcolonial *Imbokodo* Reading of the Story of Naboth's Vineyard (1 Kings 21:1–16)." In *African and European Readers of the Bible in Dialogue: In Quest of a Shared Meaning*, ed. H. de Wit and G. O. West, 223–58. Leiden: Brill.

Pleins, D. J. 2001. *The Social Visions of the Hebrew Bible: A Theological Introduction.* Louisville, Ky.: Westminster John Knox.

Ramantswana, H. 2016. "Decolonising Biblical Hermeneutics in the (South) African Context." *Acta Theologica* 36, S24: S178–203. http://www.scielo.org.za/pdf/at/v36s24/11.pdf.

———. 2017. "Decolonial Reflection on the Landlessness of the Levites." *Journal of Theology for Southern Africa*, no. 158: 72–91.

Rehmann, J. 2013. "Can Marx's Critique of Religion Be Freed from Its Fetters?" *Journal of Theology for Southern Africa*, no. 147: 5–15.

Römer, T. 2013. "Redaction Criticism: Hebrew Bible." In *The Oxford Encyclopedia of Biblical Interpretation*, ed. S. L. McKenzie, 223–32. Oxford: Oxford University Press.

Schulman, N. 1993. "Conditions of Their Own Making: An Intellectual History of the Centre for Contemporary Cultural Studies at the University of Birmingham." *Canadian Journal of Communication* 18 (1). https://doi.org/10.22230/cjc.1993v18n1a717.

Scott, J. C. 1990. *Domination and the Arts of Resistance: Hidden Transcripts*. New Haven, Conn.: Yale University Press.

Terreblanche, S. 2002. *A History of Inequality in South Africa, 1652–2002*. Pietermaritzburg, S. Afr.: University of Natal Press.

Tlhagale, B. 1985. "Culture in an Apartheid Society." *Journal of Theology for Southern Africa*, no. 51: 27–36.

Tutu, D. 1979a. "Black Theology/African Theology: Soulmates or Antagonists?" In *Black Theology: A Documentary History, 1966–1979*, ed. G. S. Wilmore and J. H. Cone, 385–92. Maryknoll, N.Y.: Orbis.

———. 1979b. "The Theology of Liberation in Africa." In *African Theology en Route: Papers from the Pan-African Conference of Third World Theologians*, ed. K. Appiah-Kubi and S. Torres. Maryknoll, N.Y.: Orbis.

Vellem, V. S. 2013. "Ecumenicity and a Black Theology of Liberation." In *South African Perspectives on Notions and Forms of Ecumenicity*, ed. E. M. Conradie, 173–84. Stellenbosch, S. Afr.: Sun.

West, C. 1984. "Religion and the Left: An Introduction." *Monthly Review* 36 (3): 9–19.

West, G. O. 1995. *Biblical Hermeneutics of Liberation: Modes of Reading the Bible in the South African Context*. 2d ed. Maryknoll, N.Y.: Orbis.

———. 2004. "Explicating Domination and Resistance: A Dialogue between James C. Scott and Biblical Scholars." In *Hidden Transcripts and the Arts of Resistance: Applying the Work of James C. Scott to Jesus and Paul*, ed. R. A. Horsley, 173–94. Atlanta: Society of Biblical Literature.

———. 2009. "The Not So Silent Citizen: Hearing Embodied Theology in the Context of HIV and AIDS in South Africa." In *Heterotopic Citizen: New Research on Religious Work for the Disadvantaged*, ed. T. Wyller, 23–42. Göttingen, Ger.: Vandenhoeck and Ruprecht.

———. 2011. "Newsprint Theology: Bible in the Context of HIV and AIDS." In *Out of Place: Doing Theology on the Crosscultural Brink*, ed. J. Havea and C. Pearson, 161–86. London: Equinox.

———. 2016. *The Stolen Bible: From Tool of Imperialism to African Icon*. Leiden: Brill.

———. 2019. "Scripture as a Site of Struggle: Literary and Socio-historical Resources for Prophetic Theology in Post-Colonial, Post-Apartheid (Neo-colonial?) South Africa." In *Scripture and Resistance*, ed. J. Havea, 149–63. New York: Lexington Books.

Wittenberg, G. H. 2007. *Resistance Theology in the Old Testament: Collected Essays*. Pietermaritzburg, S. Afr.: Cluster.

Inner Life, Politics, and the Secular: Is There a "Spirituality" of Subalterns and Dalits? Notes on Gramsci and Ambedkar

Cosimo Zene

When discussing the plight of subaltern groups, scholars often underline the economic and material troubles suffered by "the poor" through the perpetration of unjust exploitation, unequal distribution of wealth, and more generally, their being subjected to abuse and violence. This narrative frequently includes the means put in place by subalterns to regain a share of power, but the idea of "inner life" or "spirituality" has hardly been considered as part of the process through which subalterns express their agency so as to attain recognition of their "full humanity." A closer analysis of Gramsci's Notebook 11 and other works, however, highlights the relevance of an innovative, transforming, and immanent "spirituality" that necessarily reflects the historical experience of subaltern groups. This is further emphasized by the writings and activity of the Dalit leader B. R. Ambedkar.

It remains to be seen whether one can use the term "religion" when referring to a faith that does not have a personal god for an object but only impersonal or indeterminate forces.

—Antonio Gramsci, *Prison Notebooks*

Reflecting on literary criticism concerning Tolstoy, Shakespeare, and Manzoni, Gramsci (Q23§51, 1975, 2244–6; emphasis added) notes in his *Prison Notebooks* that "in the novel *The Betrothed* there is not one common person [*popolano*] who is not teased or laughed at ... They are depicted as wretched, narrow minded and *with no inner life* [*senza vita interiore*]. Only the nobles have an inner life." The concept of "inner life"—or *vita interiore* and *vita spirituale*—in fact can be translated as "spirituality" or "the life of the Spirit." While it seems to be firmly rooted in Christian theology, one must remember that this concept was already present within Greek philosophy. Following the Enlightenment, Western philosophers made reference to "the spirit," in a sense reappropriating what theology had "borrowed"; this is the case with Hegel's *Phänomenologie des Geistes* and also with Croce's idealist "philosophy of spirit." The ambiguity, however, between a human, immanent "spirit" and a theological, eternal "Spirit" has remained and still troubles our understanding and interpretation of human history.

For the purpose of our discussion, following a brief clarification of concepts, we must return to Gramsci's initial reflection so as to ascertain its validity within a specific milieu; rather than negating the existence of an inner life for nobles, Gramsci seems to vindicate the presence of an inner life for common persons—the people (*popolani*), the masses, the "simple" (*i semplici*). A first basic question must be addressed, however: why would Gramsci defend the concept of inner life per se, extending it to the masses? As a committed historical materialist, he might have simply dismissed this idea altogether, unless his understanding of inner life had something worth pursuing, notwithstanding substantial differences from both a transcendental and an idealist position. My contention is that, in fact, not only did Gramsci offer us an alternative reading of inner life but, by considering subalterns as worthy of an inner life, he also made a bold statement with revolutionary repercussions, even if today it might seem that he was stating the obvious. In order to make my point more transparent, in the second part of my essay I will extend Gramsci's assertion to those groups of people who nowadays find themselves in the very precarious position of being considered unworthy and perhaps even ontologically unable to possess an inner life: the (ex-)Untouchables or Dalits of southern Asia. A reflection on the work and thought of the Dalit leader B. R. Ambedkar will provide further evidence of a particular kind of spirituality of the subalterns.

A second question is: Why might subalterns and Dalits—the masses, the "simple"— expect or indeed demand that others recognize their having an inner life or spirituality? Are they really concerned with this, or is it rather an "intellectual" preoccupation of scholars? On the one hand, it seems clear that subalterns affirm their spirituality despite what others might think, since they simply get on with living their spirituality as part of their daily lives. On the other hand, when they become conscious of the plain refusal by others to acknowledge their spirituality, subalterns seem to insist on asserting it and making it more manifest. The reasons behind this affirmation, which springs out of self-awareness (*consapevolezza*, in Gramscian terms), must lie in the motivations offered by authors, considered in this essay, who lend their voice to all subalterns and who themselves speak as subalterns in order to affirm one fundamental truth: if inner life and spirituality represent one of the highest peaks of human achievement, then subalterns—as humans—cannot be excluded from contributing to and being an integral part of this highest accomplishment. At stake here is the primary recognition that subalterns, though "at the margins of history," should not be deprived of being considered fully human, with all the dignity and even the nobility that this implies.

It is now widely accepted that spirituality, having overcome the boundaries of Christianity, is present in all religions to the point of becoming a relevant trait of interreligious dialog, thus also prompting "inter-spirituality" (Sheldrake 2012). It is equally recognized that spirituality is also present in nonreligious contexts, hence giving origin to secular spiritualities that mostly underline the historical, philosophical, and sociological aspects of spiritual life and experience. Without disregarding the many commonalities between religion and spirituality, the present essay intends to privilege the secular aspect of spirituality for two main reasons.

First, while religion as such seems to fall under the control of those in power—religious and state power, including civil society—secular spirituality allows for a possible negotiation of power. In other words, while state hegemonic power can be exercised in the name of "religion" (through sanctions, laws, hierarchy, etc.), secular spirituality tends to escape this control, and for this very reason, hegemonic power wishes to appropriate and domesticate the "spirituality of subalterns."

Second, while there is a tendency to interpret spirituality as an individual pursuit, thus adopting the singularizing hermeneutics of those in power, I envision secular spirituality as a unifying moment and group/community effort to achieve group/class consciousness. As I will clarify, this is particularly true for subalterns and Dalits, for whom a real hope-salvation-future can be achieved mainly as a group, hardly ever as individuals, but also collaborating with other groups rather than remaining confined to one single community. Both Ambedkar and Gramsci strive to achieve this deeper meaning of an innovative, transforming, and immanent spirituality, which necessarily reflects the historical experiences of subaltern groups. Moreover, while both are opposed to the type of (often official) religion that enslaves subalterns with the promise of a future salvation, they are not ready to give up the human spirit that can animate creativity as a source of present-day transformation and new politics, especially for those excluded from transformative processes.

Discussing spirituality and the secular in China and India, Peter van der Veer (2013, 9) recently highlighted the role of Western modernity in shaping the spirituality of these two countries along the lines of what he calls the "syntagmatic chain of religion-magic-secularity-spirituality." Although in general terms I would agree with the relevance of this "chain," I also maintain that it materializes differently according to the historical milieu of a given group. Even considering, as van der Veer does, both Gandhi and Tagore as towering figures of Indian spirituality, we must allow for alternative ways in which subalterns and Dalits conceive and express their own experience of spirituality.

The Immanence of "Spirituality"

The complementarity and opposition between the material and the spiritual aspects of human life and experience has had a long history in Western thought, and it can be summarized in the binomial *mythos* and *logos*, which appeared very early in Greek philosophy, with logos becoming the "Word of God" and being adopted by Christianity in order to convey its message to a Hellenistic audience. Although the "rationality" of logos seemed to prevail over both philosophy and theology, the tensions present in the binomial were still felt by Reformation authors, despite the imminent arrival of the Enlightenment and modernity. In fact, notwithstanding the efforts of both Greek philosophy and Christian thought, Christian authors were never able to totally dispense with mythos, not even when Aquinas adopted Aristotle's philosophy so as to translate the Christian message into philosophically reasoned discourse. This mood was emphatically captured by Nietzsche at the turn of the nineteenth century, with lasting effects well into the twentieth century.

At the very beginning of Western philosophy, we are told the mythical story of Plato's allegory of the cave, regarding the meaning of Sophia (or philosophical wisdom, as depicted in Gnostic mysticism) as the goddess of darkness "who inhabits the burning womb of the earth." However, "Sophia is later saved from the realm of

Chaos and ascends again to the heavens, [but] she remains ever faithful to the material world and so divides herself into two beings ... This contrast between wisdom as light and as darkness ... gives some more depth to how we conceive philosophical wisdom" (Krebs 2004, 142). This contrast, already acknowledged in Plato's cave, is still very much a part of our philosophical and also historical and contemporary political experience since "there is no *Logos* without *Mythos*" (Jez Butterworth, quoted in Martin 2014, 173; emphasis added). Regarding the politics of logos and mythos, I would propose here a general formula that will become more evident as we proceed into our discussion: it seems clear that while those in power aim at controlling the narrative of logos so as to exercise a rational authority, this can be achieved only by skillfully taking hold of the mythos of the masses and subalterns, which is then used to feed into and sustain the logos in power.

During the twentieth century, the Czech philosopher Jan Patočka (2002, 36), proposing a critical reading of Husserl's (1970) diagnosis of the European spiritual crisis, suggests a return to the prereflective stage of Greek philosophy found in the mythological framework so as to discover the roots of a meaningful philosophy in *"caring for the soul"* in order to make "the human world a world of truth and justice," notwithstanding the violence of the two world wars. In the midst of this brutal, inhuman experience, Patočka (1996, 131; last emphasis added) invites us to rediscover *"the solidarity of the shaken,"* positing an "anguishing question": "Why has this grandiose experience ... not had a decisive effect on the history of the twentieth century ... Why has it not unfolded its saving potential?" Patočka responds to this with a new, audacious metanoia: "Here we encounter the abysmal realm of the 'prayer for the enemy,' the phenomenon of 'loving those who hate us'—*the solidarity of the shaken* for all their contradiction and conflict." Within "an economic conception of history" involving "class struggle," Patočka maintains that this is "a struggle *in the sphere of freedom for broader access to freedom.*" Moreover, "If, though, the class struggle is not an economic but a *'spiritual'* and *'existential'* matter, then it cannot be isolated from other *spiritual dimensions* which erupt in the sphere of freedom. There is not only struggle but also solidarity, there is not only society, but also community, and community has other bonds besides a common enemy" (149; emphasis added).

Patočka died in March 1977 from a brain haemorrhage following exhausting interrogations by the Czechoslovak secret police, having protested against the communist government's infringement of human rights. Although it might seem contradictory to juxtapose Patočka and Gramsci, I am inclined to do so primarily because of their intellectual integrity and the way they both strived to make their philosophy socially meaningful, often favoring a heterodox or even heretical route to achieving this. Patočka's ideal of "care for the soul," revolving around truth and justice for humanity, moves toward a politically relevant philosophy able to propose a political model conducive to human freedom for a historically situated humanity. Despite substantial differences, Gramsci's "philosophy of praxis" moves in the same direction "from the standpoint of the materialist philosophy of history" (Patočka 1996, 154), particularly when compared to Patočka's *"social being* of humans": "With this interest, not solely in *being* but in *social being*, the Czech philosopher incorporates into his study of Husserl and Heidegger a Platonically inspired devotion to the reality of human beings in community—in other words, to politics" (Findley 2002, 5).

For the purpose of the present discussion, I am mostly concerned to highlight the deep interest both Patočka and Gramsci manifest in religion and related themes such as spirituality, not solely in general terms but as part of a human-lived and histor-ical experience. At a time when the idea of God was increasingly being abandoned, it became even more urgent to reaffirm those human, moral values that once rested on divine intervention and now were to be entirely entrusted to human commitment and responsibility in order for them to survive: "Patočka uses the term *spiritual* knowing full well that it does not 'sound pleasant today.' 'It sounds,' he continues, 'in some way spiritualist and we don't like such phrases nowadays: but does there exist a better expression for what I have in mind?'" (Findley 2002, 208).[1] In other words, on what grounds does the moral/ethical accountability supported by both Gramsci and Patočka rest? Are they postulating a different and new, humanistic and historical "spirituality"? And, returning to our initial question, is there a spirituality for the subaltern? Are we in a position to discover in the history of subaltern groups those "spiritual dimensions which erupt in the sphere of freedom" (Patočka 1996, 149)?

Gramsci betrays a perplexity similar to Patočka's when using the words "spirit" and "spiritual," as attested by an early expression written in a 19 March 1927 letter to his sister-in-law, Tania, when providing her with an outline of his entire project, which later became the *Prison Notebooks*. Having listed four main subjects—the first one being "a study of the formation of public spirit in Italy during the past century" (spec-ifying this as "a study of Italian intellectuals")[2]—Gramsci (1994, 1:82–6) proposes a common ground for the four topics, which he finds in the "creative spirit of the people (*spirito popolare creativo*) in its diverse stages and degrees of development, [which] is in equal measure at [the four subjects'] base."[3] This expression was never to reappear again either in the *Letters* or the *Notebooks*. Bringing to an end his reflection on this expression, Baratta (2003, 28–32) concludes that "it should be clear by now that, given the contradictory echoes it awakens, "creative spirit of the people" represents a conceptual gridlock, even though a suggestive one, because of its somehow blasphe-mous closeness to the romantic-idealistic tradition." However, before dismissing the concept altogether, Baratta seems keen to underline that the "creative spirit of the people" is "certainly a formulation not only bold but versatile ... clearly anti-Crocean, indeed even scandalous for Croce's conception of spirit, creativity, history" but with the danger nonetheless of being interpreted in either a neoromantic or populist fashion (29). Rather than abandoning this concept altogether, Baratta sustains that Gramsci in the *Notebooks* translates it—through a "reflection on philosophy"—into a new, revolutionary tool destined to open the way toward an "intellectual progress for the masses" promoted by the "collective intellectual," as we shall see below. In this sense, Baratta is right when he explains that the "creative spirit of the people" is a formulation that "represents the irruption of the 'subaltern social groups' ... into

1. Findley was here referring to Patočka's manuscript "The Spiritual Person and the Intellectual," which Findley himself had translated.
2. The remaining three subjects are: (1) a study of comparative linguistics, (2) a study of Pirandello's theatre and the transformation of Italian theatrical taste, and (3) an essay on the serial novel and popular tastes in literature.
3. I adopt here the translation of "*spirito popolare creativo*" given by R. Rosenthal (see Gramsci 1994, 80).

the venerable temple of spirit and culture," clearly referring to the philosophy of Croce and traditional Italian intellectuals (29). Equally revealing is the expression "popular spirit," which was used by the young Gramsci and which he was later to label as "folklore." Most importantly, in the very same letter to Tania of 19 March 1927, Gramsci (1994, 1:83; last emphasis added) expresses his desire "to do something *für ewig*": "I am obsessed (this is a phenomenon typical of people in jail, I think), by this idea: that I should do something *für ewig*, following a complex concept of Goethe's ... In short, in keeping with a pre-established program, I would like to concentrate intensely and systematically on some subject that would absorb and provide a center to my *inner life* [*la mia vita interiore*]." Given the closeness of this expression (*vita interiore*) to that used by Gramsci when criticizing Manzoni for denying an inner life to the common person ("the simple"), we must assume that Gramsci is here not solely claiming the right to *possession* of an inner life but is also *caring* for it (as in "caring for the soul") and giving weight to it with the systematic intensity of a prisoner. Later, while referring to his "very hasty and quite superficial essay on southern Italy" (Gramsci 1994, 1:83), he affirms again his desire "to fully develop in depth the thesis that I sketched out then, from a 'disinterested,' '*für ewig*' point of view."[4] As we shall see, the "cultivation of inner life" for Gramsci is not a private pursuit pertaining to the intellectual as an individual, but it rather becomes a task of his as a "collective thinker," so as to aid and promote the inner life of the masses by inviting them to develop new ways of thinking and new politics, as a common effort.

Although in the *Prison Notebooks*, as we have seen, Gramsci is very cautious regarding the use of terms such as "spirit" and "spiritual," given their ambivalence, the younger Gramsci, writing on "Socialism and Culture" in *Il Grido del Popolo* in 1916,[5] seems much less hesitant. Following a quote from Novalis—who talks about the "transcendental self" (*io trascendentale—io del proprio io*) and Vico's interpretation of Solon's and Socrates's dictum to "know thyself" (see also Q11§12, Gramsci 1975, 1376; 1971, 324) in relation to human equality between plebeians and nobles[6]—Gramsci (2000, 57; first emphasis added) starts to define culture in relation to socialism as "organization, discipline of *one's inner self* [*proprio io interiore*], a coming to terms with one's own personality," and as the role of "one's own will" in shaping culture since "above all, *man is mind* [*spirito*], i.e. he is a product of history, not nature."

"Mind" is rather weak when compared to "spirito" in the original. This tells us that, for Gramsci, the attainment by humanity of a (socialist) consciousness is an eminently "spiritual" enterprise. But in order to achieve this fully (as humanity), we must

---

4. As Frank Rosengarten has rightly pointed out, "disinterested" here does not mean the achievement of a "serene and 'olympian' detachment from immediate concerns" but a "more comprehensive ... frame of reference for his studies than his early political and journalistic writing could have afforded" (see Gramsci 1994, 85–6n3).

5. See "Socialismo e Cultura," *Il Grido del Popolo*, 29 January 1916. Gramsci signed this article "Alfa Gamma." I would like to thank Marcus Green for reminding me about this relevant short article.

6. "Vico maintains that in this dictum Solon wished to admonish the plebeians, who believed themselves to be of bestial origin and the nobility to be of divine origin, to reflect on themselves and see that they had the same human nature as the nobles and hence should claim to be their equals in civil law. Vico then points to this consciousness of *human equality* between plebeians and nobles as the basis and historical reason for the rise of the democratic republics of antiquity" (Gramsci 2000, 56).

recognize the presence of this very "spirit" within subaltern (plebeian) groups as the "fighting spirit" of historical achievement (and not of nature—a given interpretation of nature is what makes these groups "untouchables"!). This of course comes to life all the stronger in the empirical experience offered by Ambedkar and other Dalits.

"All Men Are Philosophers":
Language, Common Sense, Religion, and Folklore

Gramsci does not provide a systematic or direct answer to the question raised at the beginning of our discussion concerning the *vita interiore* or spirituality of subalterns. We can nevertheless find—especially in the *Notebooks*—scattered notes and memos, at times in aphoristic form, intended for further expansion. This is the case of Notebook 8, §204, in which Gramsci sets down some general principles in preparation for "an introduction to the study of philosophy." He remarks that "one must destroy the prejudice that philosophy is a difficult thing just because it is the specific activity of a particular category of learned people, of professionals or systematic philosophers. It is therefore necessary to show that all men are philosophers, by defining the characteristics of this ['spontaneous'] philosophy that is 'everyone's,' namely, common sense and religion" (Q8§204, Gramsci 1975, 1063; 2007, 351–2).

In Notebook 11, §12, Gramsci (Q8§204, 1975, 1063; title translation mine; see also Gramsci 1971, 323) resumes the argument with "Notes for an introduction and an approach to the study of philosophy and the history of culture," thus making a relevant connection and adding that "this philosophy is contained in: 1. language itself, which is a totality of determined notions and concepts and not just of words grammatically devoid of content; 2. 'common sense' and 'good sense'; 3. popular religion and, therefore, also in the entire system of beliefs, superstitions, opinions, ways of seeing things and of acting [*modi di vedere e di operare*], which are collectively bundled together under the name of 'folklore.'"[7] With this added explanation, not only does Gramsci clarify further his notion of all people being philosophers but he places this philosophy within three interconnected spheres of everyday life: namely, language, common sense, and religion/folklore.[8]

Gramsci further elaborates on this by addressing the points enunciated in Notebook 8, starting with the movement from a spontaneous, passive, and nonreflective "intellectual activity" to one characterized by critique and self-awareness (*consapevolezza*). In the four notes following the introduction, Gramsci (Q11§12, 1975, 1376–8; 1971, 324–5) delves into the starting point of critical elaboration,[9] the contextual historicity of this process

7. I am using here the translation found in *Selections from the Prison Notebooks* (Gramsci 1971) but use text markers to refer to the original critical edition of the *Quaderni* (Gramsci 1975).
8. If we expand the role of language, common sense, religion, and "the whole system of beliefs," including also folklore, all of these become different languages through which people—the masses—express themselves. Gramsci's (Q11§13, 1975, 1396; 1971, 323) effort here is to understand and explain the place of these languages in relation to philosophy and in particular to the "philosophy of praxis," given that common sense is the "philosophy of non-philosophers" and as such "is the 'folklore' of philosophy, and like folklore presents itself in many shapes and forms."
9. "The starting-point of critical elaboration, the historicity of this process, which is 'the consciousness of what one really is,' and is 'knowing thyself' as a product of the historical process to date which has

("the real present world"), the role of language and dialect in shaping a conception of the world, and the "creation of a new culture" as a "philosophical event" shared by the masses. While reclaiming the supremacy of philosophy over common sense and religion, Gramsci advocates a "secular sense of a unity of faith"—perhaps defined as ideology or even politics?—as opposed to confessional religion.[10] This is reflected also in the relationship between science, religion, and common sense, and in the discrepancy found in "institutional philosophy" between "thought and action." For this very reason, for Gramsci, "Philosophy cannot be divorced from politics."

Gramsci (QII§12, 1975, 1379; 1971, 326) is keen to provide an explanation for his almost aphoristic affirmations—"Philosophy in general does not in fact exist. Various philosophies or conceptions of the world exist," he writes—and for how this can be clarified by analyzing the history of philosophy: "How it happens that in all periods there coexist many systems and currents of philosophical thought, how these currents are born, how they are diffused, and why in the process of diffusion they fracture along certain lines and in certain directions." Gramsci recovers also the "popular image of philosophy" present in the "healthy nucleus that exists in common sense" by addressing the central question of the "ideological unity" between the philosophy of restricted intellectual groups and that of "the mass of the simple," which Gramsci finds epitomized in "the strength of religions, and of the Catholic Church in particular," since "the Roman Church has always been the most vigorous in the struggle to prevent the 'official' formation of two religions, one for the 'intellectuals' and the other for the 'simple souls,'" although success has not always been the sole outcome of this struggle.[11] Gramsci laments, however, the failure of "immanentist philosophies" to "create an ideological unity between the bottom and the top, between the 'simple' and the intellectuals" and for their not "constituting [rather] a cultural and social bloc," not solely in Italy but "on a European scale" following either the Renaissance or the Reformation.

In other words, Gramsci (QII§12, 1975, 1382; 1971, 330; emphasis added) opposes "a specialised culture among restricted intellectual groups" in favor of one that, while overcoming common sense, "never forgets to remain in contact with the 'simple' and indeed finds in this contact the source of the problems it sets out to study and to resolve" since "only by this contact does a philosophy become 'historical,' purify itself of intellectualist elements of an individual character and become 'life.'" While Gramsci recognizes the role of the intellectual effort of the individual philosopher, the latter is invited to practice philosophy starting from common sense—as a "diffuse, uncoordinated ... generic form of thought common to a particular period and a particular popular environment"—because this common sense "is connected to and implicit in practical life, and elaborating it so that it becomes a *renewed common sense* possessing the coherence

deposited in you an infinity of traces, without leaving an inventory. Such an inventory must therefore be made at the outset" (QII§12, Gramsci 1975, 1376; 1971, 324).

10. "Note the problem of religion taken not in the confessional sense but in the secular sense of a unity of faith between a conception of the world and a corresponding norm of conduct. But why call this unity of faith 'religion' and not 'ideology', or even 'politics'?" (QII§12, Gramsci 1975, 1378; 1971, 326).

11. Gramsci is here referring mainly to the Italian experience. In this respect, his reflection on the role of the Jesuits in establishing a connection between "intellectuals and the simple" still seems pertinent today, given the presence of a very active "Jesuit pope" (see QII§12, Gramsci 1975, 1381; 1971, 329).

and the sinew of individual philosophies. *But this can only happen if the demands of cultural contact with the 'simple' are continually felt."*

There is no doubt that Gramsci was fully aware—albeit confined in a Fascist prison —of his contingent role as party leader, intent at formulating plans for the success of his party. In his planning, nevertheless, he was looking beyond an immediate victory for the philosophy of praxis while searching for the deeper causes of intellectual, philosophical, and political failures that prevent the progress of a genuine democratic process. While the philosophy of praxis presents itself as a criticism to both common sense and the philosophy of intellectuals, Gramsci lamented "the absence of a history of common sense" and thus having to rely solely on the evidence of the history of philosophy. His effort, however, was to provide at least a component of the history of common sense by discussing the example of religion, religious institutions, and in particular the Catholic Church: "The relation between common sense and the upper level of philosophy is assured by 'politics,' just as it is politics that assures the relationship between the Catholicism of the intellectuals and that of the 'simple'" (QII§12, Gramsci 1975, 1383; 1971, 331). Gramsci promptly remarks that the Church must respond to the "split in the community of the 'faithful,'" that the Church "does not even envisage such a task," and that in the past such divisions were healed by mass movements and "the creation of religious orders centred on strong personalities (Dominic, Frances)."[12]

In the remainder of Notebook II, Gramsci (QII§12, 1975, 1388; 1971, 336) tackles the necessary unity of theory and practice—still "at an early stage" within the philosophy of praxis—the role of the intellectuals in this process, a possible loss of contact with the masses, and the danger of a "deterministic, fatalistic or mechanistic element" as a "direct ideological 'aroma' emanating from the philosophy of praxis, rather like religion or drugs." Notwithstanding the fact that Gramsci, as others before and after him, hoped for a more rapid overcoming of "common sense/religion" by the masses through a process of historical self-awareness, he kept returning to reflections on Christianity, both in relation to the popular masses and to the role of Christian intellectuals and also to make use of religious vocabulary and metaphors while hoping to overcome them. In fact, according to Gramsci, the "intellectual position of the man-of-the-people [*uomo del popolo*] ... is determined not by reason but by faith," so that "in the masses *as such*, philosophy can only be experienced as a faith," albeit a faith "in the social group to which [one] belongs" (1391; 339). But if the end result is the overcoming of common sense and religion, these still remain, in the majority of cases, as unavoidable in the path ahead, given that the tension is toward the creation of "elites of intellectuals of a new type which arise directly out of the masses [those very masses imbued with common sense and religion], but remain in contact with them to become, as it were, the whalebone in the corset." Although the "culmination of this process can be a great individual philosopher," the optimum result of this Gramscian project is brought to fruition solely

---

12. Undoubtedly Gramsci would have welcomed and assessed the role of such movements as Latin American liberation theology, which was initially promoted by local intellectuals but soon became widespread among the "faithful" and "the mass of the simple," taking the illustrative name of "Ecclesial (Christian) Base Communities."

by a "collective thinker" who "must be capable of re-living concretely the demands of the massive ideological community" (1392; 340).

Elsewhere Gramsci (Q4§33, 1996, 173) explains in more depth the idea-experience of the collective thinker's "re-living concretely" when addressing "the passage from *knowing* to *understanding* to *feeling* and vice versa":

> The error of the intellectual consists in believing that one can *know* without understanding and, above all, without feeling or being impassioned [*essere appassionato*]: in other words, that the intellectual can be an intellectual if he is distinct and detached from the people. One cannot make history-politics without passion, that is, without being emotionally tied to the people, without feeling the rudimentary passions of the people, understanding them and hence explaining [and justifying] them in the specific historical situation and linking them dialectically to the laws of history, that is, to a scientifically elaborated superior conception of the world: namely, "knowledge."

Further down in this passage, Gramsci clarifies this "organic attachment in which impassioned sentiment becomes understanding and hence knowledge (not mechanically but in a living manner)." It is precisely in this "journey through experience and back" that the Gramscian intellectual encounters and comes to terms with the "spirituality of the masses of the simple" and the subalterns. To be properly substantiated, this statement should be supported by a further reflection on at least two major sources: first is Notebook 25, "At the Margins of History," in which Gramsci (Q25§1, 1975, 2279–83) discusses "the history of subaltern social groups," as he specifies in the subtitle, starting with section 1, "the drama of Lazzaretti" and his religious movement, which flourished in Tuscany in the 1860s; and second is Notebook 27, "Observations on 'Folklore'" (see Boninelli 2007), so as to develop what was said above on folklore as part of "popular religion and systems of beliefs" given that "folklore should not be conceived as bizarre, an oddity and a picturesque element, but as something that is very serious and should be taken seriously" (Q27§1, Gramsci 1975, 2314; 2000, 360–2).

Only lack of space prevents me from illustrating here my reflections thus far through the contribution of the Italian ethnographer and anthropologist Ernesto de Martino (1908–65). It suffices to underline how de Martino "succeeds in gathering the critical, dialogical and fruitful validity of Gramscian thought" and "the propulsive originality of the Gramscian laboratory on Italy" (Pizza 2013, 85).[13] Among the themes discussed by de Martino are "the problem of the relationship between Marxism and religion"; the Gramscian "creative Marxism" present within the "living tradition" of the working class; new parameters in interpreting folklore and popular traditions; and above all, "a new dimension of the southern question" as attested by de Martino (2005, 13) in *The Land of Remorse*: "In a wider sense, *La Terra del rimorso* is our whole planet, or at least that part which has entered into its bad past." As far as the present essay is concerned, Pizza's findings regarding a novel interpretation of the southern question originating from de Martino's own "south" can only confirm that

---

13. Pizza's (2013) article "Gramsci e de Martino: Appunti per una riflessione" has been reprinted and expanded in *Il tarantismo oggi: Antropologia, politica, cultura* (Pizza 2015).

the incorporation of the "many souths of the planet" is not a forcing of the Gramscian text.

A further comparison, between Gramsci and Durkheim—proposed by Massimo Rosati (2013) and aided by Bruno Karsenti's (2012) work—would also bring interesting developments to our discussion. But this too must be postponed. Besides a generalized interest in religion as a social fact, Durkheim and Gramsci share many other conceptual constructs that, notwithstanding many differences and styles of approach, point toward the achievement of a human freedom and emancipation that fundamentally resides within the "thinking person" being motivated by society. If we can appreciate a more speculative instance in Durkheim, we can certainly recognize a similar component in Gramsci's motivation to value the unity of thought and action in his formulation of the philosophy of praxis and of the role of the collective, organic thinker, albeit within a more direct political stance in Gramsci's case. For both, however, the force for transformation springs out of us as social, thinking beings. There is no external force that motivates our ability to form concepts since, according to Durkheim, "The force is created by us ... because of the mere fact that we are thinking beings. It is transcendence, but transcendence within immanence. Society is we ourselves as thinking beings, that is we ourselves *spiritually*" (Karsenti 2012, 424).

B. R. Ambedkar and Dalit Spirituality

So far, following Gramsci's dissent against Manzoni for not recognizing the presence of an inner life for common people, I have sketched a brief development of the concept of the spiritual/spirituality as interlinked with the Greek ideas of logos and mythos. Although appropriated by Christian theology, this concept returned to philosophy with the Enlightenment and modernity. Closer to our historical milieu, I have briefly highlighted the "spiritual crisis in Europe" as portrayed by Nietzsche and Husserl and have emphasized Patočka's "care for the soul" and "solidarity of the shaken." With a reflection on Notebook 11 I have attempted to substantiate Gramsci's translation of the "inner life" as the task of the "collective thinker" who, starting from and challenging common sense, religion, and folklore, endeavors to motivate the masses—the "simple" and the subaltern—to actively participate in the creation of new and emancipatory ways of thinking. The anthropological work of de Martino, particularly in southern Italy, provides a striking example of the Gramscian attempt.

In this final part, I would like to illustrate what has been discussed thus far through the experiences of Dalit groups, and in particular one of their acclaimed leaders, B. R. Ambedkar. My early work on ex-Untouchables/Dalits—the Rishi of Bengal/Bangladesh[14]—provides me with useful insights into the multilayered meanings of their experiences of untouchability and of the responses offered by them to overcome it. While the Rishi counter "religious exclusion" (e.g., injunctions against temple entry) with varied religious imagery (e.g., building their own temples, celebrating separate *pujas*, having their own priests and gurus), their final target is to achieve recognition as

14. This group, known all over Bengal and Bangladesh as Muchi-Rishi, are by tradition leatherworkers, cobblers, and musicians.

"humans" (see Zene 2000) with entitlement to human dignity. In other words, the interdiction imposed on the Rishi "not to enter the temple," as the most visible injunction that prevents them from accessing or getting "closer to the deity," represents for them the sum of all other exclusions: from social and public life, from education, from politics, from the economy, from intermarriage with other castes—in short, from "belonging to one society," or in Gramsci's words, being relegated "to the margins of history." Even though some extreme cases of exclusion have disappeared, what remains—despite the abolition and hence illegality of "untouchability"—is a generalized attitude attached to everyday experiences that a given group is de facto considered and hence treated as untouchable. Should even all traits of being untouchable disappear, the stigma—and hence continuous humiliation—both for individuals and communities is nevertheless hard to kill. The variety of names used to designate untouchability gives evidence of its ubiquity in all spheres of life.[15] It is, however, the initial overriding scriptural and religious sanction of untouchability that governs and motivates all other aspects, although our terms religious/religion fall short when trying to encapsulate and render the idea of *dharma* as the principle or law governing the whole universe but also as individual and group moral conduct conforming to this principle and the resulting obligations with respect to caste (*varna*), social custom, and civil and religious law.

From a Hindu perspective, this is better understood as *Sanatana Dharma*, or "eternal dharma," as opposed to religion as such, as a mere human endeavor. On the other hand, the totality of dharma is certainly closer to the idea of religion as a (total) social phenomenon, as underlined by Durkheim, and to the conjunction of "religion, common sense and philosophy," as expressed by Gramsci. Be that as it may, the Rishi's experiences of exclusion (as untouchables, impure, polluted, etc.) is felt primarily at the level of dharma since their a-dharmic status is the basis of the nonrecognition of their being human. All other exclusions are but a consequence of this primary permanent state of exception. Hence their determination to return to the "one *dharma*," which foretells the "oneness of humanity." Prevented from belonging to the Hindu community except as outcastes, outlaws, and outsiders, they have reverted to a foreign religion that, ideologically, allows them to be considered human.

The Rishi search for a humanity to be recognized ("We too are humans!") has guided most of my subsequent historical and anthropological research into the group's experience and in particular into their "conversion" to Christianity (Zene 2002). Expanding on this, in a more recent article (Zene 2007) I have discussed the role of myth and myth-making in the formation of the group's identity, drawing on a set of myths that purport a caste ideology according to which the Rishi in the past belonged to a noble caste who supposedly were the descendants of the very compilers of the Vedas. But their greed relegated them to the rank of skinners and leatherworkers. While recounting these myths, the Rishi themselves seem to abide to this interpretation, allegedly expressing a consensus to this hegemonic ideology. But another set of myths composed around the figure of Ruidas maintains that the Rishi and other ex-Untouchables were tricked and deprived of humanity and dignity by dominant groups in society. Although

---

15. "Untouchable" is the equivalent of the Sanskrit *asprsya* (*acchut* in Hindi). Another term, popularized by Gandhi, is *Harijan* (child of Hari/Vishnu). This was refused by Ambedkar, who preferred instead the name Dalit (crushed, oppressed).

recounted in the sphere of mythos, their struggle to regain human dignity does not dispense with logos but returns to its rational, secular, and historical dimensions without trivializing the power of dharma. Thus, "The idiom of religion and myth becomes for these ex-Untouchables and subaltern groups a 'place of resistance' from which they can hope to better themselves also in the economic, social and political spheres, as part of their overall endeavour to achieve full human dignity" (Zene 2007, 257).

Most recently, a group of colleagues and I in a common reflection on the Gramsci-Ambedkar encounter uncovered how Rishi political philosophies provide viable answers to the many questions posited by the shared plea of those at the margins of history (Zene 2013). Our common reflection has perhaps only managed to scratch at the surface of this "improbable encounter," but some unexpected hints have come to light. One of these can be found in the interconnection and multilayered dialog between Marx's (1978) "Jewish question," Gramsci's "southern question," and Ambedkar's "caste/Dalit question," which "above and beyond their specific milieus, are questions related by the substantive (even ontological) question of 'recognition' as a task for global ethics and philosophy" (5). Following the common thread of emancipation within all three questions, "The Jews become a metaphor for all (*political*) subalterns ... southern peasants turn out to be a metaphor for all (*territorial*) subalterns ... with Dalits becoming a metaphor for all (*social*) subalterns" (6). While "in all three cases we obtain universal metaphors, respectively of political, territorial and social subalternity"—which reflect a specific milieu, the political-historical—territorial and social subalternity are mostly common to all subaltern groups.

In the remainder of this discussion, I would like to concentrate on Ambedkar's role as a Dalit leader in promoting "people's emancipation as auto-emancipation" and his understanding of the religious question as part of the solution for the emancipation of Dalits and other subaltern groups. "Emancipation' stands here for the attainment of an indispensable human freedom that can guarantee full human dignity across the spectrum of human history, experience, and everyday life. Prior to moving into these considerations, however, I must also specify that the status of universality attributed to the three "questions" does not divest them of their singularity and specificity as questions that developed in a distinct social, historical, and geographical milieu concerning very concrete human groups. This is better explained by recourse to Walter Benjamin's (1968) concept of "monadological universality" as "that universality which consists in valuing as absolute each singularity [and] constitutes a colossal undertaking that goes against all the established and dominant conventions" (Mate 2001, 258), bearing in mind that "in order to reconstruct the whole, in order to advance towards [monadological] universality, the *language of the slave* is fundamental and irreplaceable" (261; emphasis added). The slave, even beyond a sociological and historical subject, stands here as a metaphor for all those excluded from or at the margins of history, whose voices are not present within a "universal history," thus representing an example of "bad, inadequate universality."

From this perspective, Ambedkar's attention to the voice of Dalits and other subaltern groups contributes to the extension of the "southern question" being applied by de Martino to the "many souths of the world." At the same time, the "caste/Dalit question" raised by Ambedkar is not a peripheral question being absorbed into wider questions (Jewish and southern) but a question that complements and clarifies the two previous questions since caste/untouchability pushes to the limit the quest for recognition and emancipation, accentuates the role of religion, and becomes a paradigm for other subaltern groups even beyond the Indian subcontinent.

Although religion—in particular, ideological/theological and ritual dimensions—plays a relevant role when addressing the caste/Dalit question, Ambedkar sought to tackle the question from a multidimensional perspective. Even when his reply to the situation was embedded within a religious/ritual wrapping, as in the case of publicly burning copies of the Manusmṛti or when prompting Dalits to enter Hindu temples, as in 1930 at Nashik, Ambedkar made it clear that "it is not true that entry into Hindu temples will solve your whole problem. Our problem is very broad. It extends into the political, social, religious and economic spheres."[16] Using a term borrowed from Gandhi, satyagraha, but applying it to the Dalits' plea, Ambedkar challenges the violence still present within Gandhian nonviolence: "Today's satyagraha is a challenge to the Hindu mind. From this true satyagraha we shall see whether Hindu society is ready to treat us *as human beings*" (last emphasis added).[17] The end result of this action in the sphere of religion is not meant to achieve religious equality but rather human equality and full human dignity. In fact, "Ambedkar often resorted in his Marathi writings to the word *manuski*, in English translated as 'humanness'" (Jaffrelot 2005, 92). Ambedkar (quoted in Jaffrelot 2005, 50) is very specific when addressing the ineffectiveness of familiar religious rituals that in themselves do not contribute to the solution of the problem: "We know that the god in the temple is of stone. *Darsan* and *puja* will not solve our problems. But we will start out, and try to make a change in the minds of the Hindus."

The complexity of the situation when addressing the Dalit question (i.e., "the problem"), is abundantly reflected in the multidimensional paths followed by Ambedkar, both from a tactical and a scholarly point of view, and this produces a constant interchange between his roles as leader and political activist and in his relentless reflection and analysis of relevant issues, which again are approached from a variety of disciplinary standpoints but with only one main purpose in mind: the Dalit question. This is echoed by the many scholars who in discussion of Ambedkar's activity emphasize his commitment to a polyhedral methodological approach. Besides devising a social theory of religion that takes into account the sociology contemporary to his time—namely Marx, Weber, and Durkheim—Ambedkar underlines the shift from a utilitarian religion in antiquity to one based on justice during modernity, closer to the moral principles of liberty, equality, and fraternity.

With the intent to provide a critical analysis of Brahmanic Hindu religion (especially in "The Philosophy of Hinduism"), Ambedkar strongly establishes that modernity contributed to "the creation/formation of a religion that treats God as universal, dissociated from a particular tribe and nationality, and which contains an equalitarian and universal morality" (Omvedt 2004, 56). This allows him to address the pressing question of the

16. These excerpts are from a speech by Dr. B. R. Ambedkar, 2 March 1930, given at the Kala Ram Mandir in Nashik (Maharashtra) in the presence of fifteen thousand Dalits.
17. While Gandhi adopted satyagraha to fight British rule in India, he did not, according to Ambedkar, extend satyagraha to oppose the violence suffered by untouchables at the hands of caste Hindus. Hence Ambedkar's appeal for a "true *satyagraha*."

lack of social revolutions in India as a direct consequence of the religious imposition of the *chaturvarṇa* (the caste system) as an unjust and premodern moral code. Morality indeed becomes the real indispensable center within the concept of religion as Ambedkar expresses it, in particular in his vision and implementation of a "new" Buddhism. This is not a transcendental and ritualistic morality, however, but one rooted in a "secular and materialistic approach" and based on "scientific rationality" and "antimysticism" (Gokhale 2004, 124).

This, however, does not imply that spirituality is absent from this sound moral basis (126–8). In order to address the novelty of his approach to morality, religion and Buddhism, Fitzgerald (2004) proposes four main concepts that help to highlight Ambedkar's originality: (1) ritual as legitimation of power and hence as opposing "ritual institutions"; (2) politics as "connected to ideas about 'scientific' rationalism and social democracy"; (3) economics that is "embedded in caste hierarchy" and that supports "bonded labour as a form of slavery"; and (4) soteriology as "liberation from inequality and exploitation." Liberation, however, "is not merely individual, it is a social, collective concern, and it is given a distinctively political emphasis" (274). Fitzgerald recognizes also that for many followers of Ambedkar "soteriology is not only political and social activism ... but has an important 'spiritual' or transcendental element as well" (274–5). This is so much so that Fitzgerald needs to clarify that "the word 'spiritual' is unsatisfactory since its range of uses is so wide that it has no clear meaning. However, there is a sense which we all have that 'there is something more' to a situation, and, in the context of practices such as meditation, the sense of 'something more' that cannot be reduced to mundane experience or states of consciousness is significant and a powerful motivation" (281).

As we have seen, the word "spiritual" proved problematic also for Gramsci and Patočka. In Durkheim's case we could say that there is transcendence, "but a transcendence within immanence," when we consider ourselves as thinking beings: "that is we ourselves *spiritually*." Should we perhaps also divest the "practice of meditation" as a total ultramundane and solely transcendental experience to make it a very human and immanent activity, as in the case of the many "philosophical meditations" with which we are acquainted? But there is also another major issue to be taken into account, which brings us back to our initial question: when individuals in power, and as part of institutions of power, express the view that "the simple"—the masses, the subalterns, the Dalits—have no inner/spiritual life, they are not only trying to prevent the latter from attaining the highest level of human potential—the ability as finite beings to think the "infinite"—but they are also preventing them from attaining any other goal in life. In other words, the control over the (symbolic) power of the "spiritual," within both so-called religious but also secular societies, is extended to every other sphere of life, thus making it impossible to gain power without securing access to the spiritual as such.

This explains why "at the end of his life Ambedkar was sceptical of whether anything much had fundamentally changed (he remained an Untouchable Mahar despite being a cabinet minister) and turned to Buddhism" (Fitzgerald 2004, 271). While in general terms I agree that "those who are ranked at the bottom of Indian society today are poor not because they lack any intrinsic qualities that others possess, but because of the power others enjoy over them under conditions of modern capitalism" (Chandra

2016, 30), a considerable degree of power and control over the economy remains in the hands of those who, controlling the sphere of the spiritual, are still able to weaken and subtract, however they can, the "intrinsic qualities" of "the poor." Ambedkar knew that in order to achieve a "true liberation" for his people, he needed power: "What I want is power—political power for my people—for if we have power we have social status." Equally, he needed to secure social status in order to attain power, as he pointed out at the end of his life: "Before I die, I must establish a definite political direction for my people. They have remained poor, oppressed and deprived and because of that, now, a new consciousness and a new anger are growing among them. That is natural. But it is also natural that this type of community becomes attracted to Communism. I do not want my people to fall under the sway of the Communists" (Ambedkar quoted in Jaffrelot 2005, 86).

Ambedkar's dissent against left-wing parties (quoted in Jaffrelot 2005, 76) seemed always to be for very contingent reasons: "If the Socialists wish to make socialism a definite reality then they must recognise that the problem of social reform is fundamental and that for them there is no escape from it." At the same time, Ambedkar always kept his "universalistic stance" open to dialog with leaders of other parties, groups, and communities so as to create a political opposition with a broader mandate, to include together with Dalits the vast majority of those affected by the violence of the caste ideology, including Shudras. Although some of his historical hypotheses might be questionable, as for instance regarding the origin of the Shudras (Ambedkar 1970), his commitment to responsibility and to uphold the principle of a "social and moral consciousness" bestowed integrity on his leadership.

At the end of his essay "Subaltern Social Groups in the *Prison Notebooks*," Joseph Buttigieg (2013, 41) reminds us of "one of Gramsci's most significant insights: one of the greatest difficulties that subaltern social groups face in challenging the prevailing hegemony is finding a way past the barriers that prevent them from being heard." Judging from the impressive amount of activity in every sphere of life that Ambedkar carried out in order to make the voices of Dalits heard, it is reasonable to believe that he was aware of—indeed, he experienced—this very difficulty.[18]

Should we take then his conversion to Buddhism at the end of his life as a final act "so as to be heard," or is there more to it? To be sure, conversion to Buddhism for Ambedkar was a process that spanned a good part of his adult life rather than only being the single act in Nagpur that took place on 14 October 1956, when he officially converted to Buddhism. The process had intensified during the previous twenty years, starting in 1935 at Nasik district, when he declared that "I was born as a Hindu but will not die as Hindu." A year later, at a Mahar conference in Mumbai in May 1936, Ambedkar (2016a) explained to the Mahar masses his views on the need for conversion ("What Path to Salvation?"), calling it a "class struggle," given the constant fight against the caste system, the permanence of untouchability, and the unwillingness of caste Hindus to reform. Ambedkar insisted also on conversion as the only path to

18. When invited by the anticaste group Jat-Pat Todak Mandal of Lahore to deliver a speech, Ambedkar (2014) wrote *The Annihilation of Caste*, but the text was found "offensive" because it criticized the Vedas and other Hindu texts, and the event was cancelled. Ambedkar, however, printed and distributed around fifteen hundred copies of the text.

true liberation and on the need to place social change before economic progress in order to make the latter more effective in terms of gaining essential political rights while securing with conversion both "material as well as spiritual gains."

The day following his conversion, Ambedkar (2016b) delivered a historical speech in Nagpur, touching upon many topics in order to justify his personal choice,[19] to motivate Dalits to follow him, and to value the cultivation of mind and education. He also explained the roots of untouchability (dealing with dead cows and eating cow meat), distanced himself from Marx, and reiterated his opposition to caste, Gandhi, and Hindu religion.[20] Since Ambedkar emphasized that "for the poor, religion is a necessity. Religion is necessary for people in distress. The poor man lives on hope," he therefore found in Navayana Buddhism the only solution because only Buddhism can guarantee immanence and radical secularism: it is based on a "social Dhamma" and on principles rather than rules, while resting on human moral grounds and not on "revelation."[21]

There is no doubt that Ambedkar's conversion was "an act of the greatest responsibility" (Skaria 2015, 451). But conversion for Ambedkar meant also a sustained criticism at different but interconnected levels: criticism toward Hinduism and caste ideology; toward ritualistic and dogmatic religions in general; toward Buddhism itself, thus proposing Navayana Buddhism as a social religion—as opposed to an individual pursuit—committed to the promotion of social and political justice. In Gramscian terms, Ambedkar proposed to convert "as a collective thinker."[22] His conversion also contained criticism of an incipient, partial Indian democracy in which Dalits and other subaltern groups did not enjoy the results of independence and self-government. For this reason, criticism was extended to both Gandhian nonviolence[23]—which still involved violence toward these minorities—and to modernity and secularism, very much in need of "re-figuring" (451). All these criticisms seem to be motivated by a common thread: opposition to various degrees of violence perpetrated against Dalits and minorities. This being the case, it seems very logical and morally motivated that, when offered a choice, Ambedkar would opt to convert to Buddhism rather than subscribe to the permanent violence, as he understood it, present within Marxism and communism when they offered freedom and equality to the masses.

Recently, Skaria (2015), in "framing Ambedkar's conversion," raised a set of questions—such as "why convert to Buddhism"?—that included "secular responsibility" and "the liberal concept of minority." Bringing together Marx's "On the Jewish Question" and Ambedkar's thinking on the "Dalit question"—both Jews and Dalits are "outside the political community"—Skaria (2015, 462) maintains that with political emancipation, (North America) "the Jew disappears" (is assimilated?) in a "spectral civil society" and the question becomes a "*secular* question" wherein "liberalism must create its concept of minority" involving "tolerance ... as a supplement to equality." Indeed, Ambedkar "could never have accepted this resolution of the minor ... what may

---

19. "This oath I made earlier, yesterday I proved it true" (Ambedkar 2016b).
20. "The *Chaturvarna* system was not created haphazardly. It is not just a popular custom. *It is religion*" (Ambedkar 2016b; emphasis added).
21. "There is no place for God and soul in the Buddhist religion" (Ambedkar 2016b).
22. "If you at all decide in favour of conversion, then you will have to promise me organised and en-masse conversion" (Ambedkar 2016a).
23. See Arundhati Roy's introduction "The Doctor and the Saint" in Ambedkar (2014).

perhaps be described as the provocation that leads to Ambedkar's massive originality, is precisely his struggle with the question of the minor who remains after political emancipation." In Ambedkar's terms, "Human emancipation must now be conceived rather as the challenge of constantly questioning and supplementing political emancipation," to include Marxism's requiring "a permanent regime of revolutionary violence" (463), as discussed in his posthumously published essay "Buddha or Karl Marx."

Skaria returns to both this essay and *The Buddha and His Dhamma* (Ambedkar 2011), indicating that Navayana Buddhism "is such a religion of reason, or how reason works when it is not a civil religion but a refuge," by highlighting the narrative of Siddharta Gautama and his "responsible" refusal to submit to the majority: that is, to political and civil society, a "participation without a part, without sovereignty—this is the first statement of the Buddha's religion" (465). Ambedkar is, of course, reflecting on his own situation and his "responsible act of conversion" as a leader and a collective thinker, but he does this with only partial recourse to logos since he finds in Siddharta's mythos a pertinent "refuge" to unmask his "homelessness" in his own country and his yearning to be included together with Dalits and other minorities in that ideal of justice present in the country's constitution, to which he so eagerly contributed. Ambedkar's effort in favor of an all-inclusive constitution was itself a "religious act" of the highest significance since, as he made clear in his speech at Nagpur, his intention was not to betray the hope of the poor: "The poor man lives on hope. 'Hope!' [in English; this is not translated]. The source of life is hope. If this hope is destroyed, then how will life go on? Religion makes one hopeful, and to those in pain, to the poor, it gives a message" (Ambedkar 2016b).

Concluding Remarks

There is one pending question that remains unanswered, which is not new but keeps resurfacing, even at present: it regards the willingness of caste Hindus to consider and keep ex-Untouchables as an integral part of the Hindu community. This goes hand in hand with the position of untouchables who by emulating the upper castes would supposedly share the latter's ideology, thus giving their consensus to their own untouchability.

To say that Brahmins have currently updated their views on untouchability and relaxed their stricter codes of conduct for mere self-interest would be to trivialize the problem. Recently, Guru, in dialog with Sarukkai, has addressed some of these issues (Guru and Sarukkai 2012, 202–10), highlighting the relevance of the phenomenology of untouchability, and in particular the difference between the "deferential or ideal untouchable Brahmins" and the "despicable or real untouchable Dalits," which comes down to the "ritually pure and the eternally impure": that is, the untouchables as "walking carrion" to be "purified" (and burnt). Indeed, it is because Dalits do not necessarily believe in the pure-impure binary, or because they reject constantly subsisting as "the repository of the impurities of the touchable" (213) that the touchables find it impossible to sit at the same table to negotiate. Even the context of the "Archaeology of Untouchability" (218–22) becomes redundant, pace Foucault, if we wish to go to the very root of the problem, which is found (in Ambedkar's terms) in "the Hindu mind."

In fact, Guru himself resorts to using the more Gramscian methodology of finding "traces" of untouchability and casteism in rural and urban India. An even more Gramscian stance would help uncover the historical traces of Dalit responses to untouchability and subalternity when they refuse to remain eternally "despicable." I agree with Guru that Ambedkar's response was preeminently political and not moral. His conversion, however, was an eminently ethical act and a moral choice: given that Brahmins were (and are) not ready to undergo a metanoia/conversion in order to integrate and welcome the "despicable untouchables" into the Hindu fold, Ambedkar resorted to undergo this metanoia himself, inviting other Dalits to follow him. In other words, rather than accept being the "walking carrion" and the "carrier of sins" for the "pure and ideal untouchables," he performed a different and more challenging religious act/karma that represented a refusal of what was expected of him, an anti- or counter-karma, so as to nullify the bad karma imposed on Dalits. At the same time, the choice of Buddhism allowed him to respond with a widely accepted nonviolent religious symbol but also to remain committed to a liberation motivated by a secular ideological stance.

Even when subalterns are crushed and oppressed, they manage to find a way to react so as to reaffirm their full humanity, including by means of making their religiosity and spirituality more manifest as a further indication of humanness. At present, the chanting of "Hindu-Hindu: Bhai-Bhai" (all Hindus are brothers)[24] might sound very appealing to Dalits' ears, but many of them are more than aware that their dignity in the cities and their land in rural India are being taken away from them, thus depriving them of both the spiritual and the material. Those who hold power not only put subalterns' abilities into question but also actively seek to prevent subalterns from achieving this reaffirmation, and when both tactics fail, the best way the powerful can hope to nullify subalterns' spirituality is to appropriate it for themselves.

According to Frosini (2013, 183), "The bourgeoisie ... takes hold of the religious myths of the subalterns and uses them as the engine of the passive inclusion of the masses in the state."[25] Once robbed of their myths, subalterns are then deprived also of the ability to interpret and recreate these myths, losing hold of their "privilege" to be human but remaining appropriated by the state—so much so that "bourgeois universalism, devoid of any proper content, absorbs the common sense of subalterns and re-organises its meaning. In this way, bourgeois power incorporates the utopian energy of popular religious universalism, rendering it functional to its own expansion" (183). At times, as we well know, both political and religious powers have played different subaltern groups against each other, with the end result being to deprive them all of their most cherished possession: the power of thinking, thus weakening the popular religious myths, which are their only source of a striving for utopia.

If I were to offer a salient metaphor—returning to Plutarch's "there are no cities without temples"—so as to enhance the worldly materiality of subalterns' spirituality, I would dare to say that the temples of all times, in all the cities of the world, could not

24. Arun Patnaik (personal communication).
25. Gramsci (Q13§1, Gramsci 1975, 1555–61) compares the utopian characteristics of Machiavelli's *The Prince* to the concept of the myth-ideology applied by Sorel to trade unionism. The utopian myth here becomes a necessary incentive for the people ("dispersed and annihilated") so as to "arouse and organise their collective will."

have been built without the contribution, the suffering, and often the death of many subalterns. No doubt many subalterns were unwilling workers, perhaps even slaves in the construction of these "temples," but this in no way diminishes their involvement in such enterprises. It is a fact that these temples would not have been possible without subalterns. Similarly and equally relevant, in my view, is subalterns' contribution to the treasures of human spirituality and the life of spirit, which sustain human thought and activity: a very human, immanent, and "secular" spirituality of which religious and political leaders of every conviction, as well as all those who hold power in society, should be very aware.

It took me some time to come to terms and to accept that "spirituality" was relevant, in different but complementary ways, to both Ambedkar and Gramsci. For both of them, spirituality is not only the driving force behind the acquisition of the consciousness of human equality and dignity but also becomes indispensable for subalterns and Dalits in order to achieve these, in a variety of degrees and via a (spiritual) critical consciousness (*consapevolezza*). In other words, Ambedkar and Gramsci reaffirm the presence of spirituality within the secular as the place (the *seculum*, within history) within which *moksha*/liberation happens. Not the postponed *moksha* proposed by Gandhi and religions in general but a present-day, historical, and local group liberation.

In this sense we can also understand and perhaps even justify the limited and at times contradictory liberation accepted by Dalits who compromise with right-wing parties so as to achieve power in some Indian states or who prefer not to annihilate caste in order to preserve "reservations." This is, however, in Gramscian and Ambedkarite terms, a "short-sighted" liberation, not informed by the spirit of consciousness and/or "conversion"; it is almost an individualistic liberation as compared to the liberation achieved by the whole group and possibly in conjunction with other such subaltern groups, as Ambedkar tried to achieve.

Far from making "Dalit a singular homogeneous social actor"[26]—I hardly use Dalit in the singular—I am pointing exactly to the opposite: homogeneity exists insofar as all share a common condition, but all preserve historical, social, political, and life-experience differences, with different degrees of fractured consciousness. For this very reason, a strict definition of "spirituality" becomes an "external tool" to achieve liberation rather than an ongoing transformative source arising from the daily, historical (secular) experience of the group. For Gramsci, this "spirit" is so very present in the "healthy nucleus" of common sense, religion, folklore, and so on, while for Ambedkar it reveals itself in the "hope of the poor" and the impulse to convert (and reconvert). For both, the "task of thinking"—as a means to achieving consciousness and self-awareness—remains paramount, thus presupposing for subalterns and Dalits the ability to "philosophize": that is, to express a vision of reality and to be able to intervene so as to transform a given reality, even in the midst of many contradictory and limiting choices. This is the real root of the "spiritual": for the human to be fully human, in all its dignity.

26. Personal communication of Anjan Chakrabarti.

Acknowledgments

I would like to thank Serap A. Kayatekin, Anjan Chakrabarti, Marcus Green, Joseph Buttigieg, Kate Crehan, Peter Thomas, Arun Patnaik, Fabio Frosini, and Anne Showstack Sassoon for their stimulating reflections on early versions of this paper.

References

Ambedkar, B. R. 2016a. Why go for conversion? Speech given at the Mahar Conference in Mumbai, 30–1 May 1936. Accessed 28 June. http://www.angelfire.com/ak/ambedkar/BRwhyconversion.html.

———. 2016b. Why was Nagpur chosen? Speech given in Nagpur, India, 14 October 1956. Accessed 28 June. http://www.columbia.edu/itc/mealac/pritchett/00ambedkar/txt_ambedkar_conversion.html.

———. 1970. *Who were the Shudras?* Bombay: Thackers.

———. 1987. Buddha or Karl Marx. In *Dr. Babasaheb Ambedkar: Writings and speeches.* Vol. 3. Bombay: Government of Maharashtra.

———. 2011. *The Buddha and his dhamma: A critical edition.* Ed. A. S. Rathore and A. Verma. New Delhi: Oxford University Press.

———. 2014. *The annihilation of caste: The annotated critical edition.* Ed. S. Anand. London: Verso.

Baratta, G. 2003. *Le rose e i quaderni: Il pensiero dialogico di Antonio Gramsci.* Rome: Carocci Editore.

Benjamin, W. 1968. *Illuminations: Essays and reflections.* New York: Harcourt Brace.

Boninelli, G. M. 2007. *Frammenti indigesti: Temi folclorici negli scritti di Antonio Gramsci.* Rome: Carocci Editore.

Buttigieg, J. A. 2013. Subaltern social groups in Antonio Gramsci's *Prison notebooks.* In *The political philosophies of Antonio Gramsci and B. R. Ambedkar: Itineraries of subalterns and Dalits,* ed. C. Zene, 35–42. London: Routledge.

Chandra, U. 2016. Kol, coolie, colonial subject: A hidden history of caste and the making of modern Bengal. In *The politics of caste in west Bengal,* ed. U. Chandra, G. Heierstad, and K. B. Nielsen, 19–34. New Delhi: Routledge.

De Martino, E. 2005. *The land of remorse: A study of southern Italian tarantism.* Trans by D. L. Zinn. London: Free Association Books.

Findley, E. F. 2002. *Caring for the soul in a postmodern age: Politics and phenomenology in the thought of Jan Patočka.* Albany, NY: State University of New York Press.

Fitzgerald, T. 2004. Analysing sects, minorities, and social movements in India: The case of Ambedkar Buddhism and Dalit(s). In *Reconstructing the world: B. R. Ambedkar and Buddhism in India,* ed. S. Jondhale and J. Beltz, 267–82. New Delhi: Oxford University Press.

Frosini, F. 2013. Why does religion matter to politics? Truth and ideology in a Gramscian approach. In *The political philosophies of Antonio Gramsci and B. R. Ambedkar: Itineraries of subalterns and Dalits,* ed. C. Zene, 173–84. London: Routledge.

Gokhale, P. P. 2004. Universal consequentialism: A note on B. R. Ambedkar's reconstruction of Buddhism with special reference to religion, morality and spirituality. In *Reconstructing the world: B. R. Ambedkar and Buddhism in India,* ed. S. Jondhale and J. Beltz, 120–31. New Delhi: Oxford University Press.

Gramsci, A. 1971. *Selections from the "Prison notebooks."* Ed. Q. Hoare and N. Smyth. London: Lawrence and Wishart.

———. 1975. *Quaderni del carcere.* 4 vols. Ed. V. Gerratana. Torino: Einaudi.

———. 1978. Some aspects of the southern question. In *Antonio Gramsci: Selections from the political writings (1921–1926)*, ed. and trans. Q. Hoare, 441–62. London: Lawrence and Wishart.

———. 1992. *Prison notebooks.* Vol. 1. Trans. J. A. Buttigieg and A. Callari, ed. J. A. Buttigieg. New York: Columbia University Press.

———. 1994. *Letters from prison.* 2 vols. Ed. F. Rosengarten. Trans. R. Rosenthal. New York: Columbia University Press.

———. 1996. *Prison notebooks.* Vol. 2. Trans. and ed. J. A. Buttigieg. New York: Columbia University Press.

———. 2000. *The Gramsci reader: Selected writings 1916–1935.* Ed. D. Forgacs. New York: New York University Press.

———. 2007. *Prison notebooks.* Vol. 3. Trans. and ed. J. A. Buttigieg. New York: Columbia University Press.

Guru, G., and S. Sarukkai. 2012. *The cracked mirror: An Indian debate on experience and theory.* New Delhi: Oxford University Press.

Husserl, E. 1970. *The crisis of European sciences and transcendental phenomenology.* Evanston, Ill. Northwestern University Press.

Jaffrelot, C. 2005. *Dr. Ambedkar and untouchability: Analysing and fighting caste.* London: Hurst and Company.

Karsenti, B. 2012. Sociology face to face with pragmatism: Action, concept and person. *Journal of Classical Sociology* 12 (3–4): 398–427.

Krebs, V. J. 2004. "Descending into primeval chaos": Philosophy, the body and the pygmalionic impulse. In *Mythos and logos: How to regain the love of wisdom*, ed. A. Anderson, S. Hicks, S. V. Witkowsi, and L. Witkowski, 141–61. Amsterdam: Rodopi Editions.

Martin, D. 2014. *Religion and power: No logos without mythos.* Furnham: Ashgate.

Marx, K. 1978. On the Jewish question. In *The Marx-Engels reader*, 2d ed., ed. R. Tucker, 26–46. New York: W. W. Norton.

Mate, R. 2001. Thinking in Spanish: Memory of logos? *Nepantla: Views from South* 2 (2): 247–64.

Omvedt, G. 2004. Confronting Brahmanic Hinduism: Dr. Ambedkar's sociology of religion and Indian society. In *Reconstructing the world: B. R. Ambedkar and Buddhism in India*, ed. S. Jondhale and J. Beltz, 49–62. New Delhi: Oxford University Press.

Patočka, J. 1996. *Heretical essays in the philosophy of history.* Trans. E. Kohák, ed. J. Dodd. Chicago: Open Court.

———. 2002. *Plato and Europe.* Trans. P. Lom. Stanford: Stanford University Press.

Pizza, G. 2013. Gramsci e de Martino: Appunti per una riflessione. *Quaderni di Teoria Sociale*, no. 13: 77–121.

———. 2015. *Il tarantismo oggi: Antropologia, politica, cultura.* Roma: Carocci Editore.

Rosati, M. 2013. Conversazioni immaginarie: Gramsci e Durkheim sulla trama del sociale. *Quaderni di Teoria Sociale*, no. 13: 23–52.

Skaria, A. 2015. Ambedkar, Marx and the Buddhist question. *South Asia: Journal of South Asian Studies* 38 (3): 450–65.

van der Veer, P. 2013. *The modern spirit of Asia: The spiritual and the secular in China and India.* Princeton: Princeton University Press.

Zene, C. 2000. "We too are Humans (Amrao je manus!)": The Rishis' struggle for human identity. Working Papers in the Study of Religions, SOAS, University of London.

———. 2002. *The Rishi of Bangladesh: A history of Christian dialogues.* London: Routledge.

————. 2007. Myth, identity and belonging: The Rishi of Bengal/Bangladesh. *Religion* 37 (4): 257–81.

————. 2013. Subalterns and Dalits in Gramsci and Ambedkar: A prologue to a posthumous dialogue. In *The political philosophies of Antonio Gramsci and B. R. Ambedkar: Itineraries of subalterns and Dalits*, ed. C. Zene, 1–32. London: Routledge.

"I am sure that you are more pessimistic than I am...": An Interview with Giorgio Agamben

Vacarme

Translated by Jason Smith

Vacarme: The specific reason we wanted to meet you was to ask you about the "flip side," so to speak, of the biopolitics you speak of. There are a certain number of movements—movements that we ourselves either come from or feel close to, such as those of the undocumented immigrants, the unemployed and those with no secure employment, the movement of people with AIDS, or even the emergent drug users' movement—that unfold in the very political space that you've identified: the zone of indistinction "of public and private, of biological body and political body, of *zoè* and *bios*," in this "state of exception that has become the rule." But you say very little about these movements, or do so only indirectly. They linger between the lines you've drawn, but more as objects (of camps, of welfare or medical power) than as subjects. You analyze with some precision the "major" biopolitics, that of the enemy whose genealogy you minutely trace, and whose center or focus would be, according to you, "*homo sacer*": naked life exposed to a sovereignty whose apparatuses, such as the camp, you also attentively examine. But you forgo the biopolitics of reappropriation or riposte, the minor biopolitics, "our" biopolitics, so to speak: the biopolitics of AC!,[1] the collectives for the undocumented, or that of Act Up. You do think both the possibility and the necessity of this minor biopolitics: "it is," you say, "starting from this uncertain terrain and from this opaque zone of indistinction that today we must once again the path of another politics, of another body, of another speech. I would not feel up to forgoing this indistinction of public and private, of biological body and political body, of *zoè* and *bios*, for any reason whatsoever. It is here that I must find my space once again—here or nowhere else. Only a politics that starts

---

1. The acronym refers to the French organization Agir ensemble contre le Chômage (Act together against Unemployment), formed in 1993, and concerned not only with a reduction of work-time combined with a guaranteed income for all, but with the analysis of new modalities of work that can no longer be characterized under the official opposition of employment and unemployment: the temporary, marginal, and "flexible" work of post-Fordism. This and all subsequent notes have been added by the translator.

from such an awareness can interest me."[2] You do not, however, explore the concrete forms of struggle that already practice a politics rooted in an awareness—and experience—of the state of exception. We ask then whether there isn't an embryonic form of this other politics you yourself call for, precisely when the unemployed stake a claim to a guaranteed income, when people with AIDS demand

Giorgio Agamben: In a way, it seems the question should be turned around: it is from the actors in question that you should expect a response. That said, if the movements and the subjects you speak of "linger between the lines I've drawn more as objects than as subjects," it's because this is for me the site of a major problem: the question of the subject itself, that I can only conceive of in terms of a process of subjectivation and desubjectivation—or rather as an interval or remainder between these processes. Who is the subject of this new biopolitics, or rather of this minor biopolitics you're speaking about? It's a problem that is always essential in classical politics, when it's a matter of finding who the revolutionary subject is, for example. There are people who continue to pose this problem in the old sense of the term: in terms of class, of the proletariat. These are not obsolete problems, but from the moment one positions oneself on the new terrain we are speaking of, that of biopower and of the biopolitical, the problem is difficult in a different sense. Because the modern state functions, it seems to me, as a kind of desubjectivation machine: it's a machine that both scrambles all the classical identities and, as Foucault shows quite well, a machine (for the most part juridical) that recodes these very same dissolved identities. There is always a resubjectivation, a reidentification of these destroyed subjects, voided as they are of all identity. Today, it seems to me that the political terrain is a kind of battlefield in which two processes unfold: the destruction of all that traditional identity was (I say this, of course, with no nostalgia) and, at the same time, its immediate resubjectivation by the State—and not only by the State, but also by the subjects themselves. It's what you evoked in your question: the decisive conflict is from now on played out—for each of its protagonists, including the new subjects you speak of—on the terrain of what I call zoè, biological life. And in fact, it is nothing other than this: I don't think there can be any question of returning to the classical political oppositions which clearly separate private and public, political body and private body, etc. But this terrain is also the one that exposes us to biopower's processes of subjection. There is therefore an ambiguity, a risk. This is what Foucault showed: the risk is that one reidentify oneself, that one invest this situation with a new identity, that one produce a new subject, if you like, but one subjected to the State; the risk that one from then on carry out again, despite oneself, this infinite process of subjectivation and subjection that precisely defines biopower. I don't believe there is any escape from this problem.

2. See G. Agamben, *Means without End: Notes on Politics*, trans. V. Binetti and C. Casarino (Minneapolis: University of Minnesota Press, 2000), p. 139.

Vacarme: Is it a risk or an aporia? Is every subjectivation fatally and without fail a subjection, or can something like a maxim or formula of subjectivation be obtained that would allow one to escape subjection?

In Foucault's last works, there is an aporia that seems very interesting to me. There is, on the one hand, all the work on the "care of self": one must care for one's self, in all the forms of the practice of self. But at the same time he often states the apparently opposite theme: the self must be let go of. He says so on many occasions: "Life is over if one questions oneself about one's identity; the art of living is to destroy identity, to destroy psychology." There is, therefore, an aporia: a care of self that should lead to a letting go of self. One way the question could be posed is: what would a practice of self be that would not be a process of subjectivation but, to the contrary, would end up only at a letting go, a practice of self that finds its identity only in a letting go of self? It is necessary to maintain or "stay," as it were, in this double movement of desubjectivation and subjectivation. Obviously, it is difficult terrain to hold. It's truly a matter of identifying this zone, this no man's land between a process of subjectivation and a process of desubjectivation, between identity and nonidentity. This terrain would have to be identified, because this would be the terrain of a new biopolitics. This is precisely what is interesting about a movement like that of people with AIDS. Why? Because it seems to me that, in this case, identification takes place only on the threshold of an absolute desubjectivation, sometimes even at the risk of death. Here, it seems that one is held right on this threshold. I have tried a little in the book on Auschwitz, with regard to testimony, to see the witness as the model of a subjectivity that would be the subject only of its own desubjectivation. The witness witnesses nothing other than its own desubjectivation. The one who survives witnesses solely for the *Muselmänner*.[3] In the last part of the book I was interested in really identifying a model of the subject as what remains between a subjectivation and a desubjectivation, speech and muteness. It's not a substantial space, but rather an interval between two processes. But this is only a beginning. A new structure of subjectivity is barely touched upon, but it's very complicated, it's a work that still remains entirely to be done. It's truly necessary . . . It's a practice, not a principle. I believe that one can have a general principle only if one makes sure not to relapse into a process of resubjectivation that would at the same time be a subjection—that is, of being a subject only within the framework of a strategy or tactic. This is why it's very important to see how, in the practice both of the movements and of each one of us, these possible zones get drawn out. This can be done everywhere, working with this notion of a care of self found in Foucault, while moving it into other domains: every practice of self there might be, including the everyday mysticism of intimacy, all these zones where one brushes against a zone of nonknowledge or a zone of desubjectivation, be it sexual life or whatever other aspect of bodily life. In these cases there are always figures of a subject attending its own downfall, brushing against its own

3. See G. Agamben, *Remnants of Auschwitz: The Witness and the Archive*, trans. D. Heller-Roazen (New York: Zone Books, 1999). The second chapter of this text is devoted to "the Muselmann."

desubjectivation—these are all everyday zones, a very banal, quotidian mysticism. We should be attentive to everything offering us a zone of this kind. It's still quite vague, but this is what would offer the paradigm of a minor biopolitics.

You present identity as a risk, an error of the subject. Isn't there all the same a material thickness of identities—even if only insofar as the adversary assigns them to us, be it through the law (think, for example, of immigration laws) or through insults (i.e., homophobic insults)—which renders these identities "objective," so to speak? In other words, how much room for desubjectivation do our social conditions leave us?

Agamben: Right now I'm working on Paul's letters.[4] Paul formulates the problem: "What is messianic life? What are we going to do now that we live in the messianic time? What are we going to do with regard to the State?" What's interesting to me is the double movement we find in Paul that has always been problematic. Paul says: "Remain in the social condition, be it juridical or cultural, in which you find yourself. You're a slave? Remain a slave. You're a doctor? Remain a doctor. You're a wife, a husband? Remain in the vocation for which you have been called." But at the same time, he says: "You're a slave? Don't worry, but make use of it, take advantage of it."[5] This means that it's not a matter of changing your juridical status, or changing your life, but of making use of it. He then specifies what he means through this very beautiful image: "as if not," or "as not." That is: "You're crying? As if you weren't crying. You're rejoicing? As if you weren't rejoicing. Are you married? As nonmarried. Have you bought something? As not bought, etc." There is this theme of the "as not." It's not even "as if," it is "as not." Literally, it's: "Crying, as not crying; married, as not married; slave, as not slave."[6] It's very interesting, because we could say that what he calls "usages" are conducts of life which, on the one hand, do not directly confront power—remain in your juridical condition, your social role—but nevertheless completely transform them in the form of an "as not." The notion of use, of usage, in this sense, interests me a great deal: it's a practice that cannot be assigned a subject. You remain a slave, but, since you make use of it in the manner of this "as not," you are no longer a slave.

Vacarme: How could such a use be properly political, or take place under political conditions? It's possible to see it as a strictly individual or ethical—even religious—conversion of thought which would, in any case, be singular and "private." How does this conversion vis-à-vis one's own status, allowing one no longer to be a subject, relate to politics? In what way does it necessitate community, struggle, conflict, and so on?

4. This book has since been published as *Il tempo che resta. Un commento alla* Lettera ai Romani (Torino: Bollati Boringhieri, 2000), and is forthcoming in an English translation from Stanford University Press.
5. Agamben refers throughout this response to Paul's 1 Cor. 7:20-30.
6. The "as not" (*comme non*) renders the Greek syntagm *"hos mè,"* which recurs throughout this sequence. The reading of this passage is developed in detail on the "Second Day" of *Il tempo che resta.*

Agamben: Of course, this theme in Paul is sometimes thought of as implying an interiorization. But I don't believe that it is a matter of interiorization at all. His problem is to the contrary that of the life of the messianic community to which he addresses himself. For example, this theme of use or usage reemerges in a very powerful form—as a critique of right—in the Franciscan movement, where the problem is that of property. These orders practice an extreme poverty while refusing all property, and yet they must nevertheless make use of certain goods. There was a severe conflict with the Church over this, insofar as the Church wanted very much to allow them to refuse a right to property, be it that of the individual or the order, but it wanted them to classify their conduct as a right of usage, a right to use. This is something that still exists: usufruct, the right to use, as separate from the right to property. To the contrary, the Franciscans insisted—this is where the conflict is— by saying: "No, it's not a right to use, it is a use without right." They call this *usus pauper*, poor usage. It's truly the idea of opening a zone of communal life that makes use, but has no right, and claims none. Moreover, the Franciscans do not critique property; they leave all property rights to the Church: "Property? We don't want any. We make use of it." This problem could therefore be said to be purely political, or at least communal.[7]

Vacarme: All the same, is it strictly by chance that the references you invoke in thinking this alternative belong to the religious sphere? Sometimes, when reading you, one finds in the designation of this other politics and this other status of the political something like a prophetic tone. For example, you write: "For this reason— to risk advancing a prophecy here—the coming politics will no longer be a struggle to conquer or to control the state on the part of either new or old social subjects, but rather a struggle between the state and the nonstate (humanity), that is, an irresolvable disjunction between whatever singularities and the state organization."[8] What role do these references and this tone play in your work?

Agamben: What interests me about Paul's text is not so much the domain of religion but a punctual domain that concerns religion without coinciding with it: the messianic, which is a domain very close to the political. Here, it is in fact another author who has been decisive for me, one who is not at all religious: Walter Benjamin. Benjamin thinks the messianic as paradigm of the political, or, let's say, of historical time. This is, for me, what's really in question. As a matter of fact, I think the way Benjamin introduces (in the first Thesis on the concept of history) theology as an entity that, even hidden, should help historical materialism win out over its enemies remains a very legitimate and timely gesture giving us, precisely, the means to think otherwise both time and the subject. So, you were speaking about the prophet . . . I was recently listening to recordings of Foucault's courses, notably the one where he distinguishes four figures of truth in our culture: the prophet, the sage, and the specialist, and then what he calls the *parrhesiastes*, the one who has the courage to say the truth. The prophet speaks of the future, and not in his own name, but in

7. On this *usus pauper*, see once again the "Second Day."
8. See *Means without end*, p. 88.

the name of something else. To the contrary, the *parrhesiastes*, with whom Foucault no doubt identifies, speaks in his own name, and must say what is true now, today. Of course, he says that these are not separate figures. But I myself would claim the figure of the *parrhesiastes* rather than the prophet. Look, the prophet is obviously important, and its disappearance from our culture is even a catastrophe: the figure of the prophet was that of the political leader until fifty years ago. It has completely disappeared. But, at the same time, it seems to me that it is no longer possible to think a discourse addressing the future. It's the messianic actuality, the *kairos*, the now-time that must be thought. That said, it's a very complicated model of time, because it is neither the time to come—the eschatological future, the eternal—nor is it exactly historical or profane time: it is a bit of time taken from the profane that, all of a sudden, is transformed. Benjamin writes somewhere that Marx secularized messianic time in a classless society. This is completely true. But at the same time, with all the aporias this engenders—the transitions, etc.—it is a type of snag on which the Revolution failed. We don't have a model of time available that permits us to think this. In any case, I believe that the messianic is always profane, never religious. It is even the ultimate crisis of the religious, the folding back of the religious onto the profane. With this in mind, I am thinking of a journal that has just been published in France, by some young people I know, called *Tiqqun*. It's really a messianic journal, since Tiqqun [or "tikkun" —*trans.*] is, in the Luria kabbala, the very term for messianic redemption, for messianic restoration. I find this interesting, because it's an extremely critical, very political journal, assuming a very messianic tone, but in an always profane manner. They therefore call the new anonymous subject Bloom, these whatever singularities that are emptied out, open for anything, which can diffuse themselves everywhere and yet remain ungraspable, without identity but reidentifiable at each instant. The problem they pose is: "How can such a Bloom be transformed, how can this Bloom perform the leap beyond himself?"[9]

Vacarme: This is probably where we have the hardest time following you. Not so much on the messianic posture as on the "whatever singularities." How can it be put? For you, the new biopolitics taking shape involves more a flight or taking leave than resistance or conflict. On the one hand, you very clearly identify an enemy, an adversary that is very much of a piece, consistent, and coherent, whose lengthy genealogies can be traced, recurrent apparatuses mapped out, etc. On the other hand, faced with the consistency of this adversary, you seem nevertheless to plead for a politics of inconsistency, of dissolution, of evasion: rather than fabricating collective subjects, we should learn to "let go" of ourselves; rather than demand rights, we should imagine "use without right"; rather than confront the State, assume the form of a "non-State," etc. But is there always the latitude to flee? It seems to us that the power of biopolitical apparatuses (think, for example, of the politics of public health, the administration of welfare, the regulation of immigration, etc.) resides precisely in their terrible force of capture. Pardon us for saying it so brutally, but it seems quite possible that desubjectivation would be a luxury

---

9. The group published a short pamphlet entitled *La Théorie du Bloom* (Paris: La fabrique, 2000).

whose possibility is offered only to those who escape the apparatuses of biopower. How can one let go of oneself, evade resubjectivation, be a non-State, etc., when one is HIV-positive, on welfare, or a drug addict—that is, literally caught in the categories and mechanisms of biopower? Isn't one most often forced to act "as such" rather than "as not," using your own terms? In short, one can have the sentiment that you plead for mobility and evasion at the very point where the power of capture and material thickness of the enemy leave us no other choice than to confront it.

Agamben: The problem seems clear to me. I think everything depends on what one understands by flight. It's a motif found in Deleuze: the "line of flight," the praise of flight. But you're right to protest. The notion of flight does not imply an elsewhere one might go. No, it's a very particular flight: a flight with no elsewhere. Where, after all, would this elsewhere be? In certain cases, for example when the Berlin wall was still standing, there were obvious flights because there was a wall (but was there an elsewhere?). For me, it's a question of thinking a flight which would not imply evasion: a movement on the spot, in the situation itself. This is the only way flight might have a political signification. Then there is another problem that seems to touch upon the question you have posed. It's the problem found in Marx in his critique of Stirner. He devotes more than a hundred pages in *The German Ideology* to the theoretician of anarchy, challenging his distinction between revolt and revolution. Stirner theorizes revolt as a personal, egoistic act of subtraction. Revolution is a political act aiming at an institution, whereas revolt is an individual act that doesn't aim at destroying institutions. It's enough simply to let the State be, no longer confronting it: it will destroy itself. It's enough to subtract oneself—a flight. Marx critiques this motif quite vigorously, but the very fact that he devotes more than a hundred pages to it proves it's a serious problem. To the opposition between revolt and revolution he opposes a sort of unity: he doesn't oppose a political concept to an anarcho-individual concept; he seeks their unity. This means that the proletarian's directly political act will always be for an egoistic reason, as a form of revolt. Even if this poses other problems, I tend to think like Marx: a kind of unity of both gestures, or indeed between them, let's say. I would not be inclined to think in terms of a cut isolating flight from revolution, as one has the tendency to do; I tend to think that every act emanating from the singular need of an individual, the proletarian, who has no identity, no substance, will also be, all the same, a political act. I believe that it is not necessary to oppose political action and flight, revolt and revolution, but to try to think what's between. But this causes problems for Marx as well. It's the whole problem of class. The class has no consciousness: the proletariat exists as subject, but with no consciousness. Whence the Leninist problem of the party: something is needed that would not be different from the class, not something other than the class but would be, so to speak, the organ of its consciousness. Here too, there is an aporia. I'm not saying that there is a solution to this problem between the line of flight as gesture of revolt and a purely political line. Neither the party model, nor the model of action without party: there is a need to invent. Because afterward one falls into the problem of political organization, of the party-class that's going to produce a "we": the party is the one who makes sure that every action is political and not personal; the class, to the contrary, is the organ of an infinite production of actions that aren't political, but individual revolts. But the problem is real.

Vacarme: It's also a problem posed, in practice, for those seeking to produce a collective—and at times even a "we"—outside the political parties that are no more than aggregating machines, and also without the help of a superior general principle, whether it be the Republic, Class or Humanity. If *Vacarme* feels close to the associations for the sick, the unemployed, or marginally employed, it's precisely because they invent something like a politics in the first person with new forms of organization, where the distinctions between the social and the political, the class and its consciousness, the singular and the universal, etc., are erased, and where the political signification of the acts is immanent to the acts themselves.

Agamben: Yes. It's necessary to invent a practice which would break the shell of these representations. Definitely not a substantial subject to be identified, but something else that it seems to me Paul discovered (I refer here once again to a work in progress). Paul was concerned with the Jewish law that divided men into Jews and non-Jews, Jews and Goyim. What does he do with this division? Paul is often presented as if he was the initiator of universalism, someone opposing a new universal principle to these divisions: Paul as father of the "Catholic"—that is, universal—Church. But when one closely examines his work, it's exactly the contrary. Confronted with this division imposed by the law (at bottom, he considered the law to be what divides Jew from non-Jew, but also citizen from noncitizen, etc.), he does not oppose, as we have the tendency to do in the epoch of the rights of man, a universal principle to an ethnic division, he does something very subtle. He divides the division itself. The law divides Jews from non-Jews? Well, I'm going to cut this division itself in two. There are many such divisions—for example, the Jew according to the flesh and Jew according to the spirit, the breath. The split between flesh and breath is going to divide the exhaustive division that shares out humanity between Jews and non-Jews. This new division will produce Jews who are not Jews, because there are Jews who are Jews according to the flesh, not the spirit, and Goyim who are Goyim according to the flesh, but not according to the spirit. He's going to produce a remnant. Paul introduces a remnant into this Jew/non-Jew division. It is a type of cut that cuts the line itself. Finally, it's a lot more interesting: it does not oppose a universal, it makes the division of the law inoperative, it introduces a remnant. Because the Jew according to the spirit is not a non-Jew, he is also a Jew— one might say that he's a kind of non-non-Jew. Everywhere, Paul works like this: instead of proposing a universal principle, he divides the division. And what remains is the new but undefinable subject, who is always left over or behind because it can be on all sides, both on the side of the non-Jews as well as the Jews.[10] This offers something valuable for the representation, today, of the notion of a people, and also perhaps for thinking what Deleuze said when he spoke of a minor people, of the people as *minoritaire*. It's not so much a matter of minorities as a presentation of the people as being always left over with relation to a division, something which

---

10. On this division of the division in Paul, see the "Third Day" of *Il tempo che resta*.

remains or resists division—not as a substance, but as an interval. One should proceed in this way, from division to division, rather than by asking oneself: "What would be the universal communal principle that would allow us to be together?" To the contrary. It is a matter, confronted with the divisions introduced by the law, of working with what disables them through resisting, through remaining—*résister*,

Vacarme: This is exactly what happened in France with the undocumented immigrants: a law defined the criteria, and all the work went not into the invocation of a general principle of hospitality, but in showing that all the criteria produced situations that no longer corresponded to anyone: people that can neither be expelled nor integrated, etc. Finally, the associations' strategy was to show how the criteria could be compounded in such a way that no one corresponded exactly to the alternative between illegal and legal. A certain angle of attack formed.

Agamben: That's what struck me about Paul. It's what is found in the Bible, in the figure of the prophet: the prophet always speaks of a remnant of Israel. He addresses himself to Israel as a whole, but pronounces "only a remnant will be saved." This is what happens in Isaiah, in Amos, in the prophetic discourse. The remnant or "remainder" here is not a numerical portion, but the figure that every people should take on in the decisive instant—in this case, salvation or election, but any other instant as well. The people should produce itself as remnant, take on the figure of this remnant. It's always necessary to see it in a determined situation: what, in such a situation, would pose itself as remnant? This does not correspond to the majority/ minority distinction. It's something else. Every people assumes this figure if the instant is truly decisive.

Vacarme: Still, in a critique of the epoch that is as radical as yours is, what's left of the "determined situations" and "decisive instants" you speak of? It seems that you focus so much more on the side of the aporia, impasse and failure—especially when you place, like Debord, the figures of totalitarianism and democracy back to back—than on the side of the opportunity, of the "shot," the *kairos*, as you put it. In your books you evoke, for example, an "experience of absolute weakness" and "the solitude and muteness there where we expected community and language." What are you referring to?

Agamben: I've often been reproached for (or at least attributed with) this pessimism that I am perhaps unaware of. But I don't see it like that. There is a phrase from Marx, cited by Debord as well, that I like a lot: "the desperate situation of society in which I live fills me with hope."[11] I share this vision: hope is given to the hopeless.

---

11. Marx, in a letter addressed to Arnold Ruge in May 1843: *"Sie werden nicht sagen, ich hielte die Gegenwart zu hoch, und wenn ich dennoch nicht an ihr verzweifle, so ist es nur ihre eigene verzweifelte Lage, die mich mit Hoffnung erfüllt"* (You won't say that I hold the present too high, and if I do not despair of it, it is only because its desperate situation fills me with hope). See Karl Marx-Friedrich Engels, *Werke*, Bd. 1 (Dietz Verlag: Berlin DDR, 1976), p. 342.

I don't see myself as pessimistic. No, in order to respond to your question, I think back to the horrible political situation of the 1980s. I also think of the Gulf war and the wars that followed, most notably in Yugoslavia. Let's say that the new figure of domination is now being sketched out well enough. It's the first time the spectacular model can be clearly seen at work. Not only in the media: it is, so to speak, put to work politically. Simone Weil says somewhere that it is wrong to consider war to be a fact concerned solely with external politics—it should also be considered a matter of internal politics. Now it seems to me that, in these wars, there is precisely an absolute indetermination, an absolute indiscernibility between internal and external politics. These days, such things have become trivial. They're heard in the mouths of experts: external and internal politics are the same thing. But I insist: there is no personal or psychological pessimism in this. It is, moreover, another manner of formulating the problem of the subject. This is, at bottom, what I like so much about Simondon: he always thinks individuation as the coexistence of an individual, personal principle and an impersonal, nonindividual principle.[12] In other words, a life is always made up of two phases at the same time, personal and impersonal. They are always in relation, even if they are clearly separated. The order of impersonal power that every life relates to could be called the impersonal, whereas desubjec-tivation would be this daily experience of brushing up against an impersonal power, something both surpassing us and giving us life. That, it seems to me, is what the question of the art of living would be: how to relate to this impersonal power? How can the subject relate to this power that doesn't belong to it, and which surpasses it? It is a problem of poetics, so to speak. The Romans called this *genius*, a fecund impersonal principle letting life be engendered. There again, a possible model. The subject would neither be the conscious subject, nor the impersonal power, but what holds itself between them. Desubjectivation does not only have a dark side. It is not simply the destruction of all subjectivity. There is also this other pole, more fecund and poetic, where the subject is only the subject of its own desubjectivation. Allow me, then, to refute your accusation: I am sure that you are more pessimistic than I am. . . .

Acknowledgement

This interview first appeared in the French journal Vacarme, no. 11, in December 1999, under the title "Une biopolitique mineure."

12. See Gilbert Simondon and his *L'individu et sa genèse physico-biologique; l'individuation à la lumière des notions de forme et d'information* (Paris: Presses Universitaires de France, 1964).

Crossing Materialism and Religion: An Interview on Marxism and Spirituality with the Fourteenth Dalai Lama

Anup Dhar, Anjan Chakrabarti, and
Serap Kayatekin

This conversation with the fourteenth Dalai Lama—the spiritual-political inspiration of the displaced Tibetan community—revolves around questions of why a practitioner of the Buddha Dharma would like to call himself Marxist, and also his views on the violence of both Marxist praxis and religion. The Dalai Lama splits Marxism into, on the one hand, violent paranoid statecraft, and, on the other, the moral principle of equal distribution. He aligns with the latter. He also displaces other-worldly religion to this-worldly moksha; he calls it spirituality. The conversation brings to dialogue the possible political consequences of a this-worldly spirituality and the possible spiritual consequences of a reflexive Marxism keenly attuned to experiences of human suffering.

The editors of this special issue of *Rethinking Marxism* on "Marxism and Spirituality" shared a few questions with the fourteenth Dalai Lama before the interview on Wednesday, 26 August 2015 at the residence of the Dalai Lama in McLeod Ganj,[1] India. Here is the questionnaire the editors shared with the Dalai Lama:

1. Religion is at the same time "the expression of real distress and also the protest against real distress. Religion is the sigh of the oppressed creature, the heart of a heartless world, just as it is the spirit of spiritless conditions"—We, from the journal, *Rethinking Marxism*, would like to seek your response on this proposition on "religion" by Marx; all the more because you have brought to a dialog Tibetan Buddhism and the Tibetan people's need for real freedom from real distress.
2. You have often marked a distinction between "religion" and "spirituality"—We would like to be enlightened on this by you; why do we need to turn away from

---

1. McLeod Ganj is a suburb of Dharamsala in Kangra district of Himachal Pradesh, India. It is known as "Little Lhasa" or "Dhasa" (a short form of Dharamshala used mainly by Tibetans) because of its large population of Tibetans. In March 1959, Tenzin Gyatso, the fourteenth Dalai Lama, fled to India. The Indian government offered him refuge in Dharamshala, where he set up the Tibetan Government in Exile in 1960, while McLeod Ganj became his official residence and also home to several Buddhist monasteries and thousands of Tibetan refugees. See https://www.mcleodganj.com/about for details.

religion and turn to spirituality to attend to the "human condition"? We would like to request you to help us see the connection of spirituality with ethics and ethical living.

3. The separation of real material experiences (say, poverty) and material needs (say, the need to be free from malnutrition) and spiritual experiences (say, experiences of communion with nature) and spiritual needs (say, the need for peaceful interdependence) has haunted humanity for some time. Can Marxism's focus on materiality and Tibetan Buddhism's focus on spiritual needs be brought to a dialog?

4. You said in 1993: "The economic system of Marxism is founded on moral principles, while capitalism is concerned only with gain and profitability. Marxism is concerned with the distribution of wealth on an equal basis ... as well as the fate of those who are underprivileged and in need, and [it] cares about the victims of minority-imposed exploitation. For those reasons, the system appeals to me, and it seems fair." You have suggested elsewhere also that you are a Marxist so far as Marxism's focus on socioeconomic conditions is concerned. You have particularly emphasized the focus in Marxism on inequality and the ethical need to move toward an equal and just world. Would you like to elaborate on this position of yours? Are you also suggesting that our present world order based on inequality and exploitation faces a spiritual crisis which Marxism (as also Tibetan Buddhism, albeit in their respective ways) holds the promise to attend to?

5. By bringing to dialog Marxism and Buddhism are you in the process reinventing Marxism as a compassionate politics and Buddhism as a social religion?

6. Do you think that there is a spirituality deficit in Marxism? Without such spirituality does Marxism become dystopic and violent? One problem common to both Marxism and religion has been its associated violence. Why do you think that is the case? Is it because of the spiritual deficit? Why does Marxism turn violent from time to time? Why is statist Marxism's history red in tooth and claw? What makes Marxism at one and the same time pro-people (speaking in other words against exploitation and inequality) and anti-people (being violent to its own people)? Would a turn to spirituality temper the violence and the aggressive modernism and Eurocentrism of much of Marxism? Why is the history of religion also the history of violence? Would you like to respond to Sri Lankan and Burmese Buddhism's history of violence? What does it mean for you then to be at the cusp of spirituality and Marxism?

7. Is there, also, in Marxism's turn to the "commune" and to communitarianism, as against individualism, a turn to the rather deeper tenets of the spiritual being—a being that foregrounds interconnectedness and interdependence of all species? Even in its apparent scientism, is there then in Marxism a "secret spirituality," all the more because many religious or faith-based orders share with Marxism similar principles?

8. What happens when China and Tibet come face to face—one armed with state-backed combative Marxism and the other disarmed with spirituality, nonviolence, and faith-based practices?

The Dalai Lama however did not respond to each question individually but offered a consolidated response to the questionnaire. Here is the transcript of his consolidated response, along with a few insertions by Anup Dhar, who represented the editors of this issue in this conversation.

ANUP DHAR: Your Holiness, I am Anup, and I teach philosophy, politics, and psycho-analysis in a university in India called Ambedkar University Delhi (AUD). I am part of an activist-academic collective that publishes a journal, *Rethinking Marxism*, and partic-ipates in anticapitalist struggle and in postcapitalist praxis. Three of us—Anjan Chak-rabarti, Serap Kayatekin, and I (and all of us are from the broader "rethinking Marxism collective")—are editing a special issue of *Rethinking Marxism* on "Marxism and Spirituality."

THE FOURTEENTH DALAI LAMA: So far as social and economic theories are concerned, I am a Marxist. I have publicly said, "I am a Marxist."

DHAR: Yes, we have read about that.

DALAI LAMA: But if you ask me on Marx or on Marxism in detail—perhaps about its detailed structure—my knowledge, I must say, is zero [laughs]; perhaps I can respond to some specific questions, if you have, on Marxism?

DHAR: Yes, I have a few; in addition to the questions we have posed to you already in writing. Perhaps you can begin by sharing your reflections on why you would say, "I am a Marxist." Would you like to elaborate a little on this statement of yours?

DALAI LAMA: First, I am a Buddhist; a *practitioner* of *Buddha Dharma*. Every day, you see, we pray for all sentient beings; we pray for all sentient beings on this planet so that all sentient beings are free from suffering; we hope all sentient beings have happiness; we pray for all sentient beings to be free from attachments, attachments causing bias. If you are serious about this, if one seriously practices these things, then one will have to think of the well-being of the billion human beings on this planet. Other beings, lim-itless number of other beings, like birds, fish, even earthworms, we have to think of their well-being as well. But you see we do not have a common language; we cannot communicate with them, so we can only pray. Now as human beings, we have languag-es of communication. We have a somewhat special apparatus: the human brain. This combination of language and brain—and I do not know for certain which should come first, which caused what—but the combination is supposed to, or at least, should be, the source of happiness. But instead, this is causing more trouble, more violence. Now, when we think of the well-being of a billion beings not only in their next life but in this life ... this very life should be a happy one, not the next one, then we have to take recourse to the Four Noble Truths. [The Four Noble Truths are: the noble truth of suffering[2] [*dukkha*, in Pali], the noble truth of the origin[3] of suffering, the noble

2. Birth is suffering, aging is suffering, illness is suffering, death is suffering; union with what is displeas-ing is suffering; separation from what is pleasing is suffering; not to get what one wants is suffering.
3. It is this craving that leads to renewed existence, accompanied by delight and lust, seeking delight here and there: that is, craving for sensual pleasures, craving for existence, craving for extermination.

truth of the cessation[4] of suffering and the origin of suffering, and the noble truth of the path that leads to the cessation of suffering and the origin of suffering.] One also has to think beyond the impermanent axis of happiness, i.e., happiness in worldly life. Impermanent happiness comes from money. The locus of impermanent happiness is in the economy, which is, however, necessary for happiness. Happiness in the long run, however, comes from *nirvana* ["Nothing can give real happiness as can *nirvana*," so said the Buddha]. The route to nirvana is in *dharma*, is in the Four Noble Truths and The Eightfold Path.[5] But then even as a Buddhist practitioner you have to think about the economy, about the economic well-being of humanity. So, uh now, and of course I am not an economist, I do not know economics, but my general impression is that the Marxian understanding of the economy is premised on and lays emphasis on "equal distribution"—equal distribution as a *moral principle*.

DHAR: You've made a similar suggestion earlier also.

DALAI LAMA: Yes! Capitalists think about profit, about only money. About gain. There is not much talk about equal distribution in capitalism. I always make this distinction between original Marxist ideology and capitalism. I think, original Marxist ideology is very much related to/with a sense of altruism, a sense of concern for the well-being of the majority. At that time, in Marx's time, Marx sees employees, farmers, workers being simply used by landlords, feudal lords, and capitalists. He sees the owner of the factory exploiting his workers. I think Marx saw a lot of hardship. So he is seriously concerned with how to tackle the extreme forms of exploitation. And he saw how exploitation perpetuates a lot of suffering for working-class people. Marx takes up the cause of that proletariat, or the workers who are a majority, even native/colonized people. So you see, Marx was right in expressing his concerns over their rights; worker's rights, their well-being. So I invest much in Marxist ideology. I invest in order to generate courage in poor peasants and workers. In India, sometimes, Dalit subjects are using this religious word, *karma* ... *karma* as destiny; "low caste" is as if due to *karma*, so nothing can be done about it; one has to accept and persevere. So you see, it is possible at that time, their religious leader or community leader could be invoking *karma* to support ruling-class ideology. Karl Marx, on the other hand, develops some sort of conception of self-creation of change. Working-class people, their hands, their work, their labor, their consciousness is the key factor to change society. So this I feel is very much related with a core moral principle. At the same time, I always make it clear that I am totally against Leninism.

DHAR: Some of us over the years have become critical of what has come to be known as Leninism.

DALAI LAMA: So then you see unfortunately this concept of the proletariat eventually becomes smeared with power. The Bolshevik revolution ... it led to a civil war in

---

4. It is the remainder-less fading away and cessation of that same craving, the giving up and relinquishing of it, freedom from it, nonreliance on it.

5. The Eightfold Path: that is, right view, right intention, right speech, right action, right livelihood, right effort, right mindfulness, right concentration.

Russia; so then, during the civil war there was also a certain practice of suspicion, distrust, and ruthless control, and secrecy. These are perhaps relevant during wartime. But unfortunately such a wartime practice and habit become part of the so-called Marxist regime in Russia, as also later Communist systems. So now in all Communist countries, they don't think much, you see, about equal distribution or exploitation. Their main concern is power.

DHAR: Not critiques of power ... but power.

DALAI LAMA: Yes ... so you see the thirst for power actually destroys their original concept and practice. So that's my view. So then I think, in a manner that is too bold perhaps, I feel I am more Marxist than those Marxist parties [laughs]. Their main concern is power and money. They don't care about equal distribution, about exploitation. I do. I do still. So then the very reason that Marxism was born and developed in the nineteenth century, the sensibility and concern for the well-being of the majority, of the needy, of the poor, of the suffering people, is lost. There is an element of altruism, a sense of concern for the other in Marxism. This Marxist ideology was developed not just for some kind of new thesis, not because Marx would need to become a doctorate or something. But I think really, you see, it expresses serious social concern, and the way Marx expresses such concern is with a certain philosophy, a certain philosophical system. So from that aspect, there is some spirituality, some kind of spirituality in Marxism.

DHAR: There is?

DALAI LAMA: Yes. Spirituality can be thought at two levels. One, spirituality with respect to certain mysterious things of life, and beliefs, and faith. So it really helps to keep the question of compassion in mind; one remains God fearing, and that's good! Useful. As a person I want to harm something, someone, but then see, "Oh God, that thing, that person was also created by God; then I cannot harm." Good! So that's one kind of spirituality, at a certain level, a certain category of spirituality premised on certain beliefs. Then there could be another level of spirituality, without talking at all about these mysterious things: spirituality as practical, spirituality as everyday practice, a sense of concern over the other's well-being. Marxism is spiritual at that level. I am remembering Karl Marx's statement on religion ... in your questionnaire, where he says "religion is the heart of heartless people, the spirit of a spiritless condition, and it is the sigh of the oppressed ... "

DHAR: At one level, Marx sees religion as the scream of the oppressed. Of the exploited.

Dalai Lama: Yes.

DHAR: You have also imparted to religion, to Tibetan Buddhism, a voice we thought, that speaks for the oppressed Tibetan people. And we saw between Marx's understanding of religion and your understanding of Tibetan Buddhism a connection.

DALAI LAMA: [Laughs] ... I don't know. I have found Buddhist monks as also some Buddhist thinkers who, as far as their socioeconomic philosophy are concerned, are sound Marxist. Then there is Rahul Sankrityayan [1893–1963],[6] who became a Buddhist monk [*Bauddha Bhikkhu*] and eventually took up Marxism. So you see people who're really thinking and who have serious concern about the well-being of others and who do not put much emphasis on the Creator, and on *karma* kind of theories, develop some kind of closer connection to Marxist revolutionary thinking.

DHAR: Marx also suggests religion is the opium of the masses ...

DALAI LAMA: That is understandable. You see, when people follow religion seriously, sincerely, then all major traditions, in spite of different philosophical views, including the concept of Creator, or even in the absence of Creator, carry the same or similar messages, which is the message of love, compassion, forgiveness, tolerance, contentment, and self-discipline. All religions, you see, anyone in any religious group is expected to seriously practice these things. Then there is not much basis of terming religion opium ... but then, these same people sometimes, unfortunately, use religious gospels, phrases, to exploit, to oppress. If someone were to think of some new ideas, in order to suppress the new one, would say, "Oh, that's against God's Word," or something like that. As I mentioned earlier, you see, religion is used to support caste oppression. The courage, the effort to change things, to overturn caste hierarchy is killed by saying, "This is your destiny, because of your *karma*." This kind of thinking restricts human revolution/evolution and creativity. Sometimes religious thinking, nowadays, also the Buddhists, I think talk much about next life and not pay much attention to this life. Religion is in that case indeed opium. Opium because of two reasons. First, I think in the Buddhist case, and this is very harmful for the general population, there are too many monks, too much ritual. People's economic development is obviously neglected. So people sometimes say, "Oh, okay, it's just for this life." The next life becomes more important.

As a Buddhist I *will* foreground The Four Noble Truths. But that doesn't mean we do not have to develop the economy, or think of livelihoods. Money not for individual pockets; money for the well being of the society. That's *socialist* thinking. At the same time, now, in today's world, in the capitalist countries, and in the economic field there are no moral principles. However, on the other side, in those capitalist countries, there is also some rule of law, some idea of equality, democracy, freedom of

6. Kedarnath Pandey, who later changed his name to Rahul Sankrityayan—after Gautam Buddha's son, Rahul, and Sankrityayan, meaning "assimilator"—did perfect justice in giving himself this new name, for he went on to become a renowned Buddhist scholar. Sankrityayan is called the "Father of Hindi Travelogue" because he played a pivotal role in giving travelogue a "literary form." Even though he had a limited formal education, Sankrityayan wrote around 150 books on sociology, history, philosophy, Buddhism, science, drama, folklore, politics, Tibetology, lexicography, biography, autobiography, essays, and pamphlets in as many as five languages: Hindi, Sanskrit, Bhojpuri, Pali, and Tibetan. In 1937–8 and in 1947–8 he was appointed professor of Indology at the University of Leningrad. Sankrityayan was also an Indian nationalist, having been arrested and jailed for three years for anti-British writings and speeches. He was both a polymath and a polyglot. Read more at http://www.iloveindia. com/indian-heroes/rahul-sankrityayan.html.

speech, a robust press, etcetera. So there is also some kind of balance in those spaces; whereas in totalitarian systems, or countries, none of the latter things, like say, the free press, exists. If these communist countries carry forward the original Marxist concept, concept of equal distribution, seriously, then it's okay; but unfortunately that's not there. So then I think the people in these countries suffer more than those in capitalist countries. That's my view.

DHAR: Coming back to the question of Marxism and spirituality ...

DALAI LAMA: Yes. So in spirituality there are, according to me, two levels. One is spirituality with a certain belief, premised on a certain belief; and another kind of spirituality, which is simply warmheartedness and a sense of concern for the other's well-being. The second kind of spirituality I usually call *secular* spirituality.

DHAR: Yes!

DALAI LAMA: India, over the last three thousand years, has developed this tradition. Not only different religious traditions but also nonbelievers have coexisted in India. That's very relevant in today's world. That's very wise of a civilization.

DHAR: A kind of secular ethics?

DALAI LAMA: Yes. Secular ethics! So according to the Indian understanding, secular means *respect*. Respect for the other. Respect for all religions.

DHAR: Even the nonbeliever?

DALAI LAMA: *Even* the nonbeliever. That's a wonderful imagination, a beautiful path [laughs]. So that's *your* tradition ... hmm? In ancient times, one found philosophy, religion, the best of religion, the best of philosophy, in Nalanda. So the Tibetan emperor invited masters and teachers from Nalanda to Tibet. Although at that time, already, Buddhism had been forged in China. But the Tibetan emperor preferred, as far as Buddhism is concerned, to bring its teachings directly from India, from Nalanda. So modern Tibetans, including myself, are now taking India's tradition seriously. Our philosophy is to serve the seven billion beings on this planet, and there are over one billion nonbelievers, and we cannot ignore these one billion people. They also have a right to achieve a happy life. So if we try to promote moral principles on *only* the basis of religion, then nonbelievers will be left out, or nonbelievers will not show any interest in our work and thinking, so we can't dialog with the nonbelievers. I wish to develop a moral philosophy that appeals to all, even nonbelievers. Secular spirituality could be the ground for that.

DHAR: What is the psychological ground for such spirituality?

DALAI LAMA: We all come from our mothers. We all receive so much affection from our mothers. So the infant learns or begins to appreciate the experience of motherly affection from very early on. They don't like the sad or angry faces of their mothers. There is no religion or religious connection in all this. It is perhaps what is *human* in us. The seven billion human beings, *all* of them, receive the mother's affection. They survive because of their mother's care and affection. If parents were to abandon the infants, they would die. And then, even if we look at human beings who come from rich and influential families, but families without much inner value, that experience of family will not be a happy one. A poor person living in poor conditions but with parents full of affection will be happier. Some affection at the infant level is so important irrespective of whether one belongs to this religion or that religion. I am talking about this very life, not the next life, not the next to next life. In order to create happy human souls, *in this life*, we need the basic experience of humanity, at least at the infant level, in childhood.

On the other hand, every day ... today, every morning, when I watch the BBC, I see people are killing people, I see terrorists, I see the brutality of the police, I see refugees, migrants, and then I see poor people. Some are facing starvation; lots of people, really facing starvation. There is violence and war. And then in India, poor people, a lot of poor people live in the countryside. In big cities, some people live very luxurious lives. The same human beings say they believe in God. But if we all are created by God, God also gives to all of us the equal right to live. We cannot discriminate amongst ourselves as God's creation. We cannot say that someone has no right, and that someone has infinite right to exploit, oppress, amass money, and some others should remain poor. How can you say that?

I want richer people to pay more attention to poorer people and their difficulties. On one occasion in Delhi, I notice some kind of decoration in an open place. I ask, "What's going on there? Is it a religious festival?" I get to know: "No, marriage." Rich people spend lakhs for marriage. Instead of spending lakhs for building impermanent structures, one can buy bread, cheese, fruits, and assist the children on the streets, the homeless; one can distribute. That's the way to a happy marriage. The show of wealth by the rich makes the poorer feel envious, jealous. Shouldn't the poorer sections of society embark on some movement, albeit in a nonviolent path, against this show of wealth and this inequality? With support from Marxist theory? [Laughs.]

DHAR: You have tried to mark a difference between religion and spirituality. Would you like to say a little more on that?

DALAI LAMA: We use the word religion in association with a certain faith, for certain beliefs. So it involves some kind of mysterious element. But then spirituality, like secular spirituality, is not involved with faith or belief, though spirituality could also be religious; religious spirituality is also one kind of spirituality. But spirituality, you see, could also be without a certain faith, or belief, or mysterious element. Some people would like to call it humanism. I think Jainism, and Buddhism, is more akin to humanism. Both religions utilize or cultivate good human qualities, and utilize or cultivate in order to achieve happiness: happiness in this life and happiness in the next life, for all beings. There is not much reliance on Buddha or God. Buddha clearly mentions, "You are your own master." Buddha also stated, "Oh my follower, you should not accept my teachings out of faith but rather thorough investigation and experiment." So Buddha never said being the head of the religious group or having power will give you happiness.

DHAR: Marxism and the practice of the Marxist state has been a history of violence.

Dalai Lama: Yes!

DHAR: Do you think there was a spiritual deficit in the way Marxism was practiced?

DALAI LAMA: Oh definitely! Hardly any moral principles in the practice of Marxism. Only the pursuit of power. Marxists in the Soviet ordered to kill all the members of the Tsar's family including children. Why would we do that? I think, it stemmed from fear, suspicion, hatred, and the total lack of respect for the other's life.

DHAR: Yes.

DALAI LAMA: Stalin killed millions of people, his own people. There was immense suffering. I feel Mao Tse-tung was a sincere Marxist; he was a true Marxist revolutionary. But then during the civil war, again, there's the practice of suspicion, ruthlessness, secrecy; that took shape and form during the wartime. But then after a certain period—after 1951, or 1952 ... 54—when I went to China, even at that time, I could see the suspicion, the distrust. But I think, it was still quite okay, still within limits. Then gradually, from 1956 ... 57, we see the birth of too much totalitarian control. Control of media. The result: over a billion people end up being ignorant, ignorant of developments elsewhere, and ignorant of other ideas. They do not know where the world is going, what is "new."

I think, in the early 1980s, an opportunity to know the truth came to the Tibetans. On one occasion in the 1980s, I met a Tibetan, his brother, his relatives, here in Dharamsala. During the Cultural Revolution he was working in one of the Chinese departments, as a staff member. He told me, only after he reached India, he developed an understanding of what really happened during the Cultural Revolution. When he was in his own department, there was no information. So I often tell my Chinese friends: nearly one billion Chinese people, actually 1.3 billion Chinese people, have every right to know reality, know truth. Once Chinese people know reality, know the truth, they also have the ability to judge what is right, what is wrong.

Censorship is immoral. This censorship affects people only within the country, not the outside world. One is then fooling one's own people. Censorship has become part of the communist country's internal system. It's sad. On one occasion in Calcutta, I met Jyoti Basu, head of another communist state in India, head of a communist state government. At that time I had hoped that they would create a free Marxist regime. I asked one Indian Marxist, what is the attitude of the Indian communist towards religion? He said, "It is the responsibility of communists to serve people. People in India are religious. Indian communists must respect people's religion." I thought this was quite an important realization. With Jyoti Basu I had some sort of closeness. I met him on a few occasions. But then my friend told me about his private life; very much bourgeois. Jai Prakash Narayan had a very simple life, very simple.

DHAR: Yes, very simple life.

DALAI LAMA: Jai Prakash Narayan was also a socialist.

DHAR: Yes.

DALAI LAMA: I think Indian Marxism—Marxism in a democratic country, free country —could be something different from, say, Marxism in China.

DHAR: One other question. The history of religion has also seen violence, and I have in mind Sri Lankan Buddhism, Buddhism in Burma, etcetera. How would you respond to this, the violence that we see in religion? The violence we see in Marxism we have discussed and critiqued. The violence in religion also cannot be condoned.

DALAI LAMA: As I mentioned earlier, whatever, whichever religion we follow we are not implementing the teachings and the tenets seriously. Religion has become lip service. Also, sometimes I think we should make a distinction between religious organizations and religion. Religious organizations, and such organizations have developed since ancient times, were all immersed in a social system that was more or less a feudal system.

DHAR: Or even slave systems.

DALAI LAMA: Yes. So these religious institutions that developed within a feudal or a slave system were also influenced by the existing social systems. So the existing religious institutions are not very democratic.

DHAR: So there is something feudal in these institutions or organizations.

DALAI LAMA: Yes. Then the worst thing is, religious people, they do not seriously practice, they just use the *name* of their religion or the name of the Son of God. And once they use the name of religion, then they, whichever religious faith they belong to, have an effect on our emotional selves. So then it becomes easy to manipulate the people who are under that particular name of the religion or Son of God. So though actually all religions will say the same thing—universal humanity, all are brothers and sisters, all created by god—at a more practical level, we shall have distinctions between *my/our* religion, *their* religion, *this* religious difference, *that* difference, helping in turn to create more and more divisions: including nationalisms, and different and contesting nationalities, differing religious faiths, different races, different family lines and backgrounds. I think that at a more fundamental level we are all human beings.

Whenever I come across some sort of problem because of different religions or because of different nationalities, or different countries, at all these moments, I think, we are after all the same human being. Even for a religious believer, we are all same and created by the same and one God. Then all these problems become less significant. But too much emphasis on the difference of religions, nations, hardens our concept of "we" and "they," "us" and "them." What follows such hardening is violence and discrimination, whereas all religions teach us universal humanity. Religious people should stress more on the fundamental sameness of human beings, rather than difference, in order to help us see the sense of *oneness* in the human and in humanity.

One of my Muslim friends, who is also a local Muslim leader, in a public meeting in one remote place in Ladakh, near the Pakistan border, stressed: a genuine Muslim, a genuine practitioner of Islam, must extend love and compassion towards the entire creation of Allah. I think there should be a distinction between, on the one hand, people's everyday practices and religion, and on the other, religious institution and religion. I am quite critical about my own institution now. I am quite critical. This institution that was born within feudalism is outdated now. There is no institution of Nāgārjuna.[7] But Nāgārjuna's teaching is still very much alive. So when people say, without the Dalai Lama, Tibetan Buddhism—I mean the *institution* of/for Tibetan Buddhism—will not survive, I always say there is no institution of Nāgārjuna, but his teaching is still very much alive. Institutions come and go; institutions are born, they also die; the teachings live on.

DHAR: Yes.

DALAI LAMA: So study and implement and practice. That is the way for the preservation of Buddha's *dharma* or Nāgārjuna's philosophy.

DHAR: Religion can be seen as an individual pursuit, as *my* happiness ...

DALAI LAMA: That's right!

DHAR: ... my *moksha*, my next life. Can we say that you have made religion *social*?

DALAI LAMA: Buddhism is *practice—Buddha chitta*; it is about altruism, *infinite* altruism. It is about thinking of the other's well-being. Śāntideva ...

DHAR: Śāntideva Bodhishanti,[8] yes ...

---

7. Nāgārjuna (ca. A.D. 150–250) is the most important Buddhist philosopher after the historical Buddha himself. His philosophy of the "middle way" (*madhyamaka*), based around the central notion of "emptiness" (*śūnyatā*), influenced the Indian philosophical debate for a thousand years after his death; with the spread of Buddhism to Tibet, China, Japan, and other Asian countries, the writings of Nāgārjuna became an indispensable point of reference for their own philosophical inquiries. A specific reading of Nāgārjuna's thought, called *Prāsaṅgika-Madhyamaka*, became the official philosophical position of Tibetan Buddhism. See http://plato.stanford.edu/entries/nagarjuna for a detailed exposition.

8. Śāntideva (literally "god of peace") was an eighth-century (ca. A.D. 685–763) Indian Buddhist monk and scholar at Nalanda and is among the most renowned and esteemed figures in the entire history of Mahayana Buddhism. He was an adherent of the Madhyamaka philosophy of Nāgārjuna. Śāntideva is the author of the *Bodhisattvacaryāvatāra* (glossed as "A Guide to the Bodhisattva's Way of Life" or "Entering the Path of Enlightenment") and the *Śikṣāsamuccaya*. The *Bodhisattvacaryāvatāra* is the primary source of most of the Tibetan Buddhist literature on the cultivation of altruism and the Spirit of Awakening. The term *Mahāyāna*, literally "Great Vehicle," came to mean the idea of attempting to become a

DALAI LAMA: Bodhishanti says that if you are able to exchange your happiness, joy, and suffering for others, then one is reaching Buddhahood—even in Samsara itself.

One will be happier if one is altruistic. Buddhism is the practice of infinite altruism. I think altruism is there in all religion; any religion which encourages the practice of love is altruistic. However, I feel there is a lack of conviction about this inner/core value of religion. That's perhaps because our existing social system, sources of culture and environment, are very much materialistic. That in turn comes from materialistic education. Existing modern education is very much oriented about material value.

DHAR: Material well-being, and not ethical value?

DALAI LAMA: The modernist vision mainly comes from the West. When modern education began in the West, when the belief took shape that with the help of science and technology more economic development could happen, education became mainly concerned with what is scientific and technological; religion or religious values were put aside. In modern times, even the serious believer among the religious does not seriously believe in or practice religion. Religion has become something like fashion right now.

However, the only hope is education. Education should include some education of moral principles. Moral principles not based on religious faith but based on common sense, common experience, and scientific findings. The scientists, some of the top scientists, have suggested that constant anger, fear, is actually eating into our immune system, and it is bad for our health. The compassionate mind ushers in inner strength, self-confidence, and that is helpful in reducing fear, I think. Some scientists have conducted experiments with infants, a few months after birth, who have not yet developed language. They show some cartoons to the infants. In one cartoon they show the young children playing together; they see the infant smiling. The other cartoon has same young children hurting each other, harming each other; they see the infant looking unhappy. I think the basic human nature is more about being compassionate, and that is also logical! We are social animals. Any social animal can survive only through care and compassion; also, to be social, to be together or to bring together, at an emotional level, the common minimum factor is love. Hatred separates. So let us educate and nurture ourselves in love and compassion.

When the British introduced modern education in India, some opportunity was lost. At that time, India's scholars who knew much about ancient Indian thought, including Indian work on the psychological, all the sciences of the mind, these should have been included in the education system with some kind of synthesis with mainstream Western education. The British introduced Western Christian education, while here in India, thousand-year-old traditions and values were still alive; a combination of the ancient and modern could have created a new curriculum.

---

bodhisattva (and eventually a buddha) oneself rather than merely following the teachings set out by Siddhārtha Gautama (considered the original Buddha). An introduction to and commentary on the *Bodhisattvacaryāvatāra* by the fourteenth Dalai Lama, called *A Flash of Lightning in the Dark of Night*, was printed in 1994 (Shambhala). A commentary on the "Patience" chapter was provided by the Dalai Lama in *Healing Anger* (Snow Lion, 1997), and his commentaries on the "Wisdom" chapter can be found in *Practicing Wisdom* (2004, Wisdom Publications). See http://www.iep.utm.edu/santideva and http://shantidevameditation.org/shantideva-story for details.

DHAR: A new imagination, perhaps.

DALAI LAMA: Yes, something new. But still, it is not too late. I think, it is possible. In India, in your thousand-year-old tradition, you have the experience or tradition of *ahimsa* that respects all religion as well as the nonbeliever. Practically all major Indian traditions, including Buddhism and Jainism, practice *samadhi, vipasana, yoga.* So there is a lot of understanding and explanation, lot of knowledge about human emotions, about the human mind. There is deeper knowledge about how to deal with emotions, pain, and suffering; about *mindfulness.* These should be included in the field of education. Through that kind of education, I think there is a possibility to create a new generation who understands the real value of compassion, and that is the way to build a happier and a loving and compassionate society. I think India should lead the way.

Tibetan thought comes from India, not from China. A fourteenth-century Tibetan scholar and practitioner felt, till the light of knowledge from India reaches Tibet, Tibet—in spite of being the land of snow and white bright light—shall remain dark. It's so true. Ancient India is our guru, not modern India. Modern India is too Westernized. Your ancient tradition is really valuable to us. But then your culture is alive now only in ceremony and ritual, not in deeper reflection on the human, what is human, who we are.

I am meeting some scholars, some spiritual practitioners, soon, in Nasik on the occasion of the Kumbh Mela. I am really excited. Now this is one opportunity to discuss seriously and revive interest and scholarship in ancient Indian knowledge, but please don't see this as yet another ceremony [laughs]. Now I think the time has come to revive ancient Indian knowledge. In the last few decades, religious harmony is still better in India than in other spaces. We should maybe go deeper into why India gave birth to the idea of *ahimsa*? How did India manage at least some form of religious harmony? What would be Marxist practice in such a culture of *ahimsa* and harmony?

You consider yourself a Marxist?

DHAR: Not in the old way.[9]

---

9. It was a moment of table turning; and "table turning" or "turning the table" is Marx's (2016, 39) metaphor (in *Capital*, vol. 1: "In the expression of value there is a complete turn of the tables"). Conventional standards of interviewing suggest that one person (the interviewer) asks/poses questions and the other person (the interviewee) answers/responds to the questions. What happens when the interviewee begins to ask questions? What happens when the other poses questions—questions that have not been already anticipated/assimilated by the self? Why would the other ask questions? When the other knows? When the other already knows that I come from and represent the journal *Rethinking Marxism*? Why would the other ask, "Are you a Marxist?" What is the other hinting at? Is the question, "Are you still a Marxist"— the stress on the *still*, with the exclamation mark: still!—"still a Marxist, after all that you have heard and seen about our suffering?" Was there a secret ethical charge in the question? I was somewhat paralyzed by the question, paralyzed as I was already by the experience of visiting the Tibet museum in McLeod Ganj, a visit that preceded the question, the shame the visit generated: What have we done? What have we, as Marxists, done in Tibet? How could we have perpetuated such brutality? A certain numbness comes to haunt one as one makes one's way through the Tibet museum. And here was the living

DALAI LAMA: What do you feel about my sort of view?

DHAR: I agree with you somewhere, because without compassion Marxism becomes very coarse, very rough. And that kind of masculinism dehumanizes us. As a perpetrator, that variant of Marxism has dehumanized itself. It is not the victim who gets dehumanized, it is the perpetrator who gets dehumanized.

DALAI LAMA: That's very true!

DHAR: We don't want to get dehumanized, because that's a very lonely and violent self. And I have always felt that the oppressed remains human even if there is suffering. It's the oppressor who gets dehumanized. The oppressor is the one losing human compassion, losing touch with love. And if Marxism puts on the cloak of an oppressor, it becomes coarse in the process. The Marxian and the spiritual also get estranged in the process.

DALAI LAMA: Yes! They themselves feel fear, loneliness, distrust ...

DHAR: Such a Marxism is always secretive; there is concealment, suspicion. But you yourself have no one to suspect because you're free, out in the open. So we don't want that kind of ideology anymore that creates and harbors secret services and paranoia.

DALAI LAMA: Thank you!

DHAR: I would like to thank you on behalf of *Rethinking Marxism* for this interview, this dialog with us, and for the way you have engaged with our questions.

Acknowledgments

The editors of this special issue of Rethinking Marxism *would like to thank Dr. Dibyesh Anand, for assistance in setting up the interview with the fourteenth Dalai Lama, and Mr. Tenzin Taklha, Secretary, Office of the fourteenth Dalai Lama, for help in conducting the interview and for constant editorial support with respect to the transcript of the interview. The editors would also like to thank Karuna Chandrasekhar for help in transcription.*

embodiment of the brutalized; here was the brutalized asking me, "Are you a Marxist? Are you *still* a Marxist," after all that you have heard and seen? Can you be one?

For a moment, I found it difficult to say with consummate ease and pride, "Yes, I am one." I felt for a moment I would be failing the brutalized, I would be failing history and the history of brutality, if I uttered, without a pause, without a moment's reflection, without doubt, and with too much confidence, "Yes, I am a Marxist." Faced with the history and experience of violence, face-to-face with the brutalized, I couldn't say with confidence, "Yes, I am." I could only manage, "Not in the old way." It was like saying, "Yes, I am. I am still. *But* not in the old way"—the "ways" that have brutalized you. It was as if to *reassure* the brutalized: I have heard you. I feel for you. I am not like them. "We"—the *Rethinking Marxism* collective—are not like them. We are in search of a *different* Marxism. Of Marxism *with a difference.*

References

The Fourteenth Dalai Lama. 1994. *A flash of lightning in the dark of night: A guide to the Bodhisattva's way of life.* Boston: Shambhala.

———. 1997. *Healing anger: The power of patience from a Buddhist perspective.* Trans. T. Jinpa. Ithaca, N.Y.: Snow Lion.

———. 2004. *Practicing wisdom: The perfection of Shantideva's Bodhisattva way.* Trans. and ed. T. Jinpa. Boston: Wisdom Publications.

Marx, K. 2016 (1965). *Capital.* Vol. I. Trans. S. Moore and E. Aveling, ed. F. Engels. Moscow: Progress Publishers. https://www.marxists.org/archive/marx/works/download/pdf/Capital-Volume-I.pdf.

Śāntideva. 1960. Bodhicaryāvatāra of Śāntideva. In *Buddhist Sanskrit Texts XII*, ed. P. L. Vaidya. Darbhanga, India: Mithila Institute.

———. 1970. *Śikṣāsamuccaya.* In *Çikshāsamuccaya: A compendium of Buddhistic teachings, compiled by Çāntideva chiefly from earlier Mahāyāna sūtras,* ed. C. Bendall. Osnabruck, Germany: Biblio Verlag.

Transcendence, Spirituality, Practices, Immanence: A Conversation with Antonio Negri

Judith Revel

Translated by Arianna Bove

Antonio Negri answers three questions posed by Judith Revel: on the necessary transcendence of spirituality, or on its potential redefinition as immanence of practices; on Francis of Assisi between mysticism and poverty; and on the possible interpretation of Spinoza as an ontology of immanence entirely built against all metaphysics of transcendence. Negri replies by retracing his own political and philosophical past and trying to reaffirm what he thinks must be defined as the "smile" of revolt.

Judith Revel's Questions

It seems to me that there are really three issues that structure your relationship to spirituality. I'll expose them rather quickly; you can then tell me what they are for you.

The first corresponds roughly to what might be called your critique of transcendence, of any form of transcendence, and religious transcendence in particular. In your work, there is this sense that religious transcendence, a separate power that hangs over and thus disqualifies the life of the men and women "down here," is a gesture of unprecedented violence. Not only because historically it was and still is used to legitimize the forms of "capture" of actual human life, to justify the exploitation imposed upon men and women, to excuse the suffering they have had to sustain, the poverty they were forced to withstand, the absolute obedience that was required of them, but also because it has nourished all of the processes of manipulation and concealment that we know of—and can still observe today.

From this point of view, despite their differences, none of the three major monotheistic religions is left unscathed: transcendence literally feeds on a life it proclaims worthless, in the name of another life that is to come. Transcendence is the weapon of the powerful: it justifies all subjection, the looting, the fleeing, the splits and fratricidal wars: all of the barbarities we know. It is a construction of power where the Greek idea of the *arche*, as principle and commandment, is reinvested in the form of a law that escapes us and decrees that one day we will be worth something on condition that we accept being worthless today.

Let me know if you have anything to add. I would like to talk about, in particular, a twofold issue intimately related to the question of transcendence—since this issue is its immediate effect—an issue that I know fascinates you: that of incarnation on the one hand and of the resurrection of the body on the other. God made man, the incarnation of Christ, and his passion, and therefore Christ cannot be king of men because he suffered in a body and a life like theirs; and also there is the issue of knowing with what body we are reborn to life. I ask you this question because this twofold issue cannot be conceived of without the idea of transcendence, of a split between here and beyond, and yet the passion of Christ as told by the texts of the Gospels is the moment when, paradoxically, transcendence vanishes: Jesus is a man among men. Similarly, the idea of the resurrection of the flesh, which is unthinkable without the idea of another life beyond our historical existence, is a moment when transcendence seems to disappear: we are reborn in the flesh, whole, living, tangible, "heavy" with our flesh.

In any case, the question is whether there might be something like spirituality without any reference to transcendence, whether it is possible to have an entirely immanent spirituality, taking the world as it is. And if so, what dimension of the mind is being deployed—the mind rather than spirit because this is what, etymologically, spirituality refers to. The problem of the concept of mind is that it is only conceivable as the difference from the body, and from matter. And one returns to thinking of spirituality as something immaterial and floating, rarefied, or secluded, even as we try to reinscribe it into the world. I wondered if instead we could not speak of spirituality as something concerning gestures, attitudes, body exercises, practices, and refer spirituality to a "making" in the world, to an action rather than some sort of very vague and disembodied spiritual ether.

That brings me to my second question. This is precisely the assumption that one could draw the very idea of spirituality close to that which the transcendent construct of religion has been trying to erase: practices, gestures, bodies, materiality of the world, intersubjective relations and the relationship with oneself, elements that are the most concrete aspect of spirituality. This is, I believe, what fascinates Foucault in the concept of "spiritual exercises" when he begins to look into ancient philosophy, particularly the Stoics: diet and pleasures, reading and remembering, physical training and self-writing, nothing is hierarchical while all helps to build oneself and to build a rapport with others (the relationship with oneself is always a relation to others, Foucault reminds us: a formidable "social relations intensifier," and spiritual exercises are never a purely individualistic matrix). I speak of Foucault because I think he is attempting a rare operation in the history of thought: to draw the spiritual dimension, which he interprets—it is no coincidence—immediately as constituent, toward practices. What is spirituality? It is to build a relationship with oneself and others that is always a practice of the self and the other, an acting with/onto oneself and others, a way of acting in and on the world.

But this practice is particular in that it constitutes, opens, transforms, and modifies only because it adds and inaugurates. The idea of practice found in spiritual exercises is both a record of what is (I "work" the reality of my body, my existence, relations that

bind me to others) and a change (I transform what is by means of the exercise I practice) and innovation (this transformation still creates a surplus, an element of novelty).

I think, speaking of spiritual exercises, Seneca wrote in one of his letters that one needs
to "digest" the world. The image of digestion is quite beautiful if it is rescued from the
images of ruminants that quarrel over power. Digestion produces something else: a
kind of incorporation that produces an energy that renews the present state of things
as it eliminates this state (it is both digested and creative of what this digestion permits).

The question becomes: is there a way for you to update the idea of "spirituality"
today as an immanent practice of the world? You often referred to Francis. I feel
that we have, in Francis, both of these two aspects just mentioned. On the one hand,
we find a very strong sense of transcendence, the divine and its superiority, in the
idea that Francis must behave *perinde hac cadaver*,[1] a concept of absolute obedience,
the stigmata, even if this comes with a very sharp criticism of the institution of the
Church and of the power it assumes, which is justified precisely on behalf of transcendence. There are really two transcendences: that of blind obedience to God, which
Francis defends, and that which establishes the worldly power of the Church, which
Francis hates. This is an obedient Francis, therefore, subjected, desperately searching
in his own life for the signs of the passion of Christ.

On the other hand is the Francis of "the *poverelli*" and the birds, who shall regulate
his own poverty, which does not mean that he decides on his own poverty as an individual gesture but that he decides to go live poor among the other poor, which is very
different. Francis the critic of his own caste who invents a completely different way of
life, always conceived as a shared one, his critique of wealth, and so on. I was wonder-
ing if you had deliberately chosen to deal with the second rather than the first—to
create a kind of monogram of your own indignation and of practices that were yours
and those of your generation. Because this is also the mystical Francis, and it seems
to me that without transcendence this figure is quite difficult to explain ...

This finally brings me to the third question, which follows on from what I am trying
to describe. I wonder whether in your work this idea of practices as a realm of the "spiritual"—the realm of transformation and invention that you often call "production"—is
not also linked to the reinsertion of an ontological perspective within the materiality of
the world. It could be said that an immanent and material ontology without transcendence that is also able to open up history at its own thresholds in order to construct the
work of creative men and women, that this ontology is actually what makes the very
matter of life both an "already there" and ever-open horizon, a future still to be forged.

I have wanted to understand what this idea, if it is right, owes to Spinoza, whether
Spinoza's thought is precisely the thought my questions were drawn to from the beginning: a philosophy of absolute immanence that nevertheless does not preclude power; a
thought of the practice of the world and its transformation based on the idea that everything opens at any moment; the need to find political forms to organize this power
without restoring the old transcendent models of metaphysics or, in political terms, of
sovereignty.

Doesn't the issue of radical democracy require that one leave the necessary transcendence of sovereignty? What is extraordinary in Spinoza is that he raised this

---

1. "In the manner of a corpse," an expression used to describe the obedience of a disciple to a master.

problematic just as modern philosophy began to raise the question of a metaphysics of sovereignty, one that is still largely our own today ... So the project of a political ontology of power would oppose a metaphysics of sovereignty, just as immanence precludes transcendence, and somehow spirituality as a set of practices and relationships, gestures and structures, would oppose a spirituality of acceptance as a renunciation of oneself and the world in the name of another life ...

Antonio Negri's Answers

I will try to answer all three of your questions at once. I could not do it separately because, in your writing, everything comes together. I hope that in mine everything will come together too.

But I will first summarize your questions to see if I understood them. First: can there be spirituality without transcendence? In this case, according to you, we always come up against aporiae that materialist discourse cannot resolve. How to deal with this problem? And how does Marx posit the relationship between critique of religion and political action? How to renew, if necessary, the critique of religious transcendence? The second question is inspired by Foucault and asks how it is possible to practice spirituality as immanent to the world. It is a question that looks favorably to religious experience. The third question poses the problem of spirituality in relation to the ontology of immanence, with a clear reference to Spinoza. I would say, therefore, that in addition to taking on the three authors (Marx, Foucault, Spinoza) around whom you articulate each problem, your questions interrogate three *dispositifs*: that of the paradoxical recognition of an effect of transcendence, immanent to history; that of a materialist production of subjectivity; and that of the definition of a political form adequate to the immanence of values (and democratic?).

On the first question of whether religion is "the opium of the people," I would note that even if it were, it would not mean that spirituality is. On the contrary, I dare to add that *ex abrupto*, the product of the imagination (in Spinoza's and Kant's sense), can certainly be defined as an effect of transcendence in immanence, as a worldly "beyond," an object of desire: provided that it does not turn into superstition. It is true that Marxism posited its distance from religion in a hyperseparation that makes it hard to rescue any spirituality. This would be "false consciousness" and surely superstition, if not mere cynical statecraft. Yet someone has rightly noted that because of this, Marxism produced a veritable "hole" in political anthropology, one that it ended up falling into because it was impossible to construct the "communist man" without taking him on as a whole. It was a painful history. Do you remember the Soviet museums of atheism? Yet even in the face of these excesses, who would dare to deny that in the class struggle experienced in the shadow cone of Marxism there was a kind of secret spirituality? That in communist militancy some experiences—such as the practice of the virtues (that some call "theological"), of solidarity, of prophecy, of poverty—are also typical of the religious experience?

Having said that, I would like to provide an initial answer to Judith: the question for me was never a denunciation of the reactionary functions of a transcendent divine. Even in my first philosophical stammering, divinity to me was immediately represented in immanence, and if I had to argue over any aporiae, it was not over those of transcendence but over those of pantheism. After all, I do not believe these difficulties to be so different from those encountered by anyone who wishes to maintain a framework of transcendence: they are two inevitably analogous opposites.

Basically, I do not believe that the negation or demystification of transcendence constitutes a major problem. But I never looked to *what is above* our existence, I always looked at *what is within* or was said to be in it. Vulgar materialism deals with criticizing what is above; Marxism unveils what's inside. Namely, my problem was never to argue directly against the idea of a divine transcendence but to directly attack any transcendent or transcendental conception of consciousness. What has always seemed unbearable to me is the constant reminder, against human pain and misery, of a supposed freedom and wealth that reside—out of all circumstances—in *interiore homine*. The objects of my criticism are the soul, identity, egoism, and individualism. And the object of my criticism is the attempt, promoted by religion, to fix values and establish a "human nature" that gives them their absoluteness and eternity.

In this case, then, in monotheistic religions this ontological transcendence and naturalist idea of consciousness serve to ensure the establishment of power, to give substance to social inequalities, to mystify human misery, and especially to conceal exploitation. If you add to this the fact that the church, or at least the theological and ecclesiastical authorities, are defined in monotheistic religions as something that corresponds to the divine order, that reproduces its form in the shape of an "ontological analogy" and that finds therein its absolute foundation, it becomes clear how unacceptable the determined and fixed subjection, slavery, and transcendence organized in churches and filtered through the consciences of individuals really is. In this regard, it is sufficient to mention what Carl Schmitt drew from the religious phenomenon (and from Catholicism in particular) with perfect consistency: an authoritarian political paradigm, capable of absolutist and fascist tendencies. If this does not make our critique of the political effects of religious transcendence necessarily true, it will at least authorize our firm denunciation of them. And I would remind the many who today lament, some even honestly, the frontal opposition between the Christian and the communist framework that has traversed and still traverses the current discontent of civilization—well, I would remind them of the wholly reactionary responsibility of this political and philosophical opposition. This opposition wished to celebrate the soul as opposed to the body, the spirit against matter, almost as if religion consisted of this opposition and had to do nothing more than safeguard it.

Yet Marxism, as we were saying, is not only the right demystification of the reactionary face of theology. Following Engels, Mehring, and many others (who would have thought!), Ernst Bloch threw light on the revolutionary religiosity at work during the Reformation and showed us the repression, or rather the damnation, to which Catholic and Protestant principles alike were united in condemning their common enemy, united against the spiritual and revolutionary conduct of the German peasants. Ernst Bloch also discovered, in hope, the deep common matrix of the *dispositif* of religion and the communist matrix of a wholly human redemption. Again, with reference to Averroè and the medieval tradition lasting up to Dante Alighieri, Bloch destroyed the infamous separation between soul and body and spirit and matter developed by Scholasticism, demonstrating how powerful and joyful their union can actually be.

As far as Bundist Marxists are concerned, their Judaic prophetic stance is certainly part and parcel of communist theory and militancy. Finally, "liberation theology" ...

You, Judith, note that the incarnation of Christ fascinates me. It is true: I believe this theological fable resonates deeply with my experience of communist militancy. But there is incarnation and incarnation.

There is a sweetish incarnation figure in the Counter-Reformation and in the colonial Conquista, one that turns the suffering of Jesus into its regal figure. When in seventeenth-century churches—in Vienna as in Quito—you look at the scenes of the Passion, you feel that the body of Jesus is paradoxically portrayed as a regal body.

The nails that pierce him do not torment the body; the crown of thorns is shown to us as a sovereign crown. There is nothing truly "embodied" in triumphant Catholicism. By contrast, there is an ancient image that fascinates me: the Lamb that absolves humanity by his sacrifice, that bears all the sins of the world, and this is indeed an ancient image already present both in the Book of Job and in the myth of Dionysus.

It is the experience of the divine conquered by man and translated into what man is rather than the illusion of a human raised to the divine, to what is not there. Then the former is the foundation of human dignity because it interprets the common of man, the innocence of a body capable of militancy, of struggle, of sacrifice for the other— that is, for everyone. It is an essential spiritual exercise because it demands humility, generosity, love; in short, it is an experience of the divine from the inside, giving it, building it for the other—that is, for everyone.

I am fascinated even more by the myth of the "resurrection of the flesh." "Liberation theology" noted that, if the body could be taken to the heavens in the Last Judgment, it was somehow sacred, and therefore its needs were sacred and holy was the action to satisfy them, which consists of the struggle of the poor against the rich, against the exploitation of workers. Therefore, whether religious or not does not matter: it is virtuous to fight for wages, in order to appropriate the land of large estates, to fight against private property and the legal organization that defends it, to build a community willing to defend life and build happiness in this world.

I am convinced of this, but I integrate it with an entirely Marxian motivation: the struggle of "living labor" against "dead labor" has sealed the fate of man's victory over death. Here atheism can no longer be confused with the polemic against transcendence or against the piety and political authority that emanate from religious power: religion shapes and produces the transcendental schema of a "being for death." Atheism rejects this.

What you say about Foucault's work on the "spiritual exercises" in the classical age and in early Christianity seems to me very important. I share the attention you give to "practical spirituality," immanent in the work (opera) and to the world. This is a spirituality that invents and reinvents itself, transforms and is transformed, always socializing the ego in us.

Here spirituality becomes productive. Unsurprisingly, this theory of "subjectivity practicing" on itself and the construction of the world investigated by Foucault in an ancient practice was immediately read as a "contemporary example," as the parable of subjectivity in the present time, both in its worldly enslavement and in its struggle for liberation in the world.

The interpretation of all of man, spirit, and matter caught in the experience of life, as an expression of free power (or as a product of power), this is a formidable image of the human condition. But there is a Foucault even more essential to recall here: the Foucault who recognizes the experience of the subject's resistance to power as an irreducible element of a domination that is intransitive and asymmetrical with respect to power.

Couldn't it be the case that this resistance, which is deepened in the immanence of the power relation, is close to class struggle? And yet in Foucault (of course, not only in Foucault but in many others of his circle, but for him with an experimental intelligence that enhances this philosophical position) the dialectic as a "mediation process" is criticized and done away with. And this is still a refusal of transcendence: because every dialectical figure, no matter its shape, contains in its concept and its operation—in its "mediation"—an element of transcendence.

There is something that is brought in from the outside, from above, to resolve the clash or the encounter between figures and/or historical powers. In Hegel every negation of transcendence is theological. On the basis of this refusal, Foucauldian practice cannot merely stop at the transformation of the spirit working on itself. It opens up a much more profound and effective perspective.

This is evidenced in the reference to the Kantian and Enlightenment motto *sapere aude*. Utopia has returned to reality, as hope returns to knowledge and power to love. Here, making is presented not only as a possibility of freedom but also as the making of the material conditions for freedom, and in this it comes close to Marxian thought. This spirituality contains a constructive materialism developed as a *dispositif* geared to affect industry, institutions, and human community, opening up the possibility of a sort of "spiritual exercise" of and in the multitude. In Foucault, power opens up to passion, the passion of making, but to this he adds a multitudinal and historical transvaluation of the productive passion. This element is no longer close to the young Marx's critique of alienation but to the mature Marx who interprets the relationship between worker and machine and the value that is produced by them.

You refer to Francis of Assisi, or the images that probably correspond to his history: the Francis of the stigmata and the poor of Assisi. One is completely absorbed in the mystical and extreme experience of religious spirituality, the other in the founders of modern humanism. Do we have to choose between these two figures? Of course we do. The second figure that emerges here is open to what is to come. But maybe in contemporaneity it is no longer necessary to choose: how is it possible to escape from the world? The world has been brought into capital; there is no possibility of an outside. Poor is the one who is exploited, indebted, exposed to the fear of living, seized by an inimical domination; the poor one is excluded, but inside the biopolitical, inside the life cage organized by capital. The Franciscan notion of poverty thus leads us to living with the poor, as you say Judith, and imposes the figure of militancy within the proletariat of our world. Francis is one of the "indignados."

The productive and constitutive element you were referring to when mentioning Foucault allows me to link to the third question, that on the ontological dimensions of atheist spirituality in the framework of critical materialism, and to draw some conclusions in the field of political philosophy.

First of all, I would like to insist on what has been said so far, and to underline the characters of a "critical materialism," of that form of historical and antagonistic immanence whose ontology was inaugurated by the recognition of the productivity of labor. Marxian materialism is clearly included in this. It is a materialism of life interpreted as a relation of man with nature and the transformation of nature and construction of the world. This historical construction operates at the pace of the productive forces that define power, that give history its direction. I thus underline that this productive force is not only mechanical, physical, and economic but also vital, immaterial (that is to say, material and cognitive, affective and cooperative), and constituent. Here, "living labor," manifest especially in a passion for the freedom of productive energies, becomes the protagonist of the historical process. There is Enlightenment in Marxism, an indomitable *sapere aude*. And there is also that love of the world that is luminously illustrated in the Spinozist passion of Being. In Spinoza, spirituality lacks all interiority; therefore, it seeks common joy, the ethical construction of happiness, and that being together in the city that expresses the power of being. The productivity of being inaugurates the politics of the multitudes, absolute democracy, and this common power destroys all metaphysics, because metaphysics is always transcendence.

I want to emphasize that, for Spinoza, spirituality—what is left of religion—is a joyous passion, knowledge, and will experienced at the threshold of a yet-to-come temporality. It is certainly exposed to the risk of nothingness, but it is not a "being in nothing" or a "being for nothing." Here, we are inside the constructive passions that push nothingness away from existence, always in the struggle of life against death. The prophecy, the reading of what is to come, becomes as important as a realistic measure of being, because we know that what is to come is conditioned by our power, our confidence in the power to build it. Class struggle is either positioned to be available for the construction of historical being or it simply does not exist. Absoluteness is not a transcendental value: the absolute is *kairos*, an insistence on every point, on each temporal intensity upon which being is constructed. Job exits tragedy by overcoming the power of a destiny that wants him enslaved, and by (literally) recognizing himself in the face of God, he recognizes human freedom: truth is construed in this act. Spinoza tends toward the maximum threshold of the thinkable, the relationship between physical *conatus*, biopolitical *cupiditas*, and *amor*. Religious passion? Why not, if it is a case of conjoining, in production, the absoluteness of knowledge and that of love?

Hence we come to the political consequences of this spirituality. Now monotheistic theology is not only the matrix of any conception of sovereignty, as we have already seen. It is also the inspiration for any restriction of democracy, freedom, and desire.

"No, we can't" is its theme and its refrain. From this perspective Carl Schmitt theorized the *katechon*, with a retinue of philosophers who, while contemplating before death their trembling souls, accompany the sad passion of servitude.

The *katechon* is a political theory of the limitation of liberty and of the relativization of the desire for justice; an insuperable limit internal to political action; a new unoriginal form of the "Machiavellianism" of the seventeenth century that is far more dangerous than that.

The sovereign as a god may impose the "state of exception," followed by a normal conception of power that preventively provides both limit and compromise because it thinks freedom impossible. The expression of the absolute sovereign follows the declaration of the impotence of the citizen and, worse, the impossibility of democracy. Marxian communism is the radical negation of all this: a negation that knows no compromise or dialectical solutions.

In the mid-90s, in discussions with Derrida around his critique of Marx's *Capital* in *Specters of Marx*, after emphasizing the dual use of "of"—the ghosts living in the letter of *Capital* and the spirit of Marxism that lives in our thinking—I noted that the intensity of "deconstruction" led to a radical dematerialization or deontologization of the communist theory of value and exploitation, thus depriving them of all passionate intensity.

The Derridean interpretation had actually been incapable of reconstructing an image of that passion in the experience of the present. In fact, it ended up erasing all relations between exploitation and revolutionary struggle and all the images of class struggle between the rich who command and the poor who rebel. What Derrida presented us with was a "postmodern" Marx in the worst sense of the term, one minus the struggle of the working class, whose poverty was marginal and whose power was not even suspected.

To conclude my critique, let me give an example. Alexis de Tocqueville's *Memoirs* tell of a day in June 1848. We are in a beautiful apartment of the Parisian Left Bank, the seventh arrondissement, at lunchtime. Tocqueville's family is gathered there and yet, in the calm of the evening, the cannons drawn by the bourgeoisie against the rebellion of the workers in revolt suddenly resonate, distant noises on the right bank. The diners pale, their faces darken.

A young waitress serving their table, fresh from the Faubourg Saint-Antoine, instinctively smiles. She is immediately fired. Isn't this true spirituality? Isn't this the real specter of communism, the spirituality expressed in this smile? What terrifies the tsar, the pope ... and the lord of Tocqueville? There is here a hint of joy that turns into a specter of liberation. That smile: how do you dematerialize or deontologize it? Let us keep this episode in mind, the smile ... in this consists that immanent spirituality that with joy, confidence, hope, and love can build a new world.

Index

Abel, Günter 69
Absolute Recoil (Žižek) 107
abstraction, alienation and 34–37
AC! 343
access, knowledge *vs.* 53–55
Act Up 343
Adorno, Theodor 110, 287
advent of nihilism 17
African Independent Churches (AICs) 299;
    sites of interpretive struggle 302–305
African National Congress (ANC) 315
African Traditional Religion 297–299
Agamben, Giorgio 164, 168–169; interview
    343–352; monasticism, views on 172–173;
    poverty 170; St. Paul's letters 346–348,
    350–351
agape 9, 182; *caritas vs.* 185, 189–190
AICs *see* African Independent Churches (AICs)
alienation 35–36, 42–43; abstraction and
    34–37; depression and 46–47
Allende, Salvador 140–141
allocation, regimes of 310
Alves, Ruben 148
Aman, Kenneth 143n16
Ambedkar, B. R. 12, 243n8, 321; Buddhism
    335–337; caste/Dalit question 332; change,
    skepticism of 334–335; Dalit spirituality
    330–337; left-wing parties *vs.* 335–336;
    modernity 333–334; originality of 334;
    spirituality 339
anamnesis 110
ANC (African National Congress) 315
Andreas-Salomé, Lou 72
animality 33
animals, becoming human 42; definition by
    Hegel 48
animism 45
anticlerical tracts 281
anti-Oedipal Marxism 11, 252–254
Anti-Oedipus (Deleuze & Guattari) 253
Anti-Oedipus (Foucault) 252–253

anti-Semitism, Nietzsche 72; *see also* "On the
    Jewish Question" (Marx)
apartheid 314–315
Aquinas, Thomas 156, 186n9, 190, 239n1
architecture of categories, political equivalent
    232–233
Argentina 141–142
Arroyo, Gónzalo 151
askesis, Foucault 11
asketic 239–259
atheism 26
Atheism in Christianity (Bloch) 111, 286
"The Attitude of the Workers Party towards
    Religion" (Lenin) 280–281
Aufhebung 104–105
Augustine, Saint 186n9
autonomous historical consciousness 215
Avineri, Shlomo 95–96, 98
Azanian People's Organization (AZAPO)
    310–311

Badiou, Alain 102, 106, 115
Baratta, G. 324
Bauman, Zygmund 122n5, 124n9
Bazarov, Vladimir 265–266, 284
being, malignancy of 136
belief, Gramsci 64–65
Benedict XVI 193–194
Benjamin, Walter 38, 65, 78–79, 286
Beradi, Franco "Bifo" 46–47
Berdiaev, Nikolai 265, 284
Betto, Frei 161
Beyond Good and Evil (Nietzsche) 77
Bhagavad Gita 246
Bhagavad Gita According to Gandhi, The 246n13
Bible: accusations of misuse 296; Levinas
    122n3; Marxist analysis 295–319
*Biblical Hermeneutics and Black Theology in
    South Africa* (Mosala) 12
biological survival, freedom as 41–42
Blanchot, M 123n6

Bloch, Ernest 6–7; anamnesis 110; charity 192; god-building 285–286; Kochi interpretation 95; liberation theology 146–147; open system Marxism 105–107; social interventions 88–89; theistic religion/faith 64–65; transformation 109; utopia 86, 87–90, 102–116; work of meditation 96–97
Block, Aleksander 272
Boer, Roland 260–261, 309–310; Bloch's god-building 285–286; charity 182–183
Boff, Clodovis 151
Boff, Leonardo 151
Bogdanov, Aleksandr 262
Bolte, Friedrich 154
Bonhoeffer, Dietrich 65
Bonino, José Míguez 150
Boothman, Derek 212
Borda, Orlando Fals 147
Border Musical, A (Delat) 29
bourgeois humanism, Marx critique of 131–135
Brecht, Berthold 106n2
Brzozowski, Stanislaw 280
Buddha and His Drum, The (Ambedkar) 337
Buddhism 2; Ambedkar 335–337
buen vivir 79
Bukharin, Nicolai 205, 205n7, 217, 218–219
Butler, Judith 7, 79, 123–124, 123n7
Buttigieg, Joseph A 227n14, 335
buyers: freedom 132

Cafiero, Carlo 282–283
Cameron, Jenny 172, 175
capitalism: Christianity and 51–52, 59; Lukács 34; Marx criticism of 118; methods of production 41; Žižek 33
capitalist alienation 47–48
Capitalist Realism (Fisher) 46
Capital (Marx) 117
Cardenal, Ernesto 152
care of the self 53–54, 62; Christianity *vs.* 55–56; complex articulation of sociality 58; religion *vs.* 61–62
caritas 9; *agape vs.* 185, 189–190; Catholic wars over 193–197
caste system 332, 334; *see also* chaturvarṇa
Castro, Fidel 147
Catholic church: charity 195–196; counter-Reformation 203; Foucault 8; Gramsci 201–202; peasant life 203, 204; philosophy of praxis *vs.* 216; unity problems 207–208; *see also* Christianity; Vatican
celibacy, monasticism 170
Centre for Contemporary Cultural Studies (CCCS) 302–305

Chalier, Catherine 124
characterization of spirituality 15–16
charity 9, 181–200; Catholic church 195–196; centrality of 185; cults of 191; Divine Grace and 188; Marxist legacy 182–186; Pascal 188–191; rejection of 183; religious generosity 197; *see also, agape; caritas*
Charpin, Frédéric 267
Charusheela, S. 190n13
chaturvarṇa 332, 334
cheapskating 173–174, 176
Christianity: appropriation of local spirituality 8; capitalism and 51–52, 59; care of the self *vs.* 55–56; individualism 209; political commitment 145; religionless 65; Roman culture and 57; theology 55; truth and 56; *see also* Catholic church
Christianity and Marxism (Bonino) 150
Ciaramelli, F. 123n8
civil society: Hegel 33
class: charity and 190–191; Derrida 94n16; division of society 226–227; Resnick & Wolff 255; struggle of 254–256; understanding of 254
class antagonism 7; Levinas 129; normativization 59n5
classless society building 187–188
clothes: religion in 171–172
Cohen, G. A. 254–255
collective life forms: spirituality 14
collective (social) consciousness 37
Comblin, José 144–145, 148
Coming Community, The (Kaufman) 178
commodities 37–40
common sense 326–330; Gramsci 206; philosophy *vs.* 209–210
community transformation 254–257
community with other, spirituality as 24
complex articulation of sociality 58
Comte, Auguste 279
concept of power, Spinoza 66
concrete utopia 107
Conditions of the Working Class in England, The (Engels) 181
Confession (Gorkii) 272–276
Congress of South African Trade unions (COSATU) 315
connaissance (intellectual knowledge) 55
consciousness: individuality and 32; movement of 58–59; reason as 40
contemporary ontology 38
Contribution to the Critique of Hegel's Philosophy of Right, A (Marx) 1, 182, 212n13, 244n10, 300
Coote, Robert 307, 308

corporality, opposition to 248
Corvalán, Luis 141–142
cosmic spirit *see* shakti
CO_2 technofetishism 168
counter-Reformation, Catholic church 203
craftsmanship 96n20
creative expression of potentials 24–25
creative spirit of the people 324
Creative Unity (Tagore) 1
crisis of negation 103–104
Critchley, Simon 119
Critique of Pure Experience (Avenarius) 263
Croce, Benedetto 223, 229; criticism of 234; faith 230–233; First World War 234; good sense 230–233
Cuban revolution 146
cults of charity 191
cultural learning 54–55
culture 216; sociality and 59

Dalai Lama, interview 13–14, 353–367
Dalits 320–342; inner life 321–322; spirituality of 330–337
Darmesteter, James 277
Davidson, Mark 167
"Debates on the law on Thefts of Wood" (Marx) 32–33
Defense of the Mendicants (Agamben) 170
Delat, Chto 29
Deleuze, Giles 66, 78, 349
de Martino, Ernesto 329–330
democratization 167
dependency theory, liberation theology 147
depression: alienation and 46–47; episodes of 46
Derrida, Jacques 81, 91–94, 241n3; class and party structure 94n16; *Geist* 255n22; Kochi interpretation 95; mourning 93; spirit 247, 248; utopia 86; work of mourning 96–97
Descartes, Rene 4, 53
developmentalist language, social scientists 149
dharma 245; eternal 331
dialectical materialism 146
dialectics of contingency 107–111
Dialectics of Power, The (Engels) 146
Dietzgen, Joseph 269, 271–272
docta spes (educated hope) 88, 106
Dombroski, Kelly 174
domination, power *vs.* 71
Durkheim, Émile 275, 334
Dussell, Enrique 130–131, 131n14, 134
dynamic power, static power *vs.* 68–70

Eagleton, Terry 93–94, 260, 304–305
Ecce Homo (Nietzsche) 71

Economic and Philosophical Manuscripts of 1844 (Marx) 38, 40–41, 48, 125–126, 301–302; humanism interpretation 42; proletarians 43
economic criticism, theology and 159–161
Ecumenical Association of African Theologists (EATWOT) 295–296
educated hope *(docta spes)* 88, 106
Elizabethan poor laws 191
emancipation: charity 184–185; secular-religious world 60
emergence of spiritual 31–32
Empire (Hardt & Negri) 67
End of Capitalism (As We Knew It), The (Gibson-Graham) 172
Engels, Friedrich 9, 181, 183
English Darwinism 69n5
enjoyment 167
epimeleia heautou 252n19
episteme, phronesis *vs.* 249–250
equality, criticism by Marx 134
Erbschaft dieser Zeit (Bloch) 103
Essence of Christianity, The (Feuerbach) 18–19, 242, 301
essence of human 37–40
estranged labor 40–44
eternal dharma 331
ethics: deficit of 260; Foucault 252–253; Levinas 118, 121–122; Marx's view 118; philanthropy of 183–184
Ethics and Community (Dussel) 160
Ethics (Spinoza) 69
Etwas fehlt 114
etymology 70
evolution 108
exchange, labor and 34–35
existential need for meaning 25
experiential knowledge, as spirituality 61–62
experimental orientation 175
Experimentum Mundi (Bloch) 109–110
exploitation: analysis of 301; humanism 132; persecution *vs.* 135; South Africa 308–309
extraction: regimes of 310

faith 228; Bloch 64–65; Croce 230–233; definition 143; Gramsci 64–65; social science and *see* social sciences and faith
fascism 78, 224, 225–228
"Father Bresciani's Progeny. Catholic Art" (Gramsci) 202–203
fetishism, geneology and 57–61
Feuerbach, Ludwig 16, 301; *Gattungswesen* 41; God definition 18–20, 21–22; spirituality 18–19; truth 242
Fidel and Religion (Betto) 161

Fiore, Joachim di 111
First World War 234
Fischer, Kuno 70
Fisher, Mark 46
Fitzgerald, T. 334
flame, spirit as 248
flexibility, utopia 98
flight, Deleuze 349
folklore 326–330
Forgacs, David 226–227n14
form of life 168–172
forward orientation 89–90
Foucault, Michel 2, 4, 164n1; *askesis* 11; *asketic* 240, 250–252; Catholicism 8; Christianity and 52; Christianity *vs.* care of the self 55–56; culture of self 54n2; ethics 252–253; governmentalization and 60–61n6; spirituality and 52, 251; truth 10–11; Western normativizing culture 58
Francis, Saint 8–9
Frank, Gunder 147
Frank, Sebastian 301
free conscious activity 22–23
freedom 132–133; biological survival 41–42; criticism by Marx 134; labor and 41; will of 133
free will 134
free workers, estranged labor 43–44
French Revolution 96n19
Frente popular (Popular Front) 140–141
Fromm, Erich 29–30, 47
Frosini, Per 299, 338
Fülöp-Miller, René 284
Función de la iglesia en la realidad rioplatense (Segundo) 149
fundamental needs 16
future: Marx's approach to 91; past and 93
"The Future of Religion" (Lunacharskii) 271
Future of Religion, The (Unger) 287

Gandhi 10–11; truth 244–246
Gasper, Phil 280
Gattungswesen 41
Gauthier, Paul 144
Gay Science, The (Nietzsche) 69
GEAR (Growth, Employment and Redistribution) 315
Geist 11, 64, 113–114 *see* spirit
genealogy, fetishism and 57–61
Geneology of Morals (Nietzsche) 67–68
Gera, Lucio 152
Geras, N. 98n22
Geremek, B. 190
German Ideology, The (Marx and Engels) 26, 241, 349

Geschichte der neuern Philosophie (Fischer) 70
Ghostly Demarcations, a Symposium on Jacques Derrida's Specters of Marx 93–94
Gibbs, Robert 127–129
Gibson, C. L. 174
Gibson, Katherine 175
Gibson-Graham, J. K. 165, 172, 173; experimental orientation 175; hybrid collective postcapitalist political theory 175–176
Girardi, Giulio 147
Giving an Account of Oneself (Butler) 123–124
global warming 176
God, definition by Feuerbach 18–20, 21–22
god-building 261, 262–266; Bloch 285–286; *Confession* (Gorkii) 272–273; criticism of 274–275; genesis of 266–268; god-seeking *vs.* 265; Lenin 283–284; necrophiliac dimensions 285
God is Love (Deus Caritas est) (Benedict XVI) 193
Goldmann, Lucien 186–191
Good Life 78–81
good life conception 79–80
good sense, Croce 230–233
Gorbachev, Mikhail 161
Gorkii, Maksim 261–263, 266–268, 269
Gotha Program 283
Gottwald, Norman 310
Gramsci, Antonio 9–10, 12, 320; charity 184; common sense 206; faith/belief 64–65; good sense conception 79; inner life 325; liberation theology 146–147; philosophy investigation 205n6; philosophy of praxis 222–238; religion, interest in 229, 234; repressive state apparatus 74; simple 201–221; southern question 332; spirit definition 324; spirituality 339
Great Upheaval, The (Lunacharskii) 286–287
Greek ethics 56n3
green consumerism 166–168, 177–178; analysis of 167
Grundrisse (Marx) 108
Guru, G. 337
Gutiérrez, Gustavo 9, 145, 149–150; Catholic church 194–195; charity 196; liberation theology 196–197
Guyau, Jean-Marie 278–279

Hadot, P. 245n12
Hall, Stuart 308
Hardt, Michael 67, 70, 74, 99n23, 164
Hart, Gillian 315–316
Harvey, David 103n1
Healy, Stephen 172

Hegel, G. W. F. 3, 31–33, 34–35, 320–321; animal 48; civil society 33; consciousness, movement of 58–59; *objektiver Geist* 112; social being change 113; spiritual animality 36; utopia 107
Heidegger, Martin 10–11, 114–115, 119; *phronesis* 240, 249, 249n17
Hellenistic/Roman civilisation: model of self 53–54
Here I am *(hineni)* 122
hermeneutical weapons, Mosala 304–305, 312
hermeneutics of innocence 66–68
Hermeneutics of the Subject, The (Foucault) 52, 253–254
Hidden God, The (Goldmann) 186
highest poverty 168–172
Hill, Ann 175
Hinduism, eternal dharma 331
hineni (Here I am) 122
Hinkelammert, Franz 147, 159–160
Historical-Critical Dictionary of Marxism 70
historical determinism 217–218
historical experience 324
historical materialism 210, 254
Historical Materialism: A System of Sociology (Bukharin) 205n7
History of Europe in the Nineteenth Century (Croce) 234
"History of the Subaltern Classes" (Gramsci) 223
Høffding, Harald 279
Holocaust, The 120–121n2
Holy Family, The (Marx & Engels) 281; speculative idealism 239–240; spiritual 241
Horkheimer, Max 262
hospitality 91–92
householding, sustainable 174–175
Howell, George 154
Hudson, Wayne 94–95
human essence 40–41; labor as 38–39, 40
humanism 95; critique by Levinas 119–122; exploitation process 132; freedom 133; Levinas 125; Lunacharskii 269–270; Marxism interpretation 42; radicalisation of 39–40
humanity, working classes *vs.* 127
humanized secularism 23, 26; essence of 37–40
humans: animals from 42; commodities *vs.* 37–38; essence of 37–40; religion construction 21
Humans, All-Too Human (Nietzsche) 71–72
Husserl, E. 323–324, 330
hybrid collective postcapitalist political theory 175–176

ideological co-optation, post-Liberation 314–316
Ideological Weapons of Death, The (Hinkelammert) 159–160
ILADES (Latin American Institute of Social Studies) 141
Ilyenkov, Evald 36–37
immanent practice 14
immanent spirituality 14, 80
individualism 209; capitalist alienation 47–48; charity 187; consciousness and 32; nonalienated existence 35–36; *potentia* 76
inhumanism 39–40
inner life 321–322, 325
inner realms 16
Instruction on Christian Liberty and Liberation 155
intellectual activity 326–327
intellectual knowledge *(connaissance)* 55
intellectuals 227–228; Catholic church, treatment of 203–204; philosophy of 211
interconnecting with nature 24
interlocutors 240–242
International Union of Social Studies 202
interrogation of self 2–3
interviews 13–14; Agamben 343–352; Dalai Lama 13–14, 353–367; Negri 14, 368–376; Revel 14, 368–376
irrational passions 228
Islam 2
Iushkevich, Pavel 263, 278–279

James, William 266
Jameson, Fredric 44, 98n21, 102
Jansenism 188
Jean Paul II 194–195
Jenaer Realphilosophie (Hegel) 34–35
Jobling, David 297n1, 310
JOC *see* Young Catholic Workers (JOC)
John XXII 176
John XXIII 139–140
John Paul II 156–159
"Judaism and Revolution" Levinas 135

Kafka, Franz 40–41, 49
Kahl, B. 280
kairos (messianic activity) 13
Kamber, T. 85n1
Karsenti, Bruno 330
Kaufman, Elanor 178
Kautsky, Karl 9, 184, 280
Kayatekin, S. A. 190n13
Kline, G. 265
Kloppenburg, Bonaventura 153
Klotzmaterialismus 105, 112

knowing thyself 215
knowledge: access *vs.* 53–55; spirituality as 62
Knowledge and Class (Resnick & Wolff) 129n11
know thyself 53
Kochi, Tarik 93n13, 95
Koigen, David 280
Kojève, Alexander 34
Kołakowski, Leszek 284
Korsch, Karl 287

labor: exchange and 34–35; freedom and 41; human essence as 38–39, 40; power market 133; spirituality and 33; theory of the soul 44–48
Laborem Exercens (John Paull II) 156–159
laborers, freedom of 132
Labriola, Antonio 210
Lacan, J. 244n9
lack of spirituality 260
La Iglesia del pueblo (Lozano) 153
Landa, Ishay 80
Land of Remorse, The (de Martino) 329–330
language 326–330; of the slave 332
La producción teórica de Marx (Dussel) 160
La Rocca, Tommaso 212
last men 65
Latin America 8, 138–142; convergence (1968–79) 140–142; historical issues 138–139; initial encounter phase (1959–68) 139–140; new contradictions (post-1984) 142–143; post-strategic alliance (1979–84) 142
Latin American Institute of Social Studies (ILADES) 141
lebendige Arbeit (living work) 154–155
Le-Dantec, Félix 264
left: right *vs.* 256
left-wing parties, Ambedkar *vs.* 335–336
Lenin, Religion and Theology (Boer) 261
Levinas, Emmanuel 117–137; ethical positions 118; humanism critique 119–122; infinite responsibility for the Other 122–124; Marx, fundamental similarity with 128–129; Marx and preliminary questions 125–127; other in 127–131
liberal ethics 191–192
liberalism 240
liberation theology 138–162; accusation of Marxism 153–156; formation of 145; Gutiérrez 196–197; 1984 instruction 153–155; Marxism incorporation 148–152; Marxism type used 146–147; Pascal 196–197; present paths 156–162; 1986 second instruction 155–156; theology &

economic criticism 159–161; Vatican 195–197; *see also* Latin America; social sciences and faith
limitless charity 189
literacy, African Independent Churches 303–304
"little daydreams" 87–88
living flower, free conscious activity as (Marx) 22–23
living work *(lebendige Arbeit)* 154–155
Long, C. P. 249–250
Losurdo, Domenico 67, 72n10
Love in Truth (Caritas in Veritate) (Benedict XVI) 193–194
Lower Depths, The (Gorkii) 267
Lozano, Javier 153
Lukács, Georg 34, 89n8
Lunacharskii, Anatolii 261–263, 265; Comte *vs.* 279; god-building 286–287; Gorkii *vs.* 269; humanism 269–270; *Mercure de France* debate 273–274; Plekhanov *vs.* 278; religion of labor 268–272

Macht 70
madness 45–46
Madodana (men's guilds) 303–304
Maduro, Otto 151
Magesterium 156–159
malignancy of Being 136
Malthus, T. R. 191–192
man as secular being 20–21
Manhood, Craig 175
Manyano (women's guilds) 303–304
MAPU 140–141
Mascat, Jamila 35–36
Marot, John Eric 262–263
Martov, Iurii 277
Marx and the Bible (Miranda) 148
Marxism, open system *see* open system Marxism
Marxism and the Muslim World (Robinson) 183n2
Marxist humanism 40
masses, religion and 228–230
mass movements 256
mass society: birth of 224–225
material existence: adjustment to 165
materialism 112; respect of 30; spiritualism incompatibility 29–30
Materialism and Empiriocriticism (Lenin) 263–264
materialistic doctrine 243
materialist metaphysics 111–115
mathematics, spiritualism 114
Max's Concept of Man (Fromm) 29–30

Mbeki, Thabo 315
meaning, existential need for 25
Means without End: Notes on Politics (Agamben) 344
medieval Christianity: charity 190
meditation, work of 96–97
Meditations of Marcus Aurelius (Hadot) 245n12
Menand, Louis 281–282
Mercure de France debate 273–274
Merezhkovskii, Dmitrii 284
messianic activity *(kairos)* 13
messianic Marxism limits 166–168
messianic promise 91
Metamorphosis (Kafka) 49
metaphysical materialism 112
Micah, Mosala, analysis by 307–311
middle class 233
mind 325–326
Mind and Face of Bolshevism, The (Fülöp-Miller) 284
Miranda, Porfirio 148
modernity 333–334
modes of spiritual 16
Mofokeng, Takatso 295–296, 316–317
moksha (personal salvation) 243n8
Molyneux, John 280
monasticism 168–172; celibacy 170; novitiates 169–170
monetarism, zombies as 35
More than Belief: A Materialist Theory of Religion (Vasquez) 67
Morrow, Otto 174
Morton, Timothy 40
Mosala, Itumeleng 12, 298–319; Bible interpretation 302; hermeneutical weapons 304–305, 312; Marxist methodology 305–312; method at work 313–314; Micah, analysis of 307–311; redactional approach rejection 306
mourning 93; work of 91–94, 96–97
movement of consciousness 58–59
mythology: Lunacharskii 276–277; religion from 233–236

nature: interconnecting with 24; religious ideology 270
necrophiliac dimensions: god-building 285
need for wholeness 25
Negarestani, Reza 39–40
negation crisis 103–104
Negative Dialectics (Adorno) 110
Negri, Antonio 6, 67, 70, 73–76, 78, 80, 99n23, 164; interviews 14, 368–376; *potentia vs. potestas* 74

Nietzsche, F. 4–5; anti-Semitism 72; fascism and 78; god-building 266, 279; last men 65; pathos of nobility 67–68; *potentia agendi* 77–78; power 77; Spinoza, departure from 71–73; Spinoza's reason orientation 68–69; spirituality 330; strong self-confident individuals 80; will to power 66, 72–73
Nietzsche and Philosophy (Deleuze) 67
nihilism 17
nobility, pathos of 67–68
nonalienated existence, individuality 35–36
nonsimultaneity *(Ungleichzeitigkeit)* 103
norm: truth and 56n3
normativization 55–57; class antagonism 59n5; secular knowledge 57
Not-Yet 87–88, 111–115
novitiates, monasticism 169–170

objektiver Geist: Hegel 112
Of Spirit (Derrida) 247
Ollman, Bertell 95
"On the Jewish Question" (Marx) 4, 128, 242, 332, 336–337; fetishism through genealogy 57–58; secular Christian state 51–52
ontology criticism: Levinas 119
On Two Fronts (Bazarov) 265–266
open system Marxism, Bloch 104, 105–107
opposition to corporality 248
oppression, analysis of 301
oppressive relations 129
organization of society 226–227
orienting world view 24
orthodoxy 228–230
The Other, Levinas 127–131
otherness elimination, Levinas 120
Otherwise Than Being, or Beyond Essence (Levinas) 117, 120n2
Otherwise Than Being (Levinas) 122, 129

Pagan individualism 209
Paganopolous, Michelangelo 169–170
Pannekoek, Anton 269
Paoli, Arthur 152
parliament reform/reorganization 227
parrhesiastes 347–348
party structure: Derrida 94n16
Pascal, Blaise 181; charity 186, 187, 188–191; liberation theology 196–197
passive revolution 226
past: future and 93; Marx's approach to 91
pathos of nobility 67–68
Patočka, Jan 323–324, 330
Patrons et ouvriers (Roguenant) 201–202
Paul's letters, Agamben on 346–348, 350–351
peasant life, Catholic church 203, 204

Pensées (Pascal) 181
Perestroika (Gorbachev) 161
persecution, exploitation *vs.* 135
person, Marxism 154–155
personal alienation 43
personal salvation *(moksha)* 243n8
Petty, William 37
Phenomenology of the Spirit (Hegel) 3, 31–33, 36–37, 320–321
philanthropy, ethics of 183–184
philosophy: common sense *vs.* 209–210; Gramsci, views on 205n6, 213, 326–327; intellectuals 211; Levinas 119; praxis *(see* philosophy of praxis; religion as 230; spirit of 210; spirituality and 252; task of 232
"Philosophy of Benedetto Croce, The" (Gramsci) 234–235
philosophy of praxis 210–211, 219, 328–329; Catholicism *vs.* 216; Gramsci 222–238
Philosophy of Right (Hegel) 112–113
phrenology 31–32
phronesis 250, 256; Heidegger 240; spiritual as 248–250
Piketty, Thomas 103n1
Pinto, Alvaro Viera 148
Pius IX 139n1, 202
Pius XII 193n15
plasticity, utopia 98
Plato 36–37; cave allegory 322–323; know thyself and care of self 53
Platonov, Andrei 44–46
plebeians 215
Pleins, David 313–314
Plekhanov, Georgii 111, 263, 267, 278
Plumwood, Val 165, 173
"Polemical Remarks on Gorkii" (Voronsky) 275
political equivalent, architecture of categories 232–233
political process, democritization of 167
political transformation 256–257
Pomfrett, Jamie 175
Popular Front (Frente popular) 140–141
Popular Manual (Bukharin) 217, 218–219
popular masses, passivity of 231
post-Liberation, ideological co-optation 314–316
potentia: individuals of 76; Spinoza 75, 76; virtue 77–78
potentia agenda: Benjamin 79; definitions 76; good sense (Gramsci) 79; Nietzsche 77–78; *potentia cogitandi* and 80; Spinoza 75–76
potentia cogitandi, potentia agendi and 80

potentials: creative expression of 24–25; *potestas vs.* 6, 73–74; Spinoza 66; usage of 74–75
potestas: potential vs. 73–74; usage of 74–75
poverty: fatalistic view 202; monasticism 170; vow of 170n5
power: definition by Weber 70; domination *vs.* 71; Nietzsche 77; sociologically amorphous concept as 70–71; Spinoza *vs.* Nietzsche 66–67
practical philosophy, Marxism and 2
praxis, philosophy of *see* philosophy of praxis
Principle of Hope, The (Bloch) 86, 88
Prison Notebooks (Gramsci) 10, 320; Catholic church 201–202; philosophy of praxis 222–238
production: capitalist methods 41; focus of 90; primacy of process 159; separation from 126–127
proletariat 113; charity as foundation 183; Marx 43; religion of 262–263
Putnam, H. 122n4

radicalisation, humanism of 39–40
Randall, Rosemary 165, 176
rationalists: charity 187; reason as prejudice 68–69
real abstraction 36
real socialism, religion 161–162
reason: consciousness as 40; rationalist prejudice as 68–69
Reclus, Elisée 270
redaction criticism 305, 306–307
reductionist materialism 7
Rée, Paul 72
Reflections on Violence (Sorel) 277
Reformation 208
regimes of allocation 310
regimes of extraction 310
Rehmann, Jan 260, 280, 300–302
reification 59–60; social, of the 61
Reiman, Jeffrey 133–134n17
relation of responsibility 130–131
religion 326–330; care of self *vs.* 61–62; clothes in 171–172; common sense 204–212; construction and human needs 21; control of leaders 321–322; definition for Marx 17; Gramsci interventions 234; history of violence 253; ideology 261–262, 270; labor of, Russian Marxism 268–272; masses and 228–230; myth to 233–236; philosophy as 230; real socialism 161–162; self-alienation 20
Religion and Socialism (Lunacharskii) 265, 274, 276–280

religionless Christianity 65
"The Religion of Social Democracy"
(Dietzgen) 271–272
Religion of Socialism (Lunacharskii) 268
Religious and Antireligious Thought in Russia
(Kline) 265
religious forces, spiritual forces *vs.* 16
religious generosity, Marxism
non-acceptance 197
*Remnants of Auschwitz: The Witness and the
Archive* (Agamben) 345
repetition, monasticism 170
repressive state apparatus 74
Resnick, Stephen 129n11, 254, 255
responsibility, relation of 130–131
Revel, Judith 80; interview 14, 368–376
revolutionary cultural workers 304
revolutionary mass: socialism and 26–27
Rhamaphosa, Cyril 316
Richard, Pablo 150–151
right, left *vs.* 256
Roberts, John 166
Roelvink, Gerda 165, 173
Rohr, Richard 170n5
Roman culture, Christianity and 57
Romero, Oscar A. 142
Rosati, Massimo 330
Rosengarten, Frank 325n4
Roguenant, Arthur 201–202
RSDLP (Russian Social Democratic Labor
Party) 264
Russian Marxism 11–12, 260–294; atheism
280–283; Lenin, showdown with 283–286;
religion of labor (Lunacharskii) 268–272;
rites and rituals 284–285
Russian Social Democratic Labor Party
(RSDLP) 264

Saar, Martin 73, 76
SACC *see* South African Council of
Churches
SACP *see* South African Communist Party
Salvation Army 192
sameness, bourgeois notion of 134
Sanders, Bernie 104
Sandinista revolution 142, 161
Santidad en la revolución (Cardenal) 152
Santos, Theotonio dos 147
Sarukkai, S. 337
Sautoy, Marcus du 114
Scannone, Juan Carlos 151–152
Scott, James 308, 309
Sea of Youth (Platonov) 45–46
Second World War 120n2
secular beings 20–21

secularization 240; spiritual form of 26;
Western culture and 3–4
secular knowledge, normativization 57
secular-religious world, emancipation from 60
secular sciences 2
secular spirituality unification 322
secular state 58
Segundo, Juan Luis 144, 145, 148, 149
self 2–3; question of 255
self-mastery 271–272
self-reference 3
self-transformation 2–3, 256
Sennett, Richard 96–97, 96n20
separation from production 126–127
Serna, Jaime 153
Sesterhenn, Raimund 266–267
sexuality 59–60
shakti 244
sharecropping 190n13
signified practices 312
Sillabo (Pius IX) 202
simple: Catholic church 208–209, 212;
Gramsci 201–221; preservation of 211–212
Skaria, A. 336–337
slavery 41–42, 120, 130–131
Sobrino, Jon 151
social, reification of 61
social being change 113
social (collective) consciousness 37
social ethics 313–314
social existence 32
social interventions 88–89
socialism, revolutionary mass and 26–27
Socialism: Utopian and Scientific (Engels)
85n1, 281
sociality 124; complex articulation of 58;
culture and 59; transformation of 135–136
social practice, spirituality and 32–33
social revolution 256
social sciences and faith 143–152; Marxist
analysis 144–146; theology and scientific
discourse 143–144
social scientists 149
social strife 264
social transformation 255–257
society: class division of 226–227; organization
of 226–227
Soloviev, Vladimir 265
sophia 11; phronesis *vs.* 249–250
Sorel, Georges 277
soul: commodity of 37–40; definition 44, 48;
labor theory of 44–48; spirituality and 47;
unconscious as 47
Soul at Work, The (Berardi) 46–47
Soul (Platonov) 45–46

South Africa 295–319; exploited classes
    308–309; ideological co-optation post-
    Liberation 314–316; sigh of the oppressed
    300–302; theology 316 see also African
    Independent Churches; Mosala, Itumeleng
South African Communist Party (SACP) 315
South African Council of Churches
    (SACC) 315
South America 12
Southern question 332
specialised cultures 327–328
specter of utopia 106–107
Specters of Marx (Derrida) 86
Specters of Marx, The (Hudson) 94–95
speculative idealism 239–240, 247
Spinoza, B. de 4–5, 6; concept of power 66;
    Nietzsche, departure from 71–73; potentia
    75, 76; potentia agendi 75–76; potentia
    cogitandi and potentia agendi 80; reason as
    rationalist prejudice 68–69; religion critique
    80–81; virtue and potentia 77–78
Spinoza for Our Time (Negri) 75, 78
spirit 247, 320–321; cosmic spirit (shakti)
    244; creative spirit of the people 324;
    definition by Gramsci 324; flame as 248;
    philosophy of 210
Spiritual Crisis of the Intelligence, The
    (Berdyaev) 265
spiritual dimensions, social strife 264
spiritual forces 17, 18; religious forces vs. 16
spiritualism 247; materialism
    incompatibility 29–30; mathematics 114
spirituality: Ambedkar 339; characterization of
    15–16; collective life forms 14; community
    with other 24; contradictory notion of 38;
    crisis of 16–17; definition for Marx 17, 18;
    emergence of 31–32; experiential knowledge
    as 61–62; Foucault 251; genesis of 31–33;
    Gramsci 339; history of 65; The Holy Family
    (Marx and Engels) 241; immanence of
    322–326; immanent spirituality 14, 80;
    interconnecting with nature 24; knowledge
    as 62; labor and 33; lack of 260; limitation
    of use 17–18; modes of 16; philosophy and
    252; phronetic as 248–250; resistance to 30;
    secularized form of 26; secular spirituality
    unification 322; social practice and 32–33;
    soul and 47
spiritualized secularism 23
spiritual life 16, 18
spiritual needs, addressing of 23–24
spiritual senses 18
Stampfer, Friedrich 269
Starkoff, Véra 272
static power, dynamic power vs. 68–70

Stern, Jakob 70
Story of My Experiments with Truth, The
    (Hadot) 245, 245n12
"strong," self-confident individuals 80
subalterns 320–342; inner life/spirituality
    321–322
Subjekt-Objekt (Bloch) 110
sumak kawsay 79
suma qamaña 79
surface unity, Catholic church 208
suspicion, poor and charity of 191
sustainable householding 174–175
sustainable urbanism 168
Swyngedouw, Erik 167–168
"Syllabus and Hegel, The" (Gramsci) 231

Tagore, Rabindranath 1
Take Back the Economy (Gibson-Graham)
    173–174
Teología de la Liberación y Cristianos para el
    socialismo (Vekemans) 153
Teología do politico e suas mediacões (Boff) 151
Terpstra, Marin 73
theistic religion 64–65
theo-economics 310
theology: aim of 144; Christianity 55;
    economic criticism and 159–161
Theology and the Church: A Response to Cardinal
    Ratzinger and a Warning to the Whole Church
    (Segundo) 149
Theology of Liberation, A (Gutiérrez) 149–150
Theory of Historical Materialism, The: A Popular
    Manual of Marxist Sociology (Bukharin) 205
"Theses on the Philosophy of History"
    (Benjamin) 78–79
Theses on Feuerbach (Marx) 30, 88n6
Tomšič, Samo 47
Toscano, Alberto 260
Todak Mandal, Jat-Pak 335n18
Totality and Infinity (Levinas) 121–122
transformation: Bloch 109; society of 135–136
Treanor, B. 119n1
truth 10–11, 242–243; Christianity and
    56; conception of 58; Ghandi 244–246;
    Ghandi vs. Marx 245–246; norm and 56n3;
    phronesis and 250

unalienated craftwork 97
unconsciousness, soul as 47
Unger, Roberto Mangabeira 287
Ungleichzeitigkeit (nonsimultaneity) 103
Unheimlich (uncanny) 91–92, 97–98
unification, secular spirituality 322
universal representation 37
urban farming 175

urbanism, sustainable 168
utopia 6–7, 85–101; Bloch 87–90;
  integration of 94; Marxism incompatibility
  with 90; specter of 106–107; spirituality of
  102–116

Vaillancourt, Ives 141n8
value perspectives 25
van der Veer, Peter 322
Varieties of Religious Experience, The (James) 266
Vasquez, Manuel 67
Vásquez, Sánchez 147
Vatican: liberation theology 195–197;
  understanding of Marxism 138–139; *see also*
  Catholic church
Vekemans, Roger 141n8, 153
Vekhi (Landmarks) (Boer) 264
Venezuela 103
violence: Marxism and 3; mitigation by
  phronesis 250; religious history 253
virtue, *potentia* 77–78
von Uexküll, Jacob 44
vow of poverty 170n5
Vperëd (Gorkii & Lunacharskii)
  262–263
Vperëdism 11–12

Wagner, R. 71
Waite, Geoff 78
weak messianic power 65

Webb, Darren 90
Weber, Max 70, 227; irrational passions 228;
  mass democracy, danger of 231n30
West, Cornel 299
Western culture: normativization of 58;
  ontology 118–119; philosophy 119
secularization and 3–4, 51–63
wholeness, need for 25
Wiesmann, Hannah Grosse 69
will to power 66, 72–73
wish-images 287
Wolff, Richard 129n11, 254, 255
Wordsworth, William 108–109
work-bread-life interrelatedness 157
working classes, humanity *vs.* 127
work of meditation 96–97
work of the mourning 91–94, 96–97
world conceptions 214–215
Worldview of Socialism, The (Koigen) 280
World War I 234
Wurzer, William 66–67

Young Catholic Workers (JOC) 139, 140

Žižek, Slavoj 6–7, 107, 109–110, 166–167;
  atheist as 112; capitalist society 33; Catholic
  church, views on 171–172; charity 184;
  Hegel and 115
zombies, monetarism as 35
Zuma, Jacob 316

For Product Safety Concerns and Information please contact our
EU representative GPSR@taylorandfrancis.com Taylor & Francis
Verlag GmbH, Kaufingerstraße 24, 80331 München, Germany